COPTIC ORTHODOX LITURGICAL HISTORY

UNCOVERING THE ORIGINS, DEVELOPMENT, AND CONTEMPORARY IMPLICATIONS OF COPTIC RITES AND TRADITIONS IN WORSHIP OF GOD

BOOK 1: REGULAR DAYS

Offering of Incense, Liturgies, and Vigil

ALBAIR MIKHAIL

Coptic Orthodox Liturgical History

Book 1: Regular Days (Offering of Incense, Liturgies, and Vigil)

Copyright © 2022 by Albair Mikhail (Albier Michaiel)

All rights reserved.

Designed & Published by:
St. Mary & St. Moses Abbey Press
101 S Vista Dr, Sandia, TX 78383
stmabbeypress.com

Cover design and illustration by Kirollos Kilada.

Library of Congress Control Number: 2022942511

CONTENTS

CHAPTER

One: Introduction..1

Two: Vespers and Prime Prayers................................6

Three: Midnight Psalmody..92

Four: The Offertory..148

Five: The Liturgy of the Word.................................202

Six: The Liturgy of the Faithful.............................273

Seven: Ancient Eucharistic Prayers..........................422

Eight: English/Arabic Terminologies....................481

References 489

Foreword

By His Grace Bishop Youssef
Bishop of the Coptic Orthodox Diocese of the Southern U.S.A.

The wise Church Fathers, over the centuries, meant to design the Church rites, with of its nuances and prayers, in a way that reflects a glorious image of our dynamic, loving God, and His magnificent kingdom. Therefore, studying the Coptic Orthodox Church rites is worthwhile and enriching. Understanding the meaning, symbol, and purpose of each movement and prayer will open the congregant's eyes and enlighten their minds so they may know our Almighty God more; this knowledge will deepen our fellowship with Him, as the ultimate purpose of any ritual practice is unity with the triune God.

Studying the history of the Church rites is another interesting, relevant field too. Many people do not realize the difference between the study of Church rites, and the study of the history of Church rites. The former scrutinizes the different orders of liturgical prayers and all their symbolical aspects. The latter tracks the different changes made to the rites along the course of its history, and is at least as valuable, if not more, than studying the rites themselves. It shows how much the rites were supple enough to accommodate the varying needs of the believers, and how much the Church Fathers were guided by the Holy Spirit to be flexible enough to develop these accommodations. This, in itself, is a strong proof that the Church is alive and dynamic.

This book is distinctive in the manner it relays its scholarly findings, shifting back and forth, smoothly, between studying the rites themselves and its history. Thus, it combines the benefits of studying both fields. Such works are scarce. Therefore, this work is definitely a valuable addition to the Coptic Orthodox Church literature. It will open the door to inspiring further research in this evolving field of study.

I pray that the Lord may reward the blessed author of this work for dedicating substantial time and effort to conduct this detailed research. May the Holy Spirit use it to enlighten its readers and bring them to a deeper fellowship with God, to Whom is glory forever. Amen

Foreword

By Very Rev Dr Geoffrey Ready
Director, Orthodox School of Theology at Trinity College, University of Toronto

Liturgy can be studied in a variety of ways. We can preoccupy ourselves as the liturgist with the minutiae of ceremony and rubrics, with getting the words and rituals correct, so that the liturgical traditions we inherit can be faithfully preserved and passed down. We can follow the liturgical historian into the complexities of the origins and development of rites and services across the centuries of the church, tracing them through both gradual evolution in relationship with the church and its culture, as well as through the occasional revolutions and reforms that have taken place. We can moreover make liturgy a "source" of theology, drawing on it for an understanding of issues of dogmatic theology or a commentary on Biblical texts, in much the same way we use patristic writings or canons as a resource for theological reflection and analysis.

The best liturgical theologians, however—people like Aidan Kavanagh and Jean Corbon for the liturgical tradition of the Latin west, or Robert Taft and Alexander Schmemann for the Byzantine rite—draw on all these approaches but finally do something altogether different. They do not merely look at liturgy, but along and through it, seeing and studying the whole sweep of our life in connection with the narrative of God enacted and interpreted within the liturgy of the church. The rites and worship services of the church, being the concentrated rehearsal of the life of the kingdom of God, are far too important to be reduced to one-dimensional "liturgics" or "theology of liturgy." They are, rather, the interpretive matrix for our whole human life within God's renewal of creation. Liturgical theology is truly that otherwise elusive "theory of everything."

In this present volume and its wider series, Albier Michaiel strives to bring this same profound approach to studying worship according to the Coptic Orthodox rite. Drawing skillfully on the convoluted history of the Alexandrian liturgical tradition, with all its interrelationships and distinctiveness in regard to other early Christian traditions, as well as on careful attention to the particularities of the services in their rubrics and contemporary practice, Michaiel paints a beautiful and detailed canvas of Coptic Orthodox Christian faith and life. For anyone who dares overlook or malign Coptic Orthodoxy for a lack of theological depth or development, its rich liturgy and the story of Christian life embedded within it tell otherwise.

We are thus indebted to Michaiel for this book, a commendable example of that principle guiding the renewal of liturgical theology over the last century, captured within the famous expression lex orandi, lex credendi, lex vivendi—expressing the fundamental interdependence of worship, faith, and life.

CHAPTER ONE

Introduction

Whenever we enter the church and draw near to the heavenly Mysteries, we ought to approach, so we must believe that they are present in the celebration of the Mysteries of His most sacred body at the time of consecration.

—**Bede the Venerable**

After the desolation of Jerusalem and the destruction of its temple, the landmark and symbol of its religious life, in AD 70, the Holy City retracted as an ecclesiastical influencer in the nascent Christian world. Hence, the leadership in the first three centuries was held by Rome, Alexandria, and Antioch. Via its Catechetical School, Alexandria was considered the epicenter of biblical and theological didactics, particularly through the teachings of Clement, and Origen. In the fourth century, however, after the Edict of Milan issued by Constantine in AD 313, Jerusalem began to rise as a pivotal center of Christendom, a theater of biblical events, where pilgrims learned its style of worship that they tried to reproduce in their local traditions. Towards the end of the same century, Constantinople emerged as a significant influencer in the Christian world as well.[1] In the midst of the old and newly emerging powers—stemmed from their civil or spiritual authority, Alexandria continued—until the fifth century—to have a substantial impact on the formation and development of liturgical and ritual practices. This influence was accomplished through two axes: theological guidance, especially the teachings of Athanasius and Cyril I, and the monastic movement (desert monasticism led by Anthony the Great, and communal monasticism headed by Pachom).

After the Council of Chalcedon in AD 451, and the resultant schism between supporters and opposers of its decisions, the influence of Alexandria dwindled, and was only limited to non-Chalcedonian churches. When the Arabs invaded Egypt in AD 642, more restrictions were imposed on the Coptic Church, and very limited access to other Christians was permitted. This level of isolation further prevented the exchange of ritual practices, *Ordos*. While dealing with these sundry

---

[1] Woolfenden, Gregory W., *Daily Liturgical Prayer: Origins and Theology*, 41-42.

traditions and how they contributed to liturgical development, this quest will primarily concentrate on the Coptic Rite.

During the liturgical year, the Coptic Orthodox Church celebrates the ecclesiastical seasons and occasions vis-à-vis Jesus' life on earth. These occasions are observed sporadically throughout the year resulting in gaps between them. The rite addressing these gaps—periods with no particular celebration (i.e., Nativity, Theophany, Lent, Good Friday, Resurrection, etc.)—is referred to as Regular Days.[2] Hence, Regular Days, which includes services of the psalmody, incense offering, and the divine liturgy, is the lengthiest season in the liturgical year. A specific set of melodies is employed to chants during this season, usually referred to as year-round tunes.[3] Regular Days include the ritual practices observed on the weekly fasting days—that is, Wednesdays, and Fridays. This weekly observance is immemorial; it was instructed by the first century *Didache*[4] and reiterated by the Syrian *Didascalia* two centuries later. The latter source provides theological exegesis of the fasting as it associates Wednesday with Jesus' betrayal and Friday with His death (5:14[21]).

The Coptic Orthodox Church, as it stands now, observes two types of psalmodies: one preceding the evening offering of incense, called Vespers Psalmody, and another, which takes place at midnight, called Vigils or Midnight Psalmody. Two incense offering services are observed: Vespers Offering of Incense, and Prime Offering of Incense.[5] The Coptic Church

---

[2] Regular Days season is like, but not the same as, Ordinary Time in the Roman Catholic Rite. However, the latter is limited to two periods only: between Christmastide and Lent, and between Eastertide and Advent.

[3] Other than the Year-round tune, the Coptic Church employs five tunes to the following seasons (periods): Feast Days, the Coptic month of Kiahk, the Fast of Nineveh and Lenten weekdays (except for the first and last days of Lent), Saturdays and Sundays of Lent in addition to the first and last days of Lent, and finally the Feasts of the Cross and Psalm Sunday (also used in Holy Crowning services).

[4] "But as for your fasts, let them not be with the hypocrites, for they fast on the second and fifth days of the week, but you should fast on the fourth and sixth days" (Did. 8:1).

[5] Some, erroneously, call it Matins Offering of Incense, but Matins is the time between 3 AM and dawn, while Prime is around 7 AM.

also celebrates three divine liturgies. The first is believed to be authored by Saint Mark the Apostle (martyred in AD 60 or 61) but was later attributed to Saint Cyril of Alexandria (AD 412–444), the 24th Patriarch of the See of Saint Mark, due to some enhancements that he introduced to the pristine liturgy. The second is credited to Saint Basil the Great (AD 370–379), and the third to Saint Gregory of Nazianzus (AD 372–390)—also referred to as Gregory the Theologian.

This study will scrutinize all these *propers*[6] according to the Coptic Rite, detailing not only the historical developments of *ordos*[7] and observances, but also theological exegeses of ritual practices and symbolism, if applicable. It also includes synopses of immemorial eucharistic prayers along with their texts. Finally, an attempt will be made to regenerate the liturgy of Saint Mark prior to the innovations introduced by Saint Cyril, the Pillar of Faith.

The purpose of this investigation is to provide insight on the origins of ritual practices, particularly of the Coptic Church, their development, and the reasons and circumstances for their development, which in many cases was purely utilitarian. Understanding the meanings and reasons for such development will provide a better chance of connecting the *church*, the body of Christ, to the Church's traditions and rites, not in a systematic or habitual manner but rather in a spiritual one that is cognizant of the very purpose of their existence. This in turn, I hope, will drive love for the church, love powered by understanding. Another advantage to understanding the original objectives for specific practices and observances is the ability to make educated decisions before making changes to existing ritual schemes. It is imperative not to address

---

[6] The word "proper" comes from the Latin origin "proprium," it is the part of the liturgy that varies depending on the occasion or liturgical season, whether in regard to orders or hymns.
[7] Latin word for "order," the set of instructions and rubrics that regulate the church's worship.

contemporary issues reactively but proactively; address them holistically having in mind the purpose of their existence, their development, and their influence on communities today, in Egypt and elsewhere.

This study will uncover some of the treasures in the Coptic Church that over the centuries, and due to diversity of seasons, were ignored or not appreciated. It is common to confuse, especially in the general public realm, the Alexandrian tradition with other rites. This ignorance drove some to attempt, perhaps unintentionally, to distort the Alexandrian character of some liturgical services by painting it with a Byzantine "brush." Understanding the differences between the Alexandrian tradition and others will engender better appreciation among Copts of their Coptic inheritance, and possibly rejuvenation of the Coptic spirit and the desire to restore its character in Coptic worship.

CHAPTER TWO

Vespers and Prime Prayers

Canonical Hours, Offering of Incense, and Veneration Services

A psalm implies serenity of soul; it is the author of peace, which calms bewildering and seething thoughts.... A psalm is a city of refuge from the demons, a means of inducing help from the angels, a weapon in fears by night, a rest from toils by day, a safeguard for infants, an adornment for those at the height of their vigor, a consolation for the elders, a most fitting ornament for women.

—**Basil the Great**[8]

When you look at the candles and lamps burning in church, rise in thought from the material fire to the immaterial fire of the Holy Spirit, "for our God is a consuming fire." When you see and smell the fragrant incense, rise in thought to the spiritual fragrance of the Holy Spirit, "for we are unto God a sweet savor of Christ."

—**John of Kronstadt**

---

[8] St. Basil, *Exegetic Homilies*, Homily 10.2, Fathers of the Church series, v. 46 (Washington DC: Catholic University of America Press, 1963), 152.

Introduction

We will begin this study with a close examination of the rites of incense offering for both Vespers and Prime. The burning of incense, as a perfume or in worship, was an ancient practice that was common among early civilizations such as in Egypt, Babylon, Assur, Uruk, Ur, Nippur, Hadhramaut, Hureidha, Mesopotamia, Yemen, and others.[9] The first recorded use of incense was by the Egyptians during the Fifth Dynasty (2345–2494 BC),[10] specifically during the reign of King Assa (c. 3580-3536 BC).[11] In Babylonia, there is evidence that incense was used in worship in c. 2000 BC. Other nations like Assyrians, Persians, and Indians used incense in worship centuries before Christ.[12] In the West, Greeks were the first to use incense in worship. Although at first they did not appreciate perfumes, around the 7th century BC, when they had more interactions with Egypt and Syria, they started to burn incense for their deities. As for the Romans, it was Plautus, in the 2nd century BC, that mentioned offering incense to the gods.[13]

It was also a common ritual among the Jews, to the extent that a special altar was designated for offering incense called the Altar of Incense, which was separate from the one on which sacrifices were offered (Exodus 30:1; 37:25; 40:5, 26, 27). The debate over whether Judaism borrowed this practice from pagan civilizations, or the latter learned it from the righteous fathers Adam, Noah, and Abraham is a long one and is not the concern of this study.

---

[9] Knowles, Melody D., *Centrality Practiced: Jerusalem in the Religious Practice of Yehud and the Diaspora in the Persian Period*, 57.
[10] Lucas, A., Harris, J.R., *Ancient Egyptian Materials and Industries*, 90.
[11] Atchley, E. G. Cuthbert, *The History of the Use of Incense in Divine Worship*, 7.
[12] Atchley, Ibid., 17, 22, 27.
[13] Atchley, Ibid., 41-42, 46.

Due to its pagan connotation, however, incense was not used in the primitive Christian worship in the first three centuries.[14] In fact, there is much evidence showing that incense was not employed by the Church in the first quarter of the fourth century.[15] In his *Legatio Pro Christianis*, Athenagoras of Athens (c. AD 133–190), for example, states, "The Creator and Father of this Universe needs neither blood nor the savor of sacrifices, nor the fragrance of flowers and incense. Himself being the perfect fragrance, needing nothing and requiring nothing more." Justin Martyr (c. AD 100–165) goes even further; he claims that burning incense was taught by devils and makes refraining from doing so a distinctive characteristic of Christians.[16] In his *Contra omnes haereses*, Irenaeus (c. AD 130–202) declares that incense offering must be symbolically understood as the prayers of the saints, an understanding that is confirmed by Tertullian (c. AD 160–220), who lucidly asserts that burning of incense is idolatry (*Apology*, Chapter 30). Along the same lines, Clement of Alexandria (c. AD 150–215) stresses that offering incense is offering prayers and acts of love (*The Instructor*, Chapter 8). Origen (c. AD 184–253) also follows his predecessors' teachings; additionally, in his *Exhortation to the Martyrs*, he compares incense to demons' food.[17]

It was not until the fourth century when the use of incense infiltrated Christian worship in Syria as a sin-offering before the other Churches in the East employed it, and from there, penetrated the West. In the fourth and fifth centuries, Christian writers ceased to express their disapprobation toward the use of incense in worship; however, the honorific use of it was accepted.[18] The first recorded incidence of

---

[14] Wybrew, Hugh. (1992). The Setting of the Liturgy—Ceremonial. In Cheslyn Jones, Geoffrey Wainwright, Edward Yarnold SJ and Paul Bradshaw (Eds.), *The Study of Liturgy*, 486.
[15] Atchley, Ibid., 92.
[16] Atchley, Ibid., 81, 82.
[17] Atchley, Ibid., 85.
[18] Davies, J.G., *A New Dictionary of Liturgy & Worship*, 265.

Christian use of incense comes from Alexandria, in AD 313, in a funeral procession—not in a worship service—of Martyr-Bishop Peter of Alexandria, the 17th patriarch of the See of Saint Mark.[19] Saint John Chrysostom, Hilary of Arles, Gregory of Tour, Paulinus of Nola, and others alluded to the honorific use of incense.[20] By the sixth century, incense was also utilized as a sacrificial offering, not only in the East but also in the West.[21]

In Christianity, offering of incense, although colored with ceremonial splendor characteristics, is a form of prayer. The book of Psalms says, "May my prayer be set before You like incense" (Psalm 141:2). Similarly, Saint John the Beloved attests, "The smoke of the incense, with the prayers of the saints, ascended before God from the angel's hand" (Revelation 8:4). Therefore, in the East, incense was given a propitiatory significance; it is understood that incense, offered before God's throne, is escorted by the prayers of the saints. It is also a symbol of the acceptable offerings before the Lord, just as the priest prays in the Litany of Offerings saying, "Remember O Lord the sacrifices, the offerings, and the thanksgivings of those who have offered to honor and glory of Your holy name. Receive them upon Your holy, rational altar of heaven as a sweet savor of incense."[22]

The practice of incense offering in Vespers and Prime finds its roots in Judaism, in which incense was burned every evening and morning before the Altar of Incense. This took place in the Tabernacle,[23] and later in the Temple of Jerusalem.[24] However, this practice was not exercised in

---

[19] Migne, Jacques-Paul, *Patrologia Graeca*, Vol. 18, 465.
[20] Atchley, Ibid., 100-105.
[21] Davies, Ibid., 265; Atchley, Ibid., 117.
[22] Salib, Abdel Massieh (Hegumen), *The Holy Euchologion*, 70.
[23] Exodus 30:7-8, 34-38, 37:29.
[24] 2 Chronicles 13:11, Leviticus 16:12-13.

a Christian context until the turn of the third century.[25] Based on its original Judaic roots, and its Christian layout, the rite of Offering of Incense is independent from the liturgy; that is, it has a beginning and an end, and can be prayed whether or not a liturgy is to follow. Eusebius of Caesarea writes, "What glorifies God's power in all the world's churches is praising Him with hymns and praises with all spiritual joy in the morning at dawn and in the evening at sunset, because God takes pleasure in the hymns that are offered to Him from his Church in every corner of the earth, at day and at evening."[26]

It seems that first-century devotional Christians, as indicated in the New Testament book of Acts, used to pray at the Temple on a daily basis (Acts 2:26), and at synagogues after the destruction of the Temple.[27] Due to both persecution, and ascetic conceptions, these gatherings became private, at homes.[28] The third-century *Apostolic Tradition* urges Christians to assemble for prayer before going to work: "The faithful, as soon as they wake up and have risen, before beginning work, shall pray to God, and then hurry to their work" (*Ap. Trad.* 35). This is not to be understood as a private prayer, but rather a communal one as the first-century Pliny the Younger indicates. Speaking of Christians, Pliny states, "were accustomed to meet on a fixed day before dawn and sing responsively a hymn to Christ as a god, and to bind themselves by oath." [29] The fourth century *Apostolic Constitutions* urges people in the following manner: "When you instruct the people, O bishop, command and exhort them to come constantly to church morning and evening every day, and by no means to forsake it on

---

[25] McGowan, Andrew B., *Ancient Christian Worship*, 113.
[26] Eusebius of Caesarea (AD 260/265-339/340) was a Church historian. He became the bishop of Caesarea in AD 314. He was a scholar of the Biblical canon and is regarded as an extremely well learned Christian of his time.
[27] Baumstark, Anton, *On the Historical Development of the Liturgy*, 53.
[28] Baumstark, *On the Historical*, Ibid., 55, 58.
[29] McGowan, Andrew B., *Ancient Christian Worship*, 188, 226.

any account, but to assemble together continually; neither to diminish the Church by withdrawing themselves, and causing the body of Christ to be without its member ... assemble yourselves together every day, morning and evening, singing psalms and praying in the Lord's house" (Ap. Const. 2:59). Hence, daily, prior to going to work, Copts continued this tradition of going to their local parishes early in the morning to participate in the Prime Offering of Incense service, and after work, returning to the parish for Vespers Offering of Incense before heading back home.[30]

In other words, incense offering has always been an independent rite regardless of whether a liturgy is to follow. This is further supported by the writings of the prominent 14th century scholar, Father Shams Al-Riyasa Abu Al-Barakat, also known as Ibn Kabar.[31] In his book, *The Lamp to Darkness and Explanation of the Service*, Ibn Kabar states, "The morning and vesper hours were reserved for the offering of incense, particularly in the morning, for it is important for every church to offer incense every day, regardless of whether or not a liturgy is to follow."[32] In the 15th century, however, Prime Offering of Incense became an optional routine unless followed by a liturgy.[33] While it is preferable to pray Vespers as well, it is not a prerequisite to celebrate the liturgy. The autonomy of the Prime Offering of Incense office remained preserved until at least the 18th century. Hence, in his AD 1735 Euchologion, Raphael Tuki at the

---

[30] Ibn Al-'Assal, Abu Is-haq Ibn Fadlallah, *The Fundamental Acts of the Ecclesiastical Etiquette (The Liturgy)*, published by Archdeacon Girgis Philotheos Awad, 20.

[31] Ibn Kabar was a 14th century scholar priest. His father is *Hegumen* Al-Asaad Ibrahim. Before priesthood, Ibn Kabar was a secretary of the Minister and Muslim historian al-Mansuri Baybars. In AD 1300, he was ordained priest by the name of "Barsum". He served at the church of Saint Mary, also referred to as "Hanging Church," which at the time, was the Papal residence. Father Barsum (Ibn Kabar) died in died in AD 1324.

[32] Ibn Kabar, *The Lamp to Darkness and Explanation of the Service*, BnF, MS Arabic 203 (c. AD 1363-1369), fol. 198v.

[33] Athanasius of Saint Macarius Monastery (Father), *Summary of the Liturgical History of the Church of Alexandria (Part 2)*, 217.

conclusion of Prime Offering of Incense instructs, "If a liturgy is not to follow, it is said 'Go in peace, the Lord be with you all.'"[34]

Assembling in the morning before going to work was an immemorial observance reported by many ancient sources. The author of the *Apostolic Traditions*, in the third century, encourages, or rather instructs, the faithful, "early in the morning, as soon as they have awaked and arisen, before they undertake their tasks shall pray to God and so may then go to their duties. But if any instruction in the word is held, let each give first place to that, that he may attend and hear the word of God, to his soul's comfort; so, let each one hurry to the church, where the Spirit abounds." In another place, more particulars were offered, "When the teacher finishes his instruction, the catechumens shall pray by themselves, apart from the believers.... And when [the catechumens] finish their prayers, they must not give the kiss of peace, for their kiss is not yet pure. Only believers shall salute one another.... At the close of their prayer, when their instructor lays his hand upon the catechumens, he shall pray and dismiss them; whoever gives the instruction is to do this, whether a cleric or a layman." [35] Although this early testimony provides evidence of the gathering of both believers and catechumens at dawn, it lacks details regarding the structure and content of the service. It, clearly, does not mention offering of incense yet prescribes edifying lessons of oratory characteristic proclaimed by talented expositors and mentors.

John Cassian,[36] who visited Egypt between AD 380 and 399, spoke about the Prime Prayers in Egypt in his work, *The Institutes*. He states that "some of the brethren who were ardent in spirit and in no slight measure

---

[34] Tuki, Raphael, *The Book of the Three Liturgies*, 157.
[35] McGowan, Andrew B., *Ancient Christian Worship*, 96-97.
[36] Saint John Cassian (AD 360–435) was a Christian monk and theologian celebrated in both the Western and Eastern Churches for his mystical writings. Cassian is noted for bringing the ideas and practices of Egyptian monasticism to the early medieval West.

disturbed by this carelessness, and it was determined by them after long discussion and anxious consideration that up till sunrise, when they could without harm be ready to read or to undertake manual labor, time for rest should be given to their wearied bodies, and after this they should all be summoned to the observance of this service and should rise from their beds, and by reciting three Psalms and prayers (after the order anciently fixed for the observance of Third and Sixth Hours, to signify the confession of the Trinity) should at the same time by a uniform arrangement put an end to their sleep and make a beginning to their work."[37]

Similarly, *The Canons of Hippolytus*[38] instructs, "Let the presbyters, deacons and readers and all the people be gathered together daily in church at cockcrow, and let them find leisure for prayer, for psalms and for reading of the Scriptures with prayers according to the command of the Apostle: 'Till I come give heed to reading.'[39] But as regards the clergy who neglect to come, being hindered neither by sickness nor travel, let them be excommunicated."[40] It seems that these early morning assemblies paved the way not only to the incense offering services, but also to the "Synaxis," the seed of what we call today the Liturgy of the Word.

The proper of Offering of Incense is considered a preparation stage for the Divine Liturgy. It consists of prayers, praises, and thanksgiving, asking for God's blessing over the service of the liturgy. In it, as a sign of humility and repentance, the priest—who represents the entire church—

---

[37] St. John Cassian, *The Institutes*, chapter 4.
[38] *The Canons of Hippolytus* is a Christian text composed of 38 decrees ("canons" or "regulations") of the genre of the Church Orders. The work has been dated to between AD 336 and 340. This collection of canons is preserved in an Arabic translation. The original text was Greek and written in Egypt; the Arabic version may depend on a Coptic translation. The author is unknown, though the work presents its author as "Hippolytus, the high/arch-bishop of Rome, according to the instructions of the Apostles."
[39] "Until I come, devote yourself to the public reading of Scripture, to preaching and to teaching." (1 Timothy 4:13).
[40] Canon 21 regarding the daily services in the Church.

stands outside the sanctuary, which resembles heaven, just as we say in the Third Hour litanies, "when we stand in Your holy sanctuary, we are considered as those standing in heaven." This rite expresses the status of humanity after the exile from Paradise. Accordingly, the priest opens the curtains with the cross, a proclamation that through the cross heaven was opened once again for us. While opening the curtain, the priest says, Ⲉⲗⲉⲏⲥⲟⲛ ⲏⲙⲁⲥ (Have mercy on us). As such, the commencement of the incense offering *Ordo* manifests our need to return to our first state in Paradise.

The fourth century marks a transitional point in Christian liturgical services; it is the time when monasticism flourished, and Christianity was initially accepted by the empire before it became the official religion of the state. These political and social developments triggered the public morning and evening services in both monastic and parochial lives. In the former, depending on the style of monastic life (i.e., eremitical, cenobitic, or lavriote), psalms were recited either privately or communally for the purposes of self-edification, contemplations, and spiritual growth. In this setting, which originated in the Egyptian deserts, all psalms are allowed—rather encouraged—to be uttered without specific appointment to certain hours of the day. In city churches, on the other hand, the emphasis was on praise, thanksgiving, and intercession. Particular psalms were assigned to specific hours as deemed appropriate, and congregational refrains were interpolated to engage the people as the main prayers were assigned to clergy and deacons.[41] Alexander Lingas suggests the following structure of the primitive morning and evening services according to the Cathedral[42] Office[43] (the rite emerged in the fourth century basilicas): Psalmody,

---

[41] Lingas, Alexander Leonidas, *Sunday Matins in the Byzantine Cathedral Rite*, 26-30.
[42] This nomenclature is attributed to Anton Baumstark.
[43] The regular public services of the church, other than the eucharist itself. See: Davies, J.G., *A New Dictionary of Liturgy and Worship*, 153.

Gloria in Excelsis Deo[44] (in the morning service) or *Nunc Dimittis*[45] (in the evening service), litanies, Prayer of Inclination, and Dismissal.[46]

From this succinct description, the illation suggesting monastic origin for the Canonical Hours and parochial (or Cathedral) roots for incense offering offices can be accepted.[47] Over time, monasteries incorporated the praise and thanksgiving into their services, while city churches integrated the psalms into theirs. Hence, redundant prayers can be found in the contemporary offices. For example, in the morning service, during the Prime Hour of the Liturgy of the Hours, the *Gloria in Excelsis Deo* followed by the Creed are recited. Yet, during Prime Offering of Incense, the same sequence is repeated. This is also similarly the case for the Trisagion, "Hail to you," "We magnify you O Mother of the True Light," and the Thanksgiving prayer. These redundancies were caused by the consolidation of both monastic and Cathedral rites in the simple manner of successive addition (psalms then incense offering) instead of reorganization or restructuring of the newly amalgamated office. In the same manner, the evening service also includes similar redundancies originated from the Compline Hour and Vespers Offering of Incense, namely, the Thanksgiving Prayer, "Graciously accord O Lord," the Trisagion, "Hail to you," "We magnify you, O Mother of the True Light," and the Creed.

As for the origin of how Vespers Offering of Incense developed, Father Matthew the Poor suggests that it was a replacement of the evening

---

[44] Latin for "Glory to God in the highest," a prayer inspired by Luke 2:14. In the Coptic Church, it commences with "Let us praise with the angels."

[45] Latin for "Now let depart," a prayer borrowed from Luke 2:29-32. Also known as the Song of Simeon.

[46] Lingas, Alexander Leonidas, *Sunday Matins in the Byzantine Cathedral Rite*, 30.

[47] Grisbrooke, W. Jardine. (1992). The Formative Period-Cathedral and Monastic Offices. In Cheslyn Jones, Geoffrey Wainwright, Edward Yarnold SJ and Paul Bradshaw (Eds.), *The Study of Liturgy*, 405.

Eucharist prayers.[48] In the early centuries, Christians used to meet at house-churches, accompanied by a bishop, or a priest (at a later date). A liturgy was prayed swiftly, analogous to that instituted by our Lord on Covenant Thursday, followed by a communal meal ("Agape"[49]). In later years, especially after the Edict of Milan in AD 313, the church combined the evening liturgy to the existing lengthier one in the morning and dedicated the Vespers Offering of Incense for the evenings. Isaac the Syrian[50] states that, in Egypt, after the departure of Saint Macarius the Great, who departed in AD 391, the Saturday evening liturgy was eliminated and only Vespers was prayed instead.[51] "After the conquest of Egypt by the Muslims, during the occasional outbreaks of persecution," De Lacy Evans O'Leary writes, "it was frequently difficult to attend celebration of the Eucharistic Liturgy; the Divine Office had never passed outside the monasteries; and so it became a common custom for lay persons to read at home the appointed lessons, censing the book used after the manner of the Priest and Deacon at the Eucharist. Thus arose the service of Daily Incense as a substitute for the Liturgy."[52]

Before delving into an exhaustive study of the incense offering prayers, I will summarize first the modern *order* practiced today. Vespers Offering of Incense is almost identical to that of Prime. In both, the prayer starts with the Thanksgiving Prayer, in an apparent message from the Church to her populace that everything should be inaugurated with thanksgiving. The hymn of the Verses of Cymbals is then chanted. It consists of stanzas

---

[48] Matthew the Poor (Father), *Eucharist of the Lord's Supper*, 52.
[49] Agape (Greek: ἀγάπη), translated as "love: the highest form of love, especially brotherly love, charity; the love of God for man and of man for God." Christianity developed Agape as the love of God or Christ for humankind.
[50] Isaac the Syrian (AD 613–700) was a 7th-century Syriac Christian bishop and theologian best remembered for his written works on Christian asceticism. He was ordained bishop of Nineveh, the former capital of Assyria, but requested to abdicate after only five months.
[51] Kyrillos Kyrillos (Father), *The Three Liturgies in Parallel with Explanation*, 31.
[52] Rev. De Lacy O'Leary, B.D., *The Daily Office and Theotokia of the Coptic Church*, 70.

of veneration of our saints. It was named as such due to using the cymbals while chanting them, since this was not the norm for most of the hymns. Then the priest prays the litanies. In vespers, he prays the Litany of the Departed; and in prime, the litanies of the Sick and the Travelers. On Sundays and feasts, the Litany of the Oblations replaces the Litany of the Travelers, as the expectation is that the faithful are not travelling in these days. This rule has one exception, which is Saturdays. On Saturdays, in prime, the Litany of the Departed is prayed. In other words, the Litany of the Departed is prayed in vespers all year long, and in prime on Saturdays unless it is a Feast of the Lord. The Litany of the Sick is employed in prime every day except for Saturdays. The Litany of the Travelers is also used in prime every day except for Saturdays, Sundays, and the Feasts of the Lord. Finally, the Litany of the Oblations is prayed in prime on Sundays and feasts, or any day of the week, if the offertory is present.

Subsequently, the priest circuits the nave with the censer while the congregation recites prayers[53] followed by chanting the Doxologies. The priest then goes back to the sanctuary and prays The Prayer of Repentance (also called The Prayer of Confession). This ritual denotes that the priest collects the confessions of the people, to offer them before Christ on the altar. Then, after the Creed, asking for God's forgiveness, the priest holds a cross with three lit candles and prays Ⲫⲛⲟⲩϯ ⲛⲁⲓ ⲛⲁⲛ (O God have mercy on us). He then prays the Litany of the Gospel, which is followed by the reading of the Psalm and the Gospel. An appropriate responsory for the Gospel reading is then chanted. One thing to note: since vespers prayer is a preparation to the liturgy, the Gospel read in this service is related to that of the following-day liturgy; yet, it is still an independent rite. Afterward, the litanies are prayed followed by the conclusion. At the end of the

---

[53] In prime, these prayers are: the Gloria, the Trisagion, and the Lord's Prayer. In vespers, however, the Gloria is replaced with "Graciously accord O Lord."

incense offering prayer, the priest recites the absolution, for us to leave the church completely forgiven. The priest confirms our spiritual state through the absolution prayers at the end of each service. We shall now inspect the incense offering rite in more details.

The Canonical Hours

Vespers office commences with uttering the Psalms, which was originally practiced in the monasteries then was adopted by city churches, as mentioned previously. During the days of fasting with abstinence, Psalms of Vespers and Compline are recited; on the other days, Psalms of the Ninth Hour precede them. In the monasteries, the Psalms of the Veil[54] are appended. During the Fast of Nineveh and Lenten days from Monday to Friday, Vespers Offering of Incense is omitted, since the liturgy is celebrated late in the day.[55] As such, all Hours from Prime to Compline precede the liturgy. As for the Vespers Offering of Incense for the Feast of Nativity or the Feast of Theophany, if the liturgy of the *Paramony*[56] was celebrated late, and thus the Hours up to Compline were accomplished, the Psalms are omitted prior to the evening incense offering office. Conversely, in the case that the *Paramony* liturgy was celebrated early, which means the Psalms up to the Ninth Hour only were performed, then the Psalms of Vespers and Compline are uttered prior to the Vespers Psalmody.[57]

---

[54] The Prayer of the Veil found its way to the Church's liturgical services in the beginning of the 11th century. See: Athanasius of Saint Macarius Monastery (Father), *Summary of the Liturgical History of the Church of Alexandria (Part 2)*, 63.

[55] The exception to this rule is the first Monday and the last Friday of the Lent in which Vespers Offering of Incense is prayed. In this case, the Ninth, Vespers and Compline Hours are uttered.

[56] *Paramony* (Greek: παραμονή) is the fasting period preceding Christmas or Epiphany. It is observed as a strict fast period, which ranges from one to three days according to the Coptic Orthodox Church.

[57] In monasteries, the Veil Hour Psalms are added after the Compline Hour.

The priest inaugurates vespers prayer saying, Ⲡ̄ⲟ̄ⲓⲥ Ⲡ̄ⲟ̄ⲓⲥ ⲛⲁⲓ ⲛⲁⲛ. Ⲁ̄ⲗⲗⲏⲗⲟⲩⲓⲁ (O Lord have mercy on us. Alleluia[58]) followed by "Ϧⲉⲛ ⲫ̄ⲣⲁⲛ ⲙ̄Ⲫⲓⲱⲧ ⲛⲉⲙ Ⲡ̄ϣⲏⲣⲓ ⲛⲉⲙ ⲡⲓⲠⲛⲉⲩⲙⲁ ⲉ̄ⲑⲟⲩⲁⲃ ⲟⲩⲛⲟⲩϯ ⲛ̄ⲟⲩⲱⲧ ⳾ ⲁ̄ⲙⲏⲛ ⳾ ⲇⲟⲝⲁ Ⲡⲁⲧⲣⲓ ⲕⲉ Ⲩ̄ⲓ̄ⲱ ⲕⲉ ⲁ̄ⲅⲓⲱ Ⲡⲛⲉⲩⲙⲁⲧⲓ ⳾ ⲕⲉ ⲛⲩⲛ ⲕⲉ ⲁ̄ⲓ̄ ⲕⲉ ⲓⲥ ⲧⲟⲩⲥ ⲉ̄ⲱⲛⲁⲥ ⲧⲱⲛ ⲉ̄ⲱⲛⲱⲛ ⲁ̄ⲙⲏⲛ" (In the Name of the Father, the Son, the Holy Spirit, One God Amen, Lord have mercy, Lord bless Amen. Glory be to the Father, the Son, and the Holy Spirit, now and forever and unto the age of all ages, amen).[59] The Lord's Prayer, the Thanksgiving prayer, and Psalm fifty are then recited, respectively. Afterwards, the Psalms are distributed among the supplicants and inaudibly prayed. The Gospel and litanies, however, are recited aloud. In Regular Days or in Fast Days with no abstinence (as the case on Saturdays and Sundays of Lent), in Vespers, the Ninth Hour prefixes Vespers and Compline.[60]

Per the contemporary practice, after reciting the Psalms, the Vespers' Gospel and litanies, as well as the Compline Gospel and litanies are all read. In the past, however, this was not the case. Up until the 1960's, only the Gospel of the Compline Office was read aloud, followed by the prayer of "Graciously accord O Lord." The Gospel of the Vesper Hour was distributed with the Psalms. In addition, the litanies were omitted; in fact, the litanies for those Hours in particular were added at a much later time

---

[58] According to Davies, J.G., A *New Dictionary of Liturgy & Worship*, 4-5: "*Alleluia* comes to English through the Greek and Latin transliterations of the Hebrew phrase *Hallelu Yah*. The Hebrew is a plural imperative with, as object, the short form of the name of God (Yahweh): 'Praise Yah.' It was adopted in the Christian liturgy at an early date as an expression of joy and praise particularly suitable for Eastertide."

[59] According to Davies, J.G., A *New Dictionary of Liturgy & Worship*, 13: *Amen* is "a Hebrew word meaning 'firm.' In synagogue worship it served as a community response of assent and confirmation. In the Eucharist the *Amen* is especially noticeable as the people's response to the prayer of consecration and, in many liturgies, to the words of administration. It is, however, not only an assent but also a proclamation of faith."

[60] In Regular Day, only the Third and Sixth Hours are prayed before the liturgy, as it is celebrated early in the morning, and as such, the rest of the Hours are prayed before vespers. In Fast Days that do not hold restrict abstinence, the liturgy commences in the Ninth Hours, which means that the Third, Sixth, and Ninth Hours precede the liturgy, which in turn, means that only Vespers and Compline Hours are said prior to Vespers. In Fast Days with restrict abstinence, where the liturgies are celebrated late, at Sunset, all Hours are prayed prior to the liturgy.

(19th century) compared to those of the other offices. Over time, the Church embraced the reading of the Vespers Hour Gospel just before that of the Compline's. Later, the Vespers Hour litanies were also read audibly, as it is practiced today.[61]

Prior to commencing the Midnight Psalmody, the three watches of the Midnight Office are uttered. In Prime Prayers, the Prime Office precedes the *Adam* Morning Doxology. Note that on the nocturnal feasts: Nativity, Theophany, and Resurrection, the Canonical Hours are omitted (the night before the feast day). On these feasts, the liturgy is celebrated around midnight, and since Canonical Hours should align with the time of the day,[62] they would have been observed in the preceding day (Nativity or Theophany Paramony, or Bright Saturday).

Vespers Psalmody

After reciting the Canonical Hours, Vespers Psalmody commences. For Prime prayers, on the other hand, the three watches of the Midnight Office are uttered, followed by the Midnight Psalmody. The Prime Office is then prayed followed by the *Adam* Morning Doxology. As mentioned earlier, Vespers Psalmody and Vigil offices are Cathedral rites, that is, having originated in city churches.

The Vespers Psalmody begins with the hymn Ⲛⲓⲉⲑⲛⲟⲥ ⲧⲏⲣⲟⲩ (All you nations), which is Psalm 116 with a glorification for the Holy Trinity appended to it. The meaning of this hymn is "Glory to our God, praise the Lord all you nations, praise the Lord all you people, for His mercy is confirmed upon us, and the truth of the Lord endures forever, Alleluia.

---

[61] Athanasius of Saint Macarius Monastery (Father), *The Prayers of Incense Offering in Vespers and Prime*, 320.

[62] For example, during the fasts, since the liturgy is usually celebrated late, the Third, Sixth, and Ninth Offices are prayed. Also, during the Fast of Nineveh and Lent (Monday through Friday) we pray up until the Compline Hour (and Veil in monasteries).

Glory be to the Father, the Son and the Holy Spirit, now and forever and unto the age of all ages, Amen."

After this, the Lauds Psalms (Psalms 148–150), referred to in the Coptic Rite as the Fourth Canticle, is chanted. The last section of this hymn, Ⲡⲓⲱⲟⲩ ⲫⲁ Ⲡⲉⲛⲛⲟⲩϯ ⲡⲉ (Glory be to our God), is optionally intoned in a melismatic melody known as *Alleluia of the Golden Hour* (Arabic: أللي العصر). This hymn is particularly chanted during the month of Kiahk but can still be sung in Regular Days if time permits. It is worth noting that there is a rare tune for the Fourth Canticle specific to the Kiahk Vespers Psalmody, while there is another for Lent. These melodies were transmitted by Cantor Habeeb Hanna Al-Merahem, who served at Saint Mark's Cathedral in Alexandria in the 20th century.

Up to this point, the tune is the same in all the days of the week. Conversely, starting from the Psaly,[63] hymns are recited in one of two musical modes, "*Adam*" and "*Watos*," respectively from the opening words of the Monday and Wednesday Theotokions.[64] The former is used for Sundays, Mondays and Tuesdays whereas the latter is assigned to the rest of the week. The *Watos* stanza has longer lines than that of the *Adam* counterpart.

In Regular Days (non-seasonal), after the Fourth Canticle, the Psaly proper for the day of the week is recited. There are seven Psalies, each of which is dedicated for a specific day of the week. Nevertheless, in the Sunday Vespers Psalmody, a Psaly for the Virgin, Ⲁⲓⲥⲱⲧⲉⲙ (I heard), is recited right before the Saturday Psaly. In Fast and Feast Days, the Psaly particular to the occasion is chanted in lieu of the one for the day of the week. As already noted, the melody for the Psaly is dependent on the day

---

[63] The Psalies and Theotokions are going to be discussed in greater detail later in this book, when we examine the Midnight Psalmody.
[64] The opening word of the Monday Theotokion is "Ⲁⲇⲁⲙ," which means Adam, and that of the Thursday one is "ⲡⲓⲃⲁⲧⲟⲥ," meaning "The fiery (or blazing) bush."

of the week, whether *Watos* or *Adam*. For instance, during Sunday Vespers Psalmody, the Saturday Psaly is recited in the *Watos* tune; nevertheless, it follows the *order* of the following day (Sunday, in this case). As such, if the following day is a Major Feast of the Lord, the Psaly is chanted in the Joyous tune, not the Year-Round one.[65]

After the Psaly, the Theotokion of the day is chanted. Like the Psalies, there are seven Theotokions, one for each day of the week. There is also a specific tune for the *Adam* days which differs from that for the *Watos* days. Unlike the Psalies, there are no Theotokions particular to the ecclesiastical seasons; therefore, the same seven Theotokions are used all year round. It should be noted that on the Monday Vespers Psalmody (Sunday evening), in most parishes, as a way of shortening the service, the Sunday Theotokion is not recited in its entirety. Instead, it is recited starting from the 11th part (**Ⲣⲁⲛ ⲛⲓⲃⲉⲛ ⲉⲧϭⲟⲥⲓ**—All the high names), which is considered by many manuscripts as the conclusion of the Sunday Theotokion.[66] Following the Theotokion, its *Lobsh* is chanted in either the *Watos* or *Adam* tune. The Theotokion *Lobsh* can be intoned in a melismatic or minor tune. There are also different melodies specific to the ecclesiastical season (i.e., Kiahk, Feasts of the Lord, Lent, Feasts of the Cross and Palm Sunday).

After this, the *Watos* or *Adam* Exposition Introduction is chanted. During Regular Days, this is followed by a reading from the Antiphonary; however, on ecclesiastical occasions, a suitable Exposition, which still follows the melody of the Antiphonary, is read instead. The word "Antiphonary" comes from the Greek word $αντίφωνο$ or the Latin word *antiphonarium*, which came from the Greek "$ἀντιφωνάριον$." The name

---

[65] For example, in Palm Sunday Vespers Psalmody, although the Psaly is recited in the *Watos* tune (following the Saturday *order*), it employs the Joyous tune attributable to the following day (Palm Sunday).
[66] Rev. De Lacy O'Leary , B.D., *The Daily Office and Theotokia of the Coptic Church*, 126.

stems from how it is delivered; two choruses hymn its lines antiphonally or alternate the singing. The Antiphonary, which encompasses a biography of the saints, is chanted on Regular Days. These stories are similar to those in the Synaxarion but written in a more abbreviated, poetic form. During Feasts and Fast Days, the Exposition is read instead. Although the Exposition and the Antiphonary share the same melody, the lyrics of the former are in relation to the ecclesiastic event in celebration. The first printed Antiphonary was published in AD 1920.

The Antiphonary is read during three rites: The Vespers Psalmody, The Veneration Service, and the Midnight Psalmody. In both psalmodies, it is recited between the Theotokion and its conclusion. The Antiphonary has an *Adam* and *Watos* Introduction. The *Adam* Introduction is used on Sundays, Mondays, and Tuesdays, whereas the *Watos* one is employed in the rest of the week. The *Adam* Introduction consists of four stanzas and is chanted in two tunes; a short tune that is prevalent in Cairo and Alexandria, and a longer one, which is predominant in Upper Egypt. The last two stanzas of the *Adam* tune can be chanted in a melismatic tune (**Ⲟⲩⲟⲛ ⲟⲩϩⲉⲗⲡⲓⲥ ⲛ̀ⲧⲁⲛ**—We have hope, in Saint Mary). The *Watos* Introduction, on the other hand, consists of two quatrains only, and its tune is faster than the *Adam* one. However, in the month of Kiahk and during Lent, on Sunday Vespers Psalmody, the *Watos* Introduction of the Exposition is intoned in a melismatic tune.

Similar to the introduction, the Antiphonary/Exposition is chanted in either the *Watos* or *Adam* tune. The tune, however, follows the *order* of the next day, whether it is Joyous, for Palm Sunday and the Feasts of the Cross, or Year-Round. In the month of Kiahk and during the Lent, the *Watos* Exposition Introduction is intoned in its melismatic tune. It is chanted on the Eve of Sunday (Saturday Night). It is noteworthy that there is also a Joyous tune for the Exposition Introduction employed for festive days. Afterwards, depending on the day of the week, the Conclusion of the *Adam* or *Watos* Theotokions is recited. The service is then concluded with the Lord's Prayer.

With regards to the Prime psalmody, after the completion of the Prime Office, the *Adam* Morning Doxology is recited, followed by Ⲛⲉⲕⲛⲁⲓ ⲱ̇ Ⲡⲁⲛⲟⲩϯ (Your mercies O my God), the Conclusion of the *Adam* Theotokions. Note that the *Adam* Morning Doxology is chanted every day of the week, regardless of its categorization, *Watos* or *Adam*. The reason being is that the word "*Adam*" in this context is in reference to the chant's musical length, not the day on which it is sung. A similar concept is the *Watos* and *Adam Aspazmos* hymns,[67] which are also chanted all year long regardless of the day of the week. Generally, the *Adam* stanza has less syllable-counts in its lines compared to that of the *Watos* one.

So far, we examined the first two parts of the Prime and Vespers prayers. The first is the Canonical Offices, which originated from the monastic tradition; and was eventually adopted by the city churches. The second is the psalmody, which unlike the Psalms, rooted in the cities and was later accepted by the monasteries. The third and last part of Vespers/Prime prayers, which is by far the most significant one, is the *offering of incense*. The *ordo* of Vespers/Prime Offering of Incense is also Cathedral—among the features of the Cathedral Office are incense, processions, lights, responsories, antiphons, and chants, which are all present in the incense offering proper—however, was later adopted by the

---

[67] The concept of *Adam* and *Watos Aspazmos* hymns appears in the liturgy and will be discussed further later in this book.

monasteries.[68] In the following pages, we will examine the *order* of this rite in substantial detail.

The Beginning of the Incense Offering

The Incense Offering prayer is performed outside the altar, like in the Tabernacle, where the Altar of Incense was in front of the Veil and outside the Holy of Holies (Exodus 40:26, 27). As previously mentioned, incense offering is a preparation of and an introduction to the liturgy; and hence, we stand in deep reverence and genuine contrition outside the altar before entering the Holy of Holies in the Divine Liturgy. The Psalms and the psalmody are recited while the veil of the sanctuary is shut. However, once ready for the offering of incense, the priest pulls the veil and commences the prayers in utmost sobriety. After the psalmody, one of the altar servers prepares the thurible and lights up the altar candles. Upon his arrival, according to rubrics, the priest washes his feet, reveals his head, and greets his brethren the priests. In his *The Priesthood Order,* Severus Ibn Al-Muqaffaʿ from the 10th century prescribes that the priest must wash his feet prior to entering the sanctuary,[69] a practice that is echoed by the 13th century scholar Ibn Sibaa, who draws parallels between this tradition and the Old Testament instructions given to Aaron and his successor priests to wash their hands and feet before offering a sacrifice (Exodus 30:17-21).[70]

Revealing the head is also an ancient tradition in the Coptic Church, which was well-documented in the Coptic ritual literature; the earliest

---

[68] Grisbrooke, W. Jardine. (1992). The Formative Period-Cathedral and Monastic Offices. In Cheslyn Jones, Geoffrey Wainwright, Edward Yarnold SJ and Paul Bradshaw (Eds.), *The Study of Liturgy*, 407-408.
[69] Severus Ibn Al-Muqaffaʿ, *The Priesthood Order*, Julius Assfalg, 39-40 (fol. 150v-r).
[70] Ibn Sibaa, *The Precious Pearl: On Ecclesiastic Science*, BnF, MS Arabic 207, fol. 117v.

reference was made by Severus Ibn Al-Muqaffaʿ.[71] In his second canon, Pope Christodoulos, the 66th Patriarch of Alexandria, who lived in the 11th century, states that "no one should enter the parish expect bare foot, with his head exposed."[72] This regulation was also reiterated in the 33rd canon of Pope Cyril II.[73] The hat of the priest symbolizes his grandeur among his people; but since the Offering of Incense is a prayer of penitence and repentance whereby the priest and the laity, alike, plead for God's mercy so that He may forgive their sins, the priest therefore, in humility before the Lord, removes his hat. This practice is simply mirroring the heavenly church, where "whenever the living creatures give glory, honor and thanks to Him who sits on the throne and who lives for ever and ever, the twenty-four priests fall down before Him who sits on the throne and worship Him who lives for ever and ever. They lay their crowns before the throne." (Revelation 4:9, 10). In other words, the priest exposes his head not only as a sign of repentance and regret for his own and his people's sins, but also as an expression of glorification and honor to our Lord and King Jesus Christ on His throne.

The 17th canon by Pope Gabriel II,[74] who lived in the 12th century, states that the priest should "stand around the altar at the time of prayer

---

[71] Severus Ibn Al-Muqaffaʿ, *The Priesthood Order*, Julius Assfalg, 40 (fol. 150r).
[72] Athanasius of Saint Macarius Monastery (Father), *Canons of the Coptic Church Patriarchs in the Middle Ages*, 35.
[73] Ibid., 63.
[74] Pope Gabriel II was the 70th Pope of Alexandria and Patriarch of the See of Saint Mark (AD 1131–1145). He was from the nobles of Cairo, and was a writer, scribe, and scholar. He transcribed many Arabic and Coptic books. His original name was (أبو العلا صاعد بن تريك). He was enthroned as the Pope of Alexandria on February 3, 1131 AD. He made a lot of enhancements to the prayers of the Passion Week and put them in booked called "The Holy Pascha." He also published three books on the Church canons. When he was first enthroned, he prayed a liturgy at the monetary of Saint Macarius; in the last Confession prayer, he added the phrase "He made it one with His divinity," but the monks of the monetary refused the addition. They discussed it with him and decided to change the phrase to "He made it one with His divinity without mingling, without confusion, and without alteration." So, he ordered all churches in Egypt to you this phrase. Pope Gabriel II is also the one who limited the use of liturgies in the Coptic Church to the three liturgies that are in use today.

bareheaded and in fear of God to listen or respond."[75] Ibn Kabar, who lived in the 14th century, also mentions this practice as a given.[76] In his book *The Ritual Order*,[77] which was published in AD 1411, Pope Gabriel V[78] states, "after a priest exposes his head and greets his brethren the priests..."[79] Likewise, Euchologions MS Lit. 147 (18th C.),[80] and MS Lit. 133 (19th C.)[81] attest to this inveterate practice.[82] Similar instruction can be found in *The Church Order* MS Not Numbered (AD 1514) of the Paromeos Monastery.[83] This tradition was transmitted from one generation to the next until it made it to the Coptic Sacramentary (Euchologion), which is in use today. In it, at the outset of the Offering of Incense, it instructs, "the priest shall expose his head and stand before the door of the sanctuary."[84] Similarly, *The Church Order*, MS Lit. 117 (AD 1910), preserved at the Old Patriarchate in Cairo, also indicated, "The Patriarch shall expose his head, and proceed inside the sanctuary. The rest of the priests will also expose their heads and follow him inside, after which the Prayer of Thanksgiving commences."[85] This document further instructs that "if the Patriarch is

---

[75] Gabriel Ibn Turaik, *Canons* (First Series), Edited and translated by O.H.E. Burmester, "The Canons of Gabriel Ibn Turaik, LXX Patriarch of Alexandria," 5-45.
[76] Ibn Kabar, *The Lamp to Darkness and Explanation of the Service*, BnF, MS Arabic 203 (c. AD 1363-1369), fol. 200r.
[77] Father Basilios Sobhy suggests that the author of this book, or at least a huge influencer of it, is *Hegumen* Jeremiah the Scribe, who lived in the 15th century; however, the work is attributed to the Pope of the time (Gabriel V). It is worth mentioning that *Hegumen* Jeremiah the Scribe is the biological father of the well-known Cantor—and later priest—Sarkis. For more details, see Sobhy, Basilios (Father), *Introduction to the History of the Coptic Rites*, 26. A more recent study suggests that *The Beginners' Guide and Discipline for Laity* as a source for both *The Ritual Order*, and the notes transcribed by Jeremiah the Scribe; see Misael of the Paromeos Monastery (Father). (2020). The Trinitarian Mystery in Priesthood Ministry. *Alexandria School*, 28(1), 103.
[78] The 88th Pope of Alexandria (AD 1409–1427).
[79] Gabriel V (Pope), *The Ritual Order*, BnF, MS 98 (AD 1411), fol. 32r.
[80] It reads, "Once the priest reveals his head... he must first clear his mind completely."
[81] "When the priest reveals his head, he first greets his brethren the priests."
[82] Athanasius of Saint Macarius Monastery (Father), *The Prayers of Incense Offering in Vespers and Prime*, 332.
[83] Samuel (Bishop), *The Church Order*, Part 1, 13.
[84] El-Massoudy, Abdel Messih (Hegumen), *The Holy Euchologion*, 17. All later printed Sacramentaries copied the same note, although this practice is now ignored.
[85] *The Church Order*, Cairo, Patriarchal Library, MS Lit. 117 (AD 1910), fol. 18v.

present at the Vespers and does not reveal his head, then he permits one of the priests to begin with the Thanksgiving prayer."[86] This suggests that head-exposing is a prerequisite necessary for administering the prayer.

The priest then utters, "Ⲉ̇ⲗⲉⲏⲥⲟⲛ ⲏ̄ⲙⲁⲥ ..." which means "Have mercy on us, O God, the Father the *Pantocrator*[87] (All-Mighty). All-Holy Trinity, have mercy on us. O Lord, God of hosts, be with us, for we have no helper in our tribulations and afflictions but You." While praying these words, he (the priest) pulls the veil of the sanctuary, and then leads the congregation in reciting the Lord's Prayer. Once finished, the chorus intones Ϧⲉⲛ Ⲡⲓⲭ̅ⲣⲓⲥⲧⲟⲥ Ⲓⲏⲥⲟⲩⲥ Ⲡⲉⲛϭⲟⲓⲥ (In Christ Jesus our Lord), which is the concluding sentence of the Lord's Prayer. This conclusion can be intoned in two ways: The Year-Round tune during the Regular and Fast Days, and the Joyous tune on the Major Feasts of the Lord, the Feasts of the Cross, the period in which the Coptic New Year is celebrated, and whenever the festive tune is used.

After this, the priest prostrates before the altar and kisses its edge, just as Pope Gabriel V directs.[88] Youhanna Ibn Abie Zakaria (also known as Ibn Sibaa), states, "the priest prostrates once on any day of the week except on Sunday. On Sundays and any major feast, the priest not only prostrates, but bow in complete worship three times."[89] As the priest prostrates, he prays, "We worship you O Christ and the Holy Spirit for you have come and saved us." After this, he prostrates before the other priests asking them for their blessing. This is followed by another prostration toward the altar

---

[86] Ibid., fol. 24r.
[87] Pantocrator (Παντοκράτωρ) is a compound word formed from the Greek words πᾶς, pas (GEN παντός pantos), i.e., "all" and κράτος, kratos, i.e., "strength," "might," "power." This is often understood in terms of potential power, i.e., ability to do anything. Originally "Pantocrator" came from the Old Testament. When the Hebrew Bible was translated into Greek as the Septuagint, Pantocrator was used both for YHWH Sabaoth "Lord of Hosts" and for El Shaddai "God Almighty".
[88] Gabriel V (Pope), *The Ritual Order*, BnF, MS 98 (AD 1411), fol. 32r.
[89] Ibn Sibaa, *The Precious Pearl: On Ecclesiastic Science*, published by Father Victor Mansour the Franciscan, chapter 62, 177-178.

servers and the people while saying, "A *metania*,⁹⁰ forgive me." Ibn Kabar prescribes that the priest prostrates toward the deacons⁹¹ first then toward the congregation,⁹² a practice that is also supported by Ibn Sibaa.⁹³ Concerning the prostration to the other priests, Pope Gabriel V writes, "The priest shall look to the right of the altar and offer a prostration."⁹⁴ The reason for this is that at the time, assistant priests used to stand at the right-side of the altar. Today, nonetheless, this practice is not necessarily followed; thus, the celebrant no longer needs to turn to the right. Following the prostration to the people, the priest approaches the rest of the priests and greets them. Some priests address the congregation saying, "I have sinned, forgive me," which is an addition that is not found in the older instructions. Asking for forgiveness at the onset of the prayer, however, has its roots in the New Testament, "And when you stand praying, if you hold anything against anyone, forgive him, so that your Father in heaven may forgive you your sins" (Mark 11:25).

After that, the priest returns and stands before the altar. Holding a cross, the altar server stands behind the priest to his right. The priest then calls for the altar server to initiate the prayer; he says, Ϣⲗⲏⲗ (Pray).⁹⁵ The altar server then instructs the worshippers saying, Ἐπι προσευχη στάθητε (Stand up for prayer). The priest then looks to the other priests and says,

---

⁹⁰ *Metania* (Greek μετάνοια) is performed by first making the Sign of the Cross; then, one bends from the waist, reaches toward the floor with the right hand open and facing outward, and touches the ground. It is used as the substitute for the prostration when it is normally prescribed, but not permitted by the Canons of the Church. Metanias are usually performed as a way of expressing respect and reverence to icons and clergy for blessing.

⁹¹ Deacons for Ibn Kabar, as well as for other medieval scholars and historians, refers to the rank of "full deacon," not just altar servers as practiced today.

⁹² Ibn Kabar, *The Lamp to Darkness and Explanation of the Service*, BnF, MS Arabic 203 (c. AD 1363-1369), fol. 209r.

⁹³ Ibn Sibaa, *The Precious Pearl: On Ecclesiastic Science*, BnF, MS Arabic 207, fol. 118r.

⁹⁴ Gabriel V (Pope), *The Ritual Order*, BnF, MS 98 (AD 1411), fol. 32r.

⁹⁵ Paromaos Monastery, MS Canon 9 (13 or 14 C.) includes an important note that sheds light on the period during which this calling was introduced. The manuscript directs the priest to remind the Servant Deacon to instruct the people to stand up for prayer; this is only if the Servant Deacon is not attentive or negligent, otherwise, "Ϣⲗⲏⲗ" is not said. This means that until the 14ᵗʰ century, this calling was optional and out of necessity, for practical reasons.

Ⲉⲩⲗⲟⲅⲓⲧⲉ (Bless). In the event that only one Assistant Priest is present, the celebrant uses the singular form "Ⲉⲩⲗⲟⲅⲏⲥⲟⲛ" instead. The priest then faces the west and while making the sign of the cross, he greets the people saying Ἰⲣⲏⲛⲏ ⲡⲁⲥⲓ (Peace be with all). This opening was not mentioned in the original Liturgy of Saint Mark and was probably borrowed from the Liturgy of Saint James.[96] The congregation then answers, Ⲕⲉ ⲧⲱ ⲡⲛⲉⲩⲙⲁⲧⲓ ⲥⲟⲩ (And with your spirit).

Nowadays, we notice that many priests have combined the words "Ⲉⲩⲗⲟⲅⲏⲥⲟⲛ/Ⲉⲩⲗⲟⲅⲓⲧⲉ" with "Ϣⲗⲏⲗ" in one phrase; however, since "Ϣⲗⲏⲗ" is directed to the altar server while "Ⲉⲩⲗⲟⲅⲓⲧⲉ/Ⲉⲩⲗⲟⲅⲏⲥⲟⲛ" is addressed to the priests, it is ideal to say "Ⲉⲩⲗⲟⲅⲏⲥⲟⲛ/Ⲉⲩⲗⲟⲅⲓⲧⲉ" after the deacon's respond, and it should be uttered, not intoned. "Ἰⲣⲏⲛⲏ ⲡⲁⲥⲓ" is the standard opening greeting in East and West. This greeting is of Jewish origin and was used by the Risen Jesus; "Jesus came and stood among them and said, 'Peace be with you!'" (John 20:19). The response "Ⲕⲉ ⲧⲱ ⲡⲛⲉⲩⲙⲁⲧⲓ ⲥⲟⲩ" is also of Semitic roots, of which there is an echo in "The Lord be with your spirit. Grace be with you all." (2 Timothy 4:22). It is noteworthy that if the Patriarch or a bishop is present, the preist will say the opening greeting "Ἰⲣⲏⲛⲏ ⲡⲁⲥⲓ" without saying "Ⲉⲩⲗⲟⲅⲓⲧⲉ" since the blessing should be given by the high priest (the Patriarch or bishop).

The Thanksgiving Prayer

Following this, the priest recites the Thanksgiving Prayer, in which he makes the sign of the cross three times. When he says, "take them away from us," the priest turns toward the other priests and bow his head while crossing himself. When he says, "and from all Your people," he looks toward the west and makes the sign of the cross on the worshippers. In the

---

[96] Cuming, Geoffrey J., *The Liturgy of St Mark*, 77.

Vespers Offering of Incense, when he says, "and this holy place," the priest makes the sign of the cross on the altar. In the Prime Offering of Incense, however, he says, "this holy Church." This, in fact, is an indicative that, in antiquity, vespers prayers (or an older evening service) used to take place in house-churches, whereas prime was prayed in churches. After the priest says, "and all the power of the enemy," he continues the Thanksgiving prayer inaudibly. Upon completion, the priest prostrates and kisses the edge of the altar, as described by H.H. Pope Gabriel V.[97] In his Euchologion published in AD 1902, Father Abd El-Messih Al-Massoody of the Paromeos Monastery provides similar, yet different, instructions. He directs that the priest bows before the entrance of the sanctuary greeting its doorstep with his hand, then bows his head to the altar and kisses it.[98]

The Circuit of Incense and the Verses of Cymbals

Following this, from the right side of the altar, the altar server presents the censer to the priest, who then takes the Coffer of Incense with his right hand and looks to the other priests in attendance, bowing his head and saying, "Ⲉⲩⲗⲟⲅⲓⲧⲉ," which means "bless,"[99] to which they respond, Ⲛ̄ⲧⲟⲕ ⲉⲩⲗⲟⲩⲏⲥⲟⲛ (You bless), at which point the Servant Priest will return the Coffer of Incense on the altar, and crossing it he says, "In the Name of the Father, the Son and the Holy Spirit, One God." Severus Ibn Al-Muqaffaʿ illustrates that the priest will make the sign of the cross upon the Coffer of Incense,[100] an instruction that Pope Gabriel V also prescribes.[101] Though,

---

[97] Gabriel V (Pope), *The Ritual Order*, BnF, MS 98 (AD 1411), fol. 33r.
[98] Salib, Abdel Massieh (Hegumen), *The Holy Euchologion*, 30.
[99] If there is only one Assistant Priest present, the Servant Priest says, "Ⲉⲩⲗⲟⲩⲏⲥⲟⲛ," in the singular form.
[100] Severus Ibn Al-Muqaffaʿ, *The Priesthood Order*, Julius Assfalg, 41 (fol. 150v).
[101] Gabriel V (Pope), *The Ritual Order*, BnF, MS 98 (AD 1411), fol. 33r.

it is interesting to note that in his Euchologion, Father Abd El-Messih Al-Massoody guides that the priest places his finger on the Coffer of Incense while saying, "In the Name of the Father, the Son and the Holy Spirit, One God."[102] Placing the finger on the Coffer of Incense while uttering the Trinitarian opening prayer, or rather name, is an indicative of the sanctification of incense by the Triune God. Escorted with three crossings, the priest will then put five spoonful of incense in the thurible. With the first spoonful he says, "Blessed be God the Father the *Pantocrator* (All-Mighty), Amen." In the second time, he says, "Blessed be His Only-begotten Son, Jesus Christ our Lord, Amen." In the third, "Blessed be the Holy Spirit, the *Paraclete*,[103] Amen." After each of these crossings, one of the altar servers[104] affirms saying, "Amen."[105]

The Servant Priest then puts the fourth and fifth spoonful of incense in the thurible without making the sign of the cross, and proclaims, "Glory and honor, honor and glory to the all-Holy Trinity, the Father, the Son and the Holy Spirit, now and at all times and unto the age of all ages, Amen." The Litany of Vespers Offering of Incense, which is prayed after, makes mention of five acceptable sacrifices offered by Abel, Noah, Abraham, Aaron, and Zachariah, proposing a reason for the choice of five spoonful. Nevertheless, the most prevalent elucidation of the five spoonful of incense replaces Abraham with Melchizedek.[106] Father

---

[102] Salib, Abdel Massieh (Hegumen), *The Holy Euchologion*, 31.
[103] Paraclete (παράκлητος) means advocate or helper. The term Paraclete refers to the Holy Spirit.
[104] Severus Ibn Al-Muqaffa' assigns this response to the congregation. See: Severus Ibn Al-Muqaffa', *The Priesthood Order*, Julius Assfalg, 41 (fol. 151v).
[105] Salib, Abdel Massieh (Hegumen), *The Holy Euchologion*, 31.
[106] Mettaos (Bishop), *The Spirituality of the Rite of the Liturgy of the Coptic Orthodox Church*, 34-35; Benjemine, Said, Domadious Bebawy (Father), *The Spiritual Meanings of the Ritual Movements in the Divine Liturgy*, 13; and Benyamine (Metropolitan), *The Rite of the Divine Liturgy*, 18-19; he also mentions it in his notes for the Catechesis School. Father Zakaria, however, keeps Abraham as in the litany; See.: AL-Soriany, Zakaria (Hegumen), *The Spiritual Meanings of the Rite of the Divine Liturgy*, 28.

Simon Ibn Kuleil,[107] on the contrary, offers a different interpretation. He explains, "When the priest offers incense, he puts five handfuls: for the Nativity, the Cross, the Resurrection, the Ascension, and the Descent of the Holy Spirit, the Comforter; five springs outpour the victorious life."[108] Ibn Sibaa records a different practice of six handfuls of incense, three representing the Holy Trinity, and three resembling the offerings of Abel, Noah, and Isaac.[109]

If more than one priest is in attendance, all Assistant Priests will put the second spoonful of incense while saying, "Blessed be His Only-begotten Son, Jesus Christ our Lord, Amen," but the Servant Priest must put in the first and third spoonful of incense into the censer. In the presence of the Patriarch or a bishop, the priest will present the Coffer of Incense, while the altar server submits the thurible. The Patriarch or bishop makes the sign of the cross on the Coffer of Incense and places the first spoonful. He then gives the incense back to the priest to place the second spoonful. However, the priest this time will not make the sign of the cross while saying, "Blessed be His Only-Begotten Son, Jesus Christ our Lord, Amen." Afterwards, the high priest places the third spoonful of incense in the thurible and makes the third sign of the cross. Subsequently, with his right hand, the Servant Priest receives the thurible from the altar server, and, while holding a cross, he offers incense before the altar while inaudibly reciting the prayers of Prime or Vespers Offering of Incense.

The Litany of Vespers Offering of Incense is such a profound, solemn, and powerful prayer with multiple references from the Holy Bible. It reads,

---

[107] Makeen Simon Ibn Kuleil Ibn Makara Ibn Abie El-Farag (Arabic: مكين سمعان بن كليل بن مقاره بن الفرج) was a monk who lived in the twelfth century at the monastery of Saint John the Short. He used to work as a scribe in the army of Saladin (An-Nasir Salah ad-Din Yusuf ibn Ayyub) before joining the monastery, where he spent the rest of his life researching and studying the Scriptures. He had several publications containing the results of his study. He departed in the early years of the thirteenth century.
[108] Bebawi, George H., *The Divine Liturgy*, 165, 166.
[109] Ibn Sibaa, *The Precious Pearl: On Ecclesiastic Science*, BnF, MS Arabic 207, fol. 124v.

for example, "In every place, incense is offered to Your Holy Name, and a pure sacrifice." Interestingly, this is taken from the Old Testament "My name will be great among the nations, from the rising to the setting of the sun. In every place incense and pure offerings will be brought to my name, because my name will be great among the nations, says the Lord Almighty." (Malachi 1:11). In this litany, we also read, "We ask you, O our Master, receive our prayers to Yourself. Let our prayers be set forth before You as incense. The lifting of our hands as the evening sacrifice," which is remarkably similar to David the Prophet's prayer, "May my prayer be set before you like incense; may the lifting up of my hands be like the evening sacrifice." (Psalm 140:2). It continues, "For you are the true evening sacrifice, who has offered Yourself upon the honored Cross for our sins," a prayer that is inspired by the words of Saint Paul, "and live a life of love, just as Christ loved us and gave himself up for us as a fragrant offering and sacrifice to God." (Ephesians 5:2).

In Prime Offering of Incense, a different litany is used. It states, "O God, who received to Yourself the offerings of the righteous Abel, the sacrifice of Noah and Abraham, and the incense of Aaron and Zachariah, receive to Yourself this incense at the hands of us sinners, as a sweet savor of incense unto the remission of our sins and with the rest of Your people. For blessed and full of glory is Your Holy Name, O Father and Son and the Holy Spirit, now and at all times, and unto the age of all ages, Amen."

As prescribed by *The Church Order* MS Lit. 73 (AD 1444),[110] until the 15th century, these litanies were uttered aloud. During the circling around the altar, the Three Minor Litanies along with the people's responsory, "Lord, have mercy," were recited audibly. The Verses of

---

[110] *The Church Order*, Cairo, Patriarchal Library, MS Lit. 73 (AD 1444), fols. 177v-178r.

Cymbals then follows.[111] However, for the sake of time, the contemporary rubric prescribes that the chanting of the Verses of Cymbals and the performance of the Circuit of Incense are done in parallel. Thus, the litany of the incense for Vespers or Prime, and the Three Minor Litanies are recited soundlessly.

After the Litany of the Incense, while circumambulating the altar (starting from his right) three times, the priest recites the three Minor Litanies, which are the Litany of Peace, the Litany of the Fathers, and the Litany of the Assemblies. Throughout the circuit, the altar server stands on the opposite side, facing the priest, and holding a cross and the Gospel. This may also involve two altar servers, where one holds a cross, and the other holds the Gospel. Circling the altar while praying the litanies is to indicate that we, represented by the priest, intercede with the Sacrifice on the altar, the True Priest, so that our prayers and petitions may be accepted. The smoke coming out of the censer represents our accepted entreaties, supplications, and pleas that raise up before the Lord.

Facing east, the priest offers incense before the altar and prays the first part of the Litany of Peace saying, "We ask You, O our Master, remember, O Lord, the peace of Your one, only, holy, catholic, and apostolic Church." The altar server says the appropriate bidding. Then the priest kisses the altar or bows his head before it, and, facing south, he proceeds around the altar and completes the litany saying, "this which exists from one end of the world to the other." He continues the circuit to the east side of the altar. He looks toward the west and prays the Litany of the Fathers saying, "Remember, O Lord, our honored patriarch and father, the high priest, Pope Abba (...)," to which the altar server recites a bidding. Facing north,

---

[111] Athanasius of Saint Macarius Monastery (Father), *The Prayers of Incense Offering in Vespers and Prime*, 368-369.

the priest completes the Litany saying, "Keep them secure for us for many years and peaceful times," which marks the completion of the first round.

Now facing the east again, he continues to offer incense and prays the Litany of the Assemblies saying, "Remember, O Lord, our assemblies; bless them," after which the altar server recites a suitable bidding. The priest will face south and proceed to the east side of the altar saying, "Grant that they may be to us without obstacle or hindrance that we may hold them according to Your holy and blessed will." Now facing the west, the priest says, "houses of prayers, houses of purity, houses of blessing. Grant them to us, O Lord, and Your servants who will come after us, forever." The priest continues walking toward the west side of the altar while offering incense, and facing east, he prays "Arise, O Lord God, let all your enemies be scattered, and let all who hate your holy name flee before Your face." He then proceeds to the east side of the altar; facing west, while continuing to offer incense, he says, "But let Your people be in blessing, thousands of thousands, and ten thousand times ten thousand, doing Your will." At the end, the priest completes his third and final round to the west side of the altar; and facing east, he prays, "Through the grace, compassion and love-of-humankind of Your only-begotten Son, our Lord, God and Savior, Jesus Christ." After this, the priest kisses the altar, or bows his head before it, and exits the sanctuary with his left foot, while facing east. Note that the altar server(s) would have exited the sanctuary before the priest.

Facing east, the priest will thrice offer incense before the sanctuary, each time, bowing his head. In the first censing the priest prays, "We worship you, O Christ, with Your Good Father, and the Holy Spirit, for You have come and saved us." The second time, he continues, "But as for me, in the abundance of Your mercy, I will enter into Your house; I will bow down in worship toward Your holy temple." On the third censing, he says, "Before the angels, I will sing [praises] to You and worship toward

Your holy temple." Addressing Saint Mary, the priest censes northward where her icon is placed on the iconostasis, and says, "We send you greetings with Gabriel the angel, saying, 'Hail, O full of grace, the Lord is with you.'" He then censes toward the west saying, "Hail to the hosts of angels, my fathers the apostles, the martyrs, and the congregation of the saints." Facing south toward the icon of Saint John the Baptist, the priest offers incense saying, "Hail to John the son of Zachariah, Hail to the priest of the Most High." Finally, he faces the east again towards our Lord Jesus and prays, "We worship our Savior the good lover-of-humankind, for He had mercy on us and saved us."

As previously mentioned, in the early centuries, as documented in several old texts, during the Circuit of Incense, the Three Minor Litanies were recited audibly, after each the altar server responds with an appropriate request, and the supplicants give credence saying, "Lord, have mercy." After the completion of the Circuit of Incense, the Verses of Cymbals were chanted. In or around the 14th or 15th century, due to time constraints (as mentioned earlier), the Verses of Cymbals took precedence over the praying of the litanies. Thus, it is uttered aloud, while the litanies and their biddings became silent prayers, with the people's rejoinder "Lord, have mercy" being totally ignored. Medieval writings show some discrepancies with the contemporary practice. Nevertheless, except for minor divergences, Pope Gabriel V agrees with the present-day practice.[112]

As practiced today, following the Thanksgiving Prayer and during the Circuit of Incense, the congregation, led by the chorus, chants the Verses of Cymbals. The name indicates a unique practice of using cymbals in worship. Inspecting manuscripts shows that the use of cymbals in worship was limited to the Verses of Cymbals and the chant attributable to the Trisagion (known as *Mohayyer*—المحير). The Verses of Cymbals were first

---

[112] Gabriel V (Pope), *The Ritual Order*, BnF, MS 98 (AD 1411), fols. 33r-34r.

mentioned in Pope Gabriel V's book *The Ritual Order* in AD 1411.[113] The original Verses of Cymbals hymn consisted of the first ten quatrains of the *Adam* Morning Doxology. This means that all parishes used to chant the same set of quatrains regardless of their patron saint(s) or the occasion being celebrated. It also indicates that there was no introduction (*Adam* or *Watos*) to or conclusion of the Verses of Cymbals. Conversely, the contemporary *ordo* prescribes three sections pertaining to the Verses of Cymbals: an introduction, a set of stanzas, and a conclusion. In the following paragraphs, further elaboration of the three sections shall be provided.

In the *Adam* days (i.e., Sunday, Monday and Tuesday), an introduction composed of four stanzas is recited. on the *Watos* days (i.e., Wednesdays, Thursdays, Fridays, and Saturdays), however, different introduction, which consists of two quatrains, is chanted. With respect to the second section, in Regular Days, stanzas for the Virgin, Angels, Apostles, Martyrs, and Saints are sung. On Feasts or Fasts, stanzas specific to the occasion are chanted first, after which the rest of the ordinary ones may follow.[114] During the Regular and Fast Days, the conclusion (the third section) is comprised of two quatrains: Ϩⲓⲧⲉⲛ ⲛⲓⲡⲣⲉⲥⲃⲓⲁ (Through the intercessions) for the Virgin, and Ⲉⲑⲣⲉⲛϩⲱⲥ ⲉⲣⲟⲕ (That we may praise You). Nevertheless, on Feasts of the Lord, the quatrain Ⲓⲏⲥⲟⲩⲥ Ⲡⲓⲭⲣⲓⲥⲧⲟⲥ (Jesus Christ)[115] is said instead, followed by the five quatrains of Ⲡⲟⲩⲣⲟ (O King of peace).

MS Lit. 117, in the chapter titled *The Priest Order for Offering Prime and Vespers Incense*, states, "after the reading of the Ϣⲉⲡϩⲙⲟⲧ,[116] if the day

---

[113] Ibid., fol. 33r.
[114] According to the recordings of Cantor Mikhail the Great, the verses for the Lent are chanted after those for Saint Mary, which is not the normal practice for other occasions.
[115] The translation of this quatrain is "Jesus Christ is the same yesterday, today and forever, One Person, we praise Him and glorify Him."
[116] The Thanksgiving Prayer.

is a Sunday or a feast, the deacons[117] chant **Ⲕⲩⲣⲓⲉ ⲉ̀ⲗⲉⲏⲥⲟⲛ** followed by **Ⲁ̀ⲙⲱⲓⲛⲓ ⲙⲁⲣⲉⲛ ⲟⲩⲱϣⲧ**[118] using the cymbals. Otherwise, on Regular Days, only **Ⲕⲩⲣⲓⲉ ⲉ̀ⲗⲉⲏⲥⲟⲛ** is chanted."[119] This same manuscript instructs that in the presence of the Patriarch at Vespers, "the deacons chant '**Ⲧⲉⲛⲟⲩⲱϣⲧ**[120] in the Year-Round tune with the cymbals."[121] It also includes information about the attendance of the Patriarch whose head is uncovered, where "he asks for the priests to proceed with the Thanksgiving Prayer. After this, **Ⲕⲩⲣⲓⲉ ⲉ̀ⲗⲉⲏⲥⲟⲛ** is not chanted, and the congregation remains silent. The priest takes the Coffer of Incense, kisses it, and presents it to the Patriarch. The Patriarch will make the sign of the Cross upon the Coffer of Incense, after which the priest will proceed normally, and only **Ⲕⲩⲣⲓⲉ ⲉ̀ⲗⲉⲏⲥⲟⲛ** will be chanted."[122]

Thus, until the beginning of the 20th century, the Verses of Cymbals chant was only chanted on Sunday mornings and Feast Days. It was also said in Vespers, provided that the Patriarch is present and is praying the Vespers Offering of Incense. Otherwise, the hymn **Ⲕⲩⲣⲓⲉ ⲉ̀ⲗⲉⲏⲥⲟⲛ** was intoned. This **Ⲕⲩⲣⲓⲉ ⲉ̀ⲗⲉⲏⲥⲟⲛ** is what is now referred to as "Lenten **Ⲕⲩⲣⲓⲉ ⲉ̀ⲗⲉⲏⲥⲟⲛ**," which, according to the present-day practice, is chanted during Prime Offering of Incense of the Fast of Nineveh and Lent (from Monday to Friday, with the exception of the first Monday and the last Friday of the Lent). Contrary to the earlier practice, the Verses of Cymbals hymn is sung every day in Prime and Vespers Offering of Incense, except for the Fast of Nineveh and Lenten days from Monday to Friday.

---

[117] Deacons in this context is referring to the chorus.
[118] Translation: "O come let us worship." This is the beginning of the *Adam* introduction to the Verses of Cymbals.
[119] *The Church Order*, Cairo, Patriarchal Library, MS Lit. 117 (AD 1910), fol. 16r.
[120] Translation: "We worship". This is the beginning of the *Watos* introduction to the Verses of Cymbals.
[121] *The Church Order*, Cairo, Patriarchal Library, MS Lit. 117 (AD 1910), fol. 18r.
[122] Ibid., fol. 24r.

When Ekladious[123] (Pek) Hanna Labib's Psalter was published in AD 1908, three types of the Verses of Cymbals were included. The first consists of a set of "Ϩⲓⲧⲉⲛ;" meaning that every quatrain starts with either "Ϩⲓⲧⲉⲛ ⲛⲓⲡⲣⲉⲥⲃⲓⲁ" or "Ϩⲓⲧⲉⲛ ⲛⲓⲉⲩⲭⲏ ," and ends with Ⲡ̄ⲟ̄ⲥ ⲁⲣⲓϩⲙⲟⲧ ⲛⲁⲛ ⲙ̄ⲡⲓⲭⲱ ⲉⲃⲟⲗ ⲛ̄ⲧⲉ ⲛⲉⲛⲛⲟⲃⲓ (O Lord, grant us the forgiveness of our sins). The Psalter provides a total of eleven quatrains following this pattern, and a concluding quatrain of "Ⲉⲑⲣⲉⲛϩⲱⲥ." The second type comprises, in essence, of four lengthy stanzas, each of which contained approximately twenty lines (*Stekhon*). Therefore, it is safe to assume a different music for this type. This type also concludes with the quatrain of "Ⲉⲑⲣⲉⲛϩⲱⲥ." As for the third type, all the stanzas start with Ⲭⲉⲣⲉ (Hail). This type is concluded with the five quatrains of "Ⲡⲟⲩⲣⲟ."

This means that the Verses of Cymbals hymn as we know it today is in fact a hybrid between the first and third types mentioned the Ekladious' Psalter. All the quatrains start with "Ⲭⲉⲣⲉ" like the third type, with the exception of the last one, which is "Ϩⲓⲧⲉⲛ ⲛⲓⲡⲣⲉⲥⲃⲓⲁ" for the Virgin, along with the conclusion of "Ⲉⲑⲣⲉⲛϩⲱⲥ" that are borrowed from the first type. As mentioned earlier, the conclusion of the third type is the five quatrains of "Ⲡⲟⲩⲣⲟ," which is now used for the Feasts of the Lord, the Nayrouz, and the Feasts of the Cross. Per the present-day practice, in the Feasts of the Lord, the quatrain of "Ⲓⲏⲥⲟⲩⲥ Ⲡⲓⲭⲣⲓⲥⲧⲟⲥ" is chanted prior to "Ⲡⲟⲩⲣⲟ."[124]

The origin of the quatrain of Ⲓⲏⲥⲟⲩⲥ Ⲡⲓⲭⲣⲓⲥⲧⲟⲥ requires more investigation as it is not found in any of the three types. In antiquity, there was a rite that used to take place for the newlyweds in the eve of their first

---

[123] Ekladious (Pek) Labib was a Coptic scholar (AD 1869–1918), who publish many valuable books on teaching the Coptic language. In 1897, Ekladious Labib was the first to publish the Holy Psalter in Cairo. He also published the Kiahk Psalter in 1911.

[124] The six quatrains (Ⲓⲏⲥⲟⲩⲥ Ⲡⲓⲭⲣⲓⲥⲧⲟⲥ and the five quatrains of Ⲡⲟⲩⲣⲟ) form the conclusion of the Verses of Cymbals in the Feasts of the Lord. The practice of chanting these six quatrains as a conclusion of the Verses of Cymbals in the Feasts of the Lord days started in the middle of the 20th century, when these changes were documented in the AD 1948 Psalter published by the Renaissance of Coptic Orthodox Churches Association.

week after the matrimony, during which they take off the wedding crowns. In his book *The Ritual Order*, Pope Gabriel V mentions that, right before the final blessing, the quatrain of Ⲓⲏⲥⲟⲩⲥ Ⲡⲓⲭⲣⲓⲥⲧⲟⲥ of the Verses of Cymbals was chanted in this rite.[125] It seems that in the twentieth century, the Church attempted to preserve her heritage. Since the rite of *Taking off the Crowns* is no longer practiced, which suggests losing prayers and hymns (including the quatrain of "Ⲓⲏⲥⲟⲩⲥ Ⲡⲓⲭⲣⲓⲥⲧⲟⲥ") used in this rite, the Church changed its vocation to precede the Conclusion of the Verses of Cymbals in the Feasts of the Lord. The same thing occurred with the first type of the Verses of Cymbals, which is now obsolete; however, two of its stanzas serve now as the Conclusion of Verses of Cymbals in the Regular and Fast Days[126].

The Verses of Cymbals chant is recited in honor of the saints. After we worship the Holy Trinity, we pay respect and give our salutations to the saints. We salute the holy Virgin, the archangels, John the Baptist, the Apostles, Saint Mark, the martyrs, and other saints. So, when entering a church, which is the house of the angels, we salute the saints. This reflects the genuine belief in our companionship with the saints; as soon as we walk into the church, we salute and pay respect to them.

The congregation chants the Verses of Cymbals while the priest and the altar server circuit the altar thrice. After the Circuit of Incense, the priest exits the sanctuary and censes first toward the east, then north, then west, then south, and finally, once again toward the east. After this, he remains at the gate of the sanctuary facing east until the Verses of Cymbals hymn is finished.

---

[125] Gabriel V (Pope), *The Ritual Order*, BnF, MS 98 (AD 1411), fol. 25v.
[126] As will be explained later on, I suggest that this could be the origin of the well-known hymn of the "Ⲃⲓⲧⲉⲛ" at the beginning of the Liturgy of the Word.

The Litanies

Afterwards the priest prays the litanies. At this point, the altar server stands behind the priest, and the priest begins the prayer saying, "Ϣⲗⲏⲗ," to which the altar server replies, "Ⲉ̇ⲡⲓ ⲡⲣⲟⲥⲉⲩⲭⲏ ⲥⲧⲁⲑⲏⲧⲉ," as usual. Facing west, the priest turns toward the populace, makes the sign of the cross on them, and says, Ⲓ̇ⲣⲏⲛⲏ ⲡⲁⲥⲓ (Peace be with all), to which they respond saying, Ⲕⲉ ⲧⲱ ⲡⲛⲉⲩⲙⲁⲧⲓ ⲥⲟⲩ (And with your spirit). The litanies then are prayed. The litanies in the Vespers Offering of Incense differ from those for Prime. We will first discuss those for Vespers.

Sunset and the evening time remind us of the end of our lives, which should trigger in us the desire to well prepared for that day. Vespers is prayed during sunset, an inevitable event. As such, it is fitting to pray the Litany of the Departed as a reminder that our lives' end is also inevitable. In this litany, the Church prays to the Lord to grant us, His people, to complete our days on earth in peace and preparation. The litany also reminds us of our resurrection and His second coming, according to the Lord's faithful promises. The Psalm says, "In the evening weeping shall have place, and in the morning gladness" (Psalm 30:5). In the evening, it is suitable for us to remember the departed, who left our earth, and have blossomed in the other world. The whole concept of reminding oneself of departure leads to repentance. Consequently, it takes us into the mood of preparation, and not to hold onto the corruptible and the temporal, but to look up toward heaven and seek forgiveness. The Litany of the Departed is a deep prayer proclaiming numerous theological concepts and Christian beliefs. For example, the priest says, "Raise up their bodies also on the day which You have appointed, according to Your true promises, which are without lie," reminding the worshippers that despite the current setting of the sun, it will rise again the next morning. So, even though the people we remember have departed, we look for their resurrection once again, and their rising up in joyous eternity.

Oral and written traditions direct that the Litany of the Departed is used in Regular and Fast Days. Although most manuscripts extend the vocation of this litany to all year long,[127] some practices, however, deal with Feast Days distinctively.

In his *The Ritual Order*, Pontiff Gabriel V states, "The priest then starts with [prays] the Litany of the Departed Ⲁⲣⲓⲕⲁⲧⲁⲍⲓⲟⲛ Ⲡ̄ⲟⲓⲥ[128] to the end."[129] He made a similar comment elsewhere.[130] The 1910 *The Church Order* preserved at the Old Patriarchate, speaking of the Nativity Vespers Offering of Incense, states, "the priest will then pray the Litany of the Dead, after which Ⲁⲣⲓⲕⲁⲧⲁⲍⲓⲟⲛ Ⲡ̄ⲟⲓⲥ is said."[131] MS Lit. 118, while explaining the rite of Easter Monday Vespers Offering of Incense, instructs, "the priest will say the Litany of the Dead."[132] Furthermore, in the first printed Euchologion published in AD 1902, Father Abd El-Messih Saleeb El-Massoody of the Paromeos Monastery explains, "some, on Festive days, have started praying the Litany of the Sick in lieu of the Litany of the Departed, and this also is happening in Prime. However, we have not found any written source indicating this as the predominant practice. On the contrary, we found that in the book titled *Order of Rites All-Year Round* that the Litany of the Departed is said in the Vespers Offering of Incense for the Feast of the Nativity and the Prime for Resurrection Sunday."[133] With regards to the Feasts of Epiphany,

---

[127] For example, *The Church Order*, Cairo, Patriarchal Library, MS Lit. 73 (AD 1444), *The Church Order*, Paromaos Monastery (AD 1514), and *The Church Order* of the Church of Archangel Michael in Tanta (AD 1868).
[128] "Graciously accord O Lord…"
[129] Gabriel V (Pope), *The Ritual Order*, BnF, MS 98 (AD 1411), fol. 35v.
[130] Ibid., fol. 35r.
[131] *The Church Order*, Cairo, Patriarchal Library, MS Lit. 117 (AD 1910), fol. 18r.
[132] *The Church Order*, Cairo, Patriarchal Library, MS Lit. 118 (AD 1911), fol. 82v.
[133] Salib, Abdel Massieh (*Hegumen*), *The Holy Euchologion*, 56-57.

Ascension and Pentecost, he says, "the Offering of Incense is conducted as usual." Father Abd El-Messih Al-Massoody's comments were made in the beginning of the 20th century, indicating that, at least, at the end of the 19th century, some priests had already started to pray the Litany of the Sick instead of the Litany of the Departed during the Vespers for Feasts and Eastertide.

Yassa Abd El-Messih (AD 1898–1959), the former Head of the Coptic Museum Library, said that among tens of manuscripts, there are two documents indicating that the Litany of the Sick is prayed during the Vespers of the feasts. The first is a 13th century manuscript found in the Monastery of the Syrians. It directs that either the Litany of the Sick or the Departed is recited during the Vespers Offering of Incense. The second one dates to AD 1820 and was found at the Church of the Virgin Mary in Haret Zweila in Cairo. It clearly demands the replacement of the Litany of the Departed with that of the Sick in festal occasions.[134] Additionally, MS Lit. 449, which was transcribed in the 16th century, reports that some parishes in Lower Egypt do not employ the Litany of the Departed during Eastertide, as such, only the Litany of the Sick is recited.[135] Codex Borg. Copto 65 (18th C.) and MS Lit. 31 (19th C.) clearly support the use of the Litany of the Sick, however, they acknowledge that other parishes, especially that of Saint Mary (the Hanging Church), assign the Litany of the Departed to Vespers service all year long even in Eastertide.[136]

Under the ritual instructions section of the 1948 Psalter authored by the Renaissance of Coptic Orthodox Churches Association, under a sub section titled the *Vespers Psalmody for the Feasts of the Nativity and*

---

[134] Athanasius of Saint Macarius Monastery (Father), *Summary of the Liturgical History of the Church of Alexandria (Part 2)*, 115-116.
[135] CM, MS Lit. 449 (16th C.), fol. 24v.
[136] Respectively, Vatican, Vat, Codex Borg. Copto 65 (18th C.), fol. 356r; and CM, MS Lit. 31 (19th C.), fol. 163v.

Epiphany, it states, "the Verses of Cymbals are sung in the Joyous tune, after which the priest says the Litany of the Sick." Interestingly, in the second half of the 20th century, H.H. Pope Cyril (Kyrillos) VI released a bulletin to standardize some unsettled ritual practices. The bulletin was in support of praying the Litany of the Sick during feasts' Vespers prayers.[137] On the other hand, Cantor Tawfik of AL-Muharraq Monastery recorded the deacon's call pertaining to the Litany of the Departed in the Joyous tune (comparable to that of the Litany of the Oblations). In his instructions to when it is chanted, he clearly declares that it is said in Eastertide, asserting a year-round use of the Litany of the Departed.

On the 25th of May 1991, headed by Pope Shenouda III, the Holy Synod of the Coptic Orthodox Church declared that the Litany of the Departed be given priority above any other litany, including the period of Eastertide (with the condition that it is chanted in the festal tune), and that there is no harm in saying the Litany of the Sick if time permits.[138] Then, on the 2nd of June, 2001, the Holy Synod made the following statement, "As requested by H.H. Pope Shenouda III, the Rites Committee advises that the previous announcement made by the Holy Synod with regards to praying the Litany of the Departed during Eastertide, is only intended for when the body of a departed person is present in the parish during the prayer, after which the Litany of the Sick can be said, as is customary during Eastertide. However, this does not mean that the Litany of the Departed during Eastertide under normal circumstances can be prayed, since during this period the Church celebrates the Resurrection of the Lord from the dead. Further, it is known

---

[137] Athanasius of Saint Macarius Monastery (Father), *The Prayers of Incense Offering in Vespers and Prime*, 400.

[138] The Holy Synod of the Coptic Orthodox Church, *The Synodical Decisions During the Epoch of H.H. Pope Shenouda the Third*, chapter 19, 85.

that litanies are prayed in correlation with the corresponding occasion."[139] In October 2017, the Holy Synod issued a list of instructions to unify the ritual practices during Offering of Incense prayers and the liturgy. One of these instructions prescribes that in Vespers Offering of Incense, the Litany of the Departed is prayed all year long.

As previously mentioned, Vespers Offering of Incense resembles the end of life. Prime Offering of Incense, on the other hand, symbolizes the everlasting hope, a new light that shines on us, and a new day that dawns. As such, with the hope of a new day, we pray for the sick that God may grant them healing. "The Church is a hospital, and not a courtroom, for souls. She does not condemn on behalf of sins, but grants remission of sins," Saint John Chrysostom says.[140] As such, she opens her doors early in the morning to receive the sinners, the needy, the disparate, the physically ill, in fact, everyone; hence, the Litany of the Sick is prayed in Prime Offering of Incense. "Come to me," says the Lord, "all you who are weary and burdened, and I will give you rest" (Matthew 11:28).

Since Christ is the head of the Church, and the true healer of our souls, bodies, and spirits, we ask Him for the gifts of spiritual and physical healing. The focus of this litany, though is spiritual healing. It reads, "The hope of those who have no hope and the help of those who have no helper; the comfort of the fainthearted; the harbor of those in the storm. All souls that are distressed or bound, grant them mercy, O Lord; grant them rest, grant them refreshment, grant them grace, grant them help, grant them salvation, grant them the forgiveness of their sins and their iniquities." Forgiveness of sins and iniquities indicates that the litany is more concerned with the spiritual sickness of the congregants. Driven by an

---

[139] Ibid., 94.
[140] Although this saying is widely known as delivered by John Chrysostom, I could not find the exact text. It might be a paraphrase of a conception that he wrote or said.

inner deep sense of spiritual poverty, the Church teaches us, her members, to walk into church feeling broken, like the tax collector, as a sinner who needs healing, while also full of hope and excitement about receiving this healing. "The Lord is calling you to the Church for a rich banquet," Saint John Chrysostom explains, "He transfers you from struggles to rest, and from tortures to relief. He relieves you from the burden of your sins. He heals worries with thanksgiving, and sadness with joy."[141] In the Litany of the Sick, the Church does not only incessantly pray for the spiritual illness, but also for the healing of the physical sickness. In the unction of the sick, for example (though a different rite, it nonetheless still holds the same concept), the priest prays for the healing of the sick; however, the priest says, "And if You will take his/her spirit, let that be on the hands of luminous angels."[142] So, even though we pray for the healing of the sick, the Church submits to His will.

In Prime Offering of Incense, the Church also prays for the travelers, so that God may guide them on their journeys and bring them back safely to their homes. It was the habit in antiquity to travel early in the morning; as such, the Church dedicated this prayer for them before and during their travels, while the Church prays for the actual means of travel, whether by road, sea or air,[143] she also prays for the traveler in a spiritual sense. The Church prays for the travelers, who will depart one day, treating their earthly life as a period of sojourn. The Litany of the Travelers reads, "keep our sojourn in this life without harm, without storm and undisturbed unto the end," which indicates that we, the faithful, are as if just traveling in this life en route to the next. The prayer, therefore, holds a subtle meaning of

---

[141] Although this has been used as a quote by John Chrysostom, I could not find the exact text. It might be a paraphrase of a conception that he wrote or said.
[142] In her wisdom, the Church made this part prayed inaudibly lest the sick person is disturbed.
[143] In June 5th, 1993, the Holy Synod added the word "air" to the original text. See: The Holy Synod of the Coptic Orthodox Church, *The Synodical Decisions During the Epoch of H.H. Pope Shenouda the Third*, chapter 19, 87.

repentance. The Church teaches her members that they are allowed a period of sojourn on earth to prepare for eternity. If this concept is prevalent before us, then our sojourn will have one purpose, that is, repentance and preparation for eternity. Failing to recognize the temporal nature of life, or even having ambiguous ideas about its purpose, Church members will be susceptible to falling into the traps of the world, which might divert them from the true Way.

On Sundays and festal days, when the faithful are not expected to be traveling, the Litany of the Travelers is substituted for that of the Oblations. As mentioned before, in the past, liturgies were limited to Sundays and feasts; however, Prime Offering of Incense was prayed daily. As such, it was expected to have oblations on Sundays and feasts. Thus, it was typical for the Church to replace the Litany of the Travelers for that of Oblations in those days. Now, since liturgies could possibly be celebrated any day of the week, the rite was supple enough to accommodate the new needs of the faithful. As such, the Litany of the Oblations could be prayed any day of the week if the oblations are present. In a footnote in his Euchologion, Father Abd El-Messih Al-Massoody of the Paromeos Monastery has pointed out this *order*; it reads, "the Litany of the Oblations is said instead of the Litany of the Travelers if the day is a Feast of the Lord, a Sunday, or if the oblations are present at the parish."[144]

The priest prays for those who brought the offerings in person or through others. It is imperative to notice that he does not pray for the gifts or doles, but for those who offer them. Therefore, what is important is how a person gives his/her alms and oblation, not the mere action of offering. The offerings include wheat, wine, church books, altar vessels, and all necessities to perform the liturgy. Since the oblations are considered a

---

[144] Salib, Abdel Massieh (*Hegumen*), *The Holy Euchologion*, 67.

sacrifice, the Litany of the Oblations is the only one prayed inside the sanctuary, before the altar. Saint Paul says, "For with such sacrifices God is well pleased" (Hebrews 13:16). The sacrifice is always offered on the altar; for this reason, the Litany of the Oblations reads, "Receive them upon Your holy, rational altar in heaven as a sweet savor of incense." In the Litany of the Oblations, after the priest completes saying, "Remember O Lord the sacrifices, the offerings, and the thanksgivings of those who have offered," he places a spoonful of incense in the censer without making the sign of the cross on the Coffer of Incense, while continuing the prayer, "to the honor and glory of Your holy name." If the Patriarch or a bishop is present, the priest presents the Coffer of Incense, and the Patriarch or bishop makes the sign of the cross upon it, after which the priest puts the spoonful of incense. The other alternative is that the senior priest prays the Litany of the Oblations. To avoid confusion regarding the Old Testament meaning of "sacrifice" with the Eucharistic one, on May 29, 1999, the Holy Synod changed the word "sacrifices" to "offerings."[145]

On Saturday mornings, in Prime Offering of Incense, only the Litany of the Departed is uttered, since Saturday, being the last day of the week, symbolizes the end of life. It is also the day on which Christ was laid in the tomb, a reason to remember our loved ones who also deceased. In doing so, we should be mindful that we too will inevitably depart. Nevertheless, we believe that, as Christ resurrected, we will also be raised again. Additionally, Saturday was the day on which the people of God rested in the Old Testament, the *Sabbath*. Finally, Saturday is the day on which God rested from the creation of the world, and therefore, considered an end. For all these reasons, in Prime Offering of Incense, it is fitting to pray the Litany of the Departed instead of any other litany.

---

[145] The Holy Synod of the Coptic Orthodox Church, *The Synodical Decisions During the Epoch of H.H. Pope Shenouda the Third*, chapter 19, 90.

This current practice slightly diverged from the older one. In his 15th century book, *The Ritual Order*, Pope Gabriel V wrote, "If a liturgy were to follow the Prime Offering of Incense, then the priest will refrain from saying the Litany of the Travelers; instead, he will pray the Litany of the Sick then enter the sanctuary and pray the Litany of the Oblations, which is Ⲛⲓⲑⲩⲥⲓⲁ. However, on Saturdays, particularly in Prime, the priest will not pray the Litany of the Sick or the Travelers. Instead, he will only pray that of the Departed."[146] As previously noted, the Copts in the past used to gather every day at their local parishes prior to going to their workplaces to pray the Prime Offering of Incense, regardless of whether or not a liturgy is to follow. Since in the past liturgies were not celebrated daily, Pope Gabriel V prescribes that the Litany of the Sick is said every day, followed by the Litany of the Travelers, in the absence of the liturgy. Nevertheless, if a liturgy is to follow, the Litany of the Oblations replaces that of the Travelers, except for Saturday mornings on which only the Litany of the Departed is recited. This arrangement makes sense, since in weekdays we pray for all those who are traveling to their workplaces, or other journeys during the daytime. On Sunday, however, the liturgy follows Prime Offering of Incense, and thus, it is expected that everyone stays to celebrate it. Consequently, there is no reason to pray the Litany of the Travelers; it is more fitting to pray the Litany of the Oblations instead.[147]

The contemporary rite has slightly evolved since then, since liturgies can now be prayed every day, and people do not gather every morning to pray Prime Offering of Incense. Now, if we are to blindly apply the old *ordo*, we would never pray the Litany of the Travelers! Because of this, the

---

[146] Gabriel V (Pope), *The Ritual Order*, BnF, MS 98 (AD 1411), fols. 43v-44r.

[147] Oblations or offerings will be present at this time since the congregation, who would have brought these gifts, would have attended Prime, i.e., already at the church.

Church has modified the rubric to adapt to the current norms and lifestyles. The *order*, as we know it today, is as follows: On Saturday Prime Offering of Incense, the Litany of the Departed is prayed. In Prime Offering of Incense of Sundays or Feasts, or when the oblations are present, the Litany of the Sick is prayed, followed by that of the Oblations. As for the rest of the week, the Litany of the Sick is prayed, followed by the Litany of the Travelers.

In an article titled *History and Origin of the Elongation of Litanies of Incense Offering, the Liturgy, and Responsories*,[148] Father Abd El-Messih Al-Massoody of the Paromeos Monastery witnessed that during his time, elongations to the melodies of the litanies—both priest and congregation parts—were introduced by Cantor Mikhail of Batanoun after AD 1901. In this article, Father Abd El-Messih reports that on November 22nd, 1932, he issued a brief explicating this matter and his appeal to curtail the melodies pertaining to the litanies per pre-1901. This brief, according to the aforementioned *Hegumen*, was widely accepted and signed by many including Cantor Mikhail himself. Additionally, a year before that, specifically on December 2nd, 1931, Pope Youannis XIX also signed the brief, yet refused to circulate it in an official Church publication. However, Cantor Mikhail retracted his approval and decided to go with the elongations.

The Major Circuit of Incense and Concomitant Prayers

After the priest has completed the litanies, whether it be in Vespers or Prime Offering of Incense, two rites will commence simultaneously; the first concerns the priest and the altar server, and the second is related to the choir and the congregation. After completing the litanies, the priest

---

[148] This article was handwritten by Father Abd El-Messih, its name in Arabic is: تاريخ وأصل تطويل أواشي رفع البخور والقداس والمردات

enters the sanctuary and kisses the edge of the altar or bows before it and then starts the Major Circuit of Incense. He makes the sign of the cross upon the Coffer of Incense, saying, "Glory and honor, honor and glory to the all-holy Trinity, the Father, the Son, and the Holy Spirit." He then places one spoonful of incense into the thurible, and, facing east, he offers incense thrice. The priest then kisses the edge of the altar again and circuits the altar once before exiting the sanctuary. After this, he offers incense thrice toward the east, north, west, south, and finally east again, as he did in the Minor Circuit of Incense (after the Thanksgiving Prayer).

Afterwards, the priest censes the Gospel located in the north side, from which lessons are delivered in Coptic, followed by the Gospel located on the south side, where lections are read in the vernacular. During this he says, "We worship the Gospel of our Lord Jesus Christ, to whom is glory forever, Amen." The priest then censes the saints' relics, if any are present in the parish, followed by censing thrice toward the Patriarch or the bishop(s) if they are present. When censing before the Patriarch or the bishop, the priest first says, "May the Lord preserve and confirm the life of our honored father, the high priest, Abba (...)." In the second time, he prays, "Keep him secure for us for many years and peaceful times." In censing the third time, the priest finally utters, "May he subdue all his enemies under his feet speedily." The priest then kisses the cross held in his hand and says, "Pray to Christ on our behalf to forgive us our sins."

The priest then censes the rest of the priests in the following manner: First, he offers incense toward the archpriests (or *hegumens*—Greek: ἡγούμενος) twice, the first time saying, "I ask you, my father the *hegumen*, to remember me in your prayer" and in the second saying, "that Christ our God may forgive me my many sins" or "the Lord keep you in peace, righteousness and strength." He then offers incense toward the presbyters once saying, "I ask you, my father the priest, to remember me in your prayer." Both *hegumens* and presbyters respond to the priest saying, "May the Lord preserve your priesthood, as He did with Melchizedek, Aaron, Zachariah, and Simeon, the priests of the Most High God, Amen." The priest then censes the entire parish and supplicants.

The priest begins from the north side, moving along the iconostasis until he reaches the northern door. He bows his head before the door saying, "Hail to the holy sanctuary of God." It is important to note that the priest should only offer incense to icons that have been anointed with the Chrism, Greek: χρῖσμα, (or *Myron*). The priest then continues toward the west. During this time, if it is Vespers Offering of Incense, he says, "The blessing of the evening incense, may its holy blessing be with us, Amen." In Prime Offering of Incense, however, he prays, "The blessing of the morning incense, may its holy blessing be with us, Amen." Upon reaching the end of the western side of the parish, the priest makes his way back in the middle aisle heading east. He will then turn southward and offer incense before the consecrated icons. The priest heads west again and repeats the same prayer as he did the first time around.

It is important to note that during this time, the congregation should be reciting prayers of repentance, asking for the forgiveness from our Lord and Savior (explained further below).[149] Once the priest has reached the end of the parish on the west side, he again returns eastward through the middle aisle, and stops in the second chorus where the Pascha prayers take place. As he walks towards the second chorus, the priest prays, "Jesus Christ is the same yesterday, today, and forever; in one hypostasis,[150] we

---

[149] It is common to use Psalm 50 or the Jesus Prayer "My Lord Jesus Christ, have mercy on me a sinner" for this purpose.
[150] The word hypostasis (Greek ὑπόστασις) means underlying state or underlying substance and is the fundamental reality that supports all else. In Early Christian writings, it is used to denote "being" or "substantive reality". It was mainly under the influence of the Cappadocian Fathers, especially Saint Basil the Great, that the terminology was clarified and standardized, so that the formula "Three Hypostases in one Ousia (substance)" came to be accepted as an epitome of the orthodox doctrine of the Holy Trinity. The Christian view of the Trinity is described as a view of one God existing in three

worship Him and glorify Him." Upon reaching the second chorus, he offers incense toward the east and says, "This is He Who offered Himself as an acceptable sacrifice upon the Cross for the salvation of our race." He then turns toward the north, and while censing he says, "His good Father smelled His aroma in the evening on Golgotha." Continuing with the censer, he turns to the west and says, "He opened the gate of Paradise and restored Adam once more to his dominion." Finally, he offers incense toward the south and says, "Through His Cross and holy Resurrection, He returned humanity once more to Paradise."

The priest then proceeds towards the sanctuary, and upon entering, he places one spoonful of incense in the censer while saying, "Glory and honor, honor and glory to the all-holy Trinity, the Father, the Son, and the Holy Spirit." He then censes above the altar as he prays for the entire congregation, a prayer known as the Prayer of Repentance. The rite of the Prayer of Repentance dates to the 12th century. In fact, the Church has always placed a great emphasis on the need for her children to continuously offer penitence and regularly practice the sacrament of repentance and confession.

The *Didache*[151] orders Christians to confess their sins before taking part in the prayer. It reads, "In your gatherings, confess your transgressions, and do not come for prayer with a guilty conscience. This is the way of life" (4:14). Saint Athanasius (AD 318–373) declares that "through confession, accompanied with repentance, the sinner is granted forgiveness by the hand of priest through the grace of Christ." This has always been the teaching instilled in the people's consciousness by the Church Fathers. However, in the 12th century, the church in Egypt was

---

distinct hypostases/personae/persons. The Three Hypostases are the Father, the Son, and the Holy Spirit.
[151] The *Didache* (Koine Greek: Διδαχή) or *The Teaching of the Twelve Apostles* (*Didachē* means "Teaching") is a brief early Christian treatise, dated by most scholars to the mid to late first century.

faced with many spiritual weaknesses. We will not discuss the details of this feebleness, but what is important to point out is that during this period many refrained from confessing their sins to clergy. Instead, they resorted to confessing their sins as the priest circled the parish with the censer. This movement was pioneered by Bishop Mikhail (Michael), Metropolitan of Damietta, who says, "The abandonment of Confession to the teacher (i.e., Auricular Confession). We say that when Mark the apostle made disciples, he did not prescribe for those who believed through him that they should confess their sins to anyone in the world, whether he be priest or other than priest. And even as the sinner under the Old (Testament) used secretly to recall his sins in the ear of his sacrifice, and the priest used to offer it and to ask pardon for him, so it was prescribed for the sinner in the New (Testament) that he should confess his sins over a censer of incense with which incense is offered, and that it is the priest who should offer incense to God and ask pardon of him."[152]

This false doctrine contradicts the teachings of the Bible, The Church Canons (i.e., Didascalia, Council of Carthage, Synod of Laodicea, Safi Collection, etc.), and the teachings of the Church Fathers (e.g., Athanasius, Cyril of Alexandria, Clement of Rome, Polycarp, Cyprian, Tertullian, Origen of Alexandria, Irenaeus of Lyons, Basil the Great, Gregory of Nyssa, Cyril of Jerusalem, John Chrysostom, Augustine of Hippo, etc.). There is no evidence that Saint Mark would have taught this, but unfortunately, the Coptic Church, as mentioned earlier, was experiencing a period of severe spiritual weakness. This false doctrine was incessant for about 70 years, during which no one would confess to a priest. It was not until the 13th century when Ibn Al-Assal opposed this ideology,

---

[152] Burmester, O.H.E., *The Sayings of Michael, Metropolitan of Damietta*, 120, 121. Ibn Kabar (14th Century) also confirms this false practice. See: Ibn Kabar, *The Lamp to Darkness and Explanation of the Service*, BnF, MS Arabic 203 (c. AD 1363-1369), fols. 271v-272r.

and as time went by, it began to fade away until it completely vanished in the 15th century. This theological belief was the driving force behind establishing the Prayer of Confession in its strongest form in the 12th century. In her wisdom, the Church kept the Prayer of Confession, also known as the Prayer of Repentance, however its meaning has fundamentally changed to reflect the sound orthodox beliefs. The priest circumambulates the parish with the censer in order to bless the congregation. During this time, he may receive special prayer requests, which he will then offer before the Lord on the altar.

After the priest has concluded the Prayer of Repentance (or the Prayer of Confession), he circles the altar once, then exits the sanctuary and offers incense in the same manner as before: three times toward the east, then once toward the north, west, south, and east again, respectively. He then censes the Coptic Gospel and the Gospel of the local language, followed by the Patriarch or bishop if present. The priest then returns to the door of the sanctuary and censes the other priests and altar servers once. Finally, he prostrates before the door of the sanctuary. Pope Gabriel V provides more details regarding the final *ordo*; he instructs that the priest should kiss the step of the sanctuary and offers a *Metania* to the other priests and altar servers present. He then stands up facing the west.[153]

It is noteworthy that this Major Circuit of Incense, which takes place in Vespers and Prime Offering of Incense after the litanies, is the same one performed after the Absolution of the Servants in the Liturgy of the Word. During the Major Circuit of Incense, the congregation, led by the chorus, says several prayers leading up to the Creed. In Vespers Offering of Incense, the first prayer uttered is "Graciously accord O Lord to keep us this day without sin." In Prime Offering of Incense, the *Gloria in Excelsis*

---

[153] Gabriel V (Pope), *The Ritual Order*, BnF, MS 98 (AD 1411), fol. 37v.

Deo "Let us praise with the angels, saying" is recited instead. The latter prayer is of immemorial antiquity—its full text was probably written in fourth-century Cappadocia—and was used in all churches in the east and the west.[154] A number of Coptic Psalters, as well as Syriac references, attribute the authorship of this profound prayer to Saint Athanasius the Apostolic.[155] In his *The Indisputable Studies in the Eastern and Western Liturgies*, Patriarch Ignatius Aphrem II Rahmani adds that although the *Gloria in Excelsis Deo* was said at the end of the evening prayer in the Alexandrian tradition, it was recited in the morning service in all other traditions. He also adds that Roman Church was the first to use it in the liturgies. It was introduced to the Nativity liturgy first, then Sundays if the bishop is presiding the service, and finally in all liturgies.[156]

After this, whether in Vespers or Prime Offering of Incense, the Trisagion is recited, followed by the Lord's Prayer. The Introduction to the Doxologies "Hail to you, we ask you"[157] is then said. This prayer is made up of eight quatrains and employs six tunes depending on the season.[158] Apart from the month of Kiahk, the first six quatrains are uttered in a recitative manner, whereas the last two are chanted in a tune applicable to the occasion. However, in the month of Kiahk, the first four are recited, and the last four are intoned. Michael Helmy suggests a Byzantine origin to this prayer, at least the first stanza, which is ascribed to Cosmas of Jerusalem, bishop of Maiuma, Gaza, in the eighth century.[159]

---

[154] McGowan, Andrew B., *Ancient Christian Worship*, 127.
[155] Ignatius Ephrem II Rahmani (Patriarch of the Syriac Catholic Church), *Les Liturgies Orientales et Occidentales*, 210.
[156] Ignatius, *Les Liturgies*, Ibid., 210.
[157] This prayer venerates Saint Mary, thus Ibn Kabar calls it the Virgin's Praise.
[158] The six tunes are attributed to: The Regular Days, the month of Kiahk, Palm Sunday and Feasts of the Cross, the Feasts Days, and Lent, which employs two tunes: one is used from Monday to Friday (except for the first Monday and last Friday of Lent), as well as during the Fast of Nineveh; and another is used during the Saturdays and Sundays of Lent (as well as the first Monday and the last Friday).
[159] Cosmas of Maiuma was a bishop (d. AD 773 or 794) and an important hymnographer in the East. He was orphaned at a young age, and was adopted by Sergius, the father of John of Damascus. Both John and Cosmas left Damascus to Jerusalem to become monks.

He also proposes a tighter nexus to the preceding Trisagion rather than the following doxologies.[160]

The 14th century scholar and priest, Father Shams El-Riyasa, known as Ibn Kabar, in his book *The Lamp to Darkness and Explanation of the Service*, states, "after 'Hail to You, we ask you,' the Psaly and Theotokion of the day are chanted. However, if they have already been chanted in the Midnight Psalmody, then it is preferable not to repeat them again."[161] He also mentions other means by which this part of the rite was abbreviated. He reports, "some people would only chant the last *Lobsh*, thus eliminating most of the Psaly and chanting the last eight quatrains only... as well as few quatrains of ⲚⲉⲕⲚⲁⲓ ⲱ̄ Ⲡⲁⲛⲟⲩϯ."[162] According to Ibn Kabar, this is followed by a reading from the Antiphonary, and the Doxologies, respectively. This 14th century practice has dramatically changed. According to the contemporary practice, "Hail to you, we ask you" is recited, and immediately followed by the Doxologies (Greek: δοξολογία). For this reason, it is now referred to as the Introduction to the Doxologies.

Many Doxologies—written in the Sahidic dialect—can be found in Morgan Collection, an indicative of their existence in worship prior to the 9th century. In a footnote, Ibn Kabar reports that the Doxologies were not used in Upper Egypt at his time,[163] suggesting a late adoption (at least the later part of the 14th century) of the Doxologies in these parishes. In the Regular Days, the purpose for the Doxologies is to venerate the Virgin Mary, the angels, the apostles, the martyrs, and the saints. In Feasts Days, however, the objective is to glorify the Lord Jesus Christ. The Doxologies chanted in the incense offering services are called *Watos* Doxologies, since

---

[160] Helmy, Michael. (2020). Byzantine Influences on a Group of Coptic Chants in the Psalter and the Antiphonary. *Alexandria School*, 29(2), 90-94.
[161] Ibn Kabar, *The Lamp to Darkness and Explanation of the Service*, BnF, MS Arabic 203 (c. AD 1363-1369), fol. 199r.
[162] Ibid., fol. 199r.
[163] Ibn Kabar, *The Lamp*, BnF, MS Arabic 203 (c. AD 1363-1369), fol. 198v.

they consist of longer stanzas than their *Adam* counterpart. In fact, there are two types of *Adam* Doxologies: The first, called the *Adam* Morning Doxology, is used every day following the Psalms of the Prime Office and prior to the Prime Offering of Incense. The second type is dedicated to the Doxologies recited in the Veneration Services[164] utilizing the same tune as that of "Ⲡⲟⲩⲣⲟ" pertaining to the Veneration Services, or the melody chanted in the vernacular (i.e., السلام لك يا مريم يا أم الله القدوس).[165]

Except for those for Saint Mary, the *Watos* Doxologies are consistent whether they are sung in Vespers or Prime. However, for the Virgin Mary, a *Watos* Doxology is assigned to Vespers Offering of Incense, another to the Midnight Psalmody, and yet a third one to Prime Offering of Incense. During the Fast and Feasts of the Virgin Mary, all three Doxologies are recited in all three services.

At the end of the Doxologies, the Conclusion of the Doxologies, which consists of four quatrains, is recited. It is worth mentioning that this conclusion was simply another Doxology for Saint Mary; however, it was assigned the conclusion vocation in around the 17th century.[166] It is noteworthy that manuscripts call the Year-round tune for the Doxologies "*Pikebernitees*," in reference to the first word of the Doxology for Patriarch Severus of Antioch, which starts with Ⲡⲓⲕⲉⲃⲉⲣⲛⲓⲧⲏⲥ ⲉⲧⲧⲁϫⲣⲏⲟⲩⲧ (The confirmed leader).

After this, the Introduction to the Creed (We magnify you O mother of the True Light) is said. The popular stance among Coptic scholars is that this prayer is of Alexandrian provenance; however, Michael Helmy

---

[164] Until the 17th century, some churches used the *Adam* Doxologies in their original place in Prime Offering of Incense. Before that time, many churches had repurposed them to be used in Veneration Services only. See: Athanasius of Saint Macarius Monastery (Father), *Summary of the Liturgical History of the Church of Alexandria (Part 2)*, 335.
[165] English translation: "Hail to You O Mary, the Mother of the Holy God."
[166] Athanasius of Saint Macarius Monastery (Father), *The Prayers of Incense Offering in Vespers and Prime*, 429-430.

challenges this notion and suggests a Byzantine origin. In a recent study, Helmy explains that the Introduction to the Creed is in fact two distinct chants, the former is addressed to Saint Mary, and the latter, which has been employed by the Coptic Rite since at least the ninth century, is addressed to the Lord. This study also suggests that this prayer, in antiquity, was the conclusion of the Doxologies not a prefix to the Creed.[167] This prayer is now recited, not chanted.

This is followed by the Creed, which must be recited sonorously, and in no rush. The congregation should take this time to fully grasp the spiritual truths of the Creed as it is being prayed. The last sentence of the Creed that reads, "We look for the resurrection of the dead and the life of the age to come. Amen" is intoned in a beautiful solemn tune.

O God Have Mercy on Us

Holding a cross and three lit candles, the priest exits the sanctuary. In reverence and humility, he faces east and prays Ⲫⲛⲟⲩϯ ⲛⲁⲓ ⲛⲁⲛ (O God have mercy on us).[168] This petitionary prayer consists of 10 supplications, which are "O God, have mercy upon us, settle mercy upon us, have compassion upon us, hear us, bless us, keep us, help us, take away Your anger from us, visit us with Your salvation, and forgive us our sins." The first to make mention of these 10 petitions was Pope Gabriel V.[169] In his 13th century book *The Precious Pearl: On Ecclesiastic Science*, Ibn Sibaa mentioned five supplications only, which are "O God have mercy on us, hear us, take away Your anger from us, have compassion upon us, and forgive us our sins." He said that the priest prays Ⲫⲛⲟⲩϯ ⲛⲁⲓ ⲛⲁⲛ holding a cross as a reminder that through the Cross, God's mercy and forgiveness

---

[167] Helmy, Michael. (2020). Byzantine Influences on a Group of Coptic Chants in the Psalter and the Antiphonary. *Alexandria School*, 29(2), 97-102.
[168] In the presence of a bishop, he is the one to pray Ⲫⲛⲟⲩϯ ⲛⲁⲓ ⲛⲁⲛ.
[169] Gabriel V (Pope), *The Ritual Order*, BnF, MS 98 (AD 1411), fols. 37v-38r.

were revealed to the whole world.[170] Father Youhanna Salama comments that the Church uses this allusion to indicate that Salvation can only be obtained through the Cross.[171]

Pope Gabriel V states, "The priest holds the cross in his right hand and raises both hands up in tears as he asks for God's mercy."[172] *The Church Orders* MS Lit. 73 (AD 1444) also supports this practice of holding a cross along with three candles while praying Ⲫⲛⲟⲩϯ ⲛⲁⲓ ⲛⲁⲛ.[173] The same details are asserted by a number of manuscripts including the 18th century MS Lit. 147 and the 19th century MS Lit. 133.[174] However, the 1902-Euchologion states, "after the Creed, the priest makes the sign of the cross three times, and in his hand are a cross and three candles. Using those, he begins praying Ⲫⲛⲟⲩϯ ⲛⲁⲓ ⲛⲁⲛ."[175] This is the *order* in effect today. The three lit candles allude to the Trinitarian work behind the Economy of Salvation fulfilled on the Cross, which brought the light of *new live* to the world.

Ibn Sibaa, on the other hand, made no reference to the priest making the sign of the cross before or while praying Ⲫⲛⲟⲩϯ ⲛⲁⲓ ⲛⲁⲛ. Similarly, Pope Gabriel V made no mention of this, but added that after Ⲫⲛⲟⲩϯ ⲛⲁⲓ ⲛⲁⲛ, the priest faces the west toward the congregation, and makes the sign of the cross upon them. Nevertheless, Father Abd El-Messih clearly instructs the priest to make the sign of the cross on the congregation three times prior to Ⲫⲛⲟⲩϯ ⲛⲁⲓ ⲛⲁⲛ. When he says, "have compassion upon us," he turns to his right and again makes the sign of the cross toward the

---

[170] Ibn Sibaa, *The Precious Pearl: On Ecclesiastic Science*, BnF, MS Arabic 207, fol. 93v.
[171] Salama, Youhanna (*Hegumen*), *The Precious Pearls: Explaining the Rites and Beliefs of the Church*, part 1, 195.
[172] Gabriel V (Pope), *The Ritual Order*, BnF, MS 98 (AD 1411), fol. 37v.
[173] Jeremiah (*Hegumen*), *The Church Order*, Cairo, Patriarchal Library, MS Lit. 73 (AD 1444), fol. 77r.
[174] Athanasius of Saint Macarius Monastery (Father), *The Prayers of Incense Offering in Vespers and Prime*, 524.
[175] Salib, Abdel Massieh (*Hegumen*), *The Holy Euchologion*, 84.

congregation. He repeats this a second time after "hear us," and a third time after "bless us."[176]

Nowadays, the priest makes the sign of the cross once toward the east after saying, "have compassion upon us." He then turns north and does the same while saying, "hear us." He duplicates the same action but this time toward the west while saying, "bless us." Facing south, he repeats the same action while saying, "keep us." Finally, he faces the east again, makes the sign of the cross, and ends the prayer saying, "and help us." Notice that when the priest says, "bless us," he is facing the populace as he makes the sign of the cross upon them.

After Ⲫⲛⲟⲩϯ ⲛⲁⲓ ⲛⲁⲛ, according to the current practice, the congregation responds saying, "Ⲁⲙⲏⲛ, Ⲕⲩⲣⲓⲉ ⲉⲗⲉⲏⲥⲟⲛ, Ⲕⲩⲣⲓⲉ ⲉⲗⲉⲏⲥⲟⲛ, Ⲕⲩⲣⲓⲉ ⲉⲗⲉⲏⲥⲟⲛ."[177] It is interesting to note that manuscripts extant do not record "Amen." Additionally, the number of (Ⲕⲩⲣⲓⲉ ⲉⲗⲉⲏⲥⲟⲛ—Lord, have mercy) varied historically, depending on the era, and perhaps even the location. In the next few lines, I will shed some light on the dissimilar local practices. It seems that the rejoinder "Lord, have mercy" is an ancient one, much older than "Ⲫⲛⲟⲩϯ ⲛⲁⲓ ⲛⲁⲛ." In his *The Priesthood Order* (10th century), Severus Ibn Al-Muqaffaʽ[178] makes no mention of "Ⲫⲛⲟⲩϯ ⲛⲁⲓ ⲛⲁⲛ," however, he prescribes that "Ⲕⲩⲣⲓⲉ ⲉⲗⲉⲏⲥⲟⲛ" is said 17 times to be completed to 41 at the end of the service.[179] To Ibn Sibaa, "the congregation then cries out saying 'Lord have mercy' 41 times."[180] Pope Gabriel V, however, states, "the congregation replies Ⲕⲩⲣⲓⲉ ⲉⲗⲉⲏⲥⲟⲛ. If the major rendition using the cymbals is chanted, it would be said three times.

---

[176] Ibid., 85.
[177] Anton Baumstark suggests a Hellenistic origin of the response "Lord, have mercy" and its three-fold pattern, possibly coming from (or at least, the oldest extant source preserved it comes from) Egypt. See Baumstark, Anton, *On the Historical Development of the Liturgy*, 82-83.
[178] Ibn Kabar (14th century) also did not know this prayer.
[179] Severus Ibn Al-Muqaffaʽ, *The Priesthood Order*, Julius Assfalg, 42 (fol. 152r).
[180] Ibn Sibaa, *The Precious Pearl: On Ecclesiastic Science*, BnF, MS Arabic 207, fol. 93v.

Otherwise, it would be chanted 17 times in the recitative tune."[181] *The Church Order* MS Lit. 73 (AD 1444) limits the number to three.[182] Euchologion MS Lit. 147 (18th century) agrees with Pope Gabriel V that, if chanted in the melismatic tune, **Ⲕⲩⲣⲓⲉ ⲉⲗⲉⲏⲥⲟⲛ** is recited three times; however, for the recitative tune it reads, "if in the recitative tune, it is said 27 times." Meanwhile, Euchologion MS Lit. 133 (19th century) instructs, "the congregation replies with **Ⲕⲩⲣⲓⲉ ⲉⲗⲉⲏⲥⲟⲛ**. If cymbals were used, it would be chanted twice. Otherwise, it would be said 27 times in the recitative tune."[183] As for Father Abd El-Messih Al-Massoody of the Paromeos Monastery, he states the following in his 1902 Euchologion, "The congregation chants '**Ⲁⲙⲏⲛ, Ⲕⲩⲣⲓⲉ ⲉⲗⲉⲏⲥⲟⲛ**.' If it is chanted in its major tune with the cymbals, it is said three times in the major tune, with an additional two in the minor tune. At the end of the prayer (the Absolution), the remaining 36 **Ⲕⲩⲣⲓⲉ ⲉⲗⲉⲏⲥⲟⲛ**'s are chanted, thus totaling 41. If cymbals are not used, it is chanted 17 times in the recitative tune, and at the end of the prayer (Offering of Incense), the remaining 24 are said (again totaling 41)."[184] It is here that we see the first mention of the word "**Ⲁⲙⲏⲛ**."

In contemporary practice, regardless of the season or the way it is chanted, preceded by "**Ⲁⲙⲏⲛ**," **Ⲕⲩⲣⲓⲉ ⲉⲗⲉⲏⲥⲟⲛ** is chanted thrice. Ibn Sibaa agrees with the explanation offered by Severus Ibn Al-Muqaffaʿ in regards to the recitation of **Ⲕⲩⲣⲓⲉ ⲉⲗⲉⲏⲥⲟⲛ** 41 times. Ibn Sibaa states, "Our Lord was flogged 39 times. He was also stricken on his head and pierced in his side. This adds to 41. Chanting **Ⲕⲩⲣⲓⲉ ⲉⲗⲉⲏⲥⲟⲛ** 41 times then reminds us

---

[181] Gabriel V (Pope), *The Ritual Order*, BnF, MS 98 (AD 1411), fol. 38r.
[182] Jeremiah (*Hegumen*), *The Church Order*, Cairo, Patriarchal Library, MS Lit. 73 (AD 1444), fol. 71r.
[183] Athanasius of Saint Macarius Monastery (Father), *The Prayers of Incense Offering in Vespers and Prime*, 534.
[184] Salib, Abdel Massieh (*Hegumen*), *The Holy Euchologion*, 86.

of these sufferings for our sake."[185] Others have mentioned that the crown of thorns should be accounted for rather than the reed beating, as well as many other opinions. As a matter of fact, though, the Gospel of Saint Mark says, "Then they struck Him on the head with a reed" (Mark 19:15), there is no mention of the number of times the Lord was hit on the head. In his book *The Prayers of Incense Offering in Vespers and Prime*, Father Athanasius of Saint Macarius Monastery provides a more rational reason. He explained that in all the other Eastern Churches, Ⲕⲩⲣⲓⲉ ⲉⲗⲉⲏⲥⲟⲛ is recited 40 times reflecting the required number of flogs stated in Deuteronomy 25:2-3. The Law of Moses stated the number of blows to be forty less one (39)—as an act of mercy. As for the Copts, according to Father Athanasius, they increased the number of requests for mercy by one, thus making it 41 as opposed to 40.[186]

There are two tunes for Ⲫⲛⲟⲩϯ ⲛⲁⲓ ⲛⲁⲛ, a melismatic melody, which when employed, the following response "Ⲁⲙⲏⲛ, Ⲕⲩⲣⲓⲉ ⲉⲗⲉⲏⲥⲟⲛ" is also chanted in its major tune; and a minor melody used if time is limited, in which case the minor tune is used for the responsory. While it is being chanted, still holding the cross and the candles, the priest may, inaudibly, recite the litany of "Healing to the sick, rest to the needy" from the Liturgy of Saint Gregory.

The Psalm and Gospel Reading

The priest then prays the Litany of the Gospel. Without making the sign of the cross, the priest places one spoonful of incense in the censer and says, "Ϣⲗⲏⲗ" (Pray), to which the altar server replies, "Ⲉⲡⲓ ⲡⲣⲟⲥⲉⲩⲭⲏ ⲥⲧⲁⲑⲏⲧⲉ"

---

[185] Ibn Sibaa, *The Precious Pearl: On Ecclesiastic Science*, BnF, MS Arabic 207, fol. 93v. This interpretation was also mentioned three centuries before Ibn Sibaa by Ibn Al-Muqaffa'. See: Severus Ibn Al-Muqaffa', *The Priesthood Order*, Julius Assfalg, 42, 43 (fol. 152r).
[186] Athanasius of Saint Macarius Monastery (Father), *The Prayers of Incense Offering in Vespers and Prime*, 522.

(Stand up for prayer). Afterward, the priest turns toward the people, makes the sign of the cross, and says, "Ⲓⲣⲏⲛⲏ ⲡⲁⲥⲓ" (Peace be with all), to which they respond, "Ⲕⲉ ⲧⲱ ⲡⲛⲉⲩⲙⲁⲧⲓ ⲥⲟⲩ" (And with your spirit). If the Patriarch or a bishop is present, then he is the one who utters this introduction.[187] After this, the priest kisses the cross and gives it to the altar server, who in turn presents the thurible to the priest. Facing east and holding the thurible, the priest prays the Litany of the Gospel at the door of the sanctuary. During this litany, the altar server will be standing behind the priest holding a cross and the Book of Gospels.

There are two litanies for the Gospel. The first litany, which used to be used in Cairo and all the cities in Egypt apart from Alexandria, starts with, "O Master, Lord Jesus Christ our God, who said to His saintly, honored disciples and holy apostles." The second litany starts with "O Master, Lord Jesus Christ, who sent His saintly, honored disciples and holy apostles into all the world," and used to be prayed only in Alexandria.[188] MS Lit. 147 (18th century) assigns the two litanies to ecclesiastical seasons; the first to Regular and Fast Days, while the second to Feast Days.[189] The contemporary *ordo*, however, does not restrict the use of any of the two litanies to a season or a location; the second is simply an alternative to the first. The Litany of the Gospel, whether the first or the second, can be chanted in a melismatic tune, if time permits, otherwise, the priest resorts to the minor melody.

After the priest concludes the Litany of the Gospel, one of the chanters reads the Psalm, which is a versicle from the Book of Psalms. It is usually uttered in a recitative manner. However, in special Regular Days (i.e., The Feast of the Virgin Mary, the Feast of the Apostles, the feasts of

---

[187] Older rubrics do not include an introduction to the Litany of the Gospel.
[188] Salib, Abdel Massieh (*Hegumen*), *The Holy Euchologion*, 93.
[189] Athanasius of Saint Macarius Monastery (Father), *The Prayers of Incense Offering in Vespers and Prime*, 542.

the saints and the martyrs, and the Paramonies), or if time permits, a melismatic tune can be employed. The Year-round tune, whether recitative or melismatic, differs from that assigned to the liturgy.[190] Ibn Kabar[191] records diverse local traditions regarding who chants the Psalm. According to him, in Cairo, Lower Egypt, and Old Cairo, it is assigned to one of the younger chanters. In Upper Egypt, however, it is allotted to one or two of the senior deacons. Yet, another tradition in Alexandria dictates that the Archdeacon recites it. Finally, the practice at Saint Macarius Monastery is to give it to the Readers.[192] During the month of Kiahk, the Psalm is intoned in a special tune for the month, which is the same all services. During the Feasts Days, the Joyous tune is used, also consistent in all services. The Joyous tune has two renditions, one syllabic and the other melismatic; the latter is called *Singarian*—the word *Singary* is derived from the ancient city of "Singar"[193] where the composition of the tune is believed to have taken place.[194]

In the meantime, the priest remains outside the sanctuary, facing the southern lectern. Once the chanter has reached the third line, the priest offers incense while praying, "Bow down before the Gospel of Jesus Christ. Through the prayers of the psalmist David the Prophet, O Lord, grant us the forgiveness of our sins."[195] When the chanter completes the fourth line, the priest proceeds back to the sanctuary, where he makes the sign of

---

[190] For the liturgy, a melismatic tune for the Psalm called the Abbreviated-Year-Round could be used, or alternatively two other minor tunes, if time is limited.
[191] Shams Al-Ri'āsa Abū Al-Barakāt Ibn Kabar (known as Ibn Kabar) was born in the 13th century and departed in AD 1324. Before ordination, he was a secretary to the Mamluk minister Baybars Al-Manṣûrî. He was ordained as a priest in AD 1300, under the name of Barsum and took office in the Church of Saint Mary known as the Hanging Church (or Mu'allaqah). He is known for his infamous ecclesiastical encyclopedia *The Lamp to Darkness and Explanation of the Service*.
[192] Ibn Kabar, *The Lamp to Darkness and Explanation of the Service*, BnF, MS Arabic 203 (c. AD 1363-1369), fol. 206r.
[193] The City of Singar was located north of the Delta before it sank under the Paralis Lake.
[194] It is also worth noting that the Psalm can be chanted in the mournful tune during the Passion Week and in funeral services.
[195] The priest asks for David's prayers here since he is the author of the Psalms.

the cross upon the Coffer of Incense, and puts one spoonful of incense in the censer as he says, "Glory and honor, etc." If the patriarch or a bishop is present, then he is the one who makes the sign of the cross. When the priest returns the Coffer of Incense on the altar, he then puts one spoonful of incense in the censer while saying, "Glory and honor, etc."

The reading of the Psalm prior to the Gospel signifies that the Psalms, from the Old Testament, prophesied of our Lord Jesus and His life-giving words, which is the Gospel. In other words, the New Testament is the fulfillment of the Old Testament's prophecies. The Gospel is the consummation of the Psalm, as Jesus Christ is the one prophesied of in the Old Testament.

Pope Gabriel V instructs that then the chanter finishes reciting the Psalm, he takes the Lectionary from which he just read the Psalm, and enters the sanctuary, where the priest is waiting. Holding the Lectionary, both the priest and the chanter circumambulate the sanctuary once. Pope Gabriel V echoes Ibn Sibaa in describing a solemn circuit around the altar where the priest censes the Gospel (the Lectionary) and the altar servers, holding lit candles, precede the priest and the Servant Deacon (who is holding the Gospel).[196] The candles symbolize the spiritual enlightenment the worshippers receive from listening to the Gospel. Also, Christ said about Himself "I am the Light of the World" (John 8:12), and through the Gospel He reveals Himself to us. Per Ibn Sibaa, circling the altar symbolizes the spreading of the Gospel to all the corners of the earth.[197] They then exit the sanctuary and stand on the sides of the lectern while the Gospel is being read. In the contemporary practice, however, a smaller Book of Gospels is used for the circuit; as such, the rite of holding the

---

[196] Ibn Sibaa, *The Precious Pearl: On Ecclesiastic Science*, BnF, MS Arabic 207, fol. 133r; Gabriel V (Pope), *The Ritual Order*, BnF, MS 98 (AD 1411), fol. 38v.
[196] Ibid., fol. 33r.
[197] Ibn Sibaa, *The Precious Pearl: On Ecclesiastic Science*, BnF, MS Arabic 207, fol. 133r.

Lectionary into the sanctuary disappeared. Instead, the altar servers, who prayed the Litany of the Gospel, enters the sanctuary. He places the cross on the Book of Gospels and performs the Gospel Circuit with the priest. Placing a cross on the Book of Gospels is an indicative that through the Cross the world was granted salvation, which is preached through the Gospel.

During this time, there were two rituals that took place in parallel. The first transpires inside the sanctuary, where the priest, inaudibly, utters the prayer of Simeon the Elder as an expression of eternal joy for Christ's promise of salvation. The prayer reads, "Lord, now you are letting your servant depart in peace, according to Your word; for my eyes have seen Your salvation which You have prepared before the face of all peoples, a light for revelation to the Gentiles, and for glory to Your people Israel." In the same manner that Simeon the Elder saw the salvation through Christ our Lord, and held Him in his hands, the priest now is reminded that in his hands is the Book of Gospels, which has brought the good news of Christ's salvation. Simultaneously, from the chancel, the second rite occurs, in which the cantor or one of the chanters recite the Circuit Psalm. As the name indicates, the Circuit Psalm is a collection of verses from the Psalms that are recited while the priest and the Servant Deacon, who read the Psalm, circuit the altar once (Gospel Circuit). Diversity of Circuit Psalms are appointed to the ecclesiastical occasion. Even Regular Days have Circuit Psalms that are intoned in incense offering services. If a bishop is present, a particular Circuit Psalm is said. Therefore, the Circuit Psalm changes based on the ecclesiastical occasion, and depending on the season, it employs the Year-round, Kiahk, or Joyous tune.

According to Pope Gabriel V, the Circuit Psalm for the Vespers is, "I call to You, Lord, come quickly to me; hear me when I call to You. May my prayer be set before You like incense; may the lifting up of my hands be like the evening sacrifice"[198] (Psalms 141 (140): 1–2). In point of fact, all the Eastern and Oriental Churches, including the Coptic Church, have been praying Psalm 140 in Vespers for a long time. As for Prime, Euchologion AD 1902 agrees with Ibn Sibaa that the Circuit Psalm is "Let the morning bring me word of Your unfailing love, for I have put my trust in You. Show me the way I should go, for to You I entrust my life. Alleluia (Psalm 143:8). May God be gracious to us and bless us and make His face shine on us so that Your ways may be known on earth, Your salvation among all nations. Alleluia (Psalm 67:1, 2)."[199] Unfortunately, due to time constraints, the Circuit Psalm is hardly chanted in any parish.

Following the Gospel Circuit, per the ancient *ordo*, the priest exits the sanctuary with his left foot facing east and stands at the door of the sanctuary. The Servant Deacon, still carrying the Lectionary, remains inside the sanctuary. The priest then censes the Gospel thrice while saying, "Bow down before the Gospel of Jesus Christ, the Son of the living God; to Him be the glory forever." The priest then takes the Gospel from the Servant Deacon and looks toward the people. The rest of the priests take off their hats and come forth one by one to greet the Gospel saying, "Bow down before the Gospel of Jesus Christ, the Son of the living God; to Him be the glory forever." Finally, the priest carrying the Gospel also kisses it and passes it on to the priest or deacon who will proceed with the reading. The person reading the Gospel, in turn, returns to the lectern or goes up to the pulpit[200] if one exists in the parish. The priest, who was carrying the Lectionary, turns back and faces east while the altar server instructs the congregation to stand up saying, Ⲥⲧⲁⲑⲏⲧⲉ (Stand).[201] Following the deacon's calling, the priest proclaims, Ϥⲥⲙⲁⲣⲱⲟⲩⲧ ⲛϫⲉ ⲫⲏⲉⲑⲛⲏⲟⲩ ϧⲉⲛ

---

[198] Ibid., 38v.
[199] Salib, Abdel Massieh (*Hegumen*), *The Holy Euchologion*, 84.
[200] The shift from using the chair to the pulpit to preach is credited to Saint John Chrysostom.
[201] The full bidding is "Stand in fear of God. Let us hear the Holy Gospel."

ϩⲣⲁⲛ ⲙⲠ̄ϭⲟⲓⲥ (Blessed is He who comes in the name of the Lord of hosts), a phrase said to our Lord when He entered Jerusalem. In her wisdom, the Church uses this phrase to draw the worshippers' attention to the words which Christ, who is among His people, is about to declare through the Gospel. When entering Jerusalem, this phrase was cried out as to a king returning to his city; as such, we, too, ask the Lord to come and reign over us and dwell in our hearts, as our God and King.

According to Pope Gabriel V, the deacon or the priest who is reading the Gospel continues, Ⲕⲩⲣⲓⲉ ⲉⲩⲗⲟⲅⲏⲥⲟⲛ ⲉⲕ ⲧⲟⲩ ⲕⲁⲧⲁ Ⲙⲁⲧⲑⲉⲟⲛ or Ⲙⲁⲣⲕⲟⲛ or Ⲗⲟⲩⲕⲁⲛ or Ⲓⲱⲁⲛⲛⲏⲛ ⲁ̀ⲅⲓⲟⲩ ⲉⲩⲁⲅⲅⲉⲗⲓⲟⲩ ⲧⲟ ⲁ̀ⲛⲁⲅⲛⲱⲥⲙⲁ (Bless, O Lord, the reading of the Holy Gospel according to Saint Matthew or Mark or Luke or John). Meanwhile, the priest offers incense three times toward the west while, inaudibly, saying, "The beginning of the Holy Gospel according to (Matthew or Mark or Luke or John), a pericope from the Holy Gospel."[202] As for the present-day *order*, after circling the altar, the priest places the Book of Gospels on his head as a sign of honor and reverence to God's word. He then stands on the northern side of the sanctuary's door facing west while the altar server stands on the southern side of the door also facing west. Holding a cross, the altar server cry out saying, "Ⲥⲧⲁⲑⲏⲧⲉ" The priest then exits the sanctuary, still keeping the Book of Gospels raised over this head, he says "Ϫ̀ⲥⲙⲁⲣⲱⲟⲩⲧ..." in the same aforementioned manner.

The congregation then chants, Ⲇⲟⲝⲁ ⲥⲓ Ⲕⲩⲣⲓⲉ (Glory to You, O Lord). By this time, one of the chanters or deacons would have reached the southern lectern from where the Gospel is read in the vernacular. The reader instructs the to stand up for the Gospel; he says, "Stand in the fear of God and listen to the Holy Gospel. A reading from the Gospel

---

[202] Gabriel V (Pope), *The Ritual Order*, BnF, MS 98 (AD 1411), fol. 39r-v.

according to our teacher Saint (...) the Evangelist. May his blessing be with us all." This is an almost exact translation of the Greek calling of "Ⲥⲧⲁⲑⲏⲧⲉ," which was earlier uttered by the altar server. As the reader chants the introduction to the Gospel, the priest offers incense toward the southern lectern thrice, inaudibly saying, "Bow down before the Gospel of Jesus Christ, the Son of the living God; to Him be the glory forever." The priest reading the Coptic Gospel, or the deacon this mission is delegated to, says, Ⲡⲉⲛϭⲟⲓⲥ ⲟⲩⲟϩ Ⲡⲉⲛⲛⲟⲩϯ ⲟⲩⲟϩ Ⲡⲉⲛⲥⲱⲧⲏⲣ ⲟⲩⲟϩ Ⲡⲉⲛⲟⲩⲣⲟ ⲧⲏⲣⲉⲛ Ⲓⲏⲥ Ⲡⲭⲥ ⲡϣⲏⲣⲓ ⲙ̇Ⲫⲛⲟⲩϯ ⲉⲧⲟⲛϧ ⲡⲓⲱⲟⲩ ⲛⲁϥ ϣⲁ ⲉ̇ⲛⲉϩ, (Our Lord, God, Savior, and King of us all, Jesus Christ, the Son of the living God, to whom be glory for forever). During this time, the priest censes three times toward the east, then once toward the other priests in attendance while soundlessly saying, "As for you, blessed are your eyes for they see, and your ears for they hear. May we be worthy to hear and to act according to Your Holy Gospels, through the prayers of Your saints." The priest then censes once toward the chorus while standing in his place, and quietly says, "Bow down before the Gospel of Jesus Christ, the Son of the living God; to Him be the glory forever." He then remains standing at the door of the sanctuary as he listens to the Coptic Gospel. When it is complete, he censes three times toward it, while the reader concludes it saying, Ⲡⲓⲱ̇ⲟⲩ ⲫⲁ Ⲡⲉⲛⲛⲟⲩϯ ⲡⲉ ϣⲁ ⲉ̇ⲛⲉϩ ⲛ̇ⲧⲉ ⲛⲓⲉ̇ⲛⲉϩ ⳾ ⲁ̇ⲙⲏⲛ (Glory is due to our God unto the age of the ages. Amen), to which the chorus responds saying, (Ⲇⲟⲝⲁ ⲥⲓ Ⲕⲩⲣⲓⲉ̇ (Glory to You, O Lord). The Gospel introduction is then repeated in the vernacular. The priest thrice censes eastward, then once toward the priests and once toward the chorus. The Gospel is then read in the vernacular, and at its conclusion, the people cry out, "Glory be to God forever."

Per rubric, following the Gospel reading, the reader presents the Lectionary to the priest, who will cense it three more times. The priest then holds the Lectionary *opened*, and all the priests in attendance step forth with their hats off to greet it.[203] The priest then kisses it himself before handing it back to the reader to put it back on the lectern.[204] If the Patriarch or one of the bishops is present, then he should read the Gospel. In that case, the Pontiff, or the bishop, will read it standing at the door of the sanctuary facing the populace. Upon completion, the Patriarch or bishop kisses the Lectionary, and no one else from the priests greets it. Afterward, Ibn Kabar states, "At the Hanging church (*Al-Moalaka*—المعلقة) as well as at others, the tradition was that upon completing the reading of the Gospel, the entire congregation would come forth to kiss it; the men first, then the women. Patriarch John, who is known as Son of the Saint, however, had advised to implement the practice of the monks instead, which is to greet the Gospel at the end of the service along with the cross."[205] The Pope referred to in this quote is Pope John VIII,[206] the 80th Patriarch of Alexandria.[207] While clergy greet the Gospel opened, the congregation kisses it *closed*. Ibn Sibaa explains that the sub-deacon covers the Gospel with a silk corporal and carries it through the parish for the worshippers to greet. It is closed as a sign of "ratification of what they have just heard and following the priests' actions."[208] Per the contemporary practice, after the Gospel reading, a particular Gospel Response for incense offering services is recited. In Regular Days, it is Ⲙⲁⲣⲉⲛⲟⲩⲱϣⲧ ⲙ̅Ⲡⲉⲛⲥⲱⲧⲏⲣ

---

[203] Ibn Sibaa, *The Precious Pearl: On Ecclesiastic Science*, BnF, MS Arabic 207, fols. 133v-134v; Ibn Kabar, *The Lamp to Darkness and Explanation of the Service*, BnF, MS Arabic 203 (c. AD 1363-1369), fol. 206r.

[204] Gabriel V (Pope), *The Ritual Order*, BnF, MS 98 (AD 1411), fols. 39r-41v.

[205] Ibn Kabar, *The Lamp to Darkness and Explanation of the Service*, BnF, MS Arabic 203 (c. AD 1363-1369), fol. 200r.

[206] Pope John (Yoannis) VIII is the 80th Patriarch of the Church of Alexandria, who served the Church from AD 1300 to 1320. His original name was Yohanna Ibn Ebsal (يوحنا بن ابسال بيامين). During the papacy of John VIII, severe tribulations befell the Christians in Egypt. They were forced to tinge their turbans with blue. Many churches were closed in Cairo and in different parts of the country. Pope John VIII was a contemporary of Saint Parsoma and presided over his funeral.

[207] Athanasius of Saint Macarius Monastery (Father), *Summary of the Liturgical History of the Church of Alexandria (Part 2)*, 161.

[208] Ibn Sibaa, *The Precious Pearl: On Ecclesiastic Science*, BnF, MS Arabic 207, fol. 134v.

(Let us worship our Savior); however, each and every occasion embraces an appropriate responsory.

In antiquity, only in Prime, following the Gospel reading in the vernacular, the Synaxarion was read.[209] This practice is confirmed by *The Church Order* of the Archangel Michael Church in Tanta (AD 1868),[210] and MS Lit. 117, which, while explicating the *order* of Prime, reads "after the Gospel is read, the Synaxarion follows, after which the prayer commences as normal."[211] On the contrary, Father Abdel Massieh Salib places the Synaxarion in Vespers Offering of Incense instead.[212] In other words, in the past, when Copts were religious about attending Vespers and Prime offering of incense, and when the liturgy was not celebrated daily (it usually was celebrated on Sundays only), the Synaxarion was read in Prime. At the commencement of the 20th century—or shortly before that, however, it became a common practice to celebrate liturgies in most of the days of the week. Additionally, Copts desisted from attending Vespers and Prime daily. Therefore, the Church innately moved the reading of the Synaxarion to the Liturgy of the Word, specifically, after the Acts lesson.[213] Nonetheless, this nascent practice was not settled yet, so if the Synaxarion was not read in the Liturgy of Word, it would be read in Vespers Offering of Incense.

Subsequently, the priest puts one spoonful of incense in the censer and stands outside the sanctuary facing east. Holding the censer, he prays five Minor Litanies for Peace, the Fathers, Place, Nature, and Assemblies,

---

[209] Ibn Kabar, *The Lamp to Darkness and Explanation of the Service*, BnF, MS Arabic 203 (c. AD 1363-1369), fol. 199v.
[210] *The Church Order*, Tanta, Church of Archangel Michael, Not Numbered (AD 1868), fol. 11v.
[211] *The Church Order*, Cairo, Patriarchal Library, MS Lit. 117 (AD 1910), fol. 16r.
[212] Salib, Abdel Massieh (*Hegumen*), *The Holy Euchologion*, 105. This is an improper placement since the Synaxarion in discussion is that of the same liturgical day whereas vespers lections follow the liturgy for the next day.
[213] This indicates that the teachings of Apostles were lived out by, and manifested in, the saints—the new placement of the Synaxarion entails that it is a continuation of the Acts of the Apostles.

respectively. With regards to the Litanies of Nature, from the 12th of Paona to the 9th of Baba, the Litany for the Waters is prayed. From the 10th of Baba to the 10th of Toba, he prays the Litany for the Seeds and the Herbs. And from the 11th of Toba to the 11th of Paona, the Litany for the Air of the Heaven and the Fruits is pleaded. This order is specific to Egypt however, in the lands of immigration, and per the Holy Synod's decision on June 3rd, 1990,[214] a combined litany for the three seasons is prayed all year long. In the Litany for the Assemblies, the priest prays, "Remember, O Lord our, assemblies," and as he says, "Bless them," he turns westward facing the people and makes the sign of the cross upon them. Toward the end of the litany, when he pleads, "Arise, O Lord God," he offers incense toward the east thrice above the altar, then turns to the west and censes the other priests, altar servers, and the congregation as he implores to the Lord saying, "But let Your people be in blessing, thousands of thousands, and ten thousand times ten thousand, doing Your will." He then turns back and faces east as he continues to offer incense and prays, "Through the grace, compassion..." If the Patriarch or one of the bishops is present, then he ought to say, "But let Your people be in blessing..." while blessing the people with the sign of the cross. In this case, the priest should not face the congregation, but rather toward the east always.

After this, the priest hands over the censer to the altar server, and the congregation recites the Lord's Prayer. Upon completion, the concluding sentence "in Christ Jesus our Lord," is repeated, this time chanted. Facing east and holding a cross, the priest prays the Absolution to the Son[215] inaudibly. The altar server calls out to the congregation saying, "Bow your

---

[214] The Holy Synod of the Coptic Orthodox Church, *The Synodical Decisions During the Epoch of H.H. Pope Shenouda the Third*, chapter 19, 84. Notice that this decision only pertains to the litanies, and did not discuss the Concluding Canon or the *Watos Aspazmos*.

[215] It starts as follows, "Yes, O Lord, the Lord who has given us authority to tread on serpents and scorpions and upon all the power of the enemy..."

heads to the Lord," to which the people, while bowing their heads in reverence, reply saying, "Before You, O Lord." Still facing east and holding a cross, the priest recites the second Absolution to the Son[216] soundlessly. The altar server calls out to the people saying, "Let us attend in the fear of God, Amen." The priest then turns westward and blesses the congregation with his cross saying, "Peace be with all," and they reply as usual saying, "and with your spirit." While the people are still bowing their heads, the priest, facing west, bends down and prays the third Absolution to the Son[217] aloud. When the priest reaches "My fathers and brethren," he blesses the people with the sign of the cross twice, and we he says, "my weakness," he crosses himself. At the end of the Absolution, the priest makes the sign of the cross three times; the first on himself while saying, "Bless us," the second toward the clergy while pleading, "Purify us, absolve us," and the third toward the supplicants while saying, "And all Your people." The congregation will then lift up their heads and say, "Amen" followed by "Lord, have mercy" thrice.[218]

Ibn Kabar explains that venerations for martyrs or saints take place immediately prior to Vespers' concluding **Κⲩⲣⲓⲉ ⲉⲗⲉⲏⲥⲟⲛ**'s. He states, "If it is the eve of a saint or martyr's feast, and there was an intention to chant and venerate before their icons, then after the deacon chants 'Let us attend' and the priest completes the absolution, the **Κⲩⲣⲓⲉ ⲉⲗⲉⲏⲥⲟⲛ**'s are not recited and instead the deacons begin chanting the veneration hymns appropriate for the day and the occasion. Further, the congregation gathers around the icon, and the Antiphonary reading pertaining to the

---

[216] It starts as follows, "You, O Lord, who bowed the heavens and descended and became man for the salvation of humankind...."

[217] It starts as follows, "O Master, Lord Jesus Christ, the only-begotten Son and Logos of God the Father...."

[218] Ibn Kabar, makes no mention of "Amen." Instead, he states, as previously mentioned, that Κⲩⲣⲓⲉ ⲉⲗⲉⲏⲥⲟⲛ is recited 37 times, or 24 times as a continuation of the ones uttered earlier after Ⲫⲛⲟⲩϯ ⲛⲁⲓ ⲛⲁⲛ, to complete 41 in total. See: Ibn Kabar, *The Lamp to Darkness and Explanation of the Service*, BnF, MS Arabic 203 (c. AD 1363-1369), fol. 199v.

occasion is read. After this, Alleluia is intoned, followed by Ⲕⲩⲣⲓⲉ ⲉ̀ⲗⲉⲏⲥⲟⲛ, the Conclusion, and the Final Blessing."²¹⁹ As such, hitherto, the Veneration Service is concluded with Ⲕⲩⲣⲓⲉ ⲉ̀ⲗⲉⲏⲥⲟⲛ three times, followed by the Concluding Canon.²²⁰ Therefore, after the three Absolutions to the Son, the veneration hymns are chanted (if any), then Ⲁ̀ⲙⲏⲛ is uttered, followed by Ⲕⲩⲣⲓⲉ ⲉ̀ⲗⲉⲏⲥⲟⲛ thrice. The Concluding Canon is then recited. During this time, the priest places the cross on the Book of Gospels for the priests, altar servers and chorus to greet. In the past, as previously noted, this involved the congregation as well.²²¹ In order to allow enough time for all the worshippers to salute the cross and the Book of Gospels, the Concluding Canons of Vespers and Prime were designed to be lengthy in comparison to those for the liturgy. The tune used for the Concluding Canons is unique. Although it is now used for all days throughout the liturgical year (except for Good Friday), this was not the case in antiquity. Originally, there were four tunes for the following seasons: Regular Days, Lenten Days, Feast Days, and Good Friday; only the first and last survived. It is worth noting that the manuscripts referred to the tune for Regular Days as the "Pauline Tune," pointing to the Canon used for the Feast of the Cross that falls during Lent, which starts with the word "Paul."

Following the Concluding Canon, the priest gives the final benediction; he blesses the congregation with the sign of the cross and says, Ⲡⲭ̅ⲥ̅ Ⲡⲉⲛⲛⲟⲩϯ (Christ our Lord), to which they reply, Ⲁ̀ⲙⲏⲛ. ⲉⲥⲉ̀ϣⲱⲡⲓ (Amen, so be it). The priest then turns toward the east and says, "O King of Peace, grant us Your peace...," after which the Lord's Prayer is recited.

---

[219] Ibid., fols. 200v-201r.
[220] The word "Canon" is the same as in Greek, "Kanèn."
[221] Severus Ibn Al-Muqaffaʻ, *The Priesthood Order*, Julius Assfalg, 43 (fol. 152r); Ibn Sibaa, *The Precious Pearl: On Ecclesiastic Science*, BnF, MS Arabic 207, fol. 134v; Ibn Kabar, *The Lamp to Darkness and Explanation of the Service*, BnF, MS Arabic 203 (c. AD 1363-1369), fol. 200r; *The Church Order*, Cairo, Patriarchal Library, MS Lit. 73 (AD 1444), fol. 72v; *The Church Order*, Cairo, Patriarchal Library, MS Lit. 117 (AD 1910), fol. 21r; Salib, Abdel Massieh (Hegumen), *The Holy Euchologion*, 139.

Then, the priest faces the people and dismisses them saying, "the love of God the Father... Go in peace, the peace of God be with you," to which they answer, "And with your spirit." It is worth noting that in antiquity and until not too long ago, the dismissal was the vocation of the deacon. *The Apostolic Constitutions* instructs, "And let the deacon say, 'depart in peace.'"[222] Ibn Kabar (14th century) attests to this immemorial tradition,[223] which can also be found in MS Hunt 572 (13th or 14th century).[224] The dismissal, however, became a function of the priest soon after. Pope Gabriel V (15th century) makes it a function of the priest,[225] which is what MS Lit. 73 (AD 1444)[226] and MS Lit. 117 (AD 1910)[227] prescribe.[228] From the aforementioned description, it seems that the dismissal up until the 14th century was the vocation of the deacon but was transferred to the priest tasks in the 15th century. In his 1902 euchologion, *Hegumen* Abd El-Messih El-Masoody introduced some confusion when he made the dismissal shared between the priest and the deacon, an odd practice probably a product of trying to reconcile instructions from manuscripts belonging to different ages. He writes, "The priest says, 'O Christ our Lord, O King of Peace... depart in peace.' Immediately after this, the deacon says 'The grace of God the Father be with you all. Depart in peace.' The congregation would then answer the priest and the deacon saying 'Amen, so be it.'"[229]

---

[222] *Apostolic Constitutions*, Section 4: Certain Prayers and Laws.
[223] Ibn Kabar, *The Lamp to Darkness and Explanation of the Service*, BnF, MS Arabic 203 (c. AD 1363-1369), fol. 200r.
[224] *Euchologion*, Oxford, Bodleian Lib., MS Hunt 572 (13th or 14th C.), fol. 141v.
[225] Gabriel V (Pope), *The Ritual Order*, BnF, MS 98 (AD 1411), fols. 43r, 73v.
[226] *The Church Order*, Cairo, Patriarchal Library, MS Lit. 73 (AD 1444), fol. 11v.
[227] *The Church Order*, Cairo, Patriarchal Library, MS Lit. 117 (AD 1910), fol. 16v.
[228] I also found the practice of the priest dismissing the people in other not-numbered euchologion manuscripts with unknown copyists and dates (probably from the 18th or 19th centuries).
[229] Salib, Abdel Massieh (*Hegumen*), *The Holy Euchologion*, 435-436.

The Veneration Service

In the Veneration Service, the Church Militant asks for the intercessions and prayers of the Church Triumphant. This is indicative of a fundamental Orthodox belief—that has its roots in the Bible— that is, the martyrs and saints are alive; "He is not the God of the dead, but of the living, for to Him all are alive" (Luke 20:38). In the Veneration Service, the saint's biography is read as a lesson for the worshippers to model after, as a testimony to Christ. Saints' lives demonstrate and confirm their profound love to Jesus to the extent that they accepted torture or even martyrdom for the sake of His Kingdom. These lessons and messages are preserved and explicated in the readings of the Antiphonary, the Hagiography, the *Adam* Doxologies, and the rest of the veneration chants and readings. Venerating Church saints is a proclamation and confession of the Church to the thoughts, faith, and teachings of these saints. In it, we assert that the celebrated martyr or saint suffered for the right reasons. Not every suffering or grief is *holy*; the Jewish leaders traveled "over land and sea to win a single convert, and when you have succeeded, you make them twice as much a child of hell as you are" (Matthew 23:15). Saint Paul the Apostle, before converting to the faith, is another example of someone who toiled in an misdirected manner before Jesus won him over to His Kingdom. Therefore, by venerating saints, the church confesses and declares that their faith was orthodox, and their tribulations were borne for a probable cause. The Veneration Service is the application and actualization of Psalm 150, which states, "Praise God in all His saints."[230] As such, by venerating the saints, we also glorify God, because He granted them the power and ability to suffer with, and for, Him. He is the One who performed miracles through them. Only through Him, the hearts of

---

[230] This translation is based on the Coptic version; others read "Praise God in His sanctuary."

the crowds seeking His love were changed when told the good news. Jesus is the All-holy One who sanctified, purified, and filled them with His Holy Spirit.

The exact date of the emergence of this rite is unknown; nevertheless, it is well-documented that it is an immemorial tradition. The annual memorial of local martyrs commenced in the second century, specifically in the year AD 155, after the martyrdom of Saint Polycarp. Baumstark writes, "The primitive sanctorale[231] was rooted in a strictly local and two-faced tradition: the *memoriae* of local martyrs and bishops, whose commemoration was inseparably connected with their place of burial. It is this connection which gave birth to the system of stations, touching all liturgical functions. This principle of stations was by nature in keeping with the primitive form of sanctorale, with its connection of a specific liturgical commemoration with a specific location."[232] Another date that is important to take note of is the establishment of the Coptic calendar system. It is probable that the church started to record the dates on which saints were martyred toward the end of the third century, in the time of Saint Cyprian.[233] Bradshaw suggests an earlier date linked to the martyrdom of Saint Polycarp.[234] This does not mean that the *ordo* for this practice were well-established as a liturgical service that early. However, these memorials could have been incorporated in existing prayers such as liturgies, meetings, reading of the hagiography of the saints, or in any other form. The rite of the Veneration Service in the Coptic Orthodox Church, as a distinguished proper, might have been instituted in the fifth century as a means to fighting the heresy of Nestorius (AD 386–450), in which

---

[231] That part of the breviary and missal which contains the offices proper for saints' days.
[232] Baumstark, Anton, *Comparative Liturgy*, 192.
[233] Dix, Dom Gregory, The Shape of the Liturgy, 325.
[234] Bradshaw, Paul, *Early Christian Worship: A Basic Introduction to Ideas and Practice*, 99.

case the rite of the Veneration Service would have started with venerating Saint Mary, not the martyrs.[235]

Before moving into explaining the details of the Veneration Service *ordo* according to the Coptic Orthodox Church, it is imperative to point out how the Early Church understood venerating saints, and how this understanding evolved overtime. Since the beginning of Christianity, through the epoch of persecution, and until the end of the third century, Christians' emphasis, whether in times of peace or persecution, was always on Christ. Any ritual practice was an expression of this focus. Therefore, it is vital to understand exultation of saints in the same Christological and eschatological perspectives.[236] In the Early Church, martyrs were viewed as servants of the Lord who witnessed to Him through their lives and deaths. By accepting the torment in their bodies, martyrs manifested their love to Christ, attested to the Church's reality, which is her eternal existence, and demonstrated their spiritual desire as heirs of the Lord's Kingdom. The Church viewed them as examples of Christ's work in His own body, the Church. He is the One who gave them strength to bear the torture and welcome the martyrdom victoriously and happily. Therefore, the focus, through this triumphal journey, was always Christ, not the saint or the martyr, who was viewed as the manifestation of God's victory in and through His Church.

Starting from the fourth century onward, the center of attention was shifted to the intercessory meaning of veneration. Christians started to view saints as mediators between God and the faithful.[237] In this view, hymnography of the Veneration Service grew, and the *ordo* associated with them expanded. Another value ascribed to the relics and tombs of the

---

[235] Athanasius of Saint Macarius Monastery (Father), *The Divine Liturgy: The Mystery of the Kingdom of God (Part 1)*, 454.
[236] Schmemann, Alexander, *Introduction to Liturgical Theology*, 187.
[237] Schmemann, Alexander, *Introduction to Liturgical Theology*, 189-190.

saints and martyrs, was sanctification. Relics of saints were regarded as sacred objects, and therefore, need to be touched or shared out with different areas or churches. In other words, the meaning of venerating saints shifted from its Christological character as the manifestation of God's power in His saints, to the intercessory and sanctifying aspect of the venerating service. This latter view is still, at least unofficially, the prevailing view inculcated in the Christian consciousness today. The Church clergy might support the first view theoretically, but practically, the second vision is preponderant.

Now, let us start our scrutiny of the Veneration Service rite per the Coptic Orthodox Church. Ibn Kabar, a prominent scholar priest of the 14th century, says that the Veneration Service should be performed after the absolution at the end of Vespers Offering of Incense, right before the chorus chants **Κⲩⲣⲓⲉ ⲉⲗⲉⲏⲥⲟⲛ** thrice and the Concluding Canon. In his book *The Lamp to Darkness and Explanation of the Service*, Ibn Kabar states, "if it is the eve of a saint or martyr's feast, and there was an intention to chant and venerate before their icons, then after the deacon recites 'Let us attend' and the priest completes the absolution, **Κⲩⲣⲓⲉ ⲉⲗⲉⲏⲥⲟⲛ** is not said; instead, the chanters begin with singing the veneration hymns appropriate for the day and the feast. Further, the people gather around the icon and the Antiphonary reading pertaining to the commemoration is read. After this, Alleluia is intoned, followed by **Κⲩⲣⲓⲉ ⲉⲗⲉⲏⲥⲟⲛ**, the Concluding Canon, and the benediction."[238] This is also affirmed by *The Church Order* MS Lit. 73 (AD 1444),[239] *The Church Order* MS 573,[240] *The Church Order* of the Archangel Michael Church in Tanta (AD 1868),[241]

---

[238] Ibn Kabar, *The Lamp to Darkness and Explanation of the Service*, BnF, MS Arabic 203 (c. AD 1363-1369), fols. 200v-201r.
[239] *The Church Order*, Cairo, Patriarchal Library, MS Lit. 73 (AD 1444), fol. 81r-v.
[240] *The Church Order*, St. Antony Monastery, MS Lit. 573, fol. 6v.
[241] *The Church Order*, Tanta, Church of Archangel Michael, Not Numbered (AD 1868), fols. 183v-188r.

The Church Order MS Lit. 118 (AD 1911),[242] and the first printed euchologion.[243]

Today, the Veneration Service is not limited to vespers, but can also be prayed in the liturgy, specifically, after the Synaxarion. In fact, it is not uncommon to perform it independently from liturgical services. In some parishes, the rite of the Veneration Service is performed in Vespers Offering of Incense during or after the procession (sometimes, due to time constraints, there is no procession). In that case, the Veneration Service takes place after Ⲫⲛⲟⲩϯ ⲛⲁⲓ ⲛⲁⲛ and its responsory. As previously demonstrated, this practice has no roots in the ritual rubrics. Instead, in the procession, chants particular to the celebrated figure can be uttered (i.e., Ⲁⲧⲁⲓ ⲡⲁⲣⲑⲉⲛⲟⲥ or *Parallaxe*[244] Ⲭⲉⲣⲉ Ⲙⲁⲣⲓⲁ for Saint Mary, Ⲛⲓⲉⲑⲛⲟⲥ ⲧⲏⲣⲟⲩ or Ϫⲉⲛⲟⲩⲉϩ ⲛⲥⲱⲕ[245] for the martyrs, etc.). The correct placement of venerating saint in vespers is, as mentioned above, between the final absolution, and Ⲕⲩⲣⲓⲉ ⲉⲗⲉⲏⲥⲟⲛ.

Another inaccurate practice is to venerate saints during Communion. Not only that this practice is not mentioned by rubrics, but it also violates two chief principles, one ritual, and the other theological. The first violation is that this practice breaks the association between hagiography and the veneration rite, a fundamental rule of the proper. The second pertains to etiquette and theological understanding of the time of administering the Holy Mysteries. During Communion, the King of Kings is on the altar, consequently, it is inappropriate to focus on someone else, even if they are angels, martyrs, or saints. As such, a more proper

---

[242] *The Church Order*, Cairo, Patriarchal Library, MS Lit. 118 (AD 1911), fol. 108r-v.
[243] Salib, Abdel Massieh (*Hegumen*), *The Holy Euchologion*, 105.
[244] The etymology of the word *Parallaxe* is uncertain; however, it most probably comes from the Ancient Greek word παράλλαξις (parállaxis, "alteration") from παραλλάσσω (parallássō, "to cause to alternate").
[245] Translation: We follow You with all our hearts.

placement of venerations, if performed during the liturgy, would be after the Synaxarion, in which case, it is usually abbreviated.

Although unpretentious, the old rite of the Veneration Service had several renditions, each with variant flavor depending on the location and epoch, but they all share the same general shape and content. *The Church Order* MS Lit. 73 (AD 1444), and *The Church Order* MS 573 provide a detailed prescription of the *ordo*. We can find detailed account of this *order* in the section depicting the Veneration Service for Saint Bartholomew the Apostle (his martyrdom is on the same day as the Coptic New Year).[246] According to *The Church Order* MS Lit. 73 (AD 1444), the veneration proper commences with the hymn Ⲕⲥⲙⲁⲣⲱⲟⲩⲧ; subsequently, the hymn Ⲭⲉⲣⲉ ⲑⲉⲟⲧⲟⲕⲉ or the last part of it, Ⲭⲉⲣⲉ ⲕⲉ ⲭⲁⲣⲓⲧⲱⲙⲉⲛⲏ,[247] is recited. After that, a particular hymn for the celebrated martyr is chanted. Church sources provide a plethora of these hymns, only a few survived. In the case of Saint Bartholomew, in honoring him, the hymn Ⲭⲉ ⲛⲏⲉⲧⲉⲛ ⲛⲁⲥⲟⲛϩⲟⲩ for the apostles is sung, followed by the *Parallexe* of Ⲕⲩⲣⲓⲟⲥ Ⲓⲏⲥ Ⲡⲭⲥ. Under a time constraint, only the *Parallexe* is said. Then the *Adam Doxology* for the Apostles is recited, and the exposition for the feast of the Coptic New Year and the Antiphonary for Saint Bartholomew are chanted. Finally, the hymn Ⲡⲟⲩⲣⲟ[248] is recited followed by the conclusion, that is, Ⲕⲩⲣⲓⲉ ⲉⲗⲉⲏⲥⲟⲛ three times, the Concluding Canon and the final benediction.[249] *The Church Order* MS 118, in prescribing the veneration order for the Feasts of the Apostles, offers an abbreviated version that basically consists of, respectively, Ⲕⲥⲙⲁⲣⲱⲟⲩⲧ, chants for the Apostles, the

---

[246] MS 73 Lit. (AD 1444), fol. 8r-v. Similar order can be found in the same manuscript in describing the order of the Veneration Service for Saint George: Ibid., fols. 27v-28r, for Archangel Michael: Ibid., fols. 31r-32-v, for the Four Heavenly Creatures: Ibid., fols. 38r-39v, for Saint Mary: Ibid., fol. 81r-v, and for the Feast of Annunciation: Ibid., fols. 196v-197r.
[247] Translation: "Rejoice O you full of grace."
[248] MS 573 is specific in mentioning that Ⲡⲟⲩⲣⲟ is said in the recitative tune.
[249] *The Church Order*, Cairo, Patriarchal Library, MS Lit. 73 (AD 1444), fols. 7r-8v.

Adam Exposition, and the conclusion. *The Church Order* MS 573 offers a similar *order*, however, includes more development. In it, the *Adam* Doxology is replaced with a list of hymns, namely: Ⲭⲉⲣⲉ ⲑⲉⲟ́ⲧⲟⲕⲉ ⲡⲁⲣⲑⲉⲛⲉ, Ⲥⲉⲙⲟⲩⲧ̀, Ⲭⲉⲣⲉ ⲛⲉ Ⲙⲁⲣⲓⲁ̀, ⲍ̄ ⲛ̀ⲥⲟⲡ ⲙ̀ⲙⲏⲛⲓ, and a particular hymn for the celebrated figure, respectively.[250]

The contemporary rite of the Veneration Service starts with the hymn Ⲕ̀ⲥⲙⲁⲣⲱⲟⲩⲧ (Blessed) followed by the hymn Ⲭⲉⲣⲉ ⲑⲉⲟ́ⲧⲟⲕⲉ (Rejoice O Theotokos). According to Cantor Tawfiq Youssef, Cantor Mikhail the Great knew a melismatic tune for Ⲕ̀ⲥⲙⲁⲣⲱⲟⲩⲧ, but never taught it to any of the other cantors at the time. The hymn Ⲭⲉⲣⲉ ⲑⲉⲟ́ⲧⲟⲕⲉ has both melismatic and minor tunes. Afterward, the hymn Ⲁ̀ⲅⲓⲟⲥ ⲓⲥⲧⲓⲛ (Holy the Father) is said. Some chanters prefix this chant with the phrase, "Ο Κυριος μετασου."[251] This is an inaccurate addition since the phrase Ο Κυριος μετασου is the concluding sentence of the hymn Ⲭⲉⲣⲉ ⲑⲉⲟ́ⲧⲟⲕⲉ, which is addressed to Saint Mary. Thus, if Ⲭⲉⲣⲉ ⲉ̀ⲟⲧⲟⲕⲉ is omitted, Ⲁ̀ⲅⲓⲟⲥ ⲓⲥⲧⲓⲛ should not be preceded with the phrase Ο Κυριος μετασου. The hymn Ⲁ̀ⲅⲓⲟⲥ ⲓⲥⲧⲓⲛ, in essence, discusses the work of the Holy Trinity, but has grammatical mistakes, which make it ambiguous and difficult to understand. A study by George Ghaly of the origins of Ⲁ̀ⲅⲓⲟⲥ ⲓⲥⲧⲓⲛ shows that the hymn was written in the late dialect of Upper Egypt, between the 13th and 18th centuries. Due to its complex structure and inclusion of Greek words, translating it based on the grammatical rules of the Greco-Bohairic dialect—the official Coptic dialect widely used in the Church today—is an intricate task. The first line of each quatrain is dedicated to glorifying God the Father, the second and the third lines describe God the Son and his salvific work, and the fourth line of each quatrain illustrates that Christ's work for the human race is accomplished through the Holy

---

[250] *The Church Order*, St. Antony Monastery, MS Lit. 573, fols. 6v-7r.
[251] It means, "The Lord be with you."

Spirit. The chant, as such, bears witness to the Trinitarian work of God in humanity.[252]

Afterward, the 8th and 9th parts of the Sunday Theotokion (Ϣⲁϣϥ ⲛⲥⲟⲡ ⲙ̇ⲙⲏⲛⲓ[253] and Ⲁⲩⲙⲟⲩϯ ⲉ̇ⲣⲟ[254]) are recited. This is followed by the Greek hymn Ⲇⲉⲩⲧⲉ ⲡⲁⲛⲧⲏⲥ,[255] the hymn Ⲁⲣⲓⲡⲣⲉⲥⲃⲉⲩⲓⲛ[256] in its melismatic tune, the Coptic hymns Ⲣⲁϣⲓ,[257] Ⲥⲉ ⲛⲁϣⲱⲟⲩ,[258] and Ⲫⲁⲓ ⲡⲉ ⲫ̇ⲗⲓⲙⲏⲛ,[259] respectively. The five hymns Ⲁ̇ⲅⲓⲟⲥ ⲓⲥⲧⲓⲛ, Ⲇⲉⲩⲧⲉ ⲡⲁⲛⲧⲏⲥ, Ⲣⲁϣⲓ, Ⲥⲉ ⲛⲁϣⲱⲟⲩ, and Ⲫⲁⲓ ⲡⲉ ⲫ̇ⲗⲓⲙⲏⲛ are designated for the rite of the Veneration Service. We should also note that the hymns Ⲇⲉⲩⲧⲉ ⲡⲁⲛⲧⲏⲥ, Ⲣⲁϣⲓ, Ⲥⲉ ⲛⲁϣⲱⲟⲩ, and Ⲫⲁⲓ ⲡⲉ ⲫ̇ⲗⲓⲙⲏⲛ were unbeknown in Cairo before Cantor Tawfiq Youseef of the Muharraq Monastery in Upper Egypt recorded them. An appropriate section of the *Adam* Morning Doxology is recited—this Doxology includes sections for the types of our intercessors: Saint Mary, angels, apostles, martyrs, saints, church fathers, and prophets. Historically, in the *Adam* days, these sections of the *Adam* Morning Doxology were said during the Vespers and Prime Offering of Incense instead of the present *Watos* Doxologies. This is followed by the conclusion of the *Adam* Doxologies, Ⲛⲉⲕⲛⲁⲓ ⲱ̇ Ⲡⲁⲛⲟⲩϯ, which is, according to the contemporary rubric, the conclusion of the *Adam* Theotokions. Afterward, a suitable hymn for the saint is chanted (i.e.,

---

[252] Ghaly, George. "Coptic Bilingualism and Hymn-Writing: A study of the Glorification Hymn *Agios Istin*." *Coptica* 10 (2011) 1–19. Published.
[253] Translation: "Seven times every day, I will praise Your name, with all my heart, O God of everyone." This hymn is also chanted during Sunday Midnight Psalmody and Monday Vespers Psalmody.
[254] Translation: "You are called, O Virgin Mary, the holy flower, of the incense." This hymn is also chanted during Sunday Midnight Psalmody and Monday Vespers Psalmody.
[255] Translation: "Come all peoples."
[256] This is the last quatrain of the *Parallaxe* Ⲭⲉⲣⲉ Ⲙⲁⲣⲓⲁ.
[257] Translation: "Rejoice O Theotokos, Mary the mother of Jesus Christ."
[258] Translation: "Yes, many are all your wonders." The word "ⲛⲁϣⲱⲟⲩ" should actually be "ⲛⲁϣⲉ" since ⲛⲁϣⲱⲟⲩ is a verb and ⲛⲉ is a copula in non-verbal sentence.
[259] Translation: "This is the image of the mother of God."

Ⲁ̀ⲧⲁⲓ ⲡⲁⲣⲑⲉⲛⲟⲥ for Saint Mary, Ⲫⲁ ⲛⲓⲧⲉⲛϩ ⲛ̀ϩⲁⲧ[260] or Ϯⲥⲧⲟⲗⲏ[261] for Archangel Michael, Ⲟⲩⲣⲁⲛ ⲛ̀ϣⲟⲩϣⲟⲩ[262] for John the Baptist, Ⲛ̀ⲓⲣⲱⲙⲓ[263] or Ⲛ̀ⲑⲱⲧⲉⲛ ⲇⲉ[264] for the Apostles, Ⲡⲓϩⲗⲟϫ[265] for the Martyrs, Ⲁ̀ⲡⲉⲕⲣⲁⲛ[266] for the Saints, and Ⲁ̀ⲇⲁⲙ Ⲁ̀ⲃⲉⲗ[267] for the prophets). The Antiphonary, along with its appropriate *Adam* or *Watos* introduction, is then read.

After the reading of the Antiphonary in the vernacular, the hymn Ⲡⲟⲩⲣⲟ is recited in the tune specific to venerations. After that, the *Adam* Doxologies, and the appropriate *Adam* melodies (مدائح) are said. Regardless of the day of the week (*Adam* or *Watos*), the *Adam* Doxologies are recited in the same tune as Ⲡⲟⲩⲣⲟ, particular to venerations. Originally, the *Adam* Doxologies were said during Prime Offering of Incense; nevertheless, starting from the 15th century they were limited to the Veneration Service.[268] Since most of the congregation no longer understands Coptic, the Church put together Arabic *Adam* Doxologies (or melodies) that employ the same tune as the *Adam* Doxologies. The *Adam* melodies can be chanted after or instead of the *Adam* Doxologies.

---

[260] Translation: "(He) who has the silver wings."

[261] Translation: "The spiritual garment, with which Michael is arrayed, and the girdle of pearls, with which Michael is adorned." This hymn is also said in matrimonies.

[262] Translation: "A name of pride is your name, O kinsman of Emmanuel." This hymn is also chanted in the feast of the Epiphany.

[263] Translation: "All you men aboard the ships upon the sea, come follow me so that I make you fishers of men." This hymn is also chanted during the fast of the Apostles.

[264] Translation: "O you who have been steadfast with Me in My temptations, I render to you My holy covenant forever." This hymn is also chanted during the fast of the Apostles.

[265] Translation: "The sweetness is the Church."

[266] Translation: "Your name is so great in the land of Egypt." *The Church Order*, Tanta, Church of Archangel Michael, Not Numbered (AD 1868), fol. 245r informs us that this hymn was originally authored by Bishop Mikhail El-Marigy (الأنبا ميخائيل المعاريجي) to venerate Saint Parsoma the Naked. Father Basilius Sobhy adds that this bishop lived in the 15th and the beginning of the 16th centuries. See: Sobhy, Basilious (Father), *Introduction to the History of Coptic Rites*, 58.

[267] Translation: "Adam and Abel." This hymn can be found in London, Bod., MS Hunt 256 (AD 1387), fols. 228v-229r among the chants addressed to our Lord Jesus Christ.

[268] Athanasius of Saint Macarius Monastery (Father), *Summary of the Liturgical History of the Church of Alexandria (Part 2)*, 217.

The final section of the Veneration proper, called *Tatkees* (Arabic: تطقيس),²⁶⁹ is the anointing of spices and perfumes on the relics of saints, if they are present in the parish. The congregation, led by the chorus, chants the hymn Ϧⲉⲛ ⲫ̀ⲣⲁⲛ followed by Coptic and Arabic hymns in the same tune. For example, the hymn Ⲥⲱⲧⲉⲙ ⲧⲁϣⲉⲣⲓ (Listen O daughter) for Saint Mary, Ⲙⲁⲣⲉⲛⲑⲱⲟⲩϯ (Let us come together), or Ⲟⲩⲭ̀ⲗⲟⲙ (A crown of gold) may be sung. At the very end, the Arabic hymn (وسلام), which translates to "May the peace of God" also employs the same tune. After the hymn Ⲡⲓⲁⲅⲅⲉⲗⲟⲥ (O angel of this day) is recited, stanzas for the saint(s) being commemorated may be appended in the same tune. After that, Ⲕⲩⲣⲓⲉ̀ ⲉ̀ⲗⲉⲏⲥⲟⲛ is uttered thrice followed by the Concluding Canon. The priest then ends the service with the Benediction and the Dismissal.²⁷⁰

Undoubtedly, the rite of the Veneration Service is a lengthy and complex one. Hence, it is usually not prayed in its entirety every time, but rather certain hymns are selected while others are skipped. There is also a short version of the rite, which comprises of the chants for the anointing the relics of the saints with spices and perfumes. This short version is widely used when the Veneration Service is performed during the Liturgy of the Word after the Synaxarion.

The Hagiography Reading Service

Although not practiced anymore, this *ordo* is of great significance in the Coptic Church, not only due to its prevalence in Coptic manuscripts, but also because of its impingement on other in-use *ordos*. Unlike Veneration

---

²⁶⁹ The name "*Tatkees*" appeared in the 17ᵗʰ century. Most probably it was derived from the key word of this part of the service, that is, "axioc" or "axia," which means "worthy." When prefixed with the definite article for singular female letter "t," it becomes "taxioc," which was pronounced *Tatkees* in Arabic. See Halim, Mina Safwat, *The Hagiography Reading Service* (unpublished), 52.

²⁷⁰ It is noteworthy that the ending of the Veneration Service (Ⲕⲩⲣⲓⲉ̀ ⲉ̀ⲗⲉⲏⲥⲟⲛ thrice, the Concluding Canon, the Benediction, and the Dismissal, respectively) is how regular Vespers Offering of Incense end (after the last Absolution). This is further proof that the correct placement for the Veneration Service is immediately after the Absolution at the end of the Vespers Offering of Incense.

Service, the Hagiography Reading Service takes place in Prime,[271] yet, in the same place of the Veneration Service (i.e., after the final absolution and before "Lord, have mercy" of the incense offering office). *The Church Order* MS Lit. 117 (AD 1910) reads, "When the Arabic Gospel is finished, the Synaxarion is read ... if it is the Morning Prayer of the Virgin Mary, one of the angels, martyrs, or saints."[272] Then the manuscript goes on and mentions the hymns for the proper. The core of this service is still the reading of the hagiography, which is a detailed biography of the celebrated martyr or saint; however, the structure and ritual content of this veneration are dissimilar to the previously described Veneration Service. In both services, though, the nexus between the story of the saint and venerating him/her is evident. It is also worth noting that hagiography, if written by some recognized saint, can be referred to as *Maymar* or Church Treatise.[273]

The Church Order manuscripts MS Lit. 73 (AD 1444), fol. 74ʳ, and MS Lit. 117, fols. 17ᵛ-18ʳ represent the basic framework of this service. Since the latter is more comprehensive, I will provide its prescription here; it reads, "The priest starts with the incense offering; he puts five handfuls of incense as usual. Meanwhile, the deacons (chanters) sing the Trinitarian hymn Ⲧⲉⲛⲟⲩⲱϣⲧ (We worship) to the end.[274] The *Parallexe* Ⲭⲉⲣⲉ

---

[271] *The Church Order*, Tanta, Church of Archangel Michael, Not Numbered (AD 1868), fols. 225v, 230r provide an incongruent practice to all other manuscripts. It prescribes reading the hagiography in the evenings, which could be a late practice introduced to this area due to low attendance at Prime service.

[272] *The Church Order*, Cairo, Patriarchal Library, MS Lit. 117 (AD 1910), fols. 16r-17v. Note the association between reading the Saint's biography (Antiphonary or Synaxarion) and the Veneration Service. Therefore, when the Synaxarion was relocated to the Liturgy of the Word, the Veneration Service also followed.

[273] For example: *The Church Order*, Cairo, Patriarchal Library, MS Lit. 73 (AD 1444), fol. 11r.

[274] This chant is currently called the Hymn of the Blessing. However, its original title, according to older sources, is (بداية السيرة), which means "Beginning of the Hagiography" as it is the hymn chanted at the commencement of the Hagiography Reading rite. In the contemporary practice, however, this hymn is chanted while the priests, altar servers, and chorus wear their liturgical vestments.

Ⲙⲁⲣⲓⲁ[275] is then said in its entirety as the priest offers incense before the altar, the icon of the saint being celebrated, and the other priests present. Afterward, he puts the thurible away and sits down. The hymn Ⲉⲣⲉ ⲡⲓⲥⲙⲟⲩ ⲛ̀ⲧϮⲡⲓⲁⲥ ⲉⲑⲟⲩⲁⲃ[276] is chanted, and subsequently the priest utters the benediction in Coptic and Arabic. Afterwards, the deacons say Ⲁ̀ⲙⲏⲛ ⲉⲥⲉ̀ϣⲱⲡⲓ followed by the hymn Ⲉ̀ϣⲱⲡ ⲛ̀ⲑⲟⲕ[277] and its *Parallexe*. They then read the saint's biography[278] or a lesson for the feast. At the end of each chapter, the hymn is chanted until it is time to start the liturgy... At the end of the reading, the priest lifts up the book—from which the saint's biography was read—before the altar and the congregation chants Ⲕⲩⲣⲓⲉ̀ ⲉ̀ⲗⲉⲏ̀ⲥⲟⲛ in its melismatic tune, and then the liturgy commences."[279] More recent manuscripts provide additional development and more comprehensive picture of this once-prayed rite.

Mina Halim, a liturgical researcher who inspected the order of the Hagiography Reading Service carefully, using a multitude of manuscripts depicting this rite, reconstructed the Hagiography Reading Service in its

---

[275] It should be noted that, according to old rubric, this *Parallaxe* is not restricted to St. Mary celebrations; it was employed for all saints as well.

[276] It means "The blessing of the holy Trinity," which is the Trinitarian stanza in the hymn of (Ⲁ̀ⲡⲓⲛⲁⲩ ϣⲱⲡⲓ—The time came to send the multitude away). Usually, this is followed by a quatrain for the celebrated saint. Contemporary rubric places this hymn at the commencement of the Offertory, as will be explained later. It is worth noting that during Bright Saturday service, at the onset of the reading of Revelations, rubric prescribes that the priest offers incense while the chorus chants the hymn of "Beginning of the Hagiography," which is Ϫⲉⲛⲟⲧⲱϣⲧ followed by *Parallaxe* Ⲭⲉⲣⲉ Ⲙⲁⲣⲓⲁ, and Ⲉⲣⲉ ⲡⲓⲥⲙⲟⲩ for Saint John the Beloved, respectively; later instructions omit the *Parallaxe*. This suggests that reading the Book of Revelations is the only extant proper still employing the order of the Hagiography Reading proper.

[277] MS Lit. 73 (AD 1444) did not make mention of either "Ⲁ̀ⲙⲏⲛ ⲉⲥⲉ̀ϣⲱⲡⲓ" or "Ⲉ̀ϣⲱⲡ ⲛ̀ⲑⲟⲕ." The latter chant is a hypothetical dialogue between the Savior and Saint Peter; the *Parallaxe*, however, is a list of promises and authoritative rights conferred to Saint Peter. Some manuscripts indicate that Ⲉ̀ϣⲱⲡ ⲛ̀ⲑⲟⲕ is a hymn for Saint Peter, others designate it to the fast and feasts of the Apostles.

[278] *The Church Order* MS Lit. 73 (AD 1444), in explaining the rite of the Veneration Service for Saint George, instructs that when the reader reaches the part pertaining to the beheading of the saint, the priest offers incense and the chorus chants the hymn "Ⲫⲛⲁⲩ ⲙ̀ⲡⲓⲥⲙⲟⲩ" (This is the time of blessing), the "Incense Hymn." See: Jeremiah (Hegumen), *The Church Order*, Cairo, Patriarchal Library, MS Lit. 73 (AD 1444), fol. 29r.

[279] *The Church Order*, Cairo, Patriarchal Library, MS Lit. 117 (AD 1910), fols. 17v-18r.

fully developed mature formation.²⁸⁰ In the following lines, I will present the shape of this *order*, based on his study. The Hagiography Reading Service commences with the priest putting five spoonsful in the thurible and censing thrice. He then, respectively, circumambulates the altar once, escorted by deacons and priests holding lit tapers, and then exits the sanctuary while censing towards the altar thrice, censes towards the people while still standing at the door of the altar, and finally censes the relics of the celebrated one—in case there is no relics, he offers incense to the icon of the celebrated one. In doing so, he, inaudibly, offers blessing to the Holy Trinity. In parallel, the chorus chants the Trinitarian hymn of Ϯⲉⲛⲟⲩⲱϣⲧ and its *Parallexe*, Ⲭⲉⲣⲉ Ⲙⲁⲣⲓⲁ. Optionally, especially in the Virgin's commemorations, *Parallexe* (Ⲁⲛⲟⲕ ⲛⲓⲙ—Who am I) is chanted.²⁸¹ This is then followed by the Ⲉⲣⲉ ⲡⲓⲥⲙⲟⲩ ⲛ̀ϯⲧⲣⲓⲁⲥ ⲉⲑⲟⲩⲁⲃ as noted above. The priest then says the benediction in Coptic and the vernacular, to which the congregation responds saying, "ⲁⲙⲏⲛ ⲉⲥⲉ̀ϣⲱⲡⲓ," which has few variant texts but in essence is the conclusion of the hymn of the Virtues. The hymn Ⲉ̀ϣⲱⲡ ⲛ̀ⲑⲟⲕ and its *Parallexe* are recited, in honoring the Pontiff, if present.

The hagiography is then read in Coptic, after each section, the chant of Ⲉⲣⲉ ⲡⲓⲥⲙⲟⲩ for the celebrated martyr or saint is recited. When completed, they chant the hymn of Ⲁⲡⲓⲛⲁⲩ ϣⲱⲡⲓ, which means, "The time came to send the multitude away. Let the scribes write, let the wise men assemble, and reveal what is in the holy Scriptures." This is then followed by reading the hagiography in the vernacular. When the reader reaches the part of the martyrdom of the celebrated saint, the priest offers

---

²⁸⁰ Halim, Mina Safwat, *The Hagiography Reading Service* (unpublished), 14-15.
²⁸¹ This hymn is now said only in the fast and feasts of Saint Mary in Communion. *Psalmody*, MS Hunt 256 (AD 1387) preserved at Bodleian Library in Oxford—London, includes 56 stanzas for this hymn—only 10 quatrains are in use today—and present it as a *Watos* Psaly for Saint Mary.

incense and the chorus chants Ⲫⲛⲁⲩ ⲙ̀ⲡⲓⲥⲙⲟⲩ.²⁸² If the celebration was for Saint Mary, they follow the hagiography with the Greek hymn (Ⲥⲏⲙⲉⲣⲟⲛ—Today),²⁸³ and a melody employing the same tune. The service is then concluded, as usual, with "Lord, have mercy" thrice followed by the Concluding Canon. As noted above, the only vestige of this rite exists in the reading of the Book of Revelations during the Bright Saturday service.

---

[282] We will examine this hymn in detail later, when we discuss the Liturgy of the Word.
[283] Writing hymns in Greek was an ancient characteristic of hymns authored in Upper Egypt. This suggests an early composition of the chant, probably before the 10th century.

CHAPTER THREE

Midnight Psalmody

Midnight and Matins Psalmodies

Prayer, fasting, vigils, and all other Christian practices, however good they are in themselves, do not constitute the goal of our Christian life, although they serve as a necessary means to its attainment. The true goal of our Christian life consists in the acquisition of the Holy Spirit of God. Fasting, vigils, prayers, alms-giving and all good deeds done for the sake of Christ are but means for the acquisition of the Holy Spirit of God. But note, my son, that only a good deed done for the sake of Christ brings us the fruits of the Holy Spirit. All that is done, if it is not for Christ's sake, although it may be good, brings us no reward in the life to come, nor does it give us God's grace in the present life.

—Seraphim of Sarov

So that psalmody, bringing about choral singing, a bond, as it were, toward unity, and joining the people into a harmonious union of one choir, produces also the greatest of blessings, charity.

—Basil the Great

Introduction

Praise is a form of worship in which the supplicant offers homage, gratitude, and thanksgiving, recited, or chanted, to God the Lord, glorifying, extolling, and honoring Him for who He is. Praise is the work of the angels in heaven, and, after departing from this world, is the vocation humans will be fulfilling in Paradise. Praise is a sacrifice of love offered by the faithful to our Lord Jesus Christ in return for His ineffable love and staggering work of salvation. When Constantine [284] came to power, he put the Edict of Milan[285] in place, which granted the church the freedom of worship. The Church enjoyed newfound peace with the Roman Empire, which in turn helped further development of the Christian worship. Moreover, with the establishment of Monasticism in the fourth century, monks saw in prayer the sole purpose of life, which led to an evolution in Hymnography and growth of religious ordos. "Pray without ceasing"[286] was often literally implemented to the extent that Saint Augustine once said, "A love of psalmody gave birth to monasticism."[287] One of the earliest references, if not the earliest, to praying at midnight is the Apostolic Tradition (third century); it reads, "At midnight arise, wash your hands with water and pray" (*Ap. Trad.* 41:11).

---

[284] Constantine the Great (**Κωνσταντῖνος ὁ Μέγας**; AD 272–337), also known as Constantine I), was a Roman Emperor from AD 306 to 337. In AD 324, Constantine became the sole ruler of both west and east. The first Roman emperor to claim conversion to Christianity, Constantine played an influential role in the proclamation of the Edict of Milan in 313, which decreed tolerance for Christianity in the empire. He called the First Council of Nicaea in 325, at which the Nicene Creed was professed by Christians. He built a new imperial residence at Byzantium and renamed the city Constantinople after himself. The Church of the Holy Sepulcher, built on his orders at the purported site of Jesus' tomb in Jerusalem, became the holiest place in Christendom.

[285] The Edict of Milan was the February 313 AD agreement to treat Christians benevolently within the Roman Empire. Western Roman Emperor Constantine I, and Licinius, who controlled the Balkans, met in Milan and among other things, agreed to change policies towards Christians. The Edict of Milan gave Christianity a legal status.

[286] or "Pray continually" (Thessalonians 5:16 NIV).

[287] Byrne, Peter, & Houlden, Leslie (1995). Spirituality and Liturgy. In *Companion encyclopedia of Theology*, 674.

One of the important services of praise in the Coptic Orthodox Church is the Midnight Psalmody, also called Vigil (or Nocturns). The concept of the Midnight Psalmody was adopted to accomplish Jesus' commandment, "Therefore, keep watch, because you do not know the day or the hour" (Matthew 25:13). For this reason, Christians in the early church spent nights in worship and praise to our Savior. In his *De vita contemplativa* (English: The Contemplative Life), Philo of Alexandria, a first century historian, attests to an all-night vigil observed by the Therapeutae, a group of devout Christians who lived close to Alexandria, during which hymns are recited.[288] Although Midnight Psalmody is directly associated with monasteries and ascetic life, we must mention that in its infancy, desert monasticism[289] discouraged singing the Psalmody in favor of reciting it.[290] Joseph Dyer explains in detail the difference between desert and urban monasticism,[291] and how the latter was not only more tolerant to music, but also greatly contributed to the success of the "Psalmodic Movement" that pervaded Christianity in the late 4th and early 5th centuries.[292] This is not to challenge the use of psalms in the desert, but rather the manner they were uttered; they were recited, not chanted. Sometimes they were hummed on an individual basis with no coordination among desert cenobites, and not practiced in communal services.[293] Urban Monasticism,[294] on the other hand, embraced singing

---

[288] Philo, *Philo of Alexandria: The Contemplative Life, The Giants, and Selections* (Winston, David, Trans.), 317-318.
[289] Examples are the monastic deserts of Nitria, Kellia, and Scetis.
[290] Dyer, Joseph, *Western Plainchant in the First Millennium: Studies in the Medieval Liturgy and its Music*, "The Desert, the City Psalmody in the Late Fourth Century", 21-24.
[291] Urban Monasticism consists of male and female ascetics who lived near the cathedrals of their home cities. Examples of these Urban Centers are Antioch, Constantinople, Jerusalem, and Asia Minor.
[292] Dyer, Joseph, *Western Plainchant in the First Millennium: Studies in the Medieval Liturgy and its Music*, "The Desert, the City Psalmody in the Late Fourth Century", 24-28.
[293] Some exceptions are the Pachomian Sunday synaxis and the incident mentioned by John Cassian of the angelic psalmist that chanted 12 psalms before assembled monks.
[294] The addition of Third, Sixth, Ninth, and Compline hours is credited to Urban Monasticism; see Talf, Robert F., *Beyond East and West: Problems in Liturgical Understanding*, 270.

psalms, which served as a bridge between city churches and the desert at a later time.[295] The transition from psalms as readings to psalms as chants was gradual and, to a certain degree, slow. It started in the mid-fifth century and was completed in the late sixth century.[296]

Talf suggests that after the Peace of Constantine in AD 313, when the green light was given to the expedition of liturgical development, desert monasticism observed Vigils (its own innovation) and Vespers as their practical implementation of praying daily, once in the morning (in this case in wee hours) and once at night. In secular churches, however, where people wake up later—once again as a practical observance—Matins, cathedral innovation, was prayed in the morning and Vespers at dusk. In other words, each system selected two offices of the three. Once again, Urban Monasticism provided the linkage between the two practices and included all three offices (Vigils, Matins, and Vespers), a practice that later prevailed.[297]

In Egypt's monasteries, Vigils were established as an independent autonomous service. It was prayed daily whether or not a liturgy is to follow on the next day. In the cities, however, Midnight Psalmody was only prayed preceding a liturgy. Nevertheless, this immemorial tradition, although was instituted by monasticism, became integral part of the city services quickly, still in the same century. In his letter to Marcellinus, Saint Athanasius, Archbishop of Alexandria, spoke about singing psalms. He writes, "By contrast, however, he who takes up this book—the Psalter—goes through the prophecies about the Savior, as is customary in other

---

[295] Between the 4th and 8th centuries, a great deal of tradition and practice homogenization between city churches and monasteries took place. Main reason for this movement toward more unified ritual practices was to protect orthodoxy from heresies. See McFarland, Jason J., *Announcing the Feast: The Entrance Song in the Mass of the Roman Rite*, 19, 20.
[296] McFarland, Jason J., *Announcing the Feast: The Entrance Song in the Mass of the Roman Rite*, 21.
[297] Talf, Robert, *The Liturgy of the Hours in East and West: The Origins of the Divine Office and Its Meaning for Today*, 193-201; and Athanasius (Monk), *Midnight and Matins Psalmody*, 202-204.

Scriptures, with admiration and adoration, but the other psalms he recognizes as being his own words. And the one who hears is deeply moved, as though he himself were speaking, and is affected by the words of the songs, as if they were his own songs."[298] Saint Athanasius keeps the emphasis on the prayers themselves not their melodies. He states, "For some of the simple among us, although they believe indeed that the phrases are divinely inspired, imagine, however, on account of sweetness of sound, that also the psalms are rendered musically for the sake of the ear's delight. But this is not so... Therefore, the Psalms are not recited with melodies because of a desire for pleasant sounds. Rather, this is a sure sign of the harmony of the soul's reflections... For thus beautifully singing praises, he brings rhythm to his soul and leads it, so to speak, from disproportion to proportion, with the result that, due to its steadfast nature, it is not frightened by something, but rather imagines positive things, even possessing a full desire for the future goods."[299] He then warns those who give precedence to music over prayer by making alterations to the tunes and sometimes lyrics, saying, "Do not let anyone amplify these words of the Psalter with the persuasive phrases of the profane, and do not let him attempt to recast or completely change the words. Rather let him recite and chant, without artifice, the things written just as they were spoken, in order for the holy men who supplied these, recognizing that which is their own, to join you in your prayer, or, rather, so that even the Spirit who speaks in the saints, seeing words inspired by Him in them, might render assistance to us."[300]

In one of his accounts attributed to his fight against Arianism, which took place on Feb 8th 356, Saint Athanasius the Apostolic was presiding at

---

[298] Athanasius, ., Gregg, R. C., & Athanasius, *The life of Antony and the letter to Marcellinus*, 109.
[299] Athanasius, Ibid., 123-126.
[300] Athanasius, Ibid., 127.

the Midnight Psalmody with the congregation in the Church of Theonas in Alexandria, when a group of Arius' partisans—some say the Eusebians[301]—stormed the church, accompanied by 500 soldiers. Saint Athanasius refused to escape. Instead, with conspicuous bravery, he calmly took his seat upon the throne, and instructed the deacon to continue chanting Psalm 135 with the supplicants responding, "His mercy endures forever."[302] (This, unequivocally, proves that the Second Canticle[303] was operative at least from the fourth century). Additionally, in his final homily, Saint Macarius the Great (c. AD 295–392), instructed his disciples to "come early to the church, so that you may listen to the psalms and the psalmody, followed by the reading of the Scriptures."[304] These are some of the many documented examples witnessing to the early origins of the Midnight Psalmody. The fact of the matter is that the Midnight Psalmody dates to early Christianity. Eusebius, the bishop of Caesarea (AD 260–340), attests, "The command to sing psalms in the name of the Lord was obeyed by everyone in every place: for the command to sing is in force in all churches which exist among the nations, not only the Greeks but also the barbarians throughout the whole world, and in towns, villages, and in the fields."[305]

Praising is the highest form of worship. Through it, we share in the service of the angels before the Lord. We exalt the Lord for He is glorified, as it is written in the Psalm, "Praise awaits You, O God, in Zion" (Psalms 65:1). Therefore, many of the Psalms begin with the word "Praise." Notably, in Psalm 150, we sing, "Praise Him for His mighty acts, praise Him in the multitude of His greatness..." and so forth. Praising elevates

---

[301] Hore, Alexander Hugh, *Eighteen Centuries of the Orthodox Greek Church*, 151.
[302] Marson, Charles Latimer, *The Psalms at Work*, 135.
[303] *Canticle* comes from the Latin *canticulum*, a little song. Canticles are songs from the Bible. See: Davies, J.G., *A New Dictionary of Liturgy & Worship*, 147.
[304] Athanasius (Monk), *Midnight and Matins Psalmody*, 34.
[305] Davies, J.G., *A New Dictionary of Liturgy & Worship*, 451.

the church to the highest form of prayer, joining the angels as described in the Divine Liturgy, "You gave to the earthly the praise of the Seraphim." Praising is also a form of offering. In it, worshippers offer their time, bodily desires, and mental energy to the Lord in humility and meekness. This desire to offer oneself as a sacrifice before the Lord stems from a profound eschatological understanding. Like the five wise virgins (Matthew 25:1-13), believers are expected to be prepared for the Day of Judgement.[306] Therefore, they spend all the night praising God lest He, unanticipatedly, comes at midnight as per the parable.

As previously mentioned, Midnight Psalmody was founded by the monks so that they can remain watchful at night, as taught in the Gospel. At first, the monks of the early church used to pray as many Psalms during Vigils as they desired or were capable of. In other words, there was no governing order. However, John Cassian[307] explained how, in Egypt, the number of Psalms is fixed at twelve in all hours.[308] He states, "the number of Psalms is fixed at twelve both at Vespers and in the office of Nocturns... because it is said that it was no appointment of man's invention, but was brought down from heaven to the fathers by the ministry of an angel."[309] This twelve-psalm practice was later used in the Gallic and Roman Churches.[310] Cassian then explains the details saying,

> At that time, therefore, when the perfection of the primitive Church remained unbroken, and was still preserved fresh in the memory by their followers and successors, and when the fervent faith of the few had not

---

[306] George of Al-Harf Monastery, *To Understand and Live the Liturgy*, 27.
[307] Saint John Cassian (AD 360–435), was a Christian monk and theologian. He is noted for his role in bringing the ideas and practices of Christian monasticism to the early medieval West.
[308] According to the contemporary practice, we pray 19 psalms in the Prime Hour. However, the original tradition of praying 12 psalms only was followed in Prime as well until the 11th century. After that, 7 more psalms were added.
[309] Cassian, John, *The Institutes*, Book 2—chapter IV.
[310] De Lacy O'Leary, D.D., *The Daily Office and Theotokia of the Coptic Church*, 29.

yet grown lukewarm by being dispersed among the many, the venerable fathers with watchful care made provision for those to come after them, and met together to discuss what plan should be adopted for the daily worship throughout the whole body of the brethren; that they might hand on to those who should succeed them a legacy of piety and peace that was free from all dispute and dissension, for they were afraid that in regard of the daily services some difference or dispute might arise among those who joined together in the same worship, and at some time or other it might send forth a poisonous root of error or jealousy or schism among those who came after. And when each man in proportion to his own fervor—and unmindful of the weakness of others—thought that *that* should be appointed which he judged was quite easy by considering his own faith and strength, taking too little account of what would be possible for the great mass of the brethren in general (wherein a very large proportion of weak ones is sure to be found); and when in different degrees they strove, each according to his own powers, to fix an enormous number of Psalms, and some were for fifty, others sixty, and some, not content with this number, thought that they actually ought to go beyond it,—there was such a holy difference of opinion in their pious discussion on the rule of their religion that the time for their Vesper office came before the sacred question was decided; and, as they were going to celebrate their daily rites and prayers, one rose up in the midst to chant the Psalms to the Lord. And while they were all sitting (as is still the custom in Egypt), with their minds intently fixed on the words of the chanter, when he had sung eleven Psalms, separated by prayers introduced between them, verse after verse being evenly enunciated, he finished the twelfth with a response of Alleluia, and then, by his sudden disappearance from the eyes of all, put an end at once to their discussion and their service.[311]

---

[311] Cassian, John, *The Institutes*, Book 2—chapter V.

Cassian continues, "the venerable assembly of the Fathers understood that by Divine Providence a general rule had been fixed for the congregations of the brethren through the angel's direction, and so decreed that this number should be preserved both in their evening and in their nocturnal services."[312]

The manner in which the Psalms were recited was also established. John Cassian testifies, "But the aforesaid number of twelve Psalms they divide in such a way that if there are two brethren, they each sing six; if there are three, then four; and if four, three each. A smaller number than this they never sing in the congregation, and accordingly, however large a congregation is assembled, not more than four brethren sing in the service."[313] John Cassian points out that not all psalms ended with Alleluia; he writes, "They also observe this with the greatest care; viz., that no Psalm should be said with the response of Alleluia except those which are marked with the inscription of Alleluia in their title."[314] At the end of the service, pericopes from the Scriptures were read. "Throughout the whole of Egypt and the Thebaid the number of Psalms is fixed at twelve both at Vespers and in the office of Nocturns, in such a way that at the close two lessons follow, one from the Old and the other from the New Testament,"[315] John Cassian proclaims.

Cassian noticed that the monks of Egypt were very respectful and attentive to the service; he attests, "they are all so perfectly silent that, though so large a number of the brethren is assembled together, you would not think a single person was present except the one who stands up and chants the Psalm in the midst; and especially is this the case when the

---

[312] Ibid., Book 2—chapter VI.
[313] Cassian, John, *The Institutes*, Book 2—chapter XI.
[314] Ibid., Book 2—chapter XI.
[315] Ibid., Book 2—chapter IV.

prayer is offered up."[316] Moreover, Cassian describes how organized the service was in the Egyptian monastery, and yet accommodating to the needs of the monks who work very hard in the morning time; he writes, "This canonical system of twelve Psalms, of which we have spoken, they render easier by such bodily rest that when, after their custom, they celebrate these services, they all, except the one who stands up in the midst to recite the Psalms, sit in very low stalls and follow the voice of the singer with the utmost attention of heart. For they are so worn out with fasting and working all day and night... when the offices of the canonical prayers have been duly finished, every one returns to his own cell, and again they offer with greater earnestness the same service of prayer, as their special private sacrifice, as it were; nor do any of them give themselves up any further to rest and sleep till when the brightness of day comes on the labors of the day succeed the labors and meditations of the night."[317]

Since the beginning, the Sunday Midnight Psalmody had a special order. John Cassian depicts the service that is celebrated on the evening preceding the Sabbath saying, "Wherefore Vigils have to be made up for with greater interest if they are prolonged with ill—considered an unreasonable length till daybreak. And so, they divide them into an office in three parts, that by this variety the effort may be distributed, and the exhaustion of the body relieved by some agreeable relaxation. For when standing they have sung three Psalms antiphonally, after this, sitting on the ground or in very low stalls, one of them repeats three Psalms, while the rest respond, each Psalm being assigned to one of the brethren, who succeed each other in turn; and to these they add three lessons while still

---

[316] Ibid., Book 2—chapter X.
[317] Ibid., Book 2—chapter XII.

sitting quietly. And so, by lessening their bodily exertion, they manage to observe their Vigils with greater attention of mind."[318]

As noted above, although the order and structure of the Midnight Psalmody was established in the monasteries, Matins Psalmody is a Cathedral Office, that is, instituted in the cities. As time elapsed, the church in the cities adopted the Midnight Psalmody from the monasteries, and the opposite was true for the Matins Psalmody. Eventually, the two offices were amalgamated to form what we know now as the Midnight Psalmody, or Vigils.[319] The service of "Praise" became universal after Emperor Justinian I had ordered all the clergy to incorporate it within the ritual scheme of their churches in all Christendom.

Overview of Vigils in the Coptic Church

The genesis of the Midnight Psalmody was primitively limited to the chanting of Psalms. The Theotokions,[320] Psalies,[321] Commemoration of the Saints, and Doxologies[322] were only added after the Council of Ephesus.[323] The consensus is that the Theotokions are somehow linked to Saint Cyril, the Pillar of Faith, probably indirectly through his writings. Ibn Kabar, a 14th-century priest and scholar, reports that a potter monk was the one composed the tunes for the Theotokions. In his book, *Lamp to Darkness and Explanation of the Service*, Ibn Kabar states that the Theotokions "are attributed—with no support—to Pope Athanasius the

---

[318] Cassian, John, *The Institutes*, Book 3—chapter VIII.
[319] Talf, *The Liturgy*, Ibid., 205.
[320] A Theotokion (Greek: Θεοτοκίον) is a hymn to Mary. The name is derived from the Greek word "Θεοτόκος," which means "Bearer or God." In the Coptic Orthodox Church, Theotokions are chanted in Vespers and Midnight Psalmodys. Each day of the week has a Theotokion dedicated for that day only.
[321] Psaly is coming from the Greek word "ψαλμός" meaning "song of praise."
[322] "Doxology" comes from the Greek word "δοξολογία," meaning "Saying Praise." In the Coptic Church, Doxologies are chants to venerate angels, martyrs, and saints.
[323] The Council of Ephesus is the third ecumenical council, which took place in Ephesus in AD 431. Emperor Theodosius II called this meeting to attain consensus regarding the teachings of Nestorius, Patriarch of Constantinople.

Midnight Psalmody

Apostolic, may God grant us his blessings, and it is said that a righteous saintly potter monk, who lived in the Wilderness of Shiheet, is the one who composed its melodies."[324]

In the Uppsala version of *The Lamp to Darkness and Explanation of the Service*, which was transcribed in AD 1546, the scribe states that "the people of Upper Egypt did not chant the Theotokions or the Doxologies, and they kept using the psalms only in Vespers and Prime prayers of the feasts, as originally established by the canons of the early church,"[325] a note that was not mentioned in the older Paris version of the document. This means that until, at least, the 15th century, parishes in Upper Egypt preserved the old practice of only using the Psalms in the Midnight Psalmody. From the above information, it seems that the primitive form of the Theotokions originated in the Scetis monasteries.

As mentioned earlier, the Midnight Psalmody was a separate service from the Matins Psalmody (also called Prayer of Daybreak). Historians have debated the Psalms that were included as part of the Prayer of Daybreak; two theories are prominent. The first clams that Lauds Psalms (Pss 148–150) were the conclusion of the Monastic Midnight Psalmody, as supported by J. Froger and Paul Bradshaw, and were then transferred to the Matins Psalmody. Supporters of the second view, such as Robert Talf, however, suggest that the three psalms were in fact the beginning of Matins Psalmody, and that the service originated in the cities before being adopted in the monasteries.[326] By the sixth century, especially in the West, Lauds Psalms (known in the Coptic Rite as the "Fourth Canticle") became the crux of the Prayer of Daybreak, viz., Matins Psalmody.[327] Paul Bradshaw

---

[324] Ibn Kabar, *The Lamp to Darkness and Explanation of the Service*, BnF, MS Arabic 203 (c. AD 1363-1369), fol. 202v.
[325] Ibn Kabar, *The Lamp to Darkness and Explanation of the Service*, Father Samuel of Syrians Monastery, 108.
[326] Talf, *The Liturgy*, Ibid., 193-201; and Athanasius (Monk), *Midnight and Matins Psalmody*, 79-82.
[327] Talf, *The Liturgy*, Ibid., 202.

writes, "Psalms 148–150 seem to have formed the nucleus of the morning praise."[328]

Psalmody in the Coptic Orthodox Church, like other offices, is based on *a cappella* chanting,[329] and can be conducted in four styles or patterns. The first style, called *responsorial*, is where one person chants a hymn, a psalm, or a versicle, and the congregation replies with an appropriate refrain or response, such as in the Grand Ode, or the *Mo-akab* (معقب) stanzas in the month of Kiahk. This chanting technique is ancient as Tertullian (end of the second century) makes mention of it: "The more diligent in prayer are wont to subjoin in their prayers the *Hallelujah*, and such kind of psalms, in the closes of which the company *respond*" (*On Prayer* 27). There is no evidence of a synagogal root for this chanting pattern, the prevalence of its use across early Christian communities, however, manifests its Hellenistic origin. Anton Baumstark writes, "we learn that this kind of responsive intercessory prayer was practiced in the Mysteries of Isis in just the same way as found in later Christianity."[330]

The second pattern is *group-singing*, which involves the entire chorus chanting in unison, and it is widely viewed that this is the oldest form of praise. Andrew McGowan suggests an inauguration of this style in second-century Syria.[331] This tends to be the normal practice with the majority of melismatic hymns, such as Ϫⲉⲛⲉⲛ, Ϫⲉⲟⲓ ⲛ̀ⲁⲅⲓⲕⲁⲛⲟⲥ, and many others not only assigned to psalmody, but to all other liturgical services.

The third technique is the *antiphonal* Psalmody, or in more generic term *antiphonal* chanting, that is, alternating the singing between two choruses, which was witnessed by Prophet Isaiah while speaking of the

---

[328] Bradshaw, Paul F., *Early Christian Worship: A Basic Introduction to Ideas and Practice*, 80.
[329] *A cappella* (Italian for "in the manner of the chapel") is a style of singing, originally employed for liturgical usage, where hymns or songs are performed without instrumental accompaniment.
[330] Baumstark, Anton, *On the Historical Development of the Liturgy*, 76.
[331] McGowan, Andrew B., *Ancient Christian Worship*, 118.

Seraphim calling to one another, "Holy, Holy, Holy, is the Lord Almighty, the whole earth is full of His glory" (Isaiah 6:3). Talf differentiates between antiphonal and alternate Psalmodies; in the former, which emerged from Cathedral worship and was evolved from its predecessor *responsorial* pattern, two soloists alternate chanting stanzas while the people, split into two groups, alternate responding to the soloist. The latter chanting style, however, is of monastic origin; the church, both chorus and congregation, is divided into two groups, each is assigned a stanza, and alternate the recitation of the psalmody.[332] In the Coptic Church, the two patterns are fused, and no distinction is made. Most of Midnight Psalmody hymns are chanted in this manner, such as the four Canticles, the Theotokions, the Psalies, the Commemoration of Saints, the Doxologies, and the Antiphonary. Saint Basil the Great states that the first-century Saint Ignatius Theophorus,[333] saw in a vision, angels chanting the hymn of the Trinity in a similar manner. For this reason, Saint Ignatius was eager to establish this form of worship, which he learned from the Jewish synagogues,[334] in the churches of Antioch. This method was eventually adopted in Egypt and Palestine, and later, specifically in the fourth century, in Europe, because of the work of Saint Ambrose, the Bishop of

---

[332] Talf, Robert F., *Beyond East and West: Problems in Liturgical Understanding*, 197-199.

[333] Saint Ignatius of Antioch (AD 35 or 50–98 to 117 (en.wikipedia.org/wiki/Ignatius_of_Antioch_-_cite_note-1), also known as Ignatius Theophorus (the God-bearing), was an Apostolic Father and the third bishop of Antioch, succeeding Saint Evodius, who was the immediate successor of Saint Peter. He heard Saint John the Beloved preach when he was a boy and knew Saint Polycarp, Bishop of Smyrna. Seven of his letters written to various Christian communities have been preserved. Eventually, he received the martyr's crown as he was thrown to wild beasts in the arena.

[334] The word "synagogue" is a Greek translation of the Hebrew 'Beit Knesset', meaning 'House of Assembly.' Jewish tradition claims that synagogues date back to the Babylonian exile; however, it is evident that they were established by the first century by Jewish communities outside Palestine, certainly in the great trading cities, such as, Alexandria in Egypt, Delos of Greece, and Ostia near Rome.

Milan.[335] Alternatively, although not preferable, these chants may be alternated between the chorus and the lead cantor.[336]

The fourth fashion in which chants can be conducted is the *solo chanting*. This is typically used for lengthy challenging chants, such as the Melismatic *Watos* Exposition, or the melismatic Midnight Alleluia. It is also appointed to the recitation of readings whether during the psalmody or the other liturgical services.

The first known reference of the existence of a Psalter dates back to the third century, during the papacy of Pope Dionysius,[337] the fourteenth Patriarch of the See of Saint Mark. The Church historian Eusebius wrote that Pope Dionysius described the work of Nepos, the Bishop of Faiyum, in such manner: "I endorse and love Nepos for his faith and industry, his study of Scriptures, and his splendid hymnody, which is still heartens the brethren, and I fully respect the man, especially now that he has gone to his rest."[338] Manuscripts of Psalters were used for centuries. It was not until AD 1744 when Raphael El-Tookhy published the first printed Psalter, titled *The Books of Theotokions and Canticles*, in Rome. In Egypt, specifically in Cairo, Ekladious (Pek) Labib is credited for the first publication of the printed Psalter in AD 1908 under the name of *The Regular Holy Psalter*. Also in AD 1908, Father Mina Mahalawy of the Paromeos Monastery published *The Holy Psalter* in Alexandria, under the auspices of Pope Youannes XIX,[339] who at the time was the Metropolitan

---

[335] Saint Ambrose (AD 340–4 April 397), was a bishop of Milan who became one of the most influential ecclesiastical figures of the 4th century. He was a staunch opponent of Arianism. Traditionally, Saint Ambrose is credited with promoting "antiphonal chant", a style of chanting in which one side of the choir responds alternately to the other.

[336] Traditionally, the lead cantor stands in the northern chorus.

[337] Saint Dionysius of Alexandria, named "the Great," 14th Pope of Alexandria from Dec. 28th, 248 until his death on March 22nd, 264. He was the first Pope to hold the title "the Great."

[338] Maier, Paul L., *Eusebius: Ecclesiastical History*, Book VII, 242.

[339] Pope John (Youannis) the nineteenth of Alexandria was born in AD 1855 in Dair Tasa, Asyut, Egypt. As a monk, he joined the Paromeos Monastery in the Nitrian Desert and was sent to Greece to study Theology. Afterwards, Pope Cyril V appointed him a Metropolitan of Al-Beheira and Menoufia. In Dec.

of Al-Beheira and Menoifia, and the acting secretary of the See of Saint Mark.

The Commencement of the Vigil Office

The contents and order of the Introduction to the Midnight Psalmody, which is the opening liturgical elements of the Vigil Office, varied over time. Originally, it was as follows: The priest commences the service by saying, Ⲡϭⲟⲓⲥ ⲛⲁⲓ ⲛⲁⲛ (O Lord have mercy on us) followed by "Alleluia." Then, he makes the sign of the cross while saying, "In the Name of the Father, the Son and the Holy Spirit, one God, Lord have mercy, Lord have mercy, Lord bless, amen." Following this, he continues, "Glory be to the Father, the Son and the Holy Spirit, now and forever and unto the age of all ages, amen," followed by the Thanksgiving Prayer. Afterward, the Trisagion, the hymn Ϫⲉⲛ ⲑⲏⲛⲟⲩ (Arise O children of the light), and Psalm 50 are recited, respectively. Subsequently, the psalms of the three watches (or nocturns) of the Midnight Office are said. We find this order in Ibn Kabar's *The Lamp to Darkness and Explanation of the Service* where he states, "We started with Ϧⲉⲛ ⲫⲣⲁⲛ, the *Doxa*,[340] 'Our Father,' Ⲙⲁⲣⲉⲛϣⲉⲡ,' and 'Ⲁ̀ⲅⲓⲟⲥ.' This is followed by Ϫⲉⲛ ⲑⲏⲛⲟⲩ, and Psalm 50, respectively. The most senior priest then commences with Psalm 3, then the next in seniority utters Psalms 6, and so on with Psalms 85, 90, and 118. Then the litanies specific to the first service ..."[341]

In accordance with the contemporary order, the priest starts with "Ⲡϭⲟⲓⲥ Ⲡϭⲟⲓⲥ ⲛⲁⲓ ⲛⲁⲛ" followed by "Alleluia," then "In the Name of the Father, the Son and the Holy Spirit, one God, Lord have mercy, Lord have

---

16th, 1928, he became the first ever Bishop/Metropolitan of a diocese to become a Pope in the history of the Coptic Orthodox Church. Pope John XIX departed in June 21st, 1942.
[340] Also known as (the Gloria Patri or the Minor Doxology).
[341] Ibn Kabar, *The Lamp*, Father Samuel of Syrians Monastery, 117. Note: BnF, MS Arabic 203 (c. AD 1363-1369), fol. 201r misses the first element, which is "Ϧⲉⲛ ⲫⲣⲁⲛ."

mercy, Lord bless, Amen," "Glory be to the Father, the Son and the Holy Spirit, now and forever and unto the age of all ages, Amen," the Thanksgiving Prayer, Psalm 50, and the three watches of the Midnight Office, respectively. Thus, incongruent to the old practice, in addition to the elimination of the Trisagion, Ϫⲉⲛ ⲑⲏⲛⲟⲩ was moved to the beginning of the Midnight Psalmody, as opposed to the Midnight Office.

The first watch of the Midnight Prayer reflects on the parable of the ten virgins, who were waiting for the Bridegroom. In the second watch, the worshipers recall the account of the woman who wept before Christ seeking forgiveness for her sins. The third watch of the Midnight Prayer focuses on the flock that is promised Paradise. All three watches are centered on humankind's salvation. Like a bride seeking her bridegroom, the spirit also seeks Christ the Lord, and upon encountering Him, kneels before Him so that He may accept her and grant her the promise of eternal life. In response, the spirit rejoices, seeking to depart to the Lord saying, "Sovereign Lord, as You have promised, You may now dismiss Your servant in peace. For my eyes have seen Your salvation, which You have prepared in the sight of all nations: a light for revelation to the Gentiles, and the glory of Your people Israel" (Luke 2:29–32).

In accordance with the contemporary practice, the hymn Ϫⲉⲛ ⲑⲏⲛⲟⲩ is recited after the three watches of the Midnight Office. This hymn is said twice; once in the local language at the beginning of the Midnight Office prayer, and the second in the melismatic tune at the commencement of the Midnight Psalmody. Ϫⲉⲛ ⲑⲏⲛⲟⲩ is the first chanted hymn in the Vigil Office; it starts with the words, "Arise O children of the Light let us praise the Lord of hosts, that He may grant us the salvation of our souls." Through this hymn, the church calls upon all the faithful to join the angels and the whole creation in praising the Lord, thereby stemming from a profound understanding of the Lord's salvific acts, experiencing the highest form of prayer.

This concludes the Introduction to the Midnight Psalmody. The priest then pleads the Lord saying, Ⲡϭⲟⲓⲥ Ⲡϭⲟⲓⲥ ⲛⲁⲓ ⲛⲁⲛ (Lord, Lord, have mercy upon us), followed by "Alleluia." During the month of Kiahk, the Feasts of Nativity and Theophany, Lent, the Feast of Palm Sunday, and the Feast of Resurrection, the word "Alleluia" is intoned in its melismatic tune known as the Melismatic Midnight Alleluia, a chant that, according to Ibn Kabar, employs three melodies: melismatic, semi-major, and minor;[342] however, only the melismatic rendition survived. Customarily, while holding a lit candle, the lead cantor or deacon chants this hymn at the door of the Sanctuary.

During the month of Kiahk, Lent, Preparation (*Paramony*) of Nativity and Epiphany, as well as the Resurrection, the Grand Ode Ϩⲱⲥ ⲡϭⲟⲓⲥ (Praise the Lord) is chanted immediately after the Midnight Alleluia. While the first strophe of the Grand Ode is common to all the above-mentioned occasions, the remaining strophes are particular to the event being celebrated. Although, as attested by many Psalter manuscripts, the Grand Ode was a standard liturgical element throughout the Coptic year,[343] the contemporary rubric excludes it from Regular Days.

During Eastertide,[344] Ⲧⲉⲛⲛⲁⲩ (We look [at the Resurrection of Christ]), also called the Canon of the Resurrection, is then recited daily; however, it is said only on Sundays during the period between Pentecost and the last Sunday of the month of Hathor.[345] Despite the fact that the

---

[342] Ibn Kabar, *The Lamp*, BnF, MS Arabic 203 (c. AD 1363-1369), fol. 201v.
[343] Examples: BnF, MS Copte 11, MS Copte 69, London, Bod., MS Hunt 256 (AD 1387), Old Cairo, CM, MS Lit. 55 (AD 1717).
[344] Eastertide, or Holy Fifty Days is the liturgical period that starts from the Feast of the Resurrection and ends with the Feast of the Pentecost.
[345] "Ⲧⲉⲛⲛⲁⲩ" is not recited in the liturgical period from Kiahk to Bright Saturday since this liturgical period depicts Jesus life from His birth to before His resurrection.

hymn Ⲧⲉⲛⲛⲁⲩ is used in other traditions, including the Byzantine and Roman rites, the prominent German liturgiologist Anton Baumstark reports that it originated in Egypt.[346] Within the lyrics of this hymn are the words, "We worship the Father, the Son and the Holy Spirit, one in essence." The statement "one in essence" started to gain popularity after the Council of Nicaea.[347] This suggests a composition after AD 325, when the council was conducted, however, no exact date can be determined. In antiquity, as the title proposes, "Ⲧⲉⲛⲛⲁⲩ" was the Concluding Canon for the Prime Offering of Incense of the Feast of Resurrection. It was not until the 15th century when, in some parishes, it was moved to its current location following Ⲧⲉⲛ ⲟⲩⲏⲟⲩ.[348] Slowly, the new placement became ubiquitous in all parishes.[349]

The emphasis on the divinity of the Lord Jesus Christ is evident in the hymn Ⲧⲉⲛⲛⲁⲩ. Being sinless, death could not defeat Him. However, His resurrection and victory over death were the greatest testimony of Jesus' divinity. The chant also reflects on humanity's jubilation and gratification as a product of the Resurrection. "Why did you mix fragrant oil, weeping and mourning with each other, O followers of the Lord? The luminous angel said to the women carrying the spices: look and be aware that the Savior has risen from the dead." We, the faithful, no longer live in sorrow, but rather in joy and thanksgiving, for through Christ's resurrection, all humankind has rejoiced at conquering death.

---

[346] Baumstark, Anton, *Comparative Liturgy*, 101.
[347] The First Council of Nicaea was a council of Christian bishops convened in Nicaea in Bithynia by the Roman Emperor Constantine I in AD 325. This first ecumenical council was the first effort to attain consensus in the church through an assembly representing all of Christendom. Its main accomplishments were settlement of the Christological issue of the nature of the Son of God and his relationship to God the Father, the construction of the first part of the Creed of Nicaea, establishing uniform observance of the date of Easter, and promulgation of early canon law.
[348] Some sources, like: Paris, BnF, MS Copte 69 (14th C.), fol. 167v, prescribe Ⲧⲉⲛⲛⲁⲩ following the recitation of the Midnight psalms. This might indicate a transitional location before its current one.
[349] Athanasius of Saint Macarius Monastery (Father), *Summary of the Liturgical History of the Church of Alexandria (Part 2)*, 209.

The hymn ⲦⲈⲚⲚⲀⲨ starts with the words, "We look at the Resurrection of Christ." As the center and chief accomplishment of our lives and existence, the Resurrection should always be before our eyes. It is our hope, power, and testimony of victory, no matter how difficult the challenges may be. Through this hymn, we, the church, declare that we are followers of Christ, who raised us up with Him, giving us a new life. Through this profound chant, we proclaim that we worship no other deity but the Lord Jesus Christ, saying, "We worship the holy Jesus Christ the Lord. We worship the holy Cross, O Christ, and we praise and glorify Your Resurrection." Along with the Resurrection, we memorialize the Cross, through which salvation became our new reality. Hence, we glorify the Lord, for He endured the cross for our salvation, and conquered death by His death.

The First Canticle

The term "Canticle," in general, refers to lyrics from the Old Testament that were included in the church's hymnody. "In practice," says James Mearns, "it means those Songs of Holy Scripture which have been selected for ecclesiastical use and are appended to, or incorporated with, the Psalter or other parts of the Divine Office."[350] In the Coptic Church, the term "Canticle" is appointed to refer to the Coptic word "Ⲑⲱⲥ" meaning "Praise." In the Coptic Orthodox Church, there are four Canticles prayed in the Midnight Psalmody.[351] In Regular Days, the first Canticle is recited immediately after "Ⲧⲉⲛ ⲟⲏⲛⲟⲩ." The First Canticle is the praise that Moses chanted during the exodus of the Israelites from Egypt after crossing the Red Sea, where they witnessed the Pharaoh's army drowning. The accounts of this miracle are found in Exodus 15, which also makes

---
[350] J. Mearns, *Canticles of the Christian Church*, 1.
[351] This is in addition to the Grand Ode (or Canticle) as will be examined later.

mention of Miriam, the sister of Moses, who, along with other women, took a timbrel in her hand, praising and rejoicing for God's salvation.

In the First Canticle, worshippers recall the Israelites crossing the Red Sea, which, as Saint Paul expounds, is a symbol of Baptism.[352] Therefore, the First Canticle allows us to reflect on Christ's victory over Satan, and accepting Jesus Christ as our Lord, thereby causing humanity to rejoice and praise God, for He is in glory glorified. Through baptism, the Lord brought humanity from darkness to light and from rejection to acceptance.

The First and Third Canticles are considered the Church's oldest praises.[353] Both were used in the East as well as in the West.[354] The First Canticle is the praise of victory. In the Old Testament, the Israelite's victory over the Egyptians and their freedom from the bondage of the Pharaoh, were powered by and stemmed from God's salvation represented by the sacrifice of a lamb. This same principle was repeated at a much larger scale in the New Testament, where the true sacrifice, Christ, granted salvation for all humanity through the Cross. For by His death, He liberated us from the bondage of Satan, and through His blood, granted us victory over sin.

Manuscripts attest that the last stanza of this canticle has a scarce melismatic tune. However, it is only mentioned in the Bright Saturday Midnight Psalmody.[355] The tune of this chant was preserved in the village of Zenia (الزينية) in Upper Egypt. After this, the *Lobsh* of the First Canticle is chanted. The word "Ⲗⲱⲃϣ" (*Lobsh*) is a Coptic word meaning "pinnacle," "peak," or "culmination;"[356] in De Lacy O'Leary's translation

---

[352] 1 Corinthians 10:1, 2.
[353] Baumstark, Anton, *Comparative Liturgy*, 112.
[354] Athanasius (Monk), *Midnight and Matins Psalmody*, 140.
[355] This subject will be discussed in further detail when we examine the order of Bright Saturday.
[356] Makar, Adeeb B., *The Abbreviated Coptic-English Dictionary*, 81.

it means "crown."³⁵⁷ The common notion of translating *Lobsh* to "explanation" has no ground in Coptic dictionaries and lexicons. Thus, the *Lobsh* of the First Canticle means the *peak* of the first praise, which is basically a summary of it. The *Lobsh* highlights the same concepts of spiritual victory as found in the First Canticle and includes prayer requests to Moses the Prophet on our behalf, as well as the intercessions of the Virgin Mary. It is concluded by worshipping the Holy Trinity, who granted us salvation, freely. Although the first mention of this chant in its current placement was by Ibn Kabar;³⁵⁸ which proposes a composition of the chant in the first half of the 14th century, Michael Helmy proposes a much older date. Helmy suggests a Jerusalem origin to this and other similar chants attributable to the First Canticle. All these chants would conclude with the phrase "for He has triumphed gloriously." At a later date, this *Lobsh* was used as a doxology for Moses the Prophet, hence, a novel stanza pertaining to Moses the Prophet was appended to the chant.³⁵⁹

Unlike the common order of Coptic prayers, the quatrain pertaining to Saint Mary in this *Lobsh*, "ϧⲉⲛ ⲟⲩϣⲱⲧ," comes after that of Prophet Moses. Inspecting Psalter manuscripts shows that documents dated before the 18th century exclude the stanza of Saint Mary.³⁶⁰ In fact, some Psalters exclude the stanza of Ⲧⲉⲛⲟⲩⲱϣⲧ (We worship) as well.³⁶¹ Even Raphael Tuki stops at the stanza pertaining to Saint Moses.³⁶² Manuscripts from the 14th and 15th centuries, like MS Cod. Vindob. Copte 3 (c. AD 1348–

---

[357] De Lacy O'Leary, D.D., *The Coptic Theotokia*, x.
[358] Ibn Kabar, *The Lamp*, BnF, MS Arabic 203 (c. AD 1363-1369), fol. 201v.
[359] Ragheb, Michael Helmy. (2021). Initial Indications Regarding Chants Attributable to the First and Third Canticles in the Coptic Rite. *Alexandria School*, 31(2), 161-166.
[360] Examples: Vienna, ONB, MS Cod. Vindob. Copte 3 (c. AD 1348-1368), Vatican, Vat, MS Copte 38 (c. AD 1370-1378), BnF, MS Copte 11 (AD 1518), MS Copte 69 (14th C.), London, Bod., MS Hunt 256 (AD 1387).
[361] BnF, MS Copte 11, fol. 27r.
[362] Tuki, Raphael (Bishop), *The Theotokions According to the Order of the Month of Kiahk*, 39.

1368),³⁶³ Bod., MS Hunt 256 (AD 1387),³⁶⁴ and MS Copte 11 (AD 1518),³⁶⁵ present this chant as a "Psaly for Moses the Prophet," not as a *Lobsh* of the First Canticle, which explains the paradox in discussion.³⁶⁶ When the quatrain of Saint Mary was introduced, it was positioned after that of Saint Moses. It also proposes the possibility that the chant once concluded with the stanza pertaining to Saint Moses before "Ϫⲉⲛⲟⲩⲱϣⲧ" was appended, then the quatrain of Saint Mary was inserted between the two.

Depending on time availability, the *Lobsh* of the First Canticle can be intoned in either a Major or Minor tune, both are applicable for all the quatrains. The Major tune comprises of two melodies. The first six stanzas utilize the first melody, which is the same as the first quatrain Ϧⲉⲛ ⲟⲩⲱⲧ (With the split). The last three stanzas, however, are chanted in the second melody. Due to time constraints, the common practice in many parishes is to chant the first two stanzas in the same manner as Ϧⲉⲛ ⲟⲩⲱⲧ, then the next four stanzas in the Minor tune, followed by the last three stanzas in the Major tune (second melody).

This prevalent practice, however, is not followed by Cantor Faheem, who directs that first melody of the Major tune (same as Ϧⲉⲛ ⲟⲩⲱⲧ) is assigned to all quatrains of the *Lobsh* in Regular Days, whereas the second melody of the Major tune (same as Ϩⲓⲧⲉⲛ ⲛⲓⲉⲩⲭⲏ—Through the prayers) is appointed to the month of Kiahk. Finally, the Major tune of Ⲙⲁⲣⲉⲛⲟⲩⲱⲛϩ (Let us give thanks), which is the *Lobsh* of the Second Canticle, is employed for ecclesiastical festal occasions. To him (Cantor Faheem), these regulations are applicable to *Lobsh* hymns of both the First

---

³⁶³ Vienna, ONB, MS Cod. Vindob. Copte 3 (c. AD 1348-1368), fol. 17r.
³⁶⁴ London, Bod., MS Hunt 256 (AD 1387), fol. 18r.
³⁶⁵ BnF, MS Copte 11, fol. 27v.
³⁶⁶ Ibn Kabar still called it *Lobsh*, which might be the reason for the wide spread of this title in later centuries. See: Ibn Kabar, *The Lamp*, BnF, MS Arabic 203 (c. AD 1363-1369), fol. 201v.

and Second Canticles. Interestingly, particular tunes for festive days and the month of Kiahk for both ϧⲉⲛ ⲟⲩⲱϣⲧ and Ⲙⲁⲣⲉⲛⲟⲩⲱⲛϩ are still preserved in the Upper Egypt heritage, precisely in Zenia.

Like the First Canticle, the chanting of the First Canticle *Lobsh* initiates from the northern chorus. Since it consists of nine stanzas, the *Lobsh* is concluded by the northern chorus, allowing the Second Canticle to commence from the southern chorus.

On all weekdays, a pericope from Luke 2:29–32[367] intercepts the Sunday sequence, and is read before the Second Canticle. This is then followed by the seventh, eighth and ninth sections of the Sunday Theotokion. However, in the Sunday Midnight Psalmody, the Second Canticle follows the First Canticle *Lobsh* at once, and the interceptor prayers are recited in their original order as part of the Sunday Theotokion. From a contemplative standpoint, the Church aims to underscore that in declaring our joy and victory in the First Canticle, we are ready to depart and be with Christ, and hence (Luke 2:29–32) is uttered. The three sections from the Sunday Theotokion reflect on Christ's salvation by His incarnation through the Holy Spirit and Virgin Mary. Recognizing the great gift of salvation prompts the supplicants to express their thankfulness and gratitude to the Lord, which are the quintessence of the Second Canticle.

The Second Canticle

Similar to the First Canticle, the Second Canticle starts with "Amen, Alleluia," Ⲕⲩⲣⲓⲉ ⲉⲗⲉⲏⲥⲟⲛ (Lord, have mercy) three times, and the Lord's Prayer. The recitation of the Second Canticle would then commence from

---

[367] Sovereign Lord, as You have promised, You may now dismiss Your servant in peace. For my eyes have seen Your salvation, which You have prepared in the sight of all nations: a light for revelation to the Gentiles, and the glory of Your people Israel.

the southern chorus, as stated earlier. Unlike the aforementioned contemporary order, Ibn Kabar directs that the Second Canticle starts with Κ̀ⲩⲣⲓⲉ ⲉ̀ⲗⲉⲏⲥⲟⲛ three times, after which the congregation, in one accord, says 'Have mercy on us O God the Father, the *Pantocrator*. O Holy Trinity, have mercy on us. O God of Powers be with us,' followed by the Lord's Prayer.[368]

The Second Canticle is Psalm 135,[369] which in the Jewish tradition is called the *Great Hallel*, meaning the Great Psalm of Praise. The Israelites chanted this praise during the days of Solomon when the construction of the temple was completed. In other words, this is considered the Psalm of praise and thanksgiving for God's work in our lives. In it, we thank God because He is good, and His mercy endures forever. This represents the period following baptism, where humanity stands before God, thanking Him for the great work He has done and His enduring mercy, as chanted in the refrain of this canticle. The refrain "for his mercy endures forever" is repeated twenty-eight times throughout Psalm 135. The Gospel of Matthew states that the number of generations from the time the Psalms were written to the coming of Christ was twenty-eight generations: "fourteen from David to the exile to Babylon, and fourteen from the exile to the Messiah" (Matthew 1:17). In the eyes of the church, God's mercy has endured throughout every generation since the Psalm was written until His mercy was fulfilled by His incarnation, death, and resurrection.

Following this, the *Lobsh* of the Second Canticle is intoned. Like the First Canticle *Lobsh*, it can be hymned in a Major or Minor tune. The first two quatrains are usually chanted in the Major tune, which form the hymn "Ⲙⲁⲣⲉⲛⲟⲩⲱⲛϩ̅." The following stanzas up to "Ϩⲓⲧⲉⲛ ⲛⲓⲉⲩⲭⲏ" are recited in the Minor tune. Alternatively, if time permits, they may be intoned in the

---

[368] Ibn Kabar, *The Lamp*, BnF, MS Arabic 203 (c. AD 1363-1369), fol. 201v.
[369] In the Hebrew (Masoretic text) Psalms numbering it is Psalm 136.

same manner as the first two. The rest of the quatrains borrow the same tune used to conclude the *Lobsh* of the First Canticle. Although Ibn Sibaa made no mention of this chant, Ibn Kabar and later manuscripts recorded it.[370] Hence, it is reasonable to deduce that this chant was developed sometime in the first half of the 14th century. It is noteworthy that manuscripts from the 14th and 15th centuries, except for Ibn Kabar,[371] dedicate this chant to David the prophet, as such, has its title "Psaly *Adam* for David."[372] Similar to the First Canticle *Lobsh*, the hymn concluded with the quatrain for David the Prophet, before more recent documents add stanzas for Saint Mary and the Holy Trinity.[373] While MS Copte 11 (AD 1518) and MS Copte 69 (14th C.) conclude the chant with the quatrain for David the Prophet, other manuscripts attest to the beginning of the amendment. Mimicking the same conclusion of the First Canticle *Lobsh*, Bod., MS Hunt 256 (AD 1387) adds the stanza of "Ϫⲉⲛⲟⲩⲱϣⲧ," while MS Cod. Vindob. Copte 3 (c. AD 1348-1368) appends the contemporary concluding quatrain "Ⲕ̀ⲥⲙⲁⲣⲱⲟⲩⲧ." In both, there is no mention of stanzas for Saint Mary or the chorus of angels, as practiced today.

The Third Canticle

After declaring victory over sin and death, and thanking the Lord for His great work, praising Him becomes the inevitable end of this sequence. This

---

[370] Ibn Kabar, *The Lamp*, BnF, MS Arabic 203 (c. AD 1363-1369), fol. 202r.
[371] Ibn Kabar still calls it *Lobsh*, which might be the reason for the spread of this title in later centuries. See: Ibn Kabar, *The Lamp*, BnF, MS Arabic 203 (c. AD 1363-1369), fol. 202r.
[372] Vienna, ONB, MS Cod. Vindob. Copte 3 (c. AD 1348-1368), fol. 20r.; BnF, MS Copte 11 (AD 1518), fol. 31r.; MS Copte 69 (14th C.), fol. 17r.; London, Bod., MS Hunt 256 (AD 1387), fol. 21r.
[373] It is probable that this *Lobsh* originally concluded with "His mercy endures forever" before it was used—like the First Canticle *Lobsh*—as a doxology for Moses the Prophet, which required an addition of a stanza pertaining to the celebrated prophet. See Ragheb, Michael Helmy. (2022). Initial Indications Regarding Chants Attributable to the First and Third Canticles in the Coptic Rite. *Alexandria School*, 31(2), 166.

is found in the Third Canticle (Daniel 3:52–90), which is the song of three young men in the fiery furnace.[374] During tribulation, the church remains committed to praising, because the salvation of the Lord, she believes, is inexorable as was witnessed in the First and Second Canticles. Likewise, we Christians, the members of this firm church, must have robust faith in the salvation of Christ, despite the worldly tribulations and the temptations of the devil, even if they were "heated seven times more than it was usually heated" (Daniel 3:19). Through our strong faith, we are reminded of Christ's salvation and victory over death. We must be assured that He stands by our side through the most difficult of times as experienced by the three youth, who praised the Lord of Hosts in the midst of the fiery furnace. Through their faith, the fire felt like a cool mist. As Christians, this is the faith and mindset the church calls us to embrace.

The Third Canticle is comprised of forty stanzas. The first six are dedicated to praising the Lord and contemplating on His glorious attributes. The refrain "exceedingly to be praised and exalted above all forever" is common in all six stanzas. In the remaining thirty-four stanzas, we praise the Lord through the glorious work of His creation, chanting the refrain "Praise Him and exalt Him above all forever."

The Third Canticle, as mentioned above, is the Song of the Three Children in the fiery furnace. After baptism, Satan continues to fight against us with various means. Figuratively, this is our fiery furnace. However, the presence of Christ in our lives (who was the fourth person appearing as the Son of God in the fiery furnace) changes the heat and pain of our sufferings and struggles to a cool and comforting mist. As such, humanity continually praises God, even at times of tribulations and anguish, knowing that the Lord God is always by our side.

---

[374] This canticle corresponds to the 8th Ode in the Byzantine Rite and is called the Song of the Three Holy Children (Daniel 3:57–88).

Rufinus,[375] a fifth century historian, witnessed that the Third Canticle "was sung by Christians throughout the world."[376] Nevertheless, the services and occasions on which the Third Canticle is assigned to differed. It is considered one of the oldest praises in the universal church.

If time permits, the last eight stanzas of the Third Canticle are chanted in a melismatic tune called Ⲥⲙⲟⲩ ⲡ̄ϭⲟⲓⲥ (Bless the Lord). This was mentioned by Ibn Kabar as well as other manuscripts.[377] This was also noted by Professor Ernest Newlandsmith[378] in his work that was based on the hymns' rendition transmitted by Master Cantor Mikhail the Great[379] and supervised by Dr. Ragheb Moftah.[380] Due to time constraints, however, chanters now employ the melismatic melody for the last two

---

[375] Rufinus was a monk, historian, and theologian, who was born in AD 344 or 345 in the Roman city of Julia Concordia. Around AD 370, he was living in a monastic community in Aquileia when he met Jerome. He studied in Alexandria under Didymus the Blind for some time, and cultivated friendly relations with Macarius the elder and other ascetics in the desert. Rufinus spent most of the first decade of the fifth century translating Origen. He translated Origen's homilies for the whole Heptateuch except Deuteronomy, and others on selected Psalms, the Song of Songs, and 1 Samuel. Rufinus also translated other works. These include Eusebius' Ecclesiastical History, translated in 401 at the request of Bishop Chromatius of Aquileia as an antidote to the terror caused by the Gothic incursions into Italy. Rufinus departed in the year AD 410.
[376] F.L. Cross and E.A. Livingstone, *The Oxford Dictionary of the Christian Church* (third edition), 183.
[377] Abba Shenouda (31 Rite)—15th century, Lectionary of the Baramous monastery (9 Coptic)—16th century, manuscript (8770 Oriental)—maybe 18th century and *The Church Order*, MS Lit. 118 (AD 1911).
[378] Ernest Newlandsmith, born AD 1875, was a musicologist with strong Christian belief who formed the Laresol Society to promote artistic vocation of a religious nature. Together with Dr. Ragheb Muftah he was instrumental in noting down and audio recording traditional Coptic Orthodox Church music in the years AD 1927 to 1936.
[379] Cantor Mikhail Girgis of Batanoun (14 September 1873–18 April 1957 AD) was the master cantor of the Coptic Orthodox Church. He was knowledgeable in Church rites, in addition to being skilled in the languages of Coptic and Arabic. Cantor Mikhail the Great was appointed to be the first instructor of hymns in the Coptic Orthodox Clerical College by Archdeacon Habib Girgis. When the Institute of Coptic Studies was established, Cantor Mikhail was appointed to be its first teacher of hymns. The hymns from Cantor Mikhail were the source of the vocal notes recorded by Professor Ernest Newlandsmith, a musicologist from Oxford University, with the help of Dr. Ragheb Moftah. In addition, Cantor Mikhail conducted the first audio recording of Coptic music.
[380] Dr. Ragheb Moftah (AD 1898–2001) was an Egyptian musicologist and scholar of the Coptic music heritage. He co-authored the article on "Coptic Music" for the Coptic Encyclopedia. He spent much of his life studying the recording and notation of Coptic liturgical texts. In 1955 he was responsible for the Music and Hymn Department at the Institute of Coptic Studies and moved the primary studio he had already made in Saint Mary Church. He began recording the hymns and all the Church services with Cantor Mikhail's voice and then published in more talented voices on cassette tapes.

stanzas only. In the last stanza, two additional chants are preserved, namely Ϩⲱⲥ ⲉ̀ⲣⲟϥ (Praise Him), and Ⲁⲣⲓϩⲟⲩ̀ⲟ ϭⲁⲥϥ (Exalt Him above all).

It is interesting to note that the hymn "Ϩⲱⲥ ⲉ̀ⲣⲟϥ" starts with a very low pitch, and progressively increases up to the last note of the chant. Some meditations compare this to the state of humanity when elevated in praise until they can offer no more at the highest pitch possible. "Ϩⲱⲥ ⲉ̀ⲣⲟϥ" begins with calm yet confident and strong tunes. The music of the hymn is festive, and increases in pitch, as if it is being offered up toward the heavens, leading the spirit to enjoy the highest spiritual levels in the presence of its Creator. The melody of "Ⲁⲣⲓϩⲟⲩ̀ⲟ ϭⲁⲥϥ," on the other hand, repeats twice, reminding the faithful that not only the Lord is exalted, but He is exalted above all. The musical notes in "Ⲁⲣⲓϩⲟⲩ̀ⲟ ϭⲁⲥϥ" are uniquely long and expressive of joy. The hymn itself ends in long and brilliantly high notes, as if to confirm that praise is forever.

It is worth noting that the second last quatrain, in the majority of manuscripts, is addressed to the three saintly youth;[381] however, some sources add Daniel the Prophet.[382] In his *The Books of Theotokions and Canticles*, the first printed psalter, Raphael El-Tookhy did not make mention of Daniel.[383] Ekladious Labib and Father Mina Mahalawy followed suit.[384] However, in his AD 1911 *The Psalter for Kiahk*, Labib added Daniel.[385] As for more recent psalters, all notable ones, except for that of the Muharraq Monastery, did not mention Daniel. Additionally, the musical notations sponsored by Dr. Moftah attesting to Cantor

---

[381] Examples: Vienna, ONB, MS Cod. Vindob. Copt. 3 (AD 1348-1368), Paris, BnF, MS Copte 11 (AD 1518), Paris, BnF, MS Copte 69 (14th C.), London, Bod., MS Hunt 256 (AD 1387), and Vienna National Library - CVP. Copt. 3 HMML 24999 (15th C.).
[382] Examples: CM, MS Lit. 55 (AD 1717), The British Lib., OR. 5284, London, Bod., OR. 653 (AD 1772), London, Bod., OR. 49 (18th C.), London, Bod., MS Ind. Inst. Copt 3 (18th C.), and CM, MS Lit. 137 (18th C.).
[383] El-Tookhy, Raphael, *The Books of Theotokions and Canticles*, 38.
[384] Labib, Ekladious (Pek), *The Regular Holy Psalter*, 56, and Mahalawy, Mina (Father), *The Holy Psalter*, 63, respectively.
[385] Labib, Ekladious (Pek), *The Psalter for Kiahk*, 499.

Mikhail's rendition, dedicates the stanza solely for the three young men. Nonetheless, Cantor Tawfik Youssef includes Daniel.

Chants Attributable to the Third Canticle

After the Third Canticle, three hymns are intoned: the *Watos* psaly Ⲁⲣⲓⲯⲁⲗⲓⲛ (O sing unto Him), the hymn Ⳓⲉⲛⲉⲛ (We therefore present an offering), and finally the chant of Ⳓⲉⲛⲟⲩⲉϩ ⲛ̀ⲥⲱⲕ (We follow You). The latter is the oldest, which, at one point, was chanted immediately after the Third Canticle. The 14th century scholar and priest Ibn Kabar attests to that; he writes, "this melody, which followed the Third Canticle, is intoned in a diversity of *Watos* tunes in accordance with the season."[386] This indicates an establishment of the chant before Ibn Kabar's time, in addition to an invaluable note vis-à-vis different renditions of the chant based on the ecclesiastical season from at least the 13th century. Therefore, Ⳓⲉⲛⲟⲩⲉϩ ⲛ̀ⲥⲱⲕ was kind of a *Lobsh* for the Third Canticle, although this title was not officially accorded to it.

It was not until the 15th century when the psaly Ⲁⲣⲓⲯⲁⲗⲓⲛ was introduced.[387] The authorship of this psaly is attributed to Cantor Sarkis.[388] The odd quatrains of Ⲁⲣⲓⲯⲁⲗⲓⲛ are in Greek whereas the even ones are in Coptic. As in all psalies, antiphonal chanting between the northern and southern choruses is exercised, with each chorus reciting two quatrains (one Greek and one Coptic) at a time. The music of Ⲁⲣⲓⲯⲁⲗⲓⲛ is unique and specific to this psaly, and remains constant throughout the

---

[386] Ibn Kabar, *The Lamp*, BnF, MS Arabic 203 (c. AD 1363-1369), fol. 202r.

[387] This psaly was introduced first to the Kiahk Psalmody then to the regular one used all year round. It is also worth noting that until the beginning of the twentieth century, this psaly was not known by all churches; its use was standardized after it was published in the printed psalmodies.

[388] Cantor Sarkis was from the area of Old Cairo. His father, Father Jeremiah, served as priest at the Church of Saint Apakir and Saint John in Old Cairo, and later went to serve in the Church of the Holy Resurrection in Jerusalem. His son, Cantor Sarkis, was also ordained as priest, and served with his father in Jerusalem, which aided him in learning Greek. Father Sarkis lived in the 15th century and departed around AD 1492.

liturgical year, regardless of the ecclesiastical season. It is interesting to note that Ⲁⲣⲓⲯⲁⲗⲓⲛ has 24 quatrains, each of which starts with a letter from the Greek alphabet.[389] Each quatrain is divided into four lines; the first three rhyme with each other, whereas the last is a refrain, which translates to "praise Him and exalt Him forever."

The Church Order, MS Lit. 117 (AD 1910) preserved at the Old Patriarchate Library states, "After Ⲧⲉⲛⲟⲩⲱϩ ⲛ̀ⲥⲱⲕ, Ⲁⲣⲓⲯⲁⲗⲓⲛ is chanted, if time permits."[390] In explaining the order of the Midnight Psalmody for the Feast of Resurrection, MS Lit. 118 (AD 1911), preserving the original placement of Ⲧⲉⲛⲟⲩⲱϩ ⲛ̀ⲥⲱⲕ immediately after the Third Canticle, skips Ⲁⲣⲓⲯⲁⲗⲓⲛ.[391] This suggests that until recently, viewing Ⲧⲉⲛⲟⲩⲱϩ ⲛ̀ⲥⲱⲕ as the *Lobsh* of the Third Canticle, the common practice was to chant it before Ⲁⲣⲓⲯⲁⲗⲓⲛ, with an option to omit the latter chant. Conversely, while explicating the order of Bright Saturday Midnight Psalmody, the same document (MS Lit. 118) made Ⲁⲣⲓⲯⲁⲗⲓⲛ precede Ⲧⲉⲛⲟⲩⲱϩ ⲛ̀ⲥⲱⲕ,[392] indicating hesitation in the order of the two hymns.

Books published in the beginning of the 20th century placed Ⲁⲣⲓⲯⲁⲗⲓⲛ before Ⲧⲉⲛⲟⲩⲱϩ ⲛ̀ⲥⲱⲕ, thereby this practice became predominant. One possible reason for placing Ⲁⲣⲓⲯⲁⲗⲓⲛ immediately after the Third Canticle is its theme; it is apparent that the lyrics of this psaly are heavily reliant on the Third Canticle text. Moreover, the melody of Ⲧⲉⲛⲟⲩⲱϩ ⲛ̀ⲥⲱⲕ is a natural lead to the Commemoration of Saint, which follows. In any case, the contemporary order places Ⲁⲣⲓⲯⲁⲗⲓⲛ immediately after the Third Canticle.

---

[389] The first quatrain starts with the letter alpha, and the last quatrain begins with omega.
[390] *The Church Order*, Cairo, Patriarchal Library, MS Lit. 117 (AD 1910), fol. 16r.
[391] *The Church Order*, Cairo, Patriarchal Library, MS Lit. 118 (AD 1911), fol. 77v.
[392] *The Church Order*, Cairo, Patriarchal Library, MS Lit. 118 (AD 1911), fols. 66r-67v.

The common practice is that after Ⲁⲣⲓⲯⲁⲗⲓⲛ, the hymn Ⲧⲉⲛⲉⲛ is chanted. However, a number of manuscripts[393] coming from Upper Egypt instruct that another hymn called Ϣⲟⲙⲧ ⲛ̀ⲣⲱⲙⲓ for the Thee Saintly Youth[394] be sung before Ⲧⲉⲛⲉⲛ, a chant that is rooted in (Daniel 3:24-25). Luckily, the melody of this chant was preserved in Zenia. As for Ⲧⲉⲛⲉⲛ, Ibn Kabar, along with all the extant manuscript predating the 15th century, did not mention this hymn. Ⲧⲉⲛⲉⲛ is comprised of four stanzas and a concluding sentence. The first two stanzas are in Greek whereas the last two are in mixed Bohairic and Sahidic Coptic, and the concluding sentence is in solely Bohairic Coptic.[395] George Ghaly suggests Fayyumic tendencies of the text,[396] and authorship sometime before the 9th century.[397] It is also worth noting that the themes of the third and fourth stanzas are analogous to the first two. This suggests different authors, particularly since various languages were employed.

In a scrupulous study of the hymn, Michael Ragheb inspected fragments belonging to the White Monastery in Upper Egypt (10th–12th centuries), which contain the hymn Ⲧⲉⲛⲉⲛ. Nonetheless, it was not consolidated as we know it today, but rather split into three distinct chants, all said during the liturgy, not vigil. The first chant consists of the first stanza, and was chanted following the Reconciliation Prayer, comparable to the contemporary *Adam* Aspasmos, on the second Sunday of Lent, according to the proper of the White Monastery, which corresponds to the current fourth Sunday of Lent. Later, the same author

---

[393] Among those documents (unfortunately not numbered), psalmodies from the monastery of Saint Mary (El-Moharraq), Zenia (Luxor), Qamoula (Luxor), Naqadah (Qena), Saint Besentaos monastery (Qena), monastery of Archangel Michael (Qena), and Cairo, CCP 8-11 (AD 1896), fol. 44v.

[394] Translation of the hymn: Three men were tied and thrown amidst fire. "I see four (men)," said Nebuchadnezzar the king.

[395] Labib, Ekladious (Pek), *The Regular Holy Psalter*, 65.

[396] Ghaly, George, *A Contextual, Historical and Grammatical Analysis of Ⲧⲉⲛⲉⲛ, A Unique Coptic Hymn*, 4, 6.

[397] Ghaly, Ibid., 29.

retracts his position and proposes a different placement of the hymn (i.e., first stanza of Ⲧⲉⲛⲉⲛ) as a chant attributable to the evening psalms.³⁹⁸ The second chant comprises of the second and third stanzas of Ⲧⲉⲛⲉⲛ, in addition to the concluding sentence "Ⲉⲣⲅⲱⲥ." It was said in the third Saturday of Lent, which is the counterpart of the fifth one in the contemporary order. Being the chief part concerned with the three saintly youth, it was also chanted on their commemoration on Bashans 10ᵗʰ. It is noteworthy that only in this chant we find the refrain (Ⲁⲛⲁⲛⲓⲁⲥ Ⲁⲍⲁⲣⲓⲁⲥ ⲕⲉ Ⲙⲓⲥⲁⲏⲗ—Hananiah Azariah and Mishael). As for the third chant, it encompasses the fourth stanza of Ⲧⲉⲛⲉⲛ preceded by its Greek translation. At the White Monastery, this hymn was used for the third Sunday of Lent, which parallels the current fifth one. It was also said on the second Sunday of Eastertide.³⁹⁹

Vatican, Vat, MS Copte 68 (15ᵗʰ C.) depicts the first appearance of the hymn in Midnight Psalmody, but only the second chant (second and third stanzas). The earliest extant manuscripts of the hymn in its current form and order are MS Copte 36 (AD 1709), London, Bodleian Library—Oxford, OR. 5284 (AD 1718), and St. Macarius Monastery, MS Lit. 98 (AD 1781).⁴⁰⁰ According to the contemporary practice, Ⲧⲉⲛⲉⲛ is chanted during the month of Kiahk, on Bright Saturday, and, if time permits, in Regular Days.

In an effort to uncover the composition date of Ⲧⲉⲛⲉⲛ, we inspected its melodic modes (Arabic: مقام, *maqām*—plural: *maqāmāt*). The hymn is mostly using the *Rast* mode, where the high parts uses *Suzidil*, a derivative

---

[398] Ragheb, Michael Helmy. (2021). Initial Indications Regarding Chants Attributable to the First and Third Canticles in the Coptic Rite. *Alexandria School*, 31(2), 171-172.
[399] This chant includes a *Trisagion*, suggesting its location after the Praxis lesson, as was the practice in Upper Egypt.
[400] Ragheb, Michael Helmy, A New Reading of the Hymn of the Three Saintly Youth According to the Most Ancient Fragments that Has it. (2018). In *The Ancestors' Heritage in the Eyes of the Descendants*, 1-27. The author also provides a more precise translation of the hymn.

of *Rast*, and the concluding part utilizes *Bayati*. These modes are all old and, unfortunately, cannot be used to determine the exact composition date. The hymn Ϯⲉⲛⲉⲛ presents praise as a rational *sacrifice*; it reads, "we bring a sacrifice and a rational worship," an essential understanding of Christian worship. It also describes tribulations, even death for Christ, as *glory*: "they were raised to take glory in their bodies"—a real application of the Christian conception presented in (Acts 5:42).[401] In the *trisagion* found in the fourth stanza, manuscripts disagreed on the attribution to the Son, some say "Immortal," and others "Invisible."

After Ϯⲉⲛⲉⲛ, the hymn Ϯⲉⲛⲟⲩⲉϩ ⲛ̀ⲥⲱⲕ follows, which comprises of six quatrains. The first two are almost identical to the Prayer of Azariah amidst the fiery furnace. This prayer is found in the continuation of the Book of Daniel as part of the Deuterocanonical Books,[402] "And now with all our hearts we follow You, we fear You and seek Your presence. Do not put us to shame but deal with us in Your patience and in Your abundant mercy" (Daniel 3:41, 42). The first two quatrains of Ϯⲉⲛⲟⲩⲉϩ ⲛ̀ⲥⲱⲕ read, "We follow You with all our hearts, and we seek Your face, O God do not forsake us. But rather deal with us according to Your meekness, and according to Your great mercy, O Lord help us."

As noted earlier, the music of this hymn changes according to the ecclesiastical season. Diversity of melodies are appointed to Regular days, the month of Kiahk, Feast Days, Lent (two tunes), and the feasts of the Cross and Palm Sunday. For this reason, Ibn Kabar states, "this melody, which followed the Third Canticle, is intoned in a diversity of *Watos* tunes

---

[401] "The apostles left the Sanhedrin, rejoicing because they had been counted worthy of suffering disgrace for the Name."
[402] Deuterocanonical books (The word deuterocanonical comes from the Greek meaning 'belonging to the second canon') is a term used since the 16th century in the Catholic Church and Eastern Christianity to describe certain books and passages of the Christian Old Testament that are not part of the current Hebrew Bible. The deuterocanonical books are considered canonical by Catholics, Eastern Orthodox, Oriental Orthodox, and the Church of the East, but are considered non-canonical by most Protestants.

in accordance with the season."⁴⁰³ The music for Regular Days is comprised of three distinct tunes: melismatic, semi-major (also known as the *Mohayer* [in Arabic]), and minor; the latter is identical to that of the Commemoration of Saints. In most parishes, the first two quatrains are intoned in the melismatic tune, the third and fourth in the semi-major tune, and the last two in the minor tune, as a lead into the Commemoration of Saints.

Thus, after chanting the Third Canticle with its three melismatic hymns, the *Watos* Psaly Ⲁⲣⲓⲯⲁⲗⲓⲛ, which Cantor (later on "Father") Sarkis authored, is recited, followed by the rare chant of ⲋ̄ ⲛ̄ⲣⲱⲙⲓ in some areas. Afterward, the hymn Ϯⲉⲛⲉⲛ is chanted, if time permits, followed by Ϯⲉⲛⲟⲩⲉϩ ⲛ̄ⲥⲱⲕ, which, perhaps, was once the *Lobsh* of the Third Canticle. After the 14ᵗʰ century, a new liturgical element entered the Midnight Psalmody following Ϯⲉⲛⲟⲩⲉϩ ⲛ̄ⲥⲱⲕ, that is, the Commemoration of the Saints.

The Commemoration of Saints

After the church, or rather the Church Militant,⁴⁰⁴ achieves the highest level of praise following the Third Canticle and its hymns, she experiences heaven on earth, and, through faith, begins to see the members of the Church Triumphant.⁴⁰⁵ We therefore rejoice in the presence of the saints, asking them to pray to the Lord on our behalf so that Christ may grant us forgiveness of our sins, and that we too may one day join them in the Paradise of Joy. The Commemoration of Saints found its way to the

---

⁴⁰³ Ibn Kabar, *The Lamp*, BnF, MS Arabic 203 (c. AD 1363-1369), fol. 202r.
⁴⁰⁴ Christians on earth who struggle as soldiers of Christ against sin, and the devil.
⁴⁰⁵ The spirits of the victorious ones who are in Paradise.

Midnight Psalmody in the 15ᵗʰ or 16ᵗʰ century,[406] initially on Sundays and in feasts.[407]

The Commemoration of Saints starts with the Virgin Mary, followed by the archangels and the heavenly orders, all of whom we ask intercessions on our behalf. After this, we ask for the prayers of the fathers the patriarchs, the prophets, and all the righteous of the Old Testament. This is followed by asking for the intercessions of Saint John the Baptist, the one hundred and forty-four thousand celibates, and Saint John the Beloved. Next, we ask for the prayers of the apostles, martyrs, saints, and patriarchs, respectively. Toward the end, quatrains dedicated to King Constantine, Queen Helen, the wise virgin ladies, and the saints of the day are recited. The second last stanza reads, "Likewise we glorify you with David the Psalmist, you are the priest forever according to the order of Melchizedek," followed by the last quatrain for the Patriarch. If the parish is part of a diocese or a bishop is present during the vigil office, a quatrain specific to the bishop is added after that of the Patriarch. The Commemoration of Saints employs six *Watos* tunes, depending on the liturgical season, which are consonant with Ϫⲉⲛⲟⲩⲉϩ ⲛ̀ⲥⲱⲕ: Year-Round, *Kiahkian*, Joyous, Lenten (two melodies), and *Hosanna*.

The Doxologies

Following the Commemoration of Saints, the *Watos* Doxologies—these are the same doxologies used during the incense offering office—are uttered. The purpose of the Doxologies is to venerate the Virgin Mary, the angels, the martyrs, and the saints, and ask them to pray on our behalf for the forgiveness of our sins. As such, the intent of the Doxologies is

---

[406] Athanasius of Saint Macarius Monastery (Father), *Summary of the Liturgical History of the Church of Alexandria (Part 2)*, 153-154.
[407] Ibid., 297.

analogous to that of the Commemoration of Saints, which is the reason for its direct succession. The *Watos* Doxologies also employ the six tunes of the preceding two chants. This concludes the Midnight Psalmody and marks the start of the Matins Psalmody. As indicated previously, the Matins Psalmody is now amalgamated with the Midnight Psalmody.

The Matins Psalmody

From time immemorial, after the Midnight Psalmody, worshippers rest a little before returning to church for Matins Psalmody. The two offices eventually were fused, probably for practical reasons. The sixth-century *Rule of the Master*[408] (33) provides a pragmatic cause for reciting both offices consecutively without a break (not amalgamated yet), "In Spring and Summer ... the brothers are to begin the Nocturns at cockcrow because of the shortness of the nights, and as soon as they have finished the set number of psalms, they are to append Matins with its full number of psalms ... so the shortness of nighttime relative to daytime requires, because of the weakness of human nature, that the psalmody of the Divine Office be curtailed and the daytime Office be joined to that of the night."[409] This early reference still makes a distinction between the two offices. Eventually, perhaps in the ninth century, the fusion occurred.

The schematic structure of the Matins Psalmody is the same as that of the Vespers Psalmody. It starts with the Fourth Canticle, followed by the Psaly of the day, the Theotokion of the day, the *Lobsh* of the Theotokion, the Antiphonary, and the Conclusion of the Theotokion, respectively. The conception here is that the incense offering office is always preceded by the psalmody (i.e., Vespers Psalmody leads Vespers Offering of Incense

---

[408] *Rule of the Master* (*Regula Magistri*) is an anonymous collection of monastic precepts, authored in the opening decades of the sixth century. Its text is found in the *Concordia Regularum* of Benedict of Aniane, who gave it its name.
[409] Talf, *The Liturgy*, Ibid., 205.

and Matins Psalmody heads Prime Offering of Incense). Since the Matins Psalmody is now part of the Midnight Psalmody, the Midnight Psalmody would be better positioned right prior to the Prime Offering of Incense, which is still the case in most of the monasteries. In city churches, however, there is a time gap between the Midnight Psalmody and Prime Offering of Incense. The only structural difference between the Matins Psalmody and the Vespers Psalmody is the fact that the latter commences with the hymn Ⲛⲓⲉⲑⲛⲟⲥ ⲧⲏⲣⲟⲩ (O praise the Lord all you, nations), which is Psalm 116, whereas this hymn is not chanted in Matins Psalmody. In fact, most churches in the East and West use this Psalm for evening and matins services.[410]

Prior to integrating the Matins Psalmody with the Midnight Psalmody, the rite of the Matins Psalmody started with the Introduction. That is, the priest's prayer of "Ⲡ̄ⲟ̄ⲓⲥ Ⲡ̄ⲟ̄ⲓⲥ ⲛⲁⲓ ⲛⲁⲛ" followed by "Alleluia," then "In the Name of the Father, the Son and the Holy Spirit, one God, Lord have mercy, Lord have mercy, Lord bless, Amen," and "Glory be to the Father, the Son and the Holy Spirit, now and forever and unto the age of all ages, Amen," and finally, the Lord's Prayer, the Prayer of Thanksgiving, then Psalm 50, respectively. After the amalgamation, however, this introduction was omitted.

The Fourth Canticle

Like in Vespers Psalmody, Lauds Psalms (Pss 148–150), which are known in the Coptic Rite as the Fourth Canticle, are recited at the commencement of Matins Psalmody. Saint Athanasius include these three psalms among those expressing praise that may be employed when God

---

[410] Athanasius (Monk), *Midnight and Matins Psalmody*, 243-248.

answers prayer.⁴¹¹ The use of these three psalms in the morning service has its roots in Jewish synagogues, a practice that was embraced in all Christendom. In Egypt, these three psalms were used in the Matins Psalmody during the pontificate of Saint Athanasius the Apostolic (AD 328–373). Saint John Chrysostom (AD 347–407), in his description of the rites of morning prayers for the Antiochian monks, corroborated the use of these psalms in the morning prayers.⁴¹² Saint John Cassian, among others, made similar references to the use of these Psalms; he says, "For the hymns which in this country they used at the Matins service at the close of the nocturnal vigils, which they are accustomed to finish after the cock-crowing and before dawn, these they still sing in like manner; viz., Ps. 148, beginning 'O praise the Lord from heaven,' and the rest which follow."⁴¹³

Ibn Kabar comments, "There were several ways of chanting Alleluia in the Fourth Canticle. There was a melismatic tune, a semi-major tune, and a minor tune."⁴¹⁴ The rubric prescribes the chanting of the last stanza of the Fourth Canticle (Ⲁⲗⲗⲏⲗⲟⲩⲓⲁ Ⲡⲓⲱⲟⲩ ⲫⲁ Ⲡⲉⲛⲛⲟⲩϯ ⲡⲉ—Alleluia. Glory be to our God) in its melismatic melody, called *Alleluia of the Golden Hour*, during the Kiahk Vespers Psalmody, Lenten Vespers Psalmody, in addition to the Sunday Vespers Psalmody in Regular Days, if time permits. In addition to the regular melody commonly employed for the Fourth Canticle, two specific tunes are optionally appointed for the month of Kiahk, and the Lenten season; both rooted in Alexandria.⁴¹⁵ These melodies are restricted to the Vespers Psalmody.

---

[411] Athanasius, ., Gregg, R. C., & Athanasius, *The life of Antony and the letter to Marcellinus*, 113, 121-122.
[412] Athanasius (Monk), *Midnight and Matins Psalmody*, 250-251.
[413] Cassian, John, *The Institutes*, Book 3—chapter VI.
[414] Athanasius (Monk), *Midnight and Matins Psalmody*, 253.
[415] These rare renditions of the Fourth Canticle were handed down by Cantor Habeeb Hanna El-Mirahem.

In Psalm 148, the psalmist calls on creation itself to praise God. Saint Basil the Great states in one of his homilies, "If sometimes, on a bright night, whilst gazing with watchful eyes on the inexpressible beauty of the stars, you have thought of the Creator of all things; if you have asked yourself who it is that has dotted heaven with such flowers, and why visible things are even more useful than beautiful; if sometimes, in the day, you have studied the marvels of light, if you have raised yourself by visible things to the invisible Being, then you are a well prepared auditor, and you can take your place in this august and blessed amphitheater."[416] Creation praises God by simply being what it was created to be in all its incredible variety. In Psalms 149 and 150, humankind is asked to praise God, because this is the will of God. This is in fulfillment of Isaiah's prophecy, where the Lord says, "I have formed these people for myself. They will praise Me" (Isaiah 43:21).

When reflecting on the Fourth Canticle, we remember humanity that was given baptism to conquer sin, that has overcome the worldly struggles and temptations of the devil and is enjoying the presence of the heavenly and joining them in praising the Lord, calling upon the whole creation to praise their Creator in all ways, with the psaltery and harp, timbrel and organs, strings, and cymbals ... let everything that has breath praise the name of the Lord our God. In the Fourth Canticle, the church offers praises to God not only for who He is, but simply that "He is." We praise Him as the self-existing, ever-existing God. This is in essence the highest level of praise and worship.

---

[416] Basil (Saint), Homily VI.

The Psalies

Following the Fourth Canticle, a specific psaly is recited. The word "psaly" takes its root from the Greek verb "ψαλλω[417]—psallo," which means "to sing praises;" the word Psaly, therefore, means "a song." The older Sahidic version of Psalies existed before the 9th century and can be found in the Morgan Collection.[418] A Psaly is typically an acrostic poem with rhyming stanzas, utilizing the 24 letters of the Greek alphabet, or the 32 of the Coptic language.[419] Each stanza is divided into four lines (forming a quatrain). Each line is divided into segments. In the *Adam* Psalies, which are said on Sunday, Monday and Tuesday, each stanza line is divided into five segments. However, each stanza line of the *Watos* Psalies (said on the other days of the week) comprises of seven segments. For this reason, the *Watos* stanzas are longer than those of the *Adam*.

Originally, the Psalies and the Theotokions were liturgical elements pertaining to the Offering of Incense; however, in the 13th century, some parishes moved them to follow the Fourth Canticle.[420] The Psalies are sung in an antiphonal manner; each chorus chants two stanzas at a time. It is important to note that there is a Psaly for each day of the week that can be chanted in the Year-Round, *Kiahkian*, or Joyous tune. The tunes of the Psaly will also vary contingent on its type (*Adam* or *Watos*). Psalies assigned to Regular Days are focused on the Lord Jesus Christ. However,

---

[417] This word was used in the New Testament in (Ephesians 5:19) and (1 Corinthians 14:15).

[418] *Pierport Morgan*, H Vol. XIII, Hermenia, Cries of the night, Acrostic hymns, 150-176. Morgan Collection consists of more than eleven hundred manuscripts as well as papyri originally acquired by Pierpont Morgan at the end of the 19th century. This collection includes medieval manuscripts that date back to the 9th century. More than fifty Coptic manuscripts from Hamouli, Egypt, nearly all of which were found in their original bindings, form the oldest and most important group of Sahidic manuscripts from a single provenance, the Monastery of St. Michael at Sôpehes.

[419] This type of psalies was not known in the Church before the 14th century. Older psalies did not abide by these rules. See: Athanasius of Saint Macarius Monastery (Father), *Summary of the Liturgical History of the Church of Alexandria (Part 2)*, 154.

[420] Athanasius of Saint Macarius Monastery (Father), *Summary of the Liturgical History of the Church of Alexandria (Part 1)*, 114.

seasonal ones are concerned about the event in celebration. In feasts, if time permits, the Psaly specific to the day can optionally be recited following that of the festival, also in the festal tune.

In Regular Days, specifically on Sundays, two Psalies are recited; one for Saint Mary, Ⲇⲓⲛⲁϩϯ (I believe)[421] and another for our Lord Jesus, Ⲇⲓⲕⲱϯ (I sought after You). It is worth mentioning that Ⲇⲓⲛⲁϩϯ was first introduced for the month of Kiahk, as attested by *MS 742 Series\73 Rites*, which dates to 1444 AD.[422] In the beginning of the 20th century, rubric instructed that it is said on Tut 21st and on the 21st of any other Coptic month.[423] Nowadays, it is used as a first Psaly on the Sunday Theotokion all year long.

The Theotokions

After this, the Introduction to the Theotokions, which varies between *Adam* and *Watos* days, is recited. In the *Watos* days, the first two quatrains of the introduction are chanted in the same manner as the Theotokion, and they start with (Ⲉϣⲱⲡ ⲁⲛϣⲁⲛⲉⲣⲯⲁⲗⲓⲛ—And whenever we sing). However, in the *Adam* days, the hymn (Ⲗⲟⲓⲡⲟⲛ—And whenever) is said instead. The latter chant has a melismatic melody and a recitative one—identical to that of the *Adam* Theotokions—optionally used if time is of a constraint. It is interesting to note that the tune of the introduction of the *Watos* Theotokions prayed during Sunday Vespers Psalmody (for the Saturday Theotokion) of Regular and Feast Days is different from the one prayed during Kiahk and Lent; the latter is lengthier.

---

[421] This Psaly was composed by Bishop John (Youannis Ibn Shinouda—يوأنس بن شنوده), bishop of Asyut, Manfalut and Abutig, from AD 1430 to 1460.
[422] Sobhy, Basilious (Father), *Introduction to the History of Coptic Rites*, 54.
[423] Philotheos El-Makary (*Hegumen*), Girgis, Mikhail (Cantor), *The Book of Watos and Adam Psalies and Expositions Used in All the Churches of the See of Saint Mark*, 66-70.

The word Theotokion (Θεοτοκίον) originates from the Greek word Theotokos (Θεοτόκος), which means "Birth-giver of God" or "Bearer of God." The purpose of the Theotokions, therefore, is to contemplate on the mystery of the incarnation of the Lord Christ from the Virgin Mary, without the seed of man. The Theotokions also refer to the symbols in the Old Testament that point to the Virgin Mary and the Lord Christ. As such, through the Theotokions, the church venerates the Virgin Mary and emphasizes her blessedness.

The Theotokions are comprised of Coptic stanzas (however, they do not rhyme) that, generally, encompass four lines each (a quatrain); however, in rare cases some stanzas are made up of five lines (a quintain). Per the Coptic Church tradition, the author of the lyrics of the Theotokions is Saint Cyril the Pillar of Faith, or at the very least, they were heavily based on and influenced by his homilies and teachings. Conversely, in his 14th century book titled *Lamp to Darkness and Explanation of the Service*, Father Shams El-Reasa Abu El-Barakat (known as Ibn Kabar), reports that the Theotokions "are attributed—with no support—to Pope Athanasius the Apostolic, may God grant us his blessings, and it is said that a righteous saintly potter monk who lived in the Wilderness of Shiheet is the one who composed its melodies."[424]

Evidence suggests that this monk is Simon the Potter, who was a sixth century Syrian monk lived at the monastery of Saint Macarius;[425] Euringer seconds this theory.[426] Simon the Potter of Geshir was a deacon whom Saint Jacob of Serugh found working as a potter in the village of Geshir near the monastery of Mar Bar Hebraeus and took as a disciple of him. The Potter was talented in composing hymns honoring the Virgin Mary and

---

[424] Ibn Kabar, *The Lamp*, BnF, MS Arabic 203 (c. AD 1363-1369), fol. 202v.
[425] Sobhy, Basilious (Father), *Introduction to the History of Coptic Rites*, 22.
[426] D'Alton, John, Youssef, Youhanna, *Severus of Antioch: His Life and Times*, 195.

assigned to each day of the week.[427] According to the 17th century *Book of Aksum*, Part II, the Syrian Potter gave these chants to the Ethiopian saint and scholar Yared.[428] Some academics credit the composition of the Theotokions to Ephrem the Syrian (also called Ephrem Syrus),[429] however, there is not enough evidence to justify the claim. Thus, father De Lacy O'Leary suggests that the latter hypothesis to be a mere confusion with the Syrian Potter; he attributes this confusion to the fact that the *Acts of Yared* claimed the potter's name to be Ephrem.[430] Others found resemblances between the Coptic Theotokions and that of the Greek ones written by Saint John Damascene and Arsenius the Monk, suggesting that the Coptic Theotokions were based on and derived from the Greek ones.[431]

Studying the Coptic Marian homilies of Severus of Antioch (homilies 14 and 67), Youhanna Youssef found resemblance between them and the Coptic Theotokions, specifically Part 6 of the Thursday Theotokion.[432] Many of the Hymns attributed to Saint Severus are Christological, six of which are categorized as hymns on the *Theotokos*, hence, could have been a principal source for the Coptic Theotokions.[433] Although the writings of Cyril of Alexandria cannot be denied as a key wellspring for the compiler of the Theotokions—as Giamberardini and Muyser indicate—the writings of Severus as another provenance must not be ignored.[434] A

---

[427] De Lacy O'Leary, D.D., *The Coptic Theotokia*, xi.
[428] Yared was a scholar, musician, and ecclesiastic who was a formative influence on the cultural life of Ethiopia. Yared, who lived in the 6th century, was born near Aksum (or Axum), the historic capital of the Ethiopian Aksumite Empire, and is considered a saint in the Ethiopian Church. According to oral tradition, Yared's collection of hymns, is the oldest literary work written in Ge'ez. It is said that before Yared there was no music in Ethiopia.
[429] De Lacy O'Leary, D.D., *The Daily Office and Theotokia of the Coptic Church*, 53.
[430] De Lacy O'Leary, D.D., *The Coptic Theotokia*, xi.
[431] De Lacy O'Leary, D.D., *The Daily Office and Theotokia of the Coptic Church*, 54, 55.
[432] Youssef, Youhanna, *The Life and Works of Severus of Antioch in the Coptic and Copto-Arabic Tradition*, 135-152.
[433] Farrington, Peter (Father) (2011), American Foundation for Syriac Studies, *The Virgin St Mary in the Hymns of St Severus of Antioch*.
[434] D'Alton, John, Youssef, Youhanna, *Severus of Antioch: His Life and Times*, 187.

comparative inspection of the hymns of Severus and the Coptic Theotokions uncovers the following correspondence between the two:[435]

Hymn	2	3	7	118	119	120
Theotokion	Thu P.3	Thu P.5	Thu P.4	Thu P.6	Sun P.1, P.3, P.4, & P.7	Tue P.4

Extracts from other Church writers like Proclus of Cyzicus[436] and Theodotus of Ancyra[437] could also have been used as sources for the Theotokions.[438] Succinctly put, the Potter was a compiler of quotations from credible sources, particularly the writings of Cyril of Alexandria and Severus of Antioch. He organized them and composed a melody for them.

Ibn Kabar also mentions that the Theotokions were used in the northern cities, but not in Upper Egypt. He states "the Theotokions, which are known to the Copts, are used in the parishes of Old Cairo, Cairo, and Lower Egypt. As for Upper Egypt, they are not used there except rarely at a few parishes in the Near Upper Egypt."[439] This testimony indicates that up until at least the 14th century, the Theotokions were not employed in liturgical services in Upper Egypt.

Like the Psalies, each of the seven Theotokions is assigned to a day of the week, hence its tune varies accordingly. On Sunday, Monday, and Tuesday, the Theotokion is recited in the *Adam* melody, whereas in the

---

[435] For text comparisons see Farrington, Ibid. and D'Alton, Ibid., 188-192. Also see Helmy, Michael. (2021). *Omonogenis* and *Agios Dimas* In the Alexandrian Coptic Rite. Alexandria School, 30(1), 160.

[436] Saint Proclus (died AD 446), a disciple of Saint John Chrysostom, was at first the bishop of Cyzicus before becoming the bishop of Constantinople in AD 434. He is known for defending the name *Theotokos* for Saint Mary.

[437] Saint Theodotus of Ancyra (died c. 446), was a theologian and bishop of Ancyra. He was a leading advocate of orthodoxy in the discussion of the nature and Person of Christ at the Council of Ephesus in AD 431. He was a supporter of his contemporary Cyril of Alexandria in his Christology against Nestorius.

[438] D'Alton, Ibid., 187.

[439] Ibn Kabar, *The Lamp*, Father Samuel of Syrians Monastery, 108.

other days of the week, the *Watos* tune, a longer melody, is appointed to the Theotokion.

The Sunday Theotokion—comprising of fifteen sections—focuses on the symbols of the Lord Christ and the Virgin Mary in the Tabernacle. Compared to the other Theotokions, the number of hymns in the Sunday Theotokion is significantly larger. After the sixth section, the Gospel reading, "Sovereign Lord, as You have promised, You may now dismiss Your servant in peace" (Luke 2:29–32) is uttered. It is likely that, in antiquity, this Gospel lesson marked the conclusion of the Sunday Theotokion, which means that the remaining nine sections were added at a later date. Older sources[440] reveal that a lection from the Gospel of Saint Luke was inserted after each of the six sections as opposed to only one at their conclusion, as currently practiced.[441] This type of interpolations is still followed during the month of Kiahk. These six sections have the same liturgical structure; the first half of each section contemplates on the symbols of the Old Testament, whereas the second half is a exegesis that reveals the connotation of those symbols (and, as previously noted, in antiquity, followed by a lection).

After reading the Gospel, the seventh section of the Sunday Theotokion commences. This section includes two melismatic hymns: Ⲭⲉⲣⲉ ⲛⲉ Ⲙⲁⲣⲓⲁ (Hail to you, O Mary) and Ⲥⲉⲙⲟⲩϯ (You are called righteous). The hymns Ⲭⲉⲣⲉ ⲛⲉ Ⲙⲁⲣⲓⲁ and Ⲥⲉⲙⲟⲩϯ venerate the Virgin Mary, for she is the rod of Aaron that budded without planting or watering, the flower of incense, and the beautiful dove, whose intercession we ask for the forgiveness of our sins. These chants contemplate on the

---

[440] For example: Paris, BnF, MS Copt. 11, MS Copte 69 (14th C.), London, Bod., MS Hunt 256 (AD 1387), Paris, BnF, MS Copte 11 (AD 1518), and Paris, BnF, MS Copte 76.
[441] The six lections are, respectively, as follows: Luke 1:45-50, Luke 1:51-55, Luke 1:68-72 (or 68-70), Luke 1:73-77 (or 71-75), Luke 1:78-79 (or 76-79), and Luke 2:29-32. See: De Lacy O'Leary, D.D., *The Coptic Theotokia*, iv, viii.

attributes of Saint Mary, who miraculously bore God the Logos,[442] who was incarnate for our salvation. David the Psalmist rejoiced and danced before the Ark of Covenant; similarly, contemplating on the Virgin, the new Ark of Covenant who carried the True Manna, the Word of God, in her womb, believers cannot but, jubilantly, praise and glorify Christ the Lord, who was incarnate of the Virgin.

The eighth section of the Sunday Theotokion Ϣⲁϣϥ ⲛ̀ⲥⲟⲡ ⲙ̀ⲙⲏⲛⲓ (Seven times every day) cannot be found in Psalters transcribed before the 15th century,[443] an indication of a different author from the original one. Per the oldest *The Church Order* extant, Ϣⲁϣϥ ⲛ̀ⲥⲟⲡ ⲙ̀ⲙⲏⲛⲓ was introduced as an interpretation of the seventh section.[444] The ninth section is a short one, and follows the same theme.

The tenth section of the Sunday Theotokion marks the beginning of the hymn Ⲧ̀ⲉⲟⲓ ⲛ̀ϩⲓⲕⲁⲛⲟⲥ (You are more worthy). This hymn can be intoned in a melismatic, semi-major, or recitative tune. The recitative tune is unique and extends to the end of the Theotokion. In the fifteenth and final section of the Sunday Theotokion, the hymn Ⲁⲩⲉⲛ ⲡⲓⲁⲣⲭⲏⲉⲣⲉⲩⲥ (They likened the high priest) is chanted. It can also employ a melismatic, a semi-major, or a recitative tune. Yet, the last two quatrains of this section, and the whole Theotokion, form another chant, that is, Ⲉ̀ⲃⲟⲗϩⲓⲧⲉⲛ Ⲙⲁⲣⲓⲁ

---

[442] Logos (Greek: λόγος) originally means "word", "speech", or "to reason". It became a technical term in philosophy, beginning with Heraclitus (535–475 B.C.), who used the term for a principle of order and knowledge. Aristotle applied the term to refer to "reasoned discourse" or "the argument" in the field of rhetoric. The Stoic philosophers identified the term with the divine animating principle pervading the Universe. Philo (20 BC–AD 50), a Hellenized Jew, used the term Logos to mean an intermediary divine being. Philo followed the Platonic distinction between imperfect matter and perfect Form, and therefore intermediary beings were necessary to bridge the enormous gap between God and the material world. The Logos was the highest of these intermediary beings and was called by Philo "the first-born of God." The Gospel of John identifies the Logos, through which all things are made, as divine (*theos*), and further identifies Jesus as the incarnate Logos. In Christology, Logos is the pre-existent Second Person (Hypostasis) of a Trinitarian God. The Logos is the Only-begotten Son of God the Father (First Person of God).

[443] Mina Safwat mentions the following examples: Vienna, National Library-Papyrus Collection, MS Coptic 3 1363 (AD1348); London, Bod., MS Hunt 256 (AD 1387); BnF, MS Coptic 69.

[444] Jeremiah (*Hegumen*), *The Church Order*, Cairo, Patriarchal Library, MS Lit. 73 (AD 1444), fol. 57r.

(Through Mary), which can also be intoned in a melismatic, semi-major, or recitative tune.

The Monday Theotokion contemplates on the fall of Adam and Eve and the coming of Christ, the Second Adam, who was born of Saint Mary, the Second Eve; through Christ, Adam, Eve, and all the creation were restored once again to Paradise. The Tuesday Theotokion ponders on the purity and righteousness of the Virgin Mary, as well as the incarnation of the Lord and His miraculous birth. The Wednesday Theotokion reflects on the prophecies that have been fulfilled. In it, the heavenly and earthly venerate the Virgin, referring to her as the Second Heaven having born the Lord of Glory in her womb. In the seventh section of the Wednesday Theotokion, the melismatic hymn ϯⲅⲁⲗⲓⲗⲉⲁ (The dignitaries of the nations) is intoned.

The Thursday Theotokion likens the fiery yet unconsumed bush that Moses saw with the Virgin Mary, who bore the Word of God in her womb—through the descent of the Holy Spirit—without being burnt by the fire of His Divinity. The Theotokion also likens the Virgin Mary to the woman clothed with the sun, whom John the Beloved spoke of in the Book of Revelation. In the eighth section of the Theotokion, the hymn Ⲡⲓⲟⲩⲁⲓ (The One of the Trinity) can be chanted in its melismatic tune. The Friday Theotokion contemplates on the honor of the Virgin Mary which has surpassed the heavenly and the earthly. In the seventh section of the Theotokion, the hymn ϯⲡⲁⲣⲑⲉⲛⲟⲥ (The Virgin Mary) can optionally be sung utilizing its melismatic melody.

The Saturday Theotokion reflects on the undefiled Virgin Mother who carried God the Logos in her arms. The Theotokion also likens the Virgin Mary to Jacob's ladder which Jacob dreamed about. The ladder was resting on the earth, with its top reaching to heaven, and the angels of God were ascending and descending on it.[445] Through her, Christ became man and lived among us to reconcile the earthly with the heavenly. This contemplation is found in the eighth section of the Theotokion (i.e., (Ⲁⲣⲉⲧⲉⲛⲟⲱⲛϯ—You were likened to the ladder) and can be chanted in its melismatic tune. It is noteworthy that all the melismatic *Watos* hymns Ϩⲅⲁⲗⲓⲗⲉⲁ, Ⲡⲓⲟⲩⲁⲓ, Ϩⲡⲁⲣⲑⲉⲛⲟⲥ and Ⲁⲣⲉⲧⲉⲛⲟⲱⲛϯ employ the same tune.

After each Theotokion, the *Lobsh* of the Theotokion is chanted in either the *Adam* or *Watos* tune, depending on the day of the week. Per MS 32 Coptic, which is preserved at the National Library of France, these *Lobsh* chants were introduced during the Papacy of John VIII (AD 1300–1320), the 80th Pope of Alexandria.[446] It is worth noting that the *Lobsh* for the Saturday Theotokion is divided into two sections referred to as the First and Second *Shere*'s. The introductory texts of the *Shere*'s are taken from Saint Cyril the Great's fourth homily, which was conducted at the Church of Saint Mary in Ephesus between June 23rd and 26th in AD 431.[447]

It is hard not to notice that the Sunday Theotokion has no *Lobsh*, but the hymn Ⲛⲓⲙ ⲅⲁⲣ (Who is likened unto You) is recited instead. For this reason, some scholars consider Ⲛⲓⲙ ⲅⲁⲣ the *Lobsh* of the Sunday Theotokion. Nevertheless, this is not necessarily true. Ibn Kabar instructs that Ⲛⲓⲙ ⲅⲁⲣ is said at the end of the *Adam* Morning Doxology, and before its conclusion section Ⲛⲉⲕⲛⲁⲓ ⲱ Ⲡⲁⲛⲟⲩϯ (Your Mercy O My God).[448] This means that originally Ⲛⲓⲙ ⲅⲁⲣ does not belong to the Theotokion, but rather it is an *Adam* Doxology for the Resurrection. This explains its melody, which is congruous with the *Adam* Morning Doxology. The hymn Ⲛⲓⲙ ⲅⲁⲣ is comprised of three sections pertaining to the Resurrection. It is chanted from the Feast of Resurrection and throughout

---

[445] Genesis 28:12,13.
[446] Sobhy, Basilious (Father), *Introduction to the History of Coptic Rites*, 44.
[447] Athanasius (Monk), *Midnight and Matins Psalmody*, 287.
[448] Ibn Kabar (Priest), *The Lamp*, BnF, MS Arabic 203 (c. AD 1363-1369), fol. 119v.

Eastertide every day, then in commemoration of the Resurrection, every Sunday thereafter to the last Sunday of the month of Hathor. It is noteworthy that the hymn Ⲛⲓⲙ ⲅⲁⲣ has two tunes that could be used interchangeably all year-round.

The Antiphonary and the Exposition

After this, in Regular Days, the Antiphonary is read to commemorate the saint or saints of the day. It is comparable to the Synaxarion but in a poetic form. In ecclesiastical seasons and occasions, however, in order to draw the worshippers' attention to the event (as opposed to the saint of the day) the Exposition is intoned instead. Interestingly, the Exposition and the Antiphonary share the same tune. Most Expositions were put in place in the 13th and 14th centuries. Still, there are a few that date back to the ninth century.

The Introduction to the Antiphonary is recited after the *Lobsh* of the Theotokion in either the *Adam* or *Watos* tune, depending on the day of the week, after which the Antiphonary is recited. The *Adam* introduction comprises of four stanzas and is chanted in either a minor or semi-major tune. The minor tune is popular in Cairo and Alexandria, whereas the semi-major tune is more common in Upper Egypt. The last two stanzas of the *Adam* introduction can also be intoned in a melismatic tune called Ⲟⲩⲟⲛ ⲟⲩϩⲉⲗⲡⲓⲥ ⲛ̀ⲧⲁⲛ (We have hope). On the other hand, The *Watos* Introduction to the Antiphonary is comprised of two quatrains only and uses a brief melody. It is noteworthy that during Kiahk and Lent, a particular melismatic melody for the *Watos* introduction may be chanted during the Sunday Vespers Psalmody.

During ecclesiastical seasons, after the *Adam* or *Watos* introduction is chanted, the Exposition of the feast, or that specific to the Sundays of Lent,

Eastertide, or the month of Kiahk, is recited, depending on the season. In Regular Days, however, the Antiphonary is recited, which is basically a biography of the saint(s) venerating their perseverance and labor. Both the Exposition and Antiphonary use the same melody of the introduction. Aside from the Year-Round tune, in Feast Days, a festal melody is employed. Additionally, a specific tune for the feasts of the Cross and Palm Sunday is used on these occasions. The Antiphonary or the Exposition is then read in its entirety in the vernacular. It is worth mentioning that before the 15th century,[449] only in the Sunday Midnight Psalmody, the Exposition of the Saintly Workers was said all year long. Now, this exposition is only recited in the month of Kiahk.

The Vigil Concluding Prayers

Thereafter, the Conclusion of the Theotokions is recited. Two conclusions can be noted: *Adam* and *Watos*. The *Adam* conclusion is the hymn Ⲛⲉⲕⲛⲁⲓ ⲱ Ⲡⲁⲛⲟⲩϯ (Your mercies O my God), whereas the *Watos* conclusion is the hymn Ⲱ Ⲡⲉⲛϭⲟⲓⲥ (O our Lord). As noted earlier, the original place for the Theotokions was during Prime Offering of Incense. At the time, the so-called Conclusion of the Theotokions was in fact the conclusion of the Doxologies. In the 14th century the Theotokions, along with the Psalies, were relocated to follow the Fourth Canticle in the Matins Psalmody,[450] and were concluded with the Exposition of the Workers.[451] In the 16th century, however, the conclusion of the Doxologies

---

[449] As attested by the 14th- century scholar and priest Ibn Kabar.
[450] Athanasius of Saint Macarius Monastery (Father), *Summary of the Liturgical History of the Church of Alexandria (Part 2)*, 157.
[451] Although this exposition was chanted daily according to the old ordos, the contemporary practice is to only sing it in Sunday Midnight Psalmody during the month of Kiahk.

was repositioned to follow the Theotokions in Matins Psalmody. Since then, they were called Conclusion of the Theotokions.[452]

This is followed by "We magnify you, O Mother of the True Light," the Creed, then the supplication prayer of Ⲫⲛⲟⲩϯ ⲛⲁⲓ ⲛⲁⲛ (O God have mercy upon us), respectively. This prayer is comprised of fifteen verses, and between each of them Ⲕⲩⲣⲓⲉ ⲉⲗⲉⲏⲥⲟⲛ (Lord, have mercy) is recited three times. The purpose of this litany is to seek God's mercy while declaring our faith in Him as the Son of God. "Holy, Holy, Holy…" is then recited, followed by the Lord's Prayer. The priest then utters the Midnight Absolution, and then the congregation prays the psalms of Prime Hour, followed by the recitation of the *Adam* Morning Doxology.

To better understand how this section evolved, I will provide a comparison between three versions of Ibn Kabar's *The Lamp to Darkness and Explanation of the Service*: The oldest is MS Arabic 203, which was inscribed between AD 1363 and AD 1369 and is currently preserved at the National Lib. of France in Paris.[453] The second document is MS OR. 486, which was copied in AD 1546, and is archived in Uppsala, Sweden.[454] The third manuscript is Arabo 623, which was transcribed in the 16th century (probably the second half of it) and is presently preserved at the Vatican Apostolic Library in the Vatican City.[455] I will also include the contemporary practice.

---

[452] Athanasius of Saint Macarius Monastery (Father), *Summary of the Liturgical History of the Church of Alexandria (Part 2)*, 298-299.
[453] Ibn Kabar, *The Lamp*, BnF, MS Arabic 203 (AD c. 1363-1369), fol. 203r.
[454] Ibn Kabar, *The Lamp*, Father Samuel of Syrian Monastery, 119.
[455] Ibn Kabar, *The Lamp*, Vatican, Vat, Arabo 623 (16th C.), fol. 172v.

	MS Arabic 203	MS OR. 486	Arabo 623	Current Practice
The Gloria in Excelsis Deo	✓	✓		
We Magnify You				✓
The Creed		✓		✓
O the begotten of the Father before all ages		✓		
Lord, have mercy	✓	✓	✓	✓
Holy, holy, holy		✓	✓	✓
The Lord's Prayer		✓	✓	✓
The Absolution	✓	✓	✓	✓
Lord, have mercy	✓			
Final Benediction	✓			

We notice from the table above that the *Gloria in Excelsis Deo* (Let us praise with the angels) was the opening of the Concluding Prayers until the first half of the 16th century, however, it was dropped later in the same century. We also notice that the Creed, "Holy, holy, holy," and the Lord's Prayer were introduced into the Vigils office sometime in the 15th or early 16th century. In the same era, the prayer "O the begotten of the Father before all ages" emerged for a short period of time but was eliminated in the same century. Sometime after the 16th century, "We magnify you" was interpolated to immediately precede the Creed. Moreover, it seems that the old tradition of reciting "Lord, have mercy" followed by the priest's delivering of the final benediction was either eliminated after the 14th century, or was still practiced as a given observance and hence was dropped from the instructions. The former seems more probable to be the case since minor details were provided in these sources; it is unlikely to skip these elements especially that they exist in the older copies being transcribed. Finally, (Ⲫⲛⲟⲩϯ ⲛⲁⲓ ⲛⲁⲛ—O God have mercy upon us) seems to have been inserted recently, specifically, in the 20th century.[456]

The Adam Morning Doxology

We should point out that the *Adam* Morning Doxology is not limited to the *Adam* days, it is said daily. We will inspect the reason for the naming shortly. The Doxology itself can be divided into four divisions. The first is comprised of ten quatrains, which are the first known set of Verses of Cymbals. In other words, the *Adam* Morning Doxology would have started with the eleventh stanza of Ⲡⲓⲟⲩⲱⲓⲛⲓ ⲛ̀ⲧⲁⲫⲙⲏⲓ (O true Light), as opposed to first one Ⲧⲉⲛⲟⲩⲱϣⲧ (We worship). However, this segment (i.e., the first ten quatrains) was later added as an introduction to the *Adam* Morning Doxology.

The second section of the *Adam* Morning Doxology starts from the stanza Ⲡⲓⲟⲩⲱⲓⲛⲓ ⲛ̀ⲧⲁⲫⲙⲏⲓ and includes the stanzas applicable to the Virgin Mary. Uppsala's *The Lamp to Darkness and Explanation of the Service*[457] mentions that the author of this section (i.e., from Ⲡⲓⲟⲩⲱⲓⲛⲓ ⲛ̀ⲧⲁⲫⲙⲏⲓ to ϧⲉⲛ ϩⲁⲛⲯⲁⲗⲙⲟⲥ) is Pope Benjamin I (AD 623–662),[458] the 38th Patriarch of the See of Saint Mark.[459]

The third segment starts from the second Doxology for Saint Mary and includes the Doxologies for the angels, the apostles, the martyrs, and

---

[456] Athanasius, *Summary*, Ibid., 424.
[457] This copy of Ibn Kabar's *The Lamp to Darkness and Explanation of the Service* is preserved at the Uppsala Library in Sweden under reference number MS OR. 486, was transcribed in AD 1546 from an older document that dates back to AD 1357.
[458] Pope Benjamin I of Alexandria, who was born around AD 590 in Barshüt, in the Beheira, is regarded as one of the greatest patriarchs of the Coptic Orthodox Church. Pope Benjamin guided the Coptic Church through a period of turmoil in Egyptian history that included the fall of Egypt to the Sassanid Empire, followed by Egypt's re-conquest under the Byzantines, and finally the Arab Islamic Conquest in AD 642.
[459] Ibn Kabar, *The Lamp*, Father Samuel of Syrians Monastery, 109.

the saints. These were, originally, the Doxologies recited in the *Adam* days, except for Sunday where "Ⲛⲓⲙ ⲅⲁⲣ," and "Ⲡⲓⲭⲣⲓⲥⲧⲟⲥ Ⲡⲉⲛⲛⲟⲩϯ" were said instead.[460] This section was developed in the 5th century, and as such, is the oldest segment of the *Adam* Morning Doxology. It is most likely that this section was written by the monks of Saint Anthony Monastery.[461] Although these immemorial stanzas were, in their primitive vocation, used in the incense offering office in the *Adam* days only, today, "Adam" is still used in its title, even when more sections were appended to it, and after its location and vocation changed.

Finally, the fourth section of the *Adam* Morning Doxology is specific to the fathers and the prophets. It is likely that the monks of the monastery of Saint Macarius added these stanzas.[462] After the *Adam* Morning Doxology is recited, the Prime Offering of Incense commences, followed by the prayer of the Liturgy.

Recap of the Order of the Vigil Office

Let us now summarize the order of the Midnight Psalmody office. At the commencement of the vigil office, the three watches of the Midnight Office are prayed. This is followed by the hymn Ϯⲉⲛ ⲑⲏⲛⲟⲩ, then Ϯⲉⲛⲛⲁⲩ if applicable. After this, the First Canticle and its *Lobsh* are chanted. Then, in all days of the week, except for Sunday, the seventh, eighth and ninth sections of the Sunday Theotokion are recited, followed by the Second Canticle and its *Lobsh*. On Sundays, however, the Second Canticle immediately follows the First Canticle *Lobsh*. Afterward, the Third Canticle and its associated hymns are sung, followed by the Psaly

---

[460] Ibn Kabar, *The Lamp*, BnF, MS Arabic 203 (c. AD 1363-1369), fols. 198v-199r.
[461] Ibn Kabar, *The Lamp*, Father Samuel of Syrians Monastery, 109. Also, Mina El-Baramosy (presbyter), *The Holy Psalmody According to the Order of the Coptic Orthodox Church*, 267.
[462] Athanasius of Saint Macarius Monastery (Father), *Summary of the Liturgical History of the Church of Alexandria (Part 1)*, 219.

Ⲁⲣⲓⲯⲁⲗⲓⲛ, the hymn Ϫⲉⲛⲉⲛ if time permits, and Ϫⲉⲛⲟⲩⲉϩ ⲛ̀ⲥⲱⲕ, respectively. The Commemoration of Saints is then recited, followed by the Doxologies. This concludes the first section (according to the original rite) of the Midnight Psalmody.

The second section, which was referred to as the Matins Psalmody, begins with the Fourth Canticle, followed by the Psaly of the day, the Introduction to the Theotokion, and the Theotokion of the day, respectively. In all days of the week, except for Sunday, the *Lobsh* of the Theotokion is chanted. On Sundays, however, there is no *Lobsh* for the Sunday Theotokion. Instead, the hymn Ⲛⲓⲙ ⲅⲁⲣ is recited according to its rite as previously explained. After this, the Exposition or Antiphonary, along with their *Adam* or *Watos* Introductions, are chanted, followed by the Conclusion of the *Adam* or *Watos* Theotokion. The Introduction to the Creed, which is "We magnify you O Mother of the True Light," is then uttered, followed by the Creed, the supplication prayer of Ⲫⲛⲟⲩϯ ⲛⲁⲓ ⲛⲁⲛ, the Sanctus, the Lord's Prayer, and finally the Midnight Absolution, which brings the second section of the Midnight Psalmody to closure. Preceded by the Prime Office, the *Adam* Morning Doxology is recited, followed by the Prime Offering of Incense, then the liturgy.

CHAPTER FOUR

The Offertory

Choosing of the Lamb and the Thanksgiving Prayer

Since then these things are manifest to us, and we have looked into the depths of the divine knowledge, we ought to do in order all things which the Master commanded us to perform at appointed times. He commanded us to celebrate sacrifices and services, and that it should not be thoughtlessly or disorderly, but at fixed times and hours. He has Himself fixed by His supreme will the places and persons whom He desires for these celebrations, in order that all things may be done piously according to His good pleasure and be acceptable to His will. So, then those who offer their oblations at the appointed seasons are acceptable and blessed, but they follow the laws of the Master and do not sin. For to the high priest his proper ministrations are allotted, and to the priests the proper place has been appointed, and on Levites their proper services have been imposed. The layman is bound by the ordinances for the laity.

—Clement of Rome

Introduction

The Offertory (from Medieval Latin *offertorium* and Late Latin *offerre*) is the section of the liturgy when the Eucharistic elements are ceremonially placed on the altar. The Offertory must be understood from its Eschatological characteristic as a sacrifice of love leading to eternal union with the Lord. It is the reality of the love of God the Father to humanity that is manifested in Him offering His Only-begotten Son, to die for us on the altar of the Cross. It is the revelation of the love of God the Son to man by offering Himself up for our salvation. This sacrifice is the spirit of love, the Spirit of God, the work of the Holy Spirit. As members of His Body, desiring to unite with Christ, the Offertory is actually offering ourselves. Athenagoras[463] explains the offertory as, "a self-sacrificial act by which each Christian offered himself in and with the bread and cup offered to God."[464] The act of offering the Eucharistic elements should be understood as a commitment to offer our bodies, souls, spirits, and even our whole lives to Him as a sacrifice of love. It is important to note that Jesus' sacrifice is complete and full and does not need anyone or anything to add to it. Therefore, our sacrifice of love is essentially a participation in His sacrifice. In light of what has been said, the Offertory should not be perceived as a simple act of placing the bread and wine on the altar, but as the sacrament of love. In it, we unite with the Lord as His own Body, and through it we offer our lives to Him. For that reason, the Offertory is an essential and vital part of the Eucharist, which cannot be detached from the other sections of the liturgy.

---

[463] Athenagoras (133—190 AD) was a Father of the Early Church, an Ante-Nicene Christian apologist who lived during the second half of the 2nd century, besides that he was Athenian (though possibly not originally from Athens), a philosopher, and a convert to Christianity. In his writings, he styles himself as "Athenagoras, the Athenian, Philosopher, and Christian". The Coptic Orthodox Church, as well as others, claims that Athenagoras was the head of the Theological School at Alexandria.

[464] Athenagoras, *Legatio*, 13:3.

It is worth noting that the first extant document that describes the Offertory in detail is the *Apostolic Tradition* of Hyppolytus. The old tradition in the pre-Nicene period, as mentioned in the Canons of the Council of Ancyra (AD 314), describes a three-phase process of the Offertory in very precise language. It explains that the communicant 'brings' the *prosphora*; the deacon 'presents' it or 'brings it up'; the bishop 'offers' it. In the light of that and what we have discussed earlier regarding the Offertory being a sacrifice of love, which is offered by communicants as a response for the love of Jesus and His Sacrifice on the Cross, each communicant gives himself on the altar desiring to unite with the rest of the church. The united oblations of all members of the church is presented by the servant (deacon) of the entire united body, the church, in the Person of Christ. This united body is offered by the bishop (or the priest) as a sacrifice to become the Body of Christ, the sacrament of oneness with Him. The Offertory, thus, expresses the unison of all members of the one Body. It is a corporal act of being participants of the Sacrifice of Jesus as being His own Body. This entrenched belief in the consciousness of the Early Fathers was reflected in their writings. Addressing the newly confirmed communicants, Saint Augustine proclaims, "There you are upon the table; there you are in the chalice."[465]

Before scrutinizing the rite of the Offertory per the Coptic Orthodox Church, let us first review the breakdown of the liturgy based on the contemporary practice. After the Prime Offering of Incense, the Canonical Hours prayers are recited followed by the Offertory. The Liturgy of the Word (also called the Liturgy of the Catechumens) follows, and then the Liturgy of the Faithful (also called the Liturgy of the

---

[465] Augustine (Saint), *Sermon 229*.

Believers) is celebrated. In this chapter, we will study the first part of the Divine Liturgy, which is the Offertory.

In the beginning of Christianity, at least for the first hundred and fifty years—some argue for the first three centuries,[466] liturgies used to take place in the evening, just like our Lord's Mystical Supper on Maundy Thursday. These events were referred to as "The breaking of the Bread."[467] The believers, led by the bishop, used to gather in one of the church-houses to pray the liturgy and receive communion.[468] The evening liturgy was based on the Jewish prayers of the *Chaburah* Meal[469] and the Jewish *Seder*,[470] which our Lord Jesus Christ used after changing some of its text to establish the Sacrament of the Eucharist.[471] The congregation of the evening liturgy was made up of Christians from Jewish background, thus, were familiar with the *ordos* of the evening liturgy. Therefore, primitive Christian worship can be described as domestic and "private."[472] Prayers were extempore; that is, each bishop, although governed by a specific framework, was not limited to an exact script. This was plainly instructed

---

[466] Bradshaw, Paul F. (1992). The Divine Office: The First Three Centuries. In Cheslyn Jones, Geoffrey Wainwright, Edward Yarnold SJ and Paul Bradshaw (Eds.), The Study of Liturgy, 400.

[467] Acts 2:42, Acts 2:46, Acts: 20:7, 11, Acts 27:33-36. In these instances, wine was not mandatory, probably for economic factors, and sometimes (like in Acts 27:33-36) the entire meal consisted mainly and solely of bread. For more details, refer to: Paul F. Bradshaw, Maxwell E. Johnson, *The Eucharistic Liturgies: Their Evolution and Interpretation*, 12, 13.

[468] In Romans, Saint Paul is alluding to these gatherings in (Romans 16:5) where he is referring to the church that meets at Priscilla and Aquila's house.

[469] A *Chaburah* or *chavurah* (חבורה Hebrew: "fellowship") is a group of friends formed for religious purposes. They often shared a common weekly meal, usually on the eves of Sabbaths or holy days. This meal is called "*Chaburah* Meal." It has been argued that Christ and His disciples formed such a *Chaburah* and that the Last Supper was a *Chaburah* Meal.

[470] *Seder* (Hebrew: סָדַר, meaning "order, arrangement") is a Jewish ritual service and ceremonial dinner for the first night or first two nights of Passover. Passover *Seder* is conducted on the evening of the 15th day of Nisan in the Hebrew calendar throughout the world. Passover lasts for 7 days in Israel and 8 days outside of Israel. The *Seder* is a ritual performed by a community or by multiple generations of a family, involving a retelling of the story of the liberation of the Israelites from slavery in ancient Egypt.

[471] Dix, Dom Gregory, *The Shape of the Liturgy*, 50-56.

[472] Dix, Dom Gregory, *The Shape of the Liturgy*, 16-18.

in the Didache, which reads, "But permit the prophets to make thanksgiving as much as they desire."[473]

Toward the end of the first century, many people from different backgrounds converted to Christianity. The converts knew little about Jewish tradition. Thus, yet still domestic in character, another morning liturgy emerged. One of the main reasons—although not the sole one—for the establishment of this incipient liturgy was to accommodate the flood of neophytes from the gentiles into Christianity, and hence was celebrated at dedicated buildings (churches), not houses. In other words, this new development—according to Richardson was instituted toward the end of the second century[474]—was the beginning of the transition of Christian worship from "private" to "public." During persecution periods, the church, the group of believers, would revert to her "private" setting.[475] This limited transformation was consummated into a full-scale "public" worship in the 4th-century basilicas. In contrast to the evening Eucharist, one of the most important particularities of the morning liturgy is its *explanatory* nature. The church leaders realized that gentile converts had limited, if any, knowledge of Jewish traditions and customs, which were essential to the Eucharistic celebration. Thus, they tasked the morning liturgy to expound what the converts from Jewish background take for granted. As such, the morning liturgy undertook the mission of describing the *ordos*, traditions and dogma of the Eucharistic prayers handed down to the early Christians. For this reason, in it, we find sentences like "For being determined to give Himself up to death for the life of the world. He took bread in His hands… He gave thanks, He blessed it, He sanctified it, and

---

[473] *The Didache* (10:7).
[474] Matthew the Poor (Father), *Eucharist of the Lord's Supper*, 51.
[475] Baumstark, Anton, *On the Historical Development of the Liturgy*, 55.

Offertory

broke it and gave it to his holy disciples… and likewise the cup after the supper he mixed it with wine and water and gave thanks…"

We will also find explanations of the redemption story from the fall of Adam and Eve, the Incarnation, the Crucifixion, the Resurrection of our Lord Jesus and His Second Coming. Therefore, the morning liturgy explains the faith, the dogma, and the old rites, which our Lord Jesus Christ used with His disciples during the Last Supper.

In the beginning of the second century, the evening liturgies started to fade out. For Tertullian (c. 160–after AD 220)—in Carthage, Tunisia—these evening assemblies were still the primary gatherings to receive the Eucharist; however, half a century later, at Cyprian's time, morning liturgies, at least in North Africa, became more prominent.[476] The evening liturgies continued to decline until they completely disappeared in the fifth century. One reason for the disappearance of the evening liturgies is the fact that some pagan rulers forbade evening Christian assemblies because they were afraid that they would evolve into political gatherings. Another reason was that, by nature, the evening prayers were short and reliant on knowledge of Jewish rituals, many of which were inaudible, and that made it difficult to accommodate the gentile converts. In addition, many ecclesiastical councils decided to remove the evening Agape meals.[477] The first of these councils was the regional synod of Laodicea (c. AD 363) in Asia Minor, which forbade domestic Eucharistic celebrations.[478]

In his *Historia Ecclesiastica*, Socrates of Constantinople (AD 380–439) attests to the existence of these evening liturgies in Egypt at his time (fifth century). He writes, "The Egyptians in the neighborhood of Alexandria, and the inhabitants of Thebaïs, hold their religious assemblies

---

[476] McGowan, Andrew B., *Ancient Christian Worship*, 48-49.
[477] Matthew the Poor (Father), *Eucharist of the Lord's Supper*, 52.
[478] Baumstark, *On the Historical*, Ibid., 55.

on the sabbath, but do not participate of the mysteries in the manner usual among Christians in general: for after having eaten and satisfied themselves with food of all kinds, in the evening making their offerings they partake of the mysteries."[479] Sozomen (c. AD 400–c. 450) also testifies that this evening Eucharist had disappeared from all churches except for Egypt; he attests, "There are several cities and villages in Egypt where, contrary to the usage established elsewhere, the people meet together on Sabbath evenings, and, although they have dined previously, partake of the mysteries."[480]

Eventually, the evening liturgies died out and the morning ones flourished. It was not easy for the Coptic Orthodox Church to just eliminate such an indispensable service from her rite; therefore, she appended it to the morning service, an addition that is referred to now as the Offertory. In other words, according to Hans Lietzmann, the Offertory was a full evening liturgy that was based on the old tradition of the Last Supper. The rite of the Offertory disappeared from all traditions, except from that of Egypt. This means that the Egyptian liturgy is the only liturgy that preserves the old rite of the Last Supper or, at least, prayers that are very similar to it. Lietzmann argues that one possible reason for that is the fact that Egypt was the only place that Saint Paul did not visit, and as such was not influenced by his innovations in this regard and preserved the primitive Jerusalem tradition.[481]

When the evening liturgy was first introduced into the morning service (the Offertory), it was placed right after the Reconciliation Prayer. As such, the order of the Liturgy was, respectively: The Liturgy of the

---

[479] Socrates, *Historia Ecclesiastica*, Book V, Chapter 22.
[480] Sozomen, *Historia Ecclesiastica*, Book VII, Chapter 19.
[481] Matthew the Poor (Father), *Eucharist of the Lord's Supper*, 29-30.

Offertory

Catechumens, the Reconciliation Prayer, the Offertory, and the Liturgy of the Faithful (or the Eucharistic Prayer).

Logically, this sequence makes sense because the catechumens were not permitted to attend the Offertory.[482] So, after the reading of the Gospel, the priest prays litanies that conclude with that of the catechumens, which marks end of the Liturgy of the Catechumens. Then, the deacon calls out for the catechumens to leave the church. Thereafter, the Reconciliation Prayer is recited, and the deacon invites the believers to "Offer in order" which means, to present their oblations according to their custom at the time. At this point, the rite of the Offertory commences, followed by the Liturgy of the Faithful. After the disappearance of the rank of the catechumenate in the 6th century, a dramatic structural change took place in the shape of the liturgy. In around the 7th or 8th century, since all attendees of the readings were Christians, the Offertory was moved to precede the Liturgy of the Catechumens.[483] In his letter to the Eusebians at Antioch, Bishop Julius[484] of Rome writes, "How could it be that Oblations were offered when catechumens were within? For if there were catechumens present, it was not yet the time for presenting the Oblations."[485] "Only the faithful being allowed to offer at mass, the catechumens properly being expelled before the Offertory."[486]

The following passage by the 10th-century Macarius, bishop of Upper Munof, talks about the service when the catechumenate was still applicable. It reads, "In the first generation… the tradition of

---

[482] Lang, Frederick K., *Ulysses and the Irish God*, 105.
[483] Athanasius of Saint Macarius Monastery (Father), *The Divine Liturgy: The Mystery of the Kingdom of God (Part 1)*, 274.
[484] Julius I served as the bishop of Rome from 6 February 337 to his death in 352. He is chiefly known by the part he took in the Arian controversy. Julius is also credited with splitting the birth of Jesus into two distinct celebrations: Epiphany stayed on the traditional date, and Nativity was added on the 25th of December.
[485] Nicene and Post-Nicene Fathers, Series II, Volume 4, chapter II.
[486] Rev. J. Charles Cox, LL.D., F.S.A., *The Reliquary and Illustrated Archaeologist*, 11.

placing the Holy of Holies on the altar at the time was right after the Gospel reading. It started with the deacon instructing the catechumens to leave the church, after which the sub-deacons would close the doors. The tradition was that the catechumens would come to the church and attend the prayers, the reading of the homilies, and listen to the reading of the books of the prophets, the epistles, and the holy Gospel. They were then instructed to leave the church and the doors were shut. The reason was that the catechumens were not baptized; therefore, they were not worthy to see the Holy of Holies that is the pure Lamb of God offered on the altar." In his footnotes, Macarius writes, "The Offertory is taken from the altar, which is the Prothesis,[487] to the place where the Gospel is read. Holding candles and incense, the clergy transfer the oblations to the High Altar. At that time, the catechumens depart. This order has ceased in Egypt among the Copts."[488] Since Ibn Sibaa also mentions this practice, we can ascertain that this tradition was effective in the Coptic Church, at least, until the 13th century.

The Offertory and the Evening Liturgy

Before proceeding any further, we shall first examine the evidence that support the theory claiming that the Coptic rite of the Offertory is in fact the immemorial evening liturgy of Jerusalem.[489] The first indication that endorses this theory is the multitude of parallels that we can draw between the rite of the Coptic Offertory and that of the

---

[487] Prothesis (Greek: Πρόθεσις "a setting forth") is the altar where the act of preparing the bread (referred to as "prosphora," which is derived from the Greek word: πρόσφορον, meaning "offering") and wine for the Eucharist takes place. In the Coptic Orthodox Church, this act of preparation used to happen in the left altar (currently used for males only).

[488] *Letter of Macarius*, Paris, BnF, MS Arabic 100 (14th C.), fols. 9r-14r.

[489] As previously mentioned, the evening liturgy was based on the Last Supper instituted by our Lord Jesus Christ on Maundy Thursday and was the first Eucharist prayed during the Apostolic Age.

Liturgy of the Faithful, which nominates the former to be a full liturgy, not mere presentation of the oblations. In the following lines, I will report some of these similarities. Both rites commence with handwashing, *lavabo*, an ancient tradition rooted in Judaism. They both start with the traditional greeting "Peace be with all," followed by a thanksgiving prayer. Both rites include the same hymn of "One is the Holy Father;" however, in the Offertory it is assigned to the altar server whereas in the Liturgy of the Faithful to the congregation.

In the Offertory, during the thanksgiving prayer, the priest mixes the wine and water, a ritual practice that was well known to Jewish converts.[490] The morning liturgy, however, describes this action; as such, the priest says, "Likewise also, the cup after supper He mixed it with wine and water." In other words, although the practice of mixing wine with water was performed silently in the Coptic Offertory, which was the case in the ancient evening liturgy, the morning liturgy had to explain this action since this liturgy was originally addressed to the gentile converts, who did not necessarily have knowledge of Jewish rituals. A similar example can be found in the Liturgy of the Faithful, specifically, the Institution Narrative when the priest proclaims, "He gave thanks… He blessed it… etc." These actions are implemented, not narrated, in the Coptic Offertory, specifically, during the Thanksgiving Prayer.

In the rite of the Coptic Offertory, after the Thanksgiving Prayer, the priest inaudibly prays the "Litany of the Oblations," which corresponds to the morning liturgy Epiclesis. In this Offertory litany, the priest prays, "Show Your face on this bread and this cup, which are put on this priestly table, which is for You. Bless it, sanctify it,

---

[490] The practice of mixing wine with water was not uncommon among Mediterranean societies. See: McGowan, Andrew B., *Ancient Christian Worship*, 42.

purify it, and transform the bread to be Your Body, and this mixture to be Your Precious Blood." That is, the priest entreats Christ Himself to transform the materials into His own Body and Blood. In the same manner, the text of the morning liturgy—particularly in the Epiclesis—implores the Holy Spirit to descend upon the materials and change them into the Holy Mysteries.

One piece of evidence that shows that the Offertory—before it was attached to the morning liturgy—was a complete liturgy, during which the bread and wine are transformed into the Body and Blood of Jesus, is what is mentioned in a manuscript preserved at the Saint Macarius monastery. This document, MS Theology 1, was transcribed by Metropolitan Mikhail of Asiout. It reads, "Then the priest covers the Body and the Cup with corporals, which symbolizes the coffins... then the priest reads the Liturgy of the Apostles, which is 'We give thanks to the beneficent;' and when he finishes it, he exits the sanctuary."[491] In other words, this document refers to the Offertory Thanksgiving Prayer as the *Liturgy of the Apostles*.

In summary, the primitive liturgies in the early centuries, imitating the Last Supper, were celebrated in the evening. Later, the morning liturgy became more popular until it eventually prevailed. In the fifth century, the Coptic Church incorporated the evening liturgy, after naming it the *Offertory*, into the morning service.[492] In this nascent arrangement, the Offertory was preceded by the Liturgy of the Catechumens and followed by the Reconciliation Prayer, which would lead the Liturgy of the Faithful. In around the seventh century, the Offertory was moved again to precede the Liturgy of the Catechumens.

---

[491] Matthew the Poor (Father), *Eucharist of the Lord's Supper*, 53.
[492] Father Matthew the Poor argues that Vespers Offering of Incense is basically a replacement of the evening liturgy after it was amalgamated with the morning one.

The Canonical Hours and the Prayers of Preparation

Historically, the Prime Offering of Incense was prayed communally every day at the church, whether or not a liturgy was to follow. The Liturgy of the Hours would then follow. In other words, until the 14th century, the Canonical Hours were associated with the Offering of Incense not to the liturgy. In non-fasting days, after the incense offering, the Third and Sixth Hours are uttered; on fasting days, however, the Ninth Hour is added.[493] In antiquity, the Ninth Hour marked the end of the business day,[494] hence, liturgies, if celebrated on these days—specifically, Wednesday and Friday, were performed on that hour. During Lent and the Fast of Nineveh, the Liturgy of the Hours further extends to include the Eleventh and Twelfth Hours. In monasteries, the Veil Hour is prayed after the Twelfth.

Ibn Kabar reports that Pope John VIII (AD 1300–1320),[495] the 80th patriarch of Alexandria, moved the Canonical Hours, during Lent, to precede the Offertory.[496] It seems that did change did not propagate to all other occasions, or maybe to all parishes. Only recently, around the 18th century, the rubric changed to permanently locate the Canonical Hours immediately after the preparation of the altar and before the Presentation of the Lamb.[497] We know about this nascent development from Father Abdel Massieh Salib's report in his AD 1902 Euchologion; in a footnote, he writes, "The present custom is for the congregation to pray the psalms

---

[493] The pattern of praying on the Third, Sixth, and Ninth Hours is an immemorial observance that was mentioned by Tertullian, Clement of Alexandria, Origen, Cyprian, and the *Apostolic Tradition*. See further McGowan, Andrew B., *Ancient Christian Worship*, 190-200.

[494] McGowan, Andrew B., *Ancient Christian Worship*, 227.

[495] Pope John VIII was born in Meniat Bani-Khosaim. His real name was Yohanna Ibn Ebsal Benjamin (Arabic: يوحنا بن إبسال بنيامين), but he was known as El-Mo'ataman Ibn El-Kedees (Arabic: المؤتمن بن القديس). He became monk at the Monastery of Shahran and was ordained Pope on February 14th, AD 1300. During his papacy, severe tribulations befell the Christians in Egypt. Many parishes were closed in Cairo and in different parts of the country.

[496] Ibn Kabar, *The Lamp to Darkness and Explanation of the Service*, BnF, MS Arabic 203 (c. AD 1363-1369), fol. 212v.

[497] Since the custom of the daily praying Prime Offering of Incense at church ceased, the Liturgy of the Hours office was correlated to the liturgy as opposed to Prime Offering of Incense.

of the Hours first. The altar preparation takes place before or during the Canonical Hours."[498] In another footnote in the same book, *Hegumen* Abdel Massieh attests, "The present custom is that the Presentation of the Lamb takes place toward the end of the Canonical Hours."[499] In the two passages, the focus on "the present custom" indicates a change that took place at his time, or a little earlier, that is incongruent to the instructions provided by the sources he is copying from. As a result of this innovation, servants dress their Sticharions[500] right before the Liturgy of the Hours, whereas in the past, only if a liturgy is to follow, Sticharions were put on following the Liturgy of the Hours.

Putting on the Sticharions before praying the liturgy is an old tradition that was inherited from the Old Testament (Leviticus 16:3, 4), and is practiced by other Churches. Wearing white Sticharions during services symbolizes holiness and glory. "Make tunics, sashes and caps for Aaron's sons to give them dignity and honor." (Exodus 28:40); "...make garments for Aaron, for his consecration, so he may serve me as priest" (Exodus 28:3). Every time we serve the Lord, we must take away our daily infirmities and weaknesses in order to put on God's bright vestments. We should leave out any malicious or impure thoughts so we may wear the crowns of chastity and righteousness, which can only be achieved through hiding in Him.

Ibn Sibaa of the 13th century, Ibn Kabar, of the 14th century, Pope Gabriel V of the 15th century, the Euchologion written by Raphael El-Tokhee in AD 1736, and other Euchologions did not recognize any orisons or blessings during the wearing of the Sticharion. However, Yessah

---

[498] Salib, Abdel Massieh (*Hegumen*), *The Holy Euchologion*, 197.
[499] Salib, Abdel Massieh (*Hegumen*), *The Holy Euchologion*, 203.
[500] It was not before the 5th century that the Sticharion became an official liturgical vestment. See: Athanasius of Saint Macarius Monastery (Father), *Summary of the Liturgical History of the Church of Alexandria (Part 1)*, 204.

Abdel Massieh found a Euchologion that was written in the first half of the 18th century with prayers uttered during the wearing of the Sticharion. The author of this Euchologion is *Hegumen* Morcos El-Ekhmimi, who departed in AD 1746. In it, he writes, "he puts it (the Sticharion) on his left forearm and bless it thrice with his right hand, draw the sign of the cross saying 'Ϧⲉⲛ ⲫⲣⲁⲛ ⲙ̇Ⲫⲓⲱⲧ ⲛⲉⲙ Ⲡϣⲏⲣⲓ ⲛⲉⲙ ⲡⲓⲠⲛⲉⲩⲙⲁ ⲉⲑⲟⲩⲁⲃ ⲟⲩⲛⲟⲩϯ ⲛ̇ⲟⲩⲱⲧ'[501] and afterwards he recites Psalm 'I will exalt you O Lord' (Psalm 29), followed by Psalm 'The Lord has reigned; He has clothed Himself with beauty' (Psalm 92). After wearing the tunic, girdles with a stole... Afterwards, he prostrates before the altar, then to his brethren the priests... He greets his brethren the priests and asks them to pray for him."[502]

In his Euchologion, *Hegumen* Abd El-Messih El-Massoody instructs, "He (the priest) then puts on the priestly vestment while uttering Psalm 29 'I will exalt you O Lord,' followed by Psalm 92, 'The Lord has reigned. He has clothed Himself with beauty.' He then greets his brethren the priests and asks them to pray for him. He then prostrates before the altar, and before his brethren the priests, respectively."[503] Per the contemporary practice, the priest blesses his own Sticharion and the servants with the three blessings. If the Pope or a Bishop is present, the person with the highest rank blesses the tunics.

After putting on the liturgical vestments, the celebrant prepares the altar.[504] The preparation of the altar is a symbol of the preparation of the upper room during the Last Supper; hence, the priest prepares the altar to

---

[501] Translation: In the name of the Father, the Son and the Holy Spirit; one God.
[502] Athanasius of Saint Macarius Monastery (Father), *The Divine Liturgy: The Mystery of the Kingdom of God (Part 1)*, 215, 216.
[503] Salib, Abdel Massieh (*Hegumen*), *The Holy Euchologion*, 195-196.
[504] In the old rite (mentioned by Pope Gabriel V in the 15th century), the priest would wash his hands before preparing the altar.

get ready for the *True Paschal* meal, who is Jesus Himself.[505] This practice should encourage all worshipers to prepare their hearts and minds to receive the Lord of Hosts. This can be achieved by repentance and confession as well as lifting up their hearts in prayers during the liturgy.

The celebrant says, "Ϧⲉⲛ ⲫⲣⲁⲛ ... Ⲧⲥⲙⲁⲣⲱⲟⲩⲧ" thrice before undoing the knots of the corporal in which the altar vessels are wrapped. Inaudibly, he then utters the first and second prayers of altar preparation, respectively.[506] Feeling unworthy to celebrate the liturgy, in these orisons, the priest implores the Lord to have mercy on him, help him, and send him power so he may be worthy to accomplish the awesome sacrament.

In the primitive order, after the preparation of the altar, the Offertory follows at once. Nevertheless, as previously noted, the contemporary rubric instructs that the Canonical Hours interjects this primeval sequence. Until the 15th century, the hymn Alleluia of the Oblations was chanted while the altar was being prepared and protracted until the priest says, "Glory and honor." The 13th century scholar Youhanna Ibn Sibaa directs, "The archdeacon, who is the head deacons, permits one of the cantors to chant the hymn *Alleluia* in the tune that is appropriate for the time, whether it is a fast then in a pensive tune, or Feast of the Lord, then joyful melody."[507] In other words, Alleluia of the Oblations was employed in every liturgy from the beginning of the preparation of the altar until the priest says, "Glory and Honor," which justifies its length. In around 18th century, when the Canonical Hours interpolated the liturgy and was placed between the preparation of the altar and the Offertory, the assignment of Alleluia of the Oblations was changed.

---

[505] The author of *The Trinitarian Mystery in Priesthood Ministry* links the covering of the altar with the covering of the Ark or the Covenant with gold (Hebrews 9:4). For more details, review *The Trinitarian Mystery in Priesthood Ministry* page 6.
[506] The author of these prayers is Saint Severus of Antioch, who lived from AD 465 to 538.
[507] Ibn Sibaa, *The Precious Pearl: On Ecclesiastic Science*, BnF, MS Arabic 207, fol. 116r.

In this recent arrangement, which is followed until now, the chanting of the hymn Ⲧⲉⲛⲟⲩⲱϣⲧ and its *Parallaxe* Ⲭⲉⲣⲉ Ⲙⲁⲣⲓⲁ replaced the recitation of Alleluia of the Oblations during the preparation of the altar. *The Church Order* MS Lit. 73 (AD 1444) sheds some light on how this happened. The manuscript explains that the hymns Ⲧⲉⲛⲟⲩⲱϣⲧ, its *Parallaxe* Ⲭⲉⲣⲉ Ⲙⲁⲣⲓⲁ, and Ⲉⲣⲉ ⲡⲓⲥⲙⲟⲩ (part of Ⲙⲡⲓⲛⲁⲩ ϣⲱⲡⲓ) were chanted during the Veneration Service at the end of the Prime Offering of Incense.[508] For the sake of time, it is possible that these hymns were fused with the altar preparation prayers deferring Alleluia of the Oblations to the time of the Presentation of the Lamb.[509] According to the current practice, Alleluia of the Oblations is given priority only in the three nocturnal festivals, which are: Nativity, Theophany, and Resurrection.

Therefore, the present-time rubric directs that the altar preparation prayers are performed first then, the Liturgy of the Hours take place. This is then followed by the rite of the Offertory, which commences with the Presentation of the Lamb.

The Presentation of the Lamb

Per the contemporary practice, upon the completion of the Canonical Hours, the priest washes his hands thrice. On the first time, he says, "Purge me with hyssop and I shall be made clean, wash me and I will be made whiter than snow" (Psalm 50:7). On the second time, he says, "Make me to hear joy and gladness; the bones You have broken, may rejoice" (Psalm 50:8). On the third time, he says, "I will wash my hands in purity, and go around Your altar, O Lord, to hear the voice of Your praise Alleluia" (Psalm 25:6, 7).

---

[508] Jeremiah (*Hegumen*), *The Church Order*, Cairo, Patriarchal Library, MS Lit. 73 (AD 1444), fol. 73r.
[509] The rite of the Presentation of the Lamb includes choosing the Lamb then placing it on the altar.

Handwashing was a Jewish custom before and after their celebratory meals, like the Passover. It was a necessary ablution before religious practices (i.e., prayer, religious meals, etc.). The Early Church inherited this custom from Judaism and practiced it before Eucharistic prayers. According to the Tractate *Bərâkhôth* of the Mishnah (viii: 2-2), Baumstark argues, the washing of hands took place at the end of the meal. This corresponds to the end of the Agape meal in Christianity and right before the Eucharistic celebration.[510]

The first to mention the tradition of the *lavabo*,[511] that is, washing the hands of the celebrant at the beginning of the Offertory, was Saint Cyril of Jerusalem in AD 348. By the fourth century, this custom was accepted and practiced by all other Churches. Saint Cyril of Jerusalem states, "You have seen then the Deacon who gives to the Priest water to wash, and to the Presbyters who stand round God's altar. He gave it not at all because of bodily defilement; it is not that; for we did not enter the Church at first with defiled bodies. But the washing of hands is a symbol that you ought to be pure from all sinful and unlawful deeds; for since the hands are a symbol of action, by washing them, it is evident, we represent the purity and blamelessness of our conduct."[512] Furthermore, the handwashing indicates preparation for receiving communion.

The staple elements of the Christian offerings are bread and wine, a tradition that was not a peculiarity of Judaism, but a common one among all ancient Mediterranean nations.[513] In antiquity, all the *Prosphora* (Offerings) were placed on the Table of Oblation (or Proskomide from the Greek word προσκομιδή meaning, "offering") in the Prothesis, which is

---

[510] Baumstark, Anton, *Comparative Liturgy*, 133.
[511] The name Latin word *lavabo*, literally meaning "I shall wash," is derived from the words of verses, which the celebrant traditionally recites while washing his hands. In the Coptic tradition, the celebrant inaudibly recites Psalms 50:7, and Psalms 25:6,7.
[512] Cyril of Jerusalem (Saint), *Catechetical Lecture 23*.
[513] McGowan, Andrew B., *Ancient Christian Worship*, 23.

Offertory

the altar located at the northern side of the High Altar. After the altar is prepared, the celebrant chooses the Lamb. This process used to take place at the Prothesis. Upon completion, escorted with censers and lit candles, the priest, who carries the chosen Lamb, and altar servers march from the Prothesis to the High Altar in a solemn procession called the Circuit of the Lamb. Meanwhile, the ceremonial hymn Alleluia of the Oblations is chanted.[514] In his book *The Precious Pearl: On Ecclesiastic Science* written in the 13th century, Ibn Sibaa says, "He (the priest) then goes to the small altar of offering and brings the Lamb from it. He inspects it lest it has an incision (defect), which is a blemish, and it is written that the lamb must be without blemish.[515] That is because this Offering resembles the Old Testament one-year-old lamb… once he (the priest) finds all what he needs from the oblations, the wine, the incense, the charcoal, and all the supplies needed for the liturgy, and that they are in a good condition, he takes the Offering and anoints it to be the Lamb. He takes the Offering and washes it as Our Lord Jesus was washed before being presented to Simeon the priest. He then rotates it in his hands as Simeon the priest, holding Him (Jesus), circumambulated the Temple. He (the priest) then places it in the paten, which symbolizes the manger. He wraps it as the Virgin swaddled Him (Jesus) upon His birth. (Thus,) the paten initially symbolizes the manger, and ultimately represents the tomb."[516] Upon arrival to the High Altar, the priest washes his hands.[517] So, per the old rite (until the 13th century), the hymn Alleluia of the Oblations used to start at the beginning of the preparation of the altar and ended after the Circuit of the Lamb.

---

[514] Paris, BnF, MS Arabic 100 (14th C.) mentions that the oblations are taken from the Prothesis to where the Gospel is read before it is offered on the altar.
[515] See: Exodus 12:5, and 1 Peter 19.
[516] Ibn Sibaa, *The Precious Pearl: On Ecclesiastic Science*, BnF, MS Arabic 207, fols. 118v-119v.
[517] Notice that the washing of the hands was done after the Lamb is selected.

In the 15th century, Pope Gabriel V instructs the Presentation of the Lamb to be performed at the door of the High Altar, not at the Prothesis. The ancient practice of choosing the Lamb at the Prothesis, nevertheless, was still observed in some areas until the 19th century.[518] In his work *The Ritual Order*, Pope Gabriel V states, "The priest turns to the left to choose the Lamb, which is the bread of offering. After he examines it carefully, to be an Offering that is a 'one-year-old without blemish,' he takes it and wipes its back with a clean corporal, and he kisses it and puts it on the right side of the altar in a silk corporal. He also examines the wine by smelling it; alternatively, he appoints someone who is not fasting to taste it in his hand. If the wine is spoiled, it will taste[519] like vinegar. If the Offering was not chosen, it will remain in its original nature, that is, mere bread."[520] The level of ritual complexity, compared to the instructions provided in the 13th century is palpable. In Ibn Sibaa's account, no specific blessings or process is assigned to Choosing the Lamb. Moreover, the Presentation of the Lamb did not include the wine but was restricted to the Lamb.[521] Videlicet, until the 13th century, when the Circuit of the Lamb was performed from the Prothesis to the High Altar, no mention was made vis-à-vis the wine in the process of choosing or offering the Lamb; it was only mentioned after the Circuit of the Lamb is accomplished; only then the wine is examined before the High Altar. Thus, this circuit was named after the Lamb only.

Before discussing the Presentation of the Lamb in further detail, let us first scrutinize the topic of *lavabo*, viz, the handwashing. As previously

---

[518] Athanasius of Saint Macarius Monastery (Father), *Summary of the Liturgical History of the Church of Alexandria (Part 2)*, 394.
[519] In his book *The Coptic Morning Service for the Lord's Day*, Marquis of Bute writes, "Then he examines the wine, smells it or causes it to be tasted, in order to be sure of its fitness."
[520] Gabriel V (Pope), *The Ritual Order*, BnF, MS 98 (AD 1411), fols. 47v-48r.
[521] The priest checked the wine when he turns to the east, while standing before the altar, not while standing at the door of the altar, facing west.

noted, until the 13th century, the washing of the hands was performed proceeding the Presentation of the Lamb. However, Pope Gabriel V states, "He turns to the west to choose the Lamb," then he continues, "The priest washes his hands thrice, and he says, 'Purge me with hyssop and I shall be made clean…',," he then writes, "He dries his hands on a clean white linen corporal."[522] According to the contemporary practice, however, the handwashing takes place prior to the Presentation of the Lamb. When the rite of *lavabo* was moved to precede the Presentation of the Lamb, rubric still preserved traces of the old tradition in its original place, that is, after the Presentation of the Lamb. Hence, after the Presentation of the Lamb, the altar server pours a little water into the hand of the priest, an action that denotes *lavabo* in its original placement. We will discuss this topic in depth shortly.

Having washed his hands, the priest holds the cross and stands at the door of the sanctuary facing west. He takes the corporal covering the paten and puts it in his left sleeve, or on his head. The servant deacon, or the most senior one, presents the basket containing the *Prosphora* (bread-offerings)[523] to the priest.[524] During the Presentation of the Lamb, two altar servers stand on both sides of the *Prosphora*. The altar server standing on the northern side will hold the decanter (wine)[525] and a lit taper while the one standing on the southern side will hold a water pitcher and a lit taper.

---

[522] Gabriel V (Pope), *The Ritual Order*, BnF, MS 98 (AD 1411), fol. 48r-v.
[523] *Prosphoron* (or the bread-offering) is round, in the shape of a circle, having no beginning and no end to symbolize the eternity of our Lord. It is stamped in the center with a large cross representing Jesus surrounded by twelve small crosses representing the 12 disciples. Around the crosses appears the stamp of the Trisagion: "Holy God, Holy Mighty, Holy Immortal." The bread is pierced in five places around the central crosses in reference to the three nails that hold Jesus on the cross, the crown of thorns and the spear that pierced His side. The bread is made from pure wheat, leavened but unsalted, because Jesus Christ is the salt of the world. The leaven symbolizes our Sins which the Lord Jesus Christ bore for us. The bread must be freshly baked.
[524] Old practice was to present the wine after the Lamb had been chosen.
[525] The wine must be grape wine, pure and red in color.

The celebrant then places the decanter (wine cruet) on the closest *Prosphoron* to him. He crosses himself saying, "In the name of the Father, the Son, and the Holy Spirit, One God Amen."[526] Then, he does the sign of the cross on the *Prosphora* and wine thrice. On the first signing he says, "Blessed be God the Father, the *Pantocrator*. Amen." On the second signing, he says, "Blessed be His Only-Begotten Son, Jesus Christ, our Lord. Amen." On the third signing he says, "Blessed be the Holy Spirit, the *Paraclete*. Amen." Although this is the prevalent practice at present time, *Hegumen* Abdel Massieh points out that he could not find them in older documents except for one that was transcribed in AD 1844.[527] The 13th-century *The Beginners' Guide and Discipline for Laity* prescribes the performance of the three signings upon each *Prosphoron* prior to Choosing the Lamb.[528] Ibn Kabar places the three signings prior to the Circuit of the Lamb, when the celebrant wipes the *Prosphora*.[529] In the 15th century, however, the same signings were postponed to follow the Circuit of the Lamb. In his *The Ritual Order*, when celebrant is presented with the basket of *Prosphora*, Pope Gabriel V instructs, "He (the priest) says 'In the name of the Father' in its entirety. He then performs the first signing while saying... during the second signing he says... he completes the third signing while saying..."[530] Same order was prescribed by Raphael Tuki.[531] In the 19th century—this is also the contemporary practice, another development emerged to accommodate both traditions.[532] In other words, the signings are performed twice, once when the Lamb is being chosen, and another after the Circuit of the Lamb.

---

[526] Mettaos (Bishop), *The Spirituality of the Rite of the Liturgy of the Coptic Orthodox Church*, 94.
[527] Salib, Abdel Massieh (*Hegumen*), *The Holy Euchologion*, 203.
[528] Misael of the Paromeos Monastery (Father). (2018). The Beginners' Guide and Discipline for Laity. *Alexandria School*, 24(1), 140.
[529] Ibn Kabar, *The Lamp*, BnF, MS Arabic 203 (c. AD 1363-1369), fols. 205r, 209v.
[530] Gabriel V (Pope), *The Ritual Order*, BnF, MS 98 (AD 1411), fol. 51v.
[531] Tuki, Raphael, *The Book of the Three Liturgies*, 17.
[532] Salib, Abdel Massieh (*Hegumen*), *The Holy Euchologion*, 203, 219.

Offertory

Following the signings, the priest examines the wine by smelling it, and then offering it to the altar server to verify that it has not gone sour. If confirmed, the alter server declares, "Good and honored." The celebrant then signs the *Prosphora* with the cross saying, "Glory and honor, honor and glory to the All-Holy Trinity, the Father, the Son, and the Holy Spirit, now and forever, and unto the age of ages, amen."[533] He then places the cross inside the *Prosphora* basket. Having his hands crossed, analogous to what Jacob did when he blessed Joseph's sons Manasseh and Ephraim (Genesis 48:13, 14), the priest starts the process of selecting the Lamb. The process of choosing the Lamb commences with the celebrant saying, "The Lord will choose a Lamb without defect." He then examines two *Prosphora* and compares between them, making certain that the better one is in his right hand. He puts the other one back and takes another *Prosphoron*. He last-selected *Prosphoron* with the one on his right hand. If it is better, he moves it into his right hand and puts the other one back in the basket. He continues to do that until he chooses the best *Prosphoron*, which becomes the Lamb. Subsequently, with the tip of the Lamb, he touches each of the *Prosphora*, denoting the fulfilment of the ultimate sacrifice of all Old Testament offerings through Jesus, the Lamb of God.

The priest then takes the corporal that he previously kept in his sleeve or on his head and places it in his left-hand upside down. Next, he places the chosen Lamb on it and, without flipping it, wipes it well with the corporal from both sides, the top and the bottom. Thereafter, he turns the corporal over and places it in his left hand and places the Lamb on it. He then dips his right thumb inside the wine and anoints the Lamb (while still in his left hand) with his thumb. While anointing the Lamb, he says, "An Offering of Blessing, an Offering of Glory." He then anoints the rest of the

---

[533] These same statements are uttered once again after the Circuit of the Lamb.

Prosphora with the sign of the cross with his right thumb saying, "An Offering of Blessing, an Offering of Abraham, an Offering of Isaac, and Offering of Jacob." He returns to the chosen Lamb and says, "An Offering of Melchizedek." Anointing the Lamb in the beginning and at the end implies that this *Prosphoron* will become the Body of Christ, who is the first and the last, the beginning and the end.

Although old sources do not dictate a specific number for the *Prosphora*, preference to odd number is discernible, as suggested by Pope Cyril III in his *The Beginners' Guide and Discipline for Laity,* which was transcribed in AD 1353 (fol. 8ᵛ).[534] Recent documents, however, suggest three, five, seven, or any odd number. Symbolic exegesis was assigned to each of these numbers. *Three* refers to the three hypostases, from which only one (the Logos) becomes the Lamb of God, the True Sacrifice. *Five* denotes the five offerings of the Old Testament, viz, Burnt Offering, Grain Offering, Peace Offering, Sin Offering, and Trespass Offering. Jesus, the True Sacrifice, encloses all these offerings in Himself, and they point to Him. *Seven* resembles the seven sacrifices of the Old Testament offerings, which are young bull, male goat, female goat, lamb, ram, dove, and pigeon. These sacrifices connote Christ's sacrifice on the Cross. The general meaning attached to these numbers refers to the sacrificial character of the Lamb of God, the True Sacrifice. As parishes grew bigger and worshippers increased in number, the limitation of seven bread-offerings became an impediment in some cases. As such, the need for new explanation when the number of *Prosphora* exceeds seven arisen. The tradition evolved to allow any odd number with the elucidation that the *Prosphora* resemble the disciples (12) and apostles (70/72) of the Lord in addition to Jesus Himself. Although this allegory deviates from the unambiguous

---

[534] Misael of the Paromeos Monastery (Father). (2018). The Beginners' Guide and Discipline for Laity. *Alexandria School, 24(1),* 140.

correlation between the number of *Prosphora* and Jesus's sacrificial work, the gist of this conception is still preserved, although implied; that is, the chosen *Prosphoron* will eventually transform into Jesus Christ Himself, the True Sacrifice.

As noted above, it was the practice to chant Alleluia of the Oblations during the Presentation of the Lamb. However, during the first third of the 20th century, another change was introduced. While the Lamb is being chosen, **Ⲕⲩⲣⲓⲉ ⲉⲗⲉⲏⲥⲟⲛ** (Lord, have mercy), the conclusion of the Canonical Hours,[535] is recited 41 times replacing Alleluia of the Oblations. If the former hymn is accomplished and the priest is not finished yet, Alleluia of the Oblations may be chanted. Later, ritual prescriptions changed again to allow for another chant to compete with Alleluia of the Oblations, that is, **Ⲁⲡⲓⲛⲁⲩ ϣⲱⲡⲓ** (The time came). As such, the formation of the current practice was completed, and can be summarized as follows: Alleluia of the Oblations is chanted during the "Choosing the Lamb" in the three nocturnal festivals. In Regular Days, however, **Ⲕⲩⲣⲓⲉ ⲉⲗⲉⲏⲥⲟⲛ** 41 times is uttered; if time permits, if the day does not mandate abstinence fasting, then Alleluia of the Oblations is said, otherwise, **Ⲁⲡⲓⲛⲁⲩ ϣⲱⲡⲓ** is chanted.

The number 41 is commonly understood as a symbolism of the prime *Arma Christi*, or the Instruments of the Passion, that is, the 39 whips that Jesus suffered, the staff that He was struck with on the head, and the lance with which a Roman soldier inflicted in His side.[536] Some sources, however, replace the staff with the crown of thorns. Yet, other explain 41 as 40 whips and the slap in Jesus' face.[537] In all construal provided,

---

[535] Since the Canonical Hours are not recited in the feasts of the Nativity, Epiphany, and Resurrection, Alleluia of the Oblations is still sung.

[536] Ibn Sibaa, *The Precious Pearl: On Ecclesiastic Science*, BnF, MS Arabic 207, fol. 93v, Mettaos (Bishop), *The Spirituality of the Rite of the Liturgy of the Coptic Orthodox Church*, 92, and Benyamine (Metropolitan), *The Rite of the Divine Liturgy*, 62.

[537] Gabriel V (Pope), *The Ritual Order*, BnF, MS 98 (AD 1411), fol. 43r.

nevertheless, the number could have been 42 (the 39 whips, the crown of thorns, and the lance), or 45 (if the 3 nails are added), or any other combination. As such, 41 is not sufficient to include all torments endured by the Lord. In the Byzantine tradition, the emphasis of **Ⲕⲩⲣⲓⲉ ⲉⲗⲉⲏⲥⲟⲛ** is strictly on the lashes, which perhaps can clue us in to the Coptic primeval construal of the number. If this is accurate, why then **Ⲕⲩⲣⲓⲉ ⲉⲗⲉⲏⲥⲟⲛ** is not recited 39 times? Father Athanasius of Saint Macarius Monastery offers a decent justification. He argues that according to the Jewish Law, the number of scourges should be 40 (Deuteronomy 25:3);[538] however, they made it 39[539] because the person that was carrying the punishment might have miscounted, hence, 39 is better than 41 in disgrace. Yes, the Jews were very legalistic; since there is a commandment regulates the maximum scourges to 40, they were always incredibly careful not to exceed this punishment. However, this was also done as a form of mercy on the person being disciplined. The Coptic Church opted to include an additional **Ⲕⲩⲣⲓⲉ ⲉⲗⲉⲏⲥⲟⲛ** to the original 40 in her count to express her need for the Lord's multitude of mercy beyond the Law.[540]

Afterwards, the servant priest, who chose the Lamb, takes his cross from the basket. Having the chosen Lamb in his hand, he says to the deacon who is presenting the basket "I have sinned forgive me." If the person holding the basket is a priest, then the principal celebrant says, "I have sinned, absolve me." Holding the Lamb, the celebrant turns toward the east, stands before the altar, and places the corporal and the cross on the altar. The entrance of the Lamb into the sanctuary is a symbol of Christ

---

[538] "But the judge must not impose more than forty lashes. If the guilty party is flogged more than that, your fellow Israelite will be degraded in your eyes" (Deuteronomy 25:3).
[539] "Five times I received from the Jews the forty lashes minus one" (2 Corinthians 11:24).
[540] Athanasius of Saint Macarius Monastery (Father), *The Prayers of Incense Offering in Vespers and Prime*, 522.

who "entered the Most Holy Place once for all by His Own Blood, thus obtaining eternal redemption" (Hebrews 9:12).[541]

The servant priest then places the Lamb in his left hand, wets his right hand with water, and wipes the Lamb from the top and bottom.[542] A common explication of this ritual—as provided by *The Mystery of the Trinity in the Priesthood*, MS Theology 84, preserved at the library of Saint Paul Monastery—likens it to the Lord's baptism in the Jordan River.[543] As mentioned previously, according to the ancient practice, the priest chooses the Lamb at the Prothesis, marches to the High Altar, washes his hands, and, per diversity of sources, partially dries them. He then rubs it with his right hand above and below. It is apparent that the intent of this unpretentious practice can hardly be understood with the aforementioned symbolism in mind. The rationale and function of the wiping was purely utilitarian; it was simply to remove any excess flour on the Lamb. When the handwashing was moved to precede the Presentation of the Lamb, the rubric preserved the original placement of the handwashing, which is after the Presentation of the Lamb.

Therefore, as it stands today, the altar server pouring little water into the priest's hands cueing the original placement of the handwashing. This is immediately followed by rubbing the Lamb from top and bottom. Two unrelated successive rituals, yet, performed uninterruptedly. This produced the illusion that the two rituals are one pertaining to washing the Lamb, especially that the priest does not fully dry his hands before wiping the Lamb.[544]

---

[541] Iskander, Athanasius (Father), *Understanding the Liturgy*, 3.
[542] While the priest is wiping the Lamb, he says, "Grant, O Lord, that our sacrifice may be accepted before You for my own sins and for the ignorance of Your people. For behold, it is pure according to the gift of Your Holy Spirit, in Christ Jesus our Lord…"
[543] Misael of the Paromeos Monastery (Father). (2020). The Trinitarian Mystery in Priesthood Ministry. *Alexandria School*, 28(1), 115.
[544] This is how the author of *The Trinitarian Mystery in Priesthood Ministry* understood it; page 4.

Accordingly, the contemporary rubric directs to two separate times Lamb-wiping; the first, during the Presentation of the Lamb using a corporal, and the second, immediately after the Lamb is chosen, in which it is performed with bare moist hands. After the second time, while keeping his right hand on top of the Lamb, the priest bows down before the altar. He then offers prayers for the needs of the people, a list of spiritual and physical exigencies called Remembrance Prayers, which includes petitions for forgiveness of the sins, the sick, travelers, departed, mourning, all faithful, and finally, for himself. This is then followed by the Three Minor Litanies, which are for the peace, the fathers, and for the liturgical assemblies. The placement of the priest hand on the Lamb while offering all these orisons a tradition that is rooted in the Old Testament, in which the penitent is instructed take his sacrifice to the officiating priest and lay his hands on the sacrifice, symbolically transferring his sins to the animal. "You are to lay your hand on the head of the burnt offering, and it will be accepted on your behalf to make atonement for you" (Leviticus 1:4). Similarly, the priest, while praying for his congregation, places his hands on the Lamb indicating that the chosen Lamb, after the sanctification, is going to carry the sins of all humanity. It is not a mere bread but will be the true Body of Jesus Himself who is, "the Lamb of God, who takes away the sin of the world" (John 1:29).

The Circuit of the Lamb

Following the wiping of the Lamb, which is the final stride of the Presentation of the Lamb, the Circuit of the Lamb commences. The priest wraps the Lamb into the corporal that was used during the process of choosing it, puts the cross on top of it slanted a little, and stands facing the congregation. Raising the wrapped Lamb above his head, he proclaims,

Offertory

"Glory and Honor..." Afterwards, the celebrant, the servant deacon, who carries the decanter wrapped in a corporal, and the rest of the altar servers, who hold lit tapers, circumambulate the sanctuary once. This solemn pageant around the altar is a symbol of carrying the body of Jesus wrapped in linen to lay it in the tomb. The celebrant and the servant deacon represent Joseph and Nicodemus who carried the body of our Lord. The whole procession becomes a beautiful icon for the short journey from Calvary to the nearby sepulcher.[545] During the Circuit of the Lamb, the altar server recites the bidding pertaining to the Litany of the Oblations, and the principal celebrant inaudibly utters, "Remember O Lord those who asked us to remember them."

Thus, the Circuit of the Lamb went through many revisions before it settled as practiced today. As previously mentioned, until approximately the 13th century, the Circuit of the Lamb was merely a simple, yet solemn, procession intended to transfer the gifts from the Prothesis to the High Altar. The next revision comes from the 14th century as testified by Ibn Kabar; he states, "(The Priest) signs the Offering and says, 'Glory and Honor...' and hands the bread-offerings to the deacon serving with him. The deacon receives it in one of the altars consecrated corporals and wraps the Lamb in it. He then circles the altar, and then, coming from his left side, gives it back to the priest. The priest then places it in the paten."[546] The next amendment took place in the 15th century and was reported by Pope Gabriel V. He writes, "The priest wraps the Lamb in the linen corporal and places it on his head. A deacon stands in front of him with a candle, another deacon holds the decanter wrapped in a linen corporal above his head. They circumambulate the sanctuary once, while the priest is saying, 'Glory and Honor, Honor and Glory to the All-holy Trinity, the

---

[545] Iskander, Athanasius (Father), *Understanding the Liturgy*, 5.
[546] Ibn Kabar, *The Lamp*, BnF, MS Arabic 203 (c. AD 1363-1369), fol. 205v.

Father, the Son, and the Holy Spirit. Peace and edification to the one, only, holy, Catholic, Apostolic Orthodox Church of God. Amen. Remember, O Lord those who have brought to you these gifts and those on whose behalf they have been brought, and those by whom they have been brought. Give them all the heavenly reward.'"[547] There are a few things to note. First, the priest is the one who wraps the Lamb, not the deacon. Second, the priest holds the Lamb and rotates the altar, and the deacon follows him holding the decanter wrapped in another corporal. Third, "Glory and Honor" was recited during the Circuit of the Lamb, as opposed to preceding it as practiced today. Fourth, Pope Gabriel V does not mention a deacon's response. Fifth, "Remember O Lord those who asked us to remember them" was delivered aloud.

The final adjustment to this ritual brings us to the contemporary practice. The priest wraps the chosen Lamb in a corporal,[548] puts it above his head to show respect and honor to it and rotates around the altar once.[549] As mentioned earlier, the Circuit of the Lamb symbolizes the burial cortege from Calvary to the sepulcher. A more recent interpretation, but still relevant, suggests that this circuit represents the spread of the good news of Salvation throughout the globe. Therefore, it is only proper that the worshippers, during the Circuit of the Lamb, bow down their heads as the Psalm instructs, "All the earth shall worship You and sing praises to You" (Psalms 66:4).

---

[547] Gabriel V (Pope), *The Ritual Order*, BnF, MS 98 (AD 1411), fol. 50r-v.
[548] Some writers compare this ritual to Saint Mary swaddling baby Jesus before handing Him to Simeon the Elder. However, the older interpretation of the burial procession from Calvary to the sepulcher is more relevant.
[549] Some writers think that the Circuit of the Lamb implies that Simeon the Elder, out of happiness because he had seen the salvation of the Lord, carried baby Jesus and walked around the Temple of Jerusalem declaring the emergence of the "light to all nations." However, the entire seen, according to older traditions, represents the burial of Jesus. The entire liturgy is actually the result of the Cross and the sacrifice of Jesus.

Afterwards, the congregation chants the hymn of Ⲁⲗⲗⲏⲗⲟⲩⲓⲁ ⲫⲁⲓ ⲡⲉ ⲡⲓ (Alleluia. This is the day), Ⲁⲗⲗⲏⲗⲟⲩⲓⲁ ⲍⲉ ⲫⲙⲉⲩⲓ (Alleluia. The thought of man), Ⲁⲗⲗⲏⲗⲟⲩⲓⲁ ⲉⲓⲉⲓ ⲉϧⲟⲩⲛ (Alleluia. I shall go in), Ⲁⲗⲗⲏⲗⲟⲩⲓⲁ ⲁⲛⲟⲕ ⲇⲉ (Alleluia. But I), or Ⲁⲗⲗⲏⲗⲟⲩⲓⲁ ⲁⲣⲓⲫⲙⲉⲩⲓ (Alleluia. Remember). Regarding the usage of these hymns, in his book *The Ritual Order*, Pope Gabriel V directs that Ⲁⲗⲗⲏⲗⲟⲩⲓⲁ ⲫⲁⲓ ⲡⲉ ⲡⲓ is sung on all non-fasting days, Sundays, and Eastertide, while Ⲁⲗⲗⲏⲗⲟⲩⲓⲁ ⲍⲉ ⲫⲙⲉⲩⲓ is employed during the Advent fast, Lent Sundays, the Apostles fast, Saint Mary's fast, and every Wednesday and Friday of Regular Days. Regarding Ⲁⲗⲗⲏⲗⲟⲩⲓⲁ ⲉⲓⲉⲓ ⲉϧⲟⲩⲛ, Pope Gabriel V prescribes it during Lenten weekdays, and Jonah's fast.[550] This order is for the most part what is recognized today. As for the hymn Ⲁⲗⲗⲏⲗⲟⲩⲓⲁ ⲁⲛⲟⲕ ⲇⲉ, MS Lit. 117—and also MS 302 agrees with it[551]—assigns it to Nineveh's fast.[552] Yet, *The Church Order* of the Paromaos monastery, 1514 AD, places it as an alternative to Ⲁⲗⲗⲏⲗⲟⲩⲓⲁ ⲁⲣⲓⲫⲙⲉⲩⲓ during Lent.[553]

According to the contemporary practice, the hymn Ⲁⲗⲗⲏⲗⲟⲩⲓⲁ ⲫⲁⲓ ⲡⲉ ⲡⲓ is said on the following occasions:

- In non-fasting days, every weekday other than Wednesday and Friday
- In Fast Days, except for Lent, in the weekend
- On Feast Days and Eastertide

The hymn Ⲁⲗⲗⲏⲗⲟⲩⲓⲁ ⲍⲉ ⲫⲙⲉⲩⲓ is chanted on the following occasions:

- In non-fasting days, on Wednesday and Friday
- In Fast Days, except for Lent, on weekdays

---

[550] Gabriel V (Pope), *The Ritual Order*, BnF, MS 98 (AD 1411), fol. 47r-v.
[551] *The Church Order*, St. Anthony Monastery, MS 302 (AD 1661), fol. 211r.
[552] *The Church Order*, Cairo, Patriarchal Library, MS Lit. 117 (AD 1910), fol. 108v.
[553] Samuel (Bishop), *The Church Order*, Part 3, 20.

- During Lent, on weekends, and on the first Monday and the last Friday of it

The hymn Ⲁⲗⲗⲏⲗⲟⲩⲓⲁ ⲉⲓⲉⲓ ⲉϧⲟⲩⲛ is recited on the following occasions:
1. During Jonah's fast
2. During Lent, in all weekdays, except for the first and last days of it

The hymns Ⲁⲗⲗⲏⲗⲟⲩⲓⲁ ⲁⲛⲟⲕ ⲇⲉ, and Ⲁⲗⲗⲏⲗⲟⲩⲓⲁ ⲁⲣⲓⲫⲙⲉⲩⲓ are alternatives to Ⲁⲗⲗⲏⲗⲟⲩⲓⲁ ⲉⲓⲉⲓ ⲉϧⲟⲩⲛ, the first during Jonah's fast, and the second in Lent.

Signings of the Lamb

Following the Circuit of the Lamb, standing before the altar facing east, the president unwraps the Lamb and places it in the palm of his left hand, the servant deacon, holding the decanter (wrapped in a corporal) in his right hand with a lit taper in his left hand, brings the decanter closer to the Lamb. Then, the celebrant makes the sign of the cross over the Lamb and the wine thrice, in the name of the Father, the Son, and the Holy Spirit. After each signing, the altar server responds saying, "Amen." Pope Gabriel instructs, "When the circuit is accomplished as mentioned, he (the priest) stands in the designated place for him facing east, and the deacon stands in his defined place facing west. The priest places the bread-offering on his left hand and blesses it along with the wine with the sign of the cross three times."[554] Subsequently, until at least the 15th century, the servant deacon stood in his primordial location east of the altar, precisely between the

---

[554] Gabriel V (Pope), *The Ritual Order*, BnF, MS 98 (AD 1411), fol. 51r-v.

Apse and the altar, facing west, as opposed to the contemporary placement at the left side of the altar.

The 13th–century scholar, Ibn Sibaa, provides the reason for the servant deacon's placement; he explains, "When the heretics, filled with the satanic hatred, attacked the parishes of those who believed in one essence and one will, slayed the priests at the altars while sanctifying the Offerings, and took the bread-offering and stepped on it. For this reason, the Copts arranged that the deacon stands opposite to the priest to watch who, from the evil ones, might come from behind the priest, looking to hurt him. If this happens, the priest will take the bread-offerings and the chalice and put them under the altar from the east side of it; this tradition has continued until now."[555] Ibn Kabar of the 14th century, however, offers a different exegesis; he writes, "They (the servant priest and the servant deacon) enter the sanctuary; the priest stands facing east and the deacon facing west toward him, because the priest is speaking to God, which to quote (Isaiah) the prophet 'I hear His voice from the east,' and the deacon receives from him (the priest) and relays to the congregation."[556]

In the 15th century *The Trinitarian Mystery in Priesthood Ministry*, attributed to Church Teachers, yet a third reason is offered. It reads, "When the priest enters the sanctuary, he stands opposite to the deacon. This is to symbolize what is mentioned in the Bible 'one at the head, and one at the feet, where the body of Jesus had lain' (John 20:12)."[557] The second and third reasons are supported by the 13th century book *The Beginners' Guide and Discipline for Laity*,[558] which also adds that the

---
[555] Ibn Sibaa, *The Precious Pearl: On Ecclesiastic Science*, BnF, MS Arabic 207, fols. 120v-121r
[556] Ibn Kabar, *The Lamp*, BnF, MS Arabic 203 (c. AD 1363-1369), fol. 206v.
[557] Church Teachers, *The Trinitarian Mystery in Priesthood Ministry*, Philotheos, Girgis (Ed.), 20.
[558] This book was published on April 19th, AD 1240 making it the earliest ritual book extant in the Coptic Orthodox Church. It is considered the chief source for many ritual books in following years like *The Beginners' Guide and Discipline for Laity* and *The Ritual Order*. For further details, review Misael of the Paromeos Monastery (Father). (2020). The Trinitarian Mystery in Priesthood Ministry. Alexandria School, 28(1), 100-111.

tradition of the servant deacon standing opposite from the celebrant facing west is a pure Alexandrian one.[559] This tradition is still practiced hitherto during the Reconciliation Prayer and the final Confession at the end of the liturgy.

As previously noted, Ibn Sibaa and Ibn Kabar attest to the old tradition of placing the signings prior to the Circuit of the Lamb. Conversely, Pope Gabriel V locates it following it. Nevertheless, the modern-day practice is to combine both traditions, viz, perform it twice as illustrated above.

Upon completion of the signings, the celebrant places the Lamb on the corporal-padded paten while inaudibly saying, "Glory and honor, honor and glory..." The altar server then responds by chanting (**Ⲓⲥ Ⲡⲁⲧⲏⲣ**—One is the Holy Father). Two renditions are known for this hymn, the shorter of which is used throughout the year, while the lengthier is designated to Feast Days. This response originates from two prayers combined, the first, which concludes with "Amen," is a confession of God's holiness and oneness in a Trinitarian configuration, while the second is Psalm 116, one of the Egyptian Hallel psalms, and hence ending with "Alleluia."

The former is in Greek and is a direct response to the celebrant's Trinitarian benediction. It seems that this type of confession in the Alexandrian tradition is compulsory before communion, an issue we will discuss in further detail later, thus, we find a corresponding response assigned to the people in the liturgy of the faithful prior to communion. The latter response is in Coptic and, as noted above, is Psalm 116 repurposed to exhort worshippers to participate in this adoration of the three Persons of the one God. This Psalm, as a Hallel psalm, was used in

---

[559] Misael of the Paromeos Monastery (Father). (2018). The Beginners' Guide and Discipline for Laity. *Alexandria School, 24(1)*, 139.

Judaism to praise God after the Passover meal, hence, it is particularly important to understand the Soteriological character of its placement immediately after the tri-benediction. Due to the formation of the Psalm using imperative verbs, it is employed as a bidding to which the people reply with the Gloria Patri,[560] a responsory that is considered the second oldest prayer—after the Lord's Prayer—by many scholars. The first part of the Gloria Patri, also called the Lesser Doxology, concerting the Trinitarian glorification is the oldest, Father Ayo claims.[561] The second portion of the doxology unites time and eternity under one act, that is, praising the Lord.

One cannot but notice how these prayers are brilliantly orchestrated: First, the president pronounces the Tri-Benediction, to which the servant deacon attributes holiness solely to the Triune God. Then, he, using Psalm 116, invites the people to exult the Lord saying, "Praise the Lord, all you gentiles! Laud Him, all you peoples!" to which they fulfill the request glorifying Him for His holiness and salvific act by reciting the Gloria Patri. This invitation to the gentiles to glorify the Lord, at the beginning of the consecratory process of the gifts is stemmed from and a fulfillment of a prophesy in the book of Malachi, where the Lord says, "'My name will be great among the nations, from where the sun rises to where it sets. In every place incense and pure offerings will be brought to Me, because My name will be great among the nations,' says the Lord Almighty" (Malachi 1:11),

---

[560] *Gloria Patri*, is a short hymn of praise to God in various Christian liturgies. The earliest Christian doxologies are addressed to God the Father alone, or to Him "through" (διὰ) the Son, or to the Father and the Holy Spirit with (μετά) the Son, or to the Son with (σύν) the Father and the Holy Spirit. The Trinitarian doxology addressed in parallel fashion to all three persons of the Trinity, joined by "and" (καί), became universal in Nicene Christianity, which became prevalent. The Greek wording of the Gloria Patri is: Δόξα Πατρὶ καὶ Υἱῷ καὶ Ἁγίῳ Πνεύματι, καὶ νῦν καὶ ἀεὶ καὶ εἰς τοὺς αἰῶνας τῶν αἰώνων. Ἀμήν. meaning: Glory to the Father, and to the Son, and to the Holy Spirit, Both now and always, and unto the ages of ages. Amen.

[561] Ayo, C.N., Nicholas. *Gloria Patri: The History and Theology of the Lesser Doxology*, 19.

a passage that is construed by the Church Fathers as a reference to the Eucharistic Sacrifice.

Hence, the Didache instructs, "But every Lord's Day do you gather yourselves together, and break bread, and give thanksgiving after having confessed your transgressions, that your sacrifice may be pure... For this is that which was spoken by the Lord: In every place and time offer to me a pure sacrifice; for I am a great King, says the Lord, and my name is wonderful among the nations." [562] Also, the Apostolic Constitution proclaims, "On the day of the resurrection of the Lord, that is, the Lord's day, assemble yourselves together, without fail, giving thanks to God, and praising Him for those mercies God has bestowed upon you through Christ, and has delivered you from ignorance, error, and bondage, that your sacrifice may be unspotted, and acceptable to God, who has said concerning His universal Church: 'In every place shall incense and a pure sacrifice be offered unto me; for I am a great King, saith the Lord Almighty, and my name is wonderful among the heathen.'" [563] Justin Martyr also comments on this prophesy saying, "In this passage God already speaks of the sacrifices which we, the gentiles offer Him in every place, namely the bread of the Eucharist and the cup, likewise, of the Eucharist. He foretells that we glorify His Name." [564] Saint Irenaeus confirms this explication saying, "Concerning which Malachi, among the twelve prophets, thus spoke beforehand: '...My name is glorified among the Gentiles, and in every place incense is offered to My name, and a pure sacrifice; for great is My name among the Gentiles, says the Lord Omnipotent'—indicating in the plainest manner, by these words, that the former people [the Jews] shall indeed cease to make offerings to God, but that in every place sacrifice

---

[562] *Didache*, chapter 14.
[563] Constitutions of the Holy Apostles, Book VII, chapter 30.
[564] Justin Martyr, *Dialogue with Trypho*, chapter 41.

Offertory

shall be offered to Him, and that a pure one; and His name is glorified among the Gentiles."[565]

Father Athanasius Iskander summarizes this understanding saying, "we, the gentiles fulfill Malachi's prophesy, by glorifying God. We glorify Him 'for his mercy is confirmed upon us,' now that our offering has become 'acceptable, being sanctified by the Holy Spirit' (Rom 15:16). We glorify Him for 'His truth endures forever,' since what He foretold of old, concerning the offering of the Gentiles, has been fulfilled, today, in our sight."[566]

The Thanksgiving Prayer

The celebrant then receives the decanter from the altar server and, addressing him, says, Ϣⲗⲏⲗ (Pray); hence, the altar server instructs the worshippers saying, Ⲉⲡⲓ ⲡⲣⲟⲥⲉⲩⲭⲏ ⲥⲧⲁⲑⲏⲧⲉ (Stand up for prayer). Holding the decanter in his right hand, the priest then blesses the congregation with the wine saying, Ⲓⲣⲏⲛⲏ ⲡⲁⲥⲓ (Peace be with all), to which they respond, Ⲕⲉ ⲧⲱ ⲡⲛⲉⲩⲙⲁⲧⲓ ⲥⲟⲩ (And with your spirit). Saluting the worshippers with the decanter delivers a vibrant message that our peace stems only from the blood of our Lord that was shed on the Cross.

Afterwards, in the shape of a cross, the celebrant pours the wine in the chalice. Then, the altar server pours between one tenth to one third of water in the decanter while it is in the priest's hand so that the water should not exceed one third of the decanter, and no less than one tenth. Next, the celebrant pours the water, in the shape of the cross, in the chalice and gives the empty decanter to the altar server flipped. In turn, the altar server

---

[565] Against the Heresies, Book IV, chapter 17, 5
[566] Iskander, Athanasius (Father), *Understanding the Liturgy*, 7.

places it on a corporal in its upside-down position. This all occurs while the priest is praying the Thanksgiving Prayer.

Historically, the altar server, not the priest, was the one who pours the wine and water in the chalice. Ibn Sibaa states, "Then the deacon, after taking permission from the priest and the congregation, says, while they are listening, 'Ⲓⲥ Ⲡⲁⲧⲏⲣ ⲁ̀ⲅⲓⲟⲥ ...,' and pours the wine in the chalice. After the wine is poured, he also pours a little bit of water forming a mix, analogous to what the Virgin Mary used to drink during pregnancy."[567] As stated by Ibn Kabar, "The deacon pours the wine in the chalice after smelling it, to ensure that it has not gone sour, and then pours it carefully in the shape of the cross. It is mixed with a tenth of drinking water. He starts saying 'Three in one and One in Three,' and Psalm 116 or a similar Psalm. The priest then recites the Thanksgiving Prayer."[568] Similar note can be found in *The Trinitarian Mystery in Priesthood Ministry*, which compares this act to the mummification of our Lord's body by Nicodemus, Joseph of Arimathea, and Gamaliel.[569]

Pope Gabriel V writes, "The deacon pours the wine in the chalice as he says 'Ⲁ̀ⲙⲏⲛ. Ⲓⲥ Ⲡⲁⲧⲏⲣ ...' He mixes the wine with a little known amount of water... and after Ⲇⲟⲝⲁ Ⲡⲁⲧⲣⲓ is said, the priest says Ⲓ̀ⲣⲏⲛⲏ ⲡⲁⲥⲓ before the Ϣⲉⲡ̀ϩⲙⲟⲧ."[570] This suggests that, at least, until the 15th century, the mixing of the wine and water in the chalice was the vocation of the altar server.[571] According to early prescriptions, this ritual was performed prior to or during the recitation of Ⲓⲥ Ⲡⲁⲧⲏⲣ; i.e. before the Thanksgiving Prayer. MS Lit. 117, *The Church Order*, which was transcribed in AD

---

[567] Ibn Sibaa, *The Precious Pearl: On Ecclesiastic Science*, BnF, MS Arabic 207, fol. 120r
[568] Ibn Kabar, *The Lamp*, BnF, MS Arabic 203 (c. AD 1363-1369), fol. 205v.
[569] Misael of the Paromeos Monastery (Father). (2020). The Trinitarian Mystery in Priesthood Ministry. *Alexandria School*, 28(1), 115.
[570] Gabriel V (Pope), *The Ritual Order*, BnF, MS 98 (AD 1411), fol. 52r.
[571] See: Ignatius Ephrem II Rahmani (Patriarch of the Syriac Catholic Church), *Les Liturgies Orientales et Occidentales*, 200-202.

1910, demonstrates a shift in this old tradition. It states, "The deacon pours the wine as usual and the Pope mixes the wine with water; and the Pope says the Thanksgiving Prayer."[572] In accordance with this passage, the deacon pours the wine in the chalice, but the celebrant is the one who mixes the wine with water. Still, the mixing is accomplished preceding the Thanksgiving Prayer. The contemporary practice, however, assigns the process of mixing wine with water to the celebrant, and makes it executed in parallel with the recitation of the Thanksgiving Prayer.

In antiquity, mixing wine with water was more for practical reasons. Wine was thicker and more potent, and it was necessary to temper it with water. "We know it is unhealthy to drink wine or water alone, whereas wine mixed with water makes a delightfully tasty drink" (2 Maccabees 15:39). Inherited from Judaism, this was a given practice at the Christian Eucharist. Hence, numerous sources from early Christianity attest to this tradition. For example, in his account of the Sunday liturgy, Saint Justin Martyr refers to the use of wine tempered with water (First Apology 65, 67).[573] Saint Irenaeus references to a mixed cup (Against Heresies 12:1; 33:3).[574] Saint Clement of Alexandria writes, "The blood of the grape—that is, the Word—desired to be mixed with water" (The Instructor 2:2).[575] And Saint Cyprian's Epistle 62 on the use of wine and water in the chalice.[576]

---

[572] *The Church Order*, Cairo, Patriarchal Library, MS Lit. 117 (AD 1910), fol. 22v.
[573] "There is then brought to the president of the brethren bread and a cup of wine mixed with water; deacons give to each of those present to partake of the bread and wine mixed with water over which the thanksgiving was pronounced" (First Apology 65). "When our prayer is ended, bread and wine and water are brought, and the president in like manner offers prayers and thanksgivings" (First Apology 67).
[574] "Wherefore also Esaias declares: 'Thy dealers mix the wine with water'" (12:1); "affirmed the mixed cup to be His blood" (33:3).
[575] Also: "as wine is blended with water, so is the Spirit with man" and "the mixture of wine and water, nourishes to faith" (The Instructor 2:2).
[576] *"Wine mixed with water, was to be offered"* (Epistle 62).

Several interpretations were provided by early church fathers. Saint Irenaeus (AD 130–200), for example, explains, "This mixture symbolizes the unity of the church with Christ in one cup."[577] Saint Clement of Alexandria (AD 150–215) provides a different exegesis; he writes, "The wine mixes with water, just as the spirit mixes with humanity."[578] Saint Cyprian (AD 200–258) agrees with former explanation. He states, "We see that in the water is understood the people, but in the wine is showed the blood of Christ. But when the water is mingled in the cup with wine, the people are made one with Christ, and the assembly of believers is associated and conjoined with Him on whom it believes; which association and conjunction of water and wine is so mingled in the Lord's cup, that that mixture cannot any more be separated. Whence, moreover, nothing can separate the Church—that is, the people established in the Church, faithfully and firmly persevering in that which they have believed—from Christ, in such a way as to prevent their undivided love from always abiding and adhering." [579] Yet, a third understanding is offered by Saint Ambrose (AD 340–397), who eloquently says, "Water to cleanse, blood to redeem." [580] Accordingly, salvation is completed through the work of water (in Baptism) and the Blood (in the Eucharist).

Another interpretation suggests that the wine points to Jesus' divinity, while the water denotes His humanity. Once the water and wine mingle, they cannot be separated. As such, Christ's divinity, and humanity, while distinct, are eternally joined in the Incarnation. Saint Augustine (AD 354–430) has his share in explaining this traditionally entrenched

---

[577] Athanasius of Saint Macarius Monastery (Father), *The Divine Liturgy: The Mystery of the Kingdom of God (Part 1)*, 332.
[578] Clement of Alexandria (Saint), *Ante-Nicene Fathers*, Vol II, chapter II.
[579] Saint Cyprian Epistle 62, 13.
[580] Ambrose (Saint), *On the Mysteries*, Book V, 1:4).

practice. He expounds, "Take this, which came out of the side, in the cup; that is the water and wine."[581] The latter explanation prevailed in the Coptic Church. Accordingly, the mixture of wine and water signifies Jesus' effusion of blood and water when pierced on the Cross (John 19:34). Scientifically speaking, a dead person's blood coagulates, so if speared, only plasma (mostly composed of water) emerges. However, if a person was speared alive, blood would come out of the body. When Jesus was speared, blood and water came out of His body, which confirmed that He is alive with his divinity—attested by the coming out of blood came out, yet dead with His humanity—thus, water came out. This profound miracle underscores the divinity of our Lord Jesus Christ; He is both fully God and fully human.

Back to the *order*, the contemporary rubric prescribes the mixing of wine with water in the chalice by the celebrant, while the Thanksgiving Prayer is being recited. The Thanksgiving Prayer finds its roots in Judaism. In the Jewish tradition, rubric directs the uttering of a thanksgiving prayer as part of the ritual meals. Our Lord Jesus used this prayer during the Passover, a tradition that was followed by the disciples and the Early Church. The two prayers (Jewish and Christian) are comparable; in fact, some parts are identical. The Offertory Thanksgiving Prayer, as noted above, is named in some manuscripts the "Liturgy of the Apostles." In other manuscripts, however, it is called "the Thanksgiving Prayer which was written by Saint Mark the Apostle." Hence, The Thanksgiving Prayer is an immemorial one that stems from Judaism and was established in its Christian format at the time of the Apostles.

After the priest pours water in the chalice and gives the empty decanter to the altar server, he holds the cross in his right hand and

---

[581] Athanasius of Saint Macarius Monastery (Father), *The Divine Liturgy: The Mystery of the Kingdom of God (Part 1)*: 334.

proceeds with reciting the Thanksgiving Prayer. The same signings performed during incense offering, are also delivered, except that on the third time, the celebrant signs on the altar and says, "and from this table."

The Litany of the Offering and the Absolution of the Servants

After the Thanksgiving Prayer, the Litany of the Offering inaudibly uttered. This is an immemorial prayer that dates to the end of the 4th century.[582] In it, the priest pleads the Lord regarding the materials (the bread and wine) saying, "bless them, sanctify them, purify them, and transform (or change) them." He signs both the Lamb and wine together with the cross thrice. Upon completion of the prayer, the celebrant covers the paten with a corporal, the chalice with another one, and finally, with the help of the servant deacon, who is standing on the east side of the altar, covers the altar with the *Prospharin*.[583] Hence, it is also called "Litany of the Covering." Covering the paten was always a function of the priest, however, covering the chalice once was assigned to the servant deacon.[584] Afterwards, the priest lays a corporal, in the shape of a triangle, on the Ark that is already covered with the *Prospharin*. This corporal is the same corporal that the priest wiped the Lamb with after it was chosen. During this time, the priest prays the third absolution for the Son inaudibly.

The altar, in this case, represents the tomb of Christ, the paten resembles the bier, and the corporals over both Offerings symbolize Christ's grave clothes. The *Prospharin* denotes the stone that was used to

---

[582] Athanasius of Saint Macarius Monastery (Father), *Summary of the Liturgical History of the Church of Alexandria (Part 1)*, 103.
[583] The *Prospharin* is a piece of silk or linen which has an icon depicted on it. It is used to cover the entire altar at the end of the Offertory and then removed at the end of the Prayer of Reconciliation. The word "*Prospharin*" is derived from the Greek work "προσφορά," which mean "Offering."
[584] Misael of the Paromeos Monastery (Father). (2018). The Beginners' Guide and Discipline for Laity. *Alexandria School, 25(2)*, 127.

Offertory

shut the tomb, and the triangular corporal that was placed over it represents the seal that was placed on the tomb. The priest and deacons surrounding the altar symbolize Joseph of Arimathea and Nicodemus who buried Christ, in addition to Gamaliel, who carried the spices for them.[585] The entire scene embodies the burial of Christ; and for this reason, the chorus chants the mournful hymn (from a musical perspective) of **Cw**.[586] Father Athanasius Iskander, on the other hand, elucidates the utilitarian function of covering the altar and uncovering it after the Prayer of Reconciliation. "The large veil that covered the altar (to conceal it from the eyes of the catechumens)," he explains, "would be removed by the priest and the deacon and brought into the assembly."[587] Once the catechumens leave the church, the *Prospharin* is removed. Hence, it is reasonable to believe that this practice was established after the 6th or 7th century when the Offertory was relocated to precede the Liturgy of the Word.

To summarize this part, after the signings that are accomplished following the Circuit of the Lamb, the altar server recites the hymn of **Ic Πathp**, and the congregation responds with **Δoza Πaτpι**. The priest then prays the Thanksgiving Prayer while pouring the wine in the chalice; he then mixes it with water. The priest then, while covering the altar, prays the Litany of the Offering inaudibly followed by the third absolution for the Son. During this time (i.e., from immediately after the Thanksgiving Prayer to right before the Absolution of the Servants), the people, led by the chorus, hum the solemn chant of **Cw**.

Marquis was confused about this hymn; he writes, "The translator believes that it is the invariable practice for the Choir to begin answering

---

[585] Misael, Ibid, 127.
[586] *Hegumen* Youhanna Salama gives a fortuitous, odd symbolism to the covering of the altar. He explains it as an allegory of Jesus hiding His divinity from the people until the age of 30.
[587] Iskander, Athanasius (Father), *Understanding the Liturgy*, page 1.

at this point, but it is contrary to the rubric, which orders the answer to be made at the end of the prayer. The respond itself is hard to understand, but seems to be a sort of acclamation, at least so it was understood by the Copts whom the translator consulted, and who advised the above translation."[588] As a matter of fact, Marquis was not precise when he said that the response "Saved amen. And with your spirit" is chanted at this point; it is only the first two letters of the first word, i.e., **Cⲱ**.

The hymn **Cⲱ** has a matronly mournful melody, which suits the simultaneous actions the priest performs inside the sanctuary—the ritual practices pertaining the burial of Christ and laying His body in the tomb. Hence, its tune serves as a funeral dirge. The hymn **Cⲱ** is the first syllable in the phrase **Cⲱⲑⲓⲥ ⲁⲙⲏⲛ ⲕⲉ ⲧⲱ ⲡⲛⲉⲩⲙⲁⲧⲓ ⲥⲟⲩ** (Saved Amen, and with your spirit). The rest of the phrase is recited after the Absolution of the Servants.[589] This phrase is composed of two parts: "Saved amen," and "And with your spirit." Historically, the former is a common greeting idiom among Copts, which means "thank you" or "God bless you." In other words, following the Absolution of the Servants, the congregation thanks the priest saying **Cⲱⲑⲓⲥ ⲁⲙⲏⲛ**, as in "thank you for the absolution and may God bless you." The attendees then continue with wishing and praying for the priest so that he may be absolved as we. Hence, they recite the second part of the responsory, "And with your spirit."[590] This hymn, i.e., **Cⲱ**, is said throughout the ecclesiastical year, regardless of the season, except in the presence of the Pope or a bishop. In that case, the hymn **Ⲛⲓⲥⲁⲃⲉⲩ ⲧⲏⲣⲟⲩ** (O all you wise men) is chanted instead. In the presence of the Pontiff or a prelate, the high priest is the one to deliver the Absolution of

---

[588] John, Marquis of Bute, *The Coptic Morning Service for the Lord's Day*, 55.
[589] "If you forgive anyone his sins, they are forgiven; if you do not forgive them, they are not forgiven." (John 20:23).
[590] Therefore, this response must be said after the Absolution of the Servants.

the Servants, after which the people chant the rest of **Ⲛⲓⲥⲁⲃⲉⲩ ⲧⲏⲣⲟⲩ** followed by **Ⲥⲱⲟⲓⲥ ⲁⲙⲏⲛ ⲕⲉ ⲧⲱ ⲡⲛⲉⲩⲙⲁⲧⲓ ⲥⲟⲩ**.

Unlike the hymn **Ⲥⲱ**, the tune for **Ⲛⲓⲥⲁⲃⲉⲩ ⲧⲏⲣⲟⲩ** is festal. It reads, "O all you wise men of Israel, the makers of golden threads, make a robe of Aaron befitting the honor of the priesthood of our honored father, the high priest, Pope Abba (...), the beloved of Christ."[591] Neither the music nor the lyrics of this hymn have any significance to the burial of Christ. Why is it then chanted instead of **Ⲥⲱ** in the presence of a bishop or Pope? Originally, as prescribed by many sources,[592] the prelate used to attire his liturgical vestment immediately before the Absolution of the Servants.[593] "The priest wears his liturgical vestments before going up to the sanctuary." Ibn Sibaa explicates, "If the high priest (Pope or bishop) is present, he wears his liturgical vestments after the Offering is chosen, but before the Absolution, to distinguish between the rank of the priesthood and that of the episcopate."[594] After the Thanksgiving Prayer, he continues, "If the servant priest is a high priest, he wears his vestments during this time, as a symbol of Aaron, and the deacons chant the applicable hymn to wearing the priesthood clothes."[595] Ibn Kabar agrees with Ibn Sibaa on this explanation. After mentioning the Thanksgiving Prayer, he states, "He (the high priest) wears his liturgical vestments as previously mentioned, and the congregation chants as appropriate for this occasion."[596] MS Lit. 117 also instructs that while the deacons chant the hymn **Ⲛⲓⲥⲁⲃⲉⲩ ⲧⲏⲣⲟⲩ** "The patriarch dresses in a white chasuble."[597]

---

[591] If a metropolitan or bishop is present, the last section of the hymn is changed to "our honored the high priest Pope Abba (...), and our father the metropolitan/bishop Abba (...), the beloved of Christ."
[592] For example: *The Church Order*, Cairo, Patriarchal Library, MS Lit. 73 (AD 1444), fols. 74v-75r.
[593] As opposed to the priests and deacons, who wear their liturgical vestments preceding the recitation of the Canonical Hours.
[594] Ibn Sibaa, *The Precious Pearl: On Ecclesiastic Science*, BnF, MS Arabic 207, fol. 117r.
[595] Ibn Sibaa, Ibid., fol. 123r
[596] Ibn Kabar, *The Lamp*, BnF, MS Arabic 203 (c. AD 1363-1369), fol. 205v.
[597] *The Church Order*, Cairo, Patriarchal Library, MS Lit. 117 (AD 1910), fol. 22v.

Thus, the relevant text and jubilant melody of this hymn are strictly correlated to the presence of the high priest, not to the burial ritual or to certain festivals, as some falsely suppose. Nowadays, the high priest attires his liturgical vestment along with the priests and deacons, an innovation that raised the question regarding the suitability of ⲚⲓⲥⲂⲉⲩ ⲧⲏⲣⲟⲩ at this part of the liturgy. A rare second stanza of the chant ⲚⲓⲥⲂⲉⲩ ⲧⲏⲣⲟⲩ is offered by a 14th-century manuscript currently preserved at the Patriarchate Library in Cairo.[598] Another document (not numbered) from the genre *Church Order*, authored by the 19th-century Bishop Gabriel of Manfalut, which was transcribed in AD 1834, currently archived at Saint Mina Monastery in Asyut (known as the Hanging Monastery)—we will refer to it in this quest as "Hanging Monastery *Church Order* (AD 1834)," also confirms this unwonted continuation. The second stanza reads, "When he gets dressed, he enters the sanctuary to pray there for this people. Say all of you 'Amen so be it.'"[599]

Notwithstanding that most sources position ⲚⲓⲥⲂⲉⲩ ⲧⲏⲣⲟⲩ as the sole possible hymn said while prelates put on their liturgical vestments, MS Lit. 50 (AD 1350) offers an alternative chant (Ⲕⲟⲩϫⲓ ⲕⲟⲩϫⲓ "Sahidic: Ⲕⲟⲩⲓ ⲕⲟⲩⲓ"—Slowly slowly)—not only an alternative but also the primary one.[600] MS Lit. 292 (AD 1708) of Saint Anthony Monastery includes this chant as well, however, as secondary.[601] Not only Hanging Monastery *Church Order* (AD 1834) includes this rare chant, but it also directs to its

---

[598] Patriarchal Library, MS Lit. 50 (AD 1350), fol. 50v.
[599] Coptic: Ⲉϣⲱⲡ ⲛ̀ⲧⲉϥⲉⲣⲫⲟⲣⲓⲛ ⲙ̀ⲙⲟϥ ϣⲁϥⲃⲱⲕ ⲉ̀ϧⲟⲩⲛ ⲉ̀ⲡⲓⲙⲁⲛⲉⲣϣⲱⲟⲩϣⲓ. Ⲛ̀ⲧⲉϥ ⲧⲱⲃϩ, ⲙ̀ⲙⲁⲩ ⲉ̀ϫⲉⲛ ⲡⲁⲓⲗⲁⲟⲥ ⲁ̀ⲭⲟⲥ ⲧⲏⲣⲟⲩ ϫⲉ ⲁ̀ⲙⲏⲛ ⲉⲥⲉϣⲱⲡⲓ.
[600] Patriarchal Library, MS Lit. 50 (AD 1350), fol. 50r.
[601] St. Antony Monastery, MS Lit. 292, fols. 91v–92r.

melody: in the tune of **Ⲛⲓⲥⲁⲃⲉⲩ ⲧⲏⲣⲟⲩ**.[602] Below is the lyrics of this scarce chant along with its English and Arabic translations.[603]

Coptic	English	Arabic
Ⲕⲟⲩϫⲓ ⲕⲟⲩϫⲓ ⲉⲕⲙⲟϣⲓ ϧⲉⲛ ϯⲥⲕⲏⲛⲏ ⁚ ⲱ Ⲁⲁⲣⲱⲛ ⲡⲓⲟⲩⲏⲃ ⲛ̀ⲁⲣⲭⲏⲉⲣⲉⲩⲥ ⁚ ⲙⲏⲡⲟⲧⲉ ⲛ̀ⲧⲉ ⲟⲩⲁⲓ ⲛ̀ϣ̀ⲕⲉⲗⲕⲓⲁ ⲛ̀ⲛⲟⲩⲃ ϩⲉⲓ ⲉ̀ⲡⲉⲥⲏⲧ ϩⲓϫⲉⲛ ⲡⲓⲕⲁϩⲓ. Ⲡⲉⲛⲓⲱⲧ ⲉⲑⲟⲩⲁⲃ ⲛ̀ⲉⲡⲓⲥⲕⲟⲡⲟⲥ ⲁⲃⲃⲁ (…).	Slow down[604] as you walk in the tabernacle, Aaron the Priest, the High Priest, lest any of the golden bells fall on the ground. O our holy father, Bishop Abba (...).	تَمَهَّل (حرفياً – عامية): واحدة واحدة وأنتَ تسير في القبة يا هارون الكاهنُ رئيسُ الكهنة، لئلا يَسقُط شيء من الجلاجل الذهب على الأرض. يا أبينا الأسقف الطاهر أنبا (…).

After the Thanksgiving Prayer, the Litany of the Offering is inaudibly said, followed by the Absolution of the Son. Pope Gabriel V states, "If it is the Liturgy of Saint Basil, they pray the Absolution of the Son... and if it is the Liturgy of Saint Gregory or Saint Cyril, they say the Absolution of the Father (O Master Lord God the *Pantocrator*, the healer...) to the end of the Litany of the Absolution."[605] Hence, the Absolution of the Son is prayed during the Liturgy of Saint Basil, and the Absolution of the Father is said during the Liturgy of Saint Gregory or Saint Cyril. Previously, these absolutions were pronounced aloud after the priest and the altar servers exit the sanctuary and before the utterance of the Absolution of the Servants. Due to time constraints, rubric now dictates the silent recitation

---

[602] The document is not categorized yet; however, its folios are given numbers as in modern books. This chant is on page 185.
[603] The presented text was redacted by Dr. Mariam Abdel-Malak and Mina Safwat after comparing all three documents and changing the Sahidic words into their Bohairic correspondents.
[604] Literally: "bit by bit" or "slowly slowly."
[605] Gabriel V (Pope), *The Ritual Order*, BnF, MS 98 (AD 1411), fol. 53v.

of these absolutions following the Litany of the Offering, while the priest is standing before the altar.

To recapitulate, the currently practice is that after the Thanksgiving prayer, the priest prays the Litany of the Offering, followed by the Absolution of the Son or the Father inaudibly, while he covers the altar with the *Prospharin*. Afterward, the priest kisses the right side of the altar. He then circuits the altar, counterclockwise, along with the other priests and altar servers. During this circuit, they bow to each other before they finally exit the altar. They then bow their heads and the priest, while standing behind them facing east, pronounces the Absolution of the Servants.[606] The priest and altar servers exiting the sanctuary symbolizes those who buried Jesus and closed the tomb; they returned to their houses and Jesus was left alone.

Rubrics prescribe that if there is more than one priest present, facing east, the most senior assistant priest delivers the Absolution of the Servants, indicating that Christ is the one providing the absolution to all, including the priest uttering it. It also has a stout humbling message to the principal celebrant that it is only with God's mercy, not his goodness, that he can celebrate the liturgy.[607] Furthermore, *The Trinitarian Mystery in Priesthood Ministry* instructs that the absolution delivering priest must stand behind all.[608] As mentioned above, if a high priest is present, representing Christ, he delivers the absolution facing west, toward the congregation. Thus, if more than one prelate is present, the most senior one delivers the Absolution of the Servants.

---

[606] The Absolution of the Saints is an ancient prayer; its shape was finalized in the 6th century. See: Athanasius of Saint Macarius Monastery (Father), *Summary of the Liturgical History of the Church of Alexandria (Part 1)*, 196.
[607] Mettaos (Bishop), *The Spirituality of the Rite of the Liturgy of the Coptic Orthodox Church*, 107-108.
[608] Misael of the Paromeos Monastery (Father). (2020). The Trinitarian Mystery in Priesthood Ministry. *Alexandria School*, 28(1), 116.

In his book *Al-Majmu' al-Mubarak (The Blessed Collection)*, Volume 2 (*History of the Saracens, which extends from the time of Mohammed to the Atabeg dynasty*), George Elmacin[609] documented that it was the norm to utter the Absolution of the Servants after the Praxis lesson until Pope Macarius II[610] moved it to its current location, preceding all readings. MS 141 Series/106 Rite (AD 1758) explains the reason for this change. It mentions the ancient practice of praying the absolution during or right after the reading of the Catholic Epistle in Arabic (i.e., before the Litany of the Praxis), but due to the emerging custom of the head deacon coming late, which caused disruption to the service and friction with other deacons, the bishops decided to move the Absolution of the Servants to its current location, that it, before the Litany of the Pauline, precluding deacons arriving after this point from serving.[611]

During the Absolution of the Servants, the priest performs specific signings with the cross. When he says, "The *hegumens*, the priests," he signs the other priests toward the east. He then continues, "the deacons" and signs, toward the east, the altar servers bowing down in front of him. He then signs the chorus on the northern side and says, "the clergy." Then, he turns to the west and signs the congregation while saying, "and all the people." Finally, facing east, he signs himself and says, "and my weakness." The priests prostrate to one another before rising to enter the sanctuary.

---

[609] George Elmacin (or Girgis Al-Makin) (AD 1205–1273), also known as Ibn al-'Amid, was a Coptic Christian historian. His full name in Arabic was Ğirğis Ibn Abī Ùl-Yāsir Ibn Abī Ùl-Mukārim Ibn Abī Ùt.-T. ayyib known as al-Makīn Ibn Al-Ameed (جرجس بن أبي الياسر بن أبي الطيب الشهير بالشيخ المكين بن العميد). His great grandfather was a merchant from Tikrit in Iraq who settled in Egypt. His sole surviving work is a world chronicle in two parts, entitled Al-Majmu` Al-Mubarak (The blessed collection). The first portion runs from Adam down to the 11th year of Heraclius. The second half is a history of the Saracens, which extends from the time of Mohammed to the accession of the Mameluke Sultan Baybars in AD 1260. This work was used by the 14-15th century Muslim historians Ibn Khaldun, Al-Qalqashandi, and Al-Maqrizi. Later, Ibn Al-Ameed moved to Damascus, where he died in AD 1273. He is not to be confused with another Coptic theologian of the 14th century that holds the same name. The latter was a physician, a monk, a priest, and the author of the famous dogmatic theology book Al-Hawy (مختصر البيان في تحقيق الإيمان المشهور بالحاوي المستفاد).
[610] Pope Macarius II of Alexandria (AD 1102-1128) is the 69th Pope of Alexandria.
[611] Sobhy, Basilious (Father), *Introduction to the History of Coptic Rites*, 32, 33.

It is noteworthy that all the saints mentioned in the Absolution of the Servants are clergy. This is important since Jesus taught us that through priesthood, He forgives our sins. He teaches, "Truly I tell you, whatever you bind on earth will be bound in heaven, and whatever you loose on earth will be loosed in heaven" (Matthew 18:18). It is also important to note that this absolution is based on the faith and beliefs of the attendees; for this reason, the names mentioned in the Absolution of the Servants are all of the Church Fathers who fought and offered their lives in order to keep the orthodox faith unchanged (such as Saint Athanasius, Saint Cyril, Saint Dioscorus, Saint Severus, etc.).[612] This is a tacit, but powerful, message underlining the importance of orthodox faith as a prerequisite for partaking of the Holy Mysteries. The author of *The Trinitarian Mystery in Priesthood Ministry* instructs that attending the Absolution of the Servants is a requirement for priests and deacons in order to participate in the service of the liturgy,[613] an instruction that was also cited in *The Beginners' Guide and Discipline for Laity*.[614]

Summary of the Offertory Office

Subsequent to Prime Offering of Incense, the priests and deacons attire their liturgical vestments. The celebrant prepares the altar. Afterwards, the appropriate Canonical Hours for the day are prayed. Next, the bread and

---

[612] This absolution mentions Saint Severus and Saint Dioscorus before Saints Athanasius and Cyril, a discernible product of the Chalcedonian conflict that left the Christian East torn. The Coptic Church affirms that the absolution is based on the faith of her Fathers, specifically, the non-Chalcedonian ones. This also sheds some light on the era in which the Absolution of the Servants was developed.

[613] Church Teachers, *The Trinitarian Mystery in Priesthood Ministry*, Philotheos, Girgis (Ed.), 10; and Misael of the Paromeos Monastery (Father). (2020). The Trinitarian Mystery in Priesthood Ministry. *Alexandria School*, 28(1), 116.

[614] Misael of the Paromeos Monastery (Father). (2018). The Beginners' Guide and Discipline for Laity. *Alexandria School*, 25(2), 128.

wine offerings are presented to the celebrant, who signs the *Prosphora*, inaudibly, and then chooses an appropriate Lamb. Meanwhile, **Ⲕⲩⲣⲓⲉ ⲉⲗⲉⲏⲥⲟⲛ** is recited 41 times. The celebrant then inaudibly utters the Remembrance Prayers, followed by **Ⲟⲩⲱⲟⲩ ⲛⲉⲙ ⲟⲩⲧⲁⲓⲟ** (Glory and honor) out loud. After that, the celebrant and the altar servers perform the Circuit of the Lamb, while the congregation chants **Ⲁ̇ⲗⲗⲏⲗⲟⲩⲓⲁ̀** ⲫⲁⲓ ⲡⲉ ⲡⲓ, **Ⲁ̇ⲗⲗⲏⲗⲟⲩⲓⲁ̀** ⲭⲉ ⲫ̀ⲙⲉⲩⲓ̀, **Ⲁ̇ⲗⲗⲏⲗⲟⲩⲓⲁ̀** ⲉⲓ̇ⲉ̀ⲓ̀ ⲉ̀ϧⲟⲩⲛ, **Ⲁ̇ⲗⲗⲏⲗⲟⲩⲓⲁ̀** ⲁ̀ⲛⲟⲕ ⲇⲉ, or **Ⲁ̇ⲗⲗⲏⲗⲟⲩⲓⲁ̀** ⲁⲣⲓⲫ̀ⲙⲉⲩⲓ̀ according to the time of year. Thereafter, the servant priest utters the signings over the Lamb and wine, followed by the Thanksgiving Prayer, during which, the priest mixes the wine with water. When it is concluded, he prays the Litany of the Offering followed by the Absolution of the Father or the Absolution of the Son. Subsequently, all clergy and altar servers circuit the altar once and then exit the sanctuary. During this time, the congregation hums the hymn **Ⲥⲱ**. If a high priest is present, the hymn **Ⲛⲓⲁⲃⲉⲩ ⲧⲏⲣⲟⲩ** is sung instead. The Absolution of the Servants is then recited and the remainder of hymn **Ⲥⲱ**, as in ⲟⲓⲥ ⲁ̀ⲙⲏⲛ ⲕⲉ ⲧⲱ ⲡⲛⲉⲩⲙⲁⲧⲓ ⲥⲟⲩ, is said. Alternatively, in the presence of a prelate, the rest of **Ⲛⲓⲁⲃⲉⲩ ⲧⲏⲣⲟⲩ** is chanted followed by **Ⲥⲱⲟⲓⲥ ⲁ̀ⲙⲏⲛ**. This marks the conclusion of the Offertory office.

Reconciliation of the Offertory with the Evening Liturgy

This analysis of the Offertory office underpins what was previously mentioned regarding it being, at one point in time, the immemorial evening liturgy. Earlier in this chapter we discussed the hypothesis in terms of historical evidence and sequence of development of the currently used liturgy; in this section, however, we will inspect the same topic from the view of its own components. The key elements of a full liturgy, which must be included in the evening liturgy, can be found in the Offertory office. If we can find enough communalities between the key elements of the full liturgy, which must be included in the evening one, and the Offertory office, then it is more likely that this hypothesis, which was developed and supported by Lietzmann, Richardson, and Father Matthew the Poor, is accurate.

The first element in common is the act of offering the materials and choosing the Lamb. The act of offering the gifts is an integral part of any Eucharist, whether evening or morning.[615] Hence, it is safe to suppose its existence in the evening liturgy. We find this proper (offering the gifts) at the commencement of the Offertory office. Additionally, it is important to point out that the practice of offering the materials on the altar is preceded with handwashing, a ritual that is common between the Offertory and the Liturgy of the Faithful offices.

The second element is the Intercessory prayers. Praying for the departed and the alive is an old tradition that is documented in most, if not all, Eucharistic prayers, whether or not still in use. At the latter part of the Presentation of the Lamb, as discussed earlier, such pleadings can be found in the inaudible devotions of the Remembrance Prayers.

The third element in common between the two offices is the blessing over the bread. In Judaism, thanksgiving prayer was offered over the bread. The blessing over the wine, on the other hand, was performed toward the end of religious meals. Christianity, in its infancy, inherited this tradition from Judaism; therefore, it is expected to find this immemorial tradition in evening liturgies. Analogous to this, in the Offertory office, the Trinitarian signings are dedicated to the Lamb. This is evident from the name of the signings (Signings of the Lamb), which points to the original custom of performing these signings over the Lamb only. These signings

---

[615] Originally, offering the gifts was part of the core Eucharist, not a distinct section.

were imported in the morning liturgy, particularly in the Institution Narrative. In it, the priest proclaims, "He took bread into His holy hands …" The priest then signs over the bread thrice and after each time the chorus and the altar servers respond saying, "Amen." We can draw parallels between this tradition and what is practice in the Offertory office. In the latter, the priest actionizes the phase "He took bread into His holy hands" by holding the Lamb before performing the three Signings of the Lamb, after each the altar server cries out, "Amen."[616]

The fourth element pertains to the blessing over the cup, which, again, stems from Judaism. In the primitive rite, when the Eucharistic meal was still under the influence of the Jewish customs of the *Chaburah* meal and the Jewish *Seder*, the blessing over the bread and that over the wine were separated by the actual meal. As such, the Liturgy of the Faithful reads, "Likewise also, the cup, after supper, He mixed it…" Correspondingly, during the Offertory office, the Thanksgiving Prayer begins with saluting the people, an indication of a time gap (allowing for a meal) between the bread blessing and the wine thanksgiving. This suggests that this Thanksgiving Prayer is an ancient one that probably stems from an even older indigenous rendition, which in turn, originates from the Jewish thanksgiving prayer. As previously noted, the priest's narration that Jesus "after supper, He mixed it (the cup) with wine and water" is actionized during the Offertory Thanksgiving Prayer when the priest mixes the wine and water in the chalice.

The fifth element is the doxology that is offered at the end of the Thanksgiving Prayer. The student of old Eucharistic prayers recognizes that it was a common tradition among liturgies of the East and the West to offer a doxology to the Lord at the end of the Eucharistic prayer, which

---

[616] Matthew the Poor (Father), *Eucharist of the Lord's Supper*, 20–23.

was, in the first three centuries, the full and complete liturgy. This can be found in the Offertory Thanksgiving Prayer, where, towards the end of it, the following Trinitarian doxology is proclaimed:[617] "Through whom the glory, the honor, the dominion, and the worship are due unto You (the Father), with Him (the Son) and the Holy Spirit, the Giver of Life, Who is of one essence with You, now and at all times and unto the age of all ages. Amen."

The sixth element is the recitation of the hymn "One is the All-Holy Father," which is, in the morning liturgies, chanted before Communion. Traces of this chant can also be found in the altar server's hymn "One is the holy Father" that is recited right after the blessings over the Lamb in the Offertory.

The seventh element is the remembrance. In most, if not all, liturgies, and to fulfil His commandment (1 Corinthians 11:26),[618] a section missioned to recall the death of the Lord is declared. Later, more actions were added (i.e., burial, passion, resurrection, ascension, second coming, etc.). Although this is uttered in the morning liturgy, the Offertory office accomplishes this commandment by acting it out. Immediately after the Thanksgiving Prayer, the gifts and the entire altar are ceremonially covered with the *Prospharin*, a solemn observance that embodies the death and burial of our Lord, Jesus.

The eighth element is the Epiclesis, or the invocation of divine power to transform the materials into the Body and Blood of the Lord. This is a distinct and prominent section of the morning liturgy. However, we can also find analogous prayer in the Offertory office. In the latter, the priest calls for the Logos to transform the bread and wine into the Body and

---

[617] This part is uttered inaudibly.
[618] "For whenever you eat this bread and drink this cup, you proclaim the Lord's death until He comes."

Blood of Jesus Christ; he entreats, "Bless them, sanctify them, purify them and change (or transform) them, in order that, on one hand, this bread may indeed become Your holy Body, and, on the other hand, the mixture which is in this Cup indeed Your precious Blood."[619] Therefore, even the culminating point of old and newer liturgies, which is the Epiclesis, is presented in the Litany of the Offering, which is prayed inaudibly at the end of the Offertory.

The ninth and final element of this study is the Absolution. In the morning liturgies, as practiced today, after the Fraction, the priest utters three absolutions immediately prior to the final Confession prayers. The altar server responds to the priest's absolutions saying, "Saved Amen. And with your spirit." In the same manner, in the Offertory, the Absolution of the Servants marks the conclusion of this office. The chorus also answers with the same responsory, that is, "Saved Amen. And with your spirit."

This brief investigation illustrates that there is a big chance that the Offertory office as practiced by the Coptic Orthodox Church was originally the Jerusalem evening liturgy that was celebrated in early Christianity. When it was decided to eliminate the use of evening liturgies, this office was amalgamated with the morning liturgy under a new name, viz., the Offertory.[620] This, in fact, highlights another important fact, which is that, according to the Orthodox tradition, the sanctification of the gifts is a process, not an instant change. This process commences at the Offertory and finds its fulfilment in the Epiclesis (end of the *Anaphora*).

---

[619] This is an Alexandrian tradition mentioned by other indigenous Coptic writers. Saint Athanasius writes, "when the great prayers and holy supplications have been sent up, the Word (Logos) comes upon the bread and the cup and they become His Body."

[620] For obvious reasons, after the amalgamation of the two liturgies (evening and morning), the Fraction and Communion were performed once at the conclusion of the morning liturgy, the Liturgy of the Faithful.

CHAPTER FIVE

The Liturgy of the Word

The Pericopes and Readings' Circuits

The Church, through the temple and Divine service, acts upon the entire man, educates him wholly; acts upon his sight, hearing, smelling, feeling, taste, imagination, mind, and will, by the splendor of the icons and of the whole temple, by the ringing of bells, by the singing of the choir, by the fragrance of the incense, the kissing of the Gospel, of the cross and the holy icons, by the prosphoras, the singing, and sweet sound of the readings of the Scriptures.

—**John of Kronstadt**

If a man should come here with earnestness—even though he does not read the Scriptures at home—and if he pays attention to what is said here, within the space of even one year he will be able to obtain a considerable acquaintance with them.

—**John Chrysostom**

Introduction

In the first and second centuries, liturgies were only prayed on Sundays and the feasts, as well as the feasts of the local saints. Nevertheless, Christians—as previously detailed—used to gather daily twice to pray; once in the morning and another in the evening. During the prayer assemblies, the Scriptures was read and expounded. As such, the Liturgy of the Word, or more precisely the teachings from the readings, played a chief role in the early church. At the time, Christians would gather to read the word of God, chant psalms, and listen to a sermon. This was first attested to by the New Testament itself; "When you come together, each of you has a hymn, or a word of instruction, a revelation, a tongue or an interpretation" (1 Corinthians 14:26). Although the notion that this practice was inherited from the Jews synagogues is common, or even given, among scholars, Andrew McGowan challenges this assumption. In his work *Ancient Christian Worship*, McGowan argues, "The first Christians would have been familiar with some of these synagogal reading practices, but that does not allow us to prejudge how those actually influenced early Christian assemblies... Christian gatherings initially arose alongside the activities of the temple and of synagogues, not as a sort of liturgical double-duty for believers in Jesus but as qualitatively different and complementary events." [621] Nevertheless, the similarities between synagogal and early Christian assemblies—as we shall see—cannot be denied or ignored.

This type of gathering is referred to as the *Synaxis* (Greek: σύναξις— "gathering together"). Ernest Burton writes about the synagogues where the *Synaxis* is held, "the synagogue was the cradle of Christianity... The early Christian churches were themselves doubtless scarcely other than

---

[621] McGowan, Andrew B., *Ancient Christian Worship*, 71.

synagogues."[622] Maximilian Rudwin agrees with this view; in his article *The Origin of Judeo-Christian Worship*, he states, "The earliest church service naturally was a synagogue service Christianized."[623] Hence, it is imperative to understand the structure and composition of the Jewish worship held at synagogues in order to draw parallels between its elements and those pertaining to the early Christian *Synaxis*. It is also essential to know that the services held two thousand years ago at the synagogues, although share the same core prayers, do not necessarily have the same shape and content of the contemporary ones.

Maximilian Rudwin believes that the Jews in exile, led by the Essenes,[624] learned the group morning worship from the Pharisees. This, according to Rudwin, emanated the synagogue worship, which flourished in the post-Exilic period.[625] The chief employment of the synagogue, after its establishment during the Exilic period, was to teach and educate the Jewish nation the law, and to preserve its traditions. Although did not exclude offering worship and praise to the Lord, the synagogue was not concerned about that since this was the prime function of the Temple. This instructional role of the synagogue was delivered through reading a section from the law, another from prophets, and rendering an exhortation.

The service at the synagogue commenced with benedictions rejoicing in the attributes of God, followed by the "*Shema*," meaning "Hear." The *Shema* was a kind of "creed," composed of the following three passages of

---

[622] Burton, Ernest De Witt (1896), The Ancient Synagogue Service, *The Biblical World*, Vol. 8, No. 2, 143.
[623] Rudwin, Maximilian J. (1919), The Origin of Judeo-Christian Worship, The Open Court: *Vol. 1919: Iss. 5, Article 4, 287*.
[624] The Essenes (Modern Hebrew: אִסִיִּים) is the third sect of Judaism besides the Pharisees and the Sadducees. This faction emerged during the Second Temple period and flourished from the 2nd century B.C. to the 1st century C.E. the Essenes lived a monastic life in the desert, adopting strict dietary laws and a commitment to celibacy.
[625] Rudwin, Maximilian J. (1919), The Origin of Judeo-Christian Worship, *The Open Court*, Vol. 1919: Iss. 5, Article 4, 292.

Scripture: Deuteronomy 6:4-9,[626] 11:13-21,[627] and Numbers 15:37-41.[628] In another rendition, the *Shema* was preceded by Psalms. After the *Shema*, another "benediction" is recited. Up until this point all prayers were recited at the lectern.

The next series of orisons are recited before "The Ark" and are headed by the service leader.[629] The "*Amidah*," meaning "standing," which comprises of eighteen eulogies (an additional eulogy was added in the 2nd century to make them nineteen blessings or eulogies), are said. According to Alfred Edersheim, "The prayers were conducted or repeated aloud by one individual,[630] specially deputed for the occasion, the congregation

---

[626] "Hear, O Israel: The Lord our God, the Lord is one. Love the Lord your God with all your heart and with all your soul and with all your strength. These commandments that I give you today are to be on your hearts. Impress them on your children. Talk about them when you sit at home and when you walk along the road, when you lie down and when you get up. Tie them as symbols on your hands and bind them on your foreheads. Write them on the doorframes of your houses and on your gates."

[627] "So, if you faithfully obey the commands I am giving you today - to love the Lord your God and to serve him with all your heart and with all your soul - then I will send rain on your land in its season, both autumn and spring rains, so that you may gather in your grain, new wine and olive oil. I will provide grass in the fields for your cattle, and you will eat and be satisfied. Be careful, or you will be enticed to turn away and worship other gods and bow down to them. Then the Lord's anger will burn against you, and he will shut up the heavens so that it will not rain, and the ground will yield no produce, and you will soon perish from the good land the Lord is giving you. Fix these words of mine in your hearts and minds; tie them as symbols on your hands and bind them on your foreheads. Teach them to your children, talking about them when you sit at home and when you walk along the road, when you lie down and when you get up. Write them on the doorframes of your houses and on your gates, so that your days and the days of your children may be many in the land the Lord swore to give your ancestors, as many as the days that the heavens are above the earth."

[628] The Lord said to Moses, "Speak to the Israelites and say to them: 'Throughout the generations to come you are to make tassels on the corners of your garments, with a blue cord on each tassel. You will have these tassels to look at and so you will remember all the commands of the Lord, that you may obey them and not prostitute yourselves by chasing after the lusts of your own hearts and eyes. Then you will remember to obey all my commands and will be consecrated to your God. I am the Lord your God, who brought you out of Egypt to be your God. I am the Lord your God.'"

[629] Edersheim, Alfred, *Sketches of Jewish Social Life in the Days of Christ*, 130.

[630] The person leading the *Amidah* was also expected to read the *Shema* and the portion from the prophets.

responding by an 'Amen.'⁶³¹"⁶³² The trice holy, *Kedushah*, which is the last section of the *Amidah*, is uttered.⁶³³ Thereafter, a reading from the law followed by a lesson from the prophets are recited. Since Aramaic was preserved in the Jewish synagogues, the verses were also repeated in the vernacular.⁶³⁴ A sermon is then conducted. This exhortation was called *derashah*, "sermon" if it was discussing theological matters, especially in academies. However, in regular settings, it was called *meamar*, "speech." As Alfred Edersheim describes them, "These addresses would be either Rabbinical expositions of Scripture, or else doctrinal discussions, in which appeal would be made to tradition and to the authority of certain great teachers."⁶³⁵

Finally, the service is concluded with the priestly benediction, "The Lord bless you and keep you" (Numbers 6:24). In another rendition of the synagogue service, probably at later time, the priestly benediction is preceded by a *Kaddish*, "Sanctification" prayer. Following the priestly benediction, another *Kaddish*, or blessing prayer is performed over wine marking the commencement of a party/meal in the synagogue hall. The following table is a depiction of the elements of the Synagogal *Synaxis* and their corresponding prayers in the Coptic Liturgy of the Word as practiced today.

---

[631] The reader can draw parallels between the supplications of the *Amidah* and how they were delivered on one hand, and the Alexandrian practice of the litanies with the congregation responding, "Lord, have mercy," a replacement of the older responsory "Amen," on the other hand. For more details, see Davies, J.G., *A New Dictionary of Liturgy and Worship*, 157.
[632] Edersheim, Alfred, *Sketches of Jewish Social Life in the Days of Christ*, 131.
[633] Baumstark, Anton, *On the Historical Development of the Liturgy*, 63.
[634] You may draw parallels between this practice and the Alexandrian tradition of uttering the periscopes in the vernacular after chanting them in Coptic.
[635] Edersheim, Alfred, *Sketches of Jewish Social Life in the Days of Christ*, 133.

Synagogal *Synaxis*	Coptic Liturgy of the Word
Benedictions	Peace be with all (now said inaudibly)
Shema	Creed
Eulogies	Litanies
Kedushah	Trisagion
Readings from the Law and the Prophets	Readings from the Pauline and Catholic epistles, Acts, and the Gospels
Derashah or *Meamar*	Sermon
Reading from Psalms	Versicles from Psalms before the Gospel

Understanding the shape of the worship at the synagogue will help us study the evolution of the Christian *Synaxis*, which will end up being the Liturgy of the Word, as currently named. Since the beginning of Christianity, the *Synaxis*, also called the Liturgy of the Spirit, was an autonomous and separate service from the Eucharist, and could be prayed even if not followed by εὐχαριστία. However, from the fourth century, the two offices gradually fused until finally, in the fifth century, the two became one indivisible liturgy. Unlike the Eucharist, the main purpose of the *Synaxis* was educational, which makes it evolve around the Scriptures and not the Body and Blood of Jesus. When the *Synaxis* became attached to the Eucharist as its first part, it was called the Ministry of the Word or Liturgy of the Catechumens. Later, precisely in the eleventh century, it was named the Liturgy of the Word.[636] This name is driven from the function of this liturgy, which is to read and elucidate the word of God. Those who are not of the faith are permitted to attend this liturgy. However, once concluded, they must leave the church. This is not to say that the faithful need not to attend, on the contrary, it is far more pertinent that the

---

[636] Cobb, Peter. G. (1992). The Liturgy of the Word in the Early Church. In Cheslyn Jones, Geoffrey Wainwright, Edward Yarnold SJ and Paul Bradshaw (Eds.), *The Study of Liturgy*, 223.

believers attend the Liturgy of the Word so they may receive it with understanding and prepare themselves spiritually for uniting with Christ in the Eucharist.

The development of both the structure and content of the *Synaxis* services differed based on time and locus for this progression. Initially, in the first two centuries, the communal education offered in these assemblies was primarily an oral discourse conducted by talented or inspired individuals regardless of their official ecclesiastical rank (clergy or laity)—as in (1 Corinthians 14:26); nonetheless, some written materials, like the Pauline letters (and those of the other apostles), were also read. In the second half of the first century, readings from the Gospels became a common practice. Shortly after, due to the need for a more scholastic approach of these communal lessons, material from the Old Testament infiltrated the *Synaxis* services. As time went by, and as more authoritative education was required—due to the emergence of heresies, the church relied more and more on written (and even canonized by the oracles of theology) texts—which were assigned to specific ranks for delivery—rather than inspired or oral teachings.[637]

At the time of persecution, some Christians turned their backs on the church and returned to idolatry. After Emperor Constantine decreed Christianity as one of the official religions in the Roman Empire, many of those who had left the church expressed their willingness to return to the Faith. The church, however, did not permit them to return until their repentance was confirmed, and as such, they were referred to as the catechumens. The catechumenate *order* also included those who wished to enter the Christian faith for the first time and were subject to a period of transition and learning. The catechumens were not permitted to attend

---

[637] McGowan, Andrew B., *Ancient Christian Worship*, 76-86.

The Liturgy of the Word

the Liturgy of the Faithful. Rather, they attended the Liturgy of the Word, which was also commonly referred to as the Liturgy of the Catechumens. There were two additional groups that were permitted to attend the Liturgy of the Word, but not the Liturgy of the Faithful. The first was the Repentant; those who were subject to a specific penance as instructed by the church because of a specific sin. The second was those who had evil spirits. The Catechumenate *order* started to fade away in the fifth century. However, the official title of "Liturgy of the Catechumens" continues to be associated with this part of the liturgy.

The church established these pericopes[638] to educate the catechumens and prepare them for accepting the faith. Every liturgy has at least nine readings. In Vespers Offering of Incense, we have a reading from the Psalms and another from the gospels, and the same is true for Prime Offering of Incense. During the liturgy of the Word, we read from the Pauline, the Catholic Epistle, the Book of Acts, the Psalms, and the Gospel. We also read from the Synaxarion, which is considered the "applied" gospel, because through it, we see how the word of God was manifested in the lives of the saints. Reading and listening to the Scriptures is not the ultimate goal of the Liturgy of the Word. The faithful should put the principles taught into practice so they become living rules that they live by. On his *On the Spiritual Law Two Hundred Texts*, Saint Mark the Ascetic advises, "Understand the words of Holy Scripture by putting them into practice, and do not fill yourself with conceit by elaborating on theoretical ideas."

The word of God cleanses the mind, just as Saint Anthony teaches "The more we read in the Scriptures, the more our minds are enlightened."

---

[638] A pericope (Greek περικοπή, "a cutting-out") is a selection from the Bible read at religious services. Lectionaries are normally made up of pericopes containing the Epistle and Gospel readings for the liturgical year.

Christ Himself said "You are already clean because of the word I have spoken to you" (John 15:3). Thus, attending the liturgy readings is key for cleansing the hearts and minds of those who wish to partake of the Eucharist. This is a reality that the church lived by since the beginning of Christianity. It is also a reality that was documented by many Coptic writers including Saint Athanasius the Apostolic, Saint Severus the Bishop, Pope Gabriel II, Ibn Kabar, and others. For this reason, the church instructs those who miss the readings not to come forth for communion. Unfortunately, many misunderstand this rule as some sort of a timing deadline that cannot be missed if you wish to partake of the Holy Mysteries. However, the intent of this canon is far more spiritual and deeper. These readings play a vital role in purifying the soul and cleaning our hearts and minds in preparation for receiving the Holy Mysteries.

The church, with great wisdom, arranged the pericopes of the liturgy based on the day of the week and her calendar. In Regular Days, we find that the pericopes are akin to the saint of the day, whether it is a monk, a martyr, a confessor, a bishop, an archangel, or Virgin Mary. The pericopes, therefore, are correlated to the life story of the saint being celebrated that day. The Sunday pericopes follow a different order; they focus on the work of the Holy Trinity toward mankind. The Sunday pericopes of Lent, however, focus on preparing the catechumens for baptism and encouraging the faithful to repent. As for the pericopes of Sundays of Eastertide, they reveal the divinity of the Lord Christ and the glory of His resurrection, as well as reflect on the Eucharist. During the readings, we ought to hark respectfully to the words being uttered, taking for ourselves a lesson to abide within our lives. In other words, we are to consider these as a direct and personal message from God for how we should live our lives. Readers of the word of God should judiciously read with clarity, good pace, and sound pronunciation; they should articulate what is being read for worshippers to clearly understand the message being delivered.

The tradition of reading lections followed by a sermon during the liturgy was present in the early church. As alluded to earlier, this practice takes root from the Jewish synagogues, in which the service included a reading from the Law and another from the Prophets, followed by the chanting of the Psalms. Origen, who departed in AD 254, testifies that the Liturgy of the Catechumens preceded the Liturgy of the Faithful. In it, pericopes from the Old and New Testaments were read, followed by a sermon expounding the readings. From this, we understand that readings from the Old Testament—per the Jewish tradition—were still used in the Coptic liturgy until, at least, the third century. We also appreciate the essential function of the sermon, after reading the pericopes, "to expound and explain the scriptures that had just been read,"[639] as Peter Cobb comments.

Saint Athanasius the Apostolic (c. AD 297–373), established the canons pertaining to the liturgy readings as follows: a chapter from the Torah, a chapter from the Historical books, and a chapter from one of the Prophets. Later, the Pauline and the Gospel pericopes were added. Robert Talf adds this important remark, "Contrary to popular misconception, there were no scripture lessons in the early cathedral office except in Egypt and Cappadocia."[640] In the fifth century, John Cassian documented the order of readings according to the Coptic rite; he reports, "At the close two lessons follow, one from the Old and the other from the New Testament,"[641] he then continues, "When they added to these two lessons, one from the Old and one from the New Testament, they added them

---

[639] Cobb, Peter. G. (1992). The Liturgy of the Word in the Early Church. In Cheslyn Jones, Geoffrey Wainwright, Edward Yarnold SJ and Paul Bradshaw (Eds.), *The Study of Liturgy*, 228.
[640] Talf, Robert F., *Beyond East and West: Problems in Liturgical Understanding*, 264.
[641] Cassian, John, *The Institutes*, Book 3—chapter IV.

simply as extras and of their own appointment, only for those who liked, and who were eager to gain by constant study a mind well stored with Holy Scripture. But on Saturday and Sunday, they read them both from the New Testament; viz., one from the Epistles or the Acts of the Apostles, and one from the Gospel."[642]

"On Egyptian soil," Anton Baumstark writes, "we come upon the first indication of a move to exclude the Old Testament reading from the assembly's celebration of the Eucharist outright."[643] Per contemporary practice, the Coptic Rite recognizes a pericope from a Pauline letter, a lection from one of the Catholic epistles, a reading from the Book of Acts, few verses from the Psalms, and finally a lesson from one of the four Gospels. Additionally, the Synaxarion is read.[644]

This highlights the intrinsic value of the Liturgy of the Word, and the fact that its content was established prior to that of the Liturgy of the Faithful. Although it was always essential for everyone to attend the Liturgy of the Word, during the Middle Ages, a special attention was given to attending the Gospel reading for those who wish to partake of the Holy Communion.[645] The result, unfortunately, was a substantial decrease in the congregation's presence during the other readings.

In their pristine arrangement, prayers (including readings) were not lengthy. Nevertheless, after the Council of Nicaea in AD 325, more readings and liturgical prayers were added to the Liturgy of the Word. The Eastern Churches established the requirement for three readings: from the Old Testament, from the Epistles or the Book of Acts, and from the

---

[642] Cassian, Ibid., Book 3—chapter VI.
[643] Baumstark, *On the Historical*, Ibid., 64.
[644] The Synaxarion is read after the Book of Acts of the Apostles.
[645] Ibn Al-'Assal, Abu Is-haq Ibn Fadlallah, *The Fundamental Acts of the Ecclesiastical Etiquette (The Liturgy)*, published by Archdeacon Girgis Philotheos Awad, 52. Also, Anonymous, *Treatise on the Holy Oblation*, Vatican, Vat, MS Arabic 123, published by Father Alfons Abdalla the Franciscan, 376.

Gospel. The church in Egypt, however, established five pericopes, in addition to the Synaxarion, and those are the Pauline, the Catholic Epistle, the Praxis, the Psalm, and the Gospel. Readings from the Old Testament, although not being part of the Liturgy of the Word, take place during the Fast of Nineveh, Lent, and Holy Week.

The readings in the Coptic Church have been established in this manner for a long time. Pope Cyril II, who departed in AD 1092, addresses one of his letters to the bishops, urging them to remind the priests in their perishes of the five pericopes. In this letter he writes, "Five readings are to be read in every liturgy, and they are the Pauline, the Catholic Epistle, the Book of Acts, the Psalm and the Gospel. A litany should follow each reading. Anyone who knowingly avoids or ignores any of these five readings will be guilty before God Almighty."[646]

Until the tenth century or shortly thereafter, liturgies in Egypt took place on Saturdays and Sundays. During the time of Saint Macarius the Great, Saturday liturgies were prayed at Sunset time, after which the monks would spend the night in church until the next morning, when they would celebrate the Sunday liturgy. This order was commonly known as Macarius' Canon. Later—according to some scholars—the Church replaced the Saturday Liturgy with the Sunday Vespers.[647] Hence, in his *Historia Ecclesiastica*, Sozomen (c. AD 400–450) writes, "There are several cities and villages in Egypt where, contrary to the usage established elsewhere, the people meet together on Sabbath evenings, and, although they have dined previously, partake of the mysteries."[648] It is worth noting that at that time there was a single Lectionary for Saturday and Sunday

---

[646] Athanasius of Saint Macarius Monastery (Father), *The Divine Liturgy: The Mystery of the Kingdom of God (Part 1)*, 437.
[647] Matthew the Poor (Father), *Eucharist of the Lord's Supper*, 51-52.
[648] Sozomen, *Historia Ecclesiastica*, Book VII, Chapter 19.

services, and the lessons for one day complemented the other, thereby maintaining consistency over both days.

Whether the priest prays the Liturgy of Saint Gregory, Saint Cyril, or Saint Basil, the order of both the Offertory, and the Liturgy of the Word offices stay the same. It is also important to note that the music of the Offertory and that of the Liturgy of the Word, as well as that of the Communion, changes according to the ecclesiastical season. So, besides the Year-round tunes that are appointed to Regular Days, Joyous melodies are assigned to Feast Days, and ascetic music are employed during Lent and the Fast of Nineveh. In the month of Kiahk, a peculiar tune is used, while another peculiar melody, named *hosanna*, is dedicated for the Feasts of the Cross and Palm Sunday. On the other hand, the Liturgy of the Faithful retains the same tunes throughout the liturgical year. Most prayers and chants in the Liturgy of the Word are assigned to the congregation led by the chorus. This is contrast to the Liturgy of the Faithful, which relies primarily on the priest, and secondarily on the congregation.

The Beginning of the Liturgy of the Word

The Liturgy of the Word commences immediately after the reading of the Absolution of the Servants, which marks the conclusion of the Offertory office. Following the Absolution of the Servants, the priest and altar servers enter the sanctuary, and, facing eastward, the priest puts five spoonsful of incense in the thurible. He then prays the Litany of Incense for the Pauline Epistle. If a high priest is present, the priest would present the Coffer of Incense to him while one of the altar servers presents the censer. The prelate would then place the incense in the censer in the first round, and the priest would put the incense in the second one.

In the book *The Trinitarian Mystery in Priesthood Ministry*, authored in AD 1493 and attributed to Church Teachers, it indicates that the assistant priest represents the priest of the New Testament, whereas the servant priest characterizes that of the Old Testament.[649] According to this document, the reason for the assistant priest putting the incense in the second time is because the priest of the New Testament became a participant with that of the Old Testament. It states, "This symbolizes Abraham's partnership with Melchizedek the priest."[650]

It is worth noting that placing five spoonsful of incense was not necessarily the common practice in the Coptic Church over the centuries. For example, Ibn Sibaa instructs six spoonsful; he states, "The offering of incense commences with three handfuls, one for each hypostasis of the Holy Trinity, the Father, the Son and the Holy Spirit. This is followed by another three handfuls, representing the offering of Abel, the incense of Noah, and the sacrifice of Isaac; these three cases took place in the Old Testament before the New Testament. As such they followed their example."[651]

Pope Gabriel V, on the other hand, states, "The Pauline incense is offered in a similar manner to that of Vesper Offering of Incense, five handfuls in total, no more or less."[652] This resolute vigorous statement appears to be addressing an issue with some parishes not adhering to the five spoonsful practice. It seems that there were competing ritual pursuits in this regard, and Pope Gabriel V wanted to ensure that the practice of five spoonsful of incense was being carried out. In the book *The*

---

[649] Church Teachers, *The Trinitarian Mystery in Priesthood Ministry*, Philotheos, Girgis (Ed.), 11.
[650] Church Teachers, Ibid., 12. Additionally, the document explicitly instructs that all contributions—all of them assigned to the handful of incense addressed to God the Son—made by any number of assistant priests are considered one, hence, the principal celebrant is assigned all remaining four spoonsful of incense.
[651] Ibn Sibaa, *The Precious Pearl: On Ecclesiastic Science*, BnF, MS Arabic 207, fol. 124v
[652] Gabriel V (Pope), *The Ritual Order*, BnF, MS 98 (AD 1411), fol. 54v.

Trinitarian Mystery in Priesthood Ministry, an explication of the five spoonsful of incense can be found. It states, "He (the priest) then enters (the sanctuary) to offer incense. He puts five handfuls, since the Old Testament mentioned that there were five individuals who offered incense and to whom an angel appeared, and announcements or instructions were provided. The first is Abel, the second is Noah, the third is Abraham through Melchizedek, the fourth is Aaron, and the fifth is Zacharias. (This means,) three preceded the Law of Moses, and two were after."[653]

After offering incense and praying the Litany of Incense for the Pauline Epistle, the Three Minor Litanies (litanies of Peace, the Fathers, and the Assemblies) are prayed. In the primitive setup, preceded by the introduction,[654] the Litany of Incense for the Pauline Epistle and the Three Minor Litanies were pronounced aloud. Similarly, the congregation responds to these orisons with "Lord have mercy" as customary. Hence, no hymns were chanted simultaneously as per the current practice. The Uppsala version of *The Lamp to Darkness and Explanation of the Service* (AD 1546) states, "After the altar server completes the biddings pertaining to the three litanies, the congregation chants 'Ⲛⲑⲟ ⲧⲉ ϯϣⲟⲩⲣⲏ.'"[655, 656] This means that these hymns were said after the Circuit of the Incense, not during it. As such, Marquis comments, "The Prayer of Incense is said in a low voice while these three anthems are sung, the Deacon answering in the same—which is obviously a corruption, as these answers are Biddings."[657]

In the past, there were two practices regarding the Litany of Incense for the Pauline Epistle. According to the first, the litany is uttered, followed by the Three Minor Litanies, and the Pauline Circuit,

---

[653] Church Teachers, *The Trinitarian Mystery in Priesthood Ministry*, Philotheos, Girgis (Ed.), 10.
[654] Priest: Ϣⲗⲏⲗ, altar server: Ⲉⲡⲓ ⲡⲣⲟⲥⲉⲩⲭⲏ ⲥⲧⲁⲑⲏⲧⲉ, priest: Ⲓⲣⲏⲛⲏ ⲡⲁⲥⲓ, and people: Ⲕⲉ ⲧⲱ ⲡⲛⲉⲩⲙⲁⲧⲓ ⲥⲟⲩ.
[655] Translation: You are the golden censer, carrying the blessed and live coal.
[656] Ibn Kabar, *The Lamp to Darkness and Explanation of the Service*, Father Samuel of Syrians Monastery, 126.
[657] John, Marquis of Bute, *The Coptic Morning Service for the Lord's Day*, 60.

respectively. The second practice comes from Ibn Sibaa, who states, "The priest begins by asking for God's acceptance of the incense offering (which is the Litany of Incense for the Pauline Epistle), and upon concluding it, the deacon responds, 'Pray for these oblations and offerings,' to which the congregation chants 'Lord have mercy.'... The priest then proceeds with circling the altar three times. Each time he is before the bread and wine, he makes the sign of the cross with the thurible. After completing the circuits, he exits the sanctuary with his left foot before the right, which is the opposite manner he entered, that is, the right foot before the left."[658]

Both practices share a rubric that instructs the priest to pray the Three Minor Litanies audibly, the altar server to respond to the litanies as usual, and the congregation to say, "Lord have mercy." Unlike the first practice that places the Pauline Circuit after the Three Minor Litanies, the second practice makes former concomitant of the latter. Ibn Kabar takes this parallelism one step further as he makes both the Litany of Incense for the Pauline Epistle and the Three Minor Litanies coincide with the Pauline Circuit. He directs: "After putting incense in the censer—with participation from the other priests—he (the priest) offers incense before the altar, and circles around it as he prays the Litany of Incense for the Pauline Epistle."[659] In other words, according to Ibn Kabar, the Litany of Incense for the Pauline Epistle and the Three Minor Litanies are prayed audibly during the Pauline Circuit.

Eventually, the priests started praying the Litany of Incense for the Pauline Epistle and the Three Minor Litanies inaudibly during the Pauline Circuit, which, on the one hand, resulted in the elimination of the altar server and congregation responses, and on the other hand, allowed for the hymns Ϫⲁⲓ ϣⲟⲣⲡ and Ⲛⲑⲟ ⲧⲉ ϯϣⲟⲣⲡ, which were originally intoned

---

[658] Ibn Sibaa, *The Precious Pearl: On Ecclesiastic Science*, BnF, MS Arabic 207, fols. 125r-126r
[659] Ibn Kabar, *The Lamp*, BnF, MS Arabic 203 (c. AD 1363-1369), fol. 205v.

after the Pauline Circuit, to be chanted during the Pauline Circuit. This is the order as practiced today. It is likely that this change was introduced as a means of shortening the service. It is worth mentioning that the stations of the Pauline Circuit are the same as that of the Major Circuit of Incense of the Vesper and Prime Offering of Incense.

According to the contemporary rubric, after the Absolution of the Servants, the congregation chants Cⲱⲟⲓⲥ ⲁⲙⲏⲛ, which is considered the conclusion of the rite of the Offertory. Immediately after this, the congregation chants the hymns Ⲧⲁⲓ ϣⲟⲩⲣⲏ,[660] Ϥϣⲟⲩⲣⲏ,[661] or Ⲛⲑⲟ ⲧⲉ ϯϣⲟⲩⲣⲏ.

In antiquity, the hymn Ⲧⲁⲓ ϣⲟⲩⲣⲏ or Ⲛⲑⲟ ⲧⲉ ϯϣⲟⲩⲣⲏ were chanted all year round. Ibn Kabar writes, "After the offering of incense, the chanters recite either Ⲧⲁⲓ ϣⲟⲩⲣⲏ ⲛⲛⲟⲩⲃ or Ⲛⲑⲟ ⲧⲉ ϯϣⲟⲩⲣⲏ."[662] The Uppsala version of the same document, MS OR. 486 (AD 1546), states, "After the altar server completes the biddings pertaining to the three litanies, the congregation chants Ⲛⲑⲟ ⲧⲉ ϯϣⲟⲩⲣⲏ."[663] This was also confirmed by Pope Gabriel V in his book *The Ritual Order*. He instructs, "If time permits, they chant either the hymn Ⲛⲑⲟ ⲧⲉ ϯϣⲟⲩⲣⲏ, or Ⲧⲁⲓ ϣⲟⲩⲣⲏ for the Virgin, then Ⲧⲉⲛⲟⲩⲱϣⲧ;[664] otherwise, they only say Ⲧⲉⲛⲟⲩⲱϣⲧ."[665]

---

[660] The common translation of this hymn is "This censer of pure gold, bearing the aroma, is in the hands of Aaron the priest, offering up incense on the altar." However, in his *Understanding the Liturgy*, page 12, Father Athanasius Iskander claims that there is a continuation to the hymn that is rarely used nowadays. It reads, "before the mercy seat, is the holy Virgin Mary; Who brought forth Jesus Christ; the Son and Logos. The Holy Spirit came upon her, purified her, sanctified her, and filled her with grace. Through her intercessions, O Lord, grant us the forgiveness of our sins."
[661] Translation: The golden censer is the Virgin; her aroma is our Savior. She gave birth to Him; He saved us and forgave us our sins.
[662] Ibn Kabar, *The Lamp*, BnF, MS Arabic 203 (c. AD 1363-1369), fol. 205v.
[663] Ibn Kabar, *The Lamp*, Father Samuel of Syrians Monastery, 126.
[664] Translation: We worship You O Christ, with Your good Father, and the Holy Spirit, for You have come and saved us. Have mercy upon us.
[665] Gabriel V (Pope), *The Ritual Order*, BnF, MS 98 (AD 1411), fols. 54v-55r.

Unlike Ϫⲁⲓ ϣⲟⲣⲡ, which was mentioned by the 13th century scholars, the hymn Ϩϣⲟⲣⲡ was first cited by the 14th century scholar Ibn Kabar. Since Ϩϣⲟⲣⲡ is an interpretation of Ϫⲁⲓ ϣⲟⲣⲡ, some manuscripts placed it to follow Ϫⲁⲓ ϣⲟⲣⲡ. For example, MS Lit. 117, preserved at the Old Patriarchate library in Cairo, states, "The Patriarch reads the absolution over them; and at the end of it, the priests start reading Ϫⲁⲓ ϣⲟⲣⲡ, followed by Ϩϣⲟⲣⲡ, and the Patriarch begins to offer incense."[666] MS 302 of Saint Anthony Monastery (transcribed in AD 1661) agrees with this practice as well. This custom, however, was not the common practice across Egypt. The question here, are these two hymns (i.e., Ϫⲁⲓ ϣⲟⲣⲡ, and Ϩϣⲟⲣⲡ) actually one chant? The transcriber of MS OR. 486 (AD 1546) comments, "He (the patriarch) reads the absolution over the servants; the congregation chants Ⲛⲓⲥⲁⲃⲉⲧ ⲧⲏⲣⲟⲩ, and when he offers incense, they chant a hymn for Saint Mary, that is, Ϫⲁⲓ ϣⲟⲣⲡ ⲛ̀ⲛⲟⲩⲃ ⲛ̀ⲕⲁⲑⲁⲣⲟⲥ, [then] the *Parallaxe* Ϩϣⲟⲣⲡ ⲛ̀ⲛⲟⲩⲃ ⲧⲉ ϯⲡⲁⲣⲑⲉⲛⲟⲥ, followed by Ϫⲉⲛⲟⲩⲱϣⲧ, then Ϩⲓⲧⲉⲛ ⲛⲓⲉⲩⲭⲏ."[667]

This perplexing comment suggests that Ϫⲁⲓ ϣⲟⲣⲡ and Ϩϣⲟⲣⲡ are one hymn, an instruction that was also mentioned by the 14th century MS 256, Huntington Collection.[668] In an effort to study this point, I reviewed over than 21 manuscripts from the 13th through the 20th century, 15 of which cited either Ϫⲁⲓ ϣⲟⲣⲡ, Ⲛⲑⲟ ⲧⲉ ϯϣⲟⲣⲡ, Ϩϣⲟⲣⲡ, or a different combination of them; the others just mentioned Ϫⲉⲛⲟⲩⲱϣⲧ. In the 15 manuscripts, 30 references to these hymns in different contexts and occasions are documented, including the Eucharist, Refilling of the Chalice, For the Patriarch, At the Presence of the Patriarch without

---

[666] *The Church Order*, Cairo, Patriarchal Library, MS Lit. 117 (AD 1910), fol. 22v-r. It is worth mentioning that this manuscript copies this *ordo* word for word from the AD 1514 *The Church Order* of the Paromeos monastery.
[667] Ibn Kabar, *The Lamp*, Father Samuel of Syrians Monastery, 138.
[668] *Psalms, the canticle of Moses, Theotokia, prayers and hymns for the Blessed Virgin Mary, archangels and martyrs*, London, Bod., MS 256, 250, Huntington Collection.

Praying, Baptism, Good Friday, Consecration of New Altars, Betrothals, the Holy Crowning, Second Marriage, Epiphany, Blessing of the Waters, and Untying the Stole of the Newly Baptized. These 15 documents represent several areas at different times in Egypt including Cairo, Alexandria, Paromeos monastery, Saint Anthony monastery, Tanta, Beni Suef, and Bayad, in addition to manuscripts from the Coptic Museum, the Euchologion authored by Raphael Tuki, Ibn Sibaa, Ibn Kabar, and Pope Gabriel V.

The following are the results of the research: Ⲧⲁⲓ ϣⲟⲣⲡ followed by Ⲧⲉⲛⲟⲩⲱϣⲧ was mentioned 15 times. Ⲧⲁⲓ ϣⲟⲣⲡ followed by Ϩϣⲟⲣⲡ then Ⲧⲉⲛⲟⲩⲱϣⲧ was stated 7 times. Ⲛⲑⲟ ⲧⲉ ϯϣⲟⲣⲡ followed by Ⲧⲉⲛⲟⲩⲱϣⲧ was mentioned twice. Ϩϣⲟⲣⲡ followed by other hymns then Ⲧⲉⲛⲟⲩⲱϣⲧ was cited twice as well. Ϩϣⲟⲣⲡ as the *Parallaxe* of Ⲧⲁⲓ ϣⲟⲣⲡ was stated twice. All other combinations were mentioned once. This suggests that the common practice was to chant one of these three hymns based on time availability; if time permits, more than one hymn can be chanted. In his AD 1735 Euchologion, Raphael Tuki writes, "This is all while the congregation chants Ⲧⲁⲓ ϣⲟⲣⲡ in the Virgin tune... and if time permits, they also say Ϩϣⲟⲣⲡ... or they say Ⲛⲑⲟ ⲧⲉ ϯϣⲟⲣⲡ..."[669] *The Church Order* (AD 1444), which explains the rite of the Patriarchate at the time, confirms this understanding. It reads, "All that while they chant Ⲧⲁⲓ ϣⲟⲣⲡ in the Virgin tune... in case there are too many priests and the three circuits are not completed, they afterward say Ϩϣⲟⲣⲡ ⲛⲛⲟⲩⲃ."[670]

From all of the above, I can confidently say that Ⲧⲁⲓ ϣⲟⲣⲡ and Ϩϣⲟⲣⲡ were treated in the Church sources over the centuries as two separate hymns. Moreover, there are certain traits of *Parallaxe* hymns that

---

[669] Tuki, Raphael, *The Book of the Three Liturgies*, 43.
[670] Jeremiah (Hegumen), *The Church Order*, Cairo, Patriarchal Library, MS Lit. 73 (AD 1444), fols. 74r-75v.

are not fulfilled in this case. The chief characteristic of *Parallaxe* hymns is that they consist of multiple stanzas chanted in the same tune. Since Ϧⲱⲟⲩⲣⲏ lacks this trait, it is not a difficult undertaking to deduce that it is not a *Parallaxe* for Ϫⲁⲓ ϣⲟⲩⲣⲏ. As for Ibn Kabar's comment, it might be a misclassification or imprecision use of the word *Parallaxe*.[671]

According to the contemporary practice, the hymn Ϫⲁⲓ ϣⲟⲩⲣⲏ is said in the following occasions:

1. In Regular Days, every day of the week except Wednesdays and Fridays
2. On Fast Days, except for Lent, on Saturdays and Sundays
3. On all feasts, except the Feasts of the Cross

The hymn Ϧⲱⲟⲩⲣⲏ[672] is chanted in the following occasions:

1. In Regular Days, on Wednesdays and Fridays
2. On Fast days, except for Lent and the fast of Nineveh, on every day of the week except Saturdays and Sundays
3. During Lent, on Saturdays and Sundays as well as the first Monday and last Friday of Lent
4. On the Feasts of the Cross

As for the hymn Ⲛⲑⲟ ⲧⲉ ϯϣⲟⲩⲣⲏ, it is chanted:

1. On the three days of the Fast of Nineveh
2. During Lent, on all days of the week from Monday to Friday expect for the first Monday and the last Friday of Lent.

---

[671] It is worth noting that *Parallaxe* hymns in all manuscripts over the centuries were always referred to as *Parallaxe*. However, to my knowledge, Ϧⲱⲟⲩⲣⲏ was never described as a *Parallaxe* except for the two times mentioned above.
[672] The hymn Ϧⲱⲟⲩⲣⲏ is also chanted in matrimonies and funerals.

We notice here a rite that once was simple and has become complex and compound over time. A possible reason for this intricacy is an attempt to preserve all these hymns from extinction. Therefore, according to the contemporary practice, the Liturgy of the Word commences with the priest praying the Litany of the Incense for the Pauline Epistle. This is followed by the Three Minor Litanies inaudibly as he, along with one or two of the altar servers, circumambulates the sanctuary thrice. During the Pauline Circuit, the congregation chants the hymn Ⲧⲁⲓ ϣⲟⲣⲡ, Ϧϣⲟⲣⲡ, or Ⲛ̄ⲑⲟ ⲧⲉ ϯϣⲟⲣⲡ, depending on the day and season.

According to the current practice, this is then followed by the hymn of the Intercessions (*Hitens*), a chant that was not mentioned by Pope Gabriel V or any of old sources. In fact, even the Euchologion authored by Father Abdel Messih in AD 1902, which is the reference of the contemporary *ordo*, did not include it. Although the first reference to this hymn in its current form is in the fifth edition of the Deacons Service book, published by the Renaissance of Coptic Orthodox Churches Association published in AD 1938, evidence show that it might have its roots from the 15th century.

MS Lit. 73 (AD 1444) instructs that in the presence of a prelate, after the hymn Ⲧⲁⲓ ϣⲟⲣⲡ is chanted, the hymn Ϧϣⲟⲣⲡ is optionally said. Following that the manuscript prescribes a hymn for the pontiff "Ⲉⲩⲗⲟⲅⲓⲥⲁⲑⲉ,"[673] then Ϩⲓⲧⲉⲛ ⲛⲓⲉⲩⲭⲏ and Ⲧⲉⲛⲟⲩⲱϣⲧ, respectively.[674] Uppsala, MS OR. 486 (AD 1546) includes similar instructions, however, places Ⲧⲉⲛⲟⲩⲱϣⲧ prior to Ϩⲓⲧⲉⲛ ⲛⲓⲉⲩⲭⲏ.[675] In other words, "Ϩⲓⲧⲉⲛ ⲛⲓⲉⲩⲭⲏ" was designated for the occasion of the Papal presence during the

---

[673] We will discuss this hymn in greater detail shortly.
[674] Jeremiah (*Hegumen*), *The Church Order*, Cairo, Patriarchal Library, MS Lit. 73 (AD 1444), fol. 76v-r.
[675] Ibn Kabar, *The Lamp*, Father Samuel of Syrians Monastery, 138. However, *The Lamp to Darkness and Explanation of the Service*, BnF, MS 203 Arabic, which is the earliest extant manuscript of this book, does not mention Ϩⲓⲧⲉⲛ ⲛⲓⲉⲩⲭⲏ after Ⲧⲉⲛⲟⲩⲱϣⲧ.

liturgy.[676] In the following centuries, the vocation of this hymn changed. Sources from the 18th century reveal that "Ϩⲓⲧⲉⲛ ⲛⲓⲉⲩⲭⲏ" was replaced by "Ϩⲓⲧⲉⲛ ⲛⲓⲡⲣⲉⲥⲃⲓⲁ" for Saint Mary.[677] That is, instead of being an occasional hymn employed at a specific event (presence of the Pope), it developed to be consistently chanted to beseech the intercessions of Saint Mary. In his AD 1902 Euchologion, Father Abd El-Messih El-Massoody documents the next progression of the order of this hymn. He attests to the oral tradition of cantors chanting multiple stanzas starting with "Ϩⲓⲧⲉⲛ ⲛⲓ" between any of the three hymns for Saint Mary[678] and Ϯⲉⲛⲟⲩⲱϣⲧ, one or two of which pertain to the day of prayer whether that be a fast or a feast.[679] This suggests that although the current shape of the (*Hitens*) hymn was only introduced in the 19th century, it has its roots from the mediaeval times.

It is clear to the student of liturgical texts and rubrics that, over the centuries, the general tendency was to reduce the length of the service. The question then arises: why would a hymn, like *Hitens*, be elaborated in the 19th century? To answer this question, it is imperative to explore the textual source of the stanzas forming the hymn in question in its present shape. Two possibilities will be presented in this study.

In his Euchologion, *Hegumen* Abd El-Messih El-Massoody includes several *Adam* Aspazmos hymns, the most notable of which is "Rejoice O Mary," which, according to the contemporary practice, is designated for Regular Days. In antiquity, however, the one assigned to Regular Days was (Ⲡⲓⲭⲣⲓⲥⲧⲟⲥ Ⲡⲉⲛⲥⲱⲧⲏⲣ—O Christ, our Savior). Starting from its fourth stanza and onwards we find a series of quatrains beginning with *Hiten*; the

---

[676] MS Lit. 73 is clear that "Ϩⲓⲧⲉⲛ ⲛⲓⲉⲩⲭⲏ" is only said if the Patriarch is praying the liturgy, otherwise, it is not chanted even if he is present but not praying. See: Jeremiah, Ibid., fol. 78r.
[677] Examples: *The Church Order*, London, British Library, MS Or. 5898 (AD 1708), fol. 26r, and *The Church Order*, St. Anthony Monastery, MS Rite 296 (AD 1781), fol. 98v.
[678] Ⲧⲁⲓ ϣⲟⲣⲡ, Ϯϣⲟⲣⲡ, or Ⲛⲑⲟ ⲧⲉ ϯϣⲟⲣⲡ.
[679] Salib, Abdel Massieh (*Hegumen*), *The Holy Euchologion*, 239.

concluding quatrain is Ϯⲉⲛⲟⲩⲱϣⲧ.[680] In other words, according to this theory, which was developed by Father Athanasius of Saint Macarius Monastery, the hymn of the Intercessions is an abbreviated version of the original *Adam* Aspazmos.[681]

Two challenges face this hypothesis: first, the interval between the two hymns (the source, and the hymn of the Intercession) is significant. Second, the aforementioned *Adam* Aspazmos is the origin of another chant, as we shall see in the next chapter, and it is unlikely to have one source for more than one chant. Another theory[682] that might shed some light on the textual origin of the hymn in question makes it derivative of the Verses of Cymbals. Printed in AD 1908, Father Mina Mahalawy's Psalter included three types of Verses of Cymbals. The first type consists of an eleven-quatrain set of "*Hitens;*" that is, each of the eleven quatrains started with either ϩⲓⲧⲉⲛ ⲛⲓⲡⲣⲉⲥⲃⲓⲁ (Through the intercessions) or ϩⲓⲧⲉⲛ ⲛⲓⲉⲩⲭⲏ (Through the prayers)[683] and ended with Ⲡ̄ⲟ̄ⲥ̄ ⲁⲣⲓϩⲙⲟⲧ ⲛⲁⲛ ⲙ̀ⲡⲓⲭⲱ ⲉⲃⲟⲗ ⲛ̀ⲧⲉ ⲛⲉⲛⲛⲟⲃⲓ (O Lord, grant us the forgiveness of our sins).[684] Since this type is no longer operated in its intended location, it is possible that the Church, in attempt to preserve its textual value, appointed its stanzas to form the hymn in question.[685]

It is noteworthy that the first stanza of the hymn of the Intercessions can be intoned in a melismatic melody, usually appointed to Feast Days. In this hymn, we ask for the intercessions and prayers of Saint Mary, the archangels, the martyrs, and the saints on our behalf, so that the Lord may

---

[680] Salib, Abdel Massieh (Hegumen), *The Holy Euchologion*, 306-308.
[681] Athanasius of Saint Macarius Monastery (Father), *The Divine Liturgy: The Mystery of the Kingdom of God (Part 2)*, 630-632.
[682] I conceptualized this hypothesis after years of studying the origins of the liturgical services.
[683] According to the Coptic Orthodox Church, intercessions are higher degree than prayers. Only Saint Mary, angles and Saint John the Baptists can intercede in our behalf. Other saints, including martyrs and patriarchs, can only pray for us.
[684] Mahalawy, Mina (Father), *The Regular Holy Psalter*, 284-286.
[685] It is not uncommon for the Church to change the order of particular hymns to preserve them from extinction.

forgive us our sins. The hymn is chanted during the Pauline Circuit while the worshippers, presumably, are reflecting on their transgressions and offering repentance to the Lord. For this reason, the priest, after completing the circuit, returns to the sanctuary and offers the Prayer of Confession (also referred to as the Returning Prayer) to the Lord. In this orison, the priest beseeches the Lord saying, "O God, who received the confession of the thief upon the honorable Cross, accept the confession of Your people and forgive them all their sins for the sake of Your holy name which is called upon us." It is appropriate that while the priest pleads to God for the forgiveness of the people's iniquities, that the worshippers offer penitence and, through the chanting of *Hitens*, implore the Lord to grant them the forgiveness of their sins.

Current rubric, analogous to Pope Gabriel V's instructions, prescribes that in the presence of a prelate, the priest first offers incense toward him thrice, then toward the *hegumen* twice, and finally toward the Assistant Priest(s) once. Then, he circumambulates the nave. The incense is a symbol of the prayers offered before God. Hence, the act of offering incense denotes the act of offering our prayers collectively before the Lord. The priests act as the representatives of their flock, offering pleas and devotions on behalf of themselves and of the people. Interestingly however, Ibn Sibaa reports a slightly different tradition. He states that the number of offerings toward the high priest is nine, and toward the *hegumen* or the presbyter is three.[686]

The priest then proceeds in the nave offering incense starting with the northern side followed by the southern. He re-enters the sanctuary and begins reciting the Prayer of Confession. In this prayer, the priest offers the confessions of the people before the Lord, uttering the words, "O God,

---

[686] Ibn Sibaa, *The Precious Pearl: On Ecclesiastic Science*, BnF, MS Arabic 207, fol. 126r

who received the confession of the thief upon the honorable Cross, accept the confession of Your people and forgive them all their sins." As previously said, it is during the Pauline Circuit that people offer repentance and confess their sins. The priest in return would take the confessions and offer them on the altar. This is analogous to the Old Testament, where the sinner laid his/her hands on the sacrifice and confess their sins, thereby transferring the sins to the sacrifice. It is said in the scriptures, "You are to lay your hand on the head of the burnt offering, and it will be accepted on your behalf to make atonement for you" (Leviticus 1:4). Likewise, the priest takes the confessions of the congregation and places them upon the True Sacrifice on the altar.

In his AD 1902 Euchologion, on page 82, *Hegumen* Abd El-Messih El-Massoody of the Paromeos Monastery had a footnote written in his own handwriting stating, "The common practice today is that upon entering the sanctuary, the priest places a spoonful of incense without making the sign of the cross. He does so while reciting the Prayer of Confession. However, this practice was not documented in any other Euchologion. For this reason, I forgot to mention this in this book even in a footnote."[687]

In *The Mystery of the Trinity in the Priesthood*, published by Girgis Philotheos Awad—from Patriarchate, MS Lit. 367 (AD 1493),[688] it states that after the Prayer of Confession, "the priest returns to the sanctuary, and proceeds to circumambulate the altar one more time, thereby a total of four circuits around the altar, symbolizing the four gospels."[689] *The*

---

[687] Athanasius of Saint Macarius Monastery (Father), *The Divine Liturgy: The Mystery of the Kingdom of God (Part 1)*, 420.

[688] In a strenuous study of this matter, Father Misael made this association; see Misael of the Paromeos Monastery (Father). (2020). The Trinitarian Mystery in Priesthood Ministry. *Alexandria School*, 28(1), 99.

[689] Athanasius, Ibid., 420; and Misael of the Paromeos Monastery (Father). (2020). The Trinitarian Mystery in Priesthood Ministry. *Alexandria School*, 28(1), 118.

Beginners' Guide and Discipline for Laity adds that the apostles (not only Saint Paul) preached them around the world.[690]

Therefore, following the Prayer of Confession, the priest, respectively, circles the altar one more time, offers incense before the prelate, exits the sanctuary to cense the Psalteria, and finally return to the sanctuary. This circuit, known as the Pauline Circuit, is preferably performed by the Servant Priest. If a high priest is present, however, he will circumambulate the altar the first three times, then pass the thurible to the Servant Priest to conclude the circuit.[691] Meanwhile, as noted above, the chancel[692] (the congregation led by the chanters recite hymns) is the theatre for a simultaneous action consisting of a series of chants led by the chorus, viz, Ⲧⲁⲓ ϣⲟⲣⲡ, Ϩϣⲟⲣⲡⲏ or Ⲛⲑⲟ ⲧⲉ ϯϣⲟⲣⲡⲏ, then the hymn of the Intercessions, and finally Ⲧⲉⲛⲟⲩⲱϣⲧ.

The Pauline Epistle

The reading of the pericopes then commences. In the East, lections are comprised of three pericopes from the Old Testament, a reading from one of the epistles or the Book of Acts, and finally a lesson from one of the Gospels. In the Coptic Church, however, the five readings are: the Pauline, which is a lection from one of the epistles of Saint Paul, the Catholic Epistle, a pericope from one of the non-Pauline epistles, the Praxis, a reading from the Book of Acts, the Psalm, few verses from the Psalms, and the Gospel, which is a pericope from one of the four Gospels. The Coptic

---

[690] Misael of the Paromeos Monastery (Father). (2018). The Beginners' Guide and Discipline for Laity. *Alexandria School, 25(2),* 129.
[691] This circuit is the same as that of Prime or Vespers Offering of Incense. However, instead of saying, "The blessing of the evening (or the morning) incense. May its holy blessing be with us, Amen," the priest says, "A blessing of Paul the apostle of Jesus Christ. May his holy blessing be with us, Amen."
[692] The chancel (Arabic: الخورس الأول), or Psalteria, is the space around the altar, including the choir.

Church limits readings from the Old Testament to special occasions, which are the Fasts of Nineveh, Lent, and Holy Week. As previously noted, Saint Paul's letters—as intended—were one of the first didactic material read in the communal Christian assemblies, even before the four Gospels were transcribed.[693] Saint Paul himself encouraged the circulation of his epistles: "After this letter has been read to you, see that it is also read in the church of the Laodiceans and that you in turn read the letter from Laodicea" (Colossians 4:16).

It is imperative to note that in antiquity, a greater attention was given to the lessons. Hence, ranks were a consideration for readings.[694] The Pauline and Praxis were often read by the third ranking deacon, the Gospel of Prime Offering of Incense is read by the second ranking deacon, and the Catholic Epistle by the first.[695] Each region, however, had their own local customs, which also varied from one era to the other. For instance, Ibn Kabar testifies that in Alexandria, the liturgy Gospel is assigned to the archdeacon.[696]

One of the chanters—Ibn Sibaa assigns it to the Reader—proceeds to the northern lectern and, while facing eastward, chants the first reading, the Pauline, in Coptic. On Feast Days, a more elaborate tune is employed for the reading.[697] Upon completion, the reader "ought to prostrate before God at the gate of the sanctuary, followed by a prostration toward the deacons in both choruses." [698] In the presence of a high priest, the congregation, led by the chorus, chants the hymn of Ⲡⲓϩⲙⲟⲧ ⲅⲁⲣ (The grace). This chant has two renditions, one for Regular Days and another

---

[693] McGowan, Andrew B., *Ancient Christian Worship*, 80.
[694] Diaconal ranks were introduced in the third century. See McGowan, Andrew B., *Ancient Christian Worship*, 92.
[695] Athanasius, Ibid., 440.
[696] Ibn Kabar, *The Lamp*, BnF, MS Arabic 203 (c. AD 1363-1369), fol. 206r.
[697] During Passion Week (except for Maundy Thursday) and in funerals, a mournful melody is used for the Pauline lesson.
[698] Ibn Sibaa, *The Precious Pearl: On Ecclesiastic Science*, BnF, MS Arabic 207, fol. 128r

with more elaborate text and lengthier music that is usually appointed for Feast Days or if time permits.[699] Most sources cite the melismatic version of the hymn Ⲡⲓϩⲙⲟⲧ ⲅⲁⲣ. Although it might seem that the short version of Ⲡⲓϩⲙⲟⲧ ⲅⲁⲣ was composed in a later date as a time-saving replacement of the original one, MS Copte 38, a 14th-century psalter, includes it, suggesting an immemorial use of this rendition despite its scarcity.[700]

Inspected documents in this study precede the melismatic rendition of Ⲡⲓϩⲙⲟⲧ ⲅⲁⲣ by a chant referred to as the *Eprologhon*,[701] which is "Ⲉⲩⲗⲟⲅⲓⲥⲁⲑⲉ" in the Coptic Sahidic dialect. The latter, which is an inspiration from the Epistle to the Hebrews, is chanted in the presence of the Pope (or a bishop) only if he is presiding over the liturgy. Having reviewed four *The Church Order* manuscripts, I found that there are slight differences in the relation between this hymn and Ⲡⲓϩⲙⲟⲧ ⲅⲁⲣ. MS Lit. 73 (AD 1444) states, "If they choose to say Ⲡⲓϩⲙⲟⲧ ⲅⲁⲣ or else part of the *Eprologhon*, any part they may choose, or the entire *Eprologhon*, which is the following; it is up to them in this matter."[702] The manuscript then mentions the entire hymn of Ⲉⲩⲗⲟⲅⲓⲥⲁⲑⲉ. Interestingly, it mentions Ⲡⲓϩⲙⲟⲧ ⲅⲁⲣ as the second last stanza of the hymn where the last one is what is now the concluding section of the hymn of the Virtues (starting from Ⲁⲙⲏⲛ ⲉⲥⲉϣⲱⲡⲓ).[703] MS Lit. 117 (AD 1910), on the other hand, treats them as different hymns; it reads, "If time permits, they commence with the *Eprologhon*, which is Ⲉⲩⲗⲟⲅⲓⲥⲁⲑⲉ. If time is of a constraint, they

---

[699] Pope Gabriel V did not mention this hymn in his order of the liturgy; however, he cites the melismatic rendition in the rite of the Baptism, and that of the Enthronement of Bishops. Ibid. 117, 207. It is important to note that there are two viewpoints with regards to this hymn. The first views it as a response for the Pauline lesson, in which case it should be recited in every liturgy. The second, which is supported by manuscripts as will be explained, considers it a hymn dedicated for the high priests, and therefore, is only used in the presence of the patriarch or a bishop. Per the second theory, which is the more popular, Ⲧⲉⲛⲟⲩⲱϣⲧ is the Pauline respond.
[700] Vatican, Vat, MS Copte 38 (AD 1370-1378), fol. 28r.
[701] *Eprologhon* is the last word of the first stanza; it means "prelude" or "introduction."
[702] Jeremiah (Hegumen), *The Church Order*, Cairo, Patriarchal Library, MS Lit. 73 (AD 1444), fol. 75v.
[703] Ibid., fol. 76v.

read (chant) **Πιϩμοτ ϭαρ μ̅Φ̅ϯ Φιωτ... Ϫ̅ενοτωϣτ.**"[704] *The Church Order* of the Paromaos monastery (AD 1514) agrees with MS Lit. 117; however, it indicates that **Πιϩμοτ ϭαρ** is the optional one chanted if time permits. Finally, MS 302 (AD 1661) places the hymn of the Virtues between **Ετλοϭιϲαθε** and **Πιϩμοτ ϭαρ**.[705]

From all of the above, we understand that **Ετλοϭιϲαθε**, **Πιϩμοτ ϭαρ**, and the hymn of the Virtues are all hymns chanted in the presence of the high priest if time permits. While agreeing on **Ετλοϭιϲαθε** being sung first, sources do not agree on the order of the other chants. Due to its significance, I will provide the full text[706] of the hymn **Ετλοϭιϲαθε** along with its English and Arabic translation.

Ετλοϭιϲαθε εκτης προς Εβρεος επιϲτολε Παυλου το αϭιο αποϲτολου προλοϭου.	Bless. From the Epistle of Saint Paul to the Hebrews. Prelude.	باركـوا. مـن رســالة العبرانيين للقــديس بــولس الرسول، مقدمة.
Εοϭον ν̅ταν οϭν μμαϭ ν̅οϭνιϣϯ ν̅αρχηερεϭϲ εαϥϲεν νιφηοϭι Ιηϲοϭϲ Π̅ϣηρι μ̅Φ̅νοϭϯ μαρεναμονι μ̅πιοϭωνϩ εβολ.	Having then a great *high priest* who passed through the heavens, Jesus the Son of God, let us lay hold on the confession.	فــإذ لنــا رئيس كهنة عظيم اجتــاز السـماوات، يســوع ابــن الله فلنتمسَّــك بالاعتراف به.
Μαρενι εϧοϭν ϧεν οϭωνϩ εβολ μ̅πεμθο μ̅πιθρονος ν̅τε πιϩμοτ ϩινα ν̅τενϭι ν̅οϭναι	Let us, therefore, come boldly to the throne of grace, that we may	فلنتقــدَّم بثقــةٍ إلى عــرشِ النعمــةِ لكــي

---

[704] *The Church Order*, Cairo, Patriarchal Library, MS Lit. 117 (AD 1910), fol. 22r.
[705] *The Church Order*, St. Anthony Monastery, MS 302 (AD 1661), fols. 366v-368v.
[706] This text is based on *The Church Order*, MS Lit. 73 (1444 AD) of the Patriarchate in Cairo. Other manuscripts provide additional stanzas, or different selection of verses.

oyog ntenxiwi noyg̀wot eỳeykepia wbohoia.	obtain mercy and find grace to help in time of need.	ننـالَ رحمـةً ونجـدَ نعمـةً وعـوناً في حينه.
Oyog wpape oyai 6i naq wpitaio wwayaty alla aqoywgew wwoq nxe Ⲫnoyt̀ kata ỳphti nAapwn.	No one takes this honor to himself, but who God called, as Aaron.	ولا يأخذُ أحدٌ هذه الكرامة بنفسِهِ، بل الـذي دعـاهُ الله مثل هرون.
Pairhti gwq Pixpictoc netaqtwoy naq wwayaty an eopeqywpi eqoi napxhpeyc alla ⲫh pe etaqcaxi newaq xe noʼok pe pashpi anok ai̓xⲫok wⲫooy.	So, Christ did not glorify Himself to become *high priest*, but it was He Who said to Him: "You are my son; today I have begotten You."	كـذلك المسيح لم يمجّـد ذاتَـه ليصيـرَ رئيسَ كهنـةٍ، بـل الـذي قـال لـه: أنـتَ ابنـي أنا اليومَ ولدتُكَ.
Kata ỳphti etaqxw wwoc ben kewa xe noʼok pe ⲫoyhb sa eneg kata t̀tazic wwelxicedek.	As He also says in another place: "You are the *priest* forever according to the order of Melchizedek."	كما يقول في موضعٍ آخر: أنتَ الكاهنُ إلى الأبدِ علـى طقـسِ ملكيصادَق.
Pi̓g̀wot ⲅap wⲪnoyt̀ Ⲫiwt piPantokpatwp : new t̀xapic nte peqwonoⲅenhc n̓shpi Ihcoyc Pixpictoc Penʼo6c : new t̀koinwnia new t̀dwpea nte	The grace of God, the Father, the Pantocrator, and the grace of His Only-Begotten Son, Jesus Christ our Lord, and the communion and	نعمـةُ الله الآب ضـابط الكلِّ وموهبة ابنِهِ الوحيـد يسـوع المسـيح ربنـا. شركـة وعطيـة

Coptic	English	Arabic
Ⲡⲓⲡⲛⲉⲩⲙⲁ ⲉⲑⲟⲩⲁⲃ ⲙ̀Ⲡⲁⲣⲁⲕⲗⲏⲧⲟⲛ: ⲉϥⲉ̀ⲓ̀ ⲉ̀ϧⲣⲏⲓ ⲉ̀ϫⲉⲛ ⲧ̀ⲁⲫⲉ ⲙ̀ⲡⲓⲙⲁⲕⲁⲣⲓⲟⲥ ⲛ̀ⲓⲱⲧ ⲉⲧⲧⲁⲓⲏⲟⲩⲧ ⲛ̀ⲁⲣⲭⲏⲉⲣⲉⲩⲥ ⲡⲁⲡⲁ ⲁⲃⲃⲁ (...)	the gift of the Holy Spirit, the Paraclete, shall come upon the head of our blessed and honorable father, the high priest, Abba (...).	الـروح القـدس المعـزِّي، تحـلُّ على رأس أبينـا الطـوباوي المكـرَّم رئيس الكهنـة أنبـا (...).
Ⲫ̀ⲛⲟⲩϯ ⲛ̀ⲧⲉ ⲧ̀ⲫⲉ ⲉϥⲉ̀ⲧⲁϫⲣⲟϥ ϩⲓϫⲉⲛ ⲡⲉϥⲑⲣⲟⲛⲟⲥ ⲛ̀ϩⲁⲛⲙⲏϣ ⲛ̀ⲣⲟⲙⲡⲓ ⲛⲉⲙ ϩⲁⲛⲥⲏⲟⲩ ⲛ̀ϩⲓⲣⲏⲛⲓⲕⲟⲛ.	May the God of heaven confirm him on his throne for many years and peaceful times.	إلـهُ السمـاء يُثبِّتـه على كرسيـه سنينـاً عديـدةً وأزمنةً سالمةً.
Ⲛ̀ⲧⲉϥⲑⲉⲃⲓⲟ ⲛ̀ⲛⲉϥϫⲁϫⲓ ⲧⲏⲣⲟⲩ ⲥⲁⲡⲉⲥⲏⲧ ⲛ̀ⲛⲉϥϭⲁⲗⲁⲩϫ ⲛ̀ⲭⲱⲗⲉⲙ: ⲧⲱⲃϩ ⲉ̀Ⲡⲭ̅ⲥ̅ ⲉ̀ϩⲣⲏⲓ ⲉ̀ϫⲱⲛ ⲛ̀ⲧⲉϥⲭⲁ ⲛⲉⲛⲛⲟⲃⲓ ⲛⲁⲛ ⲉ̀ⲃⲟⲗ.	And subdue all of his enemies under his feet speedily. Pray to Christ on our behalf that He may forgive us our sins.	ويُخضِـع جميع أعـداءه تحت قدميه سـريعاً. أطلُب من المسيح عنَّا ليغفر لنا خطايانا.

After this, from the southern lectern and facing west (toward the congregation), the Pauline is read in the vernacular. Ibn Sibaa and Ibn Kabar, among other source, outline an old custom of, following reading the Pauline in the vernacular, the priest, standing at the door of the sanctuary, and the altar server standing on his right, recites the introduction to the litanies followed by the orison of "O Lord of knowledge and provider of wisdom," to which the people respond saying, "Lord have mercy." This profound and beautiful prayer was once prayed aloud. In it, the priest entreats the Lord saying, "Grant us and all Your people a mind free from wandering and a clear understanding that we may know and understand how profitable are Your holy teachings which are now read to us through him." This wonderful petition is now uttered inaudibly, a practice that most likely arose during the pontificate of Pope Gabriel V (15th century). In his book *The Ritual Order*, Pope Gabriel V states, "The Pauline is then chanted by one of the deacons, followed by its Arabic translation, during which the Assistant Priest prays 'O Lord of knowledge.' If the Servant Priest is the only one praying, then he prays it."[707]

In the Second Litany of the Pauline, the priest prays, "O Lord of knowledge and provider of wisdom, who reveals the deep things out darkness and gives a word to those who preach with great power; who of Your kindness has called upon Paul, who was for some time a persecutor, to be a chosen vessel; and in this You were pleased that he should be called to be an apostle and a preacher of the Gospel of Your Kingdom, O Christ our God." He continues, "You also now, O Good one and Lover of Mankind, we ask You, grant us and all Your people a mind free from wandering and a clear understanding that we may know and understand how profitable are your holy teachings which are now read to us through him." Therefore, while the congregation is listening to the Pauline reading, the priest, from inside the sanctuary, is beseeching God to enlighten their hearts and bestow them with His spiritual gifts, not the least of which is a mind "free of wandering" and a "clear understanding" in order to comprehend the holy teachings of Saint Paul. The priest then continues, "Make us also worthy to be like him in deed and in faith that we may glorify Your holy name and glory in Your Cross at all times," particularly

---

[707] Gabriel V (Pope), *The Ritual Order*, BnF, MS 98 (AD 1411), fol. 55r.

since it was Saint Paul who said, "May I never boast except in the cross of our Lord Jesus Christ" (Galatians 6:14).[708]

The Catholic Epistle

After the Pauline, the responsory for the Catholic Epistle, Ⲡⲉⲧϫⲏⲕ ⲉⲃⲟⲗ (Perfect is), is chanted. This chant was not known in Cairo or documented in Lower Egypt sources. However, Cantor Mikhail Girgis of Batanoun brought it from Mallawy in El-Minya in Upper Egypt and transmitted it to his disciples. The interesting thing is that, according to the departed Dr. Ragheb Habashi Moftah,[709] Cantor Mikhail learned it from Saloma (Salome), a blind female chanter, who used to teach hymns at her parish.[710] This is then followed by chanting part of the Catholic Epistle in Coptic and then reading it in its entirety in the vernacular. This lesson is a pericope from the epistle of Saint James, the two from Saint Peter, the three written by Saint John the Beloved, or the epistle authored by Saint Jude. Ibn Sibaa states, "Then, the archdeacon of the parish, who is the head deacon, instructs one of the sub-deacons to read the Catholic Epistle, since the Catholic Epistle is of a higher position than the Pauline. Therefore, it is read by a sub-deacon who is of a higher rank than a reader. After this, the translation of the epistle is read by someone who is capable of doing very well."[711] This thirteen's century testimony reveals a different practice from

---

[708] The Coptic Orthodox Church puts huge emphasis on associating prayers with the reading of the Scriptures. This is also apparent in the Litany of the Gospel, where the priest pleads for enlightenment of the worshippers so they "may be worthy not only to be hearers but also to act according to Your holy commandments."

[709] Dr. Ragheb Moftah (AD 1898–2001) was an Egyptian musicologist and scholar of the Coptic music heritage. He sponsored and supervised the most comprehensive recordings of Coptic hymns on tapes in the twentieth century. In 1927 he invited Professor Ernest Newlandsmith from London, who transcribed most of the Coptic hymns heritage between the years 1928 and 1936. He based all this work on the teaching of Cantor Mikhail the Great.

[710] In his 1966 work *Along with the Civilian Movement* (مع التموجات المدنية), historian Anwar Al-Sanadiky (AD 1918-2007) mentioned that chanter Saloma was born in AD 1870 and departed around AD 1950.

[711] Ibn Sibaa, *The Precious Pearl: On Ecclesiastic Science*, BnF, MS Arabic 207, fol. 129r

the current one where lections are not appointed to specific ranks. It should be noted that there are no circuits during this lesson, and incense is not offered. This is a reminder of the Lord's commandment to the apostles to stay in Jerusalem until the descent of the Holy Spirit.[712]

Ibn Sibaa then continues, "After the Catholic Epistle, the altar server instructs the congregation to stand up for prayer as usual,[713] after which the priest enters the sanctuary and presents the coffer of incense to the high priest to bless it… then he says a prayer pertaining to God's acceptance to the Abraham's sacrifice."[714] This is an important attestation demonstrating that until, at least, the 13th century, the Litany of the Catholic Epistle was pronounced aloud immediately after the lesson is read in the vernacular, as opposed to the present practice of praying it inaudibly while the lection is being read. It is likely that the custom of praying this litany silently emerged in the 15th century as testified by Pope Gabriel V, who states, "After the reading of the Coptic Catholic Epistle, and while it is being read in Arabic, the Servant Priest prays the litany of the Catholic Epistle inaudibly 'O Lord our God, who through Your holy apostles…'"[715] Marquis comments, "A common, though corrupt, practice is for the Priest to say the Prayer of the Catholic Epistle immediately after that of S. Paul, and then to go and sit down until the reading of the Catholic Epistle in Arabic is over."[716] It is worth noting that, unlike the Litany of the Pauline that is directed toward God the Son, this litany is addressed to God the Father. A commonality between the two

---

[712] "I am going to send you what my Father has promised; but stay in the city until you have been clothed with power from on high" (Luke 24:49).
[713] This is an indication to the standard introduction to the litanies: the priest requests from the altar server saying, "Pray," to which he responds by instructing the congregation to "Stand up for prayer." The priest then greets the worshippers saying, "Peace be with all," to which they respond, "And with your spirit." All this proves that the following orison, which is the Litany of the Catholic Epistle, was prayed out loud at the time.
[714] Ibn Sibaa, *The Precious*, Ibid., fols. 129v-130r
[715] Gabriel V (Pope), *The Ritual Order*, BnF, MS 98 (AD 1411), fol. 55r.
[716] John, Marquis of Bute, *The Coptic Morning Service for the Lord's Day*, 68.

litanies, though, is that both are performed without accompanied by incense offering.

The Litany of the Catholic Epistle helps the worshipers recall the gifts of the Holy Spirit that the Apostles received on Pentecost so they may preach the *good news* to the whole world. In doing so, the priest prays, "...and have given to them according to the great immeasurable gift of Your grace that they should proclaim among all nations the glad tidings of the unsearchable riches of Your mercy." As such, the priest, representing the entire congregation, beseeches the Lord to grant all attendees the power of evangelizing His holy name to the world. He pleads, "Grant to us all times to walk in their footsteps and to imitate their struggle." This "struggle" refers to their evangelism—which is every true Christian's duty—that is the vocation of the faithful, as the light of the world. The priest then continues, "and to have communion with them in the sweat which they accepted for the sake of godliness." Here, the priest prays for worshippers to join the Apostles in their mission of preaching the word of God in all places. However, with this ministry, it is anticipated that, attempting to stop it, the devil's war against the children of God will ignite. Hence, the priest implores the Lord, "Watch over Your holy church which You have founded through them and bless the sheep of Your flock and make this vine to increase, which Your right hand has planted." The "vine" refers to the church that the Lord Himself instituted and entrusted to the apostles to grow and flourish.

The Praxis Epistle

Next, the people, led by the chorus, chant the Praxis response. The 14th century scholar Ibn Kabar instructs that the responsory during Regular

Days is "Ϫοτε ⲁⲗⲏⲑⲱⲥ,"[717] the sixth quatrain in the sixth section of the Sunday Theotokion.[718] In the 15th century, however, Pope Gabriel V writes, "After the reading of the translation of the Catholic Epistle, they chant the hymn 'Ϣⲁⲣⲉ Ⲫϯ ⲱⲗⲓ ⲙⲙⲁⲩ,'[719] followed by Ⲕ̀ⲥⲙⲁⲣⲱⲟⲩⲧ (Blessed are You). Otherwise, they only chant Ⲕ̀ⲥⲙⲁⲣⲱⲟⲩⲧ."[720] *The Church Order* of the Paromaos Monastery (AD 1514) agrees with Pope Gabriel's testimony; it states, "After reading the Catholic Epistle, they chant Ϣⲁⲣⲉ Ⲫϯ."[721] The use of Ϣⲁⲣⲉ Ⲫϯ ⲱⲗⲓ ⲙⲙⲁⲩ, which is the eighth quatrain in the sixth section of the Sunday Theotokion, is now limited to the Fast of Nineveh and Lenten weekdays (except for the first and last days of Lent).

It was not until AD 1899 when Father Abd El-Messih El-Massoody of the Paromeos Monastery compiled all a diversity of Praxis responds for all ecclesiastical seasons that include the renowned respond Ⲭⲉⲣⲉ ⲛⲉ Ⲙⲁⲣⲓⲁ̀ for Regular Days.[722] Yet, in his AD 1902 Euchologion, Father Abd El-Messih El-Massoody prescribes Ϣⲁⲣⲉ Ⲫϯ or Ϫοτε ⲁⲗⲏⲑⲱⲥ as primary responsories, then adds a note indicating the option to use the other emergent ones.[723] Today, we have even more responsories for the angels, apostles, martyrs, and saints. As for their melodies, other than Ϣⲁⲣⲉ Ⲫϯ, all these responses share the same tune regardless of the ecclesiastical occasion. Additionally, if time permits, a melismatic melody may optionally be employed.[724]

---

[717] Translation: Wherefore truly, I do not err, whenever I call you, the golden censer.
[718] Ibn Kabar, *The Lamp*, BnF, MS Arabic 203 (c. AD 1363-1369), fol. 206r.
[719] Translation: Wherein God takes away, the sins of the people, through the burnt offerings, and the aroma of incense.
[720] Gabriel V (Pope), *The Ritual Order*, BnF, MS 98 (AD 1411), fol. 55r.
[721] Samuel (Bishop), *The Church Order*, Part 1, 22.
[722] The Churches Revival Association, *Deacon Service Book—Third Edition*, 6.
[723] Salib, Abdel Massieh (Hegumen), *The Holy Euchologion*, 254.
[724] This melismatic tune is primarily focused on the first and fourth lines of each quatrain of the response. However, it is left to the discretion of the chanters to employ it for all quatrain or just some, and to both first and fourth lines or either one.

This is then followed by a lesson from the Book of Acts (Praxis). Andrew McGowan asserts that reading from Acts in a communal setting began at Hippo[725] probably in the fourth century.[726] In the Coptic Rite, it is first chanted in Coptic before it is read in the vernacular. The Coptic verses are delivered from the northern lectern as the chanter faces the east while the translation is uttered from the southern lectern facing west toward the people. The melody for this lection remains unchanged regardless of the season, except for Holy Thursday, during which a sorrowful—and very lengthy—tune is appointed.

While the Praxis lesson is being recited, the priest places one spoonful of incense in the censer and quietly, if was not prayed during Prime Offering of Incense, utters the Litany of the Oblations, followed by that of the Praxis. Prior to the AD 1902 Euchologion, sources did not prescribe the former litany in this location, indicating that it was a nascent innovation. As such, in a footnote in his Euchologion, *Hegumen* Abdel Messiah El-Masoody states, "there is an opinion that, if was not prayed during the Prime Offering of incense, the Litany of the Oblations is prayed prior to that of the Praxis."[727] Whether the Litany of the Oblations is said of not, the Litany of the Praxis is prayed.

This orison correlates the sacrifice of the Lord Jesus Christ to that of Abraham, since latter, like God the Father, gave up his only son Isaac as a burnt offering.[728] In the same manner that Isaac returned alive, so to was Christ who rose from the dead. In this prayer, the priest says, "O God, who accepted the burnt offering of Abraham, and prepared for him a sheep in

---

[725] Hippo, called today Annaba. Now, it is in Algeria (North Africa). Hippo was the capital city of the Vandal Kingdom from AD 435–439. until it was shifted to Carthage (today in Tunisia) following the Vandal Capture of Carthage (AD 439). Hippo was an important city in early Christianity where three church councils were held.
[726] McGowan, Andrew B., *Ancient Christian Worship*, 101.
[727] Salib, Abdel Massieh (*Hegumen*), *The Holy Euchologion*, 251.
[728] Genesis 22:2-19, Hebrews 11:17-19.

Isaac's stead, even so, again, accept at our hand, O our Master, the burnt offering of this incense, and send down upon us in return for it Your abundant mercy, cleansing us from every stench of sin, and make us worthy to serve in holiness and righteousness before Your goodness, O Lover of Mankind, all the days of our life." Through this petition, the worshippers entreat God to purify them, and accept the aroma of their prayers, incense, and repentance, and not the stench of their sins. They pray that the Lord may grant them His everlasting mercy, for without it, repentance is in vain. They earnestly plead His mercy and grace as He granted them to Isaac and brought him from death to life. Likewise, with prayerful tears, congregants importune the Lord to rescue them from the death of sin and grant them the life of genuine repentance.

Thereafter, the priest circumambulates the altar thrice before existing the sanctuary to offer incense at its door. He then offers incense, respectively, at the southern and northern lecterns, before the relics of saints, and to the bishop, if present. The priest then proceeds toward the southern portion of the parish and offers incense. Unlike the Pauline Circuit, the priest does not offer incense in the nave; hence, some interpret this a circuit as a special blessing to the *servants*.[729] While censing, the priest, inaudibly, recites the prayer, "A blessing of my lords and fathers the apostles, namely our father Peter and our teacher Paul, and the rest of the disciples. May their holy blessings be with us, Amen." He then proceeds to the northern section of the parish and offers incense in the same manner. Finally, he returns to the door of the sanctuary and, facing eastward, says the Prayer of Confession.

It is noteworthy that during the Praxis Circuit the priest first censes the southern section, where traditionally women stand, then the northern

---

[729] Misael of the Paromeos Monastery (Father). (2018). The Beginners' Guide and Discipline for Laity. *Alexandria School, 25(2)*, 130.

portion of the parish, where customarily men stand. This is the exact opposite order performed during the Pauline Circuit. Some construe this as an implementation of the verse, "In the Lord woman is not independent of man, nor is man independent of woman. For as woman came from man, so also man is born of woman. But everything comes from God." (Corinthians 11:11, 12).[730] It is also noticeable that the Praxis Circuit is only limited to the chancel, as opposed to the Pauline Circuit, which also includes the nave. This serves as a reminder that the Apostles' ministry was chiefly focused in Judea and Jerusalem, as opposed to Saint Paul's, who preached to the gentiles in a diversity of countries and cities.[731] As previously noted, the priest does not immediately return to the sanctuary, but rather prays the Litany of Confession at its door. Although, in the past this practice did not have any symbolical significance,[732] a figurative exegesis is now assigned to it; in it, not immediately returning to the sanctuary is compared to the Apostles, in preaching the gospel, not returning to Jerusalem, but rather receiving martyrdom.[733]

The Pauline Circuit includes four circumambulations around the altar, whereas Praxis Circuit encompasses three,[734] totaling seven circuits. *The Trinitarian Mystery in Priesthood Ministry*, authored in the Middle Ages, provides an exegesis of this total. It reads, "He (the priest) circles the altar to complete seven circuits, which symbolize the number of times the Israelites, led by Joshua the son of Nun, a disciple of Moses, circled Jericho before the Lord tumbled down its walls. The fathers placed the seven circuits to defeat the enemy, and the knock down of the walls of sin. Afterwards, the priest offers incense amid the chanters and the clergy only,

---

[730] Mettaos (Bishop), *The Spirituality of the Rite of the Liturgy of the Coptic Orthodox Church*, 123.
[731] Mettaos, Ibid., 123.
[732] Misael, Ibid., 130.
[733] Mettaos, Ibid., 123.
[734] Some explain this number to symbolize the four Gospels. See: Church Teachers, *The Trinitarian Mystery in Priesthood Ministry*, Philotheos, Girgis (Ed.), 13.

and does not return to the sanctuary, since he has already completed seven circuits."[735]

The Synaxarion

Afterward, the priest reads the chronicles of the saints, the Synaxarion (Latin: Synaxarium or Synexarium). The word "Synaxarion" is derived from the Greek origin Συναξάριον from (συνάγειν, synagein) meaning "to bring together." It is a book containing abbreviated hagiography and martyrology of the Church as well as the commemorations of her feasts. It is well known in the East. The first extant Synaxarion, written in Coptic, dates to the 6th century, and was found in the city of Oxyrhynchus.[736] The First Arabic Synaxarion, however, was written by Abba Peter (the Handsome), Bishop of Mileige, in the 12th or 13th century. The second oldest one was authored by Bishop Mikhail of Atirb and Melig (AD 1243–1247) and other bishops as attested by MS Arab 2139, preserved at the Austrian National Library in Vienna.[737] The first printed Synaxarion was promulgated in AD 1935. It was authored by two monks, Father Abd Al-Masseih Mikhail, and Farther Armanyos Habashi Shata Al-Barmawi.

The Synaxarion was originally read after the Prime Offering of Incense gospel lesson, which is a common practice in the East. Hence, while describing the order of reading the gospel during Prime Offering of Incense, Ibn Kabar states, "The Arabic translation is read; in Prime, this is followed by reading a chapter from the Synaxarion, which is the saints' biography and history. This is proceeded with the three prayers and what follows."[738] Additionally, while expounding the Liturgy of the Word

---

[735] Church Teachers, *The Trinitarian Mystery in Priesthood Ministry*, Philotheos, Girgis (Ed.), 14.
[736] Oxyrhynchus (Arabic: el-Bahnasa—البهنسا) is a city in Upper Egypt, located about 160 km south-southwest of Cairo, in the governorate of Al Minya.
[737] Sobhy, Basilious (Father), *Introduction to the History of Coptic Rites*, 40, 41.
[738] Ibn Kabar, *The Lamp*, BnF, MS Arabic 203 (c. AD 1363-1369), fol. 199v.

proper, Ibn Kabar instructs, "After reading the translation of the Praxis, Ⲁⲅⲓⲟⲥ (Holy) is chanted,"[739] with no mention of the Synaxarion. This same order was confirmed by Pope Gabriel V as he writes, "After the Praxis is read in Coptic and Arabic, they chant Ⲁⲅⲓⲟⲥ, that is, the Trisagion."[740]

Most probably the reading of the Synaxarion[741] was placed after the Praxis lesson in the 17th century.[742] The reordering of the service readings may have been attributed to the low attendance at Prime Offering of Incense. Another reason is perhaps to deliver a lucid message that connects both lections, that is, the Synaxarion is an extension to the Book of Acts. The preaching of the Apostles was a perquisite to the courageous martyrdoms, the monastic pursuits, and the pastoral work of patriarchs. Thus, it seemed natural to place the Synaxarion after the Praxis lesson.

The only period in which the Synaxarion is not read is Eastertide as the Church is primarily focused on the Lord's resurrection.[743] In addition, the Synaxarion is not read on Maundy Thursday or Bright Saturday, because during this time, the Church is solely preoccupied with the passion and death of the Lord. After this, the saint(s) of the day may be venerated. Formerly, the Veneration Service belongs to Prime Offering of Incense, specifically, following the gospel and Synaxarion,[744] nevertheless, as the placement of the Synaxarion changed, saints' venerations also followed.

---

[739] Ibn Kabar, Ibid., fol. 206r.
[740] Gabriel V (Pope), *The Ritual Order*, BnF, MS 98 (AD 1411), fol. 55v.
[741] In the first fifteen days of the Coptic month, the introduction to the Synaxarion reads, "May God begin it in goodness and renew it for us in peace and tranquility," whereas the later fifteen days, it is, "May God end it in goodness and renew it for us in peace and tranquility."
[742] Athanasius of Saint Macarius Monastery (Father), *The Divine Liturgy: The Mystery of the Kingdom of God (Part 1)*, 467.
[743] Festal seasons, in general, preserve ancient liturgical elements. In this case, not reading the Synaxarion during Eastertide is also a vestige of the immemorial tradition of not including it during the liturgy, as noted earlier.
[744] The original placement of the Veneration Service was at the end of the Vespers Offering of Incense, right before the conclusion of the prayer. Later, this was changed to the Prime service before moving it to its current location during the Liturgy of the Word.

The Liturgy of the Word

Chants Attributable to the Trisagion

If time permits, the hymn, Ⲫⲛⲁⲩ ⲙ̀ⲡⲓⲥⲙⲟⲩ (The time of praise), also called *Mohayyer*[745] (Arabic: مُحَيَّر), is said in Regular Days. Ⲫⲛⲁⲩ ⲙ̀ⲡⲓⲥⲙⲟⲩ was cited by Ibn Kabar[746] among others. This hymn is the derivation of all other *Mohayyer* hymns for all seasons. The last two stanzas of this chant[747] are the same for Lent. Possibly this replication occurred when this hymn was excluded from Regular Days threatening of its extinction; thence, the last two quatrains were appointed to conclude the Lenten *Mohayyer*. This explains the obvious irrelevance of these two quatrains to the other six stanzas belonging to the original Lenten *Mohayyer*.[748] Fortunately, there is a rare recording of this *Mohayyer* by Cantor Wadee El-Kommos Matta.[749] Another rendition of the hymn was preserved in the Upper Egypt village of Zenia. It was recorded by a number of chanters, the most prominent of whom is Cantor William Stephanos (AD 1938–2020).[750] Whether or not the hymn Ⲫⲛⲁⲩ ⲙ̀ⲡⲓⲥⲙⲟⲩ is chanted, Ⲁ̀ⲅⲓⲟⲥ is said.

It is imperative to note that rubric, in all sources until the beginning of the 20th century, place the *Mohayyer* following the Trisagion (Ⲁ̀ⲅⲓⲟⲥ),

---

[745] The literal translation of the word *Mohayyer* (Arabic: محير) is "confusing" or "hesitant" It is used to identify those hymns that have medium-size tunes (not recitative nor melismatic). For this reason, they are described as "hesitant." This name is fairly new (20th century) and was not mentioned in the manuscripts; it was rather called "Aspazmos" or "Stanzas chanted with the cymbals."

[746] Ibn Kabar (Priest), *The Lamp*, BnF, MS 203 Arabic, fol. 206r.

[747] "Ⲟⲩⲥ̀ⲑⲟⲓⲛⲟⲩϥⲓ" and "Ⲙⲁⲣⲉⲛϩⲱⲥ." Translation of the first stanza is "The incense is Mary, the incense is in her womb, which she will borne, to forgive us our sins." Translation of the second one is "Let us praise with the angels, proclaiming and saying, 'Worthy, worthy, worthy O Mary the Virgin.'"

[748] The first four stanzas of the *Mohayyer* of the Lent talk about how Jesus fasted for us 40 days and 40 nights; and encourage the faithful to follow His example. Then they give glory to Jesus. On the other hand, the last two stanzas talk about venerating Saint Mary.

[749] Cantor Wadee El-Kommos Matta served at the Church of Saint Mary in Tahta, Sohag in Upper Egypt. He departed in AD 2001.

[750] Cantor William Stephanos was born in AD 1938 in Zenia, Luxor in Upper Egypt. At the age of 7, he joined the village school (Arabic: كُتّاب) where he memorized all 150 psalms. He received the Church chants from his predecessors, respectively, Cantor Gabriel, Cantor Nadheer Gattas, and Cantor Mehanna Ekladius. At the age of 12, Cantor William was hired by Father Armanios as the cantor of the church of Saint Pachomius.

whereas now they are swapped. Studying the hymn Ⲫⲛⲁⲩ ⲙ̀ⲡⲓⲥⲙⲟⲩ can shed some light on a possible resolution to the discrepancy, and find the reason behind the change. Examining the meaning of the hymn Ⲫⲛⲁⲩ ⲙ̀ⲡⲓⲥⲙⲟⲩ, we can effortlessly infer that its chief subject is the "incense." Thus, rubric places it at the time the priest is about to offer incense for the Litany of the Gospel, that is, after the Trisagion. MS Lit. 73 includes Ⲫⲛⲁⲩ ⲙ̀ⲡⲓⲥⲙⲟⲩ among the hymns recited during the Hagiography Reading Service, specifically, during the reading of the biography of the saint.[751] This clue helped me develop this hypothesis which might explicate the reason for the change. In the beginning of the 20th century, when many *ordos* and hymns were revised for the purpose of unification among churches through the publication of ecclesiastical books, the reviewers might have noticed the inclusion of the hymn in study in the Hagiography Reading Service, specifically during the reading of the hagiography in the vernacular. Hence, it made since to preserve this connotation and make Ⲫⲛⲁⲩ ⲙ̀ⲡⲓⲥⲙⲟⲩ attributable to the Synaxarion as opposed to the Trisagion. Being the earliest *Mohayyer*, the new placement of Ⲫⲛⲁⲩ ⲙ̀ⲡⲓⲥⲙⲟⲩ set a precedence for all seasonal *Mohayyer* chants. Although Ⲫⲛⲁⲩ ⲙ̀ⲡⲓⲥⲙⲟⲩ had a significant vocation in the Church liturgical services, in general, and the liturgy, in specific, it is now threatened with almost total disappearance. It is this generation's responsibility to regenerate it and rediscover its importance.

In the Sahidic tradition, we find an additional old hymnic element—a group of chants, mostly written in Greek—that used the Trisagion as its framework. The syntactic flow of the hymn is interrupted with phrases from the Trisagion.

---

[751] Jeremiah (Hegumen), *The Church Order*, Cairo, Patriarchal Library, MS Lit. 73 (AD 1444), fol. 28r.

David G. Martinez comments, "We certainly have a case of *contaminatio*—a pre-existent acrostic poem with the Trisagion interposed upon it."[752] These chants precede the Trisagion. Examples of this category include, but not limited to: ἀρχὴ χαὶ τῶν μοναχὼν (Founding chief of monks),[753] ὁ διὰ τοῦ ἀρχαγγέλου (Who archangel),[754] χαῖρε Ἰωάννη (Hail to John),[755] ἀστὴρ ἐξ οὐρανοῦ (A star from heaven),[756] Ⲭⲉⲣⲉ Ⲡⲁϭⲱⲙ (Hail to Pachom),[757] Ⲙⲉⲧⲁ ⲧⲏⲛ ⲙⲉⲧⲁⲗⲩⲯⲓⲛ (Afterward, we partake),[758] Ⲇⲟⲝⲁ ⲥⲟⲓ Ⲭ̅ⲥ̅ ⲁⲡⲟⲥⲧⲟⲗⲱⲛ ⲕⲁⲩⲭⲏⲙⲁ (Glory to You, O Christ, the pride of the apostles),[759] Μεγάλος ἀρχιερεὺς (The great High Priest), Ὁ μονογενὴς (O Only-Begotten Son),[760] and ἀξιωθέντες (We

---

[752] Martinez, David G., *P. Michigan XIX. Baptized for Our Sakes: A Leather Trisagion from Egypt (P. Mich. 799)*, 44.

[753] This parchment leaf probably from the White Monastery of Shenoute at Atripe (Sohag), Vienna, MS Coptic K9740. The hymn is for Saint Shenoute the Archimandrite (AD 348-466). See: Maccoull, L.S.B. (1989), STUD. PAL. XV 250ab: A Monophysite Trisagion for the Nile Flood, *The Journal of Theological Studies*, Volume 40, Issue 1, 129-132.

[754] This chant addresses the annunciation to St. Mary, nativity of Christ, and His ascension. It is preserved on a papyrus from the 6th century (approximately). Possible origin of the manuscript is Luxor. See: Di Bitonto Kasser, Anna (1999), Due nuovi testi cristiani. *Aegyptus*, Anno 79, No. 1/2, 97.

[755] This hymn, scribed in Greek and Sahidic, is chanted in the festival of John the Baptist. The manuscript containing the text is preserved at the British Museum (or 5465[SCH 5665]). As determined by Crum, the provenance of this manuscript is the village of Duwinah, Assuit region. See: Youssef, Youhanna Nessim & Soliman, Sameh Farouk (2017), A Copto-Greek Hymn for John the Baptist. *Ephemerides Liturgicae* 131, 80-91.

[756] This chant treats the birth narrative of Christ, His baptism, passion, and ascension. It was preserved on a piece of leather, probably from the 7th century. See: Martinez, David G., *P. Michigan XIX. Baptized for Our Sakes: A Leather Trisagion from Egypt (P. Mich. 799)*, 38, 39.

[757] This hymn is for Saint Pachomius, came from White Monastery of Shenoute at Atripe (Sohag), BnF, MS Copte 20-129 (c. 9th C.).

[758] Borgia 109 Cass. XXIV, fasc. 104, fol. 4v, pag. 200, lines. 1-4.

[759] John Ryl. 20[a], fol. 1v (ⲕⲃ̅), 1-13; See Helmy, Michael. (2020). Byzantine Influences on a Group of Coptic Chants in the Psalter and the Antiphonary. *Alexandria School*, 29(2), 103.

[760] This hymn is one of the earliest chants in the Church. It was in use since the 4th or 5th century. Different Churches attribute it to different authors, including Athanasius of Alexandria (Pope from AD 328 to 373), Emperor Justinian (reigned from AD 527 to 565), and Severus of Antioch (Patriarch from 512 to 538 AD). Due to its Christological significance, the hymn of "O Only-Begotten Son" is chanted in both families of Orthodoxy. In the Eastern Orthodox Churches, it is chanted in the introductory portion of the liturgy. Some studies show that this was also the old practice in the Coptic Church before it was removed from the Eucharistic services (See: Ignatius Ephrem II Rahmani (Patriarch of the Syriac Catholic Church), *Les Liturgies Orientales et Occidentales*, 550). In the Alexandrian rendition of the hymn, a fusion of the Trisagion was added to the common part used in both Orthodox families. The extension reads, "*Holy God*, who being God, for our sake, became man without change. *Holy Mighty*, who by weakness showed forth what is greater than power. *Holy*

deserved).⁷⁶¹ Only the latter three found their way to the Lower Egypt tradition and survived extinction.⁷⁶²

The Trisagion

The congregation chants the Trisagion (Greek: Τρισάγιον),⁷⁶³ which is a substantially key hymn in all Orthodox Churches. "Trisagion" is a Greek word meaning "Trice Holy." The origin of this chant can be traced back to the Synagogue worship, specifically to a prayer called *Kedushah* (Hebrew: קְדֻשָׁה), meaning "Holiness." Whenever the *Amidah* ⁷⁶⁴ is prayed, the *Kedushah*, which was well established in the Jewish worship in the second century BC, must be recited.⁷⁶⁵ Being part of the Jewish *Synaxis*, the *Kedushah* (Isaiah 6:3, Ezekiel 3:12, and Psalms 146:10) was among other prayers borrowed, after Christianizing, by the church at an early date. Originally, the two Jewish communities (Palestinian and Babylonian) did not agree on the recitation frequency of the *Kedusha* (or Trisagion). The custom of the Jews of Palestine was to recite it only on Sabbaths and festivals; however, the Babylonian tradition instructs that it

---

Immortal, who was crucified for our sake, and endured death in his flesh, the Eternal and Immortal. O Holy Trinity have mercy on us."

⁷⁶¹ BnF, Bnf, MS Copte 129, fol. 116r. This hymn is the fourth stanza of what is known now as "Ⲧⲉⲛⲉⲛ." In antiquity, "Ⲧⲉⲛⲉⲛ," was chanted in the liturgy, not in the Midnight Psalmody, and consisted of three chants each used in a different day. For more details, see: Ragheb, Michael Helmy, A New Reading of the Hymn of the Three Saintly Youth According to the Most Ancient Fragments that Has it. (2018). In *The Ancestors' Heritage in the Eyes of the Descendants*, 1-27.

⁷⁶² "The great High Priest" is reserved for the Great Lent where as the "O only-begotten Son" chant is for Good Friday, Consecration of the Chrism, and Ordination of the Coptic Pope. As for "We deserved," together with two other chants formed the hymn "Ⲧⲉⲛⲉⲛ," which is chanted in the Midnight Psalmody.

⁷⁶³ The Latin name *Tersanctus* or *Ter Sanctus* is sometimes used to refer to this hymn, although this name is also sometimes used to refer to the Sanctus; it is the latter, a different formula, which is used in Western Christianity in the Mass.

⁷⁶⁴ The *Amidah* (Hebrew: תפילת העמידה) is the central prayer of the Jewish liturgy.

⁷⁶⁵ Rudwin, Maximilian J. (1919), The Origin of Judeo-Christian Worship, *The Open Court*, Vol. 1919: Iss. 5, Article 4, 293.

must be said daily. Eventually, the Palestinian practice was deprecated and the Babylonian one prevailed.[766]

In Christianity, the Trisagion is commonly used in the Chalcedonian and non-Chalcedonian Orthodox Churches and is also prayed in the Eastern Catholic Churches. The lyrics of the hymn, according to the Coptic Rite, are "Holy God, holy Mighty, Holy Immortal, born of a virgin, have mercy upon us. Holy God, Holy Mighty, Holy Immortal, crucified for us, have mercy upon us. Holy God, Holy Mighty, Holy immortal, risen from the dead and ascended into the heavens, have mercy upon us. Glory be to the Father, to the Son and to the Holy Spirit, now and ever and unto the ages of the ages, Amen." The text is based on the words of the Bible as written by Isaiah, "and they were calling to one another 'Holy, holy, holy is the Lord Almighty; the whole earth is full of His glory'" (Isaiah 6:3), as well as John the Beloved's account in the Book of Revelation, "each of the four living creatures had six wings and was covered with eyes all around, even under its wings. Day and night, they never stop saying 'Holy, holy, holy is the Lord God Almighty, who was, and is, and is to come'" (Revelation 4:8). The purpose of this chant is to inspire the supplicants to emulate the celestial angels in praising the Lord in reverence and holy trepidation. The intention is to motivate the terrestrial worshippers to engage in the same activity of praising the same song with the heavenly creatures in unison, a praise that was taught to humans by the celestial powers, the Seraphim.

---

[766] Korobkin, N. Daniel (2013), Kedushah, Shema, and the Difference Between Israel and the Angels, *Hakirah 16*, 23-24.

According to Saint John of Damascus,[767] during the rule of Emperor Theodosius II[768] between AD 408 and 450, Constantinople faced the threat of a major earthquake. In response to this, the emperor, along with Proclus,[769] the Patriarch of Constantinople and a disciple of Saint John Chrysostom,[770] and the people, gathered and prayed to God to lift this threat from them. As they prayed, a child was suddenly lifted into midair, to whom all cried out "Lord have mercy." The child was then seen to descend again to the earth, and in loud voice he exhorted the people to pray "Holy God, holy Mighty, holy Immortal." After giving this exhortation, the child died. The Patriarch then ordered the people to plead in this manner, and indeed the Lord responded to their prayers and lifted the danger of the earthquake from them. This tradition was reinforced by later Byzantine historians such as Theophanes, and Anastasius.[771] Other traditions, like the Chaldean's, offer minor alterations to the same Byzantine story.[772]

---

[767] Saint John of Damascus (AD 675 or 676–749) was a Syrian monk and priest. Born and raised in Damascus and died at his monastery, Mar Saba, near Jerusalem. He composed many hymns that are still used in the Eastern Churches. His work is of interest in the fields of law, theology, and philosophy.

[768] Theodosius II (Latin: *Flavius Theodosius Junior Augustus*, 10 April 401—28 July 450), commonly surnamed Theodosius the Younger, or Theodosius the Calligrapher, was Byzantine Emperor from AD 408 to 450. He presided over the outbreak of two great Christological controversies, Nestorianism and Eutychianism.

[769] Saint Proclus (died July 446 or 447 AD) was an Archbishop of Constantinople. He is venerated as a saint in the Catholic Church and the Eastern Orthodox Church. The friend and disciple of Saint John Chrysostom, Proclus became secretary to Archbishop Atticus of Constantinople (AD 406–425). In AD 429, on a festival of the Theotokos (Virgin Mary), Proclus preached his celebrated sermon on the Incarnation, which was later inserted in the beginning of the Acts of the Council of Ephesus.

[770] Saint John Chrysostom (AD 349–407), Archbishop of Constantinople, was an important Early Church Father. He is known for his preaching and public speaking, his denunciation of abuse of authority by both ecclesiastical and political leaders, the Divine Liturgy of St. John Chrysostom, and his ascetic sensibilities. The "golden-mouthed" was given because of his legendary eloquence. The Orthodox and Eastern Catholic Churches honor him as a saint and count him among the Three Holy Hierarchs, together with Basil the Great and Gregory Nazianzus. He is recognized by the Eastern Orthodox Church and the Catholic Church as a saint and as a Doctor of the Church. The Coptic Orthodox Church of Alexandria also recognizes John Chrysostom as a saint (with feast days on 16 Thout and 17 Hathor).

[771] Hanna, Malak (Father), *The Tirce-Holy (Agios), Doctrine and History*, 8, 9.

[772] Hanna, Malak (Father), *The Tirce-Holy (Agios), Doctrine and History*, 10.

Reflecting the Syrian tradition, Moses Bar-Kepha [773] claims that during the burial of our Lord Jesus Christ, Joseph heard the Seraphim praising the hymn of the Trisagion; when he heard that, he responded, "O You who was crucified, have mercy on us," since Jesus died for humankind only, not the angles. This might be the reason that the patriarchs of Antioch were the first to insist on adding these words to the hymn. According to Ibn Sibaa, when Joseph and Nicodemus prayed with this praise, the Lord opened His eyes; hence,[774] they responded, "Holy God, holy Mighty, holy Immortal."[775] This tradition is preserved in the burial hymn of Good Friday, ܓܘܠܓܘܬܐ, where it is said that Joseph and Nicodemus, after taking the Body of Christ, they anointed Him with spices, shrouded Him, and placed Him in a tomb. They praised Him, saying, "Holy God, Holy Mighty, Holy Immortal, Who was crucified for us, have mercy upon us."

The Eastern Orthodox tradition does not elaborate after the word "Holy;" meaning that the words "Who was born of the Virgin," "Who was crucified for us," "Who rose from the dead and ascended into the heavens" and "Who was baptized" are not recognized in the Byzantine Rite. The fact is that the original hymn did not include these phrases. Per the Byzantine tradition, the first to add lyrics after "Holy" was Patriarch Peter the Fuller of Antioch,[776] whose papacy extended from AD 471 to 488. John Malalas, the historian, reports that, in AD 512, Emperor Anastasius ordered the addition of the phrase "Who was crucified for us" to the Trisagion. This resulted in a tumult, in which many were killed until

---

[773] Moses Bar-Kepha (born in Balad in Nineveh, now in Iraq, about the year AD 813; died at the age of ninety, in 903) was a writer and one of the most celebrated bishops of the Syriac Orthodox Church of the ninth century.
[774] Ibn Sibaa, *The Precious*, Ibid., fol. 131v
[775] Most Coptic fathers and bishops now do not agree with Ibn Sibaa's account of the Trisagion.
[776] Patriarch Peter received his surname from his former trade as a fuller of cloth.

calmness befell the Roman Empire once more after the emperor retracted his decision.[777]

In his book *The Maronites in History*, Matti Moosa challenges this tradition affirming that the controversial phrase was in use in Syria 140 years before Peter the Fuller and dates back to the Antiochan Patriarch Euthathius (AD 325–330).[778] The preexisting tradition of using the phrase in Antioch is confirmed by subsequent historians such as Zachariah of Mitylene,[779] and Ephraim of Amida.[780] Nonetheless, there are some modern Chalcedonian writers who attribute it to others who notably also predate Peter the Fuller and Chalcedon, such as Rabbula of Edessa.[781] Isaac the Great[782] is considered one of the oldest records supporting the preexisting of the Trisagion annexation to Peter the Fuller. Isaac the Great, who predated Peter the Fuller, attests that it was the practice in Antioch at his time to chant the phrase "Who was crucified for us" attached to the Trisagion.

Moreover, Avitus of Vienne[783] believed that the original form of the Trisagion included the annexation,[784] a clear indication that the Christological Trisagion found its way to the West in the 5th century. In a letter to the king of that realm, bishop Avitus writes, ": ...It is customary in

---

[777] Menze, Volker L., *Justinian and the Making of the Syrian Orthodox Church*, 166.

[778] Moosa, Matti, *The Maronites in History*, 69-73.

[779] Zacharias of Mytilene (465—after 536 AD), was a bishop and ecclesiastical historian. He was born Gaza and studied philosophy in Alexandria where he met Severus, who was later to become a notable patriarch of Antioch. Zacharias composed several works in Greek, among which is an ecclesiastical history.

[780] Ephraim of Antioch (served from 527 to 545 AD) was the Patriarch of Antioch, and head of the Greek Orthodox Church of Antioch. He undertook a tour of Syria and Mesopotamia alongside a contingent of soldiers to enforce the Council of Chalcedon and persecute its opponents. Ephraim had non-Chalcedonian monks driven out from their monasteries in the middle of winter, imprisoned those who refused to accept the council, and erected pyres in some cases.

[781] Rabbula was a bishop of Edessa from 411 to 435 AD, noteworthy for his opposition to the views of Theodore of Mopsuestia and Nestorius.

[782] Isaac of Antioch, also called Isaac the Great, (died 460 AD), Syrian writer, is an author of a wealth of theological literature and historical verse describing events in Rome and Asia Minor.

[783] Avitus (450—519 AD) was a Latin poet and bishop of Vienne in Gaul.

[784] Hanna, Malak (Father), *The Tirce-Holy (Agios), Doctrine and History*, 15.

the East in the churches of important cities for a supplication to be made at the beginning of the mass to accompany the divine praise. The voice of the plebs raises this acclamation as one with such religious enthusiasm and alacrity that they believe—not without reason—that any plea made in the subsequent liturgical celebration will find favor as long as this dutiful expression of devotion is added at the beginning. Even though Your Piety is very familiar with it, I decided that it would be a good idea to cite the end of this supplicatory prayer here, since my argument requires it: 'Holy God, Holy Powerful One, Holy Immortal, have mercy on us! You who were crucified for us, have mercy on us!' And just as it had been whispered to the emperor, so he too made it known to the bishop: that nothing should be a cause of dissension, and that there would be no mention of dissension, if the bishop, once he had been asked to do so by the emperor, were to order or allow what used to move the souls of some in the prayer to be removed... 'You who were crucified for us, have mercy on us.'"[785]

Some monks of Romania suggested an alternative annexation, "One of the Trinity was crucified for us." Nevertheless, this suggestion was not met with success. Furthermore, Caladion (AD 481–485), the Chalcedonian patriarch of Antioch, attempted to prefix Peter the Fuller's addition "Who was crucified for us" with "Christ the King," which also failed to prevail.[786] Per Moses Bar-Kepha, Saint Ignatius Theophorus (AD 35–108) was the one who confirmed the use of the Trisagion, and was the one established the manner it should be chanted in (i.e., antiphonally)— Saint Ignatius was caught up to the heavens and witnessed the angles chanting the Trisagion antiphonally.

---

[785] Karim, Armin, "My People, What Have I Done to You?" The Good Friday Popule meus Verses in Chant and Exegesis, c. 380–880, 195.
[786] Menze, Volker L., Justinian and the Making of the Syrian Orthodox Church, 168.

In all cases, there is no doubt that Peter the Fuller profoundly contributed to the spread of the Christological extension. In the year AD 471, he enforced the use of the words "Who was crucified for us" as a sort of "test of orthodoxy against Nestorianism."[787] After this, Severus,[788] who was Patriarch of Antioch from AD 502 to 518, confirmed this addition as a mandatory requirement, ensuring that all churches across Antioch were chanting "Holy God, Holy Mighty, Holy Immortal, Who was crucified for us, have mercy on us" three times. In one of his homilies in AD 518, Patriarch Severus comments on this addition saying, "the Alexandrians, the Libyans, and the Egyptians do not sing at all in church this praise of Christ" implying that, at least, until AD 518 the Coptic Church did not recognize this Antiochan annexation.[789] The Coptic Church later[790] adopted this interpolation, however, modified the wording so that the first stanza would include "Who was born of the Virgin," the second "Who was crucified for us," and the third "Who rose from the dead and ascended into the heavens," in addition to modifying the stanzas as applicable to the feasts of Nativity, Epiphany, Maundy Thursday, Resurrection, and Ascension.

Whether the Trisagion is to be understood as addressed to the Holy Trinity or to God the Son has been a matter of contention, particularly

---

[787] Nestorianism is a Christological doctrine that emphasizes the disunion between the human and divine natures of Jesus. It was advanced by Nestorius (AD 386–450), Patriarch of Constantinople from AD 428–431, influenced by Nestorius' studies under Theodore of Mopsuestia at the School of Antioch. Nestorius's teachings brought him into conflict with other prominent church leaders, most notably Cyril of Alexandria, who criticized especially his rejection of the title Theotokos ("Bringer forth of God") for the Virgin Mary. Nestorius and his teachings were eventually condemned as heretical at the First Council of Ephesus in 431 and the Council of Chalcedon in AD 451, leading to the Nestorian Schism, in which churches supporting Nestorius broke with the rest of the Christian Church.

[788] Saint Severus the Great of Antioch was a Syriac and last non-Chalcedonian patriarch to reside in Antioch and is considered one of the founders of the Syriac Orthodox Church. Saint Severus is also considered a Church father and a saint in Oriental Orthodoxy. In Alexandria, he studied grammar and rhetoric in Latin and Greek. Severus later studied law and philosophy at the famous law school in Berytus. Severus was baptized in AD 488 in the Church of the Martyr Leontius in Tripolis.

[789] Cuming, Geoffrey J., *The Liturgy of St Mark*, 95.

[790] Possibly taught by Patriarch Severus, who fled to Egypt and lived there for 20 years.

between those who approved of the council of Chalcedon and those who were against it. Non-Chalcedonian Churches, such as the Coptic and Syriac, embraced the Christological understanding of the hymn. As such, they insisted on the insertions since they provide a firm stand against the heresies of Nestorius, thereby proclaiming that God Incarnate was crucified, and His divinity never departed from His humanity for a single moment nor even for a twinkle of an eye.[791]

The Byzantine tradition, on the other hand, held the Trinitarian understanding of the Trisagion; thus, they rejected the interpolations, which, from their perspective, will defile the unsullied orthodox faith. To them, "Holy God" is directed to God the Father, "Holy Mighty" to God the Son, who conquered death by His death, and "Holy Immortal" is addressed to God the Holy Spirit, the Giver of Life.[792] This understanding is based on the verses from (Isaiah 6:3) and (Revelation 8:4). After the Third Council of Constantinople (AD 680–681), and with the help of Emperor Constantine IV (reigned from AD 668 to 685), the Byzantine understanding and tradition of chanting the Trisagion extended to some churches in Syria.[793] In AD 692, under Justinian II, the Council in Trullo[794] anathematized anyone who adds to the hymn of the Trisagion.

Conversely, the Churches that accepted and adapted these additions direct the first part of the hymn (Trice-Holy) to God the Son. They insist that it exemplifies worship of the incarnate Logos. For this reason, the lyrics are attributed to His works in His miraculous birth, crucifixion,

---

[791] Although the account of the Trisagion in Revelation had it addressed to God the Son, this argument was never used by the Oriental Orthodox Fathers to support their view of the addition.
[792] John of Damascus, *The Orthodox Faith*, Book III Chapter 5.
[793] Hanna, Malak (Father), *The Tirce-Holy (Agios), Doctrine and History*, 20.
[794] The Coptic Church (and churches in the West) did not acknowledge this council. Dr. Fortescue says that this council showed intolerance of all other customs with the wish to make the whole Christian world conform to its own local practices. For more details on this subject, see: Shahan, T. (1908). Council in Trullo. In *The Catholic Encyclopedia*. New York: Robert Appleton Company. Retrieved October 5, 2020 from New Advent: www.newadvent.org/cathen/04311b.htm.

resurrection, and the ascension. Saint Ephraim the Syrian (AD 306–373) confirms this understanding and adds that it was the common practice in the East.[795] This group of Churches believe that the Trisagion, even before Peter the Fuller's insertions, was addressed to God the Son, not the Holy Trinity. Therefore, the additions of Peter the Fuller made it clearer as opposed to have changed its meaning. The second half of the hymn is directed to the Holy Trinity, and this is evident in the lyrics "Glory be to the Father, to the Son and to the Holy Spirit, now and ever and unto the ages of the ages, Amen."

The mention of the Trisagion in the Council of Chalcedon attests to the fact that it was in use in liturgical services prior to the year AD 451;[796] possibly between AD 430 and 450.[797] In the Coptic Orthodox Church, the Trisagion can be chanted in the Year-round, Mournful, or Joyous tune. The former is employed all year long, except for Feast Days and Holy Week.[798] The Mournful tune is assigned to Holy Thursday Prime service, Sixth and Ninth Hours of Good Friday, and funerals that take place in a Regular Days (expect Sunday). As for the Joyous tune, which has two flavors, one is lengthier than the other, is assigned to Feast Days, and the Holy Crowning office.

Ibn Sibaa reports a distinctive practice for the Trisagion. He assigns the first stanza to the most senior of the clergy, whether a priest or a bishop, being the head of the angelic hosts on earth, and the heavenly humans. The assembly of the faithful will then continue chanting the remaining

---

[795] Hanna, Malak (Father), *The Tirce-Holy (Agios), Doctrine and History*, 28.
[796] In the Council of Chalcedon, after the council condemned Dioscorus, the most devout bishops against Dioscorus proclaimed: "Many years to the senate! *Holy God, Holy Almighty, Holy Immortal, have mercy on us.* Many years to the emperors! The impious are always routed; Christ has deposed Dioscorus. Christ has deposed the murderer. This is a just sentence. This is a just council. This is a holy council. The senate is just, the council is just. God has avenged the martyrs." The use of "have mercy on us" in the Trisagion is out of place, suggesting a liturgical source for the words.
[797] Hanna, Malak (Father), *The Tirce-Holy (Agios), Doctrine and History*, 9.
[798] Holy Thursday Blessing of the Water and liturgy services are excluded since it is a Minor Feast of the Lord. Hence, in those two offices of that day, the Year-round tune is appointed.

stanzas. [799] However, neither Ibn Kabar, nor Pope Gabriel V made mention of this peculiar practice. Father Samaan Ibn Koleil, who lived in the 12th century instructs, "Every time they chant 'Ⲁ̀ⲅⲓⲟⲥ', they make the sign of the cross, a sign of the sanctification they received from the only begotten Son. For He is our mighty and living God, Who was incarnate, died, and rose. For this reason, they conclude Ⲁ̀ⲅⲓⲟⲥ with a doxology to the Trinity, thanking the Father, the Son and the Holy Spirit for the gift of eternal life. This is what prepares them to hear the word of the Gospel, with which they were preached."[800]

The Psalm and the Gospel

Reading a pericope from one of the four Gospels is the climax of the Liturgy of the Word; thus, it is preceded with a litany specific to it. Due to its significance, it is assigned to the priest, and delivered from the pulpit, if available. After hymning the Trisagion, the priest places one spoonful of incense in the censer without making the sign of the cross, and instructs the altar server saying, "Pray." The altar server then advises the worshippers to, "Stand for prayer." The congregants stand up, then the priest turns toward them and blesses them saying, "Peace be with all." In return, they respond saying, "and with your spirit." If a high priest is present, then he will be the one uttering this introduction and blessing the congregation with the sign of the cross.

The priest then kisses the bishop's cross and passes it to the altar server as he receives the thurible to proceed with the Litany of the Gospel. There are two litanies for the Gospel. The first, and most common one, begins with "O Master, Lord Jesus Christ our God, who said to His saintly,

---

[799] Ibn Sibaa, Ibid., fol. 130v.
[800] Athanasius of Saint Macarius Monastery (Father), *The Divine Liturgy: The Mystery of the Kingdom of God (Part 1)*, 477.

honored disciples and holy apostles." This litany was mostly used in Old Cairo. Per contra, the second litany, which starts with "O Master, Lord Jesus Christ our God, who sent His saintly, honored disciples and holy apostles to the whole world" was more common in Alexandria. This information is documented in *Kacmarcik Codex*.[801] On the other hand, the 18th century MS Lit. 147 offers a different prescription; it appoints the first to Regular Days and the second to Feast Days. Contemporary instructions make them interchangeable to each other. This litany (the first or the second) has two melodies, one is lengthier than the other, and is employed if time permits. Once again, except for the priest's preference, no governing rules pertain to these two renditions.

After praying the Litany of the Gospel, one of the chanters sings the Psalm. The chanting of a psalm during the Eucharist seems to have emerged first in Hippo, perhaps introduced—or at least instilled—by Augustine.[802] Ibn Sibaa writes, "The archdeacon then instructs one of the chanters to read two verses from the Old Testament, that is, from the Book of Psalms for David. They must be applicable to the season at the time of the assembly, whether it is a Feast of the Lord, a feast of the Lady Saint Mary, or a feast of a martyr. Additionally, the Psalm must also be relevant to the Gospel reading. This is then followed by the recitation of appropriate melodies,[803] whether that Mournful, Joyous, Year-round, *Kiahkian*, or specific to the Holy Fifty days."[804]

---

[801] This is a manuscript from the 14th century that was written in the Monastery of Saint Antony near the Red Sea in Egypt. It contains a unique set of prayers for the Eucharistic liturgy, displayed in parallel texts in both Greek and Arabic. These are the Order of the Liturgy, with the Anaphoras of Saint Basil, Saint Gregory the Theologian, and Saint Mark, along with prayers for the sick, the dead, and other needs.
[802] McGowan, Andrew B., *Ancient Christian Worship*, 100.
[803] Ibn Sibaa here is referring to the Psalm responsory which can employ any of these melodies according to the liturgical season.
[804] Ibn Sibaa, Ibid., fols. 132v-133r

Although Ibn Sibaa reports that it was customary in his area for a chanter (Psaltos) to recite the Psalm, Ibn Kabar attests to a different tradition. He states, "The priest prays the Litany of the Gospel, the Psalm is then recited, and they respond to it with its hymns. In Cairo, Old Cairo and Lower Egypt, the common practice is for a young chanter to read it (the Psalm), to which the chorus responds accordingly. In Upper Egypt, however, the Psalm is chanted by one or two of the senior deacons, to which the chorus responds, the first word is also intoned. In Alexandria, the archdeacon chants it. As for the Monastery of Saint Macarius, it is assigned to the chanters (psaltos) and is delivered from the center of the church, with no responsories."[805] Today, there is no specific regulations restricting the reader of these lessons based on rank.

It is noteworthy that, in Regular Days, the liturgy's Psalm can be intoned in either of two minor tunes, or a more elaborate one called the "Abbreviated Year-round." The reason it is called "abbreviated"[806] is an indicative of its original purpose as an alternative to the *Singarian* if time is a constraint. In other words, this tune was originally employed on festive days, which explains the musical similarities between its melody and that of the *Singarian*. The Abbreviated Year-round tune, however, was recently assigned to Regular Days, as such *Year-round* was appended to its title. Unlike the *Singarian* tune, the Abbreviated Year-round concludes with Alleluia as per the custom in Regular Days. This makes it a good fit for the feasts of the Virgin Mary and that of the Apostles, since both utilize the Year-round tunes, and do not have a specific Psalm reply.

---

[805] Ibn Kabar, *The Lamp*, BnF, MS Arabic 203 (c. AD 1363-1369), fol. 206r.
[806] Manuscripts show that some propers (i.e., Palm Sunday and Pentecost) treat this tune as festal. The word "Year-round" was not part of the title.

On Feast Days, the Psalm may be recited in a joyous syllabic tune, or, if time permits, in the *Singarian*[807] one, which can be rendered in either a melismatic or minor melody. During the month of Kiahk, the Psalm employs a tune specific to this month. During Lent and Holy Thursday, the Year-round tune is still assigned to it. As for Holy Week, and the funeral office on the Regular Days, the Psalm is hymned in a solemn melody called "*Edripian*."[808] An exception to that occurs in the 11th Hour of Tuesday, the 3rd Hour of the Eve of Holy Thursday, the Prime Hour of Holy Thursday, and the 12th Hour of Good Friday, when the "*Shamian*"[809] tune is appointed to the Psalm.

As previously noted, present-day rubric prescribes a circumambulation performed by the priest and the altar server—in antiquity this was assigned to the Servant Deacon—once around the altar, while the Psalm is being chanted in Coptic. In this circuit, which is called Gospel Circuit, the priest holds the gospel from one end, and the altar server, facing him and walking backwards, holds it from the other end.[810]

Unlike the current practice of conducting the Gospel Circuit while the Psalm is being chanted, in the past, the Gospel Circuit used to follow the chanting of the Psalm. Ibn Kabar states that the priest, during the recitation of the Psalm, offers incense.[811] Pope Gabriel V elucidates this further saying, "While carrying the censer, the priest looks toward the lectern as the Psalm is chanted. At the third stanza-line, he censes the

---

[807] This word is derived from "Singar," which is the name of an ancient city in Lower Egypt where it is believed that this tune was composed.
[808] This word is derived from "Idripa," which is the name of the Ancient Egyptian city (currently in Sohag) where the music of this hymn was composed. Some scholars think that the name is derived from the Coptic word "Ⲉⲧⲉⲣⲉⲙϩⲓ," which means "mournful."
[809] This word is derived from "Shama," which is the name of an ancient city in the west side of Luxor. It is believed that the music of the hymn was developed in this city.
[810] The form of this circuit as practiced today was not mentioned in the rubrics prior to the 16th century. See: Athanasius of Saint Macarius Monastery (Father), *Summary of the Liturgical History of the Church of Alexandria (Part 2)*, 305.
[811] Ibn Kabar, *The Lamp*, BnF, MS Arabic 203 (c. AD 1363-1369), fol. 199v.

gospel (the lectionary), and at the fourth stanza-line, he returns to the sanctuary and kisses the altar. He then makes the sign of the cross on the coffer of incense and places a pinch (of incense) in the censer."[812]

The 13th century scholar Ibn Sibaa describes this circuit as a celebratory pageant. He writes, "The priest and the deacon circle the altar carrying the holy gospel, and altar servers, blocking them out, precede them holding candles. The deacon still carries it (the lectionary) until they exit the sanctuary"[813] On the same folio, the following footnote is added, "the congregation chants 'Listen to my cry, for I am in desperate need; rescue me from those who pursue me, for they are too strong for me' (Psalm 142:6) Meanwhile, the deacon recites 'Show me the right path, O Lord; point out the road for me to follow' (Psalm 25:4)." Ibn Kabar goes on to say, "He (the priest) then circles the altar along with the deacon (the Servant Deacon) carrying the gospel (the lectionary) opened."[814] As such, according to the ancient practice, while listening to the psalm, the priest offers incense. When it is accomplished, the deacon carries the lectionary, and, along with the priest and the other altar servers holding candles, he circumambulates the altar once. When the Gospel Circuit is completed, the altar servers exit the sanctuary.

Afterward, Ibn Kabar instructs, "While still opened, it (the lectionary) is then greeted by the other priests."[815] Ibn Sibaa offers more details saying,[816] "He (the priest) opens the gospel and places it on the altar; a sign that this text (of the gospel) is from Christ on the altar. He then requests from the other priests to gather around it and look at it and kiss it while it

---

[812] Gabriel V (Pope), *The Ritual Order*, BnF, MS 98 (AD 1411), fol. 38r-v.
[813] Ibn Sibaa, Ibid., fol. 133r
[814] Ibn Kabar, *The Lamp*, BnF, MS Arabic 203 (c. AD 1363-1369), fol. 199v.
[815] Ibn Kabar, Ibid., fol. 199v.
[816] The original text in Arabic:

"يفتح (الكاهن) الإنجيل ويضعه على الهيكل إشارة أن هذا النص صادر عن قول المسيح على الهيكل. ثم يستحضر الكهنة الحاضرين لينظروا الكلام المسطور فيه. يُقبّلوه وهو مفتوح لتمييز الكهنة في تقبيله مفتوحاً على باقي الشعب لكهنوقم".

is open, to distinguish the way they greet it—acknowledging their priesthood—from laity."[817] In this regard, Uppsala, MS OR. 486 (AD 1546) offers an additional detail; it directs, "The attending priests greet it (the lectionary) in the order of their seniority."[818] Furthermore, Pope Gabriel V states, "The last one to kiss the gospel passes it on to the deacon so he may read it."[819] Per the present-day practice, the Gospel Circuit is performed with the priest and altar server holding a smaller gospel in a box as opposed to the lectionary. Meanwhile, the priest recites Luke 2:29 inaudibly.

In a footnote, Ibn Sibaa reports the practice of the people's recitation of Psalms 142:6 during the Gospel Circuit,[820] a practice that was also confirmed by Pope Gabriel V.[821] Since this Psalm is recited during the Gospel Circuit, it is referred to as the Circuit Psalm (Arabic: الطوّاف). Numerous Circuit Psalms are assigned to different occasions, among which the renowned Ⲙⲁⲣⲟⲩϭⲁⲥϥ (Let them exalt Him), which is uttered in the presence of a high priest. The congregation participate in concluding the Circuit Psalm saying, "Alleluia." However, on Feast Days, an occasion-specific responsory is recited following the Circuit Psalm instead. The Gospel Circuit, Ibn Sibaa explains, epitomizes the spreading of the message of the Gospel all over the world.[822] Additionally, the reason for the altar server holding a cross during this circuit is to emphasize that the message of the Gospel was only established on the salvific act of Jesus on the Cross; the cross is the cornerstone for our salvation.

---

[817] Ibn Sibaa, Ibid., fol. 133v
[818] Ibn Kabar, *The Lamp*, Father Samuel of Syrians Monastery, 112. Similar note is provided by Ibn Kabar, *The Lamp*, BnF, MS Arabic 203 (c. AD 1363-1369), fol. 206r.
[819] Gabriel V (Pope), *The Ritual Order*, BnF, MS 98 (AD 1411), fol. 39r.
[820] Ibn Sibaa, Ibid., fol. 133r
[821] Gabriel V (Pope), *The Ritual Order*, BnF, MS 98 (AD 1411), fol. 38v.
[822] Ibn Sibaa, Ibid., fol. 133r

After the Gospel Circuit is accomplished, the altar server who participated in it (who also holds the cross), stands at the southern side of the altar facing the people, and awaiting the Psalm—and perhaps the Circuit Psalm—to be completed. Upon completion, he lifts up the cross, and instructs the congregation saying, "Ⲥⲧⲁⲑⲏⲧⲉ ⲙⲉⲧⲁ ⲫⲟⲃⲟⲩ Ⲑⲉⲟⲩ ⲁⲕⲟⲩⲥⲱⲙⲉⲛ ⲧⲟⲩ ⲁⲅⲓⲟⲩ ⲉⲩⲁⲅⲅⲉⲗⲓⲟⲩ," meaning, "Stand in the fear of God. Let us hear the Holy Gospel." The priest then takes off his hat,[823] before proceeding to read the Gospel lesson in Coptic from the pulpit, if there is one. Subsequently, one of the deacons—in antiquity, only certain deacons were permitted to read the Gospel; as such, were called Anglican Deacons[824]—comes forth to read it in the vernacular.[825] Many of the old churches had pulpits from which the Gospel used to be read. Ibn Kabar impeccably summarizes this section saying, "The Gospel can be read from the pulpit, which is more appropriate due to its significance, or from the lectern. In the event the Patriarch is present, he reads the Gospel from the gate of the sanctuary facing westward, while the priest holding the thurible stands below him at the gate. The same applies to the bishop in his diocese. If a deacon reads the Gospel, he is to face eastward; meanwhile the priest stands at the gate of the sanctuary with the censer. After this, the Gospel is read in Arabic."[826]

Cyprian of Carthage (c. AD 210–258) reports that "readers" are assigned the task of uttering the Gospel. In the fourth-century *Apostolic Constitutions*, however, this duty was appointed to the presbyter or deacon.[827] As for Egypt, Marquis of Bute comments, "There can be little

---

[823] Ibn Al-'Assal, Abu Is-haq Ibn Fadlallah, *The Fundamental Acts of the Ecclesiastical Etiquette (The Liturgy)*, published by Archdeacon Girgis Philotheos Awad, 34.
[824] Ibn Sibaa, Ibid., fol. 134r
[825] At least until the 14th century, the custom of Saint Macarius Monastery was to read the Gospel in Coptic only. See: Ibn Kabar, *The Lamp*, BnF, MS Arabic 203 (c. AD 1363-1369), fol. 206r.
[826] Ibn Kabar, Ibid., fol. 206r.
[827] McGowan, Andrew B., *Ancient Christian Worship*, 92-93.

doubt that in Egypt, as in the rest of the world, it was originally the custom for the deacon to sing the Gospel, and indeed, the rubric translated by Renaudot, prescribes that he should do so, if he is capable. However, owing to the want of education in the boys who officiate as deacons, the singing of the Gospel has come by custom to be committed to the priest, and is how looked on as a privilege of the chief person officiating, so that it is even assigned to bishops when they pontificate."[828] In his *Ecclesiastical History*, Sozomen, speaking of the Alexandrian practice, attests, "The archdeacon alone reads the Gospel in this city (Alexandria), whereas in some places it is read by the deacons, and in many churches only by the priests."[829] Sources command the reader of the Gospel to expose his head as a sign of submission under Christ's feet, which is represented by the Gospel. Pope Gabriel II (Ibn Turek) states in one of his canons that, "no one (referring to clergy) is to pray the Gospel with his head covered."[830]

While the Gospel is being read, the congregation stands in reverence to listen to the word of God.[831] This practice was common in Judaism where worshippers stood during the reading of the holy books. The act of standing signifies several aspects, not the least of which, is that it shows respect and reverence to the word of God and to His divine presence. In the encounter between the Lord and Ezekiel, the Lord instructed him to, "stand up on your feet and I will speak to you" (Ezekiel 2:1). The same practice can be found in the book of Nehemiah, when the multitudes

---

[828] John, Marquis of Bute, *The Coptic Morning Service for the Lord's Day*, 78.
[829] Hartranft, Chester D., *The Ecclesiastical History of Sozomen*, 639. In the same paragraph, Sozomen also attests to a custom that is unique to the Church of Alexandria; he writes, "Another strange custom also prevails at Alexandria which I have never witnessed nor heard of elsewhere, and this is, that when the Gospel is read the bishop does not rise from his seat."
[830] Athanasius of Saint Macarius Monastery (Father), *The Divine Liturgy: The Mystery of the Kingdom of God (Part 1)*, 498.
[831] Ibn Al-'Assal, Abu Is-haq Ibn Fadlallah, *The Fundamental Acts of the Ecclesiastical Etiquette (The Liturgy)*, published by Archdeacon Girgis Philotheos Awad, 34.

gathered to read the Books of the Law. Ezra stood at a wooden pulpit made especially for this occasion. Then, "Ezra opened the book. All the people could see him because he was standing above them; and as he opened it, the people all stood up" (Nehemiah 8:5).

Standing is also a sign of preparation and attentiveness, just like the Jews did while eating the Passover when still in Egypt, as a sign of preparation.[832] Likewise, standing up prepares the faithful to receive the spiritual Passover, i.e., the word of God. Congregants, therefore, are to eat this spiritual Passover with attentiveness and readiness. Hence, the Church encourages her members to focus their attention on the personal message that Christ seeks to deliver to His children. Standing not only restricts worshippers from sitting down, but rather, avoiding any form of movement. For this reason, if a person were to enter the parish while the Gospel is being read—this is not limited to the Eucharistic service—they must stand at the entrance gate in reverence and attentiveness until the Gospel reading is completed, only at this point they may proceed to their seat.

At the time of reading the Gospel, two chanters surround the lectionary from both sides of the lectern while holding lit tapers. In antiquity, church lights were lit as well. The intention of these profound rituals is to remind the worshippers of Psalm 119:105, which reads, "Your word is a lamp for my feet, a light on my path." In AD 378, Saint Jerome[833] wrote from Bethlehem saying, "Throughout all the Church of the East when the Gospel is to read, lights are kindled...not to dispel the darkness

---

[832] Exodus 12.
[833] Saint Jerome (AD 347–420) was a priest, confessor, theologian, and historian. He was the son of Eusebius, born at Stridon, a village near Emona on the border of Dalmatia and Pannonia, then part of northeastern Italy. He is best known for his translation of most of the Bible into Latin, and his commentaries on the Gospels. Saint Jerome visited Jerusalem, Bethlehem, and the holy places of Galilee, and then went to Egypt, the home of the great heroes of the ascetic life. He spent the remainder of his life in a hermit's cell near Bethlehem until he departed on September 30th, 420 AD.

but to exhibit a token of joy." This ancient evidence confirms that kindling candles while the Gospel is being read is not merely for utilitarian motives, but rather in correlation to Psalm 119:105. "The more strictly official carrying of two lights at the Gospel," writes Gregory Dix, "is first mentioned by S. Isidore of Seville early in the seventh century."[834]

While the Gospel is being read in the vernacular, the priest, holding the thurible, utters the Prayer of the Gospel inaudibly.[835] This prayer is particular to the liturgy, and is, therefore, not used in the incense offering office. In the past, like many other inaudible prayers, it was recited aloud following the Gospel reading. It is most likely that the practice of reciting it soundlessly started around the 15th century.[836] Therefore, the author of *The Trinitarian Mystery in Priesthood Ministry* rigorously advices against silently reciting it during the reading of the Gospel.[837] The Prayer of the Gospel starts with a litany specific to the Gospel, followed by thirteen litanies, the last is for the catechumens, who, in the past, used to attend the liturgy up to the litanies following the Gospel, after which they are dismissed.

Following the Gospel reading, and as a sign of ratification of what has been uttered, the reader kisses the lectionary. In antiquity, the entire congregation would follow suit. Hence, Ibn Sibaa states, "After the reader of the Gospel comes down,[838] the clergy in attendance approach the Gospel and kiss it as well, as a sign of affirmation of their faith. After this,

---

[834] Dom Gregory Dix, *The Shape of the Liturgy*, 418.

[835] The Prayer of the Gospel starts with "O You who are longsuffering, abundant in mercy, and true."

[836] The practice of praying "O You who are longsuffering" while the Gospel is being read was fiercely condemned by *The Beginners' Guide and Discipline for Laity* since the priest, as a role model, should be the first to stand in fear and listen to the holy Gospel. See: Misael of the Paromeos Monastery (Father). (2018). The Beginners' Guide and Discipline for Laity. *Alexandria School, 25(2)*, 132-133.

[837] Misael of the Paromeos Monastery (Father). (2020). The Trinitarian Mystery in Priesthood Ministry. *Alexandria School, 28(1)*, 121.

[838] As it used to be read from the pulpit.

the sub-deacon takes the Gospel, wraps it in a silk corporal, and carries it throughout the parish for the congregants to kiss it, confirming their faith in what has been read. The bringing of the Gospel to the congregation is more appropriate than having them approach it, because it avoids the potential of overcrowding and disturbance of thought."[839] The custom of the people kissing the Gospel was eliminated in the 14th century; thus, Ibn Kabar states, "At the Hanging Church as well as at others, the tradition was that upon completing the reading of the Gospel, the entire congregation would come forth to kiss it;[840] the men first, then the women. The Patriarch John, who is known as Son of the Saint,[841] however, had advised to implement the practice of the monks instead, which is to greet the Gospel at the end of the service along with the cross."[842]

The Sermon and Following Prayers

Following the recitation of the Gospel, a relevant exhortation, in the form of a sermon, may be delivered. As an alternative, an oration, like a Homily from an approved writer, such as Saint John Chrysostom, is read.[843] The responsibility of the sermon resides with the bishop and is the privilege of a priest. Saint Justin Martyr, in the second century, confirms this responsibility saying, "The memoirs of the apostles or the writings of the prophets are read, as long as time permits; then, when the reader has ceased, the president (the bishop or the priest) verbally instructs, and

---

[839] Ibn Sibaa, Ibid., fols. 134r-135r

[840] Also see: Ibn Al-'Assal, Abu Is-haq Ibn Fadlallah, *The Fundamental Acts of the Ecclesiastical Etiquette (The Liturgy)*, published by Archdeacon Girgis Philotheos Awad, 35.

[841] Uppsala, MS OR. 486 (AD 1546) mentions the name of the Patriarch (John), however, BnF, MS Arabic 203 (c. AD 1363-1369), fol. 200r does not, it states, "The current Patriarch advised to employ the custom of the monks." Therefore, the patriarch referenced here is Pope John VIII (AD 1300–1320), the 80th Patriarch of Alexandria.

[842] Ibn Kabar, *The Lamp*, Father Samuel of Syrians Monastery, 115.

[843] John, Marquis of Bute, *The Coptic Morning Service for the Lord's Day*, 78.

exhorts to the imitation of these good things."[844] During the heresy of Arius, as mentioned by Socrates[845] and Sozomen[846] the historians,[847] Pope Athanasius the Apostolic instructed that the homilies be restricted to bishops only, thereby preventing priests from teaching. By the fourth century, a large collection of rhetorical literary—Allegorical (led by Origen's Alexandria) and exegesis (headed by Chrysostom's Antioch)—was accessible, which served as an orthodox resource of schooling.[848] This led to more relaxed rules around who delivers the discourse, providing that it is grounded on an approved source. In the fifth century, the priests' ability to exhort was reinstated. In some churches, permission was also granted to laity to conduct the sermons. The topic of the exhortation should be related to the lections read in the liturgy, particularly, the Gospel. After the sermon, the Gospel responsory is chanted.

Church sources include a plethora of Gospel responds, based on the particular Gospel reading, or the season. Contingent on the ecclesiastical season, numerous tunes are assigned to these responsories. The following are the recognized seasons to which a specific melody is appointed: Regular Days, Feast Days, the month of Kiahk, the Feasts of the Cross and Palm Sunday, and Lent. The latter is assigned two distinguished melodies, one for the Saturdays and Sundays, and the other for the rest of the week, a melody that is also employed for the Fast of Nineveh. While the Gospel responsory is being chanted, the Servant Priest approaches the gate of the sanctuary and, facing eastward, utters the Prayer of the Veil,[849] then kisses the doorstep of the sanctuary.

---

[844] Saint Justin Martyr, *First Apology*, chapter 67.
[845] Socrates of Constantinople (AD 380–440) was a 5th-century Christian church historian.
[846] Salminius Hermias Sozomenus (AD 400–450) was a historian of the Christian Church.
[847] Ignatius Ephrem II Rahmani (Patriarch of the Syriac Catholic Church), *Les Liturgies Orientales et Occidentales*, 222.
[848] McGowan, Andrew B., *Ancient Christian Worship*, 107.
[849] This prayer originated in the Syriac tradition and was then borrowed by others including the Coptic Church.

In the liturgy of Saint Basil, one of the Prayers of the Veil, directed to God the Father, starts with, "O God, who in Your ineffable love toward mankind sent Your only-begotten Son into the world." It is attributed to Saint James the Apostle. An alternate prayer, also addressed to God the Father and begins with, "O Lord our God, who saved us and granted us this life," may be recited. In the liturgy of Saint Gregory, the Prayer of the Veil, directed to the first hypostasis of the triune God, commences with, "O Lord God the *Pantocrator*, who knows the thoughts of men." There is also a surrogate prayer that is directed to God the Son, which begins with, "Again, we return to You, O God, the Good One." As for the Liturgy of Saint Cyril, the Prayer of the Veil is addressed to God the Father and starts with, "O Creator of the whole creation, visible and invisible." It is attributed to John, the Bishop of Bostra in Syria.[850] There is also a substitute orison that can be recited instead; it is also directed to first hypostasis, and begins with, "O Lord God of hosts, King of glory, who alone does wonders."

During the Middle Ages, some churches treated the Prayer of the Veil as a form of Absolution for the Servant Priest and the Servant Deacon. Ibn Kabar reports that both the Servant Priest and the Servant Deacon approach the door of the sanctuary, and another member of the clergy would recite the prayer (Prayer of the Veil) on their behalf, in the same manner as absolutions. The congregation then responds, "Cⲱⲟⲓⲥ ⲁⲙⲏⲛ ⲕⲉ ⲧⲱ ⲡⲛⲉⲩⲙⲁⲧⲓ ⲥⲟⲩ," meaning "Saved Amen, and with your spirit," which is the congregation response to absolutions.[851] However, the contemporary practice, which prescribes that the Servant Priest himself recites the Prayer

---

[850] John of Bostra was the bishop of Bostra and Arabia in the middle of the sixth century. He was contemporaneous with Saint Severus of Antioch.
[851] Ibn Kabar, *The Lamp*, BnF, MS Arabic 203 (c. AD 1363-1369), fol. 206v.

of the Veil at the door of the sanctuary, was also common in antiquity.[852] Afterwards, the priest enters the sanctuary, kisses the altar, and prays the Three Major Litanies for Peace, the Fathers, and the Assemblies, respectively.

The Three Major Litanies

Some academics consider the Three Major Litanies the last section of the Liturgy of the Word while others include them in the Liturgy of the Faithful, as they are recited after the catechumens have already left. A third categorization suggests that these litanies and up to the end of the Prayer of Reconciliation belong to neither office. The melodies employed suggest accuracy of the first hypothesis since they abide by the rules of the Liturgy of the Word. It has been the custom to perform them audibly, however, recently, it became common to utter them soundlessly. In an attempt to restore their significance, on June 1st, 1996, the Holy Synod of the Coptic Orthodox Church issued a decree mandating the recitation of the Three Major Litanies aloud.[853] Yet, not many parishes complied with or even acknowledged this precept.

The Three Major Litanies, which, according to Cuming, are "distinctively Egyptian,"[854] commence with the Litany of the Peace. Peace is vital for the church, because during times of peace the seeds of righteousness grow, and the spiritual life of the faithful can prosper, just like Saint James writes in his epistle "Peacemakers who sow in peace reap a harvest of righteousness" (James 3:18). For this reason, the Church prays for peace in all her liturgical services. The type of peace referred to in this

---

[852] This contemporary practice was also common in many churches in the Middle Ages as it was mentioned by Ibn Sibaa (13th century) and by Pope Gabriel V (15th century).
[853] The Holy Synod of the Coptic Orthodox Church, *The Synodical Decisions During the Epoch of H.H. Pope Shenouda the Third*, chapter 19, 88.
[854] Cuming, Geoffrey J., *The Liturgy of St Mark*, 100.

litany is not only external, but also internal; peace that fills the worshippers' hearts with tranquility, regardless of pains or persecutions they may be facing. As proclaimed in the hymn **Ⲡⲟⲩⲣⲟ** (O King of peace), it is the Church's conviction that the Lord Jesus Christ is the King of Peace. In the latter chant, we entreat the Lord saying, "O King of Peace, grant us Your peace, render unto us Your peace." In the Church's conscious, the source for this unique peace is Christ, as He Himself declared, "Peace I leave with you; my peace I give you. I do not give to you as the world gives" (John 14:27). Worshippers, therefore, beseech Him that He may grant them victory over sin, the chief disruption of peace. Thus, this litany is concluded with this powerful plead: "Let not the death of sins have dominion over us, we Your servants, nor over all Your people."

If the Church prays in one voice and one spirit, God will surely listen and respond. Therefore, when the altar server says, "Pray for the peace of the one holy," worshippers ought to ask the Lord to instill His peace into their hearts. When altar server says, "Catholic and Apostolic," congregants should genuinely plead for the unity of the church worldwide. When the altar server utters, "Orthodox Church of God," the faithful must pray for the Orthodox faith, which our Fathers defended with their blood, to prevail. If prayed with understanding and submission, this litany would rejuvenate the spirit of ardor within every member of the church, thus, the people would declare their affirmation to the altar server's request saying, "Lord have mercy." When saying, "all Your people," the priest turns around from his right side and faces west while blessing the congregation with the cross. If a bishop is present, he is the one who utters "all Your people," and performs the blessing.

This is then followed by the Litany of the Fathers. Praying for the Patriarch and the bishops is not simply an act of compliment, but of love and reverence. Out of love, the faithful prays for one another, especially for the church leaders, who are tasked to expand the Kingdom of God to every soul. In this litany, the Church presents a few requests before the Lord. The first is for the safety and keeping of the Patriarch and his collaborates the bishops for many years and peaceful times, fulfilling that holy high priesthood that God has entrusted them with, according to His holy and blessed will. The second is for the heavenly wisdom in teaching the word of truth, with purity and righteousness. The third is for strength in shepherding the church, the body of Christ. Finally, the fourth is for the safety of all her fathers, in peace and righteousness, for they are the shepherds and spiritual guides of the Lord's flock.

In this litany, when the altar server asks the people to pray for the Patriarch and the bishop, they should offer genuine prayers for them, so that the Lord may continue to fill their hearts with love toward His flock, lift away or help them endure tribulation that they face in their ministry, and assist them overcome the fierce attacks of the devouring enemy, Satan. Litanies were not designed to be merely poetic or religious observances, but rather to unity worshippers under specific asks that are offered to the Lord on His altar. Praying with one voice, heart, and spirit, makes God incline His ears to His people and respond to their petitions.

During the Litany of the Fathers, when the priest says, "Their prayers which they offer on our behalf, and on behalf of all Your people," he faces west, and raises the coffer of incense toward the congregation, as the incense represents prayers. The altar server brings the censer, and the priest places one spoonful of incense in it, after which he continues praying the litany. If a high priest is present, then he utters the words "all Your people," blesses the congregation with the cross, and places the spoonful of incense in the thurible.

Next is the Litany of the Assemblies. In this litany, the faithful prays for all the assemblies of the *church*, the body of Christ, that they may be spiritually fruitful and Christ serving, thereby leading people to heaven. The devil certainly targets these assemblies, causing havoc and confusion. However, the unity of prayer and spirit enables the *church* to defeat the devil and gives way for the Holy Spirit to work through these assemblies to bring forth fruit, thirty, sixty, and a hundred-fold.

Any assembly, Eucharist, psalmody, Bible study, gathering at the church or home, occurs in the presence of the Lord as He promised, "For where two or three gather in My name, there Am I with them" (Matthew 18:20). Gatherings of this nature strengthen the bond of love between the members of the body of Christ. When all members of this body are nurtured by the word of Christ and by His Body and Blood, then the verse, "For we were all baptized by one Spirit so as to form one body" (1 Corinthians 12:13) is manifested. This is how the church grows: by becoming one in spirit. At the commencement of the litany, the *church* entreats the Lord to bless all assemblies that they be without obstacle or hindrance. In it, the priest prays that these assemblies may be held according to His holy and blessed will, for the glory of His name and His Kingdom. The litany then proceeds to ask for the success of every meeting held at every Christian home so that they are fruitful and beneficial to every soul, and that attendees may be enlightened by the words of life, so that they may fulfil His commandment in their lives.

When the priest says, "Bless them," he turns toward the west and blesses the congregation. He then takes the censer from the altar server and offers incense before the altar. When he utters, "houses of prayer, houses of purity, houses of blessing," he censes the Ark, moving the thurible in the four directions in the shape of the cross: first toward the east, then west, north and south, respectively. Then, when he prays, "Arise, O Lord God," he thrice offers incense eastward, then westward in the direction of the congregation saying, "But let Your people be in blessing, thousands of thousands and ten thousand times ten thousand." Finally, facing east, he lifts the edge of the *Prospharin* and censes the oblation while covered saying, "Through the grace, compassion, and love-of-mankind…" If a bishop is present, then he would be the one to pray, "Remember, O Lord, our assemblies, bless them," and bless the congregation with the cross. He would also say, "But let Your people be in blessing, thousands of thousands and ten thousand times ten thousand."

Summary of the Liturgy of the Word Proper

After the Absolution of the Servants, the congregation chants a hymn for the Virgin subject to the season, followed by the hymn of the Intercessions, during which the priest prays the Litany of Incense for the Pauline Epistle and performs its circuit. After this, the hymn Ϯⲉⲛⲟⲩⲱϣⲧ is chanted, followed by a Pauline lesson, the response to the Catholic Epistle, and a Catholic lection. Meanwhile, the priest prays the Litany of the Catholic Epistle. The Praxis responsory is then recited, followed by a Praxis reading, during which the priest conducts the Praxis Circuit. Afterward, the Synaxarion is read, followed by, respectively, the Trisagion, the Litany of the Gospel, and the Gospel Circuit, during which the Coptic Psalm and Circuit Psalm are recited. The Gospel is then read, after which, optionally, a sermon is delivered. This is then followed by the Gospel respond. During that time, the Servant Priest utters the Prayer of the Veil inaudibly, followed by the Three Major Litanies.

CHAPTER SIX

The Liturgy of the Faithful

The Three Liturgies of Saints Cyril, Gregory, and Basil

Next, when the spiritual sacrifice, the bloodless worship has been completed, over that sacrifice of propitiation we beseech God for the public peace of the Churches... for all, in a word, who need help, we all pray and offer this sacrifice. Then we commemorate also those who have fallen asleep... for all those who have gone before us, believing that this [Eucharistic sacrifice] will be the greatest benefit to the souls of those on whose behalf our supplication is offered in the presence of the holy, of the most dread sacrifice.

—Cyril of Jerusalem

Christ held Himself in His hands when He gave His Body to His disciples saying: 'This is My Body.' No one partakes of this Flesh before he has adored it.

—Augustine

Introduction

In this section, we will have a deeper look into the order of the Liturgy of the Faithful, which takes place following the Three Major Litanies. It is referred to as the Liturgy of the Faithful because it can only be attended by baptized members of the church who could receive Holy Communion; members who believe in the Lord Jesus Christ, His salvation, death, resurrection, and second coming. For this reason, the liturgy commences with the Creed, through which the believers zealously declare their faith aloud.

The Liturgy of the Faithful itself is a journey to Heaven, where we meet with our Lord so we can receive His Body and Blood and unite with Him as participants of the Messianic Banquet. Thus, it is important that when we celebrate the liturgy, we pray with hearts lifted up to heaven, just as the priest requests from the congregation saying, "Lift up your hearts," to which they respond, "We have them with the Lord." In addition, we must be attentive to every word we utter in prayer, and actively participate in hymning the responsories, ensuring that our prayers are truly from the heart, and not mere words. In the Liturgy of the Faithful, we believe that Christ Himself is present on the altar, in His Body and Blood. We believe that the prayers we offer in the liturgy turn the bread and wine into the Body and Blood of the Lord Jesus, therefore, our communion is with Christ Himself, the New Pascha.

Communion, and what it is exactly that we receive during communion, has been a topic of great interest, and many have provided various views in attempts to explicate it. Many theologians discussed and tried to explain when and how the bread and wine become the Body and Blood of Jesus Christ.

Answering the first question as to how the Bread and Wine become the Body and Blood of Christ, the West claims that the answer resides in the words of the Institution Narrative, specifically, when the priest pronounces, "this is my body... this is my blood." Saint Ambrose of Milan[855] is an example of the traditional western view. He unequivocally states, "All that is said before are the words of the priest: praise is offered to God, the prayer is offered up, petitions are made for the people, for kings, for all others. But when the moment comes for bringing the most holy sacrament into being, the priest does not use his own words any longer; he uses the words of Christ. Therefore, it is Christ's word that brings this sacrament into being."[856] Nonetheless, the Byzantine tradition believes that the transformation is accomplished through the invocation of the Holy Spirit in the Epiclesis. "The bread... when it receives the invocation of God is no longer common bread, but the Eucharist, consisting of two realities, the earthly and the heavenly," Saint Irenaeus[857] says.[858]

As for the second question vis-à-vis the type of change or transformation that occurs to the bread and wine, western scholastics came up with few theories. One of the most notable views is Transubstantiation,[859] which came about in the 11th century and was

---

[855] Saint Ambrose (c. AD 340–4 April 397), was a bishop of Milan who became one of the most influential ecclesiastical figures of the fourth century. Saint Ambrose was a firm opponent of Arianism. Traditionally, Saint Ambrose is credited with promoting "antiphonal chant," a style of chanting in which one side of the choir responds alternately to the other. He is notable for his influence on Saint Augustine.
[856] Storey, William G., *A Prayer Book of Eucharistic Adoration*, 47.
[857] Saint Irenaeus (early second century—AD 202), was Bishop of Lugdunum in Gaul. He was an early Church Father and apologist, and his writings were formative in the early development of Christian theology.
[858] Spinks, Bryan D., *Do This in Remembrance of Me: The Eucharist from the Early Church to the Present Day*, 36.
[859] Transubstantiation (in Greek μετουσίωσις) is, according to the teaching of the Catholic Church, the change by which the bread and the wine used in the sacrament of the Eucharist become, not merely as a sign or a figure, but also in actual reality the body and blood of Christ. The Catholic Church teaches that the substance, or reality, of the bread is changed into that of the body of Christ

adopted by the Catholic Church as one of its canons. This view was based on Aristotle's [860] philosophy, [861] which argues that the substance [862] may differ from its outer appearance. [863] The main principles of Transubstantiation are:

- The entire substance (essence and substratum) of the bread and wine becomes the Body and Blood of Christ
- The original substance is no longer present
- The appearance of the original substance remains, meaning that the appearance is separate from the substance

The second theory is referred to as Consubstantiation, [864] and is a concept that the Anglican and some Protestant Churches believe in. The key principles of Consubstantiation are:

- After the descending of the Holy Spirit, the Body and Blood of Christ are both present in the bread and wine, however, the substance of the original materials (bread and wine) does not change

---

and the substance of the wine into that of his blood, while all that is accessible to the senses (the outward appearances or the physical characteristics) remains unchanged.

[860] Aristotle (384–322 BC) was a Greek philosopher and scientist born in the Macedonian city of Stagira, Chalkidice, on the northern periphery of Classical Greece. He was a student of Plato. His writings cover many subjects—including physics, biology, zoology, metaphysics, logic, ethics, aesthetics, poetry, theater, music, rhetoric, linguistics, politics and government—and constitute the first comprehensive system of Western philosophy. Shortly after Plato died, Aristotle left Athens and, at the request of Philip of Macedon, tutored Alexander the Great starting from 343 BC. In metaphysics, Aristotelianism profoundly influenced Christian theology, especially the scholastic tradition of the Catholic Church. Aristotle was well known among medieval Muslim intellectuals and revered as "The First Teacher".

[861] According to the Substance theory, a substance is distinct from its properties. A thing-in-itself is a property-bearer that must be distinguished from the properties it bears.

[862] According to Aristotle, substance is both essence (form) and substratum (matter) and may combine form and matter. Substance constitutes the reality of individual things.

[863] According to Aristotle, the appearance of something may differ from the true reality of that thing. Moreover, the appearance of something may be relative to the position of an observer and may depend on the opinions and attitudes of the observer. Things may not appear the same to everyone and may have contradictory appearances.

[864] Consubstantiation is a theological doctrine which holds that during the sacrament of the Eucharist, the fundamental "substance" of the body and blood of Christ are present alongside the substance of the bread and wine, which remain present.

- Elements or molecules of the Body and Blood of Christ are not only present with those of the original materials, but are also "in, with and under the bread."

The third conjecture is known as Impanation,[865] a hypothesis that is rejected by most Christians. In fact, the Catholic and Lutheran Churches consider it a heresy. The chief principles of Impanation are:

- The substance of the original materials does not change to that of Christ's
- The substance of Christ is united with that of the original materials, resulting in a third Eucharistic substance which we partake of in Holy Communion

What then was the answer of the early Apostolic Church to the two questions (When and How)? What is the sound Orthodox view? To answer the first question: at what moment in the liturgy the bread and wine become the Body and Blood of Jesus, the answer is: at the Divine Liturgy. The matter of when and how the transformation of the materials happens was not of interest to the Early Church Fathers, at least until the fourth century.[866] In their understanding of the Eucharist, it is one indivisible entity; one connected, unbreakable unit. The Eucharist stems from the sacrifice of Christ, which resulted in abundant mysteries to the *church* and the faithful. The Eucharist includes offering our lives to Him,

---

[865] Impanation (Latin, *impanatio*, "embodied in bread") is a high medieval theory of the Real Presence of the body of Jesus Christ in the consecrated bread of the Eucharist that does not imply a change in the substance of either the bread or the body. This doctrine, apparently patterned after Christ's Incarnation (God is made flesh in the Person of Jesus Christ), is the assertion that "God is made bread" in the Eucharist. Christ's divine attributes are shared by the Eucharistic bread via his body. Impanation is defined as the inclusion of the body of Christ in the Eucharistic bread in a hypostatic union without change in either substance. Rupert of Deutz (died in AD 1129) and John of Paris (died in AD 1306) were believed to have taught this doctrine.

[866] Halliburton, R.J. (1992). The Patristic Theology of the Eucharist. In Cheslyn Jones, Geoffrey Wainwright, Edward Yarnold SJ and Paul Bradshaw (Eds.), *The Study of Liturgy*, 249.

unity in love with Him and with each other, thanksgiving and praise with the heavenly hosts, uniting with Jesus on a spiritual level, and finally, mystically uniting with Him in Communion. So, the question that concerned the Early Church is this: What happens to the *church*, the group of believers, during the Eucharist, and not when the transformation occurs. According to the Alexandrian tradition, as we will discuss in more detail, the transformation of the elements does not happen in one exact moment, but throughout the liturgy.

As for the second question: what causes the bread and wine to become the Body and Blood of Jesus; the Orthodox answer is again different from that offered by the School Theology. The vested faith of the patristic church was simple and pure, far from the esoteric theories offered by School Theology, and accordingly, it eliminated the need for any man-made philosophies to expand on it. The faith of the Fathers was that in the Eucharist, we receive Christ, the same Christ Who was crucified for us, with no attempt to justify or explain molecular changes in the Body and Blood, or the offerings themselves. This simple belief was expressed by Saint Justin Martyr[867] who revealed the early teaching of the church saying, "We have been taught that the food over which thanks have been given by a word of prayer which is from Him, from which our flesh and blood are fed by transformation, is both the Flesh and Blood of that incarnate Jesus."[868] This straightforward and unpretentious yet fundamental and vital belief discloses that it is neither materialistic nor spiritual or symbolic transformation, but rather, a genuine, mysterious change that can only be

---

[867] Saint Justin (AD 100–165), was an early Christian apologist, and is regarded as the foremost interpreter of the theory of the Logos in the second century. Saint Justin Martyr was born at Flavia Neapolis, about AD 100, converted to Christianity about AD 130, taught and defended the Christian religion in Asia Minor and at Rome, where he suffered martyrdom about the year AD 165. Two "Apologies" bearing his name and his "Dialogue with the Jew Tryphon" have come down to us.

[868] Justin Martyr, *First Apology*, 66.2).

recognized by simple faith. "'And your floors shall be filled with wheat, and the presses shall overflow equally with wine and oil.' ... This has been fulfilled mystically by Christ," Saint Ephraim says, "who gave to the people whom He had redeemed, that is, to His Church, wheat and wine and oil in a mystic manner. For the wheat is the mystery of His Sacred Body; and the wine His Saving Blood; and again, the oil is the sweet unguent with which those who are baptized are signed, being clothed in the armaments of the Holy Spirit."[869] Saint Gregory of Nyssa[870] says "The bread is at first common bread; but when the mystery sanctifies it, it is called and actually becomes the Body of Christ."[871] Similarly, Saint Cyril of Jerusalem[872] declares, "Do not, then, regard the bread and wine as nothing but bread and wine, for they are the Body and Blood of Christ as the Master Himself has proclaimed."[873]

The Fathers' concern was how the Eucharist changes the entire *church*, the believers, not how and when the elements become the Body and Blood of Jesus Christ. This in contrast with the theology that was established in the West. These western theological philosophies are focused on "the validity and modality of the rite," as Father Alexander Schmemann says.[874] "Those who partake of it in faith are sanctified in body and in soul." Saint Clement of Alexandria articulates, "By the will of the Father, the divine mixture, man, is mystically united to the Spirit and

---

[869] SGS, Smith (Bro.), *A Monk's Topical Bible Letters E-K*, Book 2, Volume 4, 180.
[870] Saint Gregory of Nyssa, also known as Gregory Nyssen (AD 335—395), was bishop of Nyssa from 372 to AD 376 and from AD 378 until his death. Saint Gregory of Nyssa, his elder brother Basil of Caesarea, and their friend Gregory of Nazianzus are collectively known as the Cappadocian Fathers. Gregory of Nyssa was an erudite theologian who made significant contributions to the doctrine of the Trinity and the Nicene Creed.
[871] Gregory of Nyssa (Saint), *Orations and Sermons*, [Jaeger Vol 9, pp. 225-226].
[872] Saint Cyril of Jerusalem (AD 313–386) was a distinguished theologian of the early Church. About the end of AD 350 he succeeded Maximus as Bishop of Jerusalem. Saint Cyril left important writings documenting the instruction of catechumens and the order of the Liturgy in his day.
[873] Bradshaw, Paul F., *Early Christian Worship: A Basic Introduction to Ideas and Practice*, 58.
[874] Alexander Schmemann, *Liturgy and Tradition*, 19.

to the Word."[875] Saint Ignatius of Antioch says, "Come together in common, one and all without exception in charity, in one faith and in one Jesus Christ, who is of the race of David according to the flesh, the son of man, and the Son of God, so that with undivided mind you may obey the bishop and the priests and break one Bread which is the medicine of immortality and the antidote against death, enabling us to live forever in Jesus Christ."[876] Origen declares, "We also eat the bread presented to us; and this bread becomes by prayer a sacred Body, which sanctifies those who sincerely partake of it."[877] "Do we ask that our Bread, which is Christ," Saint Cyprian of Carthage[878] says, "be given to us daily, so that we who abide and live in Christ may not withdraw from His sanctification and from His Body."[879]

The pure, simple, and resilient beliefs of the Early Church in the patristic era left no room for questions to be raised around whether we receive the divine nature, or simply the human body, or perhaps the human body united with the divinity. On the contrary, the faith was of utmost simplicity, but yet very profound and solid; the bread and wine become the Body and Blood of Jesus Christ, and this is what we receive in the Eucharist. Therefore, the sacrament of the Eucharist is considered the crowing and fulfillment of the entire faith; in fact, it is what gives life to the church.

For the Early Church Fathers, the Eucharist was not merely a means of sanctification of the faithful, nor having communion of the Body and Blood of Jesus, but it was also the sacrament of oneness of the congregants;

---

[875] SGS, Smith (Bro.), *A Monk's Topical Bible Letters E-K*, Book 2, Volume 4, 193.
[876] Ignatius (Saint), *Letter to the Ephesians*, 20:1-2.
[877] Johnson, Maxwell E., *Praying and Believing in Early Christianity: The Interplay Between Christian Worship and Doctrine*, 41.
[878] Saint Cyprian (AD 200–September 14, 258) was bishop of Carthage in North Africa and an important Early Christian writer.
[879] Jurgens, William A., *The Faith of the Early Fathers*, Vol. I, 223.

through it, the *church* is lifted up to heaven, ascended before Christ, and attained her fulfillment as the Body of Christ. The concept of us, the faithful, the members of the church, being united as the Body of Christ, sanctified as a whole, and offered before God the Father in Christ, was, in the consciousness of today's theologians, reduced to individual sanctification and unity with Jesus.[880] This is a fundamental change in the *lex orandi*[881] of the church, of her liturgical belief, which, I think, should be reversed; and the original orthodox belief should be restored to its primordial state.

In honor of this sacrament, the Church spends many hours in preparation before receiving it, ahead of the Liturgy of the Faithful. In fact, preparation starts with the Vespers Psamody, followed by Vespers Offering of Incense, Vigils, Prime Offering of Incense, the Offertory office, and the Liturgy of the Word, respectively. In antiquity, the Coptic Orthodox Church employed many liturgies.[882] According to Father Antonios Makkar Ibrahim, 58 liturgies were in use among Copts.[883] The White Monastery Euchologion[884] (Sohag) mentioned the Liturgy of Saint Timothy (Pope of Alexandria), the Liturgy of Saint Gregory, prayers from the Liturgy of Saint Cyril, prayers from an Egyptian liturgy, the Liturgy of Saint John (Bishop of Bostra), the Liturgy of Saint Thomas, the Liturgy of Saint Severus of Antioch, a liturgy addressed to the Son, a Syriac liturgy, the Liturgy of Saint Matthew the Apostle, and the first part of the Liturgy of Saint James. Additionally, Father Stephanos Daniel announced that he

---

[880] In his fourth treatise, On the Lord's Prayer, Saint Cyprian says, "Our prayer is public and common; and when we pray, we pray not for one, but for the whole people, because we the whole people are one."

[881] *Lex orandi*, is a Latin term meaning "law of praying"; it refers to the beliefs of the church.

[882] Until this day, the Ethiopian Church, an offspring of the Coptic Church, still uses 14 liturgies.

[883] Ibrahim, A.M. (2013, April 13). *Liturgies of the Coptic Church*. Retrieved from coptcatholic.net/ قداسات-الكنيسة-القبطية-1

[884] Manuscript of a Euchologion in the Sahidic dialect that comes from the White Monastery in Upper Egypt. Although the dating of this fragmentary codex has been a matter of debate among scholars for a long time, many think it was written in the tenth century.

found a liturgy attributed to Saint John Chrysostom that was used in Egypt. He also added the following to the roster of liturgies once prayed in Egypt: The Liturgy of the Twelve Disciples, the Liturgy of Dionysius the Areopagite, the Liturgy of Saint Athanasius the Apostolic, the Liturgy of Saint Cyril of Jerusalem, the Liturgy of Saint Jacob of Serugh, the Liturgy of Saint Jacob of Edessa, the Liturgy of Saint Serapion, the Liturgy of Saint Mark, and the Liturgy of Saint Basil.

Conversely, Ibn Al-ʿAssāl and Ibn Sibaa (both from the 13th century), noted three liturgies only.[885] The first is the Liturgy of Saint Mark,[886] which Saint Cyril I,[887] the Pillar of Faith, adopted and added some prayers to it.[888] The second liturgy is the Liturgy of Saint Gregory, which was authored by Saint Gregory the Theologian[889] (Gregory Nazianzen).[890]

---

[885] Before the 11th century, more than twelve other liturgies were prayed in the Coptic Orthodox Church; however, Pope Gabriel II (served from AD 1131 to 1145), the 70th patriarch of Alexandria, decided to limit the use of the liturgies to the three ones that are still in use today. Ibn Sibaa noted that the Coptic Church once used 14 or more liturgies, but to shorten the service, they were limited to three.

[886] John Mark was an apostle of Jesus Christ who first served along with the Apostle Paul. After disagreements, Saint Mark found it the Lord's will to preach apart from Saint Paul. The Orthodox church of Egypt calls him "the God bearer" because he is credited with being the apostle to bear the gospel of Christ to the Egyptians. He is recognized worldwide as the writer of the second gospel named "The gospel of Saint Mark." As the first prelate to the land of Egypt, the Coptic Orthodox Church ordains its patriarch as the successor of Saint Mark. After preaching the gospel of Jesus Christ, the Apostle Mark was martyred in the year AD 68.

[887] Cyril of Alexandria (named the pillar of faith) was the 24th Bishop of Alexandria who shepherded the universal church through the third ecumenical council and defended the united nature of Christ (fully divine and fully human without confusion nor separation) against the heresy of the Nestorians. He is widely regarded as the authority on the Christological discussion. After the departure of Saint Theophilus (Saint Cyril's uncle) Cyril became patriarch. He became the forerunning defender of the mariological title "Theotokos" (meaning "bearer of God") against the Nestorian "Christotokos" (meaning "bearer of Christ") and, in so doing, became the defender of the united nature of Christ. He developed the Christological phrase "Mia Physis to Theologos Sesarkomeni" which is translated to "The united nature of the Incarnate Word of God." After shepherding the flock of Christ and teaching the Orthodox faith, Saint Cyril departed to our Lord in the year AD 444.

[888] For this reason, it is now commonly known as the Liturgy of Saint Cyril.

[889] Scholars could not find a liturgy in Saint Gregory's literature; however, according to the Coptic Church, he is the writer of the liturgy carrying his name.

[890] Gregory the theologian (also known as Gregory Nazianzen) was a close friend and beloved spiritual companion of Saint Basil the Great. He was the Bishop of Nazianzus who worked diligently to rid the church of the Arian heresy. Saint Gregory was known as a gifted theologian who was able to rid the church of Constantinople entirely of the Arianism and Appolinarianism, which had plagued it before his rule as bishop, after he has been sent there by the bishops gathered at the second ecumenical council. Further, Saint Gregory is well regarded for his astute asceticism.

The third liturgy is that of Saint Basil the Great.[891] A fourth liturgy attributed to Saint Serapion[892] was celebrated in the fourth century; however, it is no longer in use today. The liturgies of Saint Cyril and Saint Serapion are of Egyptian origin and inherit the characteristics of the Alexandrian tradition, whereas the liturgies of Saint Basil and Saint Gregory are of Byzantine roots. Due to the different cultural roots, there is a noticeable difference in the liturgical structure between the national-in-character liturgies of Saint Cyril and Saint Serapion from one hand, and that of Saint Gregory and Saint Basil from the other hand. Although the structure of each of these liturgies should be preserved, when was still the metropolitan of Asyut, Pope Makarius III, the 114th Patriarch of Alexandria (AD 1944–1945), was the first to alter the structure of the Liturgy of Saint Cyril to mimic the arrangement of the Liturgy of Saint Basil.[893] This change was a source of umbrage in the ecclesiastical forums that prevented it from spreading; hence, the pristine structure survived the subversion.

Nearing the end of his life, Saint Gregory retired from his post as Bishop, and spent his final years in ascetic seclusion, until our Lord received his soul in the year AD 390.

[891] Basil the Great was the archbishop of Caesarea. He was born into a pious family, of which, many of his siblings became noted saints in the church (Saint Macrina the younger, Saint Naucratius, Saint Peter of Sebaste and Saint Gregory of Nyssa.) He studied to be an orator and was well versed in topics ranging from philosophy to theology. He was a key figure in the defense of the faith against Arian and Appollinarian doctrines, which opposed the true apostolic teachings. Saint Basil is further noted, apart from his skill as a gifted theologian (from which skill the liturgy of Saint Basil was born), for his great asceticism and love for the poor and dejected. His struggle came to an end in AD 379 at the calling of our Lord Jesus Christ for him to enter into everlasting joy.

[892] Bishop and head of the famed Catechetical School of Alexandria, Egypt, also known as Serapion of Arsinoe. He was originally a monk in the Egyptian desert and a companion to Saint Anthony who left in his will the gift of two sheepskin cloaks, one for Serapion and the other for Saint Athanasius of Alexandria. A close friend of Athanasius, he gave support to the patriarch against the heretic Arians in Egypt especially after receiving appointment as bishop of Thmuis, in Lower Egypt, on the Nile delta (AD 339). Because of his unequivocal backing of Athanasius and his opposition to Arianism, he was exiled for a time by the ardent Arian emperor Constantius II. A brilliant scholar and theologian, he was also the author of a series of writings on the doctrine of the divinity of the Holy Spirit (addressed to the emperor), the Euchologium (a sacramentary), and a treatise against Manichacism.

[893] This was documented in exchange of letters between H.E. Makarios, Metropolitan of Asyut (later on Pope Makarius III), and the late scholar Yassa Abdel Messeh.

Another change to the liturgy in the 19th century, which is the use of Arabic—instead of Coptic—in the liturgy, was introduced by *Hegumen* Philotheos Ibrahim, the head of the Old Patriarchate at the time.[894] Unlike the former change, although it was condemned at the beginning, this alteration was widely accepted in all churches inside and outside of Egypt. This was the foundation of using the vernacular in liturgical ceremonies.

It is important to note that the Liturgy of Saint Cyril is considered the second oldest liturgy after that of Saint James the Apostle. Finally, it is noteworthy that the liturgies of Saint Cyril and Saint Basil are addressed to God the Father, whereas the Liturgy of Saint Gregory is addressed to God the Son.[895]

Hammerschmidt believes that the Liturgy of Saint Gregory has Syriac roots and was adopted in Egypt when some Syrian monks immigrated to the Scetis (Natrun Valley). Hammerschmidt also thinks that the original text of this liturgy was written between AD 350 and 400.[896] Traditionally, the Liturgy of Saint Gregory was used—in the Coptic Church—on Feast Days, as well as the festival of Saint Gregory the Theologian. The Liturgy of Saint Cyril was assigned to Lent and the Fast of Nineveh, in addition to the festivals of Saint Mark and Saint Cyril I. On all other days, the Liturgy of Saint Basil was employed. Nowadays, this order is not stringently adhered to.

As the Liturgy of Saint Basil is the most used Eucharist in the Coptic Church since early days, I shall shed some light on its origin. Since its

---

[894] Labib, Ekladious, *The First and Second Responses to the Article and Brief by Hegumen Philotheos*, 46, 47.

[895] In antiquity, based on (John 16:23), it was a common practice to address liturgical prayers to the Father through the Son. However, it was also not uncommon to address them directly to the Son. Examples: The *Anaphora* of Addai and Mari, the Liturgy of Saint Gregory, the Liturgy of Saint Matthew the Apostle (documented in the White Monastery Euchologion), the 3 Ethiopian liturgies of Saint Athanasius, Saint Jacob of Serugh, and Saint Gregory the Armenian, and finally the second Syriac liturgy of Saint Peter.

[896] Epiphaneus (bishop), *The Gregorian Liturgy*, 12, 13.

introduction to the pool of Eucharistic prayers, the Liturgy of Saint Basil was the most influential model for liturgical development.[897] Many other Eucharistic prayers fully or partially adopted its structure. The Liturgy of Saint Basil has different textual variations based on the following geographical grouping: Byzantium, Armenia, Syria and Egypt. Most of the manuscripts of this liturgy in extant are of the Byzantine Basil; however, due to its antiquarian value, the Egyptian one attracted a lot of attention from scholars. It is interesting to note that the text of the Egyptian Basil is substantially shorter than that of the other traditions. The earliest and most important group of the Egyptian Basil is the Sahidic version, which includes manuscripts date back to the seventh century. Although not as early as the Sahidic version, most of the Egyptian Basil manuscripts belong to the Bohairic version group. A third version of the Egyptian Basil is the Greek one, which is preserved in a handful of manuscripts. Although the original language of the Egyptian Basil was Greek, the Greek version in extant is relatively late and was translated from Bohairic, which suggests that the original Greek origin was lost.

In his essay *The Basilian Anaphoras*, D. Richard Stuckwisch tried to prove the influence of the Egyptian tradition of Saint Basil himself. Stuckwisch writes, "It should simply be recognized that Basil lived and worked very much within the heritage of Origen, and that he was likewise greatly influenced by the legacy of Gregory Thaumaturgus."[898] Stuckwisch found major similarities between the shape of the prayer mentioned in Origen's *Treatise on Prayer* and the Liturgy of Saint Basil. Origen spent five years (AD 233–338) in Caesarea teaching Gregory Thaumaturgus the faith, who later on became the first bishop of Pontus and who was regarded

---

[897] Stuckwisch, Richard D. (1997). The Basilian Anaphoras. In Bradshaw, Paul F. (Ed.), *Essays on Early Eastern Eucharistic Prayers*, 109.
[898] Stuckwisch, Ibid., 121.

by the Cappadocian Fathers—including Saint Basil—their master teacher and the founder of Christianity in Cappadocia. In his treatise *On the Holy Spirit*, Saint Basil writes, "We are not content in the liturgy simply to recite the words recorded by St. Paul or the Gospels,[899] but we add other words both before and after, words of great importance for this mystery." He then explains that these words are received "from unwritten teaching."[900] Therefore, it is fair to assume that the teachings of Gregory Thaumaturgus, including the Eucharist, which he received from Origen and passed down to Saint Basil have influenced the liturgy carrying his (Saint Basil's) name.

H. Engberding in AD 1931 suggested that the three non-Egyptian versions of the Liturgy of Saint Basil (Byzantine, Armenian, and Syriac) derive from a lost common source (Ω-BAS) and his conclusions were widely accepted by scholars. Studying the commonalities between the texts of these liturgies, John Fenwick reconstructed a hypothetical text of Ω-BAS. This liturgy is valuable to scholars because it provides a means to treat all non-Egyptian versions of the Liturgy of Saint Basil as one, which will ease the comparison with the Egyptian Basil. After comparing the Sahidic Egyptian Basil to Ω-BAS, Stuckwisch was able to show similarities between the Epiclesis of both liturgies, which, in turn, suggests Alexandrian tradition was the basis of the original structure of the liturgy developed by Saint Basil.[901] Furthermore, Fenwick argues that the similarities between the liturgy of Saint James and that of Saint Basil show their respective developments from a common source, now lost, but which is best preserved in the Egyptian recension of the Liturgy of Saint Basil.[902]

---

[899] Saint Basil is referring here to the Institution Narrative.
[900] Stuckwisch, Ibid., 125.
[901] Stuckwisch, Ibid., 124-129.
[902] Stuckwisch, Ibid., 117-118.

The Creed

The two pillars of the Sacrifice of Christ are faith and love, hence, at the commencement of the three liturgies, the Creed is recited followed by the Prayer of Reconciliation. Faith is declared through the Creed, and love is shown through the kiss of peace (also called the Holy Kiss). The Creed is the Christian "constitution," through which the worshippers' beliefs are proclaimed aloud. Non-believers (the catechumens) are not permitted to attend or recite the Creed as their faith has not completed yet. The Creed used today was put in place by the Church Fathers who assembled at the Council of Nicaea is AD 325. The Nicene Creed was then amended with clarifications and additions by the Church Fathers of the Council of Constantinople in AD 381. Ancient sources attest that until the 5th century, the recitation of the Creed preceding the liturgy was not a common practice. Scholars think that this tradition was introduced by Peter the Fuller[903] around AD 488 or 489 as propaganda against the council of Chalcedon; however, Jacob of Edessa mentions that it was used by the Syrians as early as right after the council of Nicaea.[904] The practice of reciting the Creed prior to celebrating the Eucharist was then adopted by Constantinople in AD 511.[905] Cuming suggests that this new practice was introduced to the Egyptian liturgy in the 6th century, at the earliest.[906]

The following is the Nicene-Constantinopolitan Creed,[907] with the Constantinople additions in bold Italic: "We believe in one God, the

---

[903] Peter the Fuller was Patriarch of Antioch for various periods from AD 465 to 488. He was an opponent of the Council of Chalcedon. Peter received his surname from his former trade as a fuller of cloth, which he practiced when he was a monk at the Monastery of Acoemeti.
[904] Ignatius Ephrem II Rahmani (Patriarch of the Syriac Catholic Church), *Les Liturgies Orientales et Occidentales*, 239.
[905] Cuming, Geoffrey J., *The Liturgy of St Mark*, 103, 104.
[906] Cuming, Geoffrey J., *The Liturgy of St Mark*, 101.
[907] The Nicene-Constantinopolitan Creed is the only authoritative ecumenical statement of the Christian faith accepted by the Roman Catholic, Eastern Orthodox, Oriental Orthodox, Anglican, and the major Protestant denominations.

Father Almighty, Maker *of heaven and earth*, and of all things visible and invisible. And in one Lord Jesus Christ, the *Only*-begotten Son of God, begotten of the Father *before all ages*, Light of Light, very God of very God, begotten, not made, being of one substance with the Father; by whom all things were made; who for us men, and for our salvation, came down *from heaven*, and was incarnate *by the Holy Spirit of the Virgin Mary*, and was made man; *he was crucified for us under Pontius Pilate*, suffered and *was buried*, and the third day, He rose again, *according to the Scriptures, and* ascended into heaven, *and sits on the right hand of the Father*; from thence he shall come *again, with glory*, to judge the quick and the dead; *whose kingdom shall have no end*. And in the Holy Spirit, *the Lord and Giver of life, who proceeds from the Father, who with the Father and the Son together is worshiped and glorified, who spoke by the prophets. In one holy catholic and apostolic Church. We acknowledge one baptism for the remission of sins. We look for the resurrection of the dead, and the life of the world to come. Amen*.[908]

The recitation of the Creed belongs originally to baptism, but in the struggle against heresies it was incorporated into the liturgies. This addition took place first in the East around the 6th century. It appears that early in the Coptic Church, as well as in some others, the recitation of the Creed was assigned to a deacon on behalf of the congregation. Therefore, the Deacons Service book, published by the Renaissance of Coptic

---

[908] The Nicene-Constantinopolitan Creed in Greek "Πιστεύομεν εἰς ἕνα θεὸν Πατέρα παντοκράτορα, ποιητὴν οὐρανοῦ καὶ γῆς, ὁρατῶν τε πάντων καὶ ἀοράτων. Καὶ εἰς ἕνα κύριον Ἰησοῦν Χριστόν, τὸν υἱὸν τοῦ θεοῦ τὸν μονογενῆ, τὸν ἐκ τοῦ Πατρὸς γεννηθέντα πρὸ πάντων τῶν αἰώνων, φῶς ἐκ φωτός, θεὸν ἀληθινὸν ἐκ θεοῦ ἀληθινοῦ, γεννηθέντα οὐ ποιηθέντα, ὁμοούσιον τῷ Πατρί· δι' οὗ τὰ πάντα ἐγένετο· τὸν δι' ἡμᾶς τοὺς ἀνθρώπους καὶ διὰ τὴν ἡμετέραν σωτηρίαν κατελθόντα ἐκ τῶν οὐρανῶν καὶ σαρκωθέντα ἐκ Πνεύματος Ἁγίου καὶ Μαρίας τῆς παρθένου καὶ ἐνανθρωπήσαντα, σταυρωθέντα τε ὑπὲρ ἡμῶν ἐπὶ Ποντίου Πιλάτου, καὶ παθόντα καὶ ταφέντα, καὶ ἀναστάντα τῇ τρίτῃ ἡμέρα κατὰ τὰς γραφάς, καὶ ἀνελθόντα εἰς τοὺς οὐρανούς, καὶ καθεζόμενον ἐκ δεξιῶν τοῦ Πατρός, καὶ πάλιν ἐρχόμενον μετὰ δόξης κρῖναι ζῶντας καὶ νεκρούς· οὗ τῆς βασιλείας οὐκ ἔσται τέλος. Καὶ εἰς τὸ Πνεῦμα τὸ Ἅγιον, τὸ κύριον, (καὶ) τὸ ζωοποιόν, τὸ ἐκ τοῦ πατρὸς ἐκπορευόμενον, τὸ σὺν Πατρὶ καὶ Υἱῷ συμπροσκυνούμενον καὶ συνδοξαζόμενον, τὸ λαλῆσαν διὰ τῶν προφητῶν. Εἰς μίαν, ἁγίαν, καθολικὴν καὶ ἀποστολικὴν ἐκκλησίαν· ὁμολογοῦμεν ἓν βάπτισμα εἰς ἄφεσιν ἁμαρτιῶν· προσδοκοῦμεν ἀνάστασιν νεκρῶν, καὶ ζωὴν τοῦ μέλλοντος αἰῶνος. Ἀμήν."

Orthodox Churches Association, states that the deacon, looking westward, recites the Creed as two other deacons hold candles on each side, during which the congregation remains silent up to the last sentence, after which they chant the concluding sentence, "we look for the resurrection of the dead, and the life of the age to come. Amen."[909] This explains why, up until now, the altar server will raise a cross and address the congregation saying, "In the wisdom of God, let us attend. Lord have mercy. Lord have mercy. Truly we believe.[910]" This bidding attests to the immemorial practice of the congregation listening to the Creed being recited by a deacon. They actively join in chanting the final phrase, as noted above. Today's rubric, however, mandates the people to join the chorus in declaiming the Creed.

To recap, the contemporary practice prescribes that after the conclusion of the Three Major litanies, one of the altar servers raises the cross and addresses the congregation saying, "In the wisdom of God, let us attend. Lord have mercy. Lord have mercy. Truly we believe." Hence, the people recite the Creed aloud. Father Samaan Ibn Koleil, a 12th century priest, elucidates, "chanting 'Lord have mercy' is a means of humility before the Lord so that God may not allow for anyone's heart to be hardened, and that everyone's faith be declared from the heart, and not only in words." Also, he writes, "The raising of the cross reminds us of Moses raising the bronze serpent, which healed those who, in need, looked at it. Therefore, healing can be accomplished by the correct reciting of the Creed, and through our Lord Jesus Christ's sign of wisdom and life, which is the honorable Cross."[911]

---

[909] The Renaissance of Coptic Orthodox Churches Association, *The Deacons Service book*, 72.
[910] "Truly we believe" is the beginning of the Creed according to the Coptic Orthodox Church.
[911] Athanasius of Saint Macarius Monastery (Father), *The Divine Liturgy: The Mystery of the Kingdom of God (Part 2)*, 590.

The last sentence of the Creed is chanted, not recited. Up until the mid-20th century, and as recorded by Cantor Mikhail the Great with the accompaniment of cantors from the Institute of Coptic Studies, there are two renditions for this phrase; either one can launch any of the three Coptic liturgies. Nevertheless, nowadays, the minor tune is usually appointed to the liturgies of Saint Cyril and Saint Basil, whereas the melismatic one is dedicated to the Liturgy of Saint Gregory.

While we are at it, let us review the key concepts—precisely confessed in the Creed—that we, Christians, believe in. In the Creed we affirm that we believe in one God. However, later, we unmistakably proclaim that this God is Trinitarian. We believe in three *Hypostases* (Persons) of our God: The Father, the Son, and the Holy Spirit. The three Persons are distinct but not separated. The three Persons of God have one and only one divine nature, will, volition, and energy. They are coequal and coeternal. The distinction of the Persons of God is genuine, eternal, and perpetual, not merely an external, temporary, or imaginary activity. Each *Hypostasis* (Person), however, possesses the entire Godhead in its totality. The three Persons are one God, not three. Bishop Kallistos explains the unity and still diversity of our Trinitarian God saying, "The Christian God is not just a unit but a union, not just unity but community."[912] We believe that God is three in one and one in three; three Persons in one divine Godhead, and one Godhead in three Persons.

God the Father is the source of and bond among the three Persons. He is the only source of the Triune God. Yet, the Father never existed without or before the other two Persons. God the Son is the *Logos* (Word) of God. He is begotten from the Father. God the Son is the Person that assumed our humanity, died, and resurrected on our behalf. God the Holy

---

[912] Ware, Kallistos (Bishop), *The Orthodox Way*, 27.

Spirit is the life of God and source of every life. He proceeds from the Father. The difference between this procession and the begetting of the Son from the Father is unknown and beyond human's recognition; yet denotes the difference between how God the Father produces the Son as opposed to the Holy Spirit. "The Threeness of God," Bishop Kallistos explains, "is something given or revealed to us in Scripture, in the Apostolic Tradition, and in the experience of the saints throughout the centuries."[913] It is worth noting that one of the essential differences between Western and Eastern Christianity is the doctrine of the *Filioque*,[914] a Latin term indicating that the Holy Spirit proceeds from the Father and the Son. This non-conciliar addition, although appeared in the fifth century, was accepted by the Roman Popes in AD 1014. The addition was repudiated by the East. In the Orthodox understanding, the *Filioque* impairs the role of the Father as well as minimizes—or could be understood that way—the role of the Holy Spirit to a mere activity, not a Person. It also propounds two sources (fathers) in the Triune God. In the East (Orthodox Churches), the *Filioque* is considered an aberration of the orthodox faith; hence, was assailed, decried, and announced by many a heresy.

In the Creed, we proclaim that God the Son was incarnate from the Holy Spirit and the Virgin Mary and became man. He took the whole of our manhood to Himself in order to restore it and save us. Therefore, Jesus Christ, the Second Person of the Holy Trinity, is a perfect man with all the elements of humanity, yet, He is the eternal God, the Creator of heaven and earth and all what therein. Jesus Christ is not two coexisting persons

---

[913] Ware, Ibid., 34.
[914] The literal meaning of the Latin clause *Filioque* is "and the Son". Although the term was first introduced in a local Syrian church in AD 410. That is, in the East, Saint Augustine of Hippo, along with other Western Fathers, adopted it and spread it in the West. This teaching was one of the reasons for the Great Schism (also called East-West Schism) that took place in AD 1054 It is also worth noting that some Roman Pope, among whom Pope Leo the Great, rejected the *Filioque*.

in one body, but one person. As such, all suffering, death, resurrection, and other events explained in the Scripture are to be ascribed to God-made-man, the incarnate Son of God, the eternal Second Person of the Holy Trinity who, for our salvation, became man within space and time. This follows, as declared in the Creed, that Virgin Mary is the *Theotokos* (God-bearer or Mother of God). Saint Mary is not the mother of a human united to the divine person of the Word of God, but rather to one undivided person, God-made-man, who is the *Logos*, the Only-Begotten Son of God, and a perfect man at once.

By assuming our human nature, Jesus Christ sanctified it and showed us the Way. In his *On the Incarnation*, Saint Athanasius writes, "He takes to Himself a body capable of death, in order that it, participating in the Word who is above all, might be sufficient for death on behalf of all, and through the indwelling Word would remain incorruptible, and so corruption might henceforth cease from all by the grace of the resurrection."[915] Through Him, and only Him, we can unite with God and be accepted once more. The incarnate God the *Logos* "shares to the full in what we are, and so He makes it possible for us to share in what He is, in His divine life and glory. He became what we are, so as to make us what He is,"[916] Bishop Kallistos writes. The Friday Theotokion echoes this very concept; it reads, "He took what is ours, and gave us what is His." As Saint Athanasius explicates, "the corruption of death, which formerly held them in its power, has simply ceased to be. For the human race would have perished utterly had not the Lord and Savior of all, the Son of God, come among us to put an end to death." He continues, "There were thus two things which the Savior did for us by becoming Man. He banished death from us and made us anew; and, invisible and imperceptible as in Himself

---

[915] Athanasius of Alexandria (Saint), *On the Incarnation*.
[916] Ware, Kallistos (Bishop), *The Orthodox Way*, 74.

He is, He became visible through His works and revealed Himself as the Word of the Father, the Ruler and King of the whole creation."[917]

The last sentence of the Creed focuses the worshippers' attention on eternal life. It states, "We look for the resurrection of the dead and the life of the age to come." The age to come is the age after Jesus' Second Coming, after His Judgment Day. The earthly death is the separation of the human spirit from the body. In the Judgement Day, the spirits will reunite with their bodies. No one knows how they will look like. Saint John testifies, "Dear friends, now we are children of God, and what we will be has not yet been made known. But we know that when Christ appears, we shall be like Him, for we shall see Him as He is" (1 John 3:2). Christians have their hope in eternity, not in this transient life. "If only for this life we have hope in Christ, we are of all people most to be pitied" (1 Corinthians 15:19). As Christians, we believe that we are sojourners awaiting going back to our true home. Therefore, the Creed ends with a note that fixes our eyes and hearts on the Lord and on His eternal Kingdom, our true home. "Our citizenship is in heaven. And we eagerly await a Savior from there, the Lord Jesus Christ" (Philippians 3:20). Therefore, "we fix our eyes not on what is seen, but on what is unseen, since what is seen is temporary, but what is unseen is eternal" (1 Corinthians 4:18).

While the congregation utters the Creed, the priest washes his hands in a rite called the *lavabo*, as a symbol of purity, then turns westward and wrings his hands before the people, then dries them. *The Apostolic Constitutions* provides an elucidation for washing the hands; it expounds, "Let one of the sub-deacons bring water to wash the hands of the priests, which is a symbol of the purity of those souls that are devoted to God."[918] In his explanation of the liturgy, the 9th century Moses Bar-Kepha

---

[917] Athanasius of Alexandria (Saint), *On the Incarnation*.
[918] *The Apostolic Constitutions VIII*, section 2, The Form of Prayer for the Faithful.

confirms this understanding. The 12th century Samaan Ibn Koleil also states that "the priest washes his hands not to imitate the Roman governor who crucified Christ...The priest (while washing his hands) recites Psalm 'purge me with hyssop and I shall be clean...' as he prays for the cleansing of his spirit. The act of washing moves the soul to ask the Holy Spirit, who dwells within the soul and the body since baptism, for purity."[919] The physical understanding of cleanliness emerged possibly in the 12th century; hence, Samaan Ibn Koleil speaks of the hand-washing symbolizing the spiritual and physical purity.[920]

In the 13th and 14th centuries, the concept of hand washing was explained as a means of sanitization prior to touching the Holy Mysteries. This is different from the spiritual connotation that was common until the 12th century. In the Late Middle Ages, specifically in the 15th century, a substitute rationalization was offered by Pope Gabriel V. He explicates that the *lavabo* signifies the celebrant's innocence of the blood of those who approach the Holy Mysteries unworthily, and without his knowledge.[921] Similarly, *The Beginners' Guide and Discipline for Laity* explicates, "The washing of the priest's hands here resembles what Moses used to do when he reads the Law to them. He used to wash his hands and say, 'I am innocent of your sins.' If you listen, obey, and keep what I have told you, you will be saved. Whoever does not listen and obey, I am innocent of him, and his blood is on himself. Similarly did Pilate when they (the Jews) came to him with our Master unto the cross. He took water, washed his hands, disowned the Jew's claims, and said, 'I am innocent of this man's blood, it is your responsibility!'"[922]

---

[919] Athanasius of Saint Macarius Monastery (Father), *The Divine Liturgy: The Mystery of the Kingdom of God (Part 2)*, 593.
[920] Bebawi, George H., *The Divine Liturgy*, 180.
[921] Gabriel V (Pope), *The Ritual Order*, BnF, MS 98 (AD 1411), fol. 59r-v.
[922] Misael of the Paromeos Monastery (Father). (2018). The Beginners' Guide and Discipline for Laity. *Alexandria School, 25(2)*, 133.

In other words, the understanding of *lavabo* evolved over time. In the first twelve centuries, the focus was on the spiritual meaning of purity prior to commencing the Eucharist. The 13th and 14th centuries understanding embraced the physical cleansing prior to the handling of the Holy Mysteries. From the 15th century onwards the washing of hands came to symbolize the priest's blamelessness from those who disparage the Holy Mysteries.

I should also note that Ibn Kabar notes an incongruously practice that is not extant in the contemporary rubric. He writes that after the *lavabo*, the assistant priest presents the thurible to the celebrant to cense his hands. Uppsala, MS OR. 486 (AD 1546) adds, "Patriarch Benjamin did not approve censing the hands at this point, but rather when the congregation says, 'According to Your mercy, O Lord, and not according to our sins.'"[923] This is probably the reason for the vanishing of this practice.

The Prayer of Reconciliation

When the People have finished the Creed, the celebrant turns westward, bows to the assistant priests,[924] and makes the sign of the cross over the people, saying, "Peace be with all," to which they respond saying, "And with your spirit." The priest then turns eastward and utters the Prayer of Reconciliation. In the Liturgy of Saint Basil, there are two Prayers of Reconciliation. The first, which starts with "O God, the Great and Eternal," was authored by Saint Basil himself in the 4th century. The second that begins with "Exalted above all power of speech," was written by Bishop Yohanna (John), the Bishop of Bostra in Syria. The Liturgy of Saint Gregory also embraces two Prayers of Reconciliation. The first is

---

[923] Ibn Kabar, *The Lamp to Darkness and Explanation of the Service*, Father Samuel of Syrians Monastery, 128. This note was not mentioned in the older Paris copy of the manuscript.

[924] The act of bowing to the other priests and the rest of the attendees is an expression of asking for forgiveness and reconciliation lest anyone in the congregation is in conflict with him.

credited to Saint Gregory of Nazianzus in the 4th century, and starts with "O you the Being, who was." The second, which commences with "O Christ our God," is attributed to the Patriarch Saint Severus of Antioch (AD 465–537). As for the Liturgy of Saint Cyril, it too includes two Prayers of Reconciliation: "O Author of Life and King of the ages," written by Saint Severus of Antioch; and "O God of love and giver of the oneness of heart," which Saint Youhanna (John) the Bishop of Bostra authored.

The faithful cannot start any prayer without having been reconciled with one another. Hence, the Didache instructs, "Let no one who is at odds with his fellow come together with you, until they be reconciled, that your sacrifice may not be profaned."[925] The worshippers can reconcile with one another because they have been reconciled with God first. Therefore, advertently, the Prayer of Reconciliation is split into two sections. The first contemplates on the fall of man by the envy of the Devil, and God's plan for the salvation of mankind through the shedding of His Blood on the Cross. The concern of this part is the separation of man from the Lord due to the commitment of sin, which served as a barrier between us, humans, and the All-Holy God. Moreover, this section exhibits God's plan to restore this relationship through the death of His Only-begotten Son on the Cross. Thus, the priest prays this section with bare hands (without corporals), a symbol of man's state prior to the reconciliation.

In the beginning, God formed man without sin or corruption. However, after "the fall,"[926] man needed redemption to return to the original state intended by God at Creation. For this to happen, God the Son was incarnated and offered Himself up to death for the salvation of the world, so that the reconciliation between God and man may be

---

[925] *The Didache* (14:2).
[926] In Christian theology, "the fall" is a term used to describe the transition of the first man and woman from a state of innocent obedience to God to a state of guilty disobedience.

accomplished, and the peace of the Lord may replace the trepidation which entered man's life after "the fall" and leaving the Garden of Eden. As sinners, Adam and Eve had lost their peace and were afraid of God. Therefore, the emphasis of this part of the prayer is on the reconciliation through the shedding of Christ's Blood on the Cross,[927] a practical prayer implementing the theological theory of Atonement.[928] "Therefore, since we have been justified through faith, we have peace with God through our Lord Jesus Christ" (Romans 5:1). "For there is one God and one mediator between God and mankind, the man Christ Jesus" (1 Timothy 2:5).

It is essential to comprehend the sacrificial nature of this prayer. The deep and profound apprehension of where we primordially belonged (i.e., paradise), what we lost, and how we were restored, is fundamental to partake of the Eucharist. That is to say, how humanity was alienated from God through transgression, and thus exiled from paradise, how God had mercy on the human feeble nature by His propitiation for our sins, and, finally, how He saved humanity and restored it to Paradise and granted us the true filial freedom. Genuinely realizing these conceptions must lead faithful to the "true" thanksgiving. Thanksgiving in this sense is not a mere thanking Him for an event or an action that He did—or kissing the back of the hands—but it is living in paradise, in union with God. Thanksgiving, in the light of this realization, is the sign of sharing God in His will, living as ambassadors to Him on earth, enjoying His fatherhood and godhead. Therefore, Thanksgiving is the fullness of the knowledge of

---

[927] It is noteworthy that the Prayer of Reconciliation is not performed on Maundy Thursday, since the reconciliation with God the Father through Christ's salvation did not take place until Good Friday.

[928] Atonement refers to the forgiving of sin in general and original sin in particular through the death and resurrection of Jesus, enabling the reconciliation between God and his creation. According to this theory, God has provided a way for humankind to come back into harmonious relation with Him, is everywhere apparent in Scripture.

God and the fulfillment of the genuine freedom in Him. It is how we live in unity with Jesus; it is the only possible result of our union with Him through the sacrifice of Him. Thanksgiving is the understanding of the essence of Paradise in relation to His sacrifice on the Cross. Lastly, it is the crowning of our genuine faith and belief in Jesus and in His ineffable plan to restore our nature and bring us back into His bosom. Experiencing this and fully living the life of thanksgiving, the Early Church Fathers called the Eucharist the *Sacrament of Sacraments*. Therefore, it was only natural—as we shall see later—to place the Thanksgiving Prayer right after that of Reconciliation.

Toward the end of the first part of the Prayer of Reconciliation in the Liturgy of Saint Cyril, the priest prays, "And make us worthy of the heavenly peace which befits Your divinity and is full of salvation, that we may give the same to one another in perfect love." In the Liturgy of Saint Basil, he states, "Glory to God in the highest, peace on earth, and good toward men." Finally, in the Liturgy of Saint Gregory, the priest pleads, "You said ... My peace I give to you; My peace I leave with you. The same also, now grant to us, O our Master." These orisons express the church's understanding of true "peace" and its source. In Jesus we, Jews and Gentiles, became one. This is what the Bible teaches; "For He Himself is our peace, who has made the two groups one and has destroyed the barrier, the dividing wall of hostility, by setting aside in his flesh the law with its commands and regulations. His purpose was to create in Himself one new humanity out of the two, thus making peace" (Ephesians 2:14-15). As such, only through our Lord Jesus Christ, perpetual peace can be conserved.

After the conclusion of the first part of the Prayer of Reconciliation, the altar server asks the people to "Pray for the perfect peace, love and holy apostolic kisses," to which they affirm saying, "Lord have mercy." In the

Basilian and Cyrilline liturgies, this affirmation employs the same melody as that of the Liturgy of the Word and the Three Major litanies.[929] This is evident in Cantor Mikhail's recordings of the Liturgy of Saint Basil, as well as that of the Institute of Coptic Studies.[930] In other words, the melody assigned to the people's responses ("And with your spirit," and "Lord have mercy"), whether during Regular Days or on Feast Days, is the same one appointed to the Offertory, the Liturgy of the Word, and the Three Major litanies.[931] This should not be a surprise considering the primitive location of the Prayer of Reconciliation between the Liturgy of the Word and the Offertory.[932]

In the second part of the Prayer of Reconciliation, the priest prays to the Lord Christ on behalf of the people for peace, and that He may make the worshippers worthy of greeting one another with a Holy Kiss, a sign of reconciliation, so that they may partake of His Body and Blood.[933] "Therefore, if you are offering your gift at the altar, and there remember that your brother or sister has something against you, leave your gift there in front of the altar. First go and be reconciled to them; then come and offer your gift" (Matthew 5:23-24). "This kiss blends souls one with another, and courts entire forgiveness for them," Saint Cyril of Jerusalem says, "The kiss therefore is the sign that our souls are mingled together and banish all remembrance of wrongs. For this cause, Christ said, 'If you are offering your gift at the altar, and

---

[929] Many chanters today inaccurately use a unique tune for this affirmation, a practice that is not supported by old sources or recordings.
[930] This tune was also used in Alexandria till the 20th century. I heard this tune in a recording of a liturgy that took place at Saint Mark's Cathedral of Alexandria in the 1950's.
[931] Same *rule* applies to the incense offering office.
[932] This explains the reason for treating the first three sections (i.e., Offertory, Liturgy of the Word, and the Prayer of Reconciliation) similarly, whereas the "rules" for the Liturgy of the Faithful, starting from the *Anaphora*, are different. In the first three sections, for example, the Joyous tunes are permitted, whereas they are not used during the Liturgy of the Faithful regardless of the occasion.
[933] The Greek word used here is "μετασχεῖν" meaning "to partake;" however, it was mistranslated in Arabic as "ننال" instead of "نتناول".

there remember that your brother has anything against time, leave there your gift upon the altar, and go your way; first be reconciled to your brother, and then come and offer your gift.' The kiss therefore is reconciliation, and for this reason holy: as the blessed Paul somewhere cried, saying, 'Greet ye one another with a holy kiss' (1 Corinthians 16:20); and Peter, 'with a kiss of charity' (1 Peter 3:15)."[934]

This part of the prayer, therefore, is concerned with the faithful reconciling with one another, since they have already been reconciled with God the Father (in the first part). Comparable to the first part, this commandment to love one another must be understood from a sacrificial perspective. In Christ, the faithful, the members of the church, are given the ability to love one another in purity and chastity. When Jesus, the Son of God and the Son of Man, gave up His life for humankind on the Cross, He gave the believers His life and spirit, the Holy Spirit. He gave them His life so they may live it; He gave them His Holy Spirit so they may enjoy His fruits. The newness of Christianity is not the commandment to love our enemies, but the staggering fact that it gave us the ability to fulfill this commandment. If we abide in Jesus, we inhale from His Holy Spirit that, in turn, shall grant us the love of Christ; and only then, we can practically implement "love your enemies" (Matthew 5:44). Reconciling with one another and loving each other is the only sign that a Christian is a true follower of Jesus. "By this everyone will know that you are my disciples, if you love one another" (John 13:35). This godly love unites the faithful, the members of His own Body (i.e., the church) in Him; thus, "there be no divisions among you, but that you be perfectly united in mind and

---

[934] Cyril of Jerusalem (Saint), *Catechetical Lecture 23*.

thought" (1 Corinthians 1:10). Failing to do so is an impediment to uniting with Jesus.

In the liturgy, we show this love, by greeting one another with a Holy Kiss, also called the Kiss of Peace.[935] "When the time comes for the exhortation of the mutual reception of the peace," writes Saint John Chrysostom, "we all kiss each other." And "the clerics greet the bishop, the laymen the men, the women the women..."[936] In his *The Instructor*, Clement of Alexandria taught that the Holy Kiss should not be a mere habit but rather an expression of genuine love to one another. He writes, "Love is not proved by a kiss, but by kindly feeling." He then warns of the abuse of this apostolic tradition. He says, "But there are those who do nothing but make the churches resound with a kiss, not having love itself within. For this very thing, the shameless use of a kiss (which should be mystical), causes foul suspicions and evil rumors. The apostle calls the kiss holy. When the kingdom is worthily tested, we express the affection of the soul with a chaste and closed mouth, by which chiefly gentle manners are expressed."[937]

Consequently, it is vital to recognize the Holy Kiss not only as a symbol of love, but also as the reality of the church, as an outcome of the sacrifice of Christ; it is the revelation of God's love to mankind. As in many other traditions, the Coptic Church inherited the Holy Kiss from Judaism. "In our Lord's time among the Jews," Gregory Dix writes, "the kiss was a courteous preliminary to any ceremonious meal."[938] In the second century, this tradition was attested to by Saint Justin Martyr, who states, "When we have completed the prayers, we salute one another with

---

[935] Tertullian places the Holy Kiss at the end of the prayer and calls it "the seal of prayer." (*On Prayer* 18). For more details, see: McGowan, Andrew B., *Ancient Christian Worship*, 55-56.
[936] Schmemann, Alexander, *The Eucharist*, 133.
[937] Clement of Alexandria (Saint), *The Paedagogus*, Book 3, Chapter 11.
[938] Dix, Dom Gregory, *The Shape of the Liturgy*, 107.

a kiss, whereupon there is brought to the president bread and a cup of wine."[939]

The Holy Kiss is now performed in a symbolic gesture[940] to signify the peace and reconciliation amongst one another, thereby preparing the congregation for partaking of the Eucharist. Each person in the church turns toward the people around him or her and greets them with the Holy Kiss. This is done by touching the fingertips of the person next to you with your own hands and returning your fingertips and the "kiss" to your lips. Repeat for all the people around you. In the past, the holy kiss used to be accompanied by one saying, "Christ is in the midst of us," to which the other replies, "He is and will be." This Holy Kiss was mentioned five times in the New Testament: "Greet one another with a holy kiss" (Romans 16:16), (1 Corinthians 16:20), (2 Corinthians 13:12); "Greet all God's people with a holy kiss" (I Thessalonians 5:26); "Greet one another with a kiss of love" (I Peter 5:14).

In this part of the prayer, the altar server, in accordance with the primeval practice, stands facing the priest and the people, and looking westward while raising a cross.[941] Meanwhile, the priest lifts the corporal covering the chalice, forms it in the shape of a triangle, and raises it between him and the chalice. This corporal represents, as noted earlier, the seal that was placed at the tomb of Christ, and therefore raising it symbolizes the breaking of this seal at the Resurrection. As it stands today, at the conclusion of the Prayer of Reconciliation, the chorus chants the

---

[939] Saint Justin Martyr, *Fist Apology*, chapter 65.
[940] In the past, the congregation may have greeted one another with an actual kiss. In order to guard against any abuse of this form of salutation, women and men were required to sit separately, and the Kiss of Peace was given only by women to women and by men to men. Today, a symbolic gesture is used instead.
[941] In his *The Beginners' Guide and Discipline for Laity*, Pope Cyril III mentions that the deacon stands across from the priest facing westward starting from beginning of the Liturgy of the Faithful (after the Gospel reading) until the end of it.

Adam Aspazmos,⁹⁴² then the altar server calls the worshippers to "Greet one another with a holy kiss." While they are satisfying this bidding, the priest places the corporal on his left, as he will be using it to cover his left hand during the prayer of the *Anaphora*. ⁹⁴³ With the altar server's assistance, the priest proceeds to lift the *Prospharin*.

To Ibn Kabar, the raising of the *Prospharin* "symbolizes the rolling of the stone from the tomb; and Christ leaving behind the linen corporals from His holy and sacred Body at His resurrection."⁹⁴⁴ For this reason, the *Prospharin* is traditionally removed slowly to allow the attaching bells to ring, declaring the resurrection of Christ from the dead and symbolizing the earthquake heard after this magnificent event.⁹⁴⁵ The narrative of the liturgy therefore transitioned from the burial of Christ at the conclusion of the Offertory, to His resurrection from the dead, thereby completing the reconciliation with God the Father.

Originally, the chanting of the *Adam* Aspazmos hymn and the bidding of "Greet one another" differed slightly from the contemporary practice. Older sources direct that after the Prayer of Reconciliation, the altar server bids the people to "Greet one another with a holy kiss." While the people are fulfilling the altar server's commandment, a hymn particular

---

⁹⁴² The most common one now is (Ⲟⲩⲛⲟϥ ⲙⲙⲟ Ⲙⲁⲣⲓⲁ—Rejoice O Mary); however, there are three other *Adam Aspazmos* hymns chanted in Regular Days. It is worth noting that Ⲟⲩⲛⲟϥ ⲙⲙⲟ Ⲙⲁⲣⲓⲁ, which for the most part borrowed from the *Lobsh* (Ⲗⲱⲃϣ) of the Tuesday Theotokion, was originally designated for the feasts of Saint Mary and the third Sunday of the month of Kiahk as indicated by older sources, for example, *The Church Order* of: Cairo, Patriarchal Library, MS Lit. 73 (AD 1444), fol. 116v; St. Antony Monastery, MS Lit. 573, fol.103r; Tanta—Not Numbered (AD 1868), fol. 247r; and Cairo, Patriarchal Library, MS Lit. 117 (AD 1910), fol. 56v. Per the earliest extant *The Church Order* sources, this *Adam Aspazmos* consisted only of the first two stanzas known today (both borrowed from the *Lobsh* of the Tuesday Theotokion). See for example: Jeremiah (Hegumen), *The Church Order*, Cairo, Patriarchal Library, MS Lit. 73 (AD 1444), fol. 116v.

⁹⁴³ "Anaphora" is a Greek word (ἀναφορά) meaning a "carrying up", and so an "offering" (hence its use in reference to the offering of sacrifice to God). The Anaphora is the core of the Divine Liturgy during which the offerings of bread and wine are consecrated as the body and blood of Christ. It starts with the Eucharistic Dialogue and ends with the Epiclesis.

⁹⁴⁴ Ibn Kabar, *The Lamp to Darkness and Explanation of the Service*, BnF, MS Arabic 203 (c. AD 1363-1369), fol. 207r.

⁹⁴⁵ Bandali, Costi, *Introduction to the Divine Liturgy*, 63.

to the day, called the *Adam Aspazmos*, is chanted. The name of the hymn is derived from the action associated with it; "Ⲁⲥⲡⲁⲥⲙⲟⲥ—*Aspazmos*" is a Greek word "ἀσπασμός" meaning "salution" or "kiss." The raising of the *Prospharin* is then performed, and the second part of the altar server's bidding is recited. If the Liturgy of Saint Basil is in session, the altar server says, "Lord have mercy, Lord have mercy. Yes, Lord who is Jesus Christ, hear us and have mercy on us." If, however, the liturgy of Saint Gregory is being celebrated, the altar server demands, "Let us stand well, let us stand reverently, let us stand earnestly, let us stand in peace, let us stand in the fear of God, trembling and stunned." The Cyrilline liturgy ignores this section of the bidding. After this, in all three liturgies, the priest uncovers[946] his head and the alter server instructs the faithful saying, "Offer in order, stand with trembling, look toward the east,[947] let us attend." In other words, this bidding was split into three sections, after each a specific action is required and consummated. The first is associated with the Holy Kiss, the second section with the raising of the *Prospharin*, and the third to the offerings.[948]

It is noteworthy that some books incorrectly translate the word "*Prospharin*" mentioned in the altar server's bidding to "approach" (تقدَّموا)

---

[946] The practice of uncovering the head before starting the *Anaphra* is not followed by most priests.
[947] The tradition of praying facing the East can be found abundantly in the Christian literature. Tertullian confirmed that churches are erected "facing the light." In his Apology (chapter 16), he wrote, "The idea no doubt has originated from our being known to turn to the east in prayer." Clement of Alexandria writes, "In correspondence with the manner of the sun's rising, prayers are made looking towards the sunrise in the east." Origen agrees with Clement saying that "the east is the only direction we turn to when we pour out prayer." According to Origen, this act "symbolizes the soul looking toward when the true light rises." The Didascalia says, "Indeed it is required that you pray towards the east, as knowing that which is written 'give thanks to God, who rides upon the heavens towards the east'. The custom of praying towards the east is connected with the belief that Christ will appear in the east at the Parousia (Second Coming)." The second book of the Apostolic Constitutions states that a church should be built "with its head to the East." Augustine speaks of this tradition as a fact and gives explanation to it. He writes, "When we rise to pray, we turn East, where heaven begins." John of Damascus, in the ninth century, says, "we worship towards the East." According to him, since "God planted a garden eastward in Eden... we worship God seeking and striving after our old fatherland."
[948] The association to the offerings will be discussed in greater detail later.

as opposed to "offer," an error that was copied from some Medieval sources.[949] "*Prospharin*" comes from the Greek word "προσφορά" meaning "offering," therefore, the proper translation is "offer" (قَدِّموا). Also, the term "in order" means "in the customary fashion." In other words, the call should be understood as "offer the oblations according to the church protocol."[950] To summarize this section per present-day rubric, the Liturgy of the Faithful commences with the recitation of the Creed; meanwhile the priest washes his hands. When the Prayer of Reconciliation is accomplished, the congregation may chant the *Adam Aspazmos*; this is followed by the altar server saying, "Greet one another with a holy kiss," during which the congregation greets one another.

As mentioned earlier, after the Prayer of Reconciliation, the altar server calls to the congregation to "greet one another with a Holy Kiss," and continues to instruct them saying, "offer in order, stand with trembling, look toward the east, let us attend." The latter part of the bidding is particularly important because it provides us with an understanding of the structure and intent of the rite of the holy liturgy. These words indicate that after the altar server calls to "offer in order," the congregation brings forth the oblations required for the liturgy, such as bread, wine, incense, books, water, etc. When everyone offers his or her oblations, the altar server instructs everyone to stand quietly in the fear of God so that they may resume the prayers. He says, "stand with trembling, look toward the east, let us attend." Yet, one more time, the text preserved in the Coptic liturgy attests to this immemorial practice: Following the Liturgy of the Word, which concludes with the Litany of the

---

[949] For example: London, Bod., MS Hunt 572 (13th or 14th C.), fol. 52r; Paris, BnF, MS Copte 82 (AD 1307), fol. 35v; Paris, BnF, MS Copte 30 (AD 1624), fol. 60v; and Paris, BnF, MS Copte 26 (18th C.), fol. 49r.

[950] The order could have been deacons first then men followed by women. However, some other traditions might have followed different orders.

Catechumens, the neophytes leave, then the faithful recite the Creed.[951] This is then followed by the Prayer of Reconciliation, and the Offertory, respectively.

Offering the oblations following the Holy Kiss was the predominant practice in the East (Eastern and Oriental Churches) and the West. Saint Justin Martyr was the first to state that the Holy Kiss precedes the Offertory. Sixty years later, this same order was echoed by Saint Hippolytus[952] of Rome.[953] This order was also documented in other sources such as the Apostolic Canons[954] (c. 336, for the patriarchate of Alexandria). After the altar server's bidding to offer the gifts, Cuming explains a solemn procession, where the deacons clear the passage for the Great Entrance.[955] The Cherubicon is then chanted, and the gifts are presented at the Prothesis.[956]

In the East, the Holy Kiss was moved to follow the Offertory. In AD 348, the Church of Jerusalem led the change,[957] after which, around the late 4th century or early 5th century, the Church of Antioch followed

---

[951] Before the 6th century, the Creed was not recited during the liturgy, as such, the Prayer of Reconciliation would directly follow the Liturgy of the Word.

[952] Hippolytus of Rome (AD 170–235) was the most important third century theologian in the Christian Church in Rome, where he was probably born. Photios I of Constantinople describes him in his Bibliotheca (cod. 121) as a disciple of Irenaeus, who was said to be a disciple of Polycarp, and from the context of this passage it is supposed that he suggested that Hippolytus himself so styled himself. However, this assertion is doubtful.

[953] Dix, Dom Gregory, *The Shape of the Liturgy*, 108.

[954] Also called *The Apostolic Constitutions*. A collection of 85 ancient ecclesiastical decrees concerning the government and discipline of the Early Christian Church, first found as last chapter of the eighth book of *The Apostolic Constitutions* and belonging to genre of the Church Orders. Most likely, the home of the author of *The Apostolic Canons* is Syria. The author makes use of the Syro-Macedonian calendar (can. 26), borrows very largely from a Syrian council (Antioch, 341), and according to Von Funk is identical with the compiler or interpolator of *The Apostolic Constitutions*, who was certainly a Syrian. *The Apostolic Canons* were translated into Syriac, Arabic, Coptic, and Armenian.

[955] The Evening Feasts of the Lord still preserve the rite of the Great Entrance.

[956] Cuming, Geoffrey J., *The Liturgy of St Mark*, 102.

[957] Athanasius of Saint Macarius Monastery (Father), *Summary of the Liturgical History of the Church of Alexandria (Part 1)*, 197.

during the time of Saint John Chrysostom.⁹⁵⁸ After this, the change was adopted by the Churches in Iraq, Turkey, and Constantinople, and finally to the remainder of the East by the 6th century. What is unique is that the Coptic Church held on to the pristine rite until that time and was the last in the East to accept the change.⁹⁵⁹ With the relocation of the Offertory office, its concomitant ritual called the Great Entrance moved along with it. This practice is now absent from the Coptic rite on Regular Days and is limited to nocturnal feasts.⁹⁶⁰ Although, in antiquity, the Cherubicon accompanied the Great Entrance, the hymn of Ⲡⲟⲩⲣⲟ (O King) is now chanted instead.

In the West, the Holy Kiss was moved from its primitive location to after the Fraction, specifically, after the Lord's Prayer. This innovation was initially a local practice of the North Africa Church toward the end of the 4th century before it was embraced by Rome in the beginning of the 5th century. From there, it spread through the rest of Italy and the other western churches.⁹⁶¹ In an attempt to resolve the secrecy behind this odd relocation of the Holy Kiss, Father Gregory Dix suggests, "By then the African churches had also adopted the custom (? From Jerusalem) of reciting the Lord's prayer between the fraction and the communion. Coming as it did in the African liturgy as the practical fulfilment of the

---

[958] Saint John Chrysostom (*Chrysostomos*, "golden-mouthed"), also called "Doctor of the Church", c. 349—407, Archbishop of Constantinople, was an important Early Church Father. He is known for his preaching and public speaking, his denunciation of abuse of authority by both ecclesiastical and political leaders, the Divine Liturgy of St. John Chrysostom, and his ascetic sensibilities. Saint John was born in Antioch in AD 349 to Greco-Syrian parents. Different scholars describe his mother Anthusa as a pagan or as a Christian, and his father was a high-ranking military officer. He was baptized in 368 or 373. Saint John studied theology under Diodore of Tarsus, founder of the re-constituted School of Antioch. Saint John lived in extreme asceticism and became a hermit in about 375. He ordained Bishop of Constantinople on 26 February, 398, in the presence of a great assembly of bishops, by Theophilus, Patriarch of Alexandria. He was considered by the Greeks and Latins as a most important witness to the Faith. Saint John died in exile at Comana Pontica on 14 September AD 407.
[959] Dix, Dom Gregory, *The Shape of the Liturgy*, 109.
[960] Nativity, Epiphany and Resurrection.
[961] Dix, Dom Gregory, *The Shape of the Liturgy*, 108-109.

clause '... as we forgive them that trespass against us,' the kiss acquired a special fittingness as a preliminary to communion."[962]

Back to the Coptic Rite. It is worth noting that after the Prayer of Reconciliation, the priest is not permitted to leave the altar on which the bread and wine rest unattended. In the event where more than one cleric is present, the second must arrive first at the altar before the first can leave. On another note, the ordinations of readers, sub-deacons, deacons, archdeacons, presbyters, and *hegumens* take place after the Prayer of the Reconciliation and prior to the altar server's bidding "Greet one another." The reason for this is rooted in the Old Testament; after the primordial fall of man, no one was permitted to enter the Holy of Holies except for the high priest once a year. However, after Christ's salvation through the Cross and His resurrection, all servants were permitted to enter the new Holy of Holies, the sanctuary. Thus, the Church places the ordination of her consecrated servants at this point of the liturgy, as a reminder of the reconciliation between mankind and God the Father through His Only-begotten Son, Jesus Christ, a reconciliation that permitted them to work in His field.

Following the Holy Kiss, the contemporary rubric dictates the recitation of the hymn "Through the intercessions of the *Theotokos*,[963] Saint Mary." Old euchologions, however, makes no mention of this hymn. The only sentence that follows the Holy Kiss is "a mercy of peace, a sacrifice of praise." So how did this transpire? As previously mentioned, originally, the *Adam Aspazmos* was a mandatory chant recited during the

---

[962] Dix, Dom Gregory, *The Shape of the Liturgy*, 108.
[963] Theotokos (Greek: Θεοτόκος) is the Greek title of Mary, the mother of Jesus used especially in the Eastern Orthodox, Oriental Orthodox, and Eastern Catholic Churches. Its literal English translations include "God-bearer", "Birth-Giver of God" and "the one who gives birth to God." Less literal translations include "Mother of God". Roman Catholics and Anglicans use the title "Mother of God" more often than "*Theotokos*". In the Coptic Orthodox Churches, the term *Theotokos* is often used, however, it is translated into "Mother of God", instead of its literal translation of "Bearer of God".

The Liturgy of the Faithful

Holy Kiss. According to Ibn Kabar, the most common one in Regular Days was "Ⲡⲓⲭⲣⲓⲥⲧⲟⲥ Ⲡⲉⲛⲥⲱⲧⲏⲣ."[964] In this *Aspazmos*, it is noticeable that from the fourth stanza onward, the quatrains are of intercessory character. They read, "Through the intercessions of the Mother of God Saint Mary, O Lord grant us the forgiveness of our sins. Through the intercessions of the three luminaries, Michael, Gabriel and Raphael, O Lord, grant us the forgiveness of our sins. Through the intercessions of the four incorporeal beasts and the twenty-four presbyters, O Lord, grant us the forgiveness of our sins. Through the intercessions of the seven archangels and the angelic hosts, O Lord grant us the forgiveness of our sins." These stanzas are then followed by ones dedicated to the Apostles, the martyrs, the saints, the patriarchs, and concluding with the quatrain "We worship You O Christ, with Your Good Father and the Holy Spirit for You have come and saved us."[965] Due to time constraints, the Church continued her efforts to shorten the service; one of the candidates for this abbreviation was the *Adam* Aspazmos. As the custom in many other hymns, the easiest way to truncate it was to relinquish all stanzas except for the first and last, which are "Through the intercessions of the *Theotokos* Saint Mary," and "We worship you O Christ." Ibn Kabar alluded to this abridgement as he writes, "If the service needs to be shortened, it (the *Adam* Aspazmos) is not said. Alternatively, it may be limited to Ⲉⲓⲧⲉⲛ ⲛⲓⲉⲩⲭⲏ on the feasts of martyrs, saints, and angels when his name is mentioned on his feast day. Or else they

---

[964] Ibn Kabar, *The Lamp*, BnF, MS Arabic 203 (c. AD 1363-1369), fol. 206v. The following is the full Coptic text of this *Adam Aspazmos*:

Ⲡⲓⲭⲣⲓⲥⲧⲟⲥ Ⲡⲉⲛⲥⲱⲧⲏⲣ ⲁⲣⲓⲧⲉⲛ ⲛⲉⲙⲡϣⲁ: ⲙⲡⲉⲕ ⲁⲥⲡⲁⲥⲙⲟⲥ ⲉⲑⲟⲩⲁⲃ ⲛ̀ϧⲣⲏⲓ ϧⲉⲛ ⲛⲓⲫⲏⲟⲩⲓ.
Ϩⲓⲛⲁ ⲛ̀ⲧⲉⲛϩⲱⲥ ⲉⲣⲟⲕ: ⲛⲉⲙ ⲛⲓⲬⲉⲣⲟⲩⲃⲓⲙ ⲛⲉⲙ ⲛⲓⲤⲉⲣⲁⲫⲓⲙ: ⲉⲛⲱϣ ⲉⲃⲟⲗ ⲉⲛϫⲱ ⲙ̀ⲙⲟⲥ.
Ϫⲉ ⲭⲟⲩⲁⲃ ⲭⲟⲩⲁⲃ ⲭⲟⲩⲁⲃ: Ⲡ̅ⲟ̅ⲥ̅ ⲡⲓⲡⲁⲛⲧⲟⲕⲣⲁⲧⲱⲣ: ⲧ̀ⲫⲉ ⲛⲉⲙ ⲡ̀ⲕⲁϩⲓ ⲙⲉϩ ⲉⲃⲟⲗ: ϧⲉⲛ ⲡⲉⲕⲱⲟⲩ ⲛⲉⲙ ⲡⲉⲕⲧⲁⲓⲟ.
Ⲉⲓⲧⲉⲛ ⲛⲓⲡⲣⲉⲥⲃⲓⲁ: ⲛ̀ⲧⲉ ϯⲑⲉⲟⲧⲟⲕⲟⲥ ⲉⲑⲟⲩ Ⲙⲁⲣⲓⲁ: Ⲡ̅ⲟ̅ⲥ̅ ⲁⲣⲓϩⲙⲟⲧ ⲛⲁⲛ: ⲙ̀ⲡⲓⲭⲱ ⲉⲃⲟⲗ ⲛ̀ⲧⲉ ⲛⲉⲛⲛⲟⲃⲓ.
Ⲉⲓⲧⲉⲛ ⲛⲓⲡⲣⲉⲥⲃⲓⲁ: ⲛ̀ⲧⲉ ⲡⲓϣⲟⲙⲧ ⲛ̀ⲣⲉϥⲉⲣⲟⲩⲱⲓⲛⲓ ⲉⲑⲩ: Ⲙⲓⲭⲁⲏⲗ ⲛⲉⲙ Ⲅⲁⲃⲣⲓⲏⲗ ⲛⲉⲙ Ⲣⲁⲫⲁⲏⲗ: Ⲡ̅ⲟ̅ⲥ̅...
Ⲉⲓⲧⲉⲛ ⲛⲓⲡⲣⲉⲥⲃⲓⲁ: ⲛ̀ⲧⲉ ⲡⲓϥ̀ⲧⲱⲟⲩ ⲛ̀ⲍⲱⲟⲛ ⲛ̀ⲁⲥⲱⲙⲁⲧⲟⲥ: ⲛⲉⲙ ⲡⲓϫⲱⲧ ⲩ̀ⲧⲱⲟⲩ ⲙ̀ⲡⲣⲉⲥⲃⲩⲧⲉⲣⲟⲥ: Ⲡ̅ⲟ̅ⲥ̅...
Ⲉⲓⲧⲉⲛ ⲛⲓⲡⲣⲉⲥⲃⲓⲁ: ⲛ̀ⲧⲉ ⲡⲓϣⲁϣϥ ⲛ̀ⲁⲣⲭⲏⲁⲅⲅⲉⲗⲟⲥ: ⲛⲉⲙ ⲛⲓⲧⲁⲅⲙⲁ ⲛ̀ⲉⲡⲟⲩⲣⲁⲛⲓⲟⲛ: Ⲡ̅ⲟ̅ⲥ̅...

Then stanzas for the apostles, martyrs, and saints; and finally concluded with the following stanza:

Ⲧⲉⲛⲟⲩⲱϣⲧ ⲙ̀ⲙⲟⲕ ⲱ̀Ⲡⲓⲭⲣⲓⲥⲧⲟⲥ: ⲛⲉⲙ Ⲡⲉⲕⲓⲱⲧ ⲛ̀ⲁⲅⲁⲑⲟⲥ: ⲛⲉⲙ Ⲡⲓⲡⲛⲉⲩⲙⲁ ⲉⲑⲟⲩⲁⲃ ϫⲉ ⲁⲕⲓ ⲁⲕⲥⲱϯ ⲙ̀ⲙⲟⲛ.

[965] The concluding sentence is "for you have come," "have risen," "were born," "were baptized," or "were crucified," according to the liturgical season.

might only say Ϯⲉⲛⲟⲩⲱϣ."⁹⁶⁶ Instead of changing the first quatrain every day, the first stanza (for Saint Mary) was standardized for all days, followed by Ϯⲉⲛⲟⲩⲱϣ. To further abbreviate the hymn, chanters employed a syllabic style to recite it as opposed to its original tune specific to the *Adam Aspazmos* chants. In other words, the formation of the hymn "Through the intercessions," which is chanted hitherto in all the liturgies after the Holy Kiss, came about through the Church's efforts to shorten the service. It is essentially an abridged version of the *Adam Aspazmos* "Ⲡⲓⲭⲣⲓⲥⲧⲟⲥ Ⲡⲉⲛⲥⲱⲧⲏⲣ."⁹⁶⁷

From the aforementioned explanation, as part of a specific *Adam Aspazmos*, "Through the intercessions," ideally, should not be chanted after any other *Adam* Aspazmos hymn.⁹⁶⁸ The elucidation above also answers the question: why do we ask for the intercession of Saint Mary at this point in the liturgy (after the Prayer of Reconciliation)? The *Adam Aspazmos* "Ⲡⲓⲭⲣⲓⲥⲧⲟⲥ Ⲡⲉⲛⲥⲱⲧⲏⲣ" reads, "O our Savior Christ, make us worthy of Your holy peace in the heavens, that we may praise You with the Cherubim and the Seraphim, proclaiming and saying: holy, holy, holy, O Lord, the Pantocrator, heaven and earth are full of Your glory and honor, through the intercessions of the *Theotokos* Saint Mary…" In other words, the focus of the hymn is not the intercessions per se, but rather on entreating the Lord to grant us His peace, which aligns with the preceding prayer (Reconciliation), through the intercessions and prayers of Saint Mary, the heavenly creatures, the apostles, the martyrs, and the saints.

---

⁹⁶⁶ Ibn Kabar, *The Lamp*, BnF, MS Arabic 203 (c. AD 1363-1369), fol. 207r.
⁹⁶⁷ This means that when any *Adam Aspazmos* other than Ⲡⲓⲭⲣⲓⲥⲧⲟⲥ Ⲡⲉⲛⲥⲱⲧⲏⲣ is chanted followed by the hymn "Through the intercessions," two *Adam Aspazmos* hymns are actually sung in a row.
⁹⁶⁸ However, the common practice now is that "Through the intercessions" is not only said following any *Adam Aspazmos*, but also even if the chanting of the *Adam Aspazmos* was skipped.

A Mercy of Peace, a Sacrifice of Praise

After the recitation of the hymn "Through the intercessions," the congregation intones "A mercy of peace, a sacrifice of praise,"[969] which marks the beginning of the *Anaphora*.[970] This sentence can be chanted in two different tunes,[971] one specific to the liturgies of Saint Basil and Saint Cyril, and another is appointed to the Liturgy of Saint Gregory. What is the meaning of this sentence, and why do we chant it prior to the *Anaphora*?

"A mercy of peace, a sacrifice of praise" refers to the Lord Christ, for, out of the abundance of His mercy, He granted us salvation. This is evident in Titus 3:5, "He saved us, not because of righteous things we had done, but because of His mercy. He saved us through the washing of rebirth and renewal by the Holy Spirit." Because of His mercy, He saved us. Christ conferred His mercy by offering us peace. In offering peace, He became the sacrifice of praise, and His Father smelled His sweet aroma on the evening at the place of Golgotha, just as indicated in the hymn "Ⲫⲁⲓ ⲉⲧⲁϥⲉⲛϥ."[972] He became the greatest and ultimate sacrifice which pleased God the Father. As such, we ought to do what Saint Paul teaches in his epistle to the Hebrews, "Through Jesus, therefore, let us continually offer to God a sacrifice of praise—the fruit of lips that openly profess His name" (Hebrews 13:15). Thus, Christ offered Himself as an acceptable sacrifice

---

[969] This sentence is the beginning of the liturgies prayed in most of the churches; whereas the hymn "Through the intercessions of Saint Mary" is particular to the Coptic Orthodox Church, which further proves that they are two separate hymns.

[970] It is worth noting here that the hymn "Through the intercessions" is in Coptic whereas the phrase "A mercy of peace, a sacrifice of praise" is in Greek. It is a Coptic tradition to keep Biblical phrases in their original form without translating them to Coptic.

[971] According to the old practice, the two tunes were chanted interchangeably in any of the three liturgies.

[972] Translation: "This is He who presented himself on the cross; an acceptable sacrifice for the salvation of our race. His good Father inhaled His sweet aroma in the evening on Golgotha."

on the Cross, and in the same spirit, we too offer a sacrifice of praise, the fruit of our lips, and our living bodies, to God the Father, in thanksgiving.

To David the Psalmist, praise is a sacrifice; hence, he says, "May my prayer be set before You like incense; may the lifting up of my hands be like the evening sacrifice" (Psalm 141:2). As such, the act of praise is, in fact, a response to the love that Christ has shown toward us, "Greater love has no one than this: to lay down one's life for one's friends" (John 15:13). This allows us to reflect on the mercy and peace as products of Christ's salvation. God, out of His abundant mercy toward us, accepted to die on the Cross for us. This is also a sacrifice of peace, for through Christ, He reconciled us to God the Father, and to one another. Christ is the sacrifice of peace, the sacrifice of mercy, and the sacrifice of praise. Consequently, the congregation affirms this by chanting, "a sacrifice of praise, a mercy of peace" prior to commencing the *Anaphora*, proclaiming that through Christ, our lips have been opened to praise His Holy Name.

In summary, "A mercy of peace" refers to the godly act of Jesus' Salvation on the Cross, which led to the state of "peace" between God the Father and mankind, and also among each other. "A sacrifice of praise" is the humanly reaction to His act of mercy. Our response should be offering Him perpetual thanksgiving and praise. Without Jesus' act of mercy and Salvation, there would be no Thanksgiving or Eucharist,[973] and therefore, there would be no *Anaphora*. As such, this sentence "A mercy of peace, a sacrifice of praise" is the viaduct between the Prayer of Reconciliation, which explains Jesus' mercy and how it resulted in peace, on the one hand, and the Eucharist (Grand Thanksgiving Prayer), which is the sacrifice of praise, on the other hand.

---

[973] Eucharist is a Greek noun **εὐχαριστία**, meaning "thanksgiving."

Eucharistic Terminologies

Before we begin discussing the core of the Liturgy of the Faithful, let us first examine some of the liturgical terminologies that are commonly used to refer to this office. The word "liturgy" is derived from the technical term in ancient Greek (λειτουργία or λητουργία, leitourgia, from λαός / Laos, "the people" and the root ἔργον / ergon, "work"); as such, the word means "the work of the people." In ancient Greece, it was a public service established by the city-state whereby its richest members (whether citizens or resident aliens), more or less voluntarily, financed the State with their personal wealth. Liturgy is a communal response to the sacred through activity reflecting praise, thanksgiving, supplication, or repentance. In fact, any church gathering for the purpose of worship is referred to as "liturgy." Nevertheless, the most common and indispensable "liturgy" among all church assemblies and offices is the Eucharist. In other words, there are many forms of liturgies in the Coptic Church beyond the *Eucharist* itself, such as the Canonical Hours, the Offering of Incense, the Midnight Psalmody, the Blessing of the Waters, the Genuflection Prayers, the Holy Week Hours, and the Veneration Services. There are also the sacraments offices and other services such as baptism, ordinations, consecrations, unction of the sick, matrimonies, and funerals. All of these are liturgies; yet the most vital one is the Eucharist.

The *Anaphora*[974] is the most solemn part of the Divine Liturgy. The word *Anaphora* is a Greek one (ἀναφορά), from ἀνά (aná, "up") and φέρω (phérō, "I carry"), meaning a "carrying up," and so an "offering" (hence its use in reference to the offering of sacrifice to God). The *Anaphora* is the

---

[974] Some of the most ancient *Anaphora*'s are the *Anaphora* of *The Apostolic Tradition*, called also the *Anaphora* of Hippolytus, the Liturgy of the seventh book of *The Apostolic Constitutions* and the Liturgy of the eighth book of *The Apostolic Constitutions* that developed in the famous Byzantine *Anaphora* now part of the Liturgy of Saint John Chrysostom, through the lost Greek version of the *Anaphora* of the Twelve Apostles (of which we have a later Syrian version).

part of the liturgy that starts with the Eucharistic Dialogue and concludes with the *Epiclesis*, the descent of the Holy Spirit. This definition is applicable to all liturgies regardless of their origin. Nevertheless, many, imprecisely, use *liturgy* and *anaphora* interchangeably. In Egypt, old *anaphora* prayers were discovered. Examples are: The *Anaphora* of Barcellona[975] (and its related Louvain Coptic Papyrus), the Prayer in the Euchologion of Serapion,[976] the Deir Balyzeh Papyrus,[977] the Strasbourg Papyrus,[978] and the ancient *Anaphora* of Saint Mark in Greek, which developed into the Coptic Liturgy of Saint Cyril.

"Eucharist" is a Greek noun εὐχαριστία (evcharistia); "εὐ" is a combining form meaning "good," "well," "χαρισ" means a spiritual power or personal quality that gives an individual influence or authority over large numbers of people. It could be translated as "grace." Finally, "ια", which forms abstract nouns of feminine gender. The noun "εὐχαριστία" means "thankfulness" or "thanksgiving." In the New Testament, εὐχαριστία was mentioned several times (i.e., Acts 24:3; 1 Corinthians 14:16; 2 Corinthians 4:15; Ephesians 5:4; 1 Thessalonians 5:18;

---

[975] The Barcelona Papyrus is a 4th-century papyrus codex, coming from Egypt and cataloged as P.Monts.Roca inv.128-178. It is the oldest liturgical manuscript containing a complete *anaphora*. This codex is for the main part conserved in the Abbey of Montserrat and it includes seven pages (154b-157b) of prayers in Greek with a complete anaphora, a related prayer to be said after receiving the Eucharist, two prayers for the sick and an acrostic hymn perhaps of baptismal type. The Codex also includes a few Latin texts and a long list of Greek words.

[976] Also known as the Sacramentary of Serapion. This fourth century Euchologion is preserved in an eleventh century manuscript, which belongs to the Lavra Monastery on Athos. It was first published in 1894 by the Russian liturgical historian Dimitrievsky in the journal of the Ecclesiastical Academy of Kiev. Apart from Rome with the rite in Hippolytus which comes from the third century there is no other liturgical text of such an early time connected with any other Church.

[977] The Deir Balyzeh Papyrus (or Der Balyzeh Euchologion) is a 6th-century papyrus, coming from Egypt. It contains early fragmentary Christian texts: three prayers, a short creed and a portion of *anaphora*.

[978] The Strasbourg Papyrus is a papyrus made of six fragments on a single leaf written in Greek and conserved at the Strasbourg National University Library, cataloged Gr. 254. It was first edited in AD 1928. The Strasbourg papyrus contains an ancient Christian prayer, probably an *anaphora*, similar to the first part of the Alexandrine Anaphora of Saint Mark. The Papyrus was probably written in the fourth or fifth century, but it may present an older text, resulting to be one of the older Eucharistic Prayer known.

Philippians 4:6; Colossians 2:7; Colossians 4:2; 1 Thessalonians 3:9; 1 Timothy 4:3; Revelation 4:9; Revelation 7:12; 2 Corinthians 9:11; 2 Corinthians 9:12; and 1 Timothy 2:1). The Holy Eucharist is a sacrament and a sacrifice. It is also called "Breaking of Bread" and the "Lord's Supper;" but the ancient title εὐχαριστία appearing in writers as early as Ignatius, Justin, and Irenaeus, has taken precedence in the technical terminology of the church and her theologians. Christ Himself instituted the Holy Eucharist at the Last Supper, the night before He died.

The Commencement of the Anaphora

After the *Anaphora* opening statement, "A mercy of peace, a sacrifice of praise," the priest takes the corporal that he had put on his left and uses it to cover his left hand. Then he takes the corporal that is on the bread and uses it to cover his right hand. Given the new state of humanity after Jesus' sacrifice—in contrary to the state of humanity epitomized by reciting the Prayer of Reconciliation bare-handed—exhibited at the beginning of the *Anaphora* as man was clothed with grace and is no longer viewed by God the Father as sinful or disobedient; unlike Adam and Eve, who felt their nakedness after they sinned against God, humanity, through the incarnate Logos, His expiation of the original sin, and after the reconciliation, is covered by the divine grace of Jesus Christ, the priest illustrates this jubilant state by covering his hands while praying the *Anaphora*. Additionally, it is practical to do so to avoid touching anything other than the Holy Body and Blood, not only as an expression of reverence but also for hygienic purposes. It is analogous to abstaining from touching materialistic elements until finally holding the Body of our Lord Jesus and the chalice containing His Holy Blood.

During the Eucharist, the priest always covers his hands while standing at the altar. This follows the example of the Cherubim and the Seraphim, who each have six wings,[979] with two they cover their faces, with two they cover their feet and with two they fly.[980] Covering one's face is a figure of speech showing reverence and solemnity before God. Covering one's feet is also an expression of respect in front of the Lord. While serving the liturgical mystery, the priest represents the angels who serve the throne of the Almighty, All-holy God. In the Liturgy of Saint Cyril, it states regarding the Seraphim, "With two wings they cover their faces on account of Your divinity that cannot be beheld or comprehended." Indeed, the angels cover their faces before the divine glory of God; and worshippers too, as weak human beings, have the opportunity to stand before Him and enjoy His glory.

In the rite as it stands today, the priest keeps his hands covered with two corporals until the Sanctification when he signs the Host and the chalice. However, in the past (at least until the 15th century), as mentioned by Pope Gabriel V, the priest used to pray with his hands exposed until the Sanctification when he says, "He took bread into his pure [hands]." At that point, it was unfitting for him to point or bless the people without corporals, as a form of respect to the Body and Blood.

The Eucharistic Dialogue

The Eucharistic Dialogue (also called the Liturgical Dialogue), *Sursum corda*,[981] is a dialogue between the priest and the people; the priest makes the sign of the cross three times: He signs the congregation, the altar

---

[979] Isaiah 6:2 and Revelation 4:8; however, Ezekiel mentions four wings "but each of them had four faces and four wings" (Ezekiel 1:6).
[980] Isaiah 6:2
[981] Latin phrase meaning "Lift up your hearts." it is used to refer to the Eucharistic Dialogue as a whole.

The Liturgy of the Faithful

servers and himself. Inscriptions until the 14th century make no mention of signings; their emphasis is on the dialogue itself. These signings were first reported by Pope Gabriel V in the 15th century.[982] Pope Gabriel documents that the priest faces the people and signs them while saying, "The Lord be with you all." Then he says, "Lift up your hearts," and turns eastward and signs the altar servers. Afterwards, he turns back again toward the congregation (westward) and crosses himself while saying, "Let us give thanks to the Lord." Facing the east, he utters the prayer which starts with, "Meet and right." Most probably, the signings during the Eucharistic Dialogue were introduced under influence of the Syriac Orthodox Church as sources attest to this as an ancient Syrian tradition.

the 4th century conspicuous work *The Apostolic Constitutions*,[983] which is of Syriac tradition, states that the priest crosses himself and then begins the Eucharistic Dialogue.[984] Saint Jacob of Edessa[985] in the 7th century remarks that the priest signs himself, the servant, and the congregation during the Eucharistic Dialogue.[986]

---

[982] Athanasius of Saint Macarius Monastery (Father), *Summary of the Liturgical History of the Church of Alexandria (Part 2)*, 243.

[983] *The Apostolic Constitutions* is an early Christian collection of eight treatises which belongs to genre of the Church Orders, intended to serve as a manual of guidance for the clergy, and to some extent for the laity. It purports to be the work of the Twelve Apostles, whose instructions, whether given by them as individuals or as a body. The work can be dated from AD 375 to 380. The provenance is usually regarded as Syria, probably Antioch. The author is unknown.

[984] "Let the high priest, therefore, together with the priests, *pray* by himself; and let him put on his shining garment, and stand at the altar, and make the sign of the cross upon his forehead with his hand, and say: The grace of Almighty God, and the love of our Lord Jesus Christ, and the fellowship of the Holy Ghost, be with you all. And let all with one voice say: And with your spirit. The high priest: Lift up your mind. All the people: We lift it up unto the Lord. The high priest: Let us give thanks to the Lord. All the people: It is meet and right so to do." See: *The Apostolic Constitutions*, Book VIII, Chapter XII, 4,5.

[985] Saint Jacob of Edessa (AD 640–5 June 708) was born in Aindaba near Aleppo, around AD 640. He studied at the monastery of Qinnasrin and later at Alexandria. On his return from Alexandria, he was appointed bishop of Edessa by his friend Athanasius II, Patriarch of Antioch. Jacob produced a revision of the bible, based on the Peshitta. This was the last attempt at a revision of the Old Testament in the Syriac Orthodox Church. Jacob produced a collection of ecclesiastical canons. He also made many contributions to Syriac liturgy, both original and as translations from Greek.

[986] Athanasius of Saint Macarius Monastery (Father), *The Divine Liturgy: The Mystery of the Kingdom of God (Part 2)*, 651.

In the presence of the Pope or a bishop, yet not presiding over the liturgy, he is still the one performing the signing on the people and the altar servers while the priest is uttering the words of the Eucharistic Dialogue. However, on the third time, the priest signs himself (despite the fact that a high priest is present). In the Basilian and Cyrilline liturgies, the Eucharistic Dialogue begins with, "The Lord be with all." According to Jacob of Edessa, this phrase is unique to Alexandria;[987] nonetheless, in the Roman rite, a similar greeting, "The Lord be with you," can be found. The Scriptures attest to this Jewish-rooted phrase. The Old Testament reports, "Just then Boaz arrived from Bethlehem and greeted the harvesters, 'The Lord be with you!' 'The Lord bless you!' they answered" (Ruth 2:4). Saint Paul the Apostle, in the New Testament, salutes the Thessalonians saying, "Now may the Lord of peace Himself give you peace at all times and in every way. The Lord be with all of you." (2 Thessalonians 3:16).

Another opening, a trinitarian formula, is assigned to the Gregorian Eucharistic Dialogue. The priest exclaims, "The love of God the Father and the grace of the Only-begotten Son, our Lord, God and Savior Jesus Christ, and the communion and gift of the Holy Spirit, be with you all," a phrase that is borrowed from (2 Corinthians 13:14).[988] The Church of Jerusalem was the first to use it in the Eucharistic Dialogue. The Liturgy of Saint James (in the Syriac rite) reads, "The love of God the Father and the grace of the Only-begotten Son and the communion of the Holy Spirit be with you all." In *The Apostolic Constitutions* (fourth century), the text for the opening of the Eucharistic Dialogue is as follows, "The grace of God the All-mighty, and the love of our Lord Jesus Christ, and the communion of the Holy Spirit be with you all." In Constantinople, as in

---

[987] Ignatius Ephrem II Rahmani (Patriarch of the Syriac Catholic Church), *Les Liturgies Orientales et Occidentales*, 539.
[988] "May the grace of the Lord Jesus Christ, and the love of God, and the fellowship of the Holy Spirit be with you all."

many other churches that followed a Syrian type of rite, this long form was substituted, probably at Antioch first, with the short form in the later fourth century.[989] Hence, both openings are immemorial and have Biblical roots. This solemn benediction (in both formulas) exists in every Eucharistic prayer without exception, in the East and the West.[990] In all three Coptic liturgies, the congregation answers, "And with your spirit," which is an old responsory used in all traditions.

The priest then says the *Sursum Corda*,[991] "Lift up your hearts," while he crosses the altar servers. A similar call can be found in the Scriptures, "Let us lift up our hearts and our hands to God in heaven" (Lamentations 3:41). Saint Augustine,[992] who lived in the 4th and 5th centuries, comments on this phrase saying, "The call 'Lift up your hearts' is a common practice among all churches all over the world, east and west."[993] This heart-moving phrase implements the fact that true worship is an ascent into God's presence. Unless our hearts and minds are lifted up, our souls cannot unite with the Lord in a mystical way. Saint Cyprian, who is the first to explicitly commented on this phrase, says, "The priest also before his prayer prepares the minds of the brethren by first uttering a preface, saying: 'Lift up your hearts,' so that when the people respond: 'We lift them up to the Lord,' they may be admonished that they should ponder on nothing other than the Lord."[994] As indicated by Saint Augustine, the phrase help Christians

---

[989] Dix, Dom Gregory, *The Shape of the Liturgy*, 126.
[990] Schmemann, Alexander, *The Eucharist*, 166.
[991] A Latin phrase meaning "lift up your hearts."
[992] Saint Augustine (AD 13 November 354–28 August 430) was an early Christian theologian and philosopher whose writings influenced the development of Western Christianity and Western philosophy. He was the bishop of Hippo Regius. Among his most important works are *City of God* and *Confessions*. In the East, many of his teachings are not accepted. Nonetheless, he is still considered a saint.
[993] This phrase is embraced in the Eucharistic Dialogue to the Preface of the Eucharistic Prayer in almost all Churches. In the Latin churches (West), it is used by Roman Catholic, Anglican, Lutheran, United Methodist, Presbyterian and others. In the East, it is used by Greek, Russian, Coptic, Armenian and other Eastern and Oriental churches.
[994] Cyprian (Saint), *The Lord's Prayer*, chapter 31.

to focus on the heavenly inheritance. In his *Mystagogical lecture V*, this was explained by Saint Cyril of Jerusalem, "The bishop commands everyone to banish worldly thoughts and workaday cares and to have their hearts in heaven with the good God."[995] As such, it is not an exaggeration to say that we commune with the Lord, not because He is brought down, but rather because we are lifted up. This statement is not to be understood as underplaying the function of Incarnation but rather to capture the state of worshippers at the liturgy that will help them unite with Jesus.

This bidding, along with its responsory, are the only part of the dialogue strictly confined to the Eucharist.[996] Father Gregory Dix attributes this to its eschatological character, which is akin to the Eucharist. He eloquently explains that the action of the Eucharist takes place beyond time and space, that is, in the "age to come," hence, the only way to be part of it is for the believers, the *ecclesia*, to meet Jesus there. This state of mind cannot be reached unless we lift up our hearts, minds, and our all to the Lord, leaving aside the worldly busyness, and releasing our thoughts in His Kingdom.[997] Any thoughts that might inadvertently infringe this state of spiritual union with the Lord must be expelled at once, that this union may only be strengthened throughout the prayer in preparation to the mystical union at Communion.

The congregation answers, "We have them with the Lord." Without the grace of our Lord, we would have continued falling into the abyss. The grace of God has lifted us up. We have become members of the body of Christ, "And he is the head of the body, the Church" (Colossians 1:18). Consequently, we always have the desire to connect with Him and be lifted up. Our teacher Paul the Apostle says, "Since, then, you have been

---

[995] Cyril of Jerusalem (Saint), *Mystagogical Lecture V*, The Dialogue.
[996] Dix, Dom Gregory, *The Shape of the Liturgy*, 127.
[997] Dix, Ibid., 127.

The Liturgy of the Faithful

raised with Christ, set your hearts on things above, where Christ is, seated at the right hand of God. Set your minds on things above, not on earthly things" (Colossians 3:1, 2). We, therefore, lift up our hearts and set our minds to what is above. It is important not to only raise our voices saying, "We have them with the Lord," but also truly raise our hearts to Him. Our hearts should not be bound to earthly matters, concerns, lusts and aspirations; our minds must be freed from distractions and tumultuous thoughts. Those who come forth to prayer without having liberated hearts and minds, Saint Paul describes as "their god is their stomach, and their glory is in their shame. Their mind is set on earthly things" (Philippians 3:19). We need to turn our hearts to the Lord with repeated, tearful plea so He may have mercy on us and set us free from all these bounds that make us cease to feel His love and, consequently, impede our union with Him.

After that, while crossing himself, the priest bids the congregation saying, "Let us give thanks to the Lord," to which they respond, "It is meet and right." The bidding and its responsory, which find their roots in the Jewish *Berakah*,[998] are the opening of the Grand Thanksgiving Prayer. The priest's order means, let us offer the Eucharist. The respond is the people's consent for the priest to offer the sacrifice. Saint Augustine says, "Let us give thanks to Him because unless He had given us His grace, our hearts would have remained clung to the earth. You therefore witness to this and say, 'Meet and right' to give thanks to Him who lifted our hearts to where our head is."[999]

It is worth noting that the precise translation of "Meet and right" is "Meet and proper,"[1000] the former emerged in the Medieval literature.

---

[998] Dix, Ibid., 127.
[999] Athanasius of Saint Macarius Monastery (Father), *The Divine Liturgy: The Mystery of the Kingdom of God (Part 2)*, 660.
[1000] Translation in Arabic (مستحقٌ ومستوجب).

Some clergy, erroneously, think that "Meet and right" is addressed to the Lord, and as such, they replaced it with, "Worthy and righteous." The original Greek phrase "Ⲁⲍⲓⲟⲛ ⲕⲉ ⲇⲓⲕⲉⲟⲛ" uses "Ⲁⲍⲓⲟⲛ," not "Ⲁⲍⲓⲟⲥ."[1001] The latter would describe the Lord. However, "Ⲁⲍⲓⲟⲛ," which is what is used here, is in the neuter declension tense, referring to the "giving of thanks." The meaning of the phrase then is, "It is proper for us to thank You" or "It is obligatory for us to thank You." Hence, the fitting translation of the phrase is "It is meet and right," not "Worthy and righteous" as some people think. The *Sursum Corda*, therefore, is the ascension of the church to the heavens, which makes her feel the presence of the Lord in her midst. This spiritual union naturally leads to offering thanks to the Almighty God through the *eucharist*. It must be noted that the tune appointed to the Liturgical Dialogue in the liturgies of Saint Basil and Saint Cyril is different from that assigned to the Liturgy of Saint Gregory.

The Grand Thanksgiving Prayer

After the Eucharistic Dialogue, the priest prays the Grand Thanksgiving Prayer—this is applicable to all pre-Nicene Eucharistic prayers—that in later centuries evolved into what is now so-called Preface.[1002] The name "Preface" in today's understanding suggests that it is a prelude to the core of the Eucharist, an orison leading up to its climax, which is the Sanctus. In the West, between the 3rd and 5th centuries, the Preface has replaced the Thanksgiving Prayer.[1003] For the purpose of this study, Thanksgiving and

---

[1001] This is in contrary to Revelation (4:11), which directly addresses the Lord, "You are worthy, our Lord and God, to receive glory and honor and power, for You created all things, and by Your will they were created and have their being."
[1002] The Grand Thanksgiving Prayer (Preface) as it is nowadays begins at the words "meet and right," and ends with the Sanctus.
[1003] Dix, Gregory, *The Shape of the Liturgy*, 537.

Preface are used interchangeably. It is worth mentioning that in the title of this prayer the word "Grand" precedes "Thanksgiving" to differentiate it from the Thanksgiving prayer pertaining to the Offertory office.

In pre-Nicene times, this prayer was the only prayer uttered at the Eucharist; it was "the prayer;" and this was the reason the entire service is called after it, that is, "the Eucharist." The Eucharistic Prayer, or the Thanksgiving Prayer, was originally in the shape of the Jewish prayers uttered at the religious meals. Later, as apparent from the *anaphora* of the *Apostolic Tradition* and the Sacramentary of Saint Serapion, the concepts of narratives for salvation or institution, as well as invocation, started to evolve, but still contained, as integral parts within the Thanksgiving Prayer.[1004] The entire liturgy was the Eucharist, viz., the Thanksgiving Prayer. Down to the third century, a wide liberty of improvisation was left to the celebrant. The president (bishop) offered extempore prayer "to the best of his power," Justin Martyr of the second century says. In the 4th, 5th, and 6th centuries, each of these notions (i.e., Institution Narrative, Epiclesis, Litanies, Diptych, etc.) started to secede from the Eucharistic Prayer, and become independent sections. This allowed theologians—firstly in the West—to assign roles and functions, and thence level of importance, to each section.

As previously mentioned, pre-Nicene Eucharistic prayers were basically Thanksgiving prayers. Dix suggests that the development of the Preface as a prayer leading up to the Angelic Praise, and the Sanctus emerged in Egypt. They were then spread in Syria and from there to the West. However, when the Syriac Church adopted the Preface, it changed its usage before exporting it to the West. In the West, it became a variable prayer, that is, its text change to fit the ecclesiastical calendar and the

---

[1004] For more details about and the text of these ancient liturgies, please review chapter 7 of this book "Ancient Eucharistic Prayers."

liturgical occasion. "The Syrian rite of the fourth century," Dix explains, "had borrowed the Preface and Sanctus from the old pre-Nicene Egyptian tradition, but it had put it to a new use. And it is the new Syrian usage, not the original Egyptian one, which spreads all over Christendom in the fifth century... and the West in turn gave a new twist to the borrowed Syrian introduction to the Sanctus by subjecting it to the influence of the calendar."[1005]

This prayer commences with the priest saying, "meet and right" three times, a pure Alexandrian tradition.[1006] In this prayer, worshippers thank God for creating the heavens, the earth, and all that is therein; the church thanks Him because He is the Creator of all things.[1007] It is worth mentioning that the Christian belief that God's presence is experienced in His creation is deeply rooted in Jewish spirituality. Hence, it is natural to start the gathering—which results in God's presence[1008]—with a thanksgiving prayer to God, the Creator of everything. In fact, it is an Alexandrian hallmark that the Thanksgiving Prayer is solely focused on God's creation, not His acts of incarnation and redemption.[1009] "The prayer's narrative," writes Paul Bradshaw, "parallels the cosmological Alexandrian vision of salvation as the return to God through the Savior."[1010] From what has been mentioned above, we understand that thanksgiving is not a mere thanking the Lord for some gifts, but rather it includes the entire worship. As such, Robert Webber declares, "Public prayer lifts up all creation to the Father through Jesus Christ by the Spirit

---

[1005] Dix, Gregory, *The Shape of the Liturgy*, 542, 544.
[1006] Ignatius Ephrem II Rahmani (Patriarch of the Syriac Catholic Church), *Les Liturgies Orientales et Occidentales*, 540.
[1007] "For in Him all things were created: things in heaven and on earth, visible and invisible, whether thrones or powers or rulers or authorities; all things have been created through Him and for Him" (Colossians 1:16).
[1008] "For where two or three gather in my name, there am I with them" (Matthew 18:20).
[1009] Ray, Walter D. (1997). The Strasbourg Papyrus. In Bradshaw, Paul F. (Ed.), *Essays on Early Eastern Eucharistic Prayers*, 44.
[1010] Ray, Walter D., Ibid., 55.

in praise and thanksgiving for the work of the Son, who has reconciled creatures and creation to God."[1011]

Studying Jewish prayers, Anton Baumstark found many parallels between the Alexandrian Grand Thanksgiving Prayer and the *Jôzêr* in the Jewish Morning Prayer. In the latter, God, the Creator, is blessed and the celestial hosts are enumerated. In addition, the citation from Isaiah is also mentioned. Baumstark proved that the *Jôzêr* as well as many early Christian anaphoric prayers emanated from the worship of the post-exilic Temple.[1012]

In the Liturgy of Saint Basil, the Grand Thanksgiving Prayer is shorter than that of the Gregorian and Cyrilline counterparts. It speaks of God the Creator, the Powerful, the Lover of Mankind. The Creator of the heaven, the earth, the sea, and all that is therein. Next, it retells the story of creation. He created man as the head of his creation and gave him the power to manage the fish of the sea, and the birds of the sky. Describing God as "the Creator" and "the Powerful" in the beginning of the liturgy, gives us hope that we are in care of a powerful, almighty, and philanthropist God. The prayer starts with a detailed explanation of the angels and their ranks. Being the Children of God, the corrupt nature, called the *old man*, has died in the sacrament of Baptism, and humanity rose with a new nature, as the Children of God. Thus, the faithful new spiritual family includes the angles and the saints. Baptism and other sacraments are the fruits of Jesus' sacrifice on the Cross. Therefore, through the Eucharist, the believers returned to their pristine rank and rejoined the heavenly family.

The Liturgy of Saint Gregory focuses more on the Only-begotten Son, the incarnate Word of God, our Lord Jesus Christ. It proclaims that He is

---

[1011] Webber, Robert E., *Ancient-Future Worship: Proclaiming and Enacting God's Narrative*, 151.
[1012] Baumstark, Anton, *Comparative Liturgy*, 49, 50.

the true eternal God, who showed humanity the Light of the Father. As Saint Paul says, "The Son is the radiance of God's glory and the exact representation of his being, sustaining all things by his powerful word" (Hebrews 1:3). He is the one who revealed to mankind the Light of the Father, gave humanity the true understanding of the Holy Spirit, disclosed to His people the great mystery of life, the mystery of Communion, and conferred His children the praise of the Seraphim. One important characteristic of this prayer is the use of apophatic descriptors like "ineffable, invisible, infinite, without beginning, timeless, immeasurable, incomprehensible, and unchangeable," a feature that finds its roots in the Hellenistic, in particular Stoicism,[1013] philosophies.[1014]

Imbedded within the Preface are three biddings assigned to the altar server:

> 1- "You who are seated stand (rise)." This must be understood from a spiritual perspective. The altar server instructs the congregation to forsake spiritual laziness and focus on prayer. The Church provides an even deeper understanding of this request. The Greek work "καθήμενοι: κάθημαι" means "to be seated," "lie idle," "sit doing nothing," "sit still," "settle," or "to be engaged or employed, especially in a sedentary business." The common theme among all these meanings is slothfulness. The Greek word "αναστῆτε" has several meanings as well, including, "rise from sleep," "rise from the

---

[1013] Stoicism or "the *Stoa*" from the Stoa Poikile (Ancient Greek: ἡ ποικίλη στοά), or "painted porch," where its followers gathered to discuss their ideas, is a philosophy that was founded by Zeno of Citium (334-262 BC) in Athens, and hence, was once called "Zenonism." The Stoics regarded the world as created and sustained in order and beauty by God, whose energy is immanent throughout it. Indeed, the order and beauty of the world were held to be manifestations of God as the divine reason, world reason, or "Logos." The Stoics are especially known for teaching that "virtue is the only good" for human beings, and those external things—such as health, wealth, and pleasure—are not good or bad in themselves but have value as "material for virtue to act upon."

[1014] Baumstark, Anton, *On the Historical Development of the Liturgy*, 83.

dead," "stand up," "raise up," "make people rise, break up an assembly by force" or "make people emigrate, transplant." Luckily, ancient Coptic writers preserved for us their understanding of this bidding in their work. The 13th century *The Beginners' Guide and Discipline for Laity* instructs, "In the liturgy of the Feast of the Resurrection to the Pentecost, the deacon must not say ⲓ̀ ⲕⲁⲑⲏⲙⲉⲛⲓ ⲁ̀ⲛⲁⲥⲑⲏⲧⲉ; instead, [he should say] Ⲕⲩⲣⲓⲉ̀ ⲉⲗⲉⲏⲥⲟⲛ."[1015] The same rubric was offered by Ibn Kabar[1016] and other manuscripts.[1017] MS Lit. 118 was more specific regarding the time ⲓ̀ ⲕⲁⲑⲏⲙⲉⲛⲓ ⲁ̀ⲛⲁⲥⲑⲏⲧⲉ is back in the liturgy. In the chapter explaining the Pentecostal liturgy, the document directs, "From this time ⲓ̀ ⲕⲁⲑⲏⲙⲉⲛⲓ ⲁ̀ⲛⲁⲥⲑⲏⲧⲉ is said."[1018] Based on the aforementioned quotes, it is palpable that the bidding of ⲓ̀ ⲕⲁⲑⲏⲙⲉⲛⲓ ⲁ̀ⲛⲁⲥⲑⲏⲧⲉ is unequivocally associated with the Resurrection. To the Church, her members, the body of Christ, are risen with Jesus during Eastertide; as such, during this festive period—according to the ancient practice, this call was suspended. Accordingly, a better translation construed from the Church's understanding is, "You who are lazy rise."

2- "Look toward [1019] the east." The Lord created a garden eastward in Eden and placed man in it (Genesis 2:8). The bidding urges the believers to long for their original home, which Adam and Eve were banished from. Ephrem the

---

[1015] Misael of the Paromeos Monastery (Father). (2018). The Beginners' Guide and Discipline for Laity. *Alexandria School, 24(1),* 169.
[1016] Ibn Kabar, *The Lamp*, BnF, MS Arabic 203 (c. AD 1363-1369), fol. 214v.
[1017] Examples: London, Bod., MS OR. 8770 (18th C.), and Paris, BnF, MS Copte 36.
[1018] *The Church Order*, Patriarchal Library, MS Lit. 118 (AD 1911), fol. 93r.
[1019] Some churches use "towards" instead of "toward." Both are correct and can be used interchangeably; however, "toward" is used more often in American English, while "towards" is more common in British English.

Syrian[1020] says, "Our holy place is the Paradise, our original place; and since it was in the east, we are told to face the east when we pray."[1021] Additionally, our Lord ascended into heaven to the east, and will come again from there. Looking toward the East is a reminiscent of our original and future home.

3- "Let us attend." Although this call was not mentioned in most old sources,[1022] it does demonstrate the prominence of the subsequent praise. Sinaiticus gr. 2148 (13th century) is addressing this bidding to the deacons. In a 14th century Euchologion, the bidding was elaborated to expound its intention. It reads, "Let us attend in silence and knowledge. The heavenly orders praise, and we also praise with them." The objective is to listen carefully and respectfully to the following hymn, which is the Sanctus (also called the Cherubic Hymn or the Cherubikon since it is the praise of the Cherubim).

The protracted Preface of the Liturgy of Saint Cyril is due to its inclusion of the Intercessory Prayers (i.e., Litanies, Supplications, Commemoration of the Saints, and the Diptych[1023]). Many examples of

---

[1020] Saint Ephrem the Syrian (AD 306–373) was a Syriac deacon and a prolific Syriac-language hymnographer and theologian of the fourth century from the region of Syria. His works are hailed by Christians throughout the world, and many denominations venerate him as a saint. Saint Ephrem wrote a wide variety of hymns, poems, and sermons in verse, as well as prose biblical exegesis. These were works of practical theology for the edification of the church in troubled times. Saint Ephrem composed over four hundred hymns.
[1021] Although this has been used as a quote by Ephrem the Syrian, I could not find the exact text. It might be a paraphrase of a conception that he wrote or said.
[1022] Athanasius of Saint Macarius Monastery (Father), *The Divine Liturgy: The Mystery of the Kingdom of God (Part 2)*, 674.
[1023] Literally, a diptych (from the Greek δίπτυχον) is any object with two flat plates attached at a hinge. In the ecclesiastical sense, the term refers to official lists of the living and departed that are commemorated by the local church. The living would be inscribed on one wing of the diptych,

this tradition can be found in the Jewish and early Christian thanksgiving prayers, such as the *Didache* and the First Epistle of Clement 59-61.[1024] This suggests that the Egyptian shape of the Grand Thanksgiving Prayer, manifested in the Liturgy of Saint Mark/Cyril, follows a very old tradition that emanates from a Jewish custom, which was adopted by the early Christians.

In the Liturgy of Saint Cyril, after the Descent of the Holy Spirit, earthly requests are not desirable; the focus, however, is solely delineated on the Lord Jesus Christ. According to the liturgical Coptic tradition,[1025] it is not proper to have the King of Kings, and the Lord of the Universe on the altar and still be concerned about secular matters. The liturgies of Saint Basil and Saint Gregory, on the other hand, are of Byzantine tradition, which places all Intercessory Prayers after the Epiclesis (Descent of the Holy Spirit).[1026] In the Liturgy of Saint Cyril, the order is as follows: Following the Eucharistic Dialogue, the priest prays the Preface, which starts with "meet and right." After "this rational sacrifice and this bloodless[1027] service," he signs the coffer of incense and places a spoonful of incense into the censer. He then takes the censer and says, "This, which all nations offer unto You." Afterward, he signs the Offerings from east to west and from north to south and says, "from the east to the west and from the north to the south." Subsequently, he offers incense over the Offerings while saying, "For great is Your name, O Lord..." The congregation

---

and the departed on the other. In the Coptic Orthodox Church, the term "diptych" is used to refer to the prayers chanted to commemorate the departed.

[1024] The First Epistle of Clement is a letter addressed to the Christians in the city of Corinth. The letter dates from the late first or early second century, and ranks with *Didache* as one of the earliest—if not the earliest—of extant Christian documents outside the canonical New Testament.

[1025] Represented in the liturgies of Saint Mark, Saint Cyril, and Deir Balyzeh.

[1026] This tradition was also documented in the Liturgy of Saint Serapion, as will be discussed later.

[1027] The phrase "bloodless service" or "bloodless sacrifice" was used by fourth century writers (first by Saint Cyril of Jerusalem) to mean the Eucharist (the Body and Blood of Jesus). However, In the Jewish tradition this phrase meant "praise to the Lord". Athenagoras, a second century Egyptian writer, theologian and the head of the catechetical school of Alexandria, as well as Origen of Alexandria had the same usage of the phase (i.e., praise to God).

responds, "Lord have mercy." Next, the priest prays a series of litanies for peace, the sick, the travelers, the nature, and the leader.[1028] This is then followed by the Commemoration of the Saints, the Litany of the Departed, and the Diptych. Another series of litanies is then recited: for the oblations, the Patriarch, the bishops (including clergy and the orders of the church), the rest of the Orthodox people, the place, those who are standing in this place, and those who have asked us for prayer.

At this point, the altar server instructs the attendees to "Worship God in fear and trembling." The priest prays the Litany of the Servant Priest inaudibly. Afterwards, the Litany of the Priesthood is uttered followed by that of the assemblies. The altar server directs, "You who are seated stand." The priest prays the Supplications; in it, the congregation punctuates each petition with "Lord have mercy." Then, the altar server bids the worshippers to "Look toward the east," after which the priest continues the rest of the Preface starting from, "For You are God, who is above every principality," a prayer that serves as an introduction to or rather a connector leading up to the Sanctus. The altar server requests, "Let us attend," and the congregation chants the Sanctus.

Obviously, this Preface has expanded over time from its primitive content. Earlier Thanksgiving texts of the Liturgy of Saint Mark demonstrate less petitions, although the core remains intact. Most old sources do not mention instructions assigned to the deacon (or the altar server); however, the Liturgy of Saint Thomas [1029] presents an early emersion of these biddings. After the Preface, and at this very point, the Church has ascended to the heavens before the Lord's throne, and as such, she has nothing to say but to glorify Him; therefore, it is natural for the worshippers to cry out chanting the Sanctus.

[1028] Also called Litany of the King or Litany of the President.
[1029] Full text of this fragment is presented in chapter 7 of this book.

The part leading to the Sanctus is commonly referred to as the Pre-Sanctus. The textual composition of the Pre-Sanctus is pretty brilliant; it quotes several verses from the Scriptures in a homogeneous manner that naturally leads to the Sanctus. The Pre-Sanctus lists the heavenly orders quoted from (Ephesians 1:21).[1030] The use of this verse in the Thanksgiving Prayer is peculiar to Egypt. Other traditions quote (Colossians 1:16)[1031] instead. The Liturgy of Saint Serapion, however, is unique in quoting both verses. This is followed by a reference to (Daniel 7:10),[1032] and finally, the Pre-Sanctus is concluded quoting (Isaiah 6:2, 3).[1033] [1034]

The Sanctus

The Sanctus,[1035] or as called by Anton Baumstark "The Biblical Trisagion,"[1036] finds its roots in the Old Testament; "Holy— *Kadosh* (Hebrew: קדוש), holy, holy is the Lord Almighty; the whole earth is full of His glory" (Isaiah 6:3). As mentioned above, the use of the Sanctus was of Jewish origin, in the Morning Prayer before echoed by the early Christian Prime Prayer.[1037] Many scholars believe that this praise, in

---

[1030] "Far above all rule and authority, power and dominion, and every name that is invoked, not only in the present age but also in the one to come."

[1031] "For in Hleim all things were created: things in heaven and on earth, visible and invisible, whether thrones or powers or rulers or authorities; all things have been created through Him and for Him."

[1032] "A river of fire was flowing, coming out from before him. Thousands upon thousands attended Him; ten thousand times ten thousand stood before Him. The court was seated, and the books were opened."

[1033] "Above Him were seraphim, each with six wings: With two wings they covered their faces, with two they covered their feet, and with two they were flying. And they were calling to one another: 'Holy, holy, holy is the Lord Almighty; the whole earth is full of His glory.'"

[1034] Cuming, Geoffrey J., *The Liturgy of St Mark*, 120.

[1035] The Sanctus (Holy), which is leniently referred to as the Cherubic Hymn, symbolically incorporates those present at the liturgy into the presence of the angels gathered around God's throne. The full text in Greek: Ἅγιος, ἅγιος, ἅγιος Κύριος Σαβαώθ· πλήρης ὁ οὐρανὸς καὶ ἡ γῆ τῆς δόξης σου, ὡσαννὰ ἐν τοῖς ὑψίστοις. Εὐλογημένος ὁ ἐρχόμενος ἐν ὀνόματι Κυρίου. Ὡσαννὰ (ὁ) ἐν τοῖς ὑψίστοις.

[1036] Baumstark, Anton, *Comparative Liturgy*, 48, 49, and others.

[1037] Baumstark, Anton, *Comparative Liturgy*, 50, 51.

its current shape and use, was first originated in Alexandria, possibly before AD 230, then adopted first by other Egyptian churches, before it spread all over Christendom. [1038] Gregory Dix suggests that the tradition of praying the Preface followed by chanting the Sanctus can be traced in the writings of Origen of Alexandria.[1039] [1040] Kretschmar believes that it was introduced into the Alexandrian liturgy by Pope Dionysius the Great[1041] in the third century, and Taft does not disagree.[1042]

Saint Ambrose of Milan (AD 340–397) says, "We, humans, cannot find a better praise to glorify the Son of God than calling Him 'Holy'."[1043] This is one of the earliest references to the Sanctus in the West. It seems that "the use of the Sanctus was in the process of spreading through the West at the beginning of the fifth century," [1044] as Yarnold writes. Although Dix's conclusion vis-à-vis the Egyptian provenance of the Sanctus is still the dominant theory, more recent studies, especially those of Bryan Spinks[1045] and Thomas Talley,[1046] argue that it is of Syrian origin.

Cuming, after comparing the ancient Egyptian liturgies with that of Saint James, believes that the Sanctus replaced the final doxology. All ancient liturgies ended with a doxology to the Lord.[1047] "The Sanctus

---

[1038] This was mentioned by Saint Athanasius the Apostolic, the 20th Pope of Alexandria (AD 298 - May 2, 373).
[1039] Dix, Dom Gregory, *The Shape of the Liturgy*, 165.
[1040] Other scholars, like Cuming and Paul Bradshaw, do not see eye to eye with Dix.
[1041] Saint Dionysius of Alexandria, named "the Great," 14th Pope of Alexandria from December 28, 248 until his death on March 22, 264 AD after seventeen years as the Pope. He was the first Pope to hold the title "the Great" (even before a Bishop of Rome). Dionysius' large surviving correspondence provides most of our information about him. Only one original letter survives to this day; the remaining letters are excerpted in the works of Eusebius.
[1042] Taft, *The Interpolation of the Sanctus*, 94-95.
[1043] Although this saying is attributed to Ambrose of Milan, I could not find the exact quotation. It might be a paraphrase of a conception that he wrote or said.
[1044] Yarnold, E.J. (1992). The Liturgy of the Faithful in the Fourth and Early Fifth Centuries. In Cheslyn Jones, Geoffrey Wainwright, Edward Yarnold SJ and Paul Bradshaw (Eds.), *The Study of Liturgy*, 232.
[1045] B. Spinks, *The Sanctus in the Eucharistic Prayer*, 87.
[1046] T. Talley, *The Literary Structure of the Eucharistic Prayer*, 414.
[1047] For more details on this topic, refer to chapter 7 "Ancient Eucharistic Prayers."

replaced the original doxology," Cumming writes, "and the rest of the *anaphora* was built up gradually by additions after the Sanctus."[1048] He also adds, "At Jerusalem it was inserted at the end of the preface."[1049] Not all scholars, however, agree with Cuming; many others believe that the original placement of the Sanctus according to the Alexandrian tradition is after the Preface, similar to the order of the Syriac and Byzantine traditions, not replacing the final doxology. If this is true, it means that the other churches not only borrowed the lyrics of the Sanctus from the Alexandrian rite, but also its placement.

This chant reflects the Church's liturgical and theological experience; her, and our, vision and purpose, which is "heaven and earth are full of Your glory." Originally, the hymn starts with the words "Holy holy holy;" nonetheless, these words are now preceded by the Cherubic Hymn,[1050] which reads, "The Cherubim worship You and the Seraphim glorify You proclaiming and saying." Today, this introduction (the Cherubic Hymn) is referred to as the *Watos Aspazmos*.[1051] The lyrics of the *Watos Aspzmos* differ from one season to another. In Regular Days, there are six *Watos Aspasmos* hymns, in addition to a specific one assigned to the Liturgy of Saint Cyril. In the past, the use of the *Watos Aspasmos* "The Cherubim worship You and the Seraphim glorify You proclaiming and saying," which was immediately followed by the Sanctus, was ubiquitous.[1052] Unlike the contemporary practice, Ibn Kabar does not limit the use of this

---

[1048] Cuming, G. J. (1997). The Anaphora of St. Mark: A Study of Development. Bradshaw, Paul F. (Ed.), *Essays on Early Eastern Eucharistic Prayers*, 71.
[1049] Cuming, Ibid., 72.
[1050] In the Syriac Church this introduction to the Sanctus, according to Patriach Ignatius Ephrem II Rahmani, exceeded 100 variations, only 11 of which are still in use today. *Les Liturgies Orientales et Occidentales*, 272.
[1051] The Cherubic Hymn is a generic term used for many churches; however, the *Watos Aspazmos* is the Coptic Church implementation of it. The name of this introductory hymn (i.e., *Watos Aspazmos*), was not mentioned in manuscripts, and might have been wrongly named since the word "Aspzmos" means "kiss," which no where can be found in this section.
[1052] Nowadays, the most common *Watos Aspazmos* in Regular Days is the one that starts with "O Lord, God of hosts, return and behold from heaven."

chant to Regular Days, but rather extends it to festivals.[1053] Eventually, the use of the *Watos Aspazmos* melody was limited to occasions; nevertheless, a syllabic style was appointed to its lyrics. In other words, the hymn "The Cherubim" that is recited hitherto after the Preface is a shortened rendition of one of the most common *Watos Aspazmos* hymns in antiquity. It is interesting to note that like the hymn (Through the intercessions) was originated from the *Adam Aspazmos* (Ⲡⲓⲭⲣⲓⲥⲧⲟⲥ Ⲡⲉⲛⲥⲱⲧⲏⲣ), the hymn "The Cherubim" was derived from the *Watos Aspazmos* (Ⲛⲓⲭⲉⲣⲟⲩⲃⲓⲙ).

In the Liturgy of Saint Gregory, as reported by Ibn Kabar,[1054] after the hymn "The Cherubim" and the Sanctus, the hymn Ⲱⲥⲁⲛⲛⲁ, meaning "Hosanna" is chanted.[1055] The meaning of the hymn is, "Hosanna in the highest. Blessed is He who comes in the name of the Lord. Hosanna in the highest." In many traditions, "Hosanna" is an integral extension of the Sanctus,[1056] nonetheless, it is now hardly used in the Coptic rite. This now-ignored hymn has a profound spiritual and theological denotation: The Sanctus is the praise of the angels (Isaiah 6:3), yet "Hosanna" is that of humans (John 12:13).[1057] Chanting the Sanctus followed by "Hosanna" confirms that through the incarnation of God the Logos, and by means of the sacrifice of Christ on the Cross, heaven and earth were united and became one indivisible entity; thus, they share the same praise.

In the Liturgy of Saint Cyril, during the *Watos Aspasmos*, the priest washes his hands while saying, "Cleanse me with hyssop, and I will be clean; wash me, and I will be whiter than snow" (Psalm 51:7), a practice that is absent from the liturgies of Saint Basil and Saint Gregory. In all

---

[1053] Ibn Kabar, *The Lamp*, BnF, MS Arabic 203 (c. AD 1363-1369), fol. 207r.
[1054] Ibn Kabar, Ibid., fol. 207r.
[1055] This hymn was recorded by the late Cantor Mikhail Girgis of Batanoun.
[1056] The hymn is used in the liturgy of Saint John Chrysostom, liturgy of Saint Basil (Byzantine), liturgy of Saint James, the Roman Rite, and the Mozarabic Rite.
[1057] The connotation is derived from the praise of the Jews while welcoming Jesus into Jerusalem.

liturgies, while chanting the Sanctus (or the *Watos Aspasmos*), the priest places the corporal covering his right hand on the left of the altar and takes the one topping the chalice to cover his right hand. He then uses the corporal covering his left hand to top the chalice. Finally, he uses the corporal on his left to cover his left hand.

There are numerous exegeses, or rather contemplations, of these actions. One compares these movements to that produced by the Cherubim around the altar moving their wings. Another suggests that uncovering the paten during the Eucharistic Dialogue while the chalice is covered alludes to Jesus' appearance to Mary Magdalene, but she did not know Him. Uncovering the chalice, while saying "Holy," as will be detailed later, indicates that He, eventually, revealed Himself to her. Topping the chalice—after has been exposed—once more symbolizes that the Lord, after declaring Himself to the disciples at Emmaus, when He broke bread, He disappeared.[1058] Yet, a third meditation proposes that, during the moving corporals, the fact that a corporal being lowered and another rising, resembles the mystery of Communion: Some people eat and drink eternal life while others receive condemnation. Another variation of the latter symbolism suggests that up and down movement of corporals is an indicative of the status of God's creatures: Some heavenly fell whereas some earthly were adopted as Children of God. In his *On the Divine Liturgy*, Nicholas Cabasilas[1059] provides yet another interpretation; he writes, "Then he (the priest) covers the paten and the chalice with luxurious covers and censes, because initially Christ's power was covered,

---

[1058] Mettaos (Bishop), *The Spirituality of the Rite of the Liturgy of the Coptic Orthodox Church*, 165.
[1059] Nicholas Cabasilas (born 1319/1323 in Thessalonica; died AD 1392) was a Byzantine mystic writer and a chief theoretician of the liturgical spiritual life masterfully leads us into the spiritual area of the Divine Liturgy. He is one of the most important representatives of 14th century Orthodox humanism. His two main spiritual works are "On the Divine Liturgy" and "Concerning Life in Christ."

until that time when He began working miracles, and God the Father gave His witness from Heaven."

Following the Sanctus, in the Basilian and Gregorian liturgies, the priest proclaims, Ⲁ̇ⲅⲓⲟⲥ (Holy) three times.[1060] On the first time, he faces east and draws the sign of the cross on himself, on the second, he signs the altar servers, and on the third, he faces west—toward the congregation—and signs them. This is the reverse order of that used during the Eucharistic Dialogue signings, an indication of equality, regardless of the rank, in needing of the purification of the Blood of Jesus and the sanctification of the Holy Spirit. As opposed to the Dialogue signings, which are performs with the priest covering his right hand with the paten corporal, these signings are accomplished with the chalice corporal, signifying equality between the Body and Blood of the Lord. The signings during Ⲁ̇ⲅⲓⲟⲥ, like the Dialogue ones, were first introduced in the 15th century.[1061]

There is a liturgical practice mentioned in the Liturgy of Saint Gregory,[1062] but absent from the other two liturgies. While the priest is reciting Ⲁ̇ⲅⲓⲟⲥ along with its associated signs, the assistant priest circuits the altar once with the censer, indicating the sacrifice of the Son that the Father inhaled its sweet aroma. In this ritual, the Church is simulating the heaven by conjoining the chanting of the word "Holy" with the offering of incense.[1063] Going around the altar is an affirmation that our sanctification, which emanates from the Holiness of Jesus, is through the sacrifice of Christ on the Cross, which was accepted by God the Father.

[1060] If the Patriarch or a bishop is present, but delegated the recitation of Ⲁ̇ⲅⲓⲟⲥ to the priest, the latter utters Ⲁ̇ⲅⲓⲟⲥ thrice but does not sign anyone except himself. The Patriarch/bishop signs himself, the altar servers, and the people without saying Ⲁ̇ⲅⲓⲟⲥ.
[1061] Athanasius of Saint Macarius Monastery (Father), *Summary of the Liturgical History of the Church of Alexandria (Part 2)*, 243.
[1062] Although this rite is mentioned in the Liturgy of Saint Gregory, it is not practiced anymore.
[1063] Praising saying "holy" (Revelation 4:8); offering incense (Revelation 8:4).

Put differently, the incense is a symbolic representation of the sacrifice of Jesus, while the chanting of the word "Holy" denotes our sanctification through the New Pascha.

In antiquity, neither the chanting of Ⲁⲅⲓⲟⲥ nor the performance of signings existed. The first time the signings were mentioned was in the 15th century work *The Ritual Order*, authored by Pope Gabriel V. According to the author, the signings take place immediately following the recitation of "The Cherubim worship you" and while the Sanctus "Ⲁⲅⲓⲟⲥ Ⲁⲅⲓⲟⲥ Ⲁⲅⲓⲟⲥ" is being chanted. Moreover, nothing is mentioned about the thrice utterance of Ⲁⲅⲓⲟⲥ.[1064] This ancient practice is still preserved in the Liturgy of Saint Cyril. To recapitulate, the development of this part of the liturgy can be traced as follows: In its primitive shape, after the Sanctus, the priest prays, "Holy, holy, holy, indeed. O Lord our God, who formed us"[1065] without signings. In the 14th or 15th century, the signings were introduced during the Sanctus. Finally, the rite matured to add the thrice utterance of Ⲁⲅⲓⲟⲥ following the Sanctus and move the three signings to parallel the thrice "Holy."

The Salvation Narrative

In the liturgies of Syro-Byzantine provenance, the Thanksgiving Prayer (preface) includes Jesus' acts of creation, incarnation, and redemption—*Christus Victor*.[1066] On the other hand, Alexandrian Thanksgiving Prayers

---

[1064] Gabriel V (Pope), *The Ritual Order*, BnF, MS 98 (AD 1411), fol. 60v.

[1065] This is a prayer of the Liturgy of Saint Basil. The same applies to the corresponding prayers in the other liturgies.

[1066] Under the *Christus Victor* theory of the Atonement in Christianity (Atonement refers to the forgiving or pardoning of sin in general and original sin in particular through the death and resurrection of Jesus, enabling the reconciliation between God and his creation), Christ's death defeated the powers of evil, which had held humankind in their dominion. The term comes from the title of Gustaf Aulén's book, first published in AD 1931 and translated into English by Gabriel Hebert, in which he drew attention back to this classic early Church understanding of the atonement. Gustav Aulén writes in description of *Christus Victor*, "the work of Christ is first and foremost a victory over the powers which hold mankind in bondage: sin, death, and the devil."

are centered solely around the act of creation, as discussed earlier; however, the acts of incarnation, redemption and the entire story of salvation are cited separately in an orison, called the Salvation Narrative, following the Sanctus.

According to the Basilian and Gregorian liturgies, the Salvation Narrative starts with the creation and fall, passes by the incarnation of God the Logos, His sufferings, resurrection and sitting at the right hand of God the Father, until it reaches the Second Coming. When accomplished, the congregation pleas to the Lord saying, "According to Your mercy O Lord, and not according to our sins." In the Liturgy of Saint Basil, the Salvation Narrative, which was once said uninterruptedly,[1067] is divided into three sections; the first is followed by the people's responsory "Amen," and the second by the congregation respond "Amen, I believe."[1068] At the outset of the second section, at the sentence "Was incarnate and became man" the priest places a spoonful of incense in the censer as a reminder of the incarnation of God in Saint Mary's womb.[1069] Some priests put this spoonful of incense holding a corporal on their hand as a way of showing honor and respect to the mystery of incarnation of God the Logos.

In the Liturgy of Saint Gregory, the Salvation Narrative is divided into four parts separated by a responsory, "Lord have mercy," which is assigned to the people. The first section is "Holy, Holy, Holy, O Lord," the second is, "You, O my Master," the third is, "You who are The Being at all times," and the fourth section is, "You have come to the slaughter." In these four

---

[1067] This is found in London, BL, OR. 1239 (12th C.), London, Bod., MS Hunt 360 (13th C.), Vatican, Vat, Copto 17 (AD 1288), London, Bod., MS Hunt 572 (13th or 14th C.), Paris, BnF, MS Copte 82 (AD 1307), Paris, BnF, MS Copte 26 (18th C.), and others. In this primitive shape of the prayer, the people's responsories "Amen" and "Amen, I believe" are absent.

[1068] From the documents inspected in this study, the oldest mention of these responsories was in the Tuki's euchologion. See: Tuki, Raphael (Bishop), *The Three Liturgies of Saints Basil, Gregory the Theologian, and Cyril, in addition to Other Holy Prayers*, 104-105.

[1069] The censer symbolizes Saint Mary's womb, the fire inside it represents the "fire" of Divinity, and the aroma of incense denotes the act of Incarnation, that is, the union between the Divinity of the Logos and humanity.

sections, the emphasis is on the fact that man is the one who necessitates the worship of God[1070] and who is in desperate need of His love and salvation. It retells about God's love and how He created man in the sixth day in order to have everything ready for him.[1071] Nonetheless, man responded to the divine love by disobeying and contravened His commandments.[1072] Hence, he became under the authority of death and was banished from Paradise; still, God, in desiring to rescue man from perdition, has "bound me with all the remedies that lead to life,"[1073] which are the Law, the holy sacraments, the gifts of the Holy Spirit, etc. These tools were granted to man to, not only help him overcome sin and eternal death, but also unite with the Creator. Through the unutterable incarnation of God the Logos, "The Son of God became a man to enable men to become sons of God," as C.S. Lewis proclaims.[1074] This is an ancient understanding of the Early Church Fathers; Saint Athanasius says, "For He was made man that we might be made God."[1075] In his sermon 192.1.1 Saint Augustine says, "To make human beings gods, He was made man who was God." Pope Cyril of Alexandria confirms this understanding saying, "For we too are sons and gods by grace, and we have surely been brought to this wonderful and supernatural dignity since we have the Only Begotten Word of God dwelling within us."[1076] Through Jesus Christ, the curse of the Law was lifted,[1077] which is a fundamental Christian belief that was underlined by Saint Paul, "Christ redeemed us from the curse of the

---

[1070] Liturgy of Saint Gregory "You have no need of my servitude, but I have need of your Lordship".
[1071] Liturgy of Saint Gregory "You have ... opened for me Paradise to enjoy and have given to me the learning of Your knowledge".
[1072] Liturgy of Saint Gregory "Of one plant have You forbidden me to eat that of which You have said to me, 'of it only do not eat.' but according to my will, I did eat. I put Your law behind me by my own counsel and became slothful towards Your commandments. I plucked for myself the sentence of death".
[1073] Liturgy of Saint Gregory.
[1074] Lewis, C.S., *Mere Christianity*, 155.
[1075] Athanasius (Saint), "Section 54", *On the Incarnation*
[1076] Cyril (Saint). *On the Unity of Christ*. Crestwood, NY: St. Vladimir's Seminary Press, 80.
[1077] Liturgy of Saint Gregory "You have lifted the curse of the Law".

law by becoming a curse for us" (Galatians 3:13). Our Lord carried our sins in His body;[1078] just as the Baptist preached saying, "Look, the Lamb of God, who takes away the sin of the world" (John 1:29). The prayer continues to confirm that death was defeated by the death of Jesus, resulting in the liberation of mankind from its bondage, [1079] and the restoration of the primitive human state, which can perpetually coexist with the Lord. Finally, with His resurrection and ascension into the heavens, He opened for us, the faithful, the door of Paradise, and now we have a share in the Kingdom of Heaven.[1080]

After the Salvation Narrative, the congregation chants, "According to Your mercy O Lord, and not according to our sins." If time permits, this pleading may be chanted in its melismatic melody, particularly in the Gregorian liturgy. Two different endings are applicable to both the minor and the melismatic tunes. Yet, another melismatic tune—borrowed from ⲁⲣⲓϩⲟⲩⲟ ⳓⲁⲥϥ of the Third Canticle— [1081] can be found, mostly in Alexandria.

The Minor Epiclesis

The Cyrilline liturgy embraces a different order. After the Sanctus, no Salvation Narrative can be found; the priest says, "Holy, Lord of hosts." This prayer, called the Post-Sanctus, capitalizes on the Sanctus: heaven and earth are full of the Lord's holy glory, and pleads the Father to fill the sacrifice with this glory by the decent of the Holy Spirit on the offerings for blessing and sanctification. Hence, the brilliant transitioning statements from the Sanctus to the words of invocation serve as a preface to the Minor Epiclesis. Since the Major Epiclesis, which takes place at the

---

[1078] Liturgy of Saint Gregory "You have abolished sin in the flesh".
[1079] Liturgy of Saint Gregory "You have slain my sin in your tomb".
[1080] Liturgy of Saint Gregory "You have brought my first fruit up to heaven".
[1081] The Third Canticle is one of the main elements of the Midnight Psalmody.

end of the Sanctification Prayers, was introduced in the 4th century, the Minor Epiclesis [1082] was the ultimate invocation of the Holy Spirit according to the Liturgy of Saint Mark. [1083] Speaking of the Major Epiclesis, Maxwell E. Johnson writes, "A development first witnessed to by Peter II of Alexandria, [1084] the immediate successor of Athanasius himself."[1085]

It is imperative to notice that the Minor Epiclesis recognizes an earlier invocation, viz., the one addressed to the Logos in the Offertory office, which reads, "Show Your face upon this bread, and upon this cup... Bless them, sanctify them, purify them, and transform them, in order that, on the one hand, this bread may indeed become Your holy Body, and, on the other hand, the mixture which is in the cup indeed Your Precious Blood." Therefore, in Mark's Minor Epiclesis, it reads, "Fill this, Your sacrifice, O Lord with Your blessing, which is from You, by the coming down upon it of Your Holy Spirit. And with blessings, bless. And with sanctification, sanctify... Your precious gifts, which are already set forth before You, this bread and this cup." The last sentence refers to the epiclesis accomplished during the Offertory office.

[1082] The Epiclesis (ἐπίκλησις "invocation" or "calling down from on high") is the part of the Anaphora by which the priest invokes God upon the Eucharistic bread and wine. According to the Byzantine tradition and in the Western rite, the epiclesis is a calling of the Holy Spirit; however, in the Alexandrian tradition, there are more than one Epiclesis and are addressed to the Father, the Son as well as to the Holy Spirit. In the Byzantine tradition, the Epiclesis comes after the Anamnesis (remembrance of Jesus' words and deeds); in the Western Rite it usually precedes. In the Coptic (Alexandrian) tradition, the first Epiclesis comes at the end of the Offertory, the second one is prayed right after the Sanctus, and the third Epiclesis takes place after the Anamnesis.

[1083] The tradition of placing the Epiclesis before the Institution Narrative was followed in Alexandria and Rome. All other churches in the East placed it after. For more details, see: Baumstark, Anton, *Comparative Liturgy*, 48.

[1084] Pope Peter II of Alexandria (AD 373–381), 21st Pope of Alexandria & Patriarch of the See of St. Mark. He was a disciple of Saint Athanasius who designated him as his successor before his death in AD 373.

[1085] Johnson, Maxwell E. (1997). The Archaic Nature of the Sanctus, Institution Narrative, and Epiclesis of the Logos in the Anaphora Ascribed to Sarapion of Thmuis. Bradshaw, Paul F. (Ed.), *Essays on Early Eastern Eucharistic Prayers*, 97.

Following the Sanctus with an invocation, instead of the Salvation Narrative, is an Alexandrian tradition. Hence, it is not surprising to find it in the Liturgy of Saint Serapion. In it, after the Sanctus, the priest is assigned the following prayer, "Fill also this sacrifice with Your power and Your partaking: for to You have we offered this living sacrifice, this bloodless[1086] oblation."[1087] As such, we can emphatically conclude that in the Egyptian liturgical tradition, characterized by the liturgies of Saint Cyril and Saint Serapion, the sanctification for transformation has started in the Offertory, and is completed in the Epiclesis prayed right after the Sanctus.

Unlike the Liturgy of Saint Cyril, however, the Liturgy of Saint Serapion invocates the Logos, not the Holy Spirit. Most scholars[1088] seem to corroborate the idea that the Logos Epiclesis represents an early Egyptian euchological and theological tradition. Writings of Saint Clement of Alexandria, Origen and Saint Athanasius were utilized to underpin this argument. In his *Adversus Haereses* of the second century, Saint Irenaeus writes, "When, therefore, the mingled cup and the manufactured bread receive the Word of God... the Eucharist becomes the Body and the Blood of Christ."[1089] Similarly, Origen of Alexandria, in his commentary on Matthew 11:14, says, "I mean by the very fact that we do not eat of the bread which has been sanctified by the word of God and prayer, are we deprived of any good thing."[1090] By the same token, Saint

---

[1086] It is worth mentioning that the phrase "bloodless" in the Liturgy of Saint Serapion comes after the Sanctus, which could mean that it is referring to praising the Lord. However, in the Liturgy of Saint Cyril, "bloodless" comes in the Grand Thanksgiving Prayer before the Sanctus. Some scholars understand that the phrase "bloodless" refers to praising God, but others think it is referring to the Eucharist that, according to the Alexandrian tradition, is present on the altar since the end of the Offertory (when the invocation of the Logos takes place).

[1087] This Epiclesis (of the Liturgy of Saint Serapion) is addressed to the Second Hypostasis, God the Son.

[1088] Such as Hans Lietzman, Johannes Quasten, Wordworth, Geoffrey Cuming, Anton Baumstark and Johannes Betz.

[1089] Irenaeus (Saint), *Against Heresies*, 5:2.

[1090] Origen, *Origen Commentary on the Gospel of Matthew*, 52.

Athanasius, in his *Sermon to the Newly Baptized*, writes, "When the great prayers and holy supplications have been sent up, the Logos comes upon the bread and the cup and they become His Body."[1091] Even in the 5th century, after the Major Epiclesis has been already introduced into the Coptic liturgies, Saint Cyril I still underscores the same concept and speaks unequivocally about the Logos being the reason for the sanctification of the elements. In the letter to Tiberius the Deacon he writes, "But we believe that the bringing of gifts celebrated in the churches are hallowed, blessed and perfected by Christ."[1092]

Western scholars, however, failed to recognize the connection between this post-Sanctus epiclesis and the one that takes place during the Offertory proper. As illustrated above, during the Litany of the Offerings, the priest invokes the Logos on the elements saying, "Bless them, sanctify them, purify them, and transform them, in order that, on the one hand, this bread may indeed become Your holy Body, and, on the other hand, the mixture which is in the cup indeed Your Precious Blood." This supports the conception that the Logos epiclesis is an old Alexandrian tradition. Inspecting the Liturgy of Saint Mark/Cyril, reveals that the Alexandrian tradition involves the three hypostases to complete the transformation of the offering materials into the Body and Blood of Jesus Christ; that is, the Epiclesis of the Son during the Offertory proper for the transformation,[1093] the presence of the Father in the Minor Epiclesis for the blessing, and the descent of the Holy Spirit, also in the Minor Epiclesis, for the sanctification.

[1091] Athanasius (Saint), *Sermon to the Newly Baptized*, ante AD 373.
[1092] Johnson, Maxwell E. (1997). The Archaic Nature of the Sanctus, Institution Narrative, and Epiclesis of the Logos in the Anaphora Ascribed to Sarapion of Thmuis. In Bradshaw, Paul F. (Ed.), *Essays on Early Eastern Eucharistic Prayers*, 98.
[1093] Saint Athanasius writes, "when the great prayers and holy supplications have been sent up, the Word comes upon the bread and the cup and they become His Body." See: Dix, *The Shape*, 168.

Back to the Liturgy of Saint Cyril. When the priest reaches "Fill this, Your sacrifice, O Lord with your blessing," he draws the sign of the cross on the paten and the chalice once and says, "which is from You, by the coming down upon it of Your Holy Spirit." The congregation responds saying, "Amen." The priest then does a second signing, and says, "And with blessings, bless" to which the people respond like the first time. The priest does a third signing on the bread and wine, and says, "And with sanctification, sanctify," and, for the third time, the congregation confirms saying, "Amen." Subsequently, the priest points to the bread and the wine with his hands, and says, "Your precious gifts, which are already set forth before You, this bread and this cup." It is noteworthy that "Amen" is an ancient responsory, which was inherited from Judaism. Saint Justin Martyr, in the 2nd century, states, "And when he (the priest) has concluded the prayers and thanksgivings, all the people present express their assent by saying Amen. This word Amen answers in the Hebrew language to γΕνοιτο (so be it)."[1094]

In summary, after the Sanctus, in the Basilian and Gregorian liturgies, the priest recite Ⲁⲅⲓⲟⲥ thrice accompanied by three signings, followed by the Salvation Narrative, after which the congregation responds saying, "According to Your mercy O Lord and not according to our sins." In the Cyrilline Liturgy, however, the thrice Ⲁⲅⲓⲟⲥ is omitted, yet the signings persist—performed during the Sanctus. This is then followed by the post-Sanctus orison and the Minor Epiclesis, respectively.

[1094] Saint Justin Martyr, *Fist Apology*, chapter 65.

The Institution Narrative

The Institution Narrative, [1095] which is the first of the three-orison Sanctification Prayers,[1096] appeared first in the *Apostolic Tradition*.[1097] In the Coptic Rite, it is consistent across all three liturgies, yet differs in its positioning. The Cyrilline liturgy places the Institution Narrative immediately after the Minor Epiclesis, however, in the other two liturgies it is preceded by the Salvation Narrative. In the West, the Institution Narrative is the culminating point of the liturgy, through which the elements are transformed to the Body and Blood of Jesus Christ; however, in the Byzantine tradition, it is the Epiclesis that is responsible for the transformation. In the Coptic Church, being influenced by the West, starting from the post-patristic era[1098] up until the Middle Ages, the Institution Narrative was viewed as the core of the liturgy.[1099] However, by the Middle Ages, and as a result of the Byzantine influence, there was more focus on the Major Epiclesis, which is the third orison of the Sanctification Prayers. In the three liturgies, the Institution Narrative starts with the conjunction word "For" indicating that it is the reason and cause for the entire Eucharist. Cuming comments, "The narrative is quoted as the ground and justification of the whole Eucharistic action."[1100]

[1095] The Words of Institution are words echoing those of Jesus Himself at His Last Supper that, when consecrating bread and wine, Christian Eucharistic liturgies include in a narrative of that event. Almost all existing ancient Christian Churches explicitly include the words of Institution in their Eucharistic celebrations and consider them necessary for the validity of the sacrament.

[1096] The Sanctification Prayers consist of three sections: The Institution Narrative, the *Anamnesis*, and the Major Epiclesis.

[1097] McGowan, Andrew B., *Ancient Christian Worship*, 39.

[1098] Patristic period is generally considered to run from the end of New Testament times or end of the Apostolic Age (AD 100) to either AD 451 (the date of the Council of Chalcedon) or to the eighth century Second Council of Nicaea.

[1099] In a fragment of a Coptic liturgy preserved in the White Monastery Euchologion, after the Institution Narrative introduction, and before the words "You took bread," the celebrant asks the assistant priests to bless, a sign of the importance of the following part. See: Epiphanius (Bishop), *The White Monastery Euchologion: Translation from Coptic and a Study*, 110, 111.

[1100] Cuming, Geoffrey J., *The Liturgy of St Mark*, 122.

The Institution Narrative contains the words spoken by the Lord Christ when He established the new covenant with His blood through bread and wine on the night of the Last Supper. In other words, it is, presumably, a dialogue with God the Father. Nevertheless, when we actually read the Institution Narrative, we note that it is not written in the form of a dialogue; rather, it is shaped in a manner that recounts the events of that night. Why is this so? and what happened to the actual Institution prayers which the Lord used to transform the bread and wine into His Holy Body and precious Blood, the prayers that He passed down to His disciples?

As previously elucidated, the Liturgy of the Faithful—which is the *morning* liturgy before the amalgamation with the *evening* one—is *explanatory*, that is, designed to describe the old Jewish customs and practices that the Lord Jesus employed; these customs that were foreign to the Gentile neophytes. On the contrary, these Jewish-based rituals are preserved in the Offertory office—originally the *evening* liturgy, as explained in chapter 4—and arranged as prayers to the Holy Trinity, as opposed to a narration. During the Offertory proper, the priest makes the sign of the cross on the bread and wine three times, and after each, the altar server confirms saying, "Amen." On the first time, the celebrant says, "Blessed be God the Father the *Pantocrator*. Amen." On the second, he says, "Blessed be His Only-begotten Son, Jesus Christ our Lord. Amen." And on the third time, he says, "Blessed be the Holy Spirit, the *Paraclete*. Amen," and again the altar server responds with "Amen."

In the Alexandrian tradition, those three signings over the bread and wine along with the Trinitarian blessing are the Institution prayers (in the *evening* liturgy). Hence, as previously noted, liturgies of Alexandrian origin (i.e., Saint Mark's and Saint Serapion's), eloquently use the past participle tense in their Minor Epiclesis prayers, understanding that the

Institution prayers have already taken place earlier. The Liturgy of Saint Serapion, for example, states, "To You have we offered this bread, the likeness of the Body of the Only-begotten Son," "Wherefore we also making the likeness of the death have offered the bread," and "we have offered also the cup, the likeness of the Blood." Likewise, in the Liturgy of Saint Cyril, we read, "Your precious gifts, which are already set forth before You, this bread and this cup." These phrases are indicative of an Alexandrian understanding of an invocation that has taken place earlier.

The faith and Tradition passed down by the Church Fathers prescribes that the sanctification of the offerings must be consummated through the invocation of God, the Holy Trinity. In this regard, Saint Clement of Alexandria[1101] of the 2nd century states in his *Excerpta ex Theodoto*, "the bread is hallowed by the power of the Name of God... it is transformed into spiritual power."[1102] Similarly, in AD 202, Saint Irenaeus of Lyons stated, "the bread, which is from the ground, once it accepts the invocation of the Name of God, it is no longer mere bread but the Eucharist."[1103] Additionally, in the 3rd century, Origen[1104] taught about "the invocation of the name of God and of Christ and of the Holy Spirit"

[1101] Titus Flavius Clemens (AD 150–215), known as Clement of Alexandria to distinguish him from the earlier Clement of Rome, was a Christian theologian who taught at the Catechetical School of Alexandria. Clement is regarded as a Church Father. Among his pupils were Origen and Alexander of Jerusalem.

[1102] Dix, Dom Gregory, *The Shape of the Liturgy*, 230.

[1103] Irenaeus (Saint), *Against Heresies*, 4:18:4-5. See: Johnson, Maxwell E. (1997). The Archaic Nature of the Sanctus, Institution Narrative, and Epiclesis of the Logos in the Anaphora Ascribed to Sarapion of Thmuis. Bradshaw, Paul F. (Ed.), *Essays on Early Eastern Eucharistic Prayers*, 102.

[1104] Origen Adamantius (AD 184/185–253/254), known as Origen or Alexandria, was a scholar and early Christian theologian who was born and spent the first half of his career in Alexandria. Origen was one of the greatest biblical scholars of the early Church, having written commentaries on most of the books of the Bible, though few are extant. He interpreted scripture both literally and allegorically. Unlike many church fathers, he was never canonized as a saint because some of his teachings directly contradicted the teachings attributed to the apostles, notably the Apostles Paul and John. His teachings on the pre-existence of souls, the final reconciliation of all creatures, including perhaps even the devil, and the subordination of the Son of God to God the Father, were extremely controversial.

over the elements.[1105] The 4th century Saint Cyril of Jerusalem also explained, "Because the bread and wine of the Eucharist before the invocation of the All-Holy Trinity were merely just bread and wine..."[1106] In other words, the liturgy is the evidence of economic Trinity;[1107] the manifestation of the act of the Holy Trinity in creation. "The liturgy in celebration introduces the believing Christian into the very life of the triune God," Crichton writes.[1108]

It is imperative to notice that the Early Church Fathers, and up until the 3rd century, only talked about the invocation of the Holy Trinity on the bread, whereas the Thanksgiving Prayer was used for the wine, a tradition that has its roots in Judaism.[1109] By the 4th century, however, the invocation of the Holy Trinity was extended to both the bread and wine, a modification that is still practiced hitherto.[1110] In summary, the Institution Narrative prayer in the Liturgy of the Faithful, according to the Coptic tradition, is in its actuality, an explanation and elaboration of the old Institution prayer buried in the Offertory office. During the Liturgy of the Faithful Institution, the priest declares, "...and when He had given thanks, He blessed it, and He sanctified it." Analogous to this, in the Offertory office, the priest prays, "Blessed is..." thrice along with three signings. The word "Bless" in Hebrew ("בָּרוּךְ," pronounced as "baruk") could mean "Give thanks," and "Sanctify."[1111] Thus, both offices are in

---

[1105] Jenkins, Claude. (1908). Origen On I Corinthians III.5., *The Journal of Theological Studies*, 9(36), 502.
[1106] Cyril of Jerusalem (Saint), *Catechetical Lectures*, 19:7.
[1107] The economic Trinity refers to the acts of the triune God with respect to the creation, history, salvation, the formation of the Church, the daily lives of believers, etc. and describes how the Trinity operates within history in terms of the roles or functions performed by each *Hypostasis* of the Trinity - God's relationship with creation.
[1108] J.D. Crichton. (1992). A Theology of Worship. In Cheslyn Jones, Geoffrey Wainwright, Edward Yarnold SJ and Paul Bradshaw (Eds.), *The Study of Liturgy*, 7.
[1109] Therefore, the name of the Coptic proper concerned with the Trinitarian blessing is called the "Presentation of the Lamb;" no mention of the wine.
[1110] In the Coptic rite, after the Circuit of the Lamb, the priest holds the bread-offering during the invocation, while the altar server carries the decanter.
[1111] Matthew the Poor (Father), *Eucharist of the Lord's Supper*, 646.

agreement on terminologies.[1112] It is hard not to notice the parallels produced in the Liturgy of the Faithful Institution, where the sign of the cross on the bread is performed thrice—imitating the Offertory Trinitarian invocation. Even the confirmation in both offices is the same, "Amen."

Returning to the Institution Narrative. An altar server holds the censer for the principal celebrant, who places a spoonful of incense in it; and holding his hands for some moments in the smoke, he points to the bread and wine saying, "He instituted for us this great mystery of godliness." Then, he turns his hands over the censer thrice. This practice is in accordance Ibn Sibaa's prescription;[1113] however, Pope Gabriel V instructs that the turning of hands takes place before saying, "He instituted..."[1114] A couple of points are worth noting:

1- The Liturgy of Saint Basil makes no mention of this spoonful of incense as the priest would have already done so earlier when he said, "was incarnate." In the Liturgy of Saint Gregory, however, he places the spoonful of incense as he says, "I offer unto You my Master..." Similarly, in the Liturgy of Saint Cyril, he does so while saying, "On the night He offered Himself for our sins..." Until this point, the priest has his hands covered with two corporals, and therefore, he holds the spoon with a corporal. After placing the incense, he exposes his hands, and censes them in preparation of holding the oblations barehanded.

2- The "washing" of the hands over the censer, for sanctification, is performed thrice, symbolizing the work of the Holy Trinity in the Economy of Salvation. The priest then brings the incense

---

[1112] This also helps clarify that the three terms do not contradict the single term used in the scripture, which is "Blessed," since, as mentioned earlier, all three words mean the same thing in Hebrew.
[1113] Ibn Sibaa, *The Precious Pearl: On Ecclesiastic Science*, BnF, MS Arabic 207, fol. 152v.
[1114] Gabriel V (Pope), *The Ritual Order*, BnF, MS 98 (AD 1411), fol. 60v.

before the bread (some clerics do this for both the bread and chalice). This practice affirms that the Offering on the altar is the same One offered on the Cross for the remission of our sins, and His Father smelled His sweet aroma. Some priests transfer the rising incense to the bread and wine thrice as opposed to once, indicating that the salvation and the redemption of Jesus on the Cross is the work of the triune God.

The phrase "great mystery of godliness" finds its roots in the Scriptures. Saint Paul says, "Beyond all question, the *mystery* from which true *godliness* springs is *great*: He appeared in the flesh, was vindicated by the Spirit, was seen by angels, was preached among the nations, was believed on in the world, was taken up in glory" (1 Timothy 3:16). Without Incarnation or Salvation, the Eucharist would have not existed. In other words, it is safe to say that the Eucharist is the merit of Incarnation and Salvation.

The congregation affirms what the priest uttered saying, Ⲁⲗⲏⲑⲟⲥ ⲡⲓⲥⲧⲉⲩⲟⲙⲉⲛ (Truly, we believe).[1115] Afterward, and in all three liturgies, the priest holds the bread, and removes the corporal that was placed underneath the bread, kisses it, and places it on the altar while saying, "He took bread into His holy hands, which are without spot or blemish, blessed and life-giving." In the Gregorian liturgy, although the same words are employed, they are addressed to the Son; hence, the priest says, "You took bread." We notice at this point that the priest picks up the bread with both hands, and then transfers it to his left hand. This is an old Jewish

---

[1115] In most Euchologions the response stated is simplified to "We believe;" however, according to the Church oral tradition, and based on what was recorded by Church cantors, the precise responsory is "Truly, we believe."

practice referred to as the Offering Waving.[1116] The Offering Waving was performed first in the Offertory proper—another proof added to the list of evidence ascertaining that the Offertory office is the *evening* liturgy, a complete liturgy that includes all elements required for the Eucharist—and second during the Institution Narrative. Once again, the congregation affirms saying, "We believe that this is true. Amen."

The priest, then, places his right hand on the bread, which he is carrying on his left, and looks up and says, "He looked up toward heaven to You, O God, who are His Father and Master of everyone." These words are taken from the scriptures: "and looking up to heaven, He gave thanks and broke the loaves" (Matthew 14:19). The previous passage is mentioned during the miracle of the feeding of the five thousand, not in association with the Last Supper, an indication that the practice of looking up to heaven and giving thanks was a usual pre-requisite to offering sacrifices or consuming meals; hence, it is reasonable to presume that it had taken place during the Last Supper. From the moment the priest holds the bread to the end of the Epiclesis, the altar servers hold up lit candles[1117] to draw the congregants' attention to the words of the Lord, the Institution, assert the prominence of the sanctification, and emphasize that the offering of Himself on the altar is what way leading to the light of resurrection and eternal life.[1118] This ceremonial splendor of the rite started first in the West, specifically in France, in the 13th century before it

---

[1116] "Put all these in the hands of Aaron and his sons and have them wave them before the Lord as a wave offering. Then take them from their hands and burn them on the altar along with the burnt offering for a pleasing aroma to the Lord, a food offering presented to the Lord. After you take the breast of the ram for Aaron's ordination, wave it before the Lord as a wave offering, and it will be your share." (Exodus 29:24-26).

[1117] Having a candle burning during prayer serves to focus the worshippers' thoughts on Jesus as the Light of the world. It is attached to prayers that emphasize the presence of the Lord. Hence, we find this ritual practiced during Gospel readings, Sanctification prayers, the Fraction, and Communion.

[1118] During the corresponding prayer in the Offertory (the invocation of the Holy Trinity), altar servers hold lighted candles as well.

was copied in the East. The reason was "to give expression," Hugh Wybrew writes, "to the theological opinion that the Host was consecrated when the relevant words of the Institution Narrative had been read."[1119]

Using his index finger, the celebrant blesses the bread saying, "And when He had given thanks," "He blessed it," and "He sanctified it." After each of these phrases, the congregation confirms on his proclamation saying, "Amen."[1120] Unlike the current structure of these statements that indicate asking the Lord to bless and sanctify the elements, older sources—stemmed from the Jewish tradition, make the three verbs bless the Lord: "He gave thanks," "He blessed," and "He sanctified." That is, "gave thanks to the Lord, blessed Him, and sanctified Him."[1121] This structure was depicted by Kacmarcik Codex (AD 1344-1345) in folios 32^{r-v} and 33^r. Therefore, all three verbs can be summed up in the first one, thanksgiving, as in "While they were eating, Jesus took bread, and when he had given thanks, he broke it and gave it to his disciples, saying, 'Take and eat; this is my body'" (Matthew 26:26). In other words, the only word that was preserved in its original form is "Gave thanks." The other two verbs, "blessed it" and "sanctified it" were adapted to be specific to the bread and wine. Still, this adaptation finds its roots in the Scripture as Saint Paul says, "Is not the cup of blessing which we bless a sharing in the blood of Christ?" (1 Corinthians 10:16), attributing "bless" to the cup, not to the Lord.

All sources agree that this thrice-benediction was performed by the Lord to transform the bread and wine into His Body and Blood; it corresponds to the thrice-benediction in the Offertory office, which, as previously noted, is the practical institution prayer and invocation of the

---

[1119] Wybrew, Hugh. (1992). The Setting of the Liturgy: Ceremonial. In Cheslyn Jones, Geoffrey Wainwright, Edward Yarnold SJ and Paul Bradshaw (Eds.), *The Study of Liturgy*, 489.

[1120] In the Liturgy of Saint Gregory, the prayer is said in the first person, and therefore, the words are "and when You had given thanks," "You blessed it," and "You sanctified it."

[1121] Athanasius of Saint Macarius Monastery (Father), *The Divine Liturgy: The Mystery of the Kingdom of God (Part 2)*, 741; Matthew the Poor (Father), *Eucharist of the Lord's Supper*, 656-658.

Holy Trinity pertaining to the immemorial *evening* liturgy: "Blessed is God the Father, the *Pantocrator*. Amen. Blessed is His Only-begotten Son, Jesus Christ. Amen. Blessed is the Holy Spirit the *Paraclete*. Amen." Interestingly, the White Monastery Euchologion provides a fourth verb. In a liturgy addressed to the Son, as well as in that of Saint Matthew, the verb "σφραγίζειν - sealed it" appears after "sanctified it."[1122] Following the thrice-benediction over the bread, the congregation chants, "We believe, we confess, and we glorify."

Subsequently, the priest breaks the bread into two pieces—one third, and two thirds—without separating them yet preserving the *Despotikon*[1123] intact. The priest does so in one bit at a time, starting from the top down, having the right-side piece always a third of the full size, whereas the left is two thirds. The one third, according to father Samaan Ibn Koleil, symbolizes the Son, where the two thirds represent the Father and the Holy Spirit.[1124] While the Trinitarian God is still united in essence, the Son took flesh and became man to save humanity. The three hypostases are united in will and inheritance,[1125] yet the Second Person is the one incarnated. While breaking the bread, the priest enunciates, "He broke it, and gave it to His own saintly disciples and holy apostles, saying 'Take, eat of it, all of you. For this is My Body...'" After he utters "broke," he opens up the oblation and insufflates into it the Breath of the Holy Spirit, and then continues with the rest of the sentence starting from "and

---

[1122] Epiphanius (Bishop), *The White Monastery Euchologion: Translation from Coptic and a Study*, 111- 112, 147-148.

[1123] *Despotikon* (**δεσποτικόν**) is the central piece of the Eucharistic Bread and is used in the rite of Consignation. *Despotikon* is a Greek word meaning "of the Lord" or "belongs to the Lord". The "Lord" is referring to the bishop. Originally, before the fourth century, the bishop was the only person who can actually pray the Eucharist. After praying the liturgy, the bishop used to send - with deacons - parts of the Body soaked in the Blood to the other churches in his diocese. Each priest would then take this piece of the Body soaked in the Blood and place it at the center of the offering bread. At the Fraction, he would elevate it and put it in the chalice. This rite has gradually vanished from the East; however, it continued to be practiced in the West until the eighth century.

[1124] Bebawi, George H., *The Divine Liturgy*, 183.

[1125] As explained by the 13th century bishop, Botros, bishop of Babylon (ancient Cairo).

gave it to His own saintly disciples..." Some clerics today peck the oblation as opposed to breathe into it.

The primitive shape of the Alexandrian Institution does not attach adjectives to the "disciples." It was the Syriac liturgy of Saint James that innovated the series of adjectives, and from there, they spread to other traditions. Starting with "saintly," these adjectives made their way into the Coptic liturgy starting from the 4th century.[1126]

The celebrant breaks the top and bottom parts of the bread without separating them. By doing this, he has essentially broken the bread in the form of a cross in four pieces without fully separating them. Moses Bar-Kepha explains that the breaking of bread without separation is analogous to the fact that when Jesus died on the Cross, His Divinity parted not from His human body nor His human spirit.[1127] The priest then says, "Which is broken for you and for many, to be given for the remission of sins.[1128] This do in remembrance of Me," to which the congregation asserts, "This is true. Amen."

After this, according to the 13th century scholar Ibn Sibaa, the priest holds the chalice in his hands;[1129] however, in today's practice, the priest uncovers the chalice and lays his right hand on its rim.[1130] Then, he says, "Likewise also, the cup, after supper, He mixed it with wine and water." Although mixing the wine with water was a Jewish inheritance that was practiced in Alexandria, like in other churches, since its acceptance of Christianity—this is clearly documented by Clement of Alexandria in his prominent work *The Instructor*—early Coptic liturgies did not make

---

[1126] Matthew the Poor (Father), *Eucharist of the Lord's Supper*, 660.
[1127] Bebawi, George H., *The Divine Liturgy*, 144.
[1128] At this point, Marquis of Bute instructs, "He (the priest) places the Sacred Host on the paten, kneels, adores It, and rises, while he continues: 'Do this in remembrance of Me,'" a note that is not prescribed by the Euchologion.
[1129] Ibn Sibaa, *The Precious Pearl: On Ecclesiastic Science*, BnF, MS Arabic 207, fol. 153r.
[1130] An alternative tradition is for the priest to only touch the lip of the chalice with the joined thumb and forefinger of his right hand.

mention of this act.[1131] Once more, we find discernable mention of it in the Syriac rite, specifically in the Liturgy of Saint James. From there, it entered the Coptic liturgy.[1132] The priest then performs the thrice-benediction over the chalice thrice; he says, "And when He had given thanks," "He blessed it," and "He sanctified it." After each benediction, the people assert saying, "Amen." Then, they conclude proclaiming, "Again, we believe, we confess, and we glorify."

The president holds the chalice up[1133] saying, "He tasted," after which, he blows the breath of the Holy Spirit, a practice that was not documented by Ibn Sibaa or Pope Gabriel V but orally passed down from one generation to another.[1134] The word "tasted," according to Hans Lietzmann, is a discerning Alexandrian tradition and is not present in any of the other traditions.[1135] It is biblically based and is founded on (Matthew 26:29).[1136] Saint Irenaeus, Saint John Chrysostom, and Jacob of Edessa also support this tradition.[1137] It is a Jewish custom that the most senior figure present at the meal is the first to drink of the wine before everyone else. The word "tasted" was introduced first to the Cyrilline liturgy in around the 7th century before it was extended to the other two liturgies.

Afterward, the priest continues, "And gave it also to His own saintly disciples and holy apostles, saying." Then, as Pope Gabriel V (15th century)

[1131] Matthew the Poor (Father), *Eucharist of the Lord's Supper*, 663.
[1132] Athanasius of Saint Macarius Monastery (Father), *The Divine Liturgy: The Mystery of the Kingdom of God (Part 2)*, 749-750.
[1133] Another rubric directs that the priest only touches the lip of the chalice with his joined right thumb and forefinger without holding it.
[1134] This tradition might have been introduced when the Institution Narrative was viewed by the Coptic Church as the core of the liturgy at which the transformation of the elements takes place. This was the view of the Church from the post-patristic era up until the Middle Ages. In the Late Middle Ages, the focus moved from the Institution Narrative to the Major Epiclesis.
[1135] Matthew the Poor (Father), *Eucharist of the Lord's Supper*, 664-665.
[1136] "But I say to you, I will not drink of this fruit of the vine from now on until that day when I drink it new with you in My Father's kingdom."
[1137] Ignatius Ephrem II Rahmani (Patriarch of the Syriac Catholic Church), *Les Liturgies Orientales et Occidentales*, 274, 543.

explains, he gently moves the chalice in the form of a cross[1138] in the four directions; east, west, north, and south, respectively, while saying, "Take, drink of it, all of you." Samaan Ibn Koleil explains that moving the chalice in all four directions signals that Christ shed His Blood on the Cross for the salvation of the whole world.[1139] After this, the priest points to the chalice and enunciates, "For this is My Blood of the New Covenant, which is shed for you and for many, to be given for the remission of sins. This do in remembrance of Me." Ibn Sibaa omits the cross-shaped movement, nonetheless, instructs that the priest, after pronouncing "shed," moves the chalice toward the south, viz., tilting it to the right as a sign of shedding the precious blood on the Cross.[1140] Afterward, the congregation confirms saying, "This is also true. Amen." Marquis of Bute offers more detailed instructions. He writes, "The Priest covers the chalice, kneels, adores the Precious Blood, and rises."[1141]

Following this, the priest points to the bread and says, "For every time you eat of this Bread," then he points to the chalice and says, "and drink of this cup," and continues, "you proclaim My death, confess My resurrection, and remember Me till I come." It is interesting to note that in his first letter to the Corinthians, Saint Paul only referred to Christ's death, "For as often as you eat this bread and drink this cup, you proclaim the Lord's death till He comes" (1 Corinthians 11:26).[1142] The Church of Alexandria maintained this tradition until around the 4th century, after which the other acts of salvation were added to the liturgical text. It is noteworthy that none of the Gospels mentioned this commandment;

[1138] Gabriel V (Pope), *The Ritual Order*, BnF, MS 98 (AD 1411), fol. 62r.
[1139] Bebawi, George H., *The Divine Liturgy*, 183.
[1140] Ibn Sibaa, *The Precious Pearl: On Ecclesiastic Science*, BnF, MS Arabic 207, fol. 153r.
[1141] John, Marquis of Bute, *The Coptic Morning Service for the Lord's Day*, 101.
[1142] Jesus' death for mankind is the central salvational action, since it demonstrates His love to humanity. "I live by faith in the Son of God, who loved me and gave Himself for me" (Galatians 2:20). "Husbands, love your wives, just as Christ loved the church and gave Himself up for her" (Ephesians 5:25).

however, it was not uncommon in the Alexandrian literature (i.e., Saint Athanasius the Apostolic and Saint Cyril I) to restructure the Pauline commandment to imply that Jesus Himself uttered these words. This concludes the prayers of the Institution Narrative. After this, the congregation chants, "Amen, Amen, Amen, Your death O Lord, we proclaim..." which is the commencement of the *Anamnesis*.[1143]

The Anamnesis

Anamnesis (Greek: ἀνάμνησις, meaning "reminiscence") is a key concept in the liturgical theology: in worship the faithful recalls God's saving deeds. This memorial aspect is not simply a passive process but one by which a Christian can enter into the Paschal mystery. For example, in the Old Testament, the Ark of the Covenant contained some manna, which of itself is an *Anamnesis*. It is not a mere symbol of an event that took place in the past, but rather a veritable part of it, which serves as a reminder of that very event. In the *Anamnesis*, the Church recalls the redemptive acts of our Lord Christ, which require His presence in the midst of the church, as He promised, "For where two or three are gathered in My name, I am there in the midst of them." (Matthew 18:20). The church is dependent on its act of *Anamnesis*: her life and witness over two thousand years has been punctuated by obedience to the command, "Do this in remembrance of me" (Luke 22:19). In the Eucharist we remember God's acts in salvation

---

[1143] Anamnesis (from the Greek word ἀνάμνησις meaning reminiscence and/or memorial sacrifice), in Christianity is a liturgical statement in which the Church refers to the memorial character of the Eucharist and/or to the Passion, Resurrection and Ascension of Christ. It has its origin in Jesus' words at the Last Supper, "Do this in memory of me". This part of the Anaphora is usually placed after the Institution Narrative. Smolarski, a liturgical scholar, suggests, Christian worship is fundamentally *anamnetic*, as an act in which "the present is brought into intimate contact with the past" and vice-versa. Dr. Frank C.Senn, a liturgical scholar, has written, "This Greek word is practically untranslatable in English. 'Memorial,' 'commemoration,' 'remembrance' all suggest a recollection of the past, whereas *Anamnesis* means making present an object or person from the past. Sometimes the term 'reactualization' has been used to indicate the force of *Anamnesis*." In other words, *Anamnesis* means "making actually present again" or "reactualizing an event".

narrative, culminating in Christ's life, death and resurrection and focusing on the Last Supper. We encounter Christ in the present to be nourished and transformed. All the redemptive visible acts of Jesus have been passed over to the church through sacraments, mainly the Eucharist. Therefore, we, as the *ecclesia*, recall His acts of salvation as present, not past.

As mentioned before, this section starts with the congregation proclamation, "Amen Amen Amen Your death, O Lord, we proclaim..." Cuming comments, "In Egypt and Syria, though not farther north, the sentence is echoed by a congregational response."[1144] According to the Egyptian tradition, the *Anamnesis* is brilliantly linked to the Institution Narrative with the sentence "For every time you eat of this bread and drink of this cup, you proclaim My death, confess My resurrection and remember Me till I come." According to Cuming, the use of the Pauline verse (1 Corinthians 11:26) to introduce the *Anamnesis* originated in Egypt and then permeated other churches.[1145] Cuming also points out that the introductory sentence in the Egyptian tradition uses "proclaiming" whereas elsewhere it is always "remembering."[1146] It is only in Egypt and Syria this sentence is echoed by a congregational affirmation. Notice that even though the liturgies of Saint Basil (Coptic) and Saint Cyril address God the Father, in this specific chant they both speak to God the Son, as it fulfills the Lord's command, which is the introductory sentence, "For every time you eat of this bread and drink of this cup, you proclaim My death, confess My resurrection and remember Me till I come." Naturally then the congregation responds to our Lord's request and says, "Your death, O Lord, we proclaim..."

[1144] Cuming, Geoffrey J., *The Liturgy of St Mark*, 124.
[1145] Cuming, G. J. (1997). The Anaphora of St. Mark: A Study of Development. In Bradshaw, Paul F. (Ed.), *Essays on Early Eastern Eucharistic Prayers*, 71.
[1146] Cuming, Geoffrey J., *The Liturgy of St Mark*, 124.

The *Anamnesis* mentioned in the Apostles Canons, attributed to Saint Clement of Alexandria (AD 150–215), is considered the source from which all the other liturgies took this prayer.[1147] Initially, the *Anamnesis* was composed of just the congregation hymn, "Your death O Lord we proclaim and Your resurrection we confess. We entreat You." later, not only the hymn evolved to include additional acts,[1148] but also the current Prayer of *Anamnesis* was added. The latter consists of three parts: the introduction, the commemoration of the redemptive acts of our Lord, followed by the Offering of Gifts.

The introduction to the *Anamnesis* in the Liturgy of Saint Basil is, "Therefore, as we also commemorate His holy passion…" In the Liturgy of Saint Cyril, it is "Therefore now, O God, the Father, the *Pantocrator*, as we proclaim the death of Your Only-begotten Son…" Notice that although the commemoration was for the death of our Lord Jesus, as Saint Paul instructs,[1149] Saint Basil's Liturgy dropped the act of death and replaced it with the holy Passion. However, the liturgies of Saint Gregory and Saint Cyril preserved the ancient tradition as the basis for the *Anamnesis*. In his *Interpreting the Liturgy*, Saint Nicholas Cabasilas explains, "Christ did not ask us to remember these things (His miraculous work), but rather those things that revealed the weakness that is the crucifixion, the passion, the death. Because the sufferings were more necessary than the miracles. The sufferings of Christ cause salvation and resurrection, whereas His miracles prove only that He is the true Savior."

The second part of the *Anamnesis* is the commemoration of the Lord Christ's redemptive acts. As mentioned earlier, the primitive text

---

[1147] Matthew the Poor (Father), *The Eucharist: The Lord's Supper*, 682.
[1148] Lietzmann suggests that these acts were introduced by Saint Basil the Great. See: Matthew the Poor (Father), *The Eucharist: The Lord's Supper*, 683.
[1149] "For whenever you eat this bread and drink this cup, you proclaim the Lord's death until he comes." (1 Corinthians 11:26).

commemorated the Lord's death only. In the early centuries, however, Resurrection was added. "In Egypt a reference to the resurrection is always added."[1150] Afterward, more acts were included. Saint Cyril the Great, in the 5th century, precisely AD 421, emulated the Syriac rite[1151] by adding Ascension to the *Anamnesis*.[1152] According to Hans Lietzmann, it was Saint Basil the Great who introduced the phrase "His sitting at Your right hand, O Father" and the adjective "fearful" describing the Second Coming to the original text.[1153] In the Coptic rite, these insertions made their way to the Cyrilline liturgy first—around the 6th century—before the other liturgies. The accreting of the *Anamnesis* acts reached its contentment as recited today around the 13th or 14th century.[1154]

The third and last part of the *Anamnesis* is the Offering of Gifts. In the Liturgy of Saint Cyril, this is preceded by the congregation responsory, "According to Your mercy, O Lord, and not according to our sins" as a natural reaction to the commemoration of Judgment—each one will be judged according to their deeds. The liturgy of Saint Mark copied this pleading from that of Saint James. It is not said in the liturgies of Saint Basil and Saint Gregory since the Judgment acts are not mentioned in them at this part of the liturgy.

The Liturgy of Saint Basil expresses the Offering of Gifts by saying, "We offer unto You Your gifts from what is Yours, for everything, concerning everything, and in everything." This same statement is mentioned in the Liturgy of Saint Gregory. The original rendering of this phrase as introduced by Saint Basil the Great is, "We offer to You what is

---

[1150] Cuming, Geoffrey J., *The Liturgy of St Mark*, 124.
[1151] Namely from *The Apostolic Constitutions*, Book VIII, which is the first to mention the act of Ascension in the liturgy.
[1152] Matthew the Poor (Father), *The Eucharist: The Lord's Supper*, 680.
[1153] Matthew, Ibid., 683.
[1154] Athanasius of Saint Macarius Monastery (Father), *The Divine Liturgy: The Mystery of the Kingdom of God (Part 2)*, 763.

Yours from what is Yours." This statement comprises of two parts: the first, "We offer You what is Yours," refers to the Body and Blood after the sancrification, as the Eucharist; and the second, "from what is Yours," refers to the elements in their simple form.[1155] Therefore, the sentence can be rephrased as, "We offer unto You Your gifts (instead of 'what is Yours') from what is Yours (since the bread and wine are God's creation)." Unlike the sacrifices of the Old Testament and pagan religions, the sacrifice we are offering on the altar is a divine, eternal, and unlimited one. A sacrifice that draws its value from the Cross, the demonstration of God's love to humanity and the merit of His Salvation. The power of this sacrifice stems from its ability to cleanse our spirits from iniquities, rinse our souls from sins, and wash our bodies from all trespasses. It is the True Sacrifice, Jesus Christ Himself.

In the Liturgy of Saint Cyril, however, the Offering of Gifts reads, "You are He before whose holy glory we have put Your own gifts, from what is Your own, O our holy Father." It is important to observe that the verb "we have put" is in the present perfect tense (not present simple tense) as the Alexandrian tradition recognizes Offertory office as the domicile for *offering* the gifts. In the 4th century, the Syriac and Byzantine traditions—represented by the Basilian and Gregorian liturgies in the Coptic rite—limited the Offertory office to a mere placement of gifts without sanctification, which shifted the emphasis to the *explanatory* liturgy; as a result, the act was put in the present tense "we offer."[1156] Therefore, while the Syriac and Byzantine rites forgo the liturgical value of the Offertory office, the Alexandrian one, exemplified by the Cyrilline liturgy, preserves the immemorial theological importance of the Offertory office.

[1155] Matthew, Ibid., 683-684.
[1156] Matthew, Ibid., 692.

After the *Anamnesis*, which in the Church's consciousness necessitates the presence of Christ according to His promise,[1157] everybody worships in adoration, reverence, and submission to the Lord Christ. Hence, in the Liturgy of Saint Basil, the altar server instructs the worshippers saying, "Worship God in fear and trembling;" and according to the Liturgy of Saint Gregory, "Worship the Lamb, the Logos of God;" while in the Liturgy of Saint Cyril, the altar server directs, "Bow to God in fear." Worship is also necessary here as a prerequisite of and in preparation to the invocation of the Holy Spirit to sanctify the offerings and transform them into the Body and Blood of our Lord Jesus. This is a mysterious act, beyond human understanding, and we cannot receive it except in worship and submission.

In the Liturgy of Saint Cyril, the priest prays an inaudible orison, full of submission and contrition to God, to forgive our sins and grant us repentance. In this prayer the priest pleads to the Lord saying, "We ask and entreat Your goodness, O Lover of Mankind, put us not to shame nor cast us away, we Your servants. Drive us not away from Your face, neither say to us, 'I know you not.'"[1158] At the end of this prayer the priest implores, "Because of my own sins and the abominations of my heart, deprive not Your people of the coming down of Your Holy Spirit." It is possible that this inaudible prayer is another innovation of Saint Basil in the late 4th century, however, it was not interpolated into Saint Mark's liturgy before the 6th century.[1159]

[1157] "For where two or three gather in my name, there am I with them" (Matthew 18:20).

[1158] The prayer is referring to "Then you will say, 'We ate and drank with you, and you taught in our streets.' But he will reply, 'I don't know you or where you come from. Away from me, all you evildoers!'" (Luke 13:26-27). As such, the prayer is indicating that attending the liturgy and partaking from the Holy Mysteries is not enough. If people do that without humble heart, sincere repentance and genuine faith, they will be like those who told the Lord 'We ate and drank with you.'

[1159] Matthew, Ibid., 694-695.

Thereafter, the congregation chants, "Have mercy upon us, O God, the Father, the *Pantocrator*," a prayer that was introduced by Saint Severus of Antioch in the 6th century[1160] when he was in Egypt.[1161] Afterward, the priest prays "For Your people and Your Church entreat You, saying, 'Have mercy upon us, O God, the Father, the *Pantocrator*.'" The altar server responds saying, "Worship God, the Father, the *Pantocrator*." Addressing the worship here to God the Father specifically makes me think that the Liturgy of Saint Cyril makes a clear distinction between two prostrations: The worship after the *Anamnesis* is for the presence of the Lord Christ as He promised, however, the worship after the inaudible prayer (and the hymn of "Have mercy upon us") is addressed to God the Father to send the Holy Spirit. On the other hand, in the liturgies of Saint Basil and Saint Gregory there is only one call by the altar server for worship, hence the two notions are fused.

In the Liturgy of Saint Basil, after the altar server's order of worship, the congregation chants, "We praise You, we bless You, we serve You, we worship You." This hymn is relatively new as it was not mentioned in the old Euchologions (Greek or Coptic); it was not even prescribed by Ibn Sibaa or Ibn Kabar. It does not conform to the spirit of that part of the liturgy. The altar server cries out saying, "Worship God in fear and trembling," and the faithful prepare, in reverence, the encounter of the decent of the Holy Spirit; yet this acclamation includes inappropriate phrases like, "We praise You, we bless You." Nonetheless, some may construe the chant as a praise to the Lord expressing the faithful's joy of receiving the sanctification of the Holy Spirit.

[1160] Matthew, Ibid., 698.
[1161] Saint Severus fled to Egypt on Sep. 25th, 518. After some years, he left Egypt for a short time, and returned to it to live there until his departure in the city of Sakha on Feb 8th, 538.

The Major Epiclesis

The Major Epiclesis is the part of third and last part of the Sanctification prayers, which is tasked to invocate the Holy Spirit to descend upon the elements to be transformed into the Body and Blood of the Lord. Describing it as "Major" is to distinguish it from the invocation following the Sanctus in the Liturgy of Saint Cyril, which is called Minor Epiclesis. According to the contemporary belief of the Coptic Church, this part is the center of and the reason for the liturgy. In it, the Holy Spirit descends upon those who are present in the church, sanctifies them, unites them, and makes them *ecclesia*, in preparation of receiving the Body and Blood. The Holy Spirit also descends upon the offerings and transforms them into the Body and Blood of our Lord Jesus Christ. Bishop Severus Ibn El-Muqaffaa[1162] (bishop of El-Ashmunein), who lived in the 10th century, confirms this dogmatic principle saying, "The Holy Spirit descends upon them before descending upon these gifts; He, therefore, descends upon the congregation before the offerings."[1163] Moses Bar-Kepha adds to this explaining that the Holy Spirit descended on Saint Mary and sanctified her so that she could receive the incarnate Logos, also descends on the elements and sanctifies them so that the Logos may unite with them; hence, they become His own Body and Blood.[1164] Thus, the Major Epiclesis is the affirmation that the transformation of the bread and wine into the Body and Blood of Jesus Christ takes place in the "age to come" of the Holy Spirit, where Christ is the very food of all life and the church

---

[1162] Severus Ibn El-Muqaffaa (in Arabic ساويرس بن المقفع) was a Coptic Orthodox Bishop, author and historian. He was bishop of Hermopolis Magna (Ashmunein), in Upper Egypt, around the end of the 10th century. He is best known as the author of the *History of the Patriarchs of the Coptic Church of Alexandria*. He is also the author of *Lamp of the Intellect* and *Affliction's physic and the cure of sorrow*. Bishop Severus departed in the year AD 987.
[1163] Athanasius of Saint Macarius Monastery (Father), *The Divine Liturgy: The Mystery of the Kingdom of God (Part 2)*, 817.
[1164] Bebawi, George H., *The Divine Liturgy*, 147.

in His Body. As such, the Eucharist makes the church the Body of Christ and the Temple of the Holy Spirit.

The invocation of the Holy Spirit (Epiclesis) in this form—in the liturgical setting—was introduced into the Egyptian rite at a relatively late date through Syro-Byzantine influence. It first appeared in the writings of Saint Cyril of Jerusalem, who departed in AD 386; but it entered the Egyptian liturgy during the era of Pope Peter II, who departed in AD 378. It then entered the Eucharistic canons in Egypt during the era of Pope Theophilus,[1165] the 23rd Patriarch of Alexandria, who departed in AD 412.[1166] We can therefore conclude that the Major Epiclesis was introduced into the Coptic liturgy at the end of the 4th century[1167] in order to defend the doctrine of the Holy Spirit, which was attacked by many of the contemporary heresies of that time.

The Major Epiclesis is split into two parts: the first invocates the Holy Spirit to descend upon those who are present and upon the offerings, and the second is the result of this descent as a response to the invocation of the Holy Spirit and His mysterious work in the Eucharist. In the next lines we will scrutinize the two parts in greater detail.

In the Liturgy of Saint Cyril, the first part commences with the celebrant inaudibly praying, "And send down from Your holy height, and from Your prepared mansion, and from Your unbounded bosom, and

---

[1165] Theophilus of Alexandria was the twenty-third Pope of Alexandria and Patriarch of the See of Saint Mark. He was a violent opponent of non-Christian religions, severe critic of heterodox influence among Christian writers and monks, and a major figure in the ecclesiastical politics of the Eastern Church of his day. After becoming Patriarch of Alexandria in AD 385, and with the permission of the emperor Theodosius I, he destroyed the renowned temples to the gods Mithra, Dionysius, and Serapis. In his persecution of Origenist monks, he commanded troops sent to destroy their desert monasteries. Successful in condemning and exiling Chrysostom at the Synod of the Oak in AD 403, Pope Theophilus continued to play a principal role in the affairs of the Eastern Church and to further the influence of Alexandria over Constantinople.

[1166] Johnson, Maxwell E. (1997). The Archaic Nature of the Sanctus, Institution Narrative, and Epiclesis of the Logos in the Anaphora Ascribed to Sarapion of Thmuis. Bradshaw, Paul F. (Ed.), *Essays on Early Eastern Eucharistic Prayers*, 97.

[1167] As mentioned before several times, the Coptic tradition recognizes other invocations of the Holy Trinity in other prayers of the liturgy.

from the throne of the kingdom of Your glory, the *Paraclete*—Your Holy Spirit, who is a hypostasis, the immutable, the unchangeable, the Lord, the Giver of Life, who spoke in the Law, the Prophets, and the Apostles; who is present in every place and who fills every place, yet no place contains Him; who, on His own authority and not as service, works sanctification on whom He wills, according to Your good pleasure; who is single in His nature and manifold in His working, the fountain of the divine graces; who is of one essence with You; who proceeds from You; the Being with You on the throne of the kingdom of Your glory, with Your Only-begotten Son, our Lord, God, Savior and King of us all, Jesus Christ—upon us, we Your servants, and upon these Your precious gifts which have been set forth before You," then he points to the offerings, and continues "upon this bread and this cup, that they may be purified and changed." The altar server then says, "Let us attend. Amen," to which the people assert saying, "Amen." The president, then, thrice makes the sign of the cross over the Sacred Host, saying aloud, "And this Bread He makes into the holy Body of Christ." The congregation responds, "Amen." He, then, makes the sign of the cross thrice over the chalice, saying aloud, "And this cup also, the precious Blood of His New Covenant,"[1168] to which the congregation responds, "Amen." The celebrant continues, "Our Lord, God, Savior, and King of us all, Jesus Christ;" and the congregation responds, "Amen." The following remarks can be made:

1. The precise and detailed description of the work of the Holy Spirit, His nature, His procession from God the Father, His work in the servants of God and His co-essentiality with the Father and the Son suggest that the purpose of this prayer is to oppose

---

[1168] Marquis of Bute mentions an additional signing over the cup, a practice that is not mentioned in any of the manuscripts or Euchologion books. He instructs, "The Priest makes the sign of the Cross over the Precious Blood, saying: 'On this cup the Glorious Blood of the New Testament.'"

heresies that were against the Holy Spirit when this prayer was introduced.

2. "The *Paraclete* Your Holy Spirit who is a hypostasis." In Greek, the words "who is a hypostasis" mean "Himself hypostatically." Hence, the sentence means "Send Your Holy Spirit *hypostatically* (or personally)," as opposed to some sort of divine *grace*, *gift*, or *power*.

3. Some Euchologions read, "Who is of one essence with You, Who proceeds from You, the sharer of the throne of the kingdom of Your glory." The word "sharer" is an inaccurate translation of the Greek word "σύνθρονον," (pronounced "synthronon") meaning, "The Being with You." As such, the proper translation of the sentence is "the Being with You on the throne of the kingdom of Your glory."

4. "That they may be purified and changed." The Coptic word for "purify" in this sentence is "ⲧⲟⲩⲃⲟ," which could either mean "sanctify" or "purify." Therefore, it is expedient to examine the Greek word to determine the original intent. The Greek word used in this sentence is a derivative of "ἁγιασμός," meaning "sanctification," as opposed to "καθαρισμός," which means "purification." Hence, the word "sanctify," in this context, is a better fit as the priest beseeches to the Holy Spirit to come down upon the elements "that they may be *sanctified* and changed."

5. Once again, there is a discernible reference to the gifts-offering process, which occurred earlier during the Offertory proper: "Your precious gifts which have been set forth before You." As a pure Alexandrian rite, the Liturgy of Saint Cyril is fully aware of the ritual and theological value of the *offering*, which took place during the Offertory office.

In the Basilian liturgy, after the congregation prostrates, [1169] a corresponding prayer is uttered. The president inaudibly says, "And we ask You, O Lord our God—we Your sinful and unworthy servants worship You by the pleasure of Your goodness—that Your Holy Spirit may descend." He crosses himself and continues, "upon us," then he points to the oblations and says, "and upon these gifts set forth."[1170] The celebrant then lifts up his hands in supplication and continues saying, "and purify (or sanctify) them, change them,[1171] and manifest them as a sanctification of Your saints." The altar server cries out saying, "Let us attend. Amen." The priest signs the bread-offering thrice and says, "And this bread He makes into His Holy Body." The congregation asserts saying, "I believe." The priest lifts up his hands, bows his head and prays inaudibly "Our Lord, God, and Savior Jesus Christ, given for the remission of sins and eternal life to those who partake of Him." The congregation responds saying "Amen." The priest then signs the chalice thrice and says, "And this cup also, the precious Blood of His New Covenant." Once again, the congregation corroborates saying, "Again, I believe." The priest lifts up his hands, bows his head and prays silently, "Our Lord, God, and Savior Jesus Christ, given for the remission of sins." Then he continues in an audible voice saying, "and eternal life to those who partake of Him," to which the congregation responds, "Amen" and then continue saying, "Lord have mercy" thrice. Practically, the responsory "Amen" is attached to both aforementioned affirmations. The primitive shape of the affirmations was

---

[1169] This prostration was not a common practice before the 17th century. See: Athanasius of Saint Macarius Monastery (Father), *Summary of the Liturgical History of the Church of Alexandria (Part 2)*, 336.

[1170] There is a certain level of disregard toward the *offering* which took place during the Offertory office when it says, "and upon these gifts set forth." This is unlike the Liturgy of Saint Cyril, which places these words in the present perfect tense to point to the earlier *offering* during that office when the celebrant says, "we have put Your own gifts."

[1171] The phrase "change them" was added after the 13th century.

simply "Amen," just like in the Liturgy of Saint Cyril. The responds "I believe" and "Again I believe" were first mentioned by the 18th century sources.[1172]

As noted above, being under the influence of the West, starting from the post-patristic era [1173] up until the Middle Ages, the Institution Narrative in the Coptic Church was viewed as the core of the liturgy. However, by the Middle Ages, and because of the Byzantine effect, this focus was shifted to the Major Epiclesis. Pope Gabriel V is a good example of scholars who talked about this change. He speaks with great precision about the Coptic Church's faith regarding the transformation time of the bread to the Body and Blood of our Lord Jesus. He writes, "As soon as he (the priest) says, 'He makes,'[1174] it is accomplished and has become the Body of Christ, He took from the Virgin Mary."[1175] Therefore, when the celebrant continues saying, "His Holy Body," the Body of our Lord is already on the altar. Pope Gabriel V then says, "As soon as he (the priest) says, 'Precious Blood,'[1176] the wine which is placed before him has become the Blood of Christ, which was shed on the wood of the Cross."[1177] Then Pope Gabriel remarks, "From now on, the priest has no authority to sign at all. Nor does he turn toward a superior or a subordinate since Christ sacrifice is before him. All orders now come from Him and all petitions are for Him firstly and lastly."[1178]

In the Liturgy of Saint Gregory, after the congregation prostrates, the priest soundlessly says, "O You, our Master, by Your voice alone, change

---

[1172] Athanasius of Saint Macarius Monastery (Father), *The Divine Liturgy: The Mystery of the Kingdom of God (Part 2)*, 794.
[1173] Patristic period is generally considered to run from the end of New Testament times or end of the Apostolic Age (AD 100) to either AD 451 (the date of the Council of Chalcedon) or to the eighth century Second Council of Nicaea.
[1174] Pope Gabriel wrote it in Coptic (ⲛ̄ⲧⲉϥ ⲁⲓϥ = He makes).
[1175] Gabriel V (Pope), *The Ritual Order*, BnF, MS 98 (AD 1411), fol. 62r.
[1176] Pope Gabriel wrote it in Coptic (ⲛ̄ⲥⲛⲟϥ ⲉⲧⲧⲁⲓⲏⲟⲩⲧ = Precious Blood).
[1177] Gabriel, Ibid., fol. 63v.
[1178] Gabriel, Ibid., fol. 63r.

these which are set forth. You who are with us, prepare for us this service, full of mystery. Implant in us by the remembrance of Your holy service. Send to us the grace of Your Holy Spirit to purify and change these gifts set forth into the Body and Blood of our salvation." The altar server cries out, "Let us attend. Amen," and the congregation confirms, "Amen." The priest signs the bread thrice and says, "And this bread He makes into Your Holy Body." The rest of the prayer is like that of the Liturgy of Saint Basil; however, it is addressed to the Lord, Christ, not the Father.[1179]

To sum up, we have been discussing thus far the first part of the Major Epiclesis. In it, the president entreats the Holy Spirit to descent upon the congregants to sanctify, unite, and prepare them before receiving Christ in Communion. He also implores the Holy Spirit to come down upon the materials and transform them into the Holy Mysteries. The second part of the Major Epiclesis is essentially the outcome of this invocation. Once again, the Cyrilline liturgy preserved for us the original rite. In it, the outcome, viz., the second part of the Major Epiclesis, follows the sanctification at once. However, liturgies of Byzantine origin (i.e., liturgies of Saint Basil and Saint Gregory) permitted the interjection of the Intercessory Prayers[1180] between the two parts, thus completely separated them. It has become an arduous task for the congregation to link the two parts or recognize the second part as the outcome and an integral part of the Major Epiclesis.

In the liturgy of Saint Cyril, the first part of the Major Epiclesis ends with the congregation saying, "Amen." Afterward, the priest immediately begins the second part of the Epiclesis saying, "That they may be unto all of us who partake of them: faith without searching; love without

---

[1179] Since the Basilian and the Gregorian liturgies have the same origin, the Byzantine tradition, they both share the same structure and traits.
[1180] The Intercessory Prayers are: The Litanies, the Commemoration of Saints, and the Diptych.

hypocrisy; perfect patience; firm hope; faith and watchfulness; health and joy; renewal for the soul, body, and spirit; glory to Your holy name; sharing in the blessedness of eternal life and incorruption; and forgiveness of sins." The congregation responds saying, "As it was and shall be, it is from generation to generation and all the ages of the ages. Amen." The priest continues, "That as in this, so also in all things, Your great and holy name may be glorified, blessed and exalted in everything honored and blessed, with Jesus Christ, Your beloved Son, and the Holy Spirit." The sentence "That as in this, so also in all things, Your great and holy name be glorified, blessed, and exalted" is an inaccurate translation that made it difficult to understand its intended meaning. The Greek word is Πανάγιον (Ⲡⲁⲛⲁⲅⲓⲟⲛ), from Πανάγιος, meaning "All-Holy." [1181] Πανάγιον was translated into Coptic as "exalted in everything." However, the Greek meaning of Πανάγιον demonstrates continuity which is lacking in the Coptic translation. Also, the Coptic translation uses the word ⲉⲧⲥⲙⲁⲣⲱⲟⲩⲧ, meaning "blessed." Although this is a correct translation of the original Greek word εὐλογημένον ὄνομα, a more precise translation is "always-exalted." The phrase then should read, "Your great, all-holy, honored, glorious, and always-exalted (or blessed) name." This prayer reveals the results of the two sentences of the first part of the Major Epiclesis: "And this bread He makes into the holy Body of Christ," and "And this cup also, the precious Blood of His New Covenant." The coordinating conjunction phrase "For that" illustrates that the following sentence is the outcome of the preceding one. In other words, since the Holy Spirit transformed the offerings into the Body and Blood of our Lord Jesus Christ, the outcome must be faith, hope, love, renewal of the soul and spirit, and glory to the name of our Lord Jesus Christ. Another product of

---

[1181] Πανάγιος is used in the hymn "One is the All-Holy Father."

the descent of the Holy Spirit is that the glorious, all-holy, honored, and always-exalted name of God be always glorified.

Older sources reveal that the entire prayer was said without interruptions, and at its conclusion, the worshippers respond, "As it was..." Later, "As it was..." was moved to follow "sharing in the blessedness of eternal life and incorruption; and forgiveness of sins," an interpolation that led to a separation between the two parts of the Major Epiclesis. Being in its antecedent original placement, the acclamation "As it was" flowed naturally, and expressed the intended meaning, which is praising the Lord, an understanding that Moses Bar-Kepha expressed saying, "As Your Name, O Father, and Your Only-begotten Son, and the Your Holy Spirit, is glorified and praised in the past, present and future, not only in these three ages, but also in the age to come."[1182] This order is also supported by a Syriac liturgy found in the White Monastery Euchologion,[1183] as well as in the Liturgy of Saint Matthew preserved in the same euchologion.[1184]

After the cleric says, "Your great, all-holy, honored, glorious, and always-exalted name," the congregation confirms what the priest has uttered saying, "As it was and shall be, it is from generation to generation and all the ages of the ages. Amen." This praise is taken from Saint Paul's Epistle to the Ephesians, "To Him be glory in the Church and in Christ Jesus throughout all generations, forever and ever! Amen." (Ephesians 3:21). The acclamation "As it was" must be understood as a prayer of absolution, praise, and glorification to God; therefore, it should be intoned in a fervent manner. This means that even though "As it was" was

---

[1182] Bebawi, George H., *The Divine Liturgy*, 148.
[1183] Epiphanius (Bishop), *The White Monastery Euchologion: Translation from Coptic and a Study*, 135. Unlike Alexandrian liturgies, in this Syriac liturgy, the transition between the Litany of the Departed and glorifying God by the living leading to "As it was" is smooth.
[1184] Epiphanius, Ibid, 165.

relocated to precede "That as in this...," it is still imperative to understand it as a prayer of praise to God and exaltation to His holy name.

For the Basilian and Gregorian liturgies, the insertion of the Intercessory Prayers is a peculiarity of the liturgies of Syro-Byzantine origin. In the Coptic rite, this interpolation created a gap between the two parts of the Major Epiclesis, resulting in difficulty to recognize the second section as being part of the Epiclesis. Being alienated from the invocation prayers, the second part of the Major Epiclesis lost its primordial significance to the point that it is now prayed by the assistant priest as opposed to the celebrant, who prays the first part of the Major Epiclesis.

It is imperative not to presume that the only explanation of the source of this interpolation is a foreign tradition; it is still reasonable to allow for the possibility that this was a local practice in some region in Egypt. Studying the Liturgy of Saint Serapion shows indication of this interpolation of the Intercessory Prayers between the two divisions of the Major Epiclesis. In fact, it might be the first documented evidence of this insertion. In the Liturgy of Saint Serapion, the first part of the Epiclesis (the invocation of the Logos) ends with the sentence, "For we have invoked You, the uncreated, through the Only-begotten in holy Spirit." this is followed by a prayer for the living then another for the deceased; then a continuation of the Epiclesis, which reads, "Through Your Only-begotten Jesus Christ in holy Spirit; as it was and is and shall be to generations of generations and to all ages of the ages. Amen." This suggests that the interpolation of the Intercessory Prayers between the two parts of the Major Epiclesis might not be a product of Syro-Byzantine influence, but rather another Alexandrian tradition adopted in certain areas in Egypt.

The liturgies of Saint Basil and Saint Gregory share the same second part of the Major Epiclesis with the Liturgy of Saint Cyril, which is, "That as in this, so also in all things, Your great and holy name may be glorified, blessed and exalted in everything honored and blessed, with Jesus Christ, Your beloved Son, and the Holy Spirit." However, in the liturgies of Saint Basil and Saint Gregory this prayer does not flow with the preceding part, which is the Diptych. The insertion of the Intercessory Prayers after the first part of the Major Epiclesis left the sentence "That as in this" hollow. In attempt to resolve this issue, the Liturgy of Saint Basil borrowed the last sentence from the Diptych "Lead us throughout the way into Your kingdom" to serve as an introduction to the phrase "That as in this." In doing so, the prayer "That as in this" became the result of "Lead us throughout the way into Your kingdom," which, in fact, further confused the meaning. In other words, instead of being the outcome of the descent of the Holy Spirit and the sanctification of the offerings, the prayer of "That as in this" became the product of the priest's request, "Lead us throughout the way into Your kingdom." Conversely, this addition before "That as in this" did not find its way into the Liturgy of Saint Gregory. Thus, being attached to neither the first part of the Major Epiclesis nor the Diptych, the phrase "That as in this" became ambiguous and opaque. This will be discussed in greater detail later.

To recapitulate, the Major Epiclesis encompasses two parts, the first is a plea entreating the Holy Spirit to descend on the people and the elements to sanctify them, and the second is to request (from God) the benefits of this decent. In the liturgy of Saint Cyril, these two parts come after each other, which is the original order; however, in the liturgies of Saint Basil and Saint Gregory, many other Intercessory Prayers were inserted between the two parts, to the degree that they can no longer be interconnected. Understanding the intended meaning of the second part in relation to the first became a laborious, if not impossible, task. This is an example of a problem when one culture or tradition embraces customs or practices of another. We will now have a closer look at these Intercessory Prayers.

The Development of the Epiclesis

As mentioned earlier, Christianity in its infancy (what is referred to as Judeo-Christian epoch) utilized Jewish worship as its foundation for developing its own worship components (i.e., prayers and *ordos*). One of the chief rituals in Judaism was the blessing over the bread. The Early Church utilized this Jewish practice in her liturgies. In the Coptic rite, this practice corresponds to the thrice-benediction of the Holy Trinity during the Offertory proper. In the Apostolic Age, the Blessing of Bread was followed by the breaking of the Body, then the distribution takes place. This was then followed by the supper, which is also called Agape. Finally, the Prayer of Thanksgiving over the chalice commences. This order is the same that was employed in the Jewish Passover, which, according to Saint Paul,[1185] our Lord Jesus utilized some of its elements in establishing the Eucharist on Holy Thursday. In other words, the Lord's Supper (or the Last Supper) consists of blessing over the bread, consuming supper, and finally uttering thanksgiving prayer over the cup, which are the same elements in the same order of the Jewish *Kiddush*.[1186]

Later, the Apostles decided not to consume a meal during the Eucharist, so, right after the blessing of the Trinity, the Thanksgiving

---

[1185] "For I received from the Lord what I also passed on to you: The Lord Jesus, on the night he was betrayed, took bread, and when he had given thanks, he broke it and said, "This is my body, which is for you; do this in remembrance of me." In the same way, after supper he took the cup, saying, "This cup is the new covenant in my blood; do this, whenever you drink it, in remembrance of me." For whenever you eat this bread and drink this cup, you proclaim the Lord's death until he comes." (1 Corinthians 11:23-26).

[1186] *Kiddush* (Hebrew: קידוש, literally, "sanctification," is a blessing recited over wine or grape juice to sanctify the Shabbat and Jewish holidays. Additionally, the word refers to a small repast held on Shabbat or festival mornings after the prayer services and before the meal. A festival *Kiddush* is used to bless over the wine for the Passover.

prayer commences. Subsequently, the prayer of the Epiclesis of the Logos for the blessing of the bread and wine to become the Body and Blood of Jesus Christ is recited. This is the exact same order preserved by the Coptic Orthodox Church in the Offertory office but is no longer practiced in other churches.

The next change occurred when converts of non-Jewish roots (Gentiles) entered Christianity. The Apostles added a longer Thanksgiving prayer (Grand Thanksgiving Prayer) that expounds the works of Jesus Christ in the New Testament. This prayer is then followed by the Epiclesis[1187] of the Holy Spirit[1188] to fill (not transform) the sacrifice and the congregation, so they may benefit from the gifts granted to them by having the Body and Blood of the Lord. It is discernable that the Epiclesis of the Holy Spirit recognizes the power of its forerunner Epiclesis of the Logos, which is meant to transform the offerings into Holy Mysteries.

So far, we have covered the three stages that affected the development of the Epiclesis in the 1st century during the time of the Apostles. The fourth and final change came about in the 4th century due to Syriac and Byzantine influence. During this time, there were many heresies against the Holy Spirit; therefore, the Syriac and Byzantine Churches, in order to restore and preserve the standing of the Holy Spirit in the church, established the Major Epiclesis of the Holy Spirit after the *Anamnesis*. By doing so, the focal point of the liturgy was shifted to the invocation of the Holy Spirit; thus, the transformation of the elements into the Body and Blood of the Lord was attributed to the Major Epiclesis. During the pontificate of Pope Peter II, the Coptic Orthodox Church accepted this

---

[1187] This Epiclesis is what we referred to today as the Minor Epiclesis.
[1188] Different liturgies have different Epiclesis prayers. The one used in the Liturgy of Saint Mark is to invocate the Holy Trinity, not just the Holy Spirit. This is to be differentiated from the Major Epiclesis, which is put in place to invocate the Holy Spirit.

change in the Alexandrian liturgy, yet, Pope Cyril I promoted the change and made it the normality, which was the paramount reason for renaming the Liturgy of Saint Mark after Saint Cyril.

Over time, the sanctification that is embedded in the prayers of the Offertory proper was ignored in the Syriac and Byzantine rites, and the focus was digressed to the sanctification of the Major Epiclesis. Although the invocation of the Holy Spirit was adopted in the Coptic Orthodox Church, it was initially never thought of as the main one. It was one among other invocations that are of equal, if not more, importance. This continued to be the case for many years; however, recently, the Coptic Church finally gave in to the surrounding churches and accepted the Holy Spirit invocation as the principal one, the central part of the entire liturgy, and is the cause for the transformation of the materials into the Holy Mysteries.

The Intercessory Prayers

The Intercessory Prayers are the Supplications, the Litanies, the Commemoration of the Saints, and the Diptych. It is crucial to comprehend the Intercessory Prayers, not as mere remembrance of the living and the dead, but rather in its sacrificial character. The essential and fundamental meaning of the Intercessory Prayers is in referring us all, still in flesh or deceased, to the Sacrifice of Christ; through which, the entire *ecclesia* is offered before God the Father. The sacrifice of Christ has closed the gap between whose who are living and those who had fallen asleep; the church in its entirety has died with Jesus and now is alive in Him. Because of the Sacrifice of Christ, the heaven and earth are united in being participants in the Kingdom of God. The Intercessory Prayers, therefore, if viewed as the manifestation of the fruits of the perpetual sacrifice of Christ, should be a source of joy and jubilation to the *ecclesia*.

The Litanies and the Supplications

As previously stated, the Sacramentary of Saint Serapion shows evidence that praying for the living was practiced in some areas in Egypt as early as the 3rd or 4th century, or maybe earlier. In the Liturgy of Saint Serapion, after the invocation of the Logos, it reads, "Let this people receive mercy, let it be counted worthy of advancement, let angels be sent forth as companions to the people for bring to naught of the evil one and for establishment of the Church." This, in fact, could be the first form of litanies known today.

In the Liturgy of Saint Basil, the priest covers both hands with two corporals, and prays the introduction to the Litanies, "Make us all worthy, O our Master, to partake of Your Holies, unto the sanctification[1189] of our souls, bodies, and spirits, that we may become one body and one spirit, and may have a share and inheritance with all the saints who have pleased You since the beginning." Pope Gabriel V did not instruct the priest to cover his hands with corporals as this was a custom of Upper Egypt only. However, after the Late Middle Ages,[1190] this tradition was also adopted by Lower Egypt parishes. Father Simon Ibn Kuleil, who lived in the 12th century, attests to this saying, "According to the custom of the clerics in Upper Egypt, they cover their hands, because the divine grace covered Adam, and allowed the priest to stand as a mediator before the Lord."[1191]

[1189] Many Euchologions use "purification" instead of "sanctification." In Coptic text, the word "ⲉⲟⲩⲧⲟⲩⲃⲟ," is a derivative of "ⲧⲟⲩⲃⲟ," which could either mean "sanctification" or "purification." As such, it is important to refer to the Greek text to understand the intended meaning. The word used in the Greek text is "εἰς ἁγιασμόν," which means "sanctification."

[1190] The Late Middle Ages comprising the 14th and 15th centuries (AD 1301–1500).

[1191] Athanasius of Saint Macarius Monastery (Father), *The Divine Liturgy: The Mystery of the Kingdom of God (Part 2)*, 822.

In this prayer, the priest pleads for three things: sanctification of the faithful, unity of the Body of Christ[1192] (i.e., the believers), and the inheritance of the heavenly kingdom. It is interesting to note that these three requests are the same ones, and in the same order, that Jesus asked for in His last prayer, after instituting the Eucharist: "Sanctify them by the truth" (John 17:17), "that all of them may be one, Father, just as You are in Me and I am in You… so that they may be brought to complete unity" (John 17:21, 23), and "Father, I want those you have given me to be with me where I am, and to see my glory" (John 17:24).

In the Liturgy of Saint Gregory, on the other hand, the priest begins with the Supplications. Supplications is a prayer that consists of a number of pleads in the form of verses; after each one (except for the last verse) the congregation responds, "Lord have mercy;" however, after the last plead, "Lord have mercy" is recited three times. Analogous to the introduction to the Basilian litanies, the Supplications in the Gregorian liturgy is for the Church and all her ranks, so that the Lord may unite the hearts of the congregants and fill them with love, faith, purity, and mercy toward one another. Moreover, it extends its domain to pray for the non-believers.

Afterward, in the Basilian and Gregorian liturgies, the litanies are prayed. As previously discussed, the primeval shape of the Eucharist included the litanies within the offering prayers, which is still preserved in the Coptic Offertory proper, where the Remembrance Prayers[1193] are

---

[1192] "Now you are the body of Christ, and each one of you is a part of it." (1 Corinthians 12:27). "So, in Christ we, though many, form one body, and each member belongs to all the others." (Romans 12:5). "For the husband is the head of the wife as Christ is the head of the church, his body, of which he is the Savior" (Ephesians 5:23). "Now I rejoice in what I am suffering for you, and I fill up in my flesh what is still lacking in regard to Christ's afflictions, for the sake of his body, which is the church." (Colossians 1:24).

[1193] The Remembrance Prayers in the Offertory office correspond to the litanies in the Liturgy of the Faithful. They consist of supplications for those who asked the priest to pray for them, for the forgiveness of the congregation's sins, for the sick, the travelers, the departed, and for the priest himself. The Remembrance Prayers also include the three Short Litanies, which are the Litany of the Peace, the Litany of the Fathers, and the Litany of the Assemblies.

performed before the thrice-benediction [1194] and the Litany of the Offering.[1195] The primitive *morning* liturgy was designed based on this very model; thus, the litanies were included in the Grand Thanksgiving Prayer (now the Preface), just as it is in the Cyrilline liturgy. The moving of the litanies to after the Sanctification prayers came from Jerusalem in the 4th century by Saint Cyril of Jerusalem,[1196] an alteration that was embraced by the Syro-Byzantine liturgies but was not accepted by the Alexandrian tradition.[1197] In other words, when the litanies were first introduced into the Markan liturgy, the Alexandrian order known at the time, portrayed by the Offertory proper, was followed (i.e., Litanies, Institution Narrative, and Epiclesis, respectively). However, in the Basilian and Gregorian liturgies, following the Byzantine tradition, the litanies were placed after the first part of the Major Epiclesis (the decent of the Holy Spirit.

Seven litanies are observed in the Liturgy of Saint Basil.[1198] The first is the Litany of Peace for the Church. In it, the priest beseeches the Lord saying, "Remember, O Lord, the peace of Your one, only, holy, catholic, and apostolic church." The church belongs to Jesus Himself "Your one...church," a biblical teaching manifested in, "on this rock I will build my church" (Matthew 16:18). In this litany, when the priest says, "This, which You have acquired to Yourself with the precious Blood of Your Christ," which refers to the church, the priest points to the Blood and then

---

[1194] The priest prays to the Holy Trinity while making the sign of the Cross three times on the bread and wine. This prayer corresponds to the Institution Narrative in the Liturgy of the Faithful.

[1195] The Litany of the Offering includes the Epiclesis of the Logos. This prayer corresponds to the Major Epiclesis of the Holy Spirit in the Liturgy of the Faithful.

[1196] Dix, *The Shape*, 508.

[1197] We must differentiate between Alexandrian and Egyptian traditions. As noted earlier, the Sacramentary of Serapion places the litanies after the Epiclesis even before the emergence of the widely adopted alterations of Saint Cyril of Jerusalem.

[1198] In Coptic texts, the prominent confirmation of litanies is "Lord, have mercy," which is assigned to the congregation. Nevertheless, Greek texts employ "Amen" instead. See: Research Center. (2012). The Liturgy of Saint Mark the Apostle (1). *Alexandria School, 12(3)*, 146.

the Body; then he continues saying, "keep her in peace." Father Samaan Ibn Koleil points out that Jesus, after dying for the church, acquired her to Himself; as such, He is the head and the master of the *ecclesia*, and she is His inheritance.[1199]

Afterward, the Litany of the Patriarch (or the Pope)[1200] is uttered. According to Ibn Kabar, Pope Cyril I, in the 5th century, was the one introduced this litany;[1201] hence, the church of Egypt was the first to remember her bishop during the liturgy, Rome came second in the 6th century.[1202] In the Litany of the Patriarch, the priest requests, "Foremost remember, O Lord, our blessed and honored father, the archbishop our patriarch, Abba …"[1203] foreign patriarchs in communion may be added after that of Alexandria.

After that, the litany for the *hegumens* and presbyters is prayed. In its primitive form, this litany was dedicated to the presbyters and deacons; the addition of *hegumens* took place after 13th century.[1204] On another note, at the onset of this prayer, some clerics say, "And those who rightly handle the word of truth with him," which is inaccurate. The error arose from the fact that both words in Arabic look the same if proper diacritics is ignored. The correct translation of the Coptic word "ϣⲱⲧ" is (يَفصِل—English: "to part," "to sever," or "to decide on") not (يُفصّل—English: "to handle," "to

---

[1199] Bebawi, George H., *The Divine Liturgy*, 185.
[1200] The title "Pope" was first emerged in Alexandria. It was first used during the pontificate of Pope Heraclas (AD 232-248), the 13th Patriarch of Alexandria. Although this title is not common in the Coptic liturgical texts, it is popular in the Greek Egyptian ones. See: Athanasius of Saint Macarius Monastery (Father), *The Divine Liturgy: The Mystery of the Kingdom of God (Part 2)*, 831; Research Center. (2012). The Liturgy of Saint Mark (1). *Alexandria School, 12(3)*, 145.
[1201] Athanasius of Saint Macarius Monastery (Father), *The Divine Liturgy: The Mystery of the Kingdom of God (Part 2)*, 834.
[1202] Dix, *The Shape*, 509.
[1203] The title "archbishop" was first used during the time of Pope Cyril I (i.e., in 5th century). Before this, the Patriarch's title was "Ⲁⲣⲭⲓⲉⲣⲉⲩⲥ", which means high-priest. The title "high-priest" is used in many hymns, like the *Adam Aspazmos* "Rejoice O Mary." The title "Patriarch" was introduced to the Liturgy after the 13th century.
[1204] Initially, the title *hegumen* was not conferred to priests, but rather to the head monk managing the monastery, even if he was not ordained a priest.

define," or "to explain"). ¹²⁰⁵ In (المعجم الوجيز), a well-known Arabic dictionary, the word (يُفَصِّل), which is "to define," means "to explain" or "to elucidate."¹²⁰⁶ Also, in (مختار الصحاح), another credible Arabic dictionary, the same word means "to clarify." ¹²⁰⁷ Thus, many assumed that the intended meaning is "to expound the word of truth," however, the fact of the matter is that the litany pleads for wisdom to church shepherds, who, in striving to protect their flock from false teachings, separate between orthodox and unorthodox doctrines. In the altar server's bidding, it adds, "the sub-deacons and the Seven Orders of the Church of God." The sub-deacon, one of the Diaconate ranks, assists the deacon. The question here is: Who are the Seven Orders of the Church?

To answer this question, we must examine the Liturgy of Saint Gregory, which follows the same order. In the first part of the litany Gregorian Litany of the Patriarchs, the priest prays for the Patriarch and Bishops, then for the *hegumens*, priest, deacons, and sub-deacons, respectively.¹²⁰⁸ Following the altar server's bidding, he resumes the litany stating the Seven Orders of the Church: The Readers, the Chanters, the Exorcists, the Monks and Virgins, the Widows and Orphans, the Ascetics, and the Laity. Unlike the detailed Gregorian account of the Seven Orders, the Basilian litany compresses them into one sentence, "The Seven Orders of the Church", and assigned it to the altar server.

Going back to the Liturgy of Saint Basil, after praying for the *hegumens*, priests, deacons, sub-deacons and the Seven Orders of the Church, the priest prays a litany for all the servants and for the purity of all Christians, to which the congregation responds saying, "Have mercy

---

[1205] Makar, Adeeb B., *The Abbreviated Coptic-English Dictionary*, 223.
[1206] The meaning in (المعجم الوجيز) is (نفصّل الأمر أي بيّنه).
[1207] The meaning in (مختار الصحاح) is (والتفصيل أيضًا التبيين).
[1208] Notice here that the priest mentions the sub-deacons, but in the Liturgy of Saint Basil, he stops at the deacons.

upon us, O God, the Father, the *Pantocrator*," a responsory that was introduced into the Egyptian liturgy by Saint Severus of Antioch.[1209]

The Litany of the Place is then pleaded followed by that of the Nature. In Egypt, in the period of the inundation of the Nile (*Akhet*), from Paonah 12th (June 19th) to Baba 9th (October 19th or 20th), the Litany of the Waters is said. In the sowing season (*Peret*), from Baba 10th to Toba 10th (January 18th or 19th), the Litany of the Herbs and the Plants is recited. In the harvesting season (*Shemu*), from Tuba 11th to Paonah 11th, the Litany of the Air of Heaven and the Fruit of the Earth is used. However, in the "lands of immigration," one combined litany is employed throughout the year.[1210] For all the litanies (except that of the nature), after the altar server bidding, the people respond, "Lord have mercy" once; however, for the Litany of the Nature "Lord have mercy" is recited thrice.

The priest then points to the sacrifice and prays the Litany of the Oblations. It seems that this plea has always played a big role in the liturgical composition of the Alexandrian rite. In the Liturgy of Saint Serapion, we find that it is the only litany mentioned distinctly.[1211] It is placed following the prayer for the living—corresponding to the contemporary litanies—which is parallel to the order of the Basilian liturgy. A particular tune, introducing the Commemoration of the Saints, is assigned to the people's responsory "Lord have mercy" succeeding this litany.

In the Liturgy of Saint Gregory, more litanies are included, namely, the Litany of the Rulers, that of those who are in government, for those

---

[1209] Matthew the Poor (Father), *The Eucharist: The Lord's Supper*, 698.
[1210] This was a decision by the Holy Synod that was rolled out in June 3rd, 1990. See: The Holy Synod of the Coptic Orthodox Church, *The Synodical Decisions During the Epoch of H.H. Pope Shenouda the Third*, chapter 19, 84-85.
[1211] The Litany of the Oblations according to the Sacramentary of Saint Seaprion: "Receive also the thanksgiving of the people and bless those who have offered the offerings and the thanksgivings, and grant health and soundness and cheerfulness and all advancement of soul and body to this whole people."

who dwell in mountains and caves, and a litany for the Captives. After the latter, the altar server cries out, "Bow before God in fear" or "Worship the Lamb, the Logos of God." The congregation prostrates and the priest inaudibly prays a litany for God not to forbid the congregation from receiving the grace of the Holy Spirit due to their sins. The congregation then chants the hymn "Have mercy upon us, O God, our Savior." The priest covers his right hand with a corporal and turns west, toward the congregation.[1212] He then points at them without any signing and says, "For Your people and Your Church ask You." He turns back to the east and continues, "and through You the Father with You, saying, 'Have mercy upon us, O God, our Savior'," to which the congregation responds thrice saying, "Have mercy upon us, O God, our Savior."[1213] Unlike the Liturgy of Saint Basil, the Gregorian liturgy does not demand the covering of hands before the litanies. Hence, at this point, rubric directs the cleric to cover his hands with corporals.

The priest then resumes the rest of the litanies. It is noteworthy that there is another set of Supplications prayed after the Litany of the Nature, after which the Litany of the Place is prayed followed by a prayer that the Lord may protect His people from famine, plagues, earthquakes, drowning, fire, the captive of barbarians,[1214] the sword of the stranger, and the rising up of heresies.

Before moving to the next section of this study, I must mention that until the papacy of Saint Athanasius the Apostolic (i.e., the 4th century),

---

[1212] In his *The Ritual Order*, Pope Gabriel V explains the Liturgy of Saint Basil, which does not include this litany. Hence, he instructs that turning toward the congregation after the transformation of the elements is not permitted.

[1213] Unlike the liturgy of Saint Gregory, other liturgies addressed to the Son still address this specific prayer to the Father. See: Epiphanius (Bishop), *The White Monastery Euchologion: Translation from Coptic and a Study*, 116, 154.

1214 The most notable raids of the barbarians on the Egyptian monasteries took place in the years AD 407, 434, 444, 570, and 817. For more details about the barbarians, refer to: Epiphaneus (bishop), *The Gregorian Liturgy*, 35.

there was no altar server biddings attached to the litanies; the addition of these requests is attributed to Saint Cyril I. Moreover, the people's responsory was "Amen," as opposed to the widely used one nowadays, viz, "Lord have mercy." [1215] In both liturgies (Basil and Gregory), the Commemoration of the Saints, and the Diptych, respectively, follow.

The Commemoration of Saints

Including the Commemoration of Saints in the Eucharistic prayers reflects the church's profound Christological understanding of herself, that is, the unity between the faithful, who are still in flesh and the deceased, the union between the Church Militant (Latin: *Ecclesia militans*) and the Church Triumphant (Latin: *Ecclesia triumphans*) as one body of Christ, *ecclesia*. The Eucharist, the Body of Christ, is the fulfillment of this unity. Saint Paul instructed the church to "Remember your leaders, who spoke the word of God to you. Consider the outcome of their way of life and imitate their faith." (Hebrews 13:7). The concept of reciting the departed in liturgical services was originally limited to local saints. However, it was Cyril of Jerusalem who extended it to enumerate apostles, saints, prophets, and patriarchs alongside the martyrs in liturgical setups.[1216] Saint Cyril's ritual innovations, including this rank-segregation of the departed, influenced local rites in all Christendom. Consequently, it is safe to accept a Jerusalem origin of the Commemoration of Saints.

As mentioned before, the Cyrilline Commemoration of Saints is located with the Litanies since, in the Alexandrian view, it is treated as a *litany* in which the church prays for the saints. However, it is a unique one, since at the end of it, the church asks for the intercessions and prayers of

---

[1215] Athanasius of Saint Macarius Monastery (Father), *The Divine Liturgy: The Mystery of the Kingdom of God (Part 2)*, 834.
[1216] Dix, Dom Gregory, *The Shape of the Liturgy*, 151.

those who she prays for. Originally, the Commemoration of the Saints only included the Patriarchs who fought for the orthodox faith; then it was extended to encompass the desert Fathers who established monasticism and ascetic-life principles.[1217] Hence, names of martyrs and female saints (with the exception of Saint Mary) are absent.

The Commemoration of Saints was developed in stages. In its inception and formulation, it was a short prayer that only mentions Saint Mary by name; the rest of the martyrs and saints were included collectively as ranks. The lyrics of the Commemoration of Saints in the White Monastery Euchologion (probably scribed end of the 10th century) states, by name, Saint Mary, John the Baptist, and Saint Stephen.[1218] The next development was the additions of Saint Mark, Saint Basil the Great, and the saint of the day. Then, it was amended to include Patriarch Severus of Antioch immediately after Saint Mark. This addition was most likely made by the monks of Saint Macarius monastery in the 7th century.[1219] The oddity here is that Saint Severus of Antioch is placed ahead of all Egyptian Popes. "The name of the departed Pope is amended to the end of the deceased patriarchs," Ibn Kabar instructs, "lastly, Pope Severus of Antioch is mentioned."[1220] Although the context of this sentence is in regard to the hymn Ⲉⲧⲭⲉⲥ (Through the prayers), in which the names of the deceased patriarchs are recited, the same concept applies to the Commemoration of Saints. The last development was the inclusion of a plethora of patriarchs, monks, and saints.

[1217] Some clergy now mention martyrs, departed Popes or bishops, and even laity; these additions are not in the scope of the Commemoration of Saints prayer and should not be made.
[1218] Epiphanius (Bishop), *The White Monastery Euchologion: Translation from Coptic and a Study*, 33, 50, and 131-132. These references are for 3 liturgies in the euchologion, consecutively: Liturgy of Saint Cyril, Egyptian liturgy (unknown author), and Syriac liturgy (unknown author).
[1219] Athanasius of Saint Macarius Monastery (Father), *The Divine Liturgy: The Mystery of the Kingdom of God (Part 2)*, 850.
[1220] Ibn Kabar, *The Lamp*, BnF, MS Arabic 203 (c. AD 1363-1369), fol. 207v.

It is worth noting that the opening statement of the Basilian Commemoration of Saints, "As this, O Lord, is the command of Your Only-begotten Son, that we share in the commemoration of Your saints," holds a unique structure. This commandment is found nowhere in any of the Gospels; it is, in fact, founded on a Pauline verse: "Remember your leaders, who spoke the word of God to you. Consider the outcome of their way of life and imitate their faith" (Hebrews 13:7). The liberty to use Saint Paul's words and attribute them to the Lord is unique to Alexandria, a tradition that is supported by another biblical verse: "Since you are demanding proof that Christ is speaking through me" (2 Corinthians 13:3).

Each of the three Coptic liturgies employs its own rendition of the commemoration. However, the altar server bidding is shared among them all. Following the commemoration, the altar server requests the recitation of the names of the late patriarchs saying, "Let those who read recite the names of our holy fathers, the patriarchs who have fallen asleep: O Lord, repose their souls and forgive us our sins."

The altar server then chants Ⲉⲩⲭⲉⲥ, in which all late patriarchs of the Coptic Orthodox Church is mentioned. The tradition of reciting the names of the departed patriarchs was originated first in Jerusalem and later adopted by other churches including Alexandria. Father Gregory Dix suggests that it is a 4th-century innovation, precisely in AD 348, of Saint Cyril of Jerusalem.[1221] Antecedent tradition of the Alexandrian Church limits the recitation of the names of the departed patriarchs to the Patriarchate. Later, this practice was generalized.[1222] This is then followed by the altar server hymn Ⲡⲓⲛⲓϣϯ (The great), after which the congregation responds saying, "May their Holy blessing be with us..." It is worth

---

[1221] Dix, Dom Gregory, *The Shape of the Liturgy*, 508.
[1222] Matthew the Poor (Father), *The Eucharist: The Lord's Supper*, 597.

mentioning that there are two renditions of the hymn Ⲡⲓⲛⲓϣϯ, one is shorter than the other. The lengthier version was first recorded by Cantor Wissa Attia,[1223] then by Cantor Wadee El-Kommos Matta.

Regarding the people's responsory "May their holy blessing," it is, in fact, a composition of two chants, the older of which is in Greek and translates to, "Glory to You, O Lord. Lord have mercy, Lord have mercy. Lord, bless us. Lord, repose them. Amen." This doxology is the people's response to the recitation of the names of the saints mentioned in the Commemoration and the hymn Ⲡⲓⲛⲓϣϯ. It is a pragmatic implementation of the biblical commandment, "Praise God in all His saints" (Psalms 150:1). The second chant, "May their holy blessing be with us. Amen," is in Coptic and is relatively new. It is simply the conclusion of the altar server hymn, Major Ⲡⲓⲛⲓϣϯ. This suggests that the use of Major Ⲡⲓⲛⲓϣϯ was common in many parishes. It seems that, for the sake of time, cantors would interrupt the lengthy conclusion of the altar server hymn and recite it in a syllabic manner followed by the people's Greek responsory, hence transformed to an introduction to the latter chant. On June 10th, 1995, the Holy Synod issued a decree demanding the use of "May their holy blessing" as a prefix to "Glory to You, O Lord." [1224] The concluding "Amen" may be intoned in its abbreviated, medium, or extended tune.

The Diptych

The people's responsory "May their holy blessing" is followed by the Diptych. The Liturgy of Saint Serapion preserves the most primitive

---

[1223] Cantor Wissa Attia (AD 1918-1975) served at the church of Saint Mary in Luxor, Upper Egypt. Besides the fact that he had a musical ear and beautiful, deep voice, Cantor Wissa was also skilled in playing the lute. He spoke Coptic fluently and was the reason for many people to learn it at the time. Cantor Wissa recorded many hymns before he departed on Thursday August 4th, 1975.

[1224] The Holy Synod of the Coptic Orthodox Church, *The Synodical Decisions During the Epoch of H.H. Pope Shenouda the Third*, chapter 19, 88.

Alexandrian form of this prayer extant. It reads, "We intercede also on behalf of all who have been laid to rest, whose memorial we are making. [after the recitation of the names:]¹²²⁵ Sanctify these souls: for You know all. Sanctify all (souls) laid to rest in the Lord; and number them with all Your holy powers and give to them a place and mansion in Your Kingdom." Comparable to the Basilian and Gregorian liturgies, and dissimilar to that of Saint Cyril, the Diptych according to Saint Serapion is located after the invocation of the Logos (Epiclesis) and the prayer for the living (litanies).

The Diptych comprises of two parts; although both parts were initially said aloud, the contemporary practice is to utter the first silently while the second is recited audibly. The first part of the Basilian Diptych starts with, "Remember also, O Lord, all those who have fallen asleep and reposed in the priesthood and in all the orders of the laity." The Gregorian one begins with, "Remember also, O Lord, our fathers and our brethren who have fallen asleep in the orthodox faith." The Cyrilline Diptych, however, is chanted out loud in a melismatic solemn tune. It begins with, "Those, O Lord, and everyone whose names we have mentioned, and those whom we have not mentioned." It is not uncommon for priests to incorporate the Cyrilline Diptych, "**Ⲟⲩⲟϩ ⲛⲁⲓ ⲛⲉⲙ**," in the Liturgy of Saint Basil. Regarding its melody, the Cyrilline Diptych employs two renditions, an original lengthy tune and a truncated one. The priest then places a spoonful of incense in the censer and mentions the names of those who have departed. The people respond saying, "Lord have mercy."¹²²⁶

It is worth noting that reciting the names of the departed or chanting **Ⲟⲩⲟϩ ⲛⲁⲓ ⲛⲉⲙ** on Sunday is indecorous and hence, not permitted. In his

---

¹²²⁵ This rubric is in the text of the Sacramentary of Saint Serapion.
¹²²⁶ This spoonful of incense, according to some exponents, is a symbol of the preaching of Resurrection and eternal life for those who are reposed in Paradise. See: Athanasius, *The Mystery*, Ibid., 862.

14th canon, Pope Gabriel II (Ibn Turek) of the 12th century states, "Some people blaspheme against God's canons and Laws, for fleeting glory, when they pray the Diptych on Sunday, the day of jubilation for the resurrection of our Lord Jesus Christ. The (Church) canons forbid this and warn of it. Those who continue to do this (after the issuing of this canon) are at fault and not absolved, they will be at loss and condemnation."[1227]

The second part of the Diptych is then said. In the Liturgy of Saint Basil, it is "Those, O Lord," and in the Liturgy of Saint Gregory, it is "Remember, O Lord, the others." After the latter, the congregation responds, **Boⲗ** ⲉⲃⲟⲗ (Loose, remit), after which the priest resumes from "For You are God the Merciful." In these two liturgies the Diptych marks the conclusion of the Intercessory Prayers. Conversely, in the Liturgy of Saint Cyril, it is followed by more litanies.

Gifts of the Major Epiclesis

As previously explained, the Major Epiclesis consists of two parts, the first is believed to be the chief Eucharistic prayer as it invocates the Holy Spirit, and the second focuses on naming the gifts of this invocation. In the Liturgy of Saint Cyril, the two parts of the Major Epiclesis come consecutively; however, in the liturgies of Saint Basil and Saint Gregory, the Intercessory Prayers were moved from its original placement—according to the Coptic tradition—in the Preface, to follow the first part of the Major Epiclesis causing a disjoint between the two parts. This disconnection resulted in difficulties to understand the Eucharistic purpose of the second part in general, and in relation to the first part in specific. In the Basilian and Gregorian liturgies, the second part of the

---

[1227] Athanasius, *The Mystery*, Ibid., 856.

The Liturgy of the Faithful

Epiclesis commences with the hymn "As it was and shall be...," after which the priest prays, "That as in this, so also in all things..."

In the Liturgy of Saint Basil, the phrase "Lead us[1228] throughout the way into Your kingdom" immediately precedes "That as in this, so also in all things..." In fact, this was neither the intent nor the location of the phrase. Old Coptic sources—from the 12th to the 14th centuries—like OR 1239, MS Copte 82, MS Hunt 572, and MS 199 (new numbering Lit. 155, Saint Macarius Monastery) agree with the Greek version of the Coptic Basilian liturgy preserved by the Kacmarcik Codex that "Those, O Lord" encompasses "Lead us," and "That as in this;" then the congregation responds with "As it was."[1229] The next development was the splitting of this prayer into two by moving up the people's responsory "As it was" to right before "That as in this," making "Lead us" the concluding statement of "Those, O Lord."[1230] This tradition lasted till the early years of the 20th century.[1231] Hence we read in Holy Thursday rubric that the Commemoration of Saints and the Diptych are not said, but the priest resumes from, "That as in this." Notice that "Lead us" is not referred to. The last development, which spread in the 20th century, was the employment of "Lead us" to prefix "That as in this," a change that is merely done for grammatical reasons. This is not to say that this development emerged in the 20th century, but rather spread. The oldest testimony of the final shape of this prayer—as far as I know—comes from Ibn Sibaa (13th

---

[1228] The Greek text used the word "ὁδήγησον," and in Coptic, it is "ϭⲓⲙⲱⲓⲧ." Both words mean "Lead us;" however, in Arabic it was mistranslated to "اهدنا!" as opposed to the more accurate translation, "قدنا". For more details, refer to: Epiphaneus (bishop), *The Basilian Liturgy*, 19, 20.

[1229] Respectively, BL, OR. 1239 (12th C.), fol. Not numbered; Paris, BnF, MS Copte 82 (AD 1307), fol. 46r-v; London, Bod., MS Hunt 572 (13th or 14th C.), fol. 69r-v; Epiphanius (Bishop), *The Basilian Liturgy* 173-174; and Kacmarcik Codex (AD 1344-1345), fols. 46v-47v.

[1230] In both the Cyrilline and Gregorian liturgies, this prayer begins with "That as in this," not "Lead us."

[1231] Respectively, London, Bod., MS Hunt 360 (13th C.), fol. 95v; Vatican, Vat, Copto 17 (AD 1288), fols. 49v-50r; Vatican, Vat, Copto 24 (14th or 15th C.), fols. 73v-74v; and Salib, Abdel Massieh (Hegumen), *The Holy Euchologion*, 381-382.

century), probably as a local custom.[1232] I also found other supporting documents of this structure, i.e., MS Copte 24, MS Copte 30, and MS Copte 26, all archived at the National Library of France.[1233]

To say it differently, "Lead us," in its pristine form, belongs to the Intercessory Prayers (precisely the Diptych) as opposed to the Major Epiclesis (second part). Once again, this problem is the product of the insertion of the Intercessory Prayers between the two parts of the Major Epiclesis. As noted above, the pristine location of the people responsory "As it was" was following "That as in this." Hence, we can understand the former as a praise to God the Father and glory to His "great and holy Name." This is lucid to the student of the Liturgy of Saint Serapion, which reads, "Through Your Only-begotten Jesus Christ in holy Spirit as it was and is and shall be to generations of generations and to all ages of the ages. Amen." Back to the contemporary rite, at the end of "That as in this," the three liturgies reconvene in the fraction prayer.

The Introduction to Fraction

In the infancy of Christianity, Fraction (the breaking of the Bread) symbolized the unity of the one Body of Christ, viz., the church. It was a direct implementation of the verse "Because there is one loaf, we, who are many, are one body, for we all share the one loaf." (1 Corinthians 10:17). The one bread embodies the oneness of the church; as members of the Body of Christ, we are one in Him. Before the end of the 2nd century, however, this meaning faded out and was substituted with another one, that is, the passion of Christ. "What led to the change of symbolism in the fraction," Gregory Dix suggests, "was probably the practical fact that the

---

[1232] Ibn Sibaa, *The Precious Pearl: On Ecclesiastic Science*, BnF, MS Arabic 207, fol. 157r.
[1233] Respectively, Paris, BnF, MS Copte 24 (14th or 15th C.), fol. 53r-v; Paris, BnF, MS Copte 30, (AD 1624) fol. 90v; and Paris, BnF, MS Copte 26 (18th C.), fol. 69r.

bread was no longer broken from a single loaf but from several."[1234] Due to the growing number of converts, the liturgy was celebrated over several loaves of bread, a practice that was later abandoned in favor of the primitive one.

The Egyptian tradition is unique in placing Fraction before the Lord's Prayer; other traditions swap this order.[1235] Another Coptic peculiarity is the high number of fraction prayers, which allows them to be employed for the purpose of catechesis. The fraction prayer commences with the priest saying, "Peace be with all," an indication of the beginning of a new section of the liturgy. Only in the liturgy of Saint Basil, this salutation is accompanied with the principal celebrant bowing his head toward the other clerics and altar servers. If a bishop is present, he is the one who gives the greeting. As usual, the congregation responds saying, "and with your spirit," after which the Introduction to the Fraction is recited. In the liturgies of Saint Basil and Saint Cyril, the Introduction to the Fraction starts with, "Again, let us give thanks to God the *Pantocrator*." Initially, this prayer was the primary official Markan Fraction; later, it was introduced into the Basilian liturgy as the sole fraction prayer. Since the fraction prayers became associated with the ecclesiastic calendar, and as they grew in number, "Again, let us give thanks" became a fixed introduction to Fraction.[1236]

In the Introduction to the Fraction, we thank God because he has allowed us to stand before Him in prayer. We also ask Him to make us worthy of partaking of His Body and Blood. In this prayer, there is a part which reads, "Let us also ask Him to make us worthy of the communion and partaking of His divine and immortal Mysteries." In Arabic, the

---

[1234] Dix, Dom Gregory, *The Shape of the Liturgy*, 132.
[1235] Cuming, Geoffrey J., *The Liturgy of St Mark*, 142.
[1236] Matthew the Poor (Father), *The Eucharist: The Lord's Supper*, 729-730.

Coptic word "†ⲙⲉⲧⲁⲗⲏⲙⲯⲓⲥ" was mistranslated to (صعود—literally "ascension"), although the act of offering has already been accomplished. The correct translation is "communion."[1237] In this prayer, the profound relationship between Fraction and communion is discernable, a relationship that is based on, "And is not the bread that we break a participation in the body of Christ?" (1 Corinthians 10:16). The act of "breaking" in this Pauline verse is clearly referring to Fraction, which is a *participation* or communion in the one body of Christ.

In the Liturgy of Saint Basil, the contemporary rubric direct that after, "partaking of His divine and immortal Mysteries," the congregation confirms saying, "Amen" and prostrates. At this point, as a sign of reverence to the Holy Mysteries, the altar servers light candles till the end of the liturgy. The celebrant leaves both corporals on the altar, picks up the Sacred Host with his right hand and places it on the palm of his left hand. He then puts the forefinger of his right index finger on the Host on the right side of the *Despotikon*, beside the broken section. He then exclaims, "The holy Body," to which the congregation confirms saying, "We worship Your holy Body." The celebrant then dips his right index finger in the Blood and draws the sign of the cross inside the chalice saying, "and the precious Blood," to which the people confess saying, "and Your precious Blood." Using his right index finger, the celebrant then anoints the Host with the Blood from front to back in the shape of a cross without lifting his finger, as in a circular motion from front to back. While doing so, he resumes his confession saying, "of His Christ, the *Pantocrator*, the Lord our God." The altar server then responds saying, "Amen. Amen. Pray," to which the congregation says, "Lord, have mercy," an acclamation that was first introduced into the liturgy in the late 4th century in Jerusalem

---

[1237] The Greek version of the Coptic Liturgy of Saint Basil use the word "μεταλήψεως," meaning "communion." See: Matthew the Poor (Father), *The Eucharist: The Lord's Supper*, 732.

and Antioch.[1238] This process of signing the Sacred Host with the Precious Blood is called the *First Consignation*.

In its primitive shape, as attested by Ibn Sibaa,[1239] the previous prayer was initially one uninterrupted orison with no responses or prostrations. The text in this primeval form reads, "For He also has made us worthy now to stand in this Holy Place, to lift up our hands and to serve His holy Name. Let us also ask Him to make us worthy of the communion and partaking of His divine and immortal Mysteries: the holy Body and the precious Blood of His Christ, the *Pantocrator*, the Lord our God."[1240] Many manuscripts attest to this ancient shape including OR. 1239, MS Hunt 360, Copto 17, and Kacmarcik Codex.[1241]

This orison remained unbroken until the 13th century when "Amen" was introduced to separate "the holy Body" from "and immortal Mysteries." This was then supplemented by a prostration. Among the early sources embracing this development are Bod., MS Hunt 572, BnF, MS Copte 82, Vat, Copto 24, BnF, MS Copte 24, BnF, MS Copte 30, and BnF, MS Copte 26.[1242] In these documents, the second part of the prayer, "the holy Body...," is sometimes assigned to the priest and others to the congregation. This structure is still followed in the Cyrilline and Gregorian liturgies where the second part remained intact without

---

[1238] McFarland, Jason J., *Announcing the Feast: The Entrance Song in the Mass of the Roman Rite*, 18.

[1239] Ibn Sibaa, *The Precious Pearl: On Ecclesiastic Science*, BnF, MS Arabic 207, fol. 157r-v.

[1240] The phrase "the *Pantocrator*, the Lord our God" is referring to God the Father who is addressed in this prayer, not Jesus. It would be better understood if the sentence is rephrased as "for He, the *Pantocrator*, the Lord our God, has made us worthy now to... Let us also ask Him to make us worthy of the communion and partaking of His divine and immortal Mysteries: the holy Body and the precious Blood of His Christ."

[1241] Respectively, BL, OR. 1239 (12th C.), fol. Not numbered; London, Bod., MS Hunt 360 (13th C.), fol. 97r-v; Vatican, Vat, Copto 17 (AD 1288), fols. 50v-51r; and Kacmarcik Codex (AD 1344-1345), fols. 57v-58r.

[1242] Respectively, London, Bod., MS Hunt 572 (13th or 14th C.), fols. 70v-71r; Paris, BnF, MS Copte 82 (AD 1307), fol. 46v-47r; Vatican, Vat, Copto 24 (14th or 15th C.), fols. 76r-v; Paris, BnF, MS Copte 24 (14th or 15th C.), fol. 54r-v; Paris, BnF, MS Copte 30 (AD 1624), fols. 92r-93r; and Paris, BnF, MS Copte 26 (18th C.), fols. 70v-71r.

responses or prostrations. It was not until the 18th century when the responses of "I believe" and "Again, I believe" were added.[1243]

In this Introduction to Fraction, the celebrant beseeches the Lord to make us worthy of uniting with Him; however, splitting the prayer into four sections and the addition of responses made it seem like a confessional prayer uttered by the celebrant and endorsed by the congregation after each section.

The Gregorian Introduction to the Fraction begins with, "O our Master and our Savior." When the principal celebrant says, "O Lord, bless" the congregation responds, "Amen." The celebrant takes the Host in his right hand and puts it on the palm of his left hand. He then puts the forefinger of his index finger on the right side of the *Despotikon*. Afterward, he places his index finger in the chalice and signs the Blood with his finger without dipping his finger inside. He then says, "O You Who did bless at that time, now also bless." and the congregation conforms saying, "Amen." The celebrant then signs the Host with the Blood using his finger, from front to back in a circular motion, and says, "O You who did sanctify at that time, now also sanctify" to which the congregation responds, "Amen." Finally, the celebrant says, "O You who did break at that time, now also break" and the congregation asserts saying, "Amen." Subsequently, the celebrant begins breaking the Host into a third and two thirds. He then puts the one third atop the two thirds in the shape of a cross. After that, he recites the prayer that starts with, "O You who did give to His holy disciples," to which the altar server responds saying, "Amen. Amen. Pray," and the people say, "Lord, have mercy." As previously explained, analogous to the primitive share of this prayer, no prostrations are required. Afterward, the Fraction is prayed.

[1243] Athanasius of Saint Macarius Monastery (Father), *Summary of the Liturgical History of the Church of Alexandria (Part 2)*, 247-248.

The earliest document that can be inspected—at least in this study—to trace back the development of this Gregorian prayer is the 12th-century OR. 1239 preserved at the British Library. In it, we find that the Gregorian Introduction to Fraction is one continuous prayer without congregation affirmations, altar server bidding, concluding responsory, or prostrations.[1244] This remained the case till the following century, as reported by MS Hunt 572 inscribed in the 13th century.[1245] Starting from the 13th century, the congregation assertation "Amen" after each of the priest's signings materialized, yet no mention of the final responsory, "We worship Your... Lord, have mercy."[1246] The earliest evidence of the emergence of the people's responsory, "Lord, have mercy," following this prayer is found in the Tuki's Euchologion published in Rome in AD 1736; still, no mention of "We worship..."[1247] In fact, the latter responsory is not even prescribed in the AD 1902 Euchologion.[1248] Therefore, we can deduce that "We worship You..." is a recent imprudent addition to the Gregorian liturgy in imitation of the Basilian one. This explains the absence of altar server bidding for prostration. Hence, it is more proper, at this point, not to use it nor perform prostrations.

The Fraction

The pristine purpose of the fraction, or *melismos*, whether in Judaism or at the Last Supper is for distribution. This, as noted earlier, changed to a symbolism, first, of oneness through and in Christ, and second—toward

---

[1244] London, BL, OR. 1239 (12th C.), fol. Not numbered.
[1245] London, Bod., MS Hunt 572 (13th or 14th C.), fols. 133v-134v.
[1246] Vatican, Vat, Copto 17 (AD 1288), fols. 96v-97r; Vatican, Vat, Copto 20 (AD 1315), fol. 52r-v; Vatican, Vat, Copto 24 (14th or 15th C.), fols. 142v-144v; London, Bod., MS Hunt 403 (13th or 14th C.), fols. 42r-43r; and Paris, BnF, MS Copte 26 (18th C.), fols. 135v-136v.
[1247] Tuki, Raphael (Bishop), *The Three Liturgies of Saints Basil, Gregory the Theologian, and Cyril, in addition to Other Holy Prayers*, 238-240.
[1248] Salib, Abdel Massieh (*Hegumen*), *The Holy Euchologion*, 529.

the end of the 2nd century—of Christ's passion. This practice almost disappeared from the West, yet is still observed in the East, especially by the Syriac and the Alexandrian rites.[1249] In the Coptic Church, the fraction is performed in two phases: The first takes place at the Institution Narrative while the second occurs during the fraction prayer. During Fraction, the actual breaking of the Sacred Host is performed in preparation for Communion. One of two techniques is used, the older of which is called the Attached Fraction (also called the Short Fraction). In this technique, the president breaks the Body without fully separating its parts, indicating that our Lord died on the Cross without breaking any bones. It is performed as follows:

1) The priest breaks the section at the bottom of the two thirds without separation[1250]
2) Then, he breaks the one third into four parts without separation
3) After that, he breaks the two thirds in half
4) Afterward, the priest breaks the left third into four parts without separation
5) Finally, he fully removes the *Despotikon*, kisses it, and puts it back in its place

The Host is now broken into twelve pieces with the *Despotikon* in the middle.

The second technique is called the Detached Fraction (or the Long Fraction).[1251] The following is how it is performed:

[1249] Zanelli, Ugo. (2011). "Fraction Prayers" in the Coptic Liturgy. *The Harp*, 27, 291.

[1250] The writer of *The Trinitarian Mystery in Priesthood Ministry* parallels this pattern to the Holy Trinity; accordingly, the one third resembles God the Son, and the two thirds represent the Father and the Holy Spirit. See Misael of the Paromeos Monastery (Father). (2020). The Trinitarian Mystery in Priesthood Ministry. *Alexandria School*, 28(1), 125.

[1251] This technique was introduced into the Coptic liturgy in the 14th century.

1) The priest places the one third atop the two thirds in the shape of a cross
2) He then takes the top third and places it on the paten
3) Then, he takes the two thirds and places it at the bottom of the paten
4) Next, he breaks the Host into four pieces and places it in the shape of a cross indicating the Sacrifice, the Lord, on the Cross
5) Afterward, he takes the middle section of the Host and breaks it into four pieces
6) The priest then takes what is left and breaks it into four pieces using three breaks, which are called "wounds" as they represent the wounds of our Lord Jesus Christ. He also breaks the other three sections
7) Finally, he takes the middle section and breaks it; he picks up the *Despotikon*, which is embodies Christ, kisses it, and then puts it back

The Sacred Host is now broken into twelve pieces and the *Despotikon* is in the middle. In both techniques, the *Despotikon* being in the middle of the twelve pieces represents the Lord among his twelve disciples.

In antiquity, precisely the first two centuries, the deacon had a much more prominent role during the liturgy, especially when it comes to Fraction and Communion, as first attested by Hippolytus.[1252] Since the fraction, in many cases, took place over three or four offerings, the servant deacon was expected to help breaking them. After the Apostolic Age, the deacon continued to have a noticeable role at the liturgy. He would not only help distributing the Blood, but also give communion to the sick who were not able to attend.[1253] As time progressed, the role of the deacon

---

[1252] Dix, *The Shape*, 131.
[1253] Matthew the Poor (Father), *Eucharist of the Lord's Supper*, 734-735.

diminished and became meager; therefore, all these responsibilities were assigned to the priest. Speaking of this new era of deterioration of the deacon's vocation, Father Alexander Schmemann eloquently states, "In this new experience of the Church the deacon proved to be in essence unneeded, certainly not obligatory; and with his gradual disappearance, his liturgical functions were for the most part transferred to the priest."[1254] To further emphasize the sanctity of these moments, Ibn Kabar reports an ancient tradition that was still practiced at his time (14th century). According to this *ordo*, right before the fraction prayer, all altar servers exit the sanctuary; only the servant deacon is allowed to stay inside it to help the celebrant.[1255]

It is worth mentioning that the fraction prayer is organized in verses. Although originally it was said uninterruptedly, the practice now is for the congregation to respond saying, "Lord, have mercy" thrice, after each verse.[1256] In his inventory of Fraction prayers, Ugo Zanetti reports 60, of which 38 are addressed to the Father, 20 to the Son, and 2 to both.[1257] One of the most theologically prominent fraction prayers is the *Syrian Fraction*. It was translated into Arabic by a Syrian monk named Isiah Dabk, then into Coptic by Father Abdel Messih Salib El-Masoody of the Paromaos monastery, who also published it in his renowned Euchologion.[1258] Another Fraction beginning with "As You have bestowed upon us the grace of sonship,"[1259] was authored by Bishop John of Bostra.[1260] There are many other fraction prayers in use today with anonymous authors. Zanetti

---

[1254] Schmemann, Alexander, *The Eucharist*, 121.
[1255] Ibn Kabar, *The Lamp*, BnF, MS Arabic 203 (c. AD 1363-1369), fol. 207v.
[1256] There are two exceptions to this rule. The first is the fraction for Eastertide, where two additional responses are said ("Christ is risen from the dead," and "Truly, He is risen from the dead"); and the second is the fraction for the feasts of Saint Mary and the Angels, where the responsory "Amen. Alleluia" is used in addition to the traditional one.
[1257] Zanelli, Ugo. (2011). "Fraction Prayers" in the Coptic Liturgy. *The Harp*, 27, 297.
[1258] Sobhy, Basilious (Father), *Introduction to the History of Coptic Rites*, 66.
[1259] This Fraction could be prayed any time of the year, particularly in the Feast of Epiphany.
[1260] Sobhy, Basilious (Father), *Introduction to the History of Coptic Rites*, 86.

identifies two peculiarities to the Coptic Fraction: first, it serves as an introduction to the Lord's Prayer. Second, the existence of large number of these prayers where the celebrant chooses the fitting one according to the ecclesiastical season and/or the circumstances.[1261]

The Lord's Prayer

At the completion of the fraction prayer, the congregation recites the Lord's Prayer, which was placed between the Fraction and the Communion at the end of the fourth century,[1262] a tradition that was possibly established in Jerusalem and adopted by the African Churches.[1263] The full text of this prayer can be found in Matthew 6:1-15 where Luke 11:2–4 reports a truncated rendition. The Lord's Prayer, which was established by our Lord Jesus Christ Himself,[1264] had its roots in Judaism.[1265] In the Jewish tradition, this prayer was called the *Shemoneh Esrei* (Hebrew:שמנה עשרה, "Eighteen Benedictions") and is said three times a day, at the appointed times—evening, morning and noon. Its original formulation is attributed to the 120 men of the Great Assembly of Ezra's time in the 5th century B.C. Among observant Jews, the *Shemoneh Esrei* is referred to as *HaTefilla* (Hebrew: תפילת העמידה, "the prayer") since it was the most important prayer of the synagogue. Sometimes it is also called *Amidah*, meaning "standing" because it is recited while standing and facing the *Aron Kodesh* (the ark that houses the Torah scrolls). A special abbreviated *Amidah* is also the core of the *Mussaf* ("Additional") service that is recited on Shabbat (the Jewish Sabbath), *Rosh Chodesh*, and Jewish

---

[1261] Zanelli, Ugo. (2011). "Fraction Prayers" in the Coptic Liturgy. *The Harp*, 27, 293.
[1262] Athanasius of Saint Macarius Monastery (Father), *The Divine Liturgy: The Mystery of the Kingdom of God (Part 2)*, 901.
[1263] Dix, Dom Gregory, *The Shape of the Liturgy*, 108.
[1264] Matthew 6:9-13, and Luke 11:2-4.
[1265] McGowan argues otherwise; see further McGowan, Andrew B., *Ancient Christian Worship*, 187.

festivals. The *Amidah* contains 19 blessings (initially 18) and takes about seven minutes to recite. Due to its length or when it is impractical to pray the entire *Amidah*, Jews are allowed to pray a shortened version of the prayer.[1266] Jesus, being a first century Jewish rabbi, would have taught His disciples a shortened version of the *Amidah* for them to recite during times when praying the entire *Amidah* was impractical.

In his book, *Back to the Sources: Reading the Classic Jewish Texts*, Barry W. Holtz outlines how the Lord's Prayer corresponds to the *Amidah*. Holtz shows that the following parts of the *Amidah* are the source of the Lord's Prayer. "Thou art holy and Thy Name is holy and the holy praise Thee daily. Blessed art Thou O Lord, the holy God. Reign thou over us O Lord, thou alone in loving kindness and tender mercy and clear us in judgment. Blessed are Thou O Lord the King who loves righteousness and judgment. Bless this year unto us O Lord our God together with every kind of the produce thereof for our welfare. Forgive us O our Father for we have sinned, pardon us O our King for we have transgressed, for Thou dost pardon and forgive. Blessed art Thou O Lord who art gracious and dost abundantly forgive. Look with compassion on all afflicted among us; be Thou our guardian and our advocate, and redeem us speedily from all evil, for in Thee do we trust as our mighty Redeemer." The invocation "Our Father" = "*Avinu*" or Abba (hence in Luke simply "Father") is one common in the Jewish liturgy (see and compare *Shemoneh Esreh*, the fourth, fifth, and sixth benedictions, especially in the New-Year's ritual the prayer "Our Father, our King! Disclose the glory of Thy Kingdom unto us speedily").

It seems that the incorporation of the Lord's Prayer into the Eucharist was one of Saint Cyril of Jerusalem's innovations. Toward the end of the

---

[1266] "Amidah." *Wikipedia*. Wikipedia.org. n.p. Web. 29 April 2016.

fourth century, it was already in use in Milan and North Africa. At the commencement of the following century, the tradition of reciting this prayer during the liturgy was spread to all churches, but Rome, which eventually—towards the end of the sixth century—conceded.[1267] In Jerusalem and Rome, it was placed immediately after the Eucharistic Prayer, and in Milan towards the end of it. However, in North Africa and Alexandria, it was positioned between the fraction and Communion.[1268]

The chief reason for reciting the Lord's Prayer right before Communion is the fact that it is the prayer that exposes the relationship between God the Father and His people, the faithful. Still being sinners and unworthy, the Father granted us the gift of fatherhood; in Christ, the believers are the Father's children "by adoption." He is their father and master, and hence they can call Him, "Our Father, Who art in heaven." This mystical relationship is what made it possible for communicants to come forth and partake of the Body and Blood of His Only-begotten Son.[1269] Another reason for this placement of the prayer, which was reported in *The Trinitarian Mystery in Priesthood Ministry*,[1270] is the sentence that reads, "Give us this day our bread for tomorrow (to come)."[1271] In the Boheric Coptic text, the phrase is translated as "ⲡⲉⲛⲱⲓⲕ ⲛ̀ⲧⲉ ⲣⲁⲥϯ" meaning "our bread for tomorrow;" whereas in Sahidic, it is "ⲡⲉⲛⲱⲓⲕ ⲉⲧⲛⲏⲩ" that means "our bread to come." Since "tomorrow" or "to come" denote the Kingdom of God and eternal life, these phrases refer to Jesus Christ Himself. Hence, communicants beseech for the bread of eternal life, Jesus Christ, that they are about to receive in Communion.

[1267] Dix, Dom Gregory, *The Shape of the Liturgy*, 131.
[1268] Dix, Ibid., 131.
[1269] For this reason, in the past, the Lord's Prayer lyrics was neither disclosed to the non-believers nor recited in their presence.
[1270] Misael of the Paromeos Monastery (Father). (2020). The Trinitarian Mystery in Priesthood Ministry. *Alexandria School*, 28(1), 128.
[1271] Matthew the Poor (Father), *The Eucharist: The Lord's Supper*, 758-759.

Saint Cyril of Jerusalem says, "The bread over there, which is ordinary bread, is not 'substantial.' But this bread on the altar, which is now holy, is indeed substantial: in other words, it has been instituted for the 'subsistence' of the soul. This bread does not enter the stomach and then pass from it in a private place, but it nourishes you in your entirety, for the good of body and soul."[1272] In his fourth treatise, *On the Lord's Prayer*, Saint Cyprian says, "For Christ is the bread of life; and this bread does not belong to all men, but it is ours... And we ask that this bread should be given to us daily, that we who are in Christ, and daily receive the Eucharist for the food of salvation, may not, by the interposition of some heinous sin, by being prevented, as withheld, and not communicating, from partaking of the heavenly bread, be separated from Christ's body, as He Himself predicts, and warns, 'I am the living bread that came down from heaven. Whoever eats this bread will live forever. This bread is My flesh, which I will give for the life of the world.'"[1273] Still some saints understood this phrase in a spiritual context, but not liturgical.[1274]

In fact, each request in the Lord's Prayer, when recited before Communion, takes a Christological meaning tightly tied to the Eucharist. Each of these requests should be understood as an outcome of Jesus' salvation that we receive through the Eucharist. Hence, Saint John Cassian comments, "The expression 'this day' can also be understood with reference to the present life - namely: Give us this bread as long as we dwell

---

[1272] Cyril of Jerusalem (Saint), *Catechetical Lecture 23*, 15.
[1273] Cyprian (Saint), *On the Lord's Prayer*, Chapter 18.
[1274] Saint Gregory of Nyssa (AD 335– after 394), for instance, wrote, "He who is attentive only to what is needful according to nature, and does not chase after vain cares beyond what is necessary, will not fall much short of the angelic way of life, imitating their attribute of needing nothing. It is for this reason that we have been commanded to seek only what suffices for the preservation of our physical body. When we say to God, 'Give bread,' we do not ask for delights, riches, and flowery robes... We pray only for bread... ask for bread to meet life's needs." Saint John Chrysostom (AD 347–407) confirms this meaning saying, "I pray thee, how even in things that are bodily, that which is spiritual abounds. For it is neither for riches, nor for delicate living, nor for costly raiment, nor for any other such thing, but for bread only, that He hath commanded us to make our prayer."

in this world. For we know that it will also be given in the world to come to those who have deserved it from You, but we beg You to give it to us this day, because unless a person deserves to receive it in this life, he will be unable to partake of it in that life."[1275]

It is to be noted that when it was first introduced in Jerusalem, the Lord's Prayer was recited by both the celebrant and the congregation, however, in the West, it was treated as part or continuation of the Eucharistic Prayer, and as such, recited by the president with the people chanting the last phrase only.[1276] This tradition seems to have been followed in Alexandria as well, since until today, only the last phrase is chanted. At a later date, even in the West, the Lord's Prayer was assigned to the congregation.

The Prayer of Inclination

After the congregation recites the Lord's Prayer, the chorus (or a chanter) intones the sentence ϧⲉⲛ Ⲡⲓⲭⲣⲓⲥⲧⲟⲥ Ⲓⲏⲥⲟⲩⲥ Ⲡⲉⲛϭⲟⲓⲥ (in Christ Jesus our Lord). This sentence was the conclusion of the Lord's Prayer before "for Yours is the kingdom, the power, the glory forever and ever. Amen" was appended. Meanwhile, the president inaudibly utters a prayer titled "The Prayer After Our Father," a petition that borrows its theme and content from the Lord's Prayer. In it, the celebrant entreats God the Father to protect the worshippers from the evil temptations, thoughts, and actions. It confirms to the congregation's plead to "not lead us into temptation but deliver us from the evil one." Then the altar server cries out, "Bow your heads before the Lord," to which the congregation—while bowing—responds saying "Before You, O Lord." It is worth noting that the

---

[1275] Cassian, John, *On the Lord's Prayer*, Chapter 21.
[1276] Dix, Ibid, 131.

instruction here is precisely for bowing not worshiping.[1277] Worshiping is preserved to showing full submission to and adoration of the Lord Himself, whereas bowing is a sign of accepting the absolution. In this part of the liturgy, we bow to receive the absolution, uttered inaudibly, from the president.

After the worshippers bow their heads, the celebrant, softly, utters a 6th-century prayer—authored by Bishop John of Bostra—titled "The Prayer of Submission Addressed to the Father."[1278] In this prayer, the celebrant confirms the communicants' belief in the works of the Lord Christ that was recited in the *Anamnesis*. It reads, "We have confessed His saving Passion; we have proclaimed His Death; we have believed in His Resurrection; and the Mystery is accomplished." Following this, the celebrant gives thanks to God the Father for preparing the Body and Blood of His Only-begotten Son, Jesus, on the altar; the Holy Mysteries that the angels desire to look at, as Saint Peter says, "Even angels long to look into these things" (1 Peter 1:12). Finally, he asks the Lord to confirm the communicants in the orthodox faith, fill then with His genuine love, and grant them to always praise and glorify Him. Indeed, a powerful and profound prayer!

The Elevation

The altar server cries out, "Let us attend in the fear of God" as an intimation of the importance of the following prayer (i.e., the absolution). Since it is a new section of the liturgy, the priest says, "Peace be with all," to which the congregation responds, "And with your spirit." The celebrant then utters the third inaudible prayer, which is the absolution. This

---

[1277] In other parts of the liturgy the altar server instructs the people saying, "Worship God in fear and trembling" or "Worship the lamb, the Word of God."
[1278] Cuming, Geoffrey J., *The Liturgy of St Mark*, 139; and Matthew the Poor (Father), *The Eucharist: The Lord's Supper*, 762.

absolution, which is now for all worshippers, was originally for people under a period of discipline by the Church and have fulfilled the chastisement. It served as an encouragement and support to them so they can approach communion without fear.[1279] During the absolution,[1280] the celebrant remembers the living and the departed as requested by the congregation, and then he continues from "every sin and every curse" till the end. After the absolution, the altar server cries out, "Saved. Amen. And with your spirit. In the fear of God, let us attend,"[1281] to which the congregation responds, "Amen. Lord have mercy, Lord have mercy, Lord have mercy."

After this, the servant priest lifts up the *Despotikon* with his right hand, and protects it with his left hand beneath, and with bowed head he exclaims aloud, "The Holies for the holy." This proclamation should be comprehended as a confirmation that the communicants, as members of the one Body of Christ, belong to Him; therefore, they can come forward to partake of His Holy Body and Precious Blood. Holiness belongs to God alone, and therefore, anything "holy" belongs to God.[1282] This means that this phrase ought to be understood as "The things that belong only to God (the Holies) are for God's people (the holy)." The *holy* are those who pursue a godly life as lead by our Lord Jesus, those who take the righteous way, even if they fall, they are still holy, particularly after the Holy Spirit has descended upon them and sanctified them, and after they have received the absolution. In brief, this statement serves as a warning to

---

[1279] Athanasius of Saint Macarius Monastery (Father), *The Divine Liturgy: The Mystery of the Kingdom of God (Part 2)*, 909.

[1280] It is important to note that the absolution comes at the end of the *explanatory* liturgy, which coincides with the Absolution of the Servants that is recited at the end of the Offertory.

[1281] This responsory did not exist in euchologions before the 15th century. See: Athanasius of Saint Macarius Monastery (Father), *Summary of the Liturgical History of the Church of Alexandria (Part 2)*, 250.

[1282] Saint Cyril of Alexandria, in the 5th century, was the first to describe the three Persons of the Trinity as "Holy" in the Coptic liturgy.

everyone. Those who wish to partake from the Holy Mysteries must be living a life of repentance and holiness, despite their short comings, lest they become unworthy and hence, not partake of the Holies.

The Commixture

The Commixture is the placing of a particle of the Sacred Host into the Blood. "The priest takes the *Despotikon* between the tips of two fingers of his right hand," the rubric of *The Divine Liturgies of Saints Basil, Gregory, and Cyril* explains, "and with It he signs the precious Blood inside the chalice in the form of the cross. Then he dips the extremity of It inside the chalice and carefully raises It soaked in the Blood, and with It signs, in the form of the cross, the pure Body which is all on the paten. Then he takes the *Despotikon* and signs with It the Blood inside the chalice in the form of the cross. He then carefully places the *Despotikon* upside down in the Blood inside the chalice, all the while with his left hand cupped under the *Despotikon* lest any of the pearls should fall or drip, while saying: Blessed be the Lord Jesus Christ, the Son of God; the sanctification is by the Holy Spirit. Amen." [1283] This process is referred to as "The Second Consignation" to distinguish it from the consignation that took place before the fraction prayer.

As mentioned earlier, *Despotikon* means "belongs to the Lord." Originally, the "lord" was referring to the bishop in a practice called *Fermentum*. The *Fermentum* is a custom that was first practiced as early as AD 120. According to this tradition, a particle of the Host was carried by a minister of the church from the bishop of one diocese to the bishop of another one. The receiving bishop would then consume the species at his next Eucharistic celebration as a sign of communion between the

---

[1283] SUS, *The Divine Liturgies of Saints Basil, Gregory, and Cyril*, Second Edition, 231.

churches. In the 2nd century, principal bishops (or patriarchs) used to send the Eucharist to other bishops as a pledge of unity of faith, this being the origin of the expression to be "in communion" with each other. On occasion, bishops also sent out *fermenti* to their priests.[1284] By the 4th century, this tradition has gradually vanished from the East; however, it continued to be practiced in the West until the 8th century.[1285] Father Gregory Dix suggests that this tradition is the root for the ritual of elevating and putting the *Despotikon* in the chalice.[1286] After the 4th century, when the *Fermentum* ceased to be practiced in the East, the utilitarian function of placing the *Despotikon* in the chalice was substituted for a symbolic meaning, which is "to show that they (the Body and Blood) are not separable, that they are one in power and that they vouchsafe the same grace to those who receive them," as Theodore of Mopsuestia[1287] explains.[1288] Later, this unpretentious but solid symbolism was replaced by another one that interprets the soaking of the *Despotikon* in the chalice as being Jesus on the Cross soaked in His own Blood. As a result, the meaning of the *Despotikon* "belongs to the *lord*" changed to refer to the *Lord* Jesus Christ, as opposed to the bishop.

The congregation then responds as they worship, "One is the all-holy Father, one is the all-holy Son, one is the all-holy Spirit. Amen."[1289] This chief acclamation declares that there is actually no one "Holy" except the

---

[1284] "Fermentum." *Wikipedia*. Wikipedia.org. n.p. Web. 22 April 2016.
[1285] Saint Basil the Great attests that the habit of keeping the Host for few days after the congregational celebration to partake from during the week existed in Egypt at his time and was practiced even by laity. See Baumstark, Anton, *On the Historical Development of the Liturgy*, 55.
[1286] Dix, Dom Gregory, *The Shape of the Liturgy*, 134.
[1287] Theodore the Interpreter (AD 350—428) was bishop of Mopsuestia (as Theodore II) from AD 392 to 428. He is also known as Theodore of Antioch, from the place of his birth. He is the best-known representative of the middle School of Antioch of hermeneutics. Theodore was an early companion and friend of John Chrysostom.
[1288] Reine, Francis Joseph, *The Eucharistic Doctrine and Liturgy of the Mystagogical Catecheses of Theodore of Mopsuestia*, 35.
[1289] It is important to note that, in the Offertory proper, the same response is recited, but this time is assigned to the altar server.

three Persons of the Holy Trinity. The pristine form of this acclamation was recorded first by Saint Cyril of Jerusalem; it reads, "One holy, our Lord Jesus Christ." This response was then adopted by all liturgies in the East and West including the Liturgy of Saint Cyril at his time. However, Theodore of Mopsuestia had an alternative acclamation that reads, "One Holy Father, one Holy Son, one Holy Spirit." The latter found its way only into the Egyptian tradition and replaced the original one in all Egyptian liturgies. It is worth mentioning that in Egypt, evidence show that in the medieval period this responsory was preceded by another one that reads, "Remember me O Lord when You come into Your Kingdom." However, in the 15th century, Pope Gabriel V relocated it to follow Communion.[1290]

The Confession

The president declares the commencement of a new section with the traditional opening, "Peace be with all," to which the communicants respond, "And with your spirit." Afterward, the priest utters the final confession. Faith is one of the cornerstone prerequisites for reaping the fruits of the Eucharist. For this reason, Jesus said, "Whoever believes in Me will never be thirsty" (John 6:35). It was also Jesus' practice to confirm one's faith before performing miracles; "Do you believe this?" (John 11:26), "Do you believe that I am able to do this?" (Matthew 9:28), "Everything is possible for one who believes" (Mark 9:23). Feeble faith limits God's work in His people. The Bible teaches, "He did not do many miracles there because of their lack of faith" (Matthew 13:58). Thus, at this point, right before Communion, the celebrant announces his faith vis-à-vis the Eucharist one last time, and the congregation confirms.

[1290] Athanasius of Saint Macarius Monastery (Father), *Summary of the Liturgical History of the Church of Alexandria (Part 1)*, 311, 312.

The celebrant says, "The Holy Body and the precious, true blood of Jesus Christ, the Son of our God. Amen," which is the faith with which communicants come forward to receive the Holy Mysteries; and hence, they assent saying, "Amen." The celebrant continues, "The Holy, precious Body and the true blood of Jesus Christ, the Son of our God. Amen." Once again, the congregation confirms saying, "Amen." He then proclaims, "The Body and the Blood of Immanuel[1291] our God; this is true. Amen." The congregation, for the third time, notarizes this belief saying, "Amen. I believe." By this, the *church* confirms that the gifts on the altar, which the communicants are about to receive, are truly the Body and Blood of our Lord Jesus Christ.

Next, the president, as a representative of the *ecclesia*, proclaims the final confession, in which he affirms that what is present on the altar is the Body and Blood of our Lord, which He took from the Virgin Mary through the Holy Spirit; the Body that is united with the Divine Logos, the Second Person (hypostasis) of the Holy Trinity. It is the same Body which was crucified on the Cross for the forgiveness of our sins; therefore, the faithful partake of it for the forgiveness of sins and for eternal life. Afterwards, he covers the paten and the chalice[1292] indicating that what is underneath the covers is the unseen God Himself.[1293]

The altar server, facing westward, stands across from the priest in the east side of the altar (in his traditional location) with a cross raised in his right hand and a candle in his left hand. He holds one end of a corporal (shaped as a triangle) with his right hand and the other end with his left hand. The cross denotes the salvation work of Jesus, the candle symbolizes

---

[1291] In the King James Version, it is spelled "Emmanuel". However, most other versions, including New International Version, it is spelled "Immanuel."
[1292] Gabriel V (Pope), *The Ritual Order*, BnF, MS 98 (AD 1411), fol. 69r.
[1293] Misael of the Paromeos Monastery (Father). (2018). The Beginners' Guide and Discipline for Laity. *Alexandria School*, 25(2), 140.

His Resurrection, and the triangular corporal indicates that all the salvatory work fulfilled by Jesus are the work of the Triune God. The congregation bow their heads while the celebrant kneels down and lifts up the paten holding the Sacred Host and recites the final confession.

Father Youhanna Salama mentions that the original text of the final confession did not include the adjective "life-giving," but was added to the text after consent from the Holy Synod headed by Pope Mikhail V[1294] in AD 1138.[1295] Since Pope Mikhail V did not preside over the See of Saint Mark until AD 1145, Father Youhanna's claim is hence inaccurate. In his *History of the Patriarchs of the Egyptian Church*, Sawīrus Ibn Al-Muḳaffa', bishop of al-Ašmūnīm, attributes the annexation "life-giving" to Pope John V[1296] (AD 1147–1166).[1297] In his book *The Precious Pearl: On the Church History*, Bishop Isidore of the Paromeos Monastery (AD 1897–1942) says that Pope Gabriel II, in his first liturgy prayed at Saint Macarius Monastery after being ordained as a pope in AD 1122, while praying the Confession, "added a sentence that was not in use in this Monastery, which is 'And He made it one with His Divinity.' The monks asked him to let go of this statement, but he revealed to them that the Holy Synod commanded this addition. The monks conditioned that in addition to this statement, 'without mingling, and without confusion' must be added as well to avoid the heresy of Eutyches.[1298] The Pope agreed and issued a

---

[1294] Pope Mikhail (Michael) V is 71st Pope of Alexandria (AD 1145–1146). During his papacy, he returned the relics of Saint Macarius of Egypt from village of Shabsheer to the Nitrian Desert.
[1295] Salama, Youhanna (Hegumen), *The Precious Pearls: Explaining the Rites and Beliefs of the Church*, part 1, 438.
[1296] Pope John V of Alexandria, 72nd Pope of Alexandria.
[1297] Gamal El-Deen, Abdel Aziz, *History of Egypt Through Manuscript 'History of the Patriarchs' by Sawīrus Ibn al-Muqaffa'*, Part 7, 75-80.
[1298] Eutyches (Greek: Εὐτυχής; AD 380–456) was a presbyter and archimandrite at Constantinople. He first came to notice in AD 431 at the First Council of Ephesus, for his vehement opposition to the teachings of Nestorius; his condemnation of Nestorianism as heresy led him to an equally extreme, although opposite view, which precipitated him being denounced as a heretic himself. Eutyches denied that Christ was 'consubstantial with us men'. He rejected Christ's dual consubstantiality (with the Father and with us men). Eutyches died in exile.

decree to all the dioceses." This incident was documented by Sawīrus Ibn Al-Muḳaffa', bishop of Al-Ašmūnīm, [1299] and quoted by *Hegumen* Youhanna Salama.[1300]

The altar server replies with a response in its melismatic form or an abbreviated one.[1301] In his *The Ritual Order* (AD 1411), Pope Gabriel V directs that after the Prayer of Confession, the congregation replies Ⲱⲉ ⲛ̀ⲣⲟⲙⲡⲓ (Hundred years).[1302] This practice is echoed by Bishop Raphael Tuki in his AD 1736 euchologion.[1303] It seems that toward the end of 19th century the Gloria Patri (also called the *Doxa*, from ancient Greek δόξα, meaning "glory") emerged as an alternate rejoinder. Therefore, in his euchologion published in AD 1902, Father Abdel Messih El-Massoudy prescribes the latter as an alternative to the former.[1304] Shortly after, the Gloria Patri, viz, Ⲇⲟⲝⲁ ⲥⲓ Ⲕ̅ⲩ̅ⲣⲓⲉ Ⲇⲟⲝⲁ ⲥⲓ (Glory to You, O Lord, glory to You), became the only rejoinder in use. While the people are intoning the Gloria Patri, the servant priest kisses the altar and then bows down to the other concelebrants, altar servers, and communicants; this marks the start of the chief part of the liturgy, that is, Communion.

The Communion

We now reach the holiest moments of the Liturgy of the Faithful and the climax of the church's entire liturgical life, that is, the partaking of the Body and Blood of our Lord Jesus Christ. The Church, through the

---

[1299] Gamal El-Deen, Abdel Aziz, *History of Egypt Through Manuscript 'History of the Patriarchs' by Sawīrus Ibn al-Muqaffa'*, Part 6, 505-507.
[1300] Salama, Youhanna (Hegumen), *The Precious Pearls: Explaining the Rites and Beliefs of the Church*, part 1, 438.
[1301] The melismatic response is usually recited on feasts; during Regular Days, the abbreviated response is more commonly used.
[1302] Gabriel V (Pope), *The Ritual Order*, BnF, MS 98 (AD 1411), fol. 69r.
[1303] Tuki, Raphael (Bishop), *The Three Liturgies of Saints Basil, Gregory the Theologian, and Cyril, in addition to Other Holy Prayers*, 160.
[1304] Salib, Abdel Massieh (Hegumen), *The Holy Euchologion*, 410.

numerous prayers that precede this moment, prepares the faithful spiritually and mentally for receiving Christ. These preparatory petitions begin with evening psalmody and incense offering, followed by vigils, morning incense offering, Offertory office, Liturgy of the Word, and that of the Faithful, respectively. During the latter, the Holy Spirit descends upon the faithful, sanctifying and preparing them to receive the heavenly Bridegroom. The Holy Spirit also descends upon the oblations transforming them into the Body and Blood of the Lord. At the end of all these orisons and supplications comes the most venerable moment, which is, uniting with the Body and Blood of our God and Savior, Jesus Christ. It is vital for us to realize the holiness and sanctity of this moment; it should not be taken lightly or out of habit; definitely not approached carelessly.

In his 13th-century book *The Fundamental Acts of the Ecclesiastical Etiquette*, Ibn Al-Assal summarizes the state of the communicant before receiving the Holy Mysteries; he identifies two conditions: believing that the materials have transformed to the Body and Blood of the Lord, and examining oneself and living a life of penitence.[1305] In addition, rubric dictates that believers should not come forth to partake of the Holies more than once a day and unless prepared, which includes abstaining from food and drink for certain number of hours (9 for healthy adults), a tradition that was introduced by Pope Damian [1306] (AD 576–605) [1307] and

---

[1305] Ibn Al-Assal, *The Fundamental Acts of the Ecclesiastical Etiquette*, published by Archdeacon Girgis Philotheos Ibrahim, 49-50.
[1306] Pope Damian of Alexandria, 35th Pope of Alexandria. Originally from Syria but became a monk in his early years and spent sixteen years in the Egyptian desert of Scete. He was very active in fighting views that he considered heretical.
[1307] Sobhy, Basilious (Father), *Introduction to the History of Coptic Rites*, 21.

confirmed by Pope Michael I[1308] (AD 743–767).[1309] However, until this era (8th century), some, especially in Upper Egypt, did not follow this preparatory period of fasting before communion.[1310] In the 10th century, Bishop Severus Ibn El-Muqaffaa reports that the pre-communion fasting time is 12 hours in Regular Days and 15 in Fast Days.[1311] However, the older custom prevailed.[1312]

After the final confession, the servant priest kisses the Sacred Host and then partakes of it. Consequently, he places a piece of the Host on the spoon for the assistant priest. Alternatively, he may also place a piece of the Host in the hand of the concelebrant.[1313] The altar servers then approach communion, followed by the rest of the chorus members. Afterward, the principal celebrant covers the paten, then holds the chalice. The order of receiving the Holy Blood is similar to that of receiving the Precious Body. The congregation then approaches communion, starting with men, followed by the women. During this time, an altar server, holding a lit taper, stands next to the Holy Mysteries.

After the principal celebrant serves the Holy Body to concelebrants, altar servers, and chorus, and prior to offering it to the congregation, he covers the Host, lifts the paten, and turns toward the people twice

---

[1308] Pope Michael I of Alexandria (also known as Khail) was the 46th Pope of Alexandria. When Pope Michael was thrown into prison by Abd al-Malik ibn Marwan ibn Musa bin Nusayr, King Kyriakos of Makuria (Nubian kingdom) marched to Egypt to free the Pope. However, once the Makurian army reached Egypt, the Pope was released from prison.
[1309] Sobhy, Ibid., 25.
[1310] Awad, Gregorius Rashidy Bishay (presbyter). (2022). Eucharistic Fasting in the Tradition of the Early Church and the Coptic Tradition. *Alexandria School*, 31(2), 198-199.
[1311] Awad, Ibid., 200.
[1312] Salib, Abdel Massieh (*Hegumen*), *The Holy Euchologion*, 195.
[1313] In the Early Church everyone, clergy and laity alike, received Holy Communion in the same manner: receiving the Body in their hands, placing it in their own mouth, and sipping directly from the chalice. In time, concern over the danger of crumbs being accidentally dropped on the floor or some of the Blood being spilt, lead to the use of tongs, with which the elements were mingled together and placed carefully into the mouths of the communicants. By the 4th century, the Church began to use the Communion spoon for the same practical reasons, and it is this practice that remains in place today (for clergy).

declaring, "the Holies for the holies, blessed be the Lord Jesus Christ, and the sanctification of the Holy Spirit, Amen." They respond saying, "Blessed is He who comes in the name of the Lord!" The significance of turning twice is to remind the faithful of the comings of our Lord Jesus Christ, the first for our salvation, and the second to judge the world.[1314]

During the distribution of the Holy Body, the priest declares to each person approaching, "The Body of Immanuel, this is true. Amen," to which the individual affirms saying, "Amen." For the Precious Blood, he proclaims, "The Blood of Immanuel our God, this is true. Amen;" the communicant confirms, "Amen." [1315] In another practice the communicant's ratification is, "I believe."[1316] After partaking of the Body and Blood, the faithful pray, "Our mouths are filled with joy, and our tongues with rejoicing for partaking in your eternal Mysteries O Lord,"[1317] after which they take a drink of water, a practice that is commonly known as "Conclusion of Communion." Father Samaan Ibn Koleil expounds that the water symbolizes the Holy Spirit;[1318] therefore, by drinking water, the Church reminds the communicants that after partaking of the Holy Mysteries, they must let the Holy Spirit, the source of life, work, and shine in them, for it is through the Spirit that we have been granted this grace and blessing.[1319]

[1314] Mettaos (Bishop), *The Spirituality of the Rite of the Liturgy of the Coptic Orthodox Church*, 211.
[1315] Pope Gabriel V mentioned another case in which the priest gives the Body soaked in the Blood to the young kids; in which case, he should say, "The Body and the Blood of Immanuel our God, this is true. Amen."
[1316] Anonymous, *Treatise on the Holy Oblation*, Vatican, MS Arabic 123, published by Father Alfons Abdalla the Franciscan, 376.
[1317] Anonymous, *Treatise*, Ibid., 377.
[1318] "Jesus answered, 'Everyone who drinks this water will be thirsty again, but whoever drinks the water I give them will never thirst. Indeed, the water I give them will become in them a spring of water welling up to eternal life.'" (John 4:13, 14). Also, "On the last and greatest day of the festival, Jesus stood and said in a loud voice, 'Let anyone who is thirsty come to me and drink. Whoever believes in me, as Scripture has said, rivers of living water will flow from within them.' By this he meant the Spirit, whom those who believed in him were later to receive. Up to that time the Spirit had not been given since Jesus had not yet been glorified." (John 7:37-39).
[1319] Bebawi, George H., *The Divine Liturgy*, 187.

The Liturgy of the Faithful

Pope Gabriel V explains the covering and then uncovering of the Holy Mysteries and turning toward the congregation, saying, "As for covering it with corporals, this denotes that John went to the tomb but did not enter; however, Peter did first. Both did not find the Lord's Body. As for uncovering it, this is a symbol of His appearance to Mary Magdalene in the garden. As for the reason that the priest turns (literally: with his face) toward the congregation, it indicates that our Master appeared to His disciples while the doors were locked."[1320]

In the early days, and until the 7th century, the priest would serve the Holy Body to the faithful in their hands, which is the reason for calling communion time "*Distribution* of the Holy Mysteries." However, some of the faithful would resort to taking the Holy Body back to their own homes, and this led to a sense of carelessness toward the Holy Mysteries. In response to this, the priests resorted to intinction[1321] and placing the Holies directly into the communicant's mouth; thereby ensuring that no one else could touch the Holy Mysteries. In the 9th century, the Church started to use the spoon for communion, which is the same rite we follow hitherto.[1322]

In antiquity, the diaconate rank was assigned more duties vis-à-vis communion. Until the 3rd century, the deacon, as noted earlier, used to assist the celebrant in dividing and distributing the Host to the communicants. This was later limited to the Precious Blood. Still, the altar servers were considered the exclusive servers of the altar. In the 4th century,

---

[1320] Gabriel V (Pope), *The Ritual Order*, BnF, MS 98 (AD 1411), fols. 72v-73r. Also, see: One of the Church Fathers, *The Trinitarian Mystery in Priesthood Ministry*, 29, 30. Seems that this was the common interpretation of this practice in the 15th century.

[1321] Intinction is the action of dipping each piece of the Body in the Blood so that a communicant receives both together.

[1322] The writer of *The Trinitarian Mystery in Priesthood Ministry* offers a symbolic reason for not giving the communicants the Holy Mysteries in their hands. He explains that this symbolizes the fact that after His resurrection, Jesus told Mary Magdalene not to touch Him (John 20:17). Review: One of the Church Fathers, *The Trinitarian Mystery in Priesthood Ministry*, 30. However, I think that this analogy is far fetched.

precisely in the Council of Nicaea (AD 325), the role of the deacon was minimized,[1323] which marked the gradual atrophy of the role and function of the diaconate order. Today, the "Full" deacon (διάκονος) is permitted to hold the chalice, but not the Host.

Communion commences with the chorus and the congregation chanting Psalm 150. The recitation of this Psalm dates to as far as the 2nd century, as documented by Saint Clement of Alexandria.[1324] Depending on the ecclesiastical season, Psalm 150 is intoned in a diversity of melodies. Specific tunes are employed for Regular Days,[1325] month of Kiahk, Fast of Nineveh and Lenten weekdays (apart from the first Monday and last Friday of Lent), Saturdays and Sunday of the Lent (which is also chanted on the first Monday and last Friday of the Lent), Palm Sunday (and the feasts of the Cross), and finally Feast Days. Next, in Regular Days, the hymn Ⲕ̀ⲥⲙⲁⲣⲱⲟⲩⲧ (Blessed are You) is sung. Cantor Tawfik Youssef reported that Cantor Mikhail the Great knew a major tune for this hymn, but unfortunately did not pass it on to any of his disciples, and as such, it was lost. This is then followed by the hymns Ⲡⲓⲱⲓⲕ (The Bread),[1326] Ⲭⲉ ϥ̀ⲥⲙⲁⲣⲱⲟⲩⲧ (Blessed be), and other applicable melodies, respectively, until communion is accomplished.

After the faithful have partaken of the Holy Body and the Precious Blood, the president washes the altar vessels in a process called Ablution of

---

[1323] The eighteenth canon of the Council of Nicaea reads, "It has come to the knowledge of the holy and great Synod that, in some districts and cities, the deacons administer the Eucharist to the elders, whereas neither canon nor custom permits that they who have no right to offer should give the Body of Christ to them that do offer. And this also has been made known, that certain deacons now touch the Eucharist even before the bishops. Let all such practices be utterly done away, and let the deacons remain within their own bounds, knowing that they are the ministers of the bishop and the inferiors of the elders. Let them receive the Eucharist according to their order, after the elders, and let either the bishop or the elder administer to them. Furthermore, let not the deacons sit among the elders, for that is contrary to canon and order. And if, after this decree, anyone shall refuse to obey, let him be deposed from the diaconate."
[1324] Clement of Alexandria (Saint), *Paedagopus* 2:4.
[1325] In Regular Days, the last part of Psalm 150, i.e., (Ⲡⲓⲱⲟⲩ ⲫⲁ Ⲡⲉⲛⲛⲟⲩϯ ⲡⲉ—glory be to our God), may be chanted in its melismatic tune, if time permits.
[1326] In other seasons, hymns specific to the occasion are chanted instead.

the Vessels.[1327] He then places some water in his hands, insufflates on it, and asks the concelebrants to do the same. After this, he sprinkles some of the water on the altar, then says, "O the angel of this sacrifice, flying up to the highest with this hymn, remember us before the Lord, that He may forgive us our sins." Still facing east, he sprinkles the remainder of the water westwards toward the congregation. From the congregations' standpoint, this scene reminds them of the River of Life flowing from the throne of God, as described by Saint John the Theologian.[1328] It is also a precise implementation of the River from the Temple described by Ezekiel, "The man brought me back to the entrance to the temple, and I saw water coming out from under the threshold of the temple toward the east. The water was coming down from under the south side of the temple, south of the altar" (Ezekiel 41:1). Placing the water on the altar and the Ark signifies the conclusion of the liturgy and the breaking of the "fast" for the altar, declaring that the altar cannot be used again until the next day. Much like communicants who abstain from food in preparation for receiving the Holy Mysteries, the altar and its vessels abstain from any other services prior to the liturgy.

The principal celebrant then wipes his hands on his beard. In the presence of assistant priests, he also touches their beards to give them the blessing of the angel's dismissal, as opposed to praying on them, since their beards represent their consecration to the ministerial life. In return, they too touch his beard, saying, "Glory to God in the highest, peace on earth, and good will toward men." After this, the celebrant sprinkles water on the

---

[1327] The author of *The Trinitarian Mystery in Priesthood Ministry* reports a lost tradition that might have been local to a specific region. He says that after the faithful have partaken of the Holy Mysteries, the priest holds the paten and circuits the altar once, as an indication of Jesus' appearance to the disciples (John 20:19-21). See: One of the Church Fathers, *The Trinitarian Mystery in Priesthood Ministry*, 30.

[1328] "Then the angel showed me the river of the water of life, as clear as crystal, flowing from the throne of God and of the Lamb" (Revelation 22:1).

congregation. It is worth noting that in ancient Egypt, sprinkling of water was understood as a means of cleansing from sins and granting life.[1329] The water also denotes the work of the Holy Spirit in the church, reminding us that after partaking of the Holy Mysteries, the gifts of the Holy Spirit work within us. It is important that communicants are reminded of this fact every time the prayer of a liturgy is concluded, realizing the significance of receiving this water and committing to allowing the Holy Spirit to work in them. Pope Cyril III mentions an older tradition than sprinkling of the water;[1330] he writes, "after washing his hands in the paten, and drinking its content, he wipes the faces of the congregants one by one according to the established custom."[1331]

During the sprinkling of water, the congregation recites the Concluding Canon. In addition to the Concluding Canons particular to Regular Days, each liturgical season has a specific one. After the recitation of the Concluding Canon, the celebrant delivers the final blessing, the people recite the Lord's Prayer, and then the celebrant dismisses the faithful. It is interesting to note that until the 16th century, it was the responsibility of the deacon to dismiss the worshippers saying, "go in peace, the peace of God be with you,"[1332] but this is now uttered by the priest.[1333] Finally, the priest distributes the antidoron[1334] (the remainder of

---

[1329] Budge, E.A. Wallis, *The Liturgy of Funerary Offerings*, 43.
[1330] Father Misael of the Paromeos Monastery believes that the author of this work (i.e., *The beginners' Guide and Discipline for Laity*) is Abu Is-haq Ibrahim Ibn Al-Assal. For more details, see *Alexandria School*, 24(1), 122-124.
[1331] Misael of the Paromeos Monastery (Father). (2018). The Beginners' Guide and Discipline for Laity. *Alexandria School*, 24(1), 142.
[1332] Athanasius of Saint Macarius Monastery (Father), *Summary of the Liturgical History of the Church of Alexandria (Part 2)*, 306.
[1333] Patriarch Ignatius Ephrem II Rahmani mentions that the congregation responds saying (literally), "Amen Amen to one hundred years." See: Ignatius Ephrem II Rahmani (Patriarch of the Syriac Catholic Church), *Les Liturgies Orientales et Occidentales*, 562. Contemporary rubrics, however, ignore this instruction.
[1334] In the Coptic Church, there is no special prayer uttered over the antidoron; however, in other traditions, as in the Syriac Church, a special blessing is recited over the antidoron before it is cut into fragments and distributed to the believers. See: Ignatius Ephrem II Rahmani (Patriarch of the Syriac Catholic Church), *Les Liturgies Orientales et Occidentales*, 329.

the *Prosphora*). The believers piously take the antidoron, kissing the priest's right hand, and exit the church.

Summary of the Liturgy of the Faithful

The Liturgy of the Faithful commences with the recitation of the Creed, followed by the Prayer of Reconciliation, during which the *Adam Aspazmos* is chanted, and the congregation greets one another with a Holy Kiss. After that, the congregation sings, "Through the Intercessions," followed by "A mercy of peace, a sacrifice of praise." Afterward, the Eucharistic Dialogue and the Preface are prayed, to which the congregation responds with the Sanctus. In the Liturgy of Saint Cyril, the Preface (also called the Grand Thanksgiving Prayer) is quite long because it contains the Intercessory Prayers, which include the Litanies, the Commemoration of Saints, the Diptych, and the Supplications.

In the liturgies of Saint Basil and Saint Gregory, after the Sanctus, the Salvation Narrative is prayed; however, in the Liturgy of Saint Cyril, the Minor Epiclesis is prayed instead. After this, in all three liturgies, the Institution Narrative, the *Anamnesis* and the Major Epiclesis are prayed. In the Liturgy of Saint Cyril, both parts of the Major Epiclesis are said consecutively. However, in the Basilian and Gregorian liturgies, the two parts of the Major Epiclesis are separated by the Intercessory Prayers (the Supplications are a peculiarity of the Gregorian liturgy). In all three liturgies, the Introduction to the Fraction is prayed, followed by the Fraction, the Prayer of Confession, and finally the partaking of the Holy Mysteries.

CHAPTER SEVEN

Ancient Eucharistic Prayers

The Structure of the Anaphora in the Ante-Nicene Era and How it Developed in the Fourth Century

For though I am alive while I write to you, yet I am eager to die. My love has been crucified, and there is no fire in me desiring to be fed; but there is within me a water that lives and speaks, saying to me inwardly, Come to the Father. I have no delight in corruptible food, nor in the pleasures of this life. I desire the bread of God, the heavenly bread, the bread of life, which is the flesh of Jesus Christ, the Son of God, who became afterwards of the seed of David and Abraham; and I desire the drink of God, namely His blood, which is incorruptible love and eternal life.

—**Ignatius of Antioch**

Introduction

In the first three centuries, stemmed from the Last Supper prayers, bishops offered Eucharistic prayers in an extemporized fashion. One of the liturgical traits of the 4th century, however, was the documentation and standardization of written texts of the liturgical prayers. This was a need more than luxury; "a process closely related to the need for liturgical texts to express orthodox teaching against Trinitarian and Christological heresy and (undoubtedly) to the increasing lack of proficient and prayerful extemporizers."[1335] As such, documented *anaphoras* before the 4th century can hardly be found.

In this chapter, I will present a succinct description of some ancient Eucharistic prayers (fragments or complete *anaphoras*), along with their full text. The purpose of this is to help the reader understand how Eucharistic prayers evolved, which elements are old, and which are more recent development, the shape and content of the early Eucharist, and how the Alexandrian structure of the *anaphora* was always different from the Syro-Byzantine one. For each *anaphora*, or fragment of it, I will have a short background about it, and where it was found with some information regarding its dating. The text of the prayer will then follow. Finally, I will have a diagram demonstrating the general structure of the prayer. Prayers under this investigation are: the Eucharistic Prayer of the Didache, Justin Martyr Prayer, the *Anaphora* of the Apostolic Tradition, the *Anaphora* of Addai and Mari, the Sacramentary of Serapion, the *Anaphora* of Saint Mark—Strasbourg Papyrus, the *Anaphora* of the Apostolic Constitutions, the *Anaphora* of the Deir Balyzeh Papyrus, and the *Anaphora* of Saint Thomas the Apostle.

[1335] Paul F. Bradshaw, Maxwell E. Johnson, *The Eucharistic Liturgies: Their Evolution and Interpretation*, 70.

Additionally, we will have a closer look at the liturgy of Saint Mark from different old manuscripts and trace its development. We will attempt to reconstruct it in its pristine format. This could assist future studies in this field and identify the parts that Saint Cyril added.

The Didache

The Didache (Koine Greek: Διδαχή) or the *Teaching of the Twelve Apostles* (Didachē means "Teaching") is a brief early Christian treatise, dated by most scholars to the mid to late first century. The author of this work is unknown. The text, parts of which constitute the oldest extant written catechism, has three main sections dealing with Christian ethics, rituals such as baptism and Eucharist (chapters 9 and 10), and Church organization. It is considered the first example of the genre of the Church Orders. The Didache is part of the category of second-generation Christian writings known as the Apostolic Fathers. Lost for centuries, a Greek manuscript of the Didache was rediscovered in AD 1873 by Philotheos Bryennios, Metropolitan of Nicomedia in the Codex Hierosolymitanus. A Latin version of the first five chapters was discovered in AD 1900 by J. Schlecht. Hitchcock and Brown produced the first English translation in March AD 1884.[1336]

THANKSGIVING

Concerning the Eucharist, give thanks this way. First, concerning the cup:
We thank You, our Father, for the holy vine of David Your servant, which You made known to us through Jesus Your servant. To You be the glory forever.

[1336] "Didache." *Wikipedia*. Wikipedia.org. n.p. Web. 15 May 2016.

Next, concerning the broken bread:
We thank You, our Father, for the life and knowledge which You made known to us through Jesus Your servant. To You be the glory forever. Even as this broken bread was scattered over the hills, and was gathered together and became one, so let Your church be gathered together from the ends of the earth into Your kingdom. To You is the glory and the power through Jesus Christ forever.

Allow no one to eat or drink of your Eucharist, unless they have been baptized in the name of the Lord. For concerning this, the Lord has said, "Do not give what is holy to dogs."

After the Eucharist when you are filled, give thanks this way:
We thank You, holy Father, for Your holy name which You enshrined in our hearts, and for the knowledge and faith and immortality that You made known to us through Jesus your servant. To You be the glory forever. You, Master Almighty, have created all things for Your name's sake. You gave food and drink to all people for enjoyment, that they might give thanks to You; but to us You freely give spiritual food and drink and life eternal through Jesus, Your servant. Before all things we thank You because You are mighty. To You be the glory forever.

LITANIES

Remember, Lord, Your church. Deliver it from all evil and make it perfect in Your love, and gather it from the four winds sanctified for Your kingdom which You have prepared for it.

DOXOLOGY

For Yours is the power and the glory forever. Let grace come, and let this world pass away! Hosanna to the Son of David!

CONCLUSION

If anyone is holy, let him come; if anyone is not holy, let him repent. Maranatha! Amen.

But permit the prophets to make thanksgiving as much as they desire.

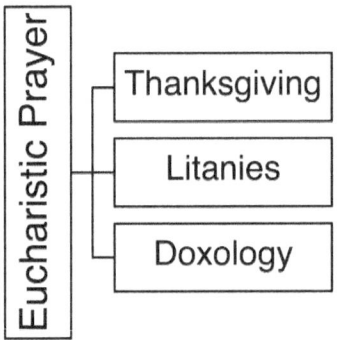

High-level structure of the Didache Eucharistic Prayer

Justin Martyr

In his First Apology chapter 67 on the "weekly worship of the Christians," Justin Martyr describes the structure of the Christian worship at his time (2nd century). The First Apology was addressed to the Roman Emperor Antoninus Pius. It is dated to AD 150 and stands today as one of the most important documents of early Christian worship. Robert Grant has claimed that it was made in response to the Martyrdom of Polycarp, which occurred around the same time as the Apology was written.[1337] The document does not include details of ceremonial practices or prayer assignments among other rituals. Yet, its general structure can be compared to that found in the early Syrian rite, precisely the *Didache*.[1338]

THE STRUCTURE OF THE EUCHARIST AT HIS TIME

And on the day called Sunday, all who live in cities or in the country gather together to one place, and the memoirs of the apostles or the writings of the prophets are read, as long as time permits; then, when the reader has ceased, the president verbally instructs, and exhorts to the imitation of these good things. Then we all rise together and pray, and, as we before said, when our prayer is ended, bread and wine and water are brought, and the president in like manner offers prayers and thanksgivings, according to his ability, and the people assent, saying "Amen;"[1339] and there is a distribution to each, and a participation of that over which thanks have been given, and to those who are absent a portion is sent by the deacons. And they who are well to do, and willing, give what each thinks fit; and what is collected is deposited with the president, who succors the orphans and widows and those who, through sickness or any other cause, are in want, and those who are in bonds and the strangers sojourning among us, and in a word takes care of all who are in need.

[1337] "First Apology of Justin Martyr." *Wikipedia*. Wikipedia.org. n.p. Web. 10 June 2016.
[1338] Bradshaw, Paul, *The Search for the Origins of Christian Worship* (2nd Ed.), 159-161.
[1339] In Chapter 65 of his *First Apology*, Justin Martyr provides more details; he explains, "There is then brought to the president of the brethren bread and a cup of wine mixed with water; and he, taking them, gives praise and glory to the Father of the universe, through the name of the Son and of the Holy Ghost, and offers thanks at considerable length for our being counted worthy to receive these things at His hands. And when he has concluded the prayers and thanksgivings, all the people present express their assent by saying "Amen." This word "Amen" answers in the Hebrew language to γένοιτο [so be it]. And when the president has given thanks, and all the people have expressed their assent, those who are called by us deacons give to each of those present to partake of the bread and wine mixed with water over which the thanksgiving was pronounced, and to those who are absent they carry away a portion."

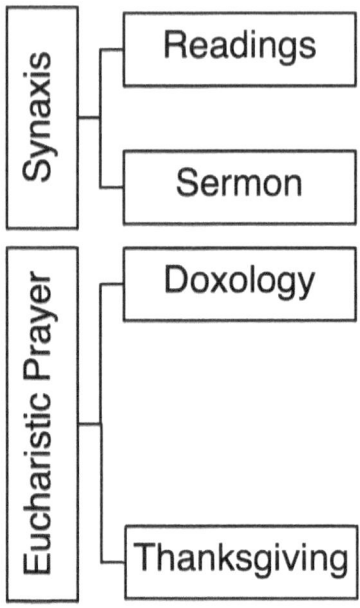

High-level structure of Justin Martyr's Eucharistic Prayer

The Anaphora of the Apostolic Tradition

The *anaphora* of the *Apostolic Tradition*, attributed to Hippolytus of Rome, is an ancient Christian anaphora, which is found in chapter four of the *Apostolic Tradition*. It should not be confused with the Syriac Orthodox *anaphora* of the Twelve Apostles. The *anaphora* of the *Apostolic Tradition* reflects the liturgical tradition of Rome in the 3rd century.[1340] However, Paul Bradshaw challenges this supposition; he states, "it is very doubtful whether the document really originates from Rome, and even if it does, whether it represents what was the actual practice of the period and not merely the unfulfilled desires of some individual or group."[1341]

[1340] "Anaphora of the Apostolic Tradition." *Wikipedia*. Wikipedia.org. n.p. Web. 10 June 2016.
[1341] Bradshaw, Paul, *The Search for the Origins of Christian Worship* (2nd Ed.), 161.

Due to its *advanced* structure (inclusion of Salvation Narrative, Institution Narrative, Anamnesis, and Epiclesis) at early date, this prayer attracted the attention scholars. Yet, some, like Paul Bradshaw, argues that the final appearance—as per the available text today—is not a product of the 3rd century but rather the mid-4th century.[1342] An example of a 4th-century interpolation is the invocation of the Holy Spirit.[1343]

EUCHARISTIC DIALOGUE

The Bishop:
The Lord be with you.

The Congregation:
And with your spirit.

The Bishop:
Lift up your hearts.

The Congregation:
We lift them up to the Lord.

The Bishop:
Let us give thanks to the Lord.

The Congregation:
It is right and proper.

[1342] Bradshaw, Paul F. (1997). Introduction: The Evolution of Early Anaphoras. In Bradshaw, Paul F. (Ed.), *Essays on Early Eastern Eucharistic Prayers*, 11.
[1343] Dix, Dom Gregory, *The Shape of the Liturgy*, 158.

THANKSGIVING

The Bishop:

We give thanks to You, O God, through Your beloved Son Jesus Christ, whom You have sent to us in former times as Savior, Redeemer, and Messenger of Your plan; who is Your inseparable Word, through whom You have created all things; and whom, in Your good pleasure, You have sent down from heaven into the womb of a virgin; and who, having been conceived, became incarnate and was shown to be Your Son, born of the Holy Spirit and the Virgin; who fulfilling Your will and acquiring for You a holy people, stretched out His hands in suffering, in order to liberate from sufferings those who believe in You;

SALVATION NARRATIVE

The Bishop:

who, when He was delivered to voluntary suffering, in order to destroy death and to break the chains of the devil, to tread down hell beneath His feet, to bring out the righteous into light, and set the limit (or term), and to manifest the resurrection.

INSTITUTION NARRATIVE

The Bishop:

Taking bread, gave thanks to You and said, "Take, eat, for this is my Body which is broken for you." Likewise, the cup, saying, "This is my Blood which is shed for you,

ANAMNESIS

The Bishop:

whenever you do this, do it in memory of me." Therefore, remembering His death and resurrection,

OFFERING

The Bishop:

we offer You this bread and this cup, giving thanks to You for accounting us worthy to stand before You and to serve as Your priests.

EPICLESIS (INVOCATION OF THE HOLY SPIRIT)

The Bishop:

And we ask You to send Your Holy Spirit upon the offering of Your Holy church. In their gathering together, grant to all those who partake of Your holy mysteries that they may be filled with the Holy Spirit for the strengthening of their faith in truth;

DOXOLOGY/RESULTS OF THE INVOCATION

The Bishop:

in order that we may praise You and glorify You through Your Son Jesus Christ, through whom be to You glory and honor with the Holy Spirit in Your holy church now and throughout all ages. Amen.

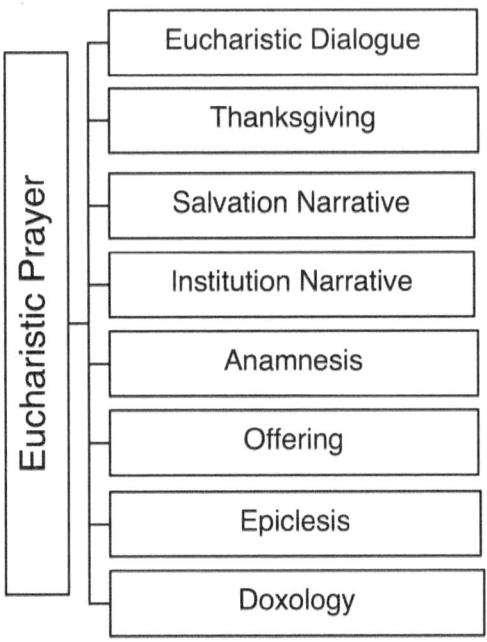

High-level structure of the Apostolic Tradition Eucharistic Prayer

The Anaphora of Addai and Mari

Christian Syria is known for its cultural diversity, primarily, West Syrian, centered in Antioch, South Syrian, in Jerusalem, and East Syrian, in Edessa.[1344] The Liturgy of Addai and Mari belongs to the East Syrians, which is in regular use, even if in different versions, in the Assyrian Church of the East and Ancient Church of the East, the Syro-Malabar Catholic Church, and the Chaldean Catholic Church.[1345] This *Anaphora* is traditionally attributed to Saint Addai (disciple of Saint Thomas the Apostle) and Saint Mari (a disciple of Saint Addai). According to a study

---

[1344] Wilson, Stephen B. (1997). The Anaphora of the Apostles Addai and Mari. In Bradshaw, Paul F. (Ed.), *Essays on Early Eastern Eucharistic Prayers*, 19.
[1345] "Liturgy of Addai and Mari." *Wikipedia*. Wikipedia.org. n.p. Web. 21 June 2016.

conducted by R.H. Connolly, this liturgy is the source of the Malabar liturgy used in India.[1346] The *Anaphora* of Addai and Mari is of particular interest, being one of the oldest in Christianity, possibly dating back to the 3rd-century. Edward Ratcliff argues that the extant text of this immemorial liturgy includes later interpolations (Intercessory Prayers, Sanctus, and Epiclesis) that were not in its pristine shape. Recent discoveries of older manuscripts confirm Ratcliff's conclusions. Additionally, he asserts that, in its primitive form, it was addressed to God the Son, an illation that Bernard Botte disagrees with; the latter argues that it was addressed to both the Father and the Son. The primitive formula of this prayer, Hieronymous Engberding argues, is the source for not only the extant text of this liturgy, but also to the Maronite liturgy.[1347]

EUCHARISTIC DIALOGUE

The Bishop:
The grace of our Lord Jesus Christ, the love of God the Father, and the fellowship of the Holy Spirit be with us all, now, at all times and forever and ever.

The Congregation:
Amen.

The Bishop:
Lift up your minds.

[1346] Wilson, Ibid., 20-21.
[1347] Wilson, Ibid., 21-23.

The Congregation:
Towards you, O God of Abraham, Isaac, and Israel, O glorious King!

The Bishop:
The oblation is offered to God, the Lord of all.

The Congregation:
It is fit and right.

THANKSGIVING

The Bishop:
Worthy of praise from every mouth and thanksgiving from every tongue is the adorable and glorious Name of the Father and the Son and the Holy Spirit, who created the world in His grace and its inhabitants in His mercifulness, and saved mankind in His compassion, and dealt very graciously with mortals. Your majesty, O my Lord, a thousand thousands of those on high bow down and worship and myriad myriads holy angels and hosts of spiritual beings, ministers of fire and spirit, praise Your name with the holy Cherubim and Seraphim, ceasing shouting, praising, calling to one another and saying: Holy holy holy Lord God of hosts heaven and earth are full of His praises.

And with these heavenly hosts we give thanks to You, O my Lord, even we, Your servants, weak and frail and miserable, for that You have given us great grace past recompense in that You put on our manhood that You might quicken it by Your godhead, and have exalted our low estate, and restored our fall, and raised our mortality, and forgiven our trespasses, and justified our sinfulness, and enlightened our knowledge, and, O our Lord and God, have condemned our enemies, and granted victory to the weakness of our frail nature in the overflowing mercies of Your grace.

OFFERING

The Bishop:

Do You, O my Lord, in Your many and unspeakable mercies make a good and acceptable memorial for all the just and righteous fathers who have been well pleasing in Your sight, in the commemoration of the body and blood of Your Christ which we offer unto You on Your pure and holy altar as You have taught us, and grant us Your tranquility and Your peace all the days of the world.

You, O our Lord and our God, grant us Your tranquility and Your peace all the days of the world that all the inhabitants of the earth may know You that You are the only true God the Father, and that You sent our Lord Jesus Christ Your Son and Your beloved. And He, our Lord and God, came and, in His life-giving gospel, taught us all the purity and holiness of the prophets and the apostles and the martyrs and the confessors and the bishops and the doctors and the presbyters and the deacons and all the children of the holy catholic church, even them that have been signed with the living sign of holy baptism.

ANAMNESIS

The Bishop:

And we also, O my Lord, the weak and frail and miserable servants who are gathered together in Your name, both stand before You at this time and have received the example which is from You delivered unto us, rejoicing and praising and exalting and commemorating and celebrating this great and fearful and holy and life-giving and divine mystery of the passion and the death and the burial and the resurrection of our Lord, our Savior, Jesus Christ.

EPICLESIS (INVOCATION OF THE HOLY SPIRIT)

The Bishop:

And may there come, O my Lord, Your Holy Spirit and rest upon this offering of Your servants and bless it and hallow it that it be to us, O my Lord, for the pardon of offences and the remission of sins and for the great hope of resurrection from the dead and for new life in the kingdom of heaven with all those who have been well pleasing in Your sight.

DOXOLOGY—SECOND PART (RESULTS) OF THE EPICLESIS

The Bishop:

And for all this great and marvelous dispensation toward us, we will give You thanks and praise You without ceasing in Your Church redeemed by the precious blood of Your Christ, with unclosed mouths and open faces lifting up praise and honor and confession and worship to Your living and holy and life-giving name now and ever and world without end.

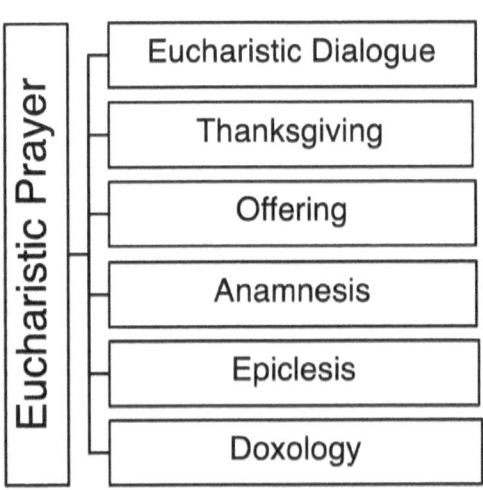

High-level structure of the Addai and Mari Eucharistic Prayer

The Anaphora of the Barcelona Papyrus

The Barcelona Papyrus is a 4th-century papyrus codex, coming from Egypt. It is the oldest extant liturgical manuscript containing a complete *anaphora*. This *anaphora* could be related to some Pachomian monastery. It includes all the typical elements of a developed *anaphora*. Following the Alexandrian tradition, the epiclesis in the *anaphora* of Barcelona is placed before the Institution Narrative.[1348] Michael Zheltov suggests that the text of the *anaphora* dates back to the 3rd century and might have been edited by Saint Athanasius the Apostolic.[1349]

EUCHARISTIC DIALOGUE

The Bishop:
Up our hearts.

The Congregation:
We have to the Lord.

The Bishop:
Let us also give thanks.

The Congregation:
Fitting and right.

[1348] "Barcelona Papyrus." *Wikipedia*. Wikipedia.org. n.p. Web. 16 August 2016.
[1349] Michael Zheltov, *The Anaphora and the Thanksgiving Prayer from the Barcelona Papyrus: An Underestimated Testimony to the Anaphoral History in the Fourth Century*, Vol. 62, No. 5 (2008), 497.

THANKSGIVING

The Bishop:

It is fitting and right to praise You, to bless You, to hymn You, to give You thanks, O Master, God Pantocrator of our Lord Jesus Christ, Who created all things from non-existence into being, all; heaven and the earth, the sea, and all that is in them, through Your beloved child Jesus Christ, our Lord, through Whom You have called us from darkness into light, from ignorance to knowledge of the glory of His name, from decay of death into incorruption, into life eternal; Who sits on the chariot, Cherubim and Seraphim before it, Who is attended by thousands of thousands and myriads of myriads of angels, archangels, thrones and dominions, hymning and glorifying, with whom we are also hymning, saying;

Holy, Holy, Holy, Lord of Sabaoth! Heaven and earth are full of Your glory, in which You have glorified us through Your Only-Begotten, the firstborn of every creature, Jesus Christ, our Lord, Who sits on the right hand of Your greatness in Heaven, Who is coming to judge the living and the dead, the remembrance of Whose death we do.

OFFERING

The Bishop:

Through Him we offer You these Your creations, the bread and the cup:

EPICLESIS (INVOCATION OF THE HOLY SPIRIT)

The Bishop:

We ask and beseech You to send onto them Your Holy and Comforter Spirit from Heaven, to represent them materially and to make the bread the Body of Christ and the cup the Blood of Christ, of the New Covenant.

INSTITUTION NARRATIVE

The Bishop:

As He Himself, when He was about to hand Himself, having taken bread and given thanks, broke it and gave it to His disciples, saying: 'Take, eat, this is My body: likewise, after supper, having taken a cup and given thanks, He gave it to them, saying: 'Take, drink the blood, which is shed for many for remission of sins.'

ANAMNESIS

The Bishop:

And we also do the same in Your remembrance, like those whenever we meet together, we make the remembrance of You, of the holy mystery of our Teacher and King and Savior Jesus Christ.

DOXOLOGY/RESULTS OF THE INVOCATION

The Bishop:

Even so, we pray to You, Master, that in blessing You will bless and in sanctifying sanctify... For all communicating from them for undivided faith, for communication of incorruption, for communion of the Holy Spirit, for perfection of belief and truth, for fulfillment of all Your will, so that in this and again we will glorify Your all-revered and all-holy name, through Your sanctified Child, our Lord Jesus Christ, through Whom glory be to You, power unto the unblended ages of ages. Amen.

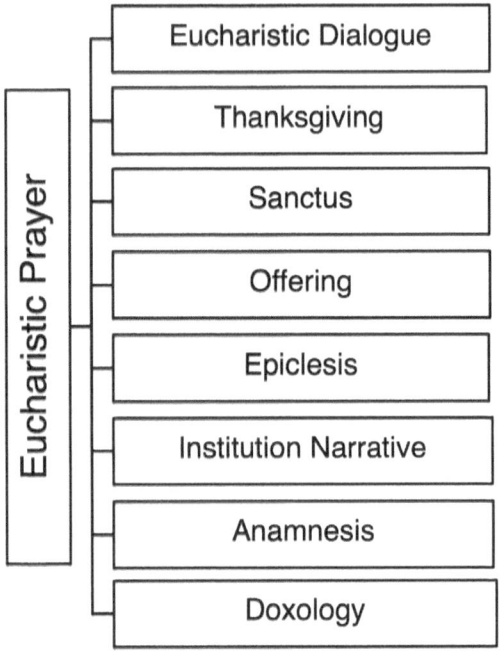

High-level structure of the Barcelona Papyrus *Anaphora*

The Sacramentary of Serapion

The Sacramentary of Serapion is a work of Saint Serapion, bishop of Thmuis (Modern: Tell el-Timai, about five miles north-west of Sinbellawein) in the Nile Delta from 339 until he died after AD 360. He was a prominent supporter of Saint Athanasius in the struggle against Arianism. This sacramentary, contained in a collection of Egyptian documents in an 11th-century manuscript at the Laura on Mount Athos, was published by A. Dmitrijewskij in AD 1894. It is a celebrant's book, containing thirty prayers belonging to the Eucharist (19-30, 1-6), baptism (7-11, 15, 16), ordination (12-14), benediction of oil, bread and water (17), and burial (18), omitting the fixed structural formulae of the rites, the parts of the other ministers, and almost all rubrication, except what is implied in the titles of the prayers. The book is important as the second earliest liturgical collection on so large a scale (after the *Anaphora* of *the Apostolic Tradition*), and as belonging to Egypt, where evidence for 4th-century ritual is scanty as compared with Syria.[1350] In his *The Shape of the Liturgy*, Father Gregory Dix suggests that, although the extant text of this liturgy comes from before AD 350, it is a revision of an even older Egyptian text from the 3rd century.[1351]

EUCHARISTIC DIALOGUE

The Bishop:
The Lord be with you.

The Congregation:
And with your spirit.

The Bishop:
Lift up your hearts.

The Congregation:
We have them with the Lord.

The Bishop:
Let us give thanks to the Lord.

The Congregation:
It is meet and right.

[1350] "Sacramentary of Serapion of Thmuis." *Wikipedia*. Wikipedia.org. n.p. Web. 25 April 2016.
[1351] Dix, Dom Gregory, *The Shape of the Liturgy*, 162.

THANKSGIVING

The Bishop:

It is meet and right to praise, to hymn, to glorify You the uncreated Father of the only begotten Jesus Christ. We praise You, uncreated God, who is unsearchable, ineffable, incomprehensible by any created substance. We praise You who are known of Your Son[1352], the only begotten, who through him is spoken of and interpreted and made known to created nature. We praise You who knows the Son and reveals to the Saints the glories that are about Him: who is known of Your begotten Word, and is brought to the sight and interpreted to the understanding of the Saints. We praise You, unseen Father, provider of immortality. You are the fount of life, the fount of light, the fount of all grace and all truth, lover of men, lover of the poor, who reconciles Yourself to all, and draws all to Yourself through the advent of Your beloved Son. We beseech You make us living men. Give us a spirit of light, that we may know You, the true (God), and Him whom You did send, (even) Jesus Christ.[1353]

Give us (the) Holy Spirit, that we may be able to tell forth and to enunciate Your unspeakable mysteries. May the Lord Jesus speak in us and (the) Holy Spirit, and hymn You through us.

For You are far above all rule and authority and power and dominion, and every name that is named, not only in this world but also in that which is to come.[1354] Beside You stand thousand thousands and myriad myriads

---

[1352] "All things have been committed to me by my Father. No one knows the Son except the Father, and no one knows the Father except the Son and those to whom the Son chooses to reveal Him" (Matthew 11:27); "just as the Father knows me and I know the Father" (John 10:15).

[1353] "Now this is eternal life: that they know you, the only true God, and Jesus Christ, whom you have sent." (John 17:3).

[1354] "far above all rule and authority, power and dominion, and every name that is invoked, not only in the present age but also in the one to come." (Ephesians 1:21).

of angels[1355], archangels, thrones, dominions, principalities, powers[1356]: by You stand the two most honorable six-winged seraphim, with two wings covering the face, and with two the feet[1357], and with two flying and crying Holy[1358], with whom receive also our cry of "holy" as we say: Holy, holy, holy, Lord of Sabaoth, full is the heaven and the earth of Your glory. Full is the heaven, full also is the earth of Your excellent glory. Lord of Hosts[1359], fill also this sacrifice with Your power and Your participation:

OFFERING

The Bishop:

To You have we offered this living sacrifice[1360], this bloodless oblation. To You we have offered this bread the likeness of the Body of the Only-begotten.

INSTITUTION NARRATIVE

The Bishop:

This bread is the likeness of the holy Body, because the Lord Jesus Christ in the night in which He was betrayed took bread and broke and gave to His disciples saying, "Take it and eat, this is my Body which is being broken for you for remission of sins". Wherefore we also making the likeness of the death have offered the bread, and beseech You through this sacrifice, be reconciled to all of us and be merciful, God of truth: and as this bread

---

[1355] "Thousands upon thousands attended Him; ten thousand times ten thousand stood before Him." (Daniel 7:10); "You have come to thousands upon thousands of angels in joyful assembly" (Hebrews 12:22).

[1356] Literally: rules, authorities.

[1357] In his work *Primitive Consecration Prayers*, Gregory Dix writes, "we can now see that Sarapion's Preface still faithfully reflects the old idea that the wings of the Seraphim veil 'The Face' (i.e., of God), while *St. Mark* was adapted to the later notion of 'their faces.'"

[1358] Isaiah 6:2, 3.

[1359] Literally: powers.

[1360] "Therefore, I urge you, brothers and sisters, in view of God's mercy, to offer your bodies as a living sacrifice, holy and pleasing to God—this is your true and proper worship." (Romans 12:1).

had been scattered on the top of the mountains and gathered together came to be one, so also gather Your holy Church out of every nation and every country and every city and village and house and make one living catholic church[1361]. We have offered also the cup, the likeness of the blood, because the Lord Jesus Christ, taking a cup after supper[1362], said to His own disciples, "Take it, drink, this is the new covenant, which is my Blood, which is being shed for you for remission of sins." Wherefore we have also offered the cup, presenting a likeness of the Blood.

EPICLESIS (INVOCATION OF THE LOGOS)

The Bishop:
God of truth, let Your holy Word come upon this bread that the bread may become body of the Word, and upon this cup that the cup may become blood of the Truth; and make all who communicate to receive a medicine of life for the healing of every sickness and for the strengthening of all advancement and virtue, not for condemnation, God of truth, and not for censure and reproach. For we have invoked You, the uncreated, through the Only-begotten in (the) Holy Spirit.

LITANIES

The Bishop:
Let this people receive mercy, let it be counted worthy of advancement, let angels be sent forth as companions to the people for bringing to naught of the evil one and for establishment of the Church.

[1361] This is a clear influence of the Thanksgiving prayer of the Didache.
[1362] Luke 22:20; 1 Corinthians 11:25.

DIPTYCH

The Bishop:

We intercede also on behalf of all who have been laid to rest, whose memorial we are making.

After the recitation of the names:

Sanctify these souls: for You know all. Sanctify all (souls) laid to rest in the Lord. And number them with all Your holy powers and give to them a place and a mansion in Your kingdom.

LITANIES

The Bishop:

Receive also the thanksgiving (Eucharist) of the people and bless those who have offered the Offerings and the thanksgivings, and grant health and soundness and cheerfulness and all advancement of soul and body to this whole people.

DOXOLOGY/RESULTS OF THE INVOCATION

The Bishop:

Through the Only-begotten Jesus Christ in (the) Holy Spirit.

The Congregation:

As it was and is and shall be to generations of generations and to all the ages of the ages. Amen.

After the (Lord's) prayer (comes) the fraction and in the fraction a prayer.

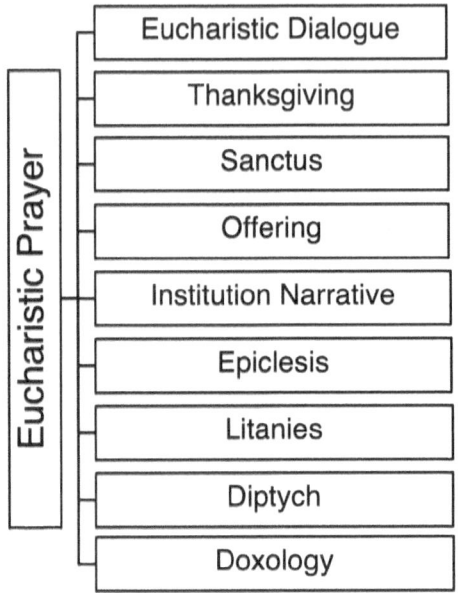

High-level structure of the Liturgy of Saint Serapion

The Anaphora of Saint Mark—Strasbourg Papyrus

The Strasbourg papyrus is a papyrus made of six fragments on a single leaf written in Greek and conserved at the Strasbourg National University Library in France, cataloged Gr. 254. It was first edited in AD 1928. The Strasbourg papyrus contains an ancient version of the Alexandrine *Anaphora* of Saint Mark. The Papyrus was probably written in the 4th or 5th century, but it probably represents an older text (Paul F. Bradshaw thinks from the 2nd century), resulting to be one of the older Eucharistic Prayer known. The Papyrus covered the part of the *anaphora* before the Sanctus. Among the supporters of this theory are M. Andrieu, P. Collomp, Klaus Gamber, R.G. Coquin and Hieronymous Engberding. In AD 1974, Edward Kilmartin suggested that the Strasbourg papyrus was a complete anaphora and located the prayer at a 3rd-century stage of development of the Eucharistic prayer. Geoffrey Cuming, in AD 1979 agreed on the same conclusion, and in AD 1985. Enrico Mazza sided with Wegman and Cuming. In this view, the prayer in the Strasbourg papyrus is regarded, just as the *Didache*, as an interim phase of the Eucharist derived from the Jewish meal benediction, the *Birkat ha-mazon*.[1363]

EUCHARISTIC DIALOGUE

The Bishop:
The Lord be with you.

The Congregation:
And with your spirit.

The Bishop:
Lift up your hearts.

The Congregation:
We have them with the Lord.

The Bishop:
Let us give thanks to the Lord.

The Congregation:
It is meet and right.

[1363] Ray, Walter D. (1997). The Strasbourg Papyrus. In Bradshaw, Paul F. (Ed.), *Essays on Early Eastern Eucharistic Prayers*, 39-44.

THANKSGIVING

The Bishop:

It is truly meet and right, holy and fitting and expedient for our souls, O Living God, Master, Lord God the Father almighty, to praise You, to hymn You, to bless You, to confess You night and day, You, the creator of heaven and all that is therein, the earth and all that is on earth, the seas and rivers and all that is in them; Who did create man according to Your own image and likeness. You did make all things by Your Wisdom, Your true light, Your Son our Lord and Savior Jesus Christ, through Whom unto You with Him and with the Holy Spirit,

OFFERING

we give thanks and offer the reasonable (λογικὴν) sacrifice of this bloodless worship[1364], which all nations offer unto You from the rising up of the sun even unto it going down, from the north even unto the south; for great is Your Name among all nations, and in every place incense is offered unto Your Holy Name and a pure offering.[1365]

LITANIES

Over this sacrifice and offering we pray and beseech You, remember Your holy and only catholic church, all Your peoples and all Your flocks. Provide the peace which is from heaven in all our hearts, and grant us also the peace of this life. The (ruler) of the land peaceful things toward us, and toward Your (holy) Name, the prefect of the province, the army, the princes, councils...

[1364] Romans 12:1.
[1365] "'My name will be great among the nations, from where the sun rises to where it sets. In every place incense and pure offerings will be brought to me, because my name will be great among the nations,' says the Lord Almighty." (Malachi 1:11).

About one-third of a page is lacking here.

(For seedtime and) harvest... preserve, for the poor of Your people, for all of us who call upon Your (holy) Name, for all who hope in You.

DIPTYCH

Give rest to the souls of those who have fallen asleep; remember those of whom we make mention today, both those whose names we say (and) whose we do not say...

LITANIES AND COMMEMORATION OF SAINTS

(Remember) our orthodox fathers and bishops everywhere; and grant us to have a part and lot with the fair... of Your holy prophets, apostles and martyrs. Receive (through) their entreats (these prayers); grant them through our Lord, through Whom be glory to You to the ages of ages.

THANKSGIVING AND SANCTUS

For You are above all principalities, power, rule, dominion and every name that is named, not only in this world but also in that which is to come. Beside You stand thousand thousands and myriad myriads of angels, archangels, thrones, dominions, principalities, powers: by You stand the two most honorable six-winged seraphim, with two wings covering the face, and with two the feet, and with two flying and crying Holy, with whom receive also our cry of "holy" as we say: Holy, holy, holy, Lord of Hosts, full is the heaven and the earth of Your glory.

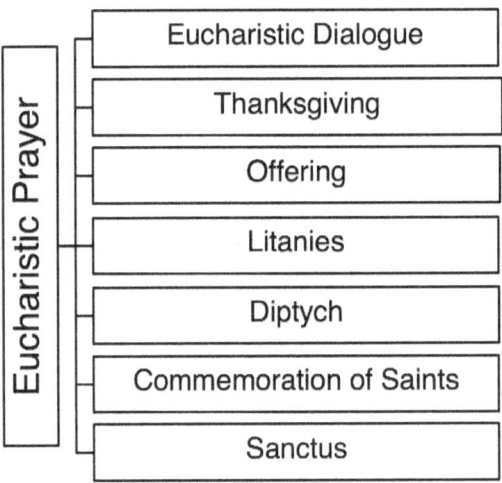

High-level structure of the Saint Mark (Strasbourg) Eucharistic Prayer

Anaphora of the Apostolic Constitutions

The Apostolic Constitutions (Latin: *Constitutiones Apostolorum*) is a composite work that consists of the *Didascalia* in its first six books (c. AD 230), plus two additional books that between AD 375 and 380, probably of Syrian origin or possibly from Constantinople, the first of which is based on the *Didache* (Book 7) while the second is stemmed from the *Apostolic Tradition* (Book 8).[1366] They include a detailed description of a liturgy, Antiochene in character but (very likely incorrectly) attributed to Pope Clement of Rome, and the Apostles. The Liturgy of the eighth book of the *Apostolic Constitutions* is a complete text of the Christian liturgy. It is the oldest known form that can be described as a complete liturgy and can be dated to the second half of the 4th century. It belongs to the Antiochene Rite.[1367]

[1366] Bradshaw, Paul, *The Search for the Origins of Christian Worship* (2nd Ed.), 84.
[1367] "Apostolic Constitutions." *Wikipedia*. Wikipedia.org. n.p. Web. 25 December 2020.

Liturgiologists pay particular attention to this liturgy vis-à-vis its linkage to the liturgical prayers of the Jewish synagogues.[1368] It was Kaufmann Kohler who first realized some Christian prayers are a version of older synagogue prayers, which triggered Anton Baumstark to investigate a Jewish origin of the liturgy in Book 8 of the *Apostolic Constitution*. He found a nexus between the liturgy in investigation and the post-exilic Temple worship. Wilhelm Bousset is another scholar argues for Jewish origin of this liturgy.[1369]

EUCHARISTIC DIALOGUE

The Bishop:
The grace of Almighty God, and the love of our Lord Jesus Christ, and the fellowship of the Holy Spirit, be with you all.

The Congregation:
And with your spirit.

The Bishop:
Lift up your mind.

The Congregation:
We lift it up unto the Lord.

The Bishop:
Let us give thanks to the Lord.

[1368] Graves, Raphael. (1997). The Anaphora of the Eighth Book of the Apostolic Constitutions. In Bradshaw, Paul F. (Ed.), *Essays on Early Eastern Eucharistic Prayers*, 173.
[1369] Graves, Ibid., 173-175.

The Congregation:

It is meet and right so to do.

THANKSGIVING

The Bishop:

It is very meet and right before all things to sing and hymn to You, who is the true God, who is before all beings, from whom the whole family in heaven and earth is named,[1370] who only is unbegotten, and without beginning, and without a ruler, and without a master; who stands in need of nothing; who is the bestower of everything that is good; who is beyond all cause and generation; who is always and immutably the same; from whom all things came into being, as from their proper original. For You are eternal knowledge, everlasting sight, unbegotten hearing, untaught wisdom, the first by nature, and the measure of being, and beyond all number; who brought all things out of nothing into being by Your only begotten Son, but begot Him before all ages by Your will, Your power, and Your goodness, without any instrument, the only begotten Son, God the Word, the living Wisdom, the First-born of every creature, the angel of Your Great Counsel, and Your High Priest, but the King and Lord of every intellectual and sensible nature, who was before all things, by whom were all things. For You, O eternal God, made all things by Him, and through Him it is that You vouchsafe Your suitable providence over the whole world; for by the very same that You bestowed being, did You also bestow well-being: the God and Father of Your only begotten Son, who by Him made before all things the Cherubim and the Seraphim, the eons and hosts, the powers and authorities, the principalities and thrones,

---

[1370] "From whom every family in heaven and on earth derives its name." (Ephesians 3:15).

the archangels and angels; and after all these, by Him made this visible world, and all things that are therein.

SALVATION NARRATIVE

The Bishop:

For You are He who framed the heaven as an arch, and stretch it out like the covering of a tent, and founded the earth upon nothing by Your mere will; who fixed the firmament, and prepare the night and the day; who brought the light out of Your treasures, and on its departure brought on darkness, for the rest of the living creatures that move up and down in the world; who appointed the sun in heaven to rule over the day, and the moon to rule over the night, and inscribed in heaven the choir of stars to praise Your glorious majesty; who made the water for drink and for cleansing, the air in which we live for respiration and the affording of sounds, by the means of the tongue, which strikes the air, and the hearings which co-operates therewith, so as to perceive speech when it is received by it, and falls upon it; who made fire for our consolation in darkness, for the supply of our want, and that we might be warmed and enlightened by it; who separated the great sea from the land, and rendered the former navigable and the latter fit for walking, and replenished the former with small and great living creatures, and filled the latter with the same, both tame and wild; furnished it with various plants, and crown it with herbs, and beautify it with flowers, and enrich it with seeds; who ordained the great deep, and on every side made a mighty cavity for it, which contains seas of salt waters heaped together[1371], yet You every way bounded them with barriers of the smallest sand[1372], who sometimes raises it to the height of mountains by the winds, and sometimes smooths it into a plain;

[1371] Job 38.
[1372] "I made the sand a boundary for the sea, an everlasting barrier it cannot cross" (Jeremiah 5:22).

sometimes enrages it with a tempest, and sometimes stills it with a calm, that it may be easy to seafaring men in their voyages; who encompassed this world, which was made by You through Christ, with rivers, and water it with currents, and moisten it with springs that never fail, and bound it round with mountains for the immoveable and secure consistence of the earth: for You have replenished Your world, and adorned it with sweet-smelling and with healing herbs, with many and various living creatures, strong and weak, for food and for labor, tame and wild; with the noises of creeping things, the sounds of various sorts of flying creatures; with the circuits of the years, the numbers of months and days, the order of the seasons, the courses of the rainy clouds, for the production of the fruits and the support of living creatures. You have also appointed the station of the winds, which blow when commanded by You, and the multitude of the plants and herbs. And You have not only created the world itself, but hast also made man for a citizen of the world, exhibiting him as the ornament of the world; for You said to Your Wisdom: Let us make man according to our image, and according to our likeness; and let them have dominion over the fish of the sea, and over the fowls of the heaven[1373]. Wherefore also You have made him of an immortal soul and of a body liable to dissolution—the former out of nothing, the latter out of the four elements—and hast given him as to his soul rational knowledge, the discerning of piety and impiety, and the observation of right and wrong; and as to his body, You have granted him five senses and progressive motion: for You, O God Almighty, by Your Christ planted a Paradise in Eden, in the east, adorned with all plants fit for food, and introduced him

---

[1373] "Then God said, 'Let us make mankind in our image, in our likeness, so that they may rule over the fish in the sea and the birds in the sky, over the livestock and all the wild animals, and over all the creatures that move along the ground.'" (Genesis 1:26).

into it, as into a rich banquet[1374]. And when You made him, You gave him a law implanted within him, that so he might have at home and within himself the seeds of divine knowledge; and when You had brought him into the Paradise of pleasure, You allowed him the privilege of enjoying all things, only forbidding the tasting of one tree, in hopes of greater blessings; that in case he would keep that command, he might receive the reward of it, which was immortality.

But when he neglected that command, and tasted of the forbidden fruit, by the seduction of the serpent and the counsel of his wife, You justly cast him out of Paradise.

Yet of Your goodness You did not overlook him, nor suffer him to perish utterly, for he was Your creature; but You subjected the whole creation to him and granted him liberty to procure himself food by his own sweat and labors, while You caused all the fruits of the earth to spring up, to grow, and to ripen. But when You had laid him asleep for a while, You with an oath called him to a restoration again, loosed the bond of death, and promise him life after the resurrection. And not this only; but when You had increased his posterity to an innumerable multitude, those that continued with You, You glorified, and those who did apostatize from You, You punished. And while You accepted of the sacrifice of Abel[1375] as of a holy person, You rejected the gift of Cain, the murderer of his brother, as of an abhorred wretch. And besides these, You accepted of Seth and Enos,[1376] and translated Enoch: for You are the Creator of men, and the giver of life, and the supplier of want, and the giver of laws, and the rewarder of those that observe them, and the avenger of those that

---

[1374] "Now the Lord God had planted a garden in the east, in Eden; and there he put the man he had formed" (Genesis 2:8).
[1375] Genesis 4.
[1376] "Shem and Seth were honored among human beings, and above every living thing in creation was Adam" (Sirach 49:16).

transgress them; who brought the great flood upon the world by reason of the multitude of the ungodly, and delivered righteous Noah from that flood by an ark, with eight souls[1377], the end of the foregoing generations, and the beginning of those that were to come; who kindled a fearful fire against the five cities of Sodom, and turned a fruitful land into a salt lake for the wickedness of them that dwelt therein, but snatched holy Lot out of the conflagration. You are He who delivered Abraham from the impiety of his fore-fathers, and appointed him to be the heir of the world, and discovered to him Your Christ; who a forehand ordained Melchizedek an high priest for Your worship; who rendered Your patient servant Job the conqueror of that serpent who is the patron of wickedness; who made Isaac the son of the promise, and Jacob the father of twelve sons, and increased his posterity to a multitude, and bring him into Egypt with seventy-five souls. You, O Lord, did not overlook Joseph, but granted him, as a reward of his chastity for Your sake, the government over the Egyptians. You, O Lord, did not overlook the Hebrews when they were afflicted by the Egyptians, on account of the promises made unto their fathers; but You delivered them and punish the Egyptians. And when men had corrupted the law of nature, and had sometimes esteemed the creation the effect of chance, and sometimes honored it more than they ought, and equaled it to the God of the universe, You did not, however, suffer them to go astray, but raised up Your holy servant Moses, and by him gave the written law for the assistance of the law of nature, and showed that the creation was Your work, and banished away the error of polytheism. You adorned Aaron and his posterity with the priesthood, and punished the Hebrews when they sinned, and receive

---

[1377] "To those who were disobedient long ago when God waited patiently in the days of Noah while the ark was being built. In it only a few people, eight in all, were saved through water" (1 Peter 3:20).

them again when they returned to You. You punished the Egyptians with a judgment of ten plagues, and divided the sea, and bring the Israelites through it, and drown and destroy the Egyptians who pursued after them. You sweetened the bitter water with wood; You brought water out of the rock of stone; You rained manna from heaven, and quails, as meat out of the air; You afforded them a pillar of fire by night to give them light, and a pillar of a cloud by day to overshadow them from the heat; You declared Joshua to be the general of the army, and overthrew the seven nations of Canaan by him; You divided Jordan, and dry up the rivers of Etham; You overthrew walls without instruments or the hand of man.

DOXOLOGY

The Bishop:
For all these things, glory be to You, O Lord Almighty. You do the innumerable hosts of angels, archangels, thrones, dominions, principalities, authorities, and powers, Your everlasting armies, adore.

THANKSGIVING AND SANCTUS

The Bishop:
The Cherubim and the six-winged Seraphim, with two covering their feet, with two their heads, and with two flying, say, together with thousand thousands of archangels, and ten thousand times ten thousand of angels, incessantly, and with constant and loud voices, and let all the people say it with them: Holy, holy, holy, Lord of hosts, heaven and earth are full of His glory: be blessed forever. Amen.[1378]

And afterwards let the high priest say:

[1378] Isaiah 6:3; and Romans 1:25.

SALVATION NARRATIVE

The Bishop:
For You are truly holy, and most holy, the highest and most highly exalted forever. Holy also is Your only begotten Son our Lord and God, Jesus Christ, who in all things ministered to His God and Father, both in Your various creation and Your suitable providence, and has not overlooked lost mankind. But after the law of nature, after the exhortations in the positive law, after the prophetical reproofs and the government of the angels, when men had perverted both the positive law and that of nature, and had cast out of their mind the memory of the flood, the burning of Sodom, the plagues of the Egyptians, and the slaughters of the inhabitant of Palestine, and being just ready to perish universally after an unparalleled manner, He was pleased by Your good will to become man, who was man's Creator; to be under the laws, who was the Legislator; to be a sacrifice, who was an High Priest; to be a sheep, who was the Shepherd. And He appeased You, His God and Father, and reconciled You to the world, and freed all men from the wrath to come, and was made of a virgin, and was in flesh, being God the Word, the beloved Son, the first-born of the whole creation, and was, according to the prophecies which were foretold concerning Him by Himself, of the seed of David and Abraham, of the tribe of Judah. And He was made in the womb of a virgin, who formed all mankind that are born into the world; He took flesh, who was without flesh; He who was begotten before time, was born in time; He lived holily, and taught according to the law; He drove away every sickness and every disease from men, and wrought signs and wonders among the people; and He was partaker of meat, and drink, and sleep, who nourishes all that stand in need of food, and fills every living creature with His

goodness; He manifested His name to those that knew it not[1379]; He drove away ignorance; He revived piety, and fulfilled Your will; He finished the work which You gave Him to do; and when He had set all these things right, He was seized by the hands of the ungodly, of the high priests and priests, falsely so called, and of the disobedient people, by the betraying of him who was possessed of wickedness as with a confirmed disease; He suffered many things from them, and endured all sorts of ignominy by Your permission; He was delivered to Pilate the governor, and He that was the Judge was judged, and He that was the Savior was condemned; He that was impassible was nailed to the cross, and He who was by nature immortal died, and He that is the giver of life was buried, that He might loose those for whose sake He came from suffering and death, and might break the bonds of the devil, and deliver mankind from his deceit. He arose from the dead the third day; and when He had continued with His disciples forty days, He was taken up into the heavens, and is sat down on the right hand of You, who art His God and Father.

THANKSGIVING

The Bishop:
Being mindful, therefore, of those things that He endured for our sakes, we give You thanks, O God Almighty, not in such a manner as we ought, but as we are able, and fulfill His constitution:

[1379] "I have revealed you to those whom you gave me out of the world" (John 17:6).

INSTITUTION NARRATIVE

The Bishop:

For in the same night that He was betrayed, He took bread[1380] in His holy and undefiled hands, and, looking up to You His God and Father, He broke it, and gave it to His disciples, saying, This is the mystery of the new covenant: take of it, and eat. This is my Body, which is broken for many, for the remission of sins. In like manner also He took the cup, and mixed it of wine and water, and sanctified it, and delivered it to them, saying: Drink all of this; for this is my Blood which is shed for many, for the remission of sins: do this in remembrance of me.

ANAMNESIS

The Bishop:

For as often as you eat this bread and drink this cup, you do show forth my death until I come.

OFFERING

The Bishop:

Being mindful, therefore, of His passion, and death, and resurrection from the dead, and return into the heavens, and His future second appearing, wherein He is to come with glory and power to judge the quick and the dead, and to recompense to everyone according to his works, we offer to You, our King and our God, according to His constitution, this bread and this cup, giving You thanks, through Him, that You have thought us worthy to stand before You, and to sacrifice to You.

[1380] "The Lord Jesus, on the night he was betrayed, took bread" (1 Corinthians 11:23).

EPICLESIS

The Bishop:

And we beseech You that You will mercifully look down upon these gifts which are here set before You, O God, who stands in need of none of our offerings. And accept them, to the honored Your Christ, and send down upon this sacrifice Your Holy Spirit, the Witness of the Lord Jesus' sufferings, that He may show this bread to be the Body of Your Christ, and the cup to be the Blood of Your Christ, that those who are partakers thereof may be strengthened for piety, may obtain the remission of their sins, may be delivered from the devil and his deceit, may be filled with the Holy Spirit, may be made worthy of Your Christ, and may obtain eternal life upon Your reconciliation to them, O Lord Almighty.

LITANIES

The Bishop:

We further pray unto You, O Lord, for your holy Church spread from one end of the world to another, which You have purchased with the precious blood of Your Christ, that You will preserve it unshaken and free from disturbance until the end of the world; for every episcopate who rightly divides the word of truth. We further pray to You for me, who am nothing, who offer to You, for the whole presbytery, for the deacons and all the clergy, that You will make them wise, and replenish them with the Holy Spirit. We further pray to You, O Lord, for the king and all in authority[1381], for the whole army, that they may be peaceable towards us, that so, leading the whole time of our life in quietness and unanimity, we

---

[1381] "for kings and all those in authority, that we may live peaceful and quiet lives in all godliness and holiness" (1 Timothy 2:2).

may glorify You through Jesus Christ, who is our hope. We further offer to You also for all those holy persons who have pleased You from the beginning of the world—patriarch, prophets, righteous men, apostles, martyrs, confessors, bishops, presbyters, deacons, sub-deacons, readers, singers, virgins, widows, and lay persons, with all whose names You know. We further offer to You for this people, that You will render them, to the praise of Your Christ, a royal priesthood and a holy nation;[1382] for those that are in virginity and purity; for the widows of the Church; for those in honorable marriage and childbearing; for the infants of Your people, that You will not permit any of us to become castaways. We further beseech You also for this city and its inhabitants; for those that are sick; for those in bitter servitude; for those in banishments; for those in prison; for those that travel by water or by land; that You, the helper and assister of all men, will be their supporter. We further also beseech You for those that hate us and persecute us for Your name's sake; for those that are without and wander out of the way; that You will convert them to goodness and pacify their anger. We further also beseech You for the catechumens of the Church, and for those that are vexed by the adversary, and for our brethren the penitents, that You will perfect the first in the faith, that You will deliver the second from the energy of the evil one, and that You will accept the repentance of the last and forgive both them and us our offenses. We further offer to You also for the good temperature of the air, and the fertility of the fruits, that so, partaking perpetually of the good things derived from You, we may praise You without ceasing, who gives food to all flesh. We further beseech You also for those who are absent on a just cause, that You will keep us all in piety, and gather

---

[1382] "But you are a chosen people, a royal priesthood, a holy nation, God's special possession, that you may declare the praises of him who called you out of darkness into his wonderful light" (1 Peter 2:9).

us together in the kingdom of Your Christ, the God of all sensible and intelligent nature, our King that You would keep us immoveable, unblameable, and unreprovable:

DOXOLOGY

The Bishop:

For to You belongs all glory and worship, and thanksgiving, honor and adoration, the Father, with the Son, and to the Holy Spirit, both now and always, and for everlasting, and endless ages forever. And let all the people say, Amen.

And let the bishop say: the peace of God be with you all.
And let all the people say: And with your spirit.

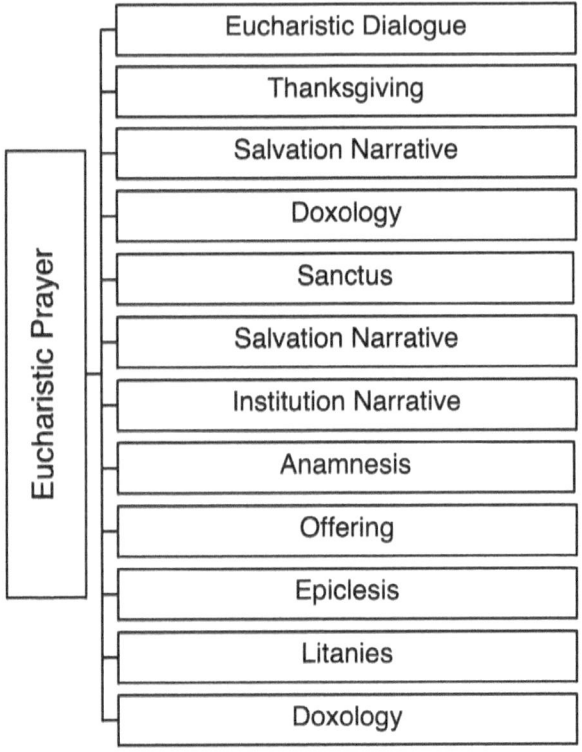

High-level structure of the Liturgy of the Apostolic Constitutions

Anaphora of the Deir Balyzeh Papyrus

The Deir Balyzeh Papyrus is a 6th-century papyrus, coming from Upper Egypt. It contains early fragmentary Christian texts: three prayers, a short creed, and a portion of *Anaphora*. It was found in AD 1907 in the ruins of the Deir Balyzeh monastery in the village of Al-Balyzeh in the Asyut governorate. The fragments are in Greek written in uncial script, and are dated to the end of the 6th-century. These fragments were published by P. de Puniet in AD 1909. Other fragments were later discovered and the texts were re-edited in AD 1949 by C.H. Roberts and B. Capelle. Due to similarities with the *Anaphora* of Serapion, Cuming suggests that the content of the papyrus dates back to the 4th century.[1383] The significance of this papyrus stems from the fact that it starts where the Strasbourg papyrus finishes, which helps reconstructing the early Egyptian liturgy of the 4th century. Another interesting point is that it quotes the "corn prayer" of the *Didache*, as in the *Anaphora* of Saint Serapion.[1384]

PEACE (Three Prayers)

...who hate....bless (Your) people...raise the fallen, turn back the wanderers, comfort the weak-hearted.

THANKSGIVING

The Bishop:

For You are far above every principality and power and virtue and dominion and every name that is named, not only in this age but also (in the age to come. By You) stand (thousands) of the holy (angels and archangels) unnumbered... the...stand in a circle... (six) wings to one and six to the other, and with two they veiled the face, and with two the feet, and with two they flew.

Everything at all times hallows You, but with all that hallow You, receive also our hallowing, as we say to You: Holy, holy, holy, Lord of Sabaoth; heaven and earth are full of Your glory.

[1383] "Deir Balyzeh Papyrus." *Wikipedia*. Wikipedia.org. n.p. Web. 18 August 2016.
[1384] Jasper, R.C.D., and G.J. Cuming, *Prayers of the Eucharist: Early and Reformed*, 79.

EPICLESIS (INVOCATION OF THE HOLY SPIRIT)

The Bishop:

Fill us also with the glory from (You), and vouchsafe to send down Your Holy Spirit upon these creatures (and) make the bread the body of our (Lord and) Savior Jesus Christ, and the cup the blood ... of our Lord and ... (And) as this bread was scattered on (the mountains) and hills and fields and was mixed together and became one body...so this wine which came from the vine of David and the water from the spotless lamb also mixed together became one mystery, gather the catholic church.

INSTITUTION NARRATIVE

The Bishop:

For (our Lord Jesus) Christ Himself (in the night when) he handed (Himself) over... His disciples (and) apostles, saying, "Take, (eat) from it; this (is) My body, which is given for you for forgiveness of sins." Likewise, after supper He took the cup, blessed, drank, and gave it to them, saying, "Take, drink from it, all of you; this is My blood, which is shed for you for forgiveness of sins."

ANAMNESIS

The Bishop:

"As often as you eat this bread and drink this cup, you proclaim My death, you make My remembrance."

The Congregation:

We proclaim Your death, we confess Your resurrection, and we pray...
(At least fifteen lines are missing here.)

DOXOLOGY/RESULTS OF THE INVOCATION

The Bishop:

... and provide us Your servants with the power of the Holy Spirit, for strengthening and increasing of faith, for the hope of the eternal life to come; through our Lord Jesus Christ, (through Whom) be glory to You, the Father, with the Holy (Spirit) to the ages. Amen.

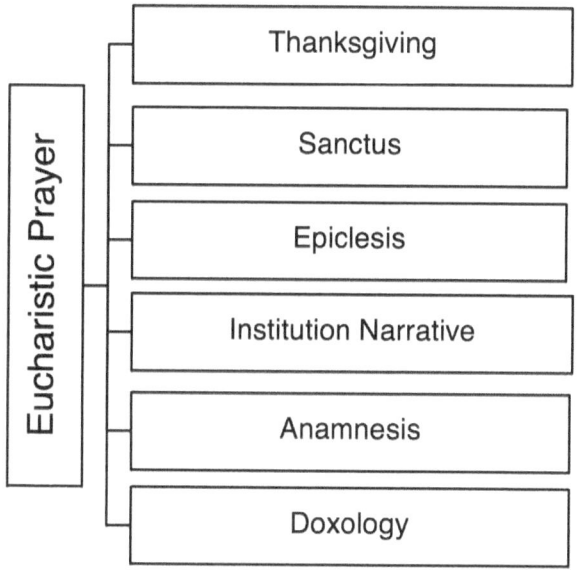

High-level structure of the *Anaphora* of Deir Balyzeh

The *Anaphora* of Saint Thomas the Apostle

The *anaphoral* fragment ascribed to Saint Thomas the Apostle was found in the Euchologion of the White Monastery (copied in the 10th century), which is basically a compilation of earlier Eucharistic prayers. This *anaphora* follows the Egyptian pattern, which is an early testimony of the

Egyptian textual tradition.[1385] Michael Zheltov has an important observation; the transition between the Sanctus and the Minor Epiclesis, the petition to "fill" the offerings with the Lord's blessing, is very smooth, a characteristic of the Egyptian type, especially Mark/Cyril's Liturgy.[1386] The following translation of the fragment is given by Mary Farag.[1387]

Although some challenged its attribution to Thomas the Apostle and credited it to the 7th century Thomas of Harqel, bishop of Mabbug in Syria, who left his diocese and lived in the Coptic monastery of the Enaton west of Alexandria, a careful study of the text and its structure defies this suggestion. However, the extant text of the liturgy suggests Syro-Byzantine interpolations, precisely with the repetition of the word *Holy*, and the delay of the Intercessory Prayers to after the Epiclesis.[1388]

(*Eucharistic Dialogue and the beginning of the Thanksgiving Prayer are missing*)

THANKSGIVING

The Bishop:
Who can make his mind heavenly and place his thoughts in Paradise and place his heart in the heavenly Jerusalem and see God the invisible, the incomprehensible, the unattainable, the uncreated, the immeasurable? As for He who accurately measured the entire creation, His workmanship no one comprehends, except He Himself and (His) good Father and the Holy Spirit. (These) three are one, a single divinity, a single lordship, three

---

[1385] Spinks, Bryan D., *Do This in Remembrance of Me: The Eucharist from the Early Church to the Present Day*, 102.
[1386] Zheltov, Michael, *Studia Patristica: Vol. XLV*, 108.
[1387] I added titles and subtitles for clarifications (not in the original text).
[1388] Epiphanius (Bishop), *The White Monastery Euchologion: Translation from Coptic and a Study*, 71-73.

hypostases, a perfect Trinity in a single divinity. These three are one: He who collected all the waters that were upon the earth into a single gathering and called it the sea and established the four river-branches flowing into it, (a sea that) can neither become overfilled nor lack (for water), He who bounded the waters in three parts and placed one part in heaven, one part upon the earth, and one part under the earth, He who created the sun and the moon and the stars and appointed the sun to shine upon His creations by day and the moon by night, the evening (star) and Arcturus and the morning star to shine upon the earth. And You also created the angels and the archangels, the principalities and the authorities, the powers and all the powers that are in the heavens. And by Your hands, along with Your good Father and the Holy Spirit, You also created man according to Your image and according to Your likeness. And you also created Paradise and placed the man whom You created in it to cultivate it and to praise You, You whom the angels praise, You whom the archangels worship.

The Deacon:
Those who are seated stand

The Bishop:
You whom the powers hymn, You whose holy glory the authorities sing, You to whom the thrones sing the doxology of victory.

The Deacon:
Look toward the east

The Bishop:
You before whom stand Your tow honored creatures, the Cherubim and the Seraphim, each of them with six wings, with two wings they cover their faces on account of the great glory of Your divinity, and with two they cover their feet on account of the great fire emanating from around Your throne, O God, the Creator.

The Deacon:
Let us attend

The Bishop:
And with two they fly, while hymning and praising You, glorifying You with unwearying mouth and unceasing tongue and never-silent lips, hymning You, glorifying You, saying:

The Congregation:
Holy, holy, holy, Lord Sabaoth. Heaven and earth are full of Your holy glory.

EPICLESIS

The Bishop:
Holy are You, holy are You, holy are You, Lord Sabaoth. Truly heaven and earth are full of Your glory. Fill now this sacrifice also with the joy of Your Holy Spirit.

SALVATION NARRATIVE

The Bishop:
You placed the man whom You had created in the Paradise of Delight and commanded him that from every tree in...

(The rest of the liturgy is missing)

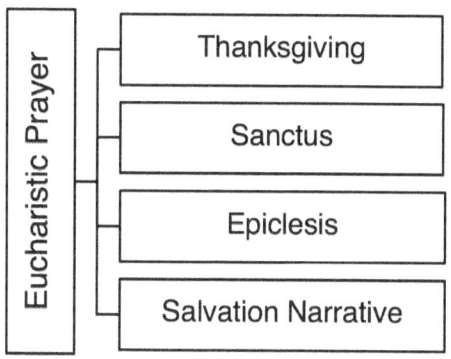

High-level structure of the *Anaphora* of Saint Thomas

Characteristics of the Egyptian Liturgy

One of the peculiar characteristics of the Egyptian liturgical tradition is the Thanksgiving-Sanctus-Epiclesis unit. As shown above, this order is the most common one among most Egyptian *anaphoras*. In some cases, this unit is broken by the interpolation of the offering between the Sanctus and the Epiclesis. Nevertheless, The Epiclesis always comes before the Institution Narrative. The Egyptian Thanksgiving Prayer is concerned, firstly, with thanking the Lord for His creation. The redemptive work of Jesus is not mentioned in this prayer, but deferred to later orisons. The inclusion of the Pre-Sanctus in the Thanksgiving Prayer is discerning to the Egyptian tradition, which serves as a linkage between the thanksgiving and the Sanctus, which, in the Egyptian tradition, concludes the Thanksgiving Prayer. The Post-Sanctus statement to "fill" the gifts is also a smooth transition from the Sanctus to the Egyptian Epiclesis.

In the Egyptian (more precisely Alexandrian) liturgical tradition, Intercessory Prayers are ordinarily included in the Thanksgiving Prayer. This is manifested in the Strasbourg's MARK, Deir Balyzeh Papyrus, and the Liturgy of Saint Cyril. Although missing from the Barcelona Papyrus and the *Anaphora* of Saint Thomas, the Intercessory prayers come after the Epiclesis in the Liturgy of Saint Serapion, which suggests a parallel tradition, although not commonly used, in different areas in Egypt.

As previously noted, in several occasions, the Egyptian liturgies, especially Saint Mark's (and later on Saint Cyril's), recognizes another epiclesis before the Thanksgiving. This tradition, I think, is a product of the amalgamation of the evening liturgy with the morning one. Numerous evidence supporting that the Egyptian Offertory office was a complete *anaphora* (probably the *evening* one) have been presented. Many scholars attribute the Offertory Thanksgiving to Saint Mark himself, as such, it is logical to expect his liturgy to acknowledge the rudimentary epiclesis that comes after it.

The Epiclesis, according to the Egyptian tradition, is not necessarily an invocation of the Holy Spirit, but rather of the Logos or sometimes of the Holy Trinity. This can be found in the Offertory proper, the *Anaphora* of Saint Serapion, and the Liturgy of Saint Mark/Cyril.

Table of Different Sections of the Egyptian Liturgy

When studying the Egyptian liturgies, it is important to notice that the Barcelona Papyrus and the *anaphora* of Saint Serapion are the only complete 4th-century *anaphoras* extant. Saint Mark's, MARK (Strasbourg Papyrus), captures the *anaphora* from its commencement to the Sanctus. The Deir Balyzeh Papyrus, on the other hand, contains part of the *anaphora* starting from the Pre-Sanctus (last part of the Thanksgiving Prayer) to the end of the liturgy. Many scholars think, however not confirmed, that the liturgy preserved in the Deir Balyzeh papyrus is of Saint Mark's. The surviving fragments of the *anaphora* of Saint Thomas encloses the Pre-Sanctus, Sanctus, Epiclesis, and an introduction to the Salvation Narrative; other parts of the liturgy are missing.

The following table presents the high-level structure of the five Egyptian *anaphora* prayers manifesting the ancient shape of the Egyptian liturgy before the 5th century (i.e., before the changes introduced by Saint Cyril I).

Barcelona	**Serapion**	**MARK**	**Balyzeh**	**Thomas**
Dialogue	Dialogue	Dialogue		
Thanksgiving	Thanksgiving	Thanksgiving	(Missing)	(Missing)
		Offering		
		Intercessory P	Intercessory P	
Pre-Sanctus	Pre-Sanctus	Pre-Sanctus	Pre-Sanctus	Pre-Sanctus
Sanctus	Sanctus	Sanctus	Sanctus	Sanctus
Offering	Offering			
Epiclesis			Epiclesis	Epiclesis
Institution	Institution	(Missing)	Institution	Salvation
Anamnesis	Epiclesis		Anamnesis	
	Intercessory P		(Missing)	(Missing)
Doxology	Doxology		Doxology	

Reconstruction of the Egyptian Liturgy

In this section, I will present a hypothetical reconstruction of the Liturgy of Saint Mark before the changes introduced by Saint Cyril I. I will rely mainly on the Strasbourg Papyrus since it is the only old, confirmed document depicting Saint Mark's liturgy. Unluckily it falls short of capturing the entire liturgy; it stops at the Sanctus. Fortunately, the rest of the liturgy was documented in other manuscripts from the same era, namely, the Barcelona Papyrus and the Deir Balyzeh Papyrus. It is not inveterate, however, that both depict the Liturgy of Saint Mark; it is possible that they could be for other Egyptian *anaphoras* that are no longer in use.

Comparing the common parts of the two texts with the corresponding sections in the Strasbourg Papyrus, I found that Pre-Sanctus of the Deir-Balyzeh is much closer in structure and lyrics to that of the Strasbourg Papyrus. Also, the Barcelona *anaphora* does not have Intercessory prayers in its structure whereas the Deir Balyzeh one has them in the same section as in the Strasbourg Papyrus, i.e., before the Pre-Sanctus. Unlike the Strasbourg *anaphora*, the offering in the Barcelona *anaphora* comes after the Sanctus. As such, I will use the Deir Balyzeh Papyrus as the primary complementary source for the Strasbourg Papyrus Mark's.

From the table above, there is a conspicuous absence of the Salvation Narrative suggesting that it was unequivocally unknown in Egyptian liturgies prior to the 5th century. Hence, for the purpose of this exercise, I will not include it. As needed, sections from other Egyptian sources are used to reconstruct all sections of the liturgy as we know it today. These sections will be identified in square brackets and referenced in footnotes. Remaining gaps were filled with words not in the original text (indicated by brackets). Moreover, titles and subtitles are not in the original text, but I added them to illustrate the shape of the Liturgy of Saint Mark in the 4th century.

EUCHARISTIC DIALOGUE[1389]

The Bishop:
The Lord be with you.

The Congregation:
And with your spirit.

The Bishop:
Lift up your hearts.

The Congregation:
We have them with the Lord.

The Bishop:
Let us give thanks to the Lord.

The Congregation:
It is meet and right.

THANKSGIVING

The Bishop:
It is truly meet and right, holy and fitting and expedient for our souls, O Living God, Master, Lord God the Father almighty, to praise You, to hymn You, to bless You, to confess You night and day; You, the creator of

---

[1389] From the Eucharistic Dialogue to the Sanctus the text is from the Strasbourg Papyrus unless indicated in the footnotes.

heaven and all that is therein, the earth and all that is on earth, the seas and rivers and all that is in them; Who did create man according to Your own image and likeness. You did make all things by Your Wisdom, Your true light, Your Son our Lord and Savior Jesus Christ, through Whom unto You with Him and with the Holy Spirit,

OFFERING

The Bishop:

we give thanks and offer the reasonable sacrifice of this bloodless worship, which all nations offer unto You from the rising up of the sun even unto it going down, from the north even unto the south; for great is Your Name among all nations, and in every place incense is offered unto Your Holy Name and a pure offering.

LITANIES

The Bishop:

Over this sacrifice and offering, we pray and beseech You; remember Your holy and only catholic church, all Your peoples and all Your flocks. Provide the peace which is from heaven in all our hearts, and grant us also the peace of this life. The (emperor/ruler) of the land (may think) peaceful things toward us, and toward Your (holy) Name; the prefect of the province, the army, the princes, (and the) councils. [The sick among Your people, visit them with mercy and compassion; heal them.][1390] [Give a good journey to our brothers who are abroad; or are going abroad. Send down Your rains; cheer the face of the earth; provide Your fruits for seedtime and][1391] harvest. [Bless the crown of the year with Your goodness][1392] for the poor

---

[1390] The section in square brackets is borrowed from the Liturgy of Saint Cyril.
[1391] The section in square brackets is borrowed from the Coptica Lovaniensia fragment 29.
[1392] The section in square brackets is borrowed from the Liturgy of Saint Cyril.

of Your people, for all of us who call upon Your (holy) Name, for all who hope in You.

DIPTYCH

The Bishop:

Give rest to the souls of those who have fallen asleep; remember those of whom we make mention today, both those whose names we say (and) whose we do not say.

[*After the recitation of the names:*
Sanctify these souls: for You know all. Sanctify all (souls) laid to rest in the Lord. And number them with all Your holy powers and give to them a place and a mansion in Your kingdom.][1393]

LITANIES

The Bishop:

[Receive also the thanksgiving of the people, and bless those who have offered the Offerings and the thanksgivings, and grant health and soundness and cheerfulness and all advancement of soul and body to this whole people.] [1394] (Remember) our orthodox fathers and bishops everywhere; and grant us to have a part and lot with the fair (church).

COMMEMORATION OF SAINTS

The Bishop:

[Remember also all the saints who have pleased You since the beginning, our holy fathers the patriarchs, the][1395] prophets, apostles and martyrs.

[1393] The section in square brackets is borrowed from the Liturgy of Saint Serapion.
[1394] The section in square brackets is borrowed from the Liturgy of Saint Serapion.
[1395] The section in square brackets is borrowed from the Liturgy of Saint Cyril.

Receive (through) their entreats (these prayers); grant them through our Lord, through Whom be glory to You to the ages of ages.

PRE-SANCTUS AND SANCTUS

The Bishop:

For You are above all principalities, power, rule, dominion and every name that is named, not only in this world but also in that which is to come. Beside You stand thousand thousands and myriad myriads of angels, archangels, thrones, dominions, principalities, powers: by You stand the two most honorable six-winged seraphim, with two wings covering the face, and with two the feet, and with two flying and crying Holy, with whom receive also our cry of "holy" as we say:

The Congregation:

Holy, holy, holy, Lord of Hosts, full is the heaven and the earth of Your glory.[1396]

EPICLESIS (INVOCATION OF THE HOLY SPIRIT)[1397]

The Bishop:

[Holy are You, holy are You, holy are You, Lord Sabaoth. Truly heaven and earth are full of Your glory.][1398] Fill us also with the glory from (You), and vouchsafe to send down Your Holy Spirit upon these creatures (and) make the bread the body of our (Lord and) Savior Jesus Christ, and the cup the blood of our Lord and (Savior Jesus Christ). (And) as this bread was scattered on [the top of the mountains][1399] and hills and fields, and was mixed together and became one body, (and) so this wine which came

---

[1396] The Strasbourg *anaphora* stops at this point.
[1397] From this part to the end of the liturgy, unless indicated, the text is from the Deir Balyzeh papyrus.
[1398] The section in square brackets is borrowed from the Liturgy of Saint Thomas.
[1399] The section in square brackets is borrowed from the Liturgy of Saint Serapion.

from the vine of David and the water from the spotless lamb also mixed together became one mystery, gather the catholic church.

INSTITUTION NARRATIVE

The Bishop:

For (our Lord Jesus) Christ Himself [in the night in which][1400] He handed [Himself][1401] up [to death,][1402] [having taken bread and given thanks, broke it and gave it to][1403] His disciples (and) apostles, saying, "Take, [eat][1404] from it; this [is][1405] My body, which is given for you for forgiveness of sins." Likewise after supper He took the cup, blessed, drank, and gave it to them, saying, "Take, drink from it, all of you; this is My blood, which is shed for you for forgiveness of sins."

ANAMNESIS

The Bishop:

"As often as you eat this bread and drink this cup, you proclaim My death, you make My remembrance."

The Congregation:

We proclaim Your death, we confess Your resurrection, and we pray (to) [You, O our God][1406].

[1400] The section in square brackets is borrowed from the Liturgy of Saint Cyril.
[1401] The section in square brackets is borrowed from the Liturgy of Saint Cyril.
[1402] The section in square brackets is borrowed from the Liturgy of Saint Cyril.
[1403] The section in square brackets is borrowed from the Barcelona Papyrus.
[1404] The section in square brackets is borrowed from the Barcelona Papyrus.
[1405] The section in square brackets is borrowed from the Barcelona Papyrus.
[1406] The section in square brackets is borrowed from the Liturgy of Saint Cyril.

DOXOLOGY/RESULTS OF THE INVOCATION

The Bishop:

[Even so, we pray to You, Master, that in blessing You will bless and in sanctifying sanctify,][1407] and provide us, Your servants, with the power of the Holy Spirit, for strengthening and increasing of faith, for the hope of the eternal life to come; through our Lord Jesus Christ, [through Whom][1408] be glory to You, the Father, with the Holy (Spirit) to the ages. Amen.

The Congregation:

[As it was and is and shall be to generations of generations and to all the ages of the ages. Amen.][1409]

[1407] The section in square brackets is borrowed from the Barcelona Papyrus.
[1408] The section in square brackets is borrowed from the Barcelona Papyrus.
[1409] The section in square brackets is borrowed from the Liturgy of Saint Serapion.

CHAPTER EIGHT

English/Arabic Terminologies

Vestments, Church Sections, Altar Supplies, Books, Hymnody Titles, and Liturgical Terms

Do you know what a hymn is? It is singing to the praise of God. If you praise God and do not sing, you utter no hymn. If you praise anything which does not pertain to the praise of God -- though in singing you praise, you utter no hymn. A hymn then contains these three things: song, and praise, and that of God. Praise then of God in song is called a hymn.

—Augustine

Vestments

English	Arabic
Amice	شملة
Sticharion	تونية
Hat	عِمَّة
Orarion	بطرشيل
Priestly Breastplate/Epitrachelion	صَدرة
Mitre	طيلسانة
Chasuble/Phenolion	بُرنُس (حُلة)
Stole/Girdle	زنار

Church Sections

English	Arabic
Baptistery	غرفة المعمودية
Nave	صحن الكنيسة
Atrium	الجزء الخلفي من صحن الكنيسة، مكان الموعوظين أثناء خدمة القداس الإلهي
Pew	دِكَّة
Psalteria/Chancel	الخورس الأول
Lectern	منجلية
Pulpit	إنبل
Cathedra	كرسي البابا أو الأسقف
Veil	الستر أو الحجاب
Iconostasis	حامل الأيقونات
Sanctuary	هيكل
Prothesis	هيكل التقدمة (الرجال)
Altar	مذبح

English	Arabic
High Altar	المذبح الرئيسي
Apse	حضن الأب

Altar Supplies

English	Arabic
Altar Vessels	أواني المذبح
Altar Board	اللوح المكرَّس
Paten	الصينية
Chalice	كأس
Spoon	المستير
Ark	كرسي الكأس
Decanter	قارورة الخمر
Censer/Thurible	الشورية
Coffer of Incense	درج البخور
Pinch of Incense/handful of Incense	يد بخور
Pyx	حُق الذَخيرة
Prospharin	بروسفارين
Corporal	لفافة

Liturgical Books

English	Arabic
Book of Hours/Horologion	الأجبية
Lectionary	قطمارس
Euchologion/ Sacramentary/ Missal	الخولاجي
Antiphonary	الدفنار
Synaxarion	السنكسار
Psalter	كتاب الإبصالمودية

| Deacon's Service Book/The Hymnal | كتاب خدمة الشماس |
| Holy Week Book | كتاب البصخة المقدسة |

Ancient Ritual Books

English	Arabic
Didache	الديداخي
Didascalia of the Apostles	الدسقولية
The Apostolic Constitutions	المراسيم الرسولية
The Institutes	المعاهد
The Ecclesiastical History	التاريخ الكنسي
The Precious Scroll: On the Church History	الخريدة النفيسة في تاريخ الكنيسة
The Beginners' Guide and Discipline for Laity	دلال المبتدئين وتهذيب العلمانيين
The Precious Pearl: On Ecclesiastic Science	الجوهرة النفيسة في علوم الكنيسة
The Lamp to Darkness and Explanation of the Service	مصباح الظلمة وإيضاح الخدمة
The Ritual Order	الترتيب الطقسي
The Trinitarian Mystery in Priesthood Ministry	سر الثالوث في خدمة الكهنوت
Treatise on the Holy Oblation	مقالة في القربان المقدس
The Fundamental Acts of the Ecclesiastical Etiquette	الأعمال الرئيسية في الآداب الكنسية

Hymnody Terms and Prayers

English	Arabic
Hymn	لحن
Hymnody	ترديد وترتيل الألحان
Response/Responsory/Respond	مرد
Response/Bidding	مرد الشماس
Hymnology	علم أو دراسة الألحان
Hymnography	تأليف الألحان
Canonical Hours/Liturgy of the Hours	صلاة السواعي
The Gloria Patri	الذوكصا
The Gloria in Excelsis Deo	تسبحة الملائكة
Year-Round Tune	اللحن السَّنوي
Regular Days	الأيام السَّنوي
Feast Days	الأيام الفرايحي
Feasts of the Lord	أعياد سيدية
Fast Days	أيام الأصوام
Paramony	البرمون
Holy Quarantine	الأربعين المقدسة
Eastertide/Holy Fifty Days	الخمسين المقدسة
Canticle/Ode	هُوس
Psaly	إبصالية
Theotokion	ثيؤطوكية
Adam Morning Doxology	ذكصولوجية باكر الآدام
Doxology	ذكصولوجية
Parallaxe	باراليكس

English	Arabic
Abbreviated-Year-Round Psalm	المزمور الملخَّص السنوي
Circuit Psalm	مزمور الطواف
Concluding Canon	قانون الختام
Sanctus	التسبحة الشيروبيمية
Stanza	ربع مكون من ستيخونات
Quatrain	ربع مكون من أربع ستيخونات
Quintain	ربع مكون من خمس ستيخونات
Strophe	ربع مكون من ستيخونات مختلفة الطول
Line	ستيخون
Cymbals	دُف
Triangle	ترianto
Prostration	ميطانية
Servant Priest/Principal Celebrant	الكاهن الخديم
Assistant Priest/Concelebrant	الكاهن الشريك
Servant Deacon	الشماس الخديم
Altar Server	شماس الهيكل
Diaconate	رتبة الشماسية
Hagiography	سير القديسين
Church Treatise	ميمر

Liturgical Terms and Sections

English	Arabic
Vespers Psalmody	تسبحة العشية
Vespers Offering of Incense	رفع بخور عشية
Prime Offering of Incense	رفع بخور باكر
Thanksgiving Prayer	صلاة الشكر

English/Arabic Terminologies

Minor Circuit of Incense	دورة البخور الصغرى
Major Circuit of Incense	دورة البخور الكبرى
Circuit of the Gospel	دورة الإنجيل
Veneration Service	التمجيد
Midnight Psalmody	تسبحة نصف الليل
Matins Psalmody	تسبحة السحر
The Offertory	تقديم الحَمل
Choosing of the Lamb	إختيار الحَمل
Circuit of the Lamb	دورة الحَمل
Offering Waving	ترديد التقدمة
The Absolution of the Servants	تحليل الخدّام
The Liturgy of the Word	قداس الكلمة
Lections	القراءات
Pericope	فصل (قراءة مختارة من القطمارس)
Circuit of the Pauline/Pauline Circuit	دورة البولس
Praxis Circuit	دورة الإبركسيس
The Creed	قانون الإيمان
The Prayer of Reconciliation	صلاة الصلح
The Liturgy of the Faithful	قداس المؤمنين
The Eucharistic Dialogue	الحوار الإفخارستي
The Grand Thanksgiving/The Preface	صلاة الشكر الكبرى
The Salvation Narrative	قصة الخلاص
The Minor Epiclesis	الإستدعاء الصغير
The Sanctification Prayers	صلوات التقديس
The Institution Narrative	صلوات التأسيس
The Epiclesis/The Major Epiclesis	الإستدعاء أو الإستدعاء الكبير

English	Arabic
The Intercessory Prayers	الصلوات التوسلية
The Litanies	الأواشي
The Supplications	الطلبات
The Commemoration of the Saints	مجمع القديسين
The Diptych	الترحيم
The Fraction	القسمة
Inclination	صلاة الخضوع
The Confession Prayers	الإعتراف
Consignation	رشم أحد عناصر الذبيحة بالآخر
The Communion	التناول أو التوزيع
Dismissal	التسريح
Antidoron	لقمة البركة

Others

English	Arabic
Manuscript	مخطوط
Imposition of Hands	وضع اليد
Inauguration	تدشين
Patron Saint	شفيع
Relics	رفات
Locum Tenens/Surrogate	قائم مقام
Aspersorium/Fountain	وعاء اللقان
Epact	الأبقطي

References

1- Atchley, E. G. Cuthbert, *The History of the Use of Incense in Divine Worship*, London: Longmans, Green, and Co, 1909.

2- Athanasius, ., Gregg, R. C., & Athanasius, *The life of Antony and the letter to Marcellinus*, New York: Paulist Press, 1980.

3- Ayo, C.N., *Gloria Patri: The History and Theology of the Lesser Doxology*, Notre Dame: University of Notre Dame Press, 2007.

4- Awad, Gregorius Rashidy Bishay (presbyter). (2021). Eucharistic Fasting in the Tradition of the Early Church and the Coptic Tradition. *Alexandria School*, 31(2), Cairo: Paromaos Monastery, 2021.

5- Baumstark, Anton, *Comparative Liturgy*, Maryland: Newman Press, 1958.

6- Baumstark, Anton, *On the Historical Development of the Liturgy*, Minnesota: Liturgical Press, 1989.

7- Bradshaw, Paul F., *Early Christian Worship: A Basic Introduction to Ideas and Practice*, Minnesota: The Liturgical Press, 2010.

8- Bradshaw, Paul F. (1997). Introduction: The Evolution of Early Anaphoras. In Bradshaw, Paul F. (Ed.), *Essays on Early Eastern Eucharistic Prayers*, Minnesota: The Liturgical Press, 1997.

9- Bradshaw, Paul F. (1992). The Divine Office: The First Three Centuries. In Cheslyn Jones, Geoffrey Wainwright, Edward Yarnold SJ and Paul Bradshaw (Eds.), *The Study of Liturgy*, New York: Oxford University Press.

10- Bradshaw, Paul, *The Search for the Origins of Christian Worship* (2nd Ed.), New York: Oxford University Press, 2002.Budge, E.A. Wallis, *The Liturgy of Funerary Offerings*, New York: Dover Publications Inc., 1994.

11- Burmester, O.H.E., *The Canons of Gabriel Ibn Turaik, LXX Patriarch of Alexandria*, Orientalia Christiana Periodica 1, 1935.

12- Burmester, O.H.E., *The Sayings of Michael, Metropolitan of Damietta*, Orientalia Christiana Periodica 2, 1936.

13- Burton, Ernest De Witt (1896), The Ancient Synagogue Service, *The Biblical World*, Vol. 8, No. 2, 143-148, The University of Chicago Press, Retrieved from www.jstor.org/stable/3140264.

14- Byrne, P., & Houlden, J. L. (1995). *Companion Encyclopedia of Theology*. London: Routledge.

15- Cabasilas, Nicholas (Saint), *Commentary on the Divine Liturgy*, New York: St. Vladimir's Seminary Press, 1960.

16- Cassian, John (Saint), *The Twelve Books of John Cassian on the Institutes of Coenobia, and the Remedies for the Eight Principal Faults*, from: *Nicene and Post-Nicene Fathers*, Second Series, Volume 11, New York: Christian Literature Publishing Co., 1894.

17- Cheslyn Jones, Geoffrey Wainwright, Edward Yarnold SJ and Paul Bradshaw, *The Study of Liturgy*, New York: Oxford University Press, 1992.

18- Cobb, Peter. G. (1992). The Liturgy of the Word in the Early Church. In Cheslyn Jones, Geoffrey Wainwright, Edward Yarnold SJ and Paul Bradshaw (Eds.), *The Study of Liturgy*, New York: Oxford University Press.

19- Cross and E.A. Livingstone, *The Oxford Dictionary of the Christian Church* (third edition), New York: Oxford University Press, 2005.

20- Cuming, G. J. (1997). The Anaphora of St. Mark: A Study of Development. In Bradshaw, Paul F. (Ed.), *Essays on Early Eastern Eucharistic Prayers*, Minnesota: The Liturgical Press, 1997.

21- Cuming, Geoffrey J., *The Liturgy of St Mark*, Roma: Orientalia Christiana Analecta, 1990.

22- Cyril of Jerusalem (Saint), *Nicene and Post-Nicene Fathers, Second Series, Volume 7: Catechetical Lecture 23*, Buffalo, NY: Christian Literature Publishing Co., 1894.

23- D'Alton, John, Youssef, Youhanna, *Severus of Antioch: His Life and Times*, Boston: Brill, 2016.

24- Davies, J.G., *A New Dictionary of Liturgy and Worship*, London: SCM Press LTD, 1989.

25- De Lacy O'Leary, D.D., *The Coptic Theotokia*, London: LUZAC & Co., 1923.

26- De Lacy O'Leary, D.D., *The Daily Office and Theotokia of the Coptic Church*, London: Simpkin, Marshall, Hamilton, Kent & Co., Ltd., 1911.

27- Di Bitonto Kasser, Anna (1999), Due nuovi testi cristiani. *Aegyptus, Anno 79, No. ½,* 93-106.

28- Dix, Dom Gregory, *The Shape of the Liturgy*, London: Bloomsbury Publishing, 1945.

29- Dyer, Joseph, *Western Plainchant in the First Millennium: Studies in the Medieval Liturgy and its Music, "The Desert, the City Psalmody in the Late Fourth Century"*, NY: Ashgate Publishing, 2003.

30- Edersheim, Alfred, *Sketches of Jewish Social Life in the Days of Christ*, London: Religious Tract Society, 1876.

31- Farrington, Peter (Father) (2011), American Foundation for Syriac Studies, *The Virgin St Mary in the Hymns of St Severus of Antioch*, Retrieved from http://www.syriacstudies.com/AFSS/Syriac_Articles_in_English/Entries/2011/1/8_The_Virgin_St_Mary_in_the_Hymns_of_St_Severus_of_Antioch_By_Father_Peter_Farrington_.html.

32- Ghaly, George. (2016). *A Contextual, Historical and Grammatical Analysis of ϫⲉⲛⲉⲛ, A Unique Coptic Hymn*. Unpublished raw data.

33- Ghaly, George. "Coptic Bilingualism and Hymn-Writing: A study of the Glorification Hymn *Agios Istin*." *Coptica* 10 (2011) 1–19. Published.

34- Graves, Raphael. (1997). The Anaphora of the Eighth Book of the Apostolic Constitutions. In Bradshaw, Paul F. (Ed.), *Essays on Early Eastern Eucharistic Prayers*, Minnesota: The Liturgical Press, 1997.

35- Grisbrooke, W. Jardine. (1992). The Formative Period-Cathedral and Monastic Offices. In Cheslyn Jones, Geoffrey Wainwright, Edward Yarnold SJ and Paul Bradshaw (Eds.), *The Study of Liturgy*, New York: Oxford University Press.

36- Halim, Mina Safwat, *The Hagiography Reading Service* (unpublished).

37- Helmy, Michael. (2020). Byzantine Influences on a Group of Coptic Chants in the Psalter and the Antiphonary. *Alexandria School*, 29(2), Cairo: Paromaos Monastery, 2020.

38- Helmy, Michael. (2021). *Omonogenis* and *Agios Dimas* In the Alexandrian Coptic Rite. *Alexandria School*, 30(1), Cairo: Paromaos Monastery, 2021.

39- Ragheb, Michael Helmy. (2021). Initial Indications Regarding Chants Attributable to the First and Third Canticles in the Coptic Rite. *Alexandria School*, 31(2), Cairo: Paromaos Monastery, 2021.

40- Holtz, Barry W., *Back to the Sources: Reading the Classic Jewish Texts*, New York: Simon & Schuster Paperbacks, 1984.

41- Jenkins, C. (1908). Origen on I Corinthians. III. *The Journal of Theological Studies*, 9(36), 502-514.

42- Jurgens, William A., *The Faith of the Early Fathers*, Vol. I, Minnesota: The Liturgical Press, 1970.

43- Johnson, Maxwell E., *Praying and Believing in Early Christianity: The Interplay Between Christian Worship and Doctrine*, Minnesota: The Liturgical Press, 2013.

44- Johnson, Maxwell E. (1997). The Archaic Nature of the Sanctus, Institution Narrative, and Epiclesis of the Logos in the Anaphora Ascribed to Sarapion of Thmuis. In Bradshaw, Paul F. (Ed.), *Essays on Early Eastern Eucharistic Prayers*, Minnesota: The Liturgical Press, 1997.

45- Knowles, Melody D., *Centrality Practiced: Jerusalem in the Religious Practice of Yehud and the Diaspora in the Persian Period*, Atlanta: Society of Biblical Literature, 2006.

46- Lewis, C.S., *Mere Christianity*, London: Collins, 2012.

47- Lingas, Alexander Leonidas, *Sunday Matins in the Byzantine Cathedral Rite*, Vancouver: The University of British Columbia, 1996.

48- Lucas, A., Harris, J.R., *Ancient Egyptian Materials and Industries*, New York: Dover Publications, Inc., 1999.

49- Maccoull, L.S.B. (1989), STUD. PAL. XV 250ab: A Monophysite Trisagion for the Nile Flood, *The Journal of Theological Studies, Volume 40, Issue 1,* 129-135.

50- Makar, Adeeb B., *The Abbreviated Coptic-English Dictionary*, California: St. Antonius Coptic Orthodox Church, 2001.

51- Marson, Charles Latimer, *The Psalms at Work*, Philadelphia: George W. Jacobs and Co., 1895.

52- Martinez, David G., *P. Michigan XIX. Baptized for Our Sakes: A Leather Trisagion from Egypt (P. Mich. 799)*, Michigan: B. G. Teubner Stuttgart and Leipzig, 1999.

53- Maier, Paul L., *Eusebius: The Church History*, Michigan: Kregel Publications, 2007.

54- McGowan, Andrew B., *Ancient Christian Worship*, Michigan: Baker Academic, 2014.

55- Menze, Volker L., *Justinian and the Making of the Syrian Orthodox Church*, New York: Oxford University Press, 2008.

56- Migne, Jacques-Paul, *Patrologia Graeca*, Vol. 18, Paris: Imprimerie Catholique, 1848.

57- Halliburton, R.J. (1992). The Patristic Theology of the Eucharist. In Cheslyn Jones, Geoffrey Wainwright, Edward Yarnold SJ and Paul Bradshaw (Eds.), *The Study of Liturgy*, New York: Oxford University Press.

58- Hartranft, Chester D., *The Ecclesiastical History of Sozomen*, downloaded from http://www.ccel.org/ccel/schaff/npnf202.html.

59- Hore, Alexander Hugh, *Eighteen Centuries of the Orthodox Greek Church*, London: James Parker and CO., 1899.

60- Iskander, Athanasius (Father), *Understanding the Liturgy*, Ontario: Parousia, 1993.

61- Jasper, R.C.D., and G.J. Cuming, *Prayers of the Eucharist: Early and Reformed*, Third Edition, Minnesota: A Pueblo Book, 1987.

62- J. Charles Cox, LL.D., F.S.A., *The Reliquary and Illustrated Archaeologist*, London: Bemrose and Sons, 1889.

63- J.D. Crichton. (1992). A Theology of Worship. In Cheslyn Jones, Geoffrey Wainwright, Edward Yarnold SJ and Paul Bradshaw (Eds.), *The Study of Liturgy*, New York: Oxford University Press.

64- John, Marquis of Bute, *The Coptic Morning Service for the Lord's Day*, London: Cope and Fenwick, 1908.

65- Karim, Armin (2014), *"My People, What Have I Done to You?" The Good Friday Popule meus Verses in Chant and Exegesis, c. 380–880* (Doctoral dissertation). Case Western Reserve University, Cleveland, Ohio.

66- Korobkin, N. Daniel (2013), Kedushah, Shema, and the Difference Between Israel and the Angels, *Hakirah 16*, 19-46.

67- Lang, Frederick K., *Ulysses and the Irish God*, Cranbury: Associated University Presses, 1993.

68- McFarland, Jason J., *Announcing the Feast: The Entrance Song in the Mass of the Roman Rite*, Minnesota: Liturgical Press, 2011.

69- Moosa, Matti, *The Maronites in History*, Syracuse: Syracuse University Press, 1986.

70- Origen, *Origen Commentary on the Gospel of Matthew*, New Apostolic Bible Covenant, 2019.

71- Paul F. Bradshaw, Maxwell E. Johnson, *The Eucharistic Liturgies: Their Evolution and Interpretation*, Minnesota: The Liturgical Press, 2012.

72- Phillips, Charles Stanley, *Hymnody Past and Present*, London: Society for Promoting Christian Knowledge, 1937.

73- Philo, *Philo of Alexandria: The Contemplative Life, The Giants, and Selections* (Winston, David, Trans.), New Jersey: Paulist Press, 1981.

74- *Psalms, the canticle of Moses, Theotokia, prayers and hymns for the Blessed Virgin Mary, archangels and martyrs*, London: Bodleian Library—Oxford, MS 256, Huntington Collection.

75- Rattenbury, J. Ernest, *Thoughts on Holy Communion*, London: Epworth Press, 1958.

76- Ray, Walter D. (1997). The Strasbourg Papyrus. In Bradshaw, Paul F. (Ed.), *Essays on Early Eastern Eucharistic Prayers*, Minnesota: The Liturgical Press, 1997.

77- Reine, Francis J., *The Eucharistic Doctrine and Liturgy of the Mystagogical Catecheses of Theodore of Mopsuestia*, Washington, D.C.: The Catholic University of America Press, 1942.

78- Rudwin, Maximilian J. (1919), The Origin of Judeo-Christian Worship, *The Open Court*, Vol. 1919: Iss. 5, Article 4, Southern Illinois University, Retrieved from https://opensiuc.lib.siu.edu/ocj/vol1919/iss5/4.

79- Schaff, Philip, *Nicene and Post-Nicene Fathers, Series II, Volume 4*, Grand Rapids, Michigan: Christian Classics Ethereal Library.

80- Schmemann, Alexander, *Liturgy and Life: Christian Development through Liturgical Experience*, New York: Orthodox Church in America, 1993.

81- Schmemann, Alexander, *Introduction to Liturgical Theology*, New York: St. Vladimir's Seminary Press, 1986.

82- Schmemann, Alexander, *The Eucharist*, New York: Orthodox Church in America, 1987.

83- Schmemann, Alexander, *Liturgy and Tradition*, New York: Orthodox Church in America, 1990.

84- SGS, Smith (Bro.), *A Monk's Topical Bible Letters E-K*, Book 2, Volume 4, Florida: Revelation Insight Publishing Co., 2012.

85- Shahan, T. (1908). Council in Trullo. In *The Catholic Encyclopedia*. New York: Robert Appleton Company. Retrieved October 5, 2020 from New Advent: http://www.newadvent.org/cathen/04311b.htm.

86- Spinks, Bryan D., *Do This in Remembrance of Me: The Eucharist from the Early Church to the Present Day*, London: SCM Press, 2013.

87- Storey, William G., *A Prayer Book of Eucharistic Adoration*, Chicago: Loyola Press, 2010.

88- Stuckwisch, Richard D. (1997). The Basilian Anaphoras. In Bradshaw, Paul F. (Ed.), *Essays on Early Eastern Eucharistic Prayers*, Minnesota: The Liturgical Press, 1997.

89- SUS, *The Divine Liturgies of Saints Basil, Gregory and Cyril*, Second Edition, USA: Coptic Orthodox Diocese of the Southern United States, 2007.

90- Talf, Robert F., *Beyond East and West: Problems in Liturgical Understanding*, Second Revised and Enlarged Edition, Rome: Pontifical Oriental Institute, 1997.

91- Talf, Robert F., *The Liturgy of the Hours in East and West: The Origins of the Divine Office and Its Meaning for Today*, Minnesota: The Liturgical Press, 1986.

92- Webber, Robert E., *Ancient-Future Worship: Proclaiming and Enacting God's Narrative*, Michigan: Baker Books, 2008.

93- *Wikipedia: The free encyclopedia*. FL: Wikimedia Foundation, Inc. Retrieved February 5, 2016, from http://www.wikipedia.org

94- Wilson, Stephen B. (1997). The Anaphora of the Apostles Addai and Mari. In Bradshaw, Paul F. (Ed.), *Essays on Early Eastern Eucharistic Prayers*, Minnesota: The Liturgical Press, 1997.

95- Wobbermin, Dr. G., *Bishop Sarapion's Prayer-Book*, London: Society for Promoting Christian Knowledge, 1922.

96- Woolfenden, Gregory W., *Daily Liturgical Prayer: Origins and Theology*, New York and London: Routledge, 2016.

97- Wybrew, Hugh. (1992). The Setting of the Liturgy: Ceremonial. In Cheslyn Jones, Geoffrey Wainwright, Edward Yarnold SJ and Paul Bradshaw (Eds.), *The Study of Liturgy*, New York: Oxford University Press.

98- Yarnold, E.J. (1992). The Liturgy of the Faithful in the Fourth and Early Fifth Centuries. In Cheslyn Jones, Geoffrey Wainwright, Edward Yarnold SJ and Paul Bradshaw (Eds.), *The Study of Liturgy*, New York: Oxford University Press.

99- Youssef, Youhanna, *The Life and Works of Severus of Antioch in the Coptic and Copto-Arabic Tradition: Texts and Commentaries*, New Jersey, Gorgias Press, 2014.

100- Youssef, Youhanna Nessim & Soliman, Sameh Farouk (2017), A Copto-Greek Hymn for John the Baptist. *Ephemerides Liturgicae* 131, 80-91.

101- Zanelli, Ugo. (2011). "Fraction Prayers" in the Coptic Liturgy. *The Harp*, 27, 291-302, Kottayam: St. Ephrem Ecumenical Research Institute (SEERI).

102- Zheltov, Michael, *The Anaphora and the Thanksgiving Prayer from the Barcelona Papyrus: An Underestimated Testimony to the Anaphoral History in the Fourth Century*, Vol. 62, No. 5, The Netherlands: Brill, 2008.

103- Zheltov, Michael, *Studia Patristica: Vol. XLV*, Paris: Peeters, 2010.

104- الأب متى المسكين، **الإفخارستيا عشاء الرب: بحث في الأصول الأولى لليتورجيا ومدخل لشرح القداس وتطوره من القرن الأول حتى عصرنا الحالي**، الطبعة الثانية، مطبعة دير أنبا مقار بوادي النطرون، ٢٠٠٠م.

105- الأب متى المسكين، **إفخارستيا عشاء الرب: قداس الرسل الأول وهو نواة جميع القداسات**، الطبعة الأولى، مطبعة دير أنبا مقار بوادي النطرون، ٢٠٠٠م.

106- الراهب القس أثناسيوس المقاري، **القداس الإلهي سر ملكوت الله** (جزئين)، دار نوبار بشبرا، ٢٠٠٨م.

107- الراهب القس أثناسيوس المقاري، **موجز التاريخ الليتورجي لكنيسة الإسكندرية** (جزئين)، مطابع صحارا بمدينة نصر، ٢٠١٨م.

108- الراهب القس أثناسيوس المقاري، **صلوات رفع البخور في عشية وباكر**، الطبعة الثانية، دار نوبار بشبرا، ٢٠١١م.

109- الراهب القس أثناسيوس المقاري، **تسبحة نصف الليل والسحر**، دار نوبار بشبرا، ٢٠٠٥م.

110- الشماس ألبير جمال ميخائيل، **الأساس في خدمة الشماس**، الطبعة الثالثة، مكتبة مار جرجس بشكولاني، ٢٠١٣م.

111- الأنبا غبريال الخامس (القرن ١٥)، **الترتيب الطقسي**، مطبوعات المركز الفرنسيسكاني للدراسات الشرقية بالقاهرة، ١٩٦٢م.

112- البابا غبريال الخامس (القرن ١٥)، **الترتيب الطقسي**، مخطوط رقم ٩٨، المكتبة الوطنية بباريس، ١٤١١م.

113- الأنبا صموئيل (أسقف شبين القناطر وتوابعها)، **ترتيب البيعة: عن مخطوطات البطريركية بمصر والإسكندرية ومخطوطات الأديرة والكنائس** (ثلاثة أجزاء)، النعام للطباعة والتوريدات، ٢٠٠٠م.

114- الراهب القس صموئيل السرياني، ابن كَبَر (القرن ١٤)، **مصباح الظلمة وإيضاح الخدمة** (جزء ١ وجزء ٢)، ١٩٩٨م.

115- يوحنا بن زكريا المعروف بابن سباع (القرن ١٣)، **الجوهرة النفيسة في علوم الكنيسة**، ٢٠٠١م.

116- الشيخ المكين بن العميد (القرن ١٣)، تاريخ المسلمين من صاحب شريعة الإسلام أبي القاسم محمد إلى الدولة الأتابكية، دار العواصم للنشر والتوزيع، ٢٠١٠م.

117- مخطوط رقم ١١٧ طقوس (ترتيب البيعة) بالدار البطريركية بالقاهرة، ١٩١٠م.

118- مخطوط رقم ١١٨ طقوس (ترتيب البيعة) بالدار البطريركية بالقاهرة، ١٩١١م.

119- مخطوط رقم ٧٣ طقس (ترتيب البيعة) بالدار البطريركية بالقاهرة، ١٤٤٤م.

120- مخطوط رقم ٣٠٢ (ترتيب البيعة) بدير الأنبا أنطونيوس، ١٦٦١م.

121- مخطوط رقم ٦٧ طقس (الإكليل) بدير العذراء مريم بياض – بني سويف، ١٥٦٧م.

122- مخطوط رقم ٦٩ طقس (الإكليل) بدير العذراء مريم بياض – بني سويف. تاريخ النساخة غير معروف.

123- مخطوط رقم ٧٠ طقس (الإكليل) بدير العذراء مريم بياض – بني سويف. تاريخ النساخة غير معروف.

124- مخطوط رقم ٨١ طقس (خولاجي قبطي-عربي) بدير العذراء مريم بياض – بني سويف. تاريخ النساخة غير معروف.

125- مخطوط رقم ٨٢ طقس (خولاجي قبطي) بدير العذراء مريم بياض – بني سويف. تاريخ النساخة غير معروف.

126- مخطوط رقم ٢٦٨ بالمتحف القبطي، ١٨٩٥م.

127- مخطوط رقم ١٠٠ عربي بالمكتبة الأهلية بباريس، القرن ١٤.

128- مخطوط رقم ٥٥ طقس (الإبصالمودية السنوية) بالمتحف القبطي، ١٧١٧م.

129- مخطوط رقم ١١ قبطي (الإبصالمودية السنوية) بالمكتبة الأهلية بباريس.

130- مخطوط رقم ٦٩ قبطي (الإبصالمودية السنوية) بالمكتبة الأهلية بباريس.

131- مخطوط رقم ٢٥٦ هانت (الإبصالمودية السنوية) بمكتبة بودلين بلندن، ١٣٨٧م.

132- مخطوط رقم ٤٩ شرقيات (الإبصالمودية الكيهكية) بمكتبة بودلين بلندن.

133- مخطوط رقم ٣ قبطي (الإبصالمودية الكيهكية) بمكتبة بودلين بلندن.

134- مخطوط رقم ٦٥٣ شرقيات (الإبصالمودية الكيهكية) بمكتبة بودلين بلندن، ١٧٧٢م.

135- مخطوط رقم ٣ قبطي بالمكتبة الأهلية بالنمسا بفيينا، ١٣٤٨–١٣٦٨م.

136- مخطوط رقم ٥٢٨٤ شرقيات بالمكتبة البريطانية بلندن.

137- مخطوط رقم ١٢٣٩ شرقيات (خولاجي) بالمكتبة البريطانية بلندن، القرن ١٢.

138- مخطوط رقم ٨٢ قبطي (خولاجي) بالمكتبة الأهلية بباريس، القرن ١٤.

139- مخطوط رقم ٢٤ قبطي (خولاجي) بالمكتبة الأهلية بباريس.

140- مخطوط رقم ٣٠ قبطي (خولاجي) بالمكتبة الأهلية بباريس.

141- مخطوط رقم ٥٧٢ هانت (خولاجي) بمكتبة بودلين بلندن، القرن ١٣ أو ١٤.

142- مخطوط رقم ٣٦٠ هانت (خولاجي) بمكتبة بودلين بلندن، القرن ١٣.

143- مخطوط رقم ٤٠٣ هانت (خولاجي) بمكتبة بودلين بلندن.

144- مخطوط رقم ١٧ قبطي (خولاجي) بمكتبة الفاتيكان، القرن ١٣.

145- مخطوط رقم ٢٠ قبطي (خولاجي) بمكتبة الفاتيكان، القرن ١٤.

146- مخطوط رقم ٢٤ قبطي (خولاجي) بمكتبة الفاتيكان، القرن ١٤ أو ١٥.

147- مخطوط رقم ١٣٧ بالمتحف القبطي، القرن ١٨.

148- مخطوط رقم ٩ قانون بدير البرموس، القرن ١٣ أو ١٤.

149- مخطوط رقم ٣٨ قبطي بمكتبة الفاتيكان، ١٣٧٠-١٣٧٨.

150- مخطوط رقم ٤٤٩ طقس (دلال دير أبو سيفين بطموه) بالمتحف القبطي، القرن ١٥ أو ١٦.

151- مخطوط رقم ٣١ طقس (دلال الأنبا شنوده) بالمتحف القبطي، القرن ١٩.

152- مخطوط رقم ٥٠ طقس (بصخة) بالدار البطريركية بالقاهرة، ١٣٥٠م.

153- مخطوط رقم ٦٥ قبطي بورجيا بالفاتيكان، القرن ١٨.

154- مخطوط رقم ٢٩٢ طقس بدير الأنبا أنطونيوس بالبرية الشرقية، ١٧٠٨م.

155- مخطوط رقم ١٢٣ عربي (١٣٩٦)، **مقالة في القربان المقدس**، الأب ألفونس عبد الله الفرنسيسكاني، مؤلفات المركز الفرنسيسكاني للدراسات الشرقية المسيحية، القاهرة، ١٩٦٧م.

156- مخطوط رقم ٥٧٢ هانت (خولاجي للقداسات الثلاثة) بمكتبة بودليان بلندن، القرن ١٣ أو ١٤.

157- سيفين بطرس ابراهيم هارون، مخطوط (غير مرقم) كتاب تمجيد لربي يسوع والعدري والملايكة والرسل والشهدا والقديسين (بخط المرحوم بقطر جرجس المخربط)، بيع نقادة، سنة ١٩١٤م.

158- مخطوط ترتيب مردات وألحان ووهمات السنة القبطية (بدون رقم) بدير مار مينا (المعلق) بأسيوط، ١٨٣٤م.

159- معلمي البيعة (القرون الوسطى)، **سر الثالوث في خدمة الكهنوت**، الأرشي دياكون جرجس فيلوثاؤس عوض، ١٩٤٢م.

160- القمص عبد المسيح صليب المسعودي البراموسي (دير السيدة العذراء برموس)، **الخولاجي المقدس**، الطبعة الأولى، مطبعة عين شمس، ١٩٠٢م.

161- القمص عبد المسيح صليب المسعودي البراموسي (دير السيدة العذراء برموس)، **الخولاجي المقدس**، الطبعة الثانية، دار نوبار للطباعة، ٢٠٠٢م.

162- القمص عبد المسيح صليب (لجنة التحرير والنشر بمطرانية بني سويف والبهنسا)، **الخولاجي المقدس**، دار الجيل الجديد، ١٩٩٣م.

163- دير السيدة العذراء مريم (المحرق)، **الثلاثة القداسات**، الطبعة الرابعة، مطبعة دير الشهيد العظيم مار مينا العجائبي بمريوط، ٢٠٠٦م.

164- الأنبا متاؤس، **روحانية طقس القداس في الكنيسة القبطية الأرثوذكسية**، الطبعة الرابعة، لجنة التحرير والنشر بمطرانية بني سويف والبهنسا ١٩٩٣م.

165- الشماس ألبير جمال ميخائيل، **القداسات الثلاثة: روحياً، لاهوتياً، طقسياً، موسيقياً** ١٩٩٩م.

166- الأنبا أبيفانيوس، **القداس الباسيلي: النص اليوناني مع الترجمة العربية**، الطبعة الثانية، دار مجلة مرقس، ٢٠١٥م.

167- الأنبا أبيفانيوس، **القداس الغريغوري: النص اليوناني مع الترجمة العربية**، الطبعة الثانية، دار مجلة مرقس، ٢٠١٥م.

168- الأنبا أبيفانيوس، **قداس القديس مرقس: القداس الكيرلسي**، الطبعة الأولى، دار مجلة مرقس، ٢٠١٥م.

169- القس كيرلس كيرلس، **القداسات الثلاثة متقابلة مع الضبط والشرح**، كنيسة مار جرجس بخماروية، ١٩٨٧م.

170- مؤتمن الدولة أبو اسحق بن العسال (القرن ١٣)، **الأعمال الرئيسية في الآداب الكنسية**، الأرشي دياكون جرجس فيلوثاؤس عوض، المطبعة المصرية الأهلية الحديثة بالقاهرة ١٩٤٢م.

171- المجمع المقدَّس للكنيسة القبطية الأرثوذكسية، **القرارات المجمعية في عهد صاحب الغبطة والقداسة البابا شنوده الثالث**، الطبعة الثانية، بريا جرافيك بحلمية الزيتون، ٢٠٠١م.

172- الأنبا متاؤس، **القرارات المجمعية الخاصة بالطقوس الكنسية**، تاتش برس، ٢٠١٠م.

173- القمص يوحنا سلامه، **اللآلئ النفيسة في شرح طقوس ومعتقدات الكنيسة** (جزئين)، مكتبة مار جرجس بشكولاني، ١٩٩٩م.

174- القمص فيلوثاوس المقاري، المعلم ميخائيل جرجس، **كتاب الإبصاليات والطروحات الواطس والأدام المُستعمل تلاوتها في جميع كنائس الكرازة المرقسية**، مطبعة القديس مكاريوس بمصر القديمة، ١٩١٣م.

175- دكتور چورچ حبيب بباوي، **القداس الإلهي: تعليقات وتفاسير لكثير من أقوال الآباء**، چي سي سنتر، ٢٠١٣م.

176- جمعية نهضة الكنائس القبطية الأرثوذكسية المركزية بالقاهرة، **خدمة الشماس والألحان**، الطبعة العاشرة، مكتب النعام، ١٩٩٣م.

177- القس مينا البرموسي، **الإبصلمودية المقدسة السنوية، حسب طقس وترتيب الكنيسة القبطية الأرثوذكسية**، مطبعة الكمال، الإسكندرية، ١٩٠٨م.

178- دكتور سامح فاروق حنين، **الكنيسة وثقافة العصر**، مركز بانـاريون للتراث الآبائي، ٢٠١٥م.

179- أغناطيوس إفرام الثاني (بطريرك السريان الأنطاكي)، **المباحث الجلية في الليتورجيات الشرقية والغربية**، المطبعة البطريركية في دير الشرفة، ١٩٢٤م.

180- أنور أحمد الصناديقي، **مع التموجات المدنية**، دار الثقافة ملوي ١٩٦٦م.

181- إقلاديوس يوحنا لبيب الميري، **الرَّد الأول والثاني على مقالة ونبذة الإيغومانوس فيلوثاوس**، مطبعة التوفيق بالفجالة، ١٨٩١م.

182- رهبنة دير مار جرجس الحرف (منشورات النور)، **من أجل فهم الليتورجيا وعيشها**، مطبعة النور في بيروت، ١٩٨١م.

183- إقلاديوس يوحنا لبيب الميري، **كتاب الإبصلمودية السنوية المقدسة**، مطبعة عين شمس بمصر، ١٩٠٨م.

184- إقلاديوس يوحنا لبيب الميري، **الإبصلمودية المقدسة الكيهكية**، مطبعة عين شمس بمصر، ١٩١١م.

185- القس مينا البرموسي المحلاوي، **كتاب الإبصلمودية السنوية المقدسة**، مطبعة ومكتبة الكمال عبد المسيح تادرس، ١٩٠٨م.

186- البابا كيرلس الثالث (القرن ١٣)، **دلال المبتدئين وتهذيب العلمانيين**، مخطوط قانون ٩ بدير البرموس (١٣٥٣م)، تحقيق ودراسة الراهب ميصائيل البرموسي، مدرسة الإسكندرية—العدد ٢٤، ٢٠١٨م.

187- البابا كيرلس الثالث (القرن ١٣)، **دلال المبتدئين وتهذيب العلمانيين**، مخطوط قانون ١٢ بالدير المحرق، تحقيق ودراسة الراهب ميصائيل البرموسي، مدرسة الإسكندرية—العدد ٢٥، ٢٠١٨م.

188- أحد معلمي البيعة (تاريخ النساخة غير معروف)، **سر الثالوث في خدمة الكهنوت**، مخطوط لاهوت ٨٤ بدير الأنبا بولا، تحقيق ودراسة الراهب ميصائيل البرموسي، مدرسة الإسكندرية—العدد ٢٨، ٢٠٢٠م.

189- الأنبا ساويرس بن المقفع، **ترتيب الكهنوت**، تحقيق Julius Assfalg، مطبوعات مركز الدراسات الشرقية لحراسة الأراضي المقدسة، القاهرة، ١٩٥٥م.

190- روفائيل الطوخي، **كتاب الثلاثة قداسات**، روما: ١٧٣٦م.

191- روفائيل الطوخي، **كتاب الثاودوكيات وكترتيب شهر كيهك**، روما، ١٧٤٦م.

192- الأب ملاك حنا، **الثلاث تقديسات "أجيوس" في العقيدة والتاريخ**، الفجالة ١٩٥٤م.

193- الأنبا أبيفانيوس، **خولاجي الدير الأبيض: ترجمة عن اللغة القبطية ودراسة**، مدرسة الإسكندرية، ٢٠١٤م.

194- عبد العزيز جمال الدين، **تاريخ مصر من خلال مخطوطة تاريخ البطاركة لساويرس بن المقفع** (جزء ٦ وجزء ٧)، الهيئة العامة لقصور الثقافة، القاهرة، ٢٠١٢م.

195- البطريرك أغناطيوس أفرام الثاني، **المباحث الجلية في الليتورجيات الشرقية والغربية**، المطبعة البطريركية السريانية في دير الشرفة، ١٩٢٤م.

196- القس باسيليوس صبحي، **مقدمة في تاريخ الطقوس القبطية**، الطبعة الثانية، كنيسة السيدة العذراء بالزيتون، ٢٠١٦م.

197- مايكل حلمي راغب، **قراءة جديدة للحن الثلاثة فتية القديسين طبقاً لأقدم شذرات تحتويه**، تراث الأجداد في عيون الأحفاد، مطبعة نوبار ديجيتال بالقاهرة، ٢٠١٨م.

198- الراهب القس أثناسيوس المقاري، **قوانين بطاركة الكنيسة القبطية في العصور الوسطى**، دار نوبار بشبرا، ٢٠٠٩م.

199- الراهب زكريا السرباني، **المعاني الروحية في طقس القداس الإلهي**، ٢٠٠٣م.

200- القس دوماديوس بيباوي سعيد، **المعاني الروحية للحركات الطقسية في القداس الإلهي**، Good Shepherd Group، ٢٠٠٣م.

201- مركز الأبحاث، **ليتورجية القديس مرقس الرسول (١)**، مدرسة الإسكندرية—العدد ١٢، ٢٠١٢م.

202- الأنبا بنيامين، **طقس القداس الإلهي**، مطبعة الكرنك بالإسكندرية.

203- كوستي باندلي، **مدخل إلى القداس الإلهي**، منشورات النور ١٩٩٥م.

www.ingramcontent.com/pod-product-compliance
Lightning Source LLC
Chambersburg PA
CBHW021953160426
43197CB00007B/124